AN INTERNATIONAL READER'S DICTIONARY

New Edition

An International Reader's Dictionary

NEW EDITION

Michael West, M.A., D.Phil.
and
James Gareth Endicott, M.A.

Revised for this edition by
Ian Elliott
and
Lloyd Humberstone

Longman

Longman Group Limited
London

Associated companies, branches and representatives
throughout the world

First published 1965
Twenty-first impression 1975
Second edition 1977

ISBN 0 582 55535 5

Printed in Great Britain by
Richard Clay (The Chaucer Press) Ltd, Bungay, Suffolk

Contents

About this dictionary

This English dictionary is written specially for those who have learnt (or who are learning) English as a foreign language. It explains to them, in words that they know, the meaning of words and expressions that they may not know.

In this SECOND EDITION of *An International Reader's Dictionary*, we have tried to keep all the special qualities of the first edition, which was similar in many ways to the well known *New Method English Dictionary* by Dr Michael West and J. G. Endicott. At the same time, we have added some new ways of helping the user, and we have generally brought the dictionary up to date. For example, we have kept the list of DEFINING words to make the DEFINITIONS simple; but we have improved the way of showing the PRONUNCIATION of each word; and we have added a note to tell the user which part of speech (noun, verb, etc.) is being defined. See the tables below.

The Defining Vocabulary

At the back of the dictionary there is a list of 1,490 common or important words. For all the definitions in the dictionary we use the words in that list (with words defined under them, like *happiness* defined under *happy*; words regularly formed from them, like *unhappy* and *happiest*; personal PRONOUNS, like *I*, *you*, *his*; the names of days, months and countries, and number words like *four* and *fourth*). Where it is possible, no other words are used, but in a few cases it would be silly not to use a word that is outside the list, so the single outside word is used, and it appears in the definition in SMALL CAPITAL LETTERS. We have made sure that where that outside word is itself defined, no other outside word is used.

Pronunciation

The pronunciation of every main word is shown between strokes, / /, using the form of the INTERNATIONAL PHONETIC ALPHABET that is used in other Longman dictionaries. The form of British speech that we show is 'Received Pronunciation' (RP). We do not offer it as the only 'correct' pronunciation, but as a pronunciation which is widely accepted and understood everywhere that English is spoken. The table shows the SYMBOLS, or signs, that we use for RP in this book.

CONSONANTS		VOWELS	
Symbol	Key Word	Symbol	Key Word
p	pay	iː	sheep
b	boy	ɪ	ship
t	tea	e	bed
d	day	æ	bad
k	key	ɑː	calm
g	gay	ɒ	pot
		ɔː	caught
tʃ	cheer	ʊ	put
dʒ	jump	uː	boot
		ʌ	cut
f	few	ɜː	bird
v	view	ə	away
θ	thing		
ð	then	eɪ	make
s	soon	əʊ	note
z	wise	aɪ	bite
ʃ	fishing	aʊ	now
ʒ	pleasure	ɔɪ	joy
h	hot	ɪə	here
		eə	there
m	sum	ʊə	poor
n	sun		
ŋ	sung		
		eɪə	player
l	let	əʊə	lower
r	red	aɪə	tire
		aʊə	tower
j	yet	ɔɪə	employer
w	wet		

/ʳ/ —This means that the sound /r/ is heard only when the next word begins with a vowel sound. For example, *far* /fɑː ʳ/ means that no /r/ is heard in *far down* /ˌfɑːˈdaʊn/, but *far away* would be /ˌfɑːrəweɪ/.

/ə/ is shown before /m, n, ŋ, l, r/ to show that the sound /ə/ may or may not be heard. For example, travel /'trævəl/ means that RP speakers may say /'trævəl/ or they may say /'trævl/.

/'/ means that the SYLLABLE following the main STRESS in the word; it is heard more noticeably than the rest. Some words also have a syllable with weaker stress, and this is shown by /ˌ/ before the syllable: *understand* /ˌʌndə'stænd/.

/./ —Some expressions are made up of two or more words whose pronunciation has already been given. In this case stress is shown by using one /./ for each of the syllables: *single-minded* /ˌ. ˈ. ./.

Special Use and the Parts of Speech

Some words are used in a special way, and we have marked them:

> *sl* for 'slang'
>
> *infml* for 'INFORMAL' (not used in very careful speech or writing)
>
> *derog* for 'DEROGATORY' (showing dislike and lack of respect).

We have also used the following for the parts of speech:

> *n* for nouns (words like *book, goat*)
>
> *adj* for adjectives (like *good, lazy*)
>
> *pron* for pronouns (like *them, we*)
>
> *det* for determiners (words like *a, the, some*, which come before all the adjectives there may be before a noun)
>
> *adv* for adverbs (words like *soon, happily*)
>
> *prep* for prepositions (like *at, of*)
>
> *conj* for conjunctions (like *and, but, while*)
>
> *interj* for interjections (like *ouch!*)
>
> *vi* for intransitive verbs (like *disappear*: 'The fairy disappeared.')
>
> *vt* for transitive verbs (like *kill*: 'They killed *their enemies*.')

If a verb is (like *be* or *shall*) neither intransitive nor transitive, or if (like *move* or *boil*) it can be both transitive and intransitive, it has been marked simply *v*.

Lastly, we have sometimes used these short forms of words in our definitions of other words:

> esp. for 'especially'
>
> etc. for 'ETCETERA' (and others of that kind)
>
> e.g. for 'for example'.

Gordon Walsh of the Longman Resource and Development Unit has written the pronunciation signs for this new edition.

A

a /ə/; *strong* eɪ/, **an** /ən/; *strong* æn/ *det* [indefinite article] some; one; any. *prep* for each, e.g. *He earns £1 a day.*

aback /ə'bæk/ *adv* backwards. **taken aback** = surprised.

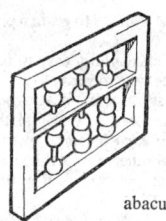

abacus

abacus /'æbəkəs/ *n* frame with balls on wires, used for teaching children to count; instrument used in calculating.

abandon /ə'bændən/ *vt* give up; leave, esp. someone in need of help. *n* lack of SELF-CONTROL.

abase /ə'beɪs/ *vt* make low—in office, honour, or in one's self-respect.

abash /ə'bæʃ/ *vt* make ashamed.

abate /ə'beɪt/ *v* make or become less.

abattoir /'æbətwɑː/ *n* place where animals are killed for food.

abbey /'æbɪ/ *n* place where religious men (or women) live apart, giving their lives to God; church used or once used by such people. *n* **abbot** /'æbət/ head of an abbey.

abbreviate /ə'briːvɪeɪt/ *vt* make shorter. *n* **abbreviation** /ə,briːvɪ'eɪʃən/ shortening, esp. of a word, e.g. 'adj' for 'adjective'.

abdicate /'æbdɪkeɪt/ *v* give up a power or right; cease to be king.

abdomen /'æbdəmən, æb'dəʊmən/ *n* stomach. *adj* **abdominal** /æb'dɒmɪnəl/.

abduct /æb'dʌkt/ *vt* wrongfully carry away a person, e.g. a child or young woman.

aberration /,æbə'reɪʃən/ *n* wandering from the right or expected course, e.g. of a star.

abet /ə'bet/ *vt* help in doing something, usually bad.

abeyance /ə'beɪəns/ **in abeyance** = not in use, not at present in force, e.g. *That law is in —.*

abhor /əb'hɔː/ *vt* to hate. *n* **abhorrence** /əb'hɒrəns/.

abide /ə'baɪd/ *v* stay. **I cannot abide him** = I cannot bear him; I hate him. **To abide by** an agreement = do what was promised.

ability /ə'bɪlɪtɪ/ *n* state of being able; cleverness.

abject /'æbdʒekt/ *adj* without value; without self-respect. **in abject poverty** = very poor.

abjure /əb'dʒʊə/ *vt* swear to give up.

ablaze /ə'bleɪz/ *adj, adv* burning.

able /'eɪbəl/ *adj* **1** I **am able to** = I can. **2** having the skill, etc. *adj* **able-bodied** /,eɪbəl 'bɒdɪd/ strong, in good health.

abnormal /æb'nɔːməl/ *adj* different from the NORMAL.

aboard /ə'bɔːd/ *adj, adv* on a ship, train, etc. **all aboard!** = all must now get aboard.

abode[1] /ə'bəʊd/ *p.t.* of **abide.**

abode[2] /ə'bəʊd/ *n* home; place in which people (or animals) live.

abolish /ə'bɒlɪʃ/ *vt* destroy; put an end to. *n* **abolition** /,æbə'lɪʃən/.

abominate /ə'bɒmɪneɪt/ *vt* feel great hatred for. *adj* **abominable** /ə'bɒmɪnəbəl, ə'bɒmnəbəl/ very bad, hateful.

aborigines /,æbə'rɪdʒɪniːz/ *n* people who have lived in a country from the beginning. *adj* **aboriginal** /,æbə'rɪdʒɪnəl/.

abortive /ə'bɔːtɪv/ *adj* unsuccessful.

abound /ə'baʊnd/ *vi* be in plenty; contain plenty, e.g. *The river abounds in fish.*

about /ə'baʊt/ *adv, prep* **1** on some or all sides of (a place). **2** in the area of (a place), e.g. *They walked about in the dark.* *prep* **1** on the subject of, e.g. *A book about birds.* **2** roughly; perhaps a little more or less than, e.g. *It will take about six hours.* **about turn** = turn round to face in the opposite direction. **to come about** = happen. **to bring about** = cause. **to set about** (a piece of work) = begin. **be about to** = be going to (do something) very soon.

above /ə'bʌv/ *adv, prep* higher (than); over. **above all** = most importantly.

abrasion /ə'breɪʒən/ *n* rubbing away; painful place on the skin. *adj* **abrasive** /ə'breɪsɪv/ rubbing.

abreast /ə'brest/ *adv* side by side. **abreast of the times** = knowing the latest things that are being done.

abridge /ə'brɪdʒ/ *vt* make (a book or story) shorter.

abroad /ə'brɔːd/ *adj, adv* out of one's own country.

abrogate /'æbrəgeɪt/ *vt* cause (a law or power) to cease.

abrupt /ə'brʌpt/ *adj* **1** sudden; steep. **2** using very few words; rude.

abscess /'æbses/ *n* painful poisoned place in or on the body.

abscond /æb'skɒnd/ *vi* run away quickly and secretly, e.g. *He absconded with the money.*

absent /'æbsənt/ *adj* not here, not present. **absent-minded** = not thinking of what one is doing. *n* **absence** /'æbsəns/ state of being absent. *n* **absentee** /,æbsən'tiː/ one who is absent (e.g. owner of land).

absolute /'æbsəluːt/ *adj* **1** free, uncontrolled, e.g.

1

absolution

An absolute ruler. **2** perfect, complete, e.g. *An absolute fool*; real, e.g. *An absolute fact.*

absolution /ˌæbsə'luːʃən/ *n* forgiveness.

absolve /əb'zɒlv/ *vt* set free, e.g. from blame or debt.

absorb /əb'sɔːb/ *vt* drink in or take in (liquid) through the surface, e.g. *The dry earth absorbs water.* **absorbed in** = giving one's whole mind to. *n* **absorption** /əb'sɔːpʃən/.

abstain /əb'steɪn/ *vi* **1** keep away (from something generally thought pleasant but which one feels is bad or harmful), e.g. *Abstain from strong drink.* **2** not VOTE for either side. *adj* **abstemious** /əb'stiːmɪəs/ not drinking or eating much. *n* **abstinence** /'æbstɪnəns/ keeping oneself from food or drink.

abstract /əb'strækt/ *vt* take out. *adj* **abstract** /'æbstrækt/ not directly concerned with experience, e.g. *Abstract ideas.* *n* a short account of the main ideas of a piece of written work. *n* **abstraction** /əb'strækʃən/ idea in the mind only, e.g. goodness, beauty, not the thought of any actual thing. **abstract art** = patterns and carvings that are not like real things but are meant to show the artist's ideas and feelings.

abstruse /əb'struːs/ *adj* hidden; hard to understand.

absurd /əb'sɜːd/ *adj* very foolish; unreasonable; causing people to laugh.

abundance /ə'bʌndəns/ *n* plenty. *adj* **abundant** /ə'bʌndənt/ plentiful.

abuse /ə'bjuːz/ *vt* **1** make a wrong use of. **2** speak rudely to. *n* **abuse** /ə'bjuːs/.

abyss /ə'bɪs/ *n* very deep hole. *adj* **abysmal** /ə'bɪzməl/ very deep; very serious (usually of something bad).

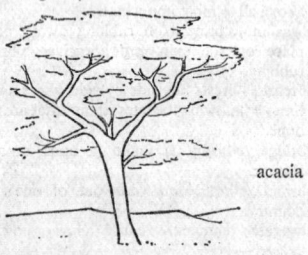

acacia

acacia /ə'keɪʃə/ *n* plant found mainly in hot countries.

academy /ə'kædəmɪ/ *n* **1** school for higher learning. **2** group of learned men. *adj* **academic** /ˌækə'demɪk/ **1** of or relating to a university. **2** not having any real importance in practice.

accede /ək'siːd/ *vi* **1** agree. **2** yield to a person's wishes. **3** come into an office.

accelerate /ək'seləreɪt/ *v* go more quickly or make (something) go more quickly. *n* **accelerator** /ək'seləreɪtə/ small handle, or PEDAL, which increases the speed of a car.

accent /'æksənt/ *n* **1** special weight given by the voice to one part of a word. **2** mark (') showing this. **3** peculiar way of speaking, e.g. *He has a foreign accent.* *vt* **accent** /ək'sent/ or **accentuate** /ək'sentʃʊeɪt/ place special weight or importance on.

accept /ək'sept/ *vt* **1** take or receive (something offered). **2** believe; agree to. *adj* **acceptable** /ək'septəbəl/ pleasant to receive; accepted gladly.

access /'ækses/ *n* ability to get to a place, person, etc.

accessible /ək'sesəbəl/ *adj* easy to reach; whom one can easily go and see.

accession /ək'seʃən/ *n* act of ACCEDING.

accessory /ək'sesərɪ/ *n* **1** helpful thing added. **accessories of a car** = lamps, instruments used in repair, and other special things added to the car. **2** someone who gives help to one acting wrongfully.

accident /'æksɪdənt/ *n* **1** event, esp. an unfortunate event, that happens by chance. **2** something not necessary or important.

acclaim /ə'kleɪm/ *vt* receive with shouts of joy or praise. *n* **acclamation** /ˌæklə'meɪʃən/.

acclimatize /ə'klaɪmətaɪz/ *vt* accustom (someone) to the CLIMATE of a place.

acclivity /ə'klɪvətɪ/ *n* a slope up, e.g. the side of a hill.

accolade /'ækəleɪd/ *n* act of making a person a KNIGHT by laying a sword on his shoulder; any act of recognition for greatness.

accommodate ə'kɒmədeɪt/ *vt* **1** make (something) fit. **2** settle (a quarrel). **3** supply as a kindness, e.g. money. **4** give lodgings to. *adj* **accommodating** /ə'kɒmədeɪtɪŋ/ kind; helpful. *n* **accommodation** /ə,kɒmə'deɪʃən/ lodgings.

accompany /ə'kʌmpənɪ/ *vt* go with. *n* **accompaniment** /ə'kʌmpənɪmənt/.

accomplice /ə'kʌmplɪs/ *n* companion in wrongdoing.

accomplish /ə'kʌmplɪʃ/ *vt* do or finish successfully. *adj* **accomplished** /ə'kʌmplɪʃt/ very able, esp. in one of the arts.

accord /ə'kɔːd/ *vi* agree. *n* agreement. **of one's own accord** = by one's own wish. **in accordance** /ə'kɔːdəns/ **with** = in agreement with. **according to** = as claimed by. *adv* **accordingly** /ə'kɔːdɪŋlɪ/ for that reason.

accordion

accordion /ə'kɔːdɪən/ *n* musical instrument played by pulling the ends out and pressing them together, thus forcing air under thin metal plates which make the musical sounds.

accost /ə'kɒst/ vt greet; speak to.

account /ə'kaʊnt/ n story; description; explanation. n (pl) **accounts** report of money received and spent. **on account of** = because of. **to take into account** = consider. **of no account** = not important. **to account for** = explain. adj **accountable** /ə'kaʊntəbəl/ expected to account for something and perhaps be blamed for its happening.

accountant /ə'kaʊntənt/ n one who keeps accounts of money. n **accountancy** /ə'kaʊntənsɪ/ art of keeping accounts.

accoutrements /ə'kuːtəmənts/ n all the things used by a soldier in war except his clothes and weapons.

accredit /ə'kredɪt/ vt show (someone) to be trustworthy.

accrue /ə'kruː/ vi increase; ACCUMULATE.

accumulate /ə'kjuːmjʊleɪt/ vi grow into a mass; become greater in amount. vt collect more and more of. n **accumulator** /ə'kjuːmjʊleɪtə/ instrument used for storing electricity.

accurate /'ækjʊrət/ adj exact; correct.

accursed /ə'kɜːsɪd/, **accurst** /ə'kɜːst/ adj under a curse; hateful.

accuse /ə'kjuːz/ vt say that (someone) has done wrong; blame. n **accusation** /,ækjʊ'zeɪʃən/.

accustom /ə'kʌstəm/ vt get (someone) used (to something).

ace (1)

ace /eɪs/ n 1 playing card with one spot. 2 CHAMPION.

acetic /ə'siːtɪk/ adj of an acid present in VINEGAR.

acetylene /ə'setəliːn/ n gas which burns with a bright white light.

ache /eɪk/ n continuous or repeated dull pain. vi cause one such pain, e.g. My leg aches.

achieve /ə'tʃiːv/ vt finish successfully; gain. n. **achievement** /ə'tʃiːvmənt/.

acid /'æsɪd/ adj 1 sour; sharp-tasting. 2 illtempered or sharp in speech. n powerful liquid, often able to cause burning.

acknowledge /ək'nɒlɪdʒ/ vt recognize; allow as being true, important, or great. **to acknowledge receipt of** = say that one has received. n **acknowledgment**.

acme /'ækmɪ/ n highest point; the greatest amount.

acne /'æknɪ/ n condition of having small hard spots on the skin of the face.

acorn /'eɪkɔːn/ n fruit of the OAK tree.

acoustic /ə'kuːstɪk/ adj having to do with hearing. n **acoustics** science of sound.

acquaint /ə'kweɪnt/ vt make known. n **acquaintance** /ə'kweɪntəns/ person whom one knows, but not a close friend.

acquiesce /,ækwɪ'es/ vi agree silently; not express disagreement.

acquire /ə'kwaɪə/ vt gain; get. adj **acquisitive** /ə'kwɪzətɪv/ eager to get and own. n **acquisition** /,ækwɪ'zɪʃən/ act of acquiring something; thing acquired.

acquit /ə'kwɪt/ vt set a prisoner free in a court of law. n **acquittal** /ə'kwɪtl/.

acre /'eɪkə/ n 4840 square yards (0.405 hectares) of land. n **acreage** /e'ɪkərɪdʒ/ number of acres in a piece of land.

acrid /'ækrɪd/ adj sour; bad-tempered; (of a smell) bitter and unpleasant.

acrobat /'ækrəbæt/ n person who can do clever things with his body, e.g. throwing and twisting himself about, walking on a rope, etc. n **acrobatics** /,ækrə'bætɪks/ doing such things. adj **acrobatic**.

across /ə'krɒs/ adv, prep from one side of (a place) to the other; over. **to come across** = find by chance.

acrostic /ə'krɒstɪk/ n game in which one has to find certain words which, written one below another, make other words with their letters.

act /ækt/ v 1 behave; do something. 2 perform in a play, film, etc.; pretend. n 1 something done. 2 a law passed by PARLIAMENT. 3 part of a play. 4 pretence.

action /'ækʃən/ n 1 movement; work; the producing of an effect. **to take action** = begin to do something. 2 natural working, e.g. The action of the heart; way of acting, e.g. The horse has a graceful action. **out of action** = not able to work or be used.

active /'æktɪv/ adj quick and full of life; full of action. n **activity** /æk'tɪvətɪ/ 1 state of being active. 2 something one does, esp. often or regularly; (kind of) action.

actor /'æktə/ n man who acts in plays or films. n **actress** /'æktrəs/ woman who acts in plays or films.

actual /'æktʃʊəl/ adj real; as a fact. adv **actually** /'æktʃʊəlɪ/ really, in fact, e.g. He actually ran = he really did run, though you would not have expected it.

actuary /'æktʃʊərɪ/ n person who calculates how much must be paid for INSURANCE.

acumen /'ækjʊmən/ n keenness of mind; cleverness and quick understanding.

acute /ə'kjuːt/ adj sharp. **an acute angle** = angle that is less than 90°. **an acute mind** = keen mind.

adage /'ædɪdʒ/ n wise saying.

adamant /'ædəmənt/ adj unyielding.

3

Adam's apple

Adam's apple /ˌædəmz ˈæpəl/ *n* part of a man's throat which stands out and moves during speech and swallowing.

adapt /əˈdæpt/ *vt* change and fit to a new use.

add /æd/ *vt* join one thing to another; find the whole amount of several numbers, e.g. *2 added to 2 makes 4*. *n* **addendum** /əˈdendəm/ thing to be added, e.g. to a book.

adder

adder /ˈædə/ *n* a kind of small poisonous snake.

addicted (to) /əˈdɪktɪd/ *adj* so accustomed to something that to be without it causes suffering, e.g. *He is addicted to drink*. *n* **addict** /ˈædɪkt/ person who is addicted to something.

addition /əˈdɪʃən/ *n* **1** act of adding. **2** that which is added. *adj* **additional** /əˈdɪʃənəl/.

addle /ˈædl/ **an addled egg** = bad egg.

address /əˈdres/ *vt* **1** write on (a letter, etc.) where it is to be sent. **2** speak to or begin to speak to. *n* **1** writing on a letter, etc., showing where it is to be sent; place where a person lives, a building stands, etc. **2** a public speech. *n* **addressee** /ˌædreˈsiː/ person to whom a letter is addressed.

adduce /əˈdjuːs/ *vt* bring forward (reasons, etc.).

adenoids /ˈædənɔɪdz/ *n* soft masses growing at the back of the nose.

adept /ˈædept, əˈdept/ *n*, *adj* (one who is) very skilled.

adequate /ˈædɪkwət/ *adj* enough; good enough.

adhere /ədˈhɪə/ *vi* stick (to something); believe (in something). *n* **adherent** /ədˈhɪərənt/ one who holds a certain opinion. *adj* **adhesive** /ədˈhiːsɪv/ sticky. *n* substance used for sticking things together.

ad hoc /ˌæd ˈhɒk/ *Latin adv, adj* for this special purpose.

adieu /əˈdjuː/ *interj* goodbye.

ad infinitum /ˌæd ɪnfɪˈnaɪtəm/ *Latin adv* for ever; without stopping.

adjacent /əˈdʒeɪsənt/ *adj* lying near or next to something, e.g. *The fire spread to an adjacent building*.

adjective /ˈædʒɪktɪv/ *n* word used with a noun telling more about it, e.g. 'big', 'soft', 'happy'.

adjoin /əˈdʒɔɪn/ *vt* be next to or joined on to.

adjourn /əˈdʒɜːn/ *v* stop (something) with the intention of continuing at a later time, e.g. *The meeting is adjourned*.

adjudicate /əˈdʒuːdɪkeɪt/ *v* give a judgment settling (a claim or quarrel).

adjunct /ˈædʒʌŋkt/ *n* something added, or joined on.

adjust /əˈdʒʌst/ *vt* set right; make a thing fit. *n* **adjustment** /əˈdʒʌstmənt/.

adjutant /ˈædʒʊtənt/ *n* officer who helps a Commanding Officer in the army.

ad lib /ˌæd ˈlɪb/ *adv* freely. *v* make up (something) as one goes along.

administer /ədˈmɪnɪstə/ *vt* look after, govern, carry on the business of. *adj* **administrative** /ədˈmɪnɪstrətɪv/. *n* **administration** /ədˌmɪnɪˈstreɪʃən/ that part of a government which carries out the laws.

admiral /ˈædmərəl/ *n* highest rank of officer in the NAVY. *n* **admiralty** /ˈædmərəltɪ/ office that controls the navy.

admire /ədˈmaɪə/ *vt* respect; look upon with wonder and pleasure. *adj* **admirable** /ˈædmərəbəl/ worthy of respect. **admirably done** = very well done. *n* **admiration** /ˌædmɪˈreɪʃən/.

admit /ədˈmɪt/ *vt* **1** allow (someone) to enter, e.g. *Admit a boy into a school*. **2** agree that (something unfavourable to oneself) is true, e.g. *I admit I deceived her*. *n* **admission** /ədˈmɪʃən/ act of admitting. *n* **admittance** /ədˈmɪtəns/ right to enter. *adj* **admissible** /ədˈmɪsəbəl/ which may be admitted.

admixture /ədˈmɪkstʃə/ *n* act of mixing; things mixed; one thing mixed in with others.

admonish /ədˈmɒnɪʃ/ *vt* warn, advise, tell (someone) that he is doing wrong.

ado /əˈduː/ *n* trouble and excitement.

adolescent /ˌædəˈlesənt/ *n, adj* (boy or girl) aged about 12 to 17.

adopt /əˈdɒpt/ *vt* take and bring up (another person's child) as one's own; accept (an idea).

adore /əˈdɔː/ *vt* love very much. *adj* **adorable** /əˈdɔːrəbəl/ very nice; very lovable. *n* **adoration** /ˌædəˈreɪʃən/ feeling of great love and respect; the act of showing love and respect.

adorn /əˈdɔːn/ *vt* make beautiful or ornament, e.g. *The room was adorned with roses*.

adrift /əˈdrɪft/ *adv, adj* floating about freely.

adroit /əˈdrɔɪt/ *adj* clever, skilful.

adulation /ˌædʒʊˈleɪʃən/ *n* giving praise in which one does not believe, in order to gain favour.

adult /ˈædʌlt, əˈdʌlt/ *n, adj,* fully grown (person).

adulterate /əˈdʌltəreɪt/ *vt* make impure by mixing in other cheaper things. *n* **adulteration** /əˌdʌltəˈreɪʃən/.

adultery /əˈdʌltərɪ/ *n* sexual unfaithfulness of a husband or wife. *n* **adulterer** /əˈdʌltərə/ one who is unfaithful to a husband or wife.

advance /ədˈvɑːns/ *v* move forward; raise to a higher rank or position. *adj* early, e.g. *An advance warning*. *n* forward movement; PROGRESS. **in advance of** = in front of; before. **to make advances to** = try to gain the friendship of. *adj* **advanced** /ədˈvɑːnst/ at a late, rather than early, level (in education, thought etc.). **an advanced idea** = very new, not generally accepted.

advantage /ədˈvɑːntɪdʒ/ *n* gain; anything likely to produce gain or success, e.g. being stronger or wiser. **to gain an advantage over** = do better than. **take advantage of** = make use of, esp. make improper use of (another person). adj **advantageous** /ˌædvən'teɪdʒəs/ helpful.

advent /'ædvent/ n coming; the act of arriving; coming of Christ. n Advent time from the 4th Sunday before Christmas to Christmas Day.

adventitious /ˌædven'tɪʃəs/ adj happening by chance.

adventure /əd'ventʃə / n dangerous or exciting deed or event. n **adventurer** /əd'ventʃərə / one who lives a dangerous (and perhaps dishonest) life. adj **adventurous** /əd'ventʃərəs/ eager for adventure.

adverb /'ædvɜ:b/ n word used with a verb, an adjective or another adverb to tell us something about it, e.g. run *quickly*, *very* big, *very* slowly.

adverse /'ædvɜ:s/ adj working against one, e.g. *Adverse fate, wind* etc. n **adversary** /'ædvəsərɪ/ enemy. n **adversity** /əd'vɜ:sətɪ/ unhappiness; misfortune.

advertise /'ædvətaɪz/ vt make known; bring to people's notice (esp. something one wishes to sell) e.g. by notices in the newspapers, pictures on walls, etc. n **advertisement** /əd'vɜ:tɪsmənt/ act of advertising; a printed notice, short film, etc., in which something is advertised.

advise /əd'vaɪz/ vt tell (someone) what you think he ought to do. n **advice** /əd'vaɪs/ opinion so given. adj **advisable** /əd'vaɪzəbəl/ which should be done.

advocate

advocate /'ædvəkət/ n one who speaks for another, e.g. in a law court. vt **advocate** /'ædvəkeɪt/ speak in favour of (an idea).

aegis /'i:dʒɪs/ **under the aegis of** = under the protection of.

aerate /'eəreɪt/ vt drive air, or gas, into. **aerated water** = water filled with gas.

aerial /'eərɪəl/ n wire or metal instrument in the air to receive radio or television waves.

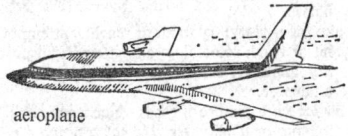

aeroplane

aero- /'eərəʊ/ having to do with the air. n **aeroplane** /'eərəpleɪn/ flying machine which is heavier than air. adj **aeronautical** /ˌeərə'nɔ:tɪkəl/ having to do with aeroplanes; n **aerodrome** /'eərədrəʊm/ place where

aeroplanes come to earth, or from which they set out on journeys.

aesthetic /i:s'θetɪk/ adj having to do with beauty or art.

afar /ə'fɑ: / adv at a distance.

affable /'æfəbəl/ adj easy to talk to; friendly. n **affability** /ˌæfə'bɪlətɪ/.

affair /ə'feə / n 1 matter of business; event. 2 relationship between a man and a woman, esp. when either is married to someone else.

affect /ə'fekt/ vt 1 act on; have a result on. 2 move the feelings. 3 pretend. adj **affected** /ə'fektɪd/ not natural, pretending. n **affectation** /ˌæfek'teɪʃən/ unnatural way of behaving, pretending to be different from one's real self, pretending to feel, e.g. *An affectation of kindness.*

affection /ə'fekʃən/ n love. **an affection of (the throat)** = illness or disease. adj **affectionate** /ə'fekʃənət/ loving.

affidavit /ˌæfɪ'deɪvɪt/ n written account of an event declared in the presence of an officer of the law to be true.

affiliate /ə'fɪlɪeɪt/ vt join (one group, etc.) on to (another), e.g. *Our school is affiliated to the university.*

affinity /ə'fɪnətɪ/ n nearness in blood or in natural character; being of the same family.

affirm /ə'fɜ:m/ v say with certainty; say solemnly. adj **affirmative** /ə'fɜ:mətɪv/ **answer in the affirmative** = say "yes". n **affirmation** /ˌæfə'meɪʃən/.

affix /ə'fɪks/ vt fix to; add part of a word onto the beginning or end of another word. n **affix** /'æfɪks/ part of a word so added.

afflict /ə'flɪkt/ vt give pain to. n **affliction** /ə'flɪkʃən/ pain; sorrow.

affluent /'æflʊənt/ adj rich; enjoying the comforts of wealth. n **affluence** /'æflʊəns/.

afford /ə'fɔ:d/ vt be able to pay for, e.g. *I can't afford a car* = I don't have enough money to buy a car.

affray /ə'freɪ/ n fight.

affront /ə'frʌnt/ vt be very rude and impolite to. n impolite act or saying.

afield /ə'fi:ld/ adv, adj in the field; far away from home.

afire /ə'faɪə / adv, adj on fire.

aflame /ə'fleɪm/ adv, adj in flames, burning.

afloat /ə'fləʊt/ adv, adj floating; on a ship.

afoot /ə'fʊt/ adv, adj on foot, walking; being planned or done, e.g. *There is mischief afoot* = some evil is being planned.

afraid /ə'freɪd/ adj frightened (by something); fearing (something), e.g. *Afraid of the dark.*

afresh /ə'freʃ/ adv from the beginning; again.

aft /ɑ:ft/ adv towards the back of a ship.

after /'ɑ:ftə / adv, prep later in time (than); behind. conj later than the time when. **to look after** = take care of, be in charge of. **to ask after** = ask for news about. **after all** = when everything is considered.

aftermath /ˈɑːftəmæθ/ n result of some event, esp. when this result is unfortunate and was not intended.

afternoon /ˌɑːftəˈnuːn/ n time of day between the morning and the evening.

afterthought /ˈɑːftəθɔːt/ n something thought of after an act or a speech; something thought of too late, after the chance of saying it or doing it has gone.

afterwards /ˈɑːftəwədz/ adv later.

again /əˈgeɪn, əˈgen/ adv for a second time; one more time. **now and again** = sometimes. **again and again** = often. **and again; but then again** = as a further thought.

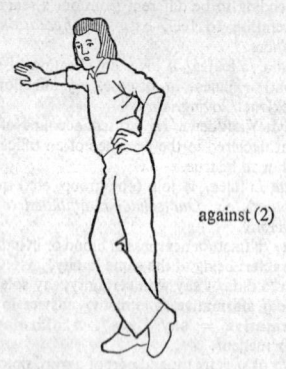

against (2)

against /əˈgemst, əˈgenst/ prep 1 in opposition to. 2 leaning on, e.g. A ladder against the wall.

agape /əˈgeɪp/ adv, adj with the mouth open.

agate /ˈægɪt/ n a kind of very hard stone used as a jewel.

age /eɪdʒ/ n 1 length of time, esp. if great. 2 length of a person's life or a thing's existence, esp. if great. v make or become old. adj **aged** /ˈeɪdʒɪd/ old or very old. adj **ageless** /ˈeɪdʒləs/ never becoming old.

agency /ˈeɪdʒənsɪ/ n 1 power or means by which something is done. 2 work of an AGENT; place where this work is done.

agenda /əˈdʒendə/ n list of things to be settled at a meeting.

agent /ˈeɪdʒənt/ n 1 person who acts for another. 2 cause, e.g. Water is the agent that wears away the rocks.

aggravate /ˈægrəveɪt/ vt make worse; make angry.

aggregate /ˈægrɪgɪt/ n whole amount.

aggression /əˈgreʃən/ n an attack; the tendency to attack, fight, etc. adj **aggressive** /əˈgresɪv/ quick to attack. n **aggressor** /əˈgresə/ the first to attack; the one who starts a fight.

aggrieved /əˈgriːvd/ adj feeling that one has good reason for complaint.

aghast /əˈgɑːst/ adj struck with sudden surprise or terror.

agile /ˈædʒaɪl/ adj quick-moving. n **agility** /əˈdʒɪlətɪ/ quickness of movement.

agitate /ˈædʒəteɪt/ vt cause to move; shake; excite; cause people to fight against the government.

aglow /əˈgləʊ/ adj, adv shining; heated; excited.

agnostic /ægˈnɒstɪk/ n one who believes that nothing can be known about God or the future life.

ago /əˈgəʊ/ adv in the past, e.g. Three years ago.

agog /əˈgɒg/ adv, adj eager, excited.

agony /ˈægənɪ/ n great pain; terrible struggle. adj **agonizing** /ˈægənaɪzɪŋ/ causing terrible pain or sorrow.

agrarian /əˈgreərɪən/ adj having to do with land that is farmed.

agree /əˈgriː/ vi have the same opinion (as someone else), e.g. I don't agree with him about that. adj **agreeable** /əˈgriːəbəl/ nice; ready to agree. n **agreement** /əˈgriːmənt/ agreeing; written promise made by two or more people.

agriculture /ˈægrɪkʌltʃə/ n art of making things grow on the land; farming. n **agriculturist** /ˌægrɪˈkʌltʃərɪst/ farmer. adj **agricultural** /ˌægrɪˈkʌltʃərəl/.

aground

aground /əˈgraʊnd/ adv, adj (of a ship) stuck on the ground.

ahead /əˈhed/ adv in front, e.g. To go ahead of the rest; forward. **go ahead** = continue your story (work etc.).

ahoy /əˈhɔɪ/ interj shout used at sea for calling a ship.

aid /eɪd/ n, vt help.

aide-de-camp /ˌeɪd də ˈkɑ̃/ n officer who attends on the leader of an army or officer of high rank and carries his orders.

ail /eɪl/ vt trouble. vi be ill. n **ailment** /ˈeɪlmənt/ illness.

aim /eɪm/ vi try; try to hit or reach. n attempt to hit or reach something; any attempt; purpose. adj **aimless** /ˈeɪmləs/ (of a person) without a purpose.

air /eə/ n 1 mixture of gases which we breathe. 2 manner or quality, e.g. He has a proud air. 3 music of a song vt 1 put out in the air so as to dry. 2 express (one's opinions). **on the air** = now being BROADCAST on radio or television.

airborne /ˈeəbɔːn/ adj carried in aeroplanes or by air.

air-conditioning /ˌeə kənˈdɪʃənɪŋ/ *n* equipment for keeping the heat and wetness of a room at a comfortable level.

aircraft /ˈeəkrɑːft/ *n* aeroplane; aeroplanes.

air force /ˈ. ./ *n* the strength of a country in machines and men for fighting in the air.

airgun /ˈeəgʌn/ *n* gun powered by air.

airline /ˈeəlaɪn/ *n* group of aeroplanes carrying goods and people at regular times from one place to another.

airlock /ˈeəlɒk/ *n* small amount of air in a pipe which prevents the regular flow of liquid.

airmail /ˈeəmeɪl/ *n* post carried by aeroplanes.

airport /ˈeəpɔːt/ *n* place where aeroplanes come to earth, set off, are repaired, etc.

air raid /ˈ. ./ *n* attack by aeroplanes.

airstrip /ˈeəˌstrɪp/ *n* long hard road along which aeroplanes go up or come down.

airtight /ˈeətaɪt/ *adj* keeping air in (or out).

aisle /aɪl/ *n* way for walking along, between blocks of seats, in a church, theatre, etc.

ajar /əˈdʒɑː/ ʲ *adv, adj* not quite shut, e.g. door, window.

akimbo

akimbo /əˈkɪmbəʊ/ *adv* with the arms bent and hands on the sides.

akin /əˈkɪn/ *adj* of the same family; alike.

à la carte /ˌɑː lɑː ˈkɑːt/ *French adj* (of a meal) ordered dish by dish, not as a whole.

alacrity /əˈlækrəti/ *n* quickness.

alarm /əˈlɑːm/ *n* warning of danger; feeling of fear. *vt* give warning of danger; frighten. *n, adj* **alarmist** /əˈlɑːmɪst/ (one) who is always warning people that terrible things are going to happen.

alarm clock /ˈ. ./ *n* clock that rings a bell to waken one in the morning.

alas /əˈlæs/ *interj* cry of grief.

albatross /ˈælbətrɒs/ *n* a kind of large white seabird.

albino /ælˈbiːnəʊ/ *n, adj* (person or animal) lacking colouring matter in the body.

album /ˈælbəm/ *n* book of plain, unprinted pages for collecting stamps, pictures, etc.

albumen /ˈælbjʊmən/ *n* white liquid in an egg; material of the same kind as this.

alchemist /ˈælkəmɪst/ *n* one who in old times studied the nature of matter, chiefly with the aim of changing other materials into gold, or of finding a liquid that would make men live for ever. *n* **alchemy** /ˈælkəmɪ/ study of such things.

alcohol /ˈælkəhɒl/ *n* pure form of that liquid which gives wine, beer, and other such drinks

their power to change one's state of mind. *adj*

alcoholic /ˌælkəˈhɒlɪk/ containing alcohol. *n* one who is ADDICTED to alcohol.

alcove /ˈælkəʊv/ *n* part of a room cut off from the rest, e.g. for a bed.

alderman /ˈɔːldəmən/ *n* one of a group of men who used to govern a city.

ale /eɪl/ *n* drink with a bitter taste made from grain.

alert /əˈlɜːt/ *adj* watchful. *vt* warn (someone) to be watchful. *n* such a warning.

alfresco /ælˈfreskəʊ/ *adj* (of a meal) eaten in the open air.

algebra /ˈældʒɪbrə/ *n* way of calculating in which letters stand for numbers and quantities. *adj* **algebraic** /ˌældʒɪˈbreɪ‑ɪk/.

alias /ˈeɪlɪəs/ *prep* also known as.

alibi /ˈælɪbaɪ/ *n* claim that one could not have done what one is blamed for because one was in another place.

alien /ˈeɪlɪən/ *adj* foreign. *n* foreigner. *vt* **alienate** /ˈeɪlɪəneɪt/ make (someone) dislike one.

alight[1] /əˈlaɪt/ *vi* get down from a carriage, horse, etc.; (of a bird) come to earth, settle.

alight[2] /əˈlaɪt/ *adj, adv* on fire.

align /əˈlaɪn/ *vt* bring into line.

alike /əˈlaɪk/ *adj, adv* like each other.

alimony /ˈælɪmənɪ/ *n* money that must be paid to a woman by her husband to support her after she has been separated from him by law.

alive /əˈlaɪv/ *adj* living; active.

alkali /ˈælkəlaɪ/ *n* substance that NEUTRALIZES an acid. *adj* **alkaline** /ˈælkəlaɪn/.

all /ɔːl/ *pron, det, adj* whole amount; the whole number of; without exception, e.g. *All the children were drowned.* **once and for all** = one last time. **all over** = over the whole surface. **after all** = after considering everything. **not at all** = certainly not; to no degree.

Allah /ˈælə/ *n* Arabic word for God.

allay /əˈleɪ/ *vt* make less, make calm, e.g. *To allay pain.*

allege /əˈledʒ/ *vt* say as a fact, e.g. *He alleges that he was there.* *n* **allegation** /ˌælɪˈgeɪʃən/.

allegiance /əˈliːdʒəns/ *n* loyalty, duty to one's ruler (king, etc.).

allegory /ˈælɪgərɪ/ *n* story in which persons and things stand for special ideas; lesson taught in the form of a story. *adj* **allegorical** /ˌælɪˈgɒrɪkəl/.

allergy /ˈælədʒɪ/ *n* condition of one for whom even small quantities of some substance, harmless to most people, cause suffering. *adj* **allergic** /əˈlɜːdʒɪk/ having an allergy.

alleviate /əˈliːvɪeɪt/ *vt* make less, or easier to bear, e.g. *To alleviate pain.*

alley /ˈælɪ/ *n* narrow path or road between buildings. **a blind alley** = road that leads nowhere.

alliance /əˈlaɪəns/ *n* friendship between governments promising to help each other, esp. in time of war.

alligator

alligator /'ælɪgeɪtə/ *n* American reptile with four legs, a long tail and a large mouth, living in rivers.

alliteration /ə,lɪtə'reɪʃən/ *n* beginning several words with the same sound, e.g. Sing a Song of Sixpence. *vi* **alliterate** /ə'lɪtəreɪt/.

allocate /'æləkeɪt/ *vt* set apart for a special person, or special purpose. *n* **allocation** /,ælə'keɪʃən/.

allot /ə'lɒt/ *vt* give a part to each person. *n* **allotment** /ə'lɒtmənt/ part of a field divided up among persons, so as to give each a small vegetable garden.

allow /ə'laʊ/ *vt* permit, let (someone) have or do. *n* **allowance** /ə'laʊəns/ payment of money other than for work done. **make allowances for, allow for** = not forget (something) when judging.

alloy /'ælɔɪ/ *n* mixture of metals. *vt* /ə'lɔɪ/ mix (metals).

allude to /ə'luːd/ *vt* speak of indirectly, e.g. *He did not say Mr Smith's name, but it was clear he was alluding to him.* *n* **allusion** /ə'luːʒən/.

allure /ə'lʊə/ *vt* charm; draw on; win the love of.

alluvial /ə'luːvɪəl/ *adj* (of soil) left by rivers or FLOODS.

ally /ə'laɪ/ *vt* form an ALLIANCE with or between; unite, e.g. families in marriage, countries in making war. **closely allied to** = very like, of the same kind. *adj* **allied** related; alike. *n* /'ælaɪ/ member of an ALLIANCE.

almanac /'ɔːlmənæk/ *n* list of days, months, etc.

almighty /ɔːl'maɪtɪ/ *adj* having all power, e.g. *Almighty God.*

almond

almond /'ɑːmənd/ *n* a kind of tree; the nut of this tree.

almost /'ɔːlməʊst/ *adv* nearly.

alms /ɑːmz/ *n* gifts to the poor. *n* **almshouse** /'ɑːmzhaʊs/ house used as a home for the old poor.

aloe /'æləʊ/ *n* a kind of plant with thick leaves, growing chiefly in hot countries, from which a very bitter liquid is obtained and used as a medicine.

aloft /ə'lɒft/ *adj, adv* high up, especially on a ship, up among the sails.

alone /ə'ləʊn/ *adj, adv* separate; not with others. **to leave alone** = not to trouble. **he did not speak to me, let alone help me** = did not help me, did not even speak to me.

along /ə'lɒŋ/ *prep* following the length of, from end to end of, e.g. *To walk along the road.* *adv* on, forward, e.g. *Move along.* **all along** = all the time. **along with** = together with.

alongside /ə'lɒŋsaɪd/ *adv, prep* by the side (of).

aloof /ə'luːf/ *adj* proudly keeping oneself separate from others.

aloud /ə'laʊd/ *adv* so as to be heard.

Alps /ælps/ high mountains in Switzerland and neighbouring countries. *adj* **Alpine** /'ælpaɪn/.

alpaca /æl'pækə/ *n* **1** South American animal, like a sheep, with long fine wool. **2** cloth made from this wool—often mixed with silk or cotton.

alpha /'ælfə/ *n* first Greek letter, often used to mark work as being of good or very good quality.

alphabet /'ælfəbet/ *n* list of letters used in writing a language; in English A, B, C, D, etc. **alphabetical order** = in the order of the letters of the alphabet.

already /ɔːl'redɪ/ *adv* even before this time.

alright /ɔːl'raɪt/ *sl* all right.

also /'ɔːlsəʊ/ *adv* too; further.

altar /'ɔːltə/ *n* raised place on which offerings are made to a god; table at the end of a Christian church. **to lead to the altar** = marry.

alter /'ɔːltə/ *v* change. *n* **alteration** /,ɔːltə'reɪʃən/.

altercation /,ɔːltə'keɪʃən/ *n* quarrel.

alternate /ɔːl'tɜːnət/ *adj* every other /'ɔːltəneɪt/ *v* pass from one to another, then back to the first, and so on. *n* **alternation** /,ɔːltə'neɪʃən/. *n* **alternating current** /'.... ,../ flow of electricity to and fro along a wire about 50 times per second.

alternative /ɔːl'tɜːnətɪv/ *n* choice. *adj* other; able to be chosen instead.

although /ɔːl'ðəʊ/ *conj* though, e.g. *Although it is raining, I shall go* = it is raining, but I shall still go.

altitude /'æltɪtjuːd/ *n* height, e.g. of mountains.

alto /'æltəʊ/ *n* very deep voice of a boy, or very high voice of a man.

altogether /,ɔːltə'geðə/ *adv* **1** completely. **2** all things considered.

altruist /'æltruɪst/ *n* one who thinks of the good of others rather than of his own. *adj* **altruistic** /,æltru'ɪstɪk/.

aluminium /,æljʊ'mɪnɪəm/ *n* a white metal of light weight.

always /'ɔːlweɪz/ *adv* at all times; for ever.

am /m, əm/ *strong* æm/ *v* (present form of **be** used after 'I').

amalgam /ə'mælgəm/ *n* MERCURY mixed with another metal; any mixture. *v* **amalgamate** /ə'mælgəmeɪt/ mix together; unite.

amass /ə'mæs/ *vt* collect a large quantity of.

amateur /'æmətə, 'æmətʃə/ *n* one who studies an art, or plays a game, for the love of it, not for money. *adj* **amateurish** /'æmətərɪʃ/ done by an unpractised person.

amaze /əˈmeɪz/ vt surprise greatly.

ambassador /æmˈbæsədə/ n officer of the government sent to another country to act for his own government.

amber /ˈæmbə/ n clear yellow stone-like material, formed of the liquid of a tree changed in the course of thousands of years into this stone-like condition.

ambidextrous /ˌæmbɪˈdekstrəs/ adj able to do things equally well with either hand.

ambiguous /æmˈbɪgjʊəs/ adj not clear as to meaning; which may be understood in more than one way.

ambition /æmˈbɪʃən/ n desire for success and power; the success desired, e.g. It is my ambition to be a great singer. adj **ambitious** /æmˈbɪʃəs/.

amble /ˈæmbəl/ vi (of a horse) move the two right legs, then the two left; go at an easy speed.

ambulance /ˈæmbjʊləns/ n carriage for the sick or wounded.

ambush /ˈæmbʊʃ/ vt hide in a secret place in order to attack (someone) by surprise. n such an attack.

ameliorate /əˈmiːlɪəreɪt/ vt make better.

amen /ɑːˈmen, eɪˈmen/ interj word said at the end of a prayer, meaning "So may it be".

amenable /əˈmiːnəbəl/ adj able to be controlled or led.

amend /əˈmend/ vt make (something) better; change the words of (a law or rule) which is being considered in a meeting. n **amendment** /əˈmendmənt/ such a change. **to make amends** = do something to pay for, or make good, some harm done to another.

amenity /əˈmiːnɪtɪ/ n advantage (of a place or object), esp. in respect of CONVENIENCE.

amethyst /ˈæməθɪst/ n a kind of red-blue jewel.

amiable /ˈeɪmɪəbəl/ adj friendly, kind.

amicable /ˈæmɪkəbəl/ adj friendly.

amid(st) /əˈmɪd(st)/ prep in the middle of. adv **amidships** /əˈmɪdˌʃɪps/ in the middle of a ship.

amiss /əˈmɪs/ adv wrong, wrongly. **nothing comes amiss to him** = he is prepared for, able to deal with, anything.

amity /ˈæmɪtɪ/ n friendship.

ammeter /ˈæmɪtə, ˈæmˌmiːtə/ n instrument for measuring electric flow in AMPERES.

ammonia /əˈməʊnɪə/ n strong-smelling gas, often used in making ice.

ammonium /əˈməʊnɪəm/ n AMMONIA mixed with water or an acid; liquid used for cleaning clothes.

ammunition /ˌæmjʊˈnɪʃən/ n powder and shot for guns.

amnesia /æmˈniːzɪə/ n loss of memory.

amnesty /ˈæmnəstɪ/ n setting free of all prisoners, a general forgiving of wrongdoers by a ruler (e.g. king).

amoeba /əˈmiːbə/ n simplest living creature, found in water.

amok /əˈmɒk/ adv see **amuck**.

among(st) /əˈmʌŋ(st)/ prep mixed with; in the middle of; between.

amorous /ˈæmərəs/ adj easily moved to love.

amorphous /əˈmɔːfəs/ adj shapeless.

amount /əˈmaʊnt/ vi add up to; become equal to, e.g. Your words amount to this = this is the real meaning of all that you have said. n the whole; the result of adding; certain quantity or number.

ampere /ˈæmpeə/ n measure of the amount of electricity passing along a wire.

ampersand /ˈæmpəsænd/ n the sign **&**, meaning 'and'.

amphibious /æmˈfɪbɪəs/ adj living both on land and in water. n **amphibian** /æmˈfɪbɪən/ amphibious creature.

amphitheatre /ˈæmfɪˌθɪətə/ n building used for public games and shows.

ample /ˈæmpəl/ adj big enough, large. adv **amply** /ˈæmplɪ/ fully.

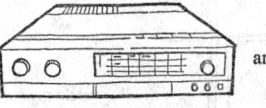
amplifier

amplify /ˈæmplɪfaɪ/ vt make larger or louder. n **amplifier** /ˈæmplɪfaɪə/ electric instrument used to make sounds louder.

amputate /ˈæmpjʊteɪt/ vt cut off (a limb).

amuck, amok /əˈmʌk/ **to run amuck** = become mad and try to kill people.

amulet /ˈæmjʊlət/ n thing worn as a magic charm.

amuse /əˈmjuːz/ vt cause time to pass pleasantly for (someone); make (someone) laugh. n **amusement** /əˈmjuːzmənt/ feeling of laughter; pleasant way of passing time.

an /ən; strong æn/ det (form of **a** used before VOWELS).

anachronism /əˈnækrənɪzəm/ n thing that could not happen at the date supposed, e.g. "Julius Caesar got into his motor-car."

anaemia /əˈniːmɪə/ n lack of blood; weakness or bad quality of the blood.

anaesthesia /ˌænɪsˈθiːzɪə/ n loss of all the senses in a deep sleep, caused by doctors before they cut open the body of a sick person. n **anaesthetic** /ˌænɪsˈθetɪk/ substance which causes such a state. vt **anaesthetize** /əˈniːsθətaɪz/ cause such a state. n **anaesthetist** /əˈniːsθətɪst/ one who causes this state.

anagram /ˈænəgræm/ n new word made up out of the letters of another, e.g. Name—Mean.

analogy /əˈnælədʒɪ/ n agreement or likeness in certain ways, e.g. On the analogy of Though, Through should be said as Throw.

analyse /ˈænəlaɪz/ vt divide up a thing into the parts of which it is made; separate out the different materials of which a mixed material is made up, e.g. The scientist analysed the liquid

9

and found that it was made up of A, B, and C (various materials). n **analysis** /ə'næləsɪs/ act of or result of analysing something n **analyst** /'ænəlɪst/ one who analyses. adj **analytical** /ˌænə'lɪtɪkəl/.

anarchy /'ænəkɪ/ n state of having no government at all. n **anarchist** /'ænəkɪst/ one who wishes to destroy all government.

anathema /ə'næθɪmə/ n solemn curse; thing cursed.

anatomy /ə'nætəmɪ/ n study of the parts of the body. n **anatomist** /ə'nætəmɪst/ one who studies or teaches anatomy. adj **anatomical** /ˌænə'tɒmɪkəl/.

ancestor /'ænsestə, 'ænsəstə/ n person from whom one is descended, e.g. Great-great-grandfather, etc. adj **ancestral** /æn'sestrəl/ n (sing) **ancestry** /ænsəstrɪ/ one's ancestors.

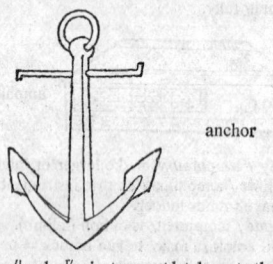

anchor

anchor /'æŋkə/ n instrument let down to the bottom of the sea to prevent a ship from moving. v fix (a ship) in one place with an anchor. **anchorage** /'æŋkərɪdʒ/ n good place in which to anchor a ship.

anchovy /'æntʃəvɪ/ n small fish having a very strong taste, salted and used for food.

ancient /'eɪnʃənt/ adj old, belonging to a time long ago. **the ancients** = those who lived long ago.

and /ənd, ən; strong ænd/ conj (word used to join two sentences).

anecdote /'ænɪkdəʊt/ n short story.

anemone /ə'nemənɪ/ n a kind of flower. n **sea-anemone** /'. . ˌ. . ./ creature like a flower, living in the sea.

anew /ə'njuː/ adv again.

angel /'eɪndʒəl/ n spirit who carries God's messages. adj **angelic** /æn'dʒelɪk/.

anger /'æŋgə/ n feeling that makes people want to quarrel, fight and do harm. vt cause this feeling (in someone).

angler

angle[1] /'æŋgəl/ v catch (fish) with a hook. **to angle for** = try to lead a person on to give one (some desired thing). n **angler** /'æŋglə/ man who catches fish with a hook.

angle[2] /'æŋgəl/ n meeting of two lines; corner.

Anglican /'æŋglɪkən/ adj having to do with the Church of England.

anglicize /'æŋglɪsaɪz/ vt make English in form or custom.

Anglo- /'æŋgləʊ/ English. n, adj **Anglo-Saxon** /ˌæŋgləʊ 'sæksən/ (one) of a group of early settlers in England from Northern Europe, or of their descendants.

angry /'æŋgrɪ/ adj being in a state of anger.

anguish /'æŋgwɪʃ/ n great pain, or sorrow.

angular /'æŋgjʊlə/ adj having many sharp corners.

animal /'ænɪməl/ n living thing which is not a plant; creature. **animal desires** = like those of an animal.

animate /'ænɪmeɪt/ vt give life to. **animated talk** = talk that is full of life, clever, amusing. **animated cartoon** or n **animation** /ˌænɪ'meɪʃən/ cinema film of drawings that move, e.g. Donald Duck.

animosity /ˌænɪ'mɒsətɪ/ n strong hatred.

aniseed /'ænɪsiːd/ n seeds used in making sweets and strong drink.

ankle /'æŋkəl/ n part of the leg where the foot is joined on. n **anklet** /'æŋklət/ jewelled band worn on the ankle.

annals /'ænəlz/ n history written down year by year.

annex /ə'neks/ vt add; join on; (of governments) add to one's own country. n **annexe** /'æneks/ small building added to, or used as well as, a larger one, e.g. The annexe of a hotel.

annihilate /ə'naɪəleɪt/ vt destroy completely.

anniversary /ˌænɪ'vɜːsərɪ/ n return each year of a certain date; date on which some great event is remembered each year.

Anno Domini /ˌænəʊ 'dɒmɪnaɪ/ (shortened to AD) in the year of Our Lord, e.g. AD 1900 = 1900 years since Christ was born.

annotate /'ænəteɪt/ vt add notes to (a written work) explaining parts of it.

announce /ə'naʊns/ make something known publicly. n **announcement** /ə'naʊnsmənt/ act of announcing; thing announced. n **announcer** /ə'naʊnsə/ one who gives news of what is on the radio or television.

annoy /ə'nɔɪ/ vt trouble; make angry. n **annoyance** /ə'nɔɪəns/ feeling of anger.

annual /'ænjʊəl/ adj happening every year. n plant which grows up and dies in a year; book of facts, stories or pictures printed and sold every year.

annuity /ə'njuːətɪ/ n amount of money paid every year.

annul /ə'nʌl/ vt bring to nothing; destroy.

anoint /ə'nɔɪnt/ vt put oil on; make holy by putting oil on.

anomalous /ə'nɒmələs/ adj unusual, irregular or

not according to natural law. *n* **anomaly** /ə'nɒmǝlɪ/, e.g. *A wingless bird is an anomaly.*

anonymous /ə'nɒnɪməs/ *adj* nameless; without the name of the writer. *n* **anonymity** /ˌænə'nɪmǝtɪ/.

answer /'ɑːnsə/ *v* speak or write in return. **to answer the bell** = go to the door when the door bell rings. **I can answer for his skill** = I can promise that he is skilful. *n* **1** something said or written in return. **2** correct result of a sum, problem, etc. *adj* **answerable** /'ɑːnsǝrǝbǝl/ ACCOUNTABLE, e.g. *You will be answerable for this* = you will be asked to explain this, may be blamed for this.

ant /ænt/ *n* small insect which builds its nest in the ground, or above the ground in the shape of a small hill.

antagonist /æn'tægǝnɪst/ *n* person on the opposite side. *vt* **antagonize** /æn'tægǝnaɪz/ make (someone) one's enemy.

antarctic /æn'tɑːktɪk/ *n*, *adj* (of the) very cold part in the farthest southern part of the earth.

ante- /'æntɪ/ before.

antecedent /ˌæntɪ'siːdǝnt/ *adj* going before, before in time.

antedate /ˌæntɪ'deɪt/ *vt* give an earlier date than the real date; PRECEDE.

antelope /'æntɪlǝʊp/ *n* a kind of animal like a deer.

ante meridiem /ˌæntɪ mǝ'rɪdɪǝm/ (shortened to **a.m.**) in the morning, before 12 o'clock.

antenatal /ˌæntɪ'neɪtl/ *adj* before birth.

antenna →
AERIAL

antenna /æn'tenǝ/ *n* **1** one of the long hairs at the front of an insect's head, used in feeling. **2** AERIAL.

anterior /æn'tɪǝrɪǝ/ *adj* earlier.

anteroom /'æntɪrʊm, -ruːm/ *n* small room through which one enters a larger room; waiting-room.

anthem /'ænθǝm/ *n* piece of music sung in a church. **the National Anthem** = special song of a country, e.g. "God save the Queen" is the British national anthem.

anther /'ænθǝ/ *n* that part of a flower which carries the POLLEN.

anthology /æn'θɒlǝdʒɪ/ *n* collection of poems or other written pieces.

anthracite /'ænθrǝsaɪt/ *n* very hard coal.

anthrax /'ænθræks/ *n* dangerous disease of cattle, sometimes also attacking man.

anthropoid /'ænθrǝpɔɪd/ *adj* like a man, e.g. *An anthropoid* APE.

anthropology /ˌænθrǝ'pɒlǝdʒɪ/ *n* study of the races of man.

anti- /'æntɪ/ against, e.g. *Anti-smoking* = not in favour of people smoking pipes or cigarettes.

antibiotic /ˌæntɪbaɪ'ɒtɪk/ *n* substance produced by a living thing that prevents the growth of other living things, e.g. as PENICILLIN prevents growth of germs.

antibody /'æntɪbɒdɪ/ *n* material formed in the body to fight against a disease.

antic /'æntɪk/ *n* strange trick, peculiar movement.

anticipate /æn'tɪsɪpeɪt/ *vt* think of (something) before it actually comes; expect.

anticlimax /ˌæntɪ'klaɪmæks/ *n* sudden and laughable loss of force, e.g. in a speech; foolish saying following good sense.

antidote /'æntɪdǝʊt/ *n* something given to prevent the effects of a poison or disease.

antipathy /æn'tɪpǝθɪ/ *n* dislike.

antipodes /æn'tɪpǝdiːz/ *n* that part of the world just on the opposite side to our own part.

antiquarian /ˌæntɪ'kweǝrɪǝn/, **antiquary** /æn'tɪkwǝrɪ, 'æntɪkwǝrɪ/ *n* one who studies or collects old things. *adj*, *n* **antique** /æn'tiːk/ old (thing) esp. if valuable because of age. *adj* **antiquated** /'æntɪkweɪtɪd/ old, not such as is used today. *n* **antiquity** /æn'tɪkwǝtɪ/ thing that is of value or interest because of its age. **in antiquity** = long ago.

antiseptic /ˌæntɪ'septɪk/ *adj*, *n* (liquid or powder) which kills the seeds of disease.

antithesis /æn'tɪθǝsɪs/ *n* exact opposite. *adj* **antithetical** /ˌæntɪ'θetɪkǝl/.

antler /'æntlǝ/ *n* horn of a deer.

antonym /'æntǝnɪm/ *n* word meaning the opposite, e.g. "bad" is the antonym of "good".

anus /'eɪnǝs/ *n* opening through which waste matter leaves the body.

anvil /'ænvɪl/ *n* large mass of iron on which pieces of hot iron (etc.) are hammered into shape.

anxiety /æŋ'zaɪǝtɪ/ *n* feeling of fear and doubt about the future. *adj* **anxious** /'æŋkʃǝs/ feeling anxiety; causing anxiety.

any /'enɪ/ *det* **1** no matter what or which, e.g. *He'll drink any wine.* **2** some (in questions, in NEGATIVE sentences, and after 'if') e.g. *I didn't see any smoke.* *pron* **anybody** /'enɪbɒdɪ/ or **anyone** /'enɪwʌn/ any person. *adv* **anyhow** /'enɪhaʊ/ in any way; no matter what happens. *pron* **anything** /'enɪθɪŋ/ any thing. *adv* **anywhere** /'enɪweǝ/ in or to any place.

apart /ǝ'pɑːt/ *adv* separately. **to set apart** = keep for some special purpose. **joking apart** = speaking seriously. **apart from** = other than.

apartheid /ǝ'pɑːtheɪt/ *n* separation of white and coloured peoples in South Africa.

apartment /ǝ'pɑːtmǝnt/ *n* room or lodgings.

apathetic /ˌæpǝ'θetɪk/ *adj* lacking feeling or interest. *n* **apathy** /'æpǝθɪ/.

ape /eɪp/ *n* large monkey-like creature with no

tail. *vt* behave just like (another person); to copy exactly.

aperture /ˈæpətʃə'/ *n* opening.

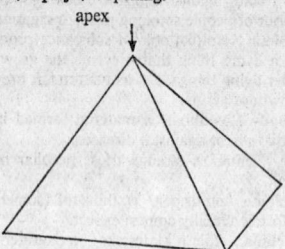

apex

apex /ˈeɪpeks/ *n* pointed top of anything.

aphorism /ˈæfərɪzəm/ *n* short wise saying.

apiece /əˈpiːs/ *adv* for each one, e.g. *A penny apiece.*

aplomb /əˈplɒm/ *n* boldness and faith in oneself, in speaking or manner.

apocryphal /əˈpɒkrɪfəl/ *adj* of doubtful truth; not contained in that part of the Bible which is generally accepted.

apogee /ˈæpədʒiː/ *n* greatest distance of a star (etc.) from the Earth.

apologize /əˈpɒlədʒaɪz/ *vi* say that one is sorry for something that one has done. *n* **apology** /əˈpɒlədʒɪ/ act of apologizing. *adj* **apologetic** /əˌpɒləˈdʒetɪk/.

apoplexy /ˈæpəpleksɪ/ *n* bursting of a blood-vessel in the brain, causing loss of power to move or feel.

apostle /əˈpɒsəl/ *n* person sent to teach men about God.

apostrophe /əˈpɒstrəfɪ/ *n* the written or printed mark, ', e.g. as in **isn't.**

appal /əˈpɔːl/ *vt* make very frightened or shock greatly.

apparatus /ˌæpəˈreɪtəs/ *n* instruments and machines, esp. those used by doctors and scientists.

apparel /əˈpærəl/ *n* clothing.

apparent /əˈpærənt/ *adj* seeming; very clear to see or understand. *adv* **apparently** /əˈpærəntlɪ/ as it seems.

apparition /ˌæpəˈrɪʃən/ *n* appearance, e.g. of the spirit of a dead man.

appeal /əˈpiːl/ *vi* **1** ask eagerly and anxiously. **2** ask a higher court of law to change the judgment given already by a lower court. **does not appeal to** = does not interest. *adj* **appealing** worthy of pity; moving the heart.

appear /əˈpɪə'/ *vi* come before; be seen by; seem. *n* **appearance** /əˈpɪərəns/ act of appearing; way something appears.

appease /əˈpiːz/ *vt* make peaceful; satisfy. *n* **appeasement** /əˈpiːzmənt/ trying to keep peace by giving way to an enemy.

appellation /ˌæpəˈleɪʃən/ *n* name.

append /əˈpend/ *vt* join on or add. *n* **appendage** /əˈpendɪdʒ/ thing added to or hanging from another thing.

appendix /əˈpendɪks/ (*pl* **appendices** /əˈpendɪsiːz/) *n* **1** long note added at the end of a book. **2** small pipe leading off the bowel. *n* **appendicitis** /əˌpendɪˈsaɪtɪs/ disease of the appendix.

appertain /ˌæpəˈteɪn/ *vi* belong.

appetite /ˈæpətaɪt/ *n* desire (esp. for food). *adj* **appetizing** /ˈæpətaɪzɪŋ/ causing desire (for food). *n* **appetizer** /ˈæpətaɪzə'/ something that causes desire for food.

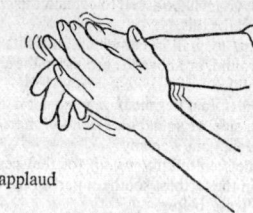

applaud

applaud /əˈplɔːd/ *v* praise; praise (someone) loudly by shouting or **CLAPPING.** *n* **applause** /əˈplɔːz/ praises, shouts of praise.

apple /ˈæpəl/ *n* a kind of fruit; the tree from which this fruit comes. **apple of my eye** = most dearly loved person.

appliance /əˈplaɪəns/ *n* instrument used for some special purpose.

apply /əˈplaɪ/ *vt* **1** cause to touch, put on, e.g. *To apply paint.* **2** put into practice. *vi* **1** ask (for something, e.g. employment or permission to do something), e.g. *This doesn't apply to you* = this does not concern you, this has nothing to do with you. *adj* **applicable** /ˈæplɪkəbəl, əˈplɪkəbəl/ able to be applied. *n* **applicant** /ˈæplɪkənt/ one who asks for employment, etc. *n* **application** /ˌæplɪˈkeɪʃən/ act of applying.

appoint /əˈpɔɪnt/ *vt* choose (someone) for an office. *n* **appointment** /əˈpɔɪntmənt/ **1** meeting arranged, e.g. *To keep an appointment* = be present as arranged. **2** office for which one is chosen.

apportion /əˈpɔːʃən/ *vt* divide out into shares.

apposite /ˈæpəzɪt/ *adj* well chosen; just right, e.g. word or saying.

apposition /ˌæpəˈzɪʃən/ *n* putting of one thing or word next to another.

appraise /əˈpreɪz/ *vt* set a value on. *n* **appraisal** /əˈpreɪzəl/.

appreciate /əˈpriːʃɪeɪt/ *vt* **1** judge the value of; feel that a thing is good and understand in what way it is good. **2** understand, e.g. *I appreciate your difficulty.* *vi* increase in price. *adj* **appreciable** /əˈpriːʃəbəl/ enough to be noticed. *n* **appreciation** /əˌpriːʃɪˈeɪʃən/ favourable judgment showing pleasure. *adj* **appreciative** /əˈpriːʃətɪv/ able to understand and be pleased by things.

apprehend /ˌæprɪˈhend/ *vt* 1 take hold of, seize. 2 understand. 3 fear. *n* **apprehension** /ˌæprɪˈhenʃən/ understanding; fear. *adj* **apprehensive** /ˌæprɪˈhensɪv/ afraid.

apprentice /əˈprentɪs/ *n* one who has promised to work for someone for a number of years in order to learn an art or trade.

approach /əˈprəʊtʃ/ *vt* move towards; come near to. **approach him on the matter** = ask him about it.

approbation /ˌæprəˈbeɪʃən/ *n* thinking well of something.

appropriate /əˈprəʊprɪət/ *adj* proper; right for the purpose. *vt* **appropriate** /əˈprəʊprɪeɪt/ take as one's own. *n* **appropriation** /əˌprəʊprɪˈeɪʃən/ 1 act of taking for oneself. 2 act of setting a thing apart for a special person or purpose.

approve /əˈpruːv/ *v* think well (of); say that a thing is good. *n* **approval** /əˈpruːvəl/ (act of) thinking well of something. **goods on approval** = goods that may be sent back to the shop if not liked.

approximate /əˈprɒksɪmət/ *adj* nearly exact; not exact. *vi* **approximate** /əˈprɒksɪmeɪt/ be near (to the truth).

apricot /ˈeɪprɪkɒt/ *n* orange-yellow fruit with a large stone in it.

April /ˈeɪprəl/ *n* the fourth month of the year.

apron /ˈeɪprən/ *n* piece of cloth worn in front to protect the clothes. **tied to his mother's apron strings** = too long dependent on his mother.

apropos /ˌæprəˈpəʊ/ *French adj* well suited to the subject which is being spoken about. **apropos of** = in regard to, about (some subject on which we have just been speaking).

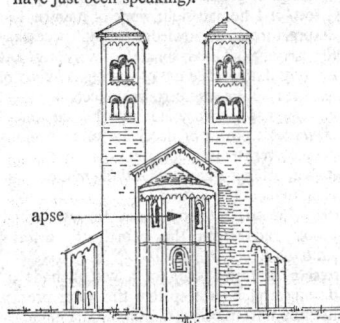

apse

apse /æps/ *n* east end of a church which is half-round, instead of square.

apt /æpt/ *adj* well suited. **apt to give trouble** = that will probably give trouble. *n* **aptitude** /ˈæptɪtjuːd/ natural cleverness in some particular work.

aqualung /ˈækwəlʌŋ/ *n* instrument used for breathing under water.

aquarium /əˈkweərɪəm/ *n* place specially made for keeping fishes, water-plants and water-animals.

aquatic /əˈkwætɪk/ *adj* having to do with water; living in water.

aqueduct /ˈækwədʌkt/ *n* pipe or path made for bringing water.

arable /ˈærəbəl/ *adj* (of land) fit for PLOUGHING.

arbiter /ˈɑːbɪtə/ or **arbitrator** /ˈɑːbɪtreɪtə/ *n* man who judges or decides. *vi* **arbitrate** /ˈɑːbɪtreɪt/ judge; decide who is right or wrong. *n* **arbitration** /ˌɑːbɪˈtreɪʃən/. *adj* **arbitrary** /ˈɑːbɪtrərɪ/ not according to any rule; freely chosen.

arbour /ˈɑːbə/ *n* seat or walk in a garden shaded by trees.

arc /ɑːk/ *n* part of the edge of a circle. *n* **arc-light** /ˈɑːk laɪt/ electric lamp that gives a very powerful white light.

arcade /ɑːˈkeɪd/ *n* row of arches; covered street with shops on both sides.

arch¹ /ɑːtʃ/ *n* curved part of a building which carries weight, e.g. above a door or window; curved part of the bottom of the foot. *vt* cause to have the shape of an arch, e.g. *A cat arches its back.*

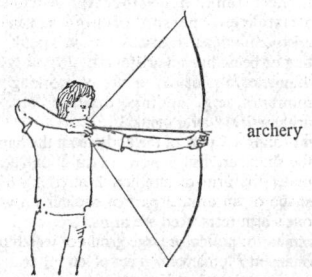

archery

arch² /ɑːtʃ/ *adj* chief; head, e.g. *My arch-enemy* = chief enemy. **an arch look** = an inviting look.

archaeology /ˌɑːkɪˈɒlədʒɪ/ *n* study of ancient things, e.g. art, graves, ruins etc. *adj* **archaeological** /ˌɑːkɪəˈlɒdʒɪkəl/.

archaic /ɑːˈkeɪɪk/ *adj* very old; not used any more. *n* **archaism** /ˈɑːkeɪˌɪzəm, ɑːˈkeɪɪzəm/ use of an old word or form of words no longer in common use.

archangel /ˈɑːkˌeɪndʒəl/ *n* chief ANGEL.

archbishop /ˌɑːtʃˈbɪʃəp/ *n* high officer in the Christian Church.

archer /ˈɑːtʃə/ *n* one who shoots with a BOW and arrows. *n* **archery** /ˈɑːtʃərɪ/ art of shooting with bows and arrows.

archipelago /ˌɑːkɪˈpeləgəʊ/ *n* group of small islands.

architect /ˈɑːkɪtekt/ *n* man who makes the plans for new buildings. *n* **architecture** /ˈɑːkɪtektʃə/ art of planning buildings, esp. beautiful buildings.

archives /ˈɑːkaɪvz/ *n* government reports and notes.

archway /ˈɑːtʃweɪ/ *n* way by which one passes under an arch.

arctic /'ɑːktɪk/ *adj, n* (of the) very cold part in the farthest north.

ardent /'ɑːdənt *l adj* hot; eager. *n* **ardour** /'ɑːdə *l* eagerness.

arduous / ɑːdjʊəs/ *adj* difficult; causing much hard work.

are /ə *l* strong ɑː *l v* (form of **be** used after 'you', and in the plural).

area /'eərɪə/ *n* amount of space (on a surface); place.

arena /ə'riːnə/ *n* central space with seats all round it, used for games or public shows.

argue /'ɑːgjuː/ *v* talk to a person trying to prove or disprove (something). *n* **argument** /'ɑːgjʊmənt/ talk of this kind; reason for a belief. *adj* **argumentative** /ˌɑːgjʊ'mentətɪv/ eager to argue.

arid /'ærɪd/ *adj* receiving no rain; uninteresting or useless.

arise /ə'raɪz/ *vi* rise up; appear or be noticed.

aristocracy /ˌærɪs'tɒkrəsɪ/ *n* **1** government by persons of noble rank. **2** lords and people of highest rank. *n* **aristocrat** /'ærɪstəkræt, ə'rɪstəkræt/ person of high rank. *adj* **aristocratic** /ˌærɪstə'krætɪk, əˌrɪstə'krætɪk/ acting or being like an aristocrat.

arithmetic /ə'rɪθmətɪk/ *n* art of working with numbers, e.g. adding, dividing etc. *adj* **arithmetical** /ˌærɪθ'metɪkəl/.

arm /ɑːm/ *n* **1** part of the body from the hand to the shoulder. **arm in arm** = arm of one person under the arm of another. **2** anything of the shape of an arm. **3** part of a chair on which one's arm rests. And see **arms**.

armada /ɑː'mɑːdə/ *n* large group of warships.

armament /'ɑːməmənt/ *n* act of getting ready for war; a nation's armies, warships; guns on a ship or in a fort.

armadillo /ˌɑːmə'dɪləʊ/ *n* South American animal which has a ringed shell.

armistice /'ɑːmɪstɪs/ *n* agreement to stop fighting for a time.

armour /'ɑːmə *l n* iron covering to protect against weapons or shot. *n* **armourer** /'ɑːmərə *l* one who makes and repairs armour. *n* **armoury** /'ɑːmərɪ/ place where weapons are made or stored.

armpit /'ɑːmˌpɪt/ *n* hollow under the arm near the shoulder.

arms /ɑːmz/ *n* (*pl*) weapons. **small arms** = guns that are carried in the hand. **take up arms against** = get ready to fight against. **lay down arms** = stop fighting. **up in arms against** = complaining angrily against. **coat of arms** = figures on a shield or flag as a sign of noble birth, rank and good family. *vt* arm give weapons to. **armed forces** = the army, AIR FORCE, and NAVY of a country.

army /'ɑːmɪ/ *n* large group of soldiers.

aroma /ə'rəʊmə/ *n* sweet smell. *adj* **aromatic** /ˌærə'mætɪk/.

arose /ə'rəʊz/ p.t. of **arise**.

around /ə'raʊnd/ *prep, adv* about; in a circle; near.

arouse /ə'raʊz/ *vt* awaken; excite to action.

arrange /ə'reɪndʒ/ *vt* set in order; settle or decide; change a thing so as to suit it to a new purpose, e.g. *To arrange a story as a play in the theatre.* *n* **arrangement** /ə'reɪndʒmənt/.

array /ə'reɪ/ *vt* put in order, e.g. soldiers for battle; to dress, e.g. *She arrayed herself in all her finery* = dressed herself in all her fine clothes.

arrears /ə'rɪəz/ *n* (*pl*) work left undone; money owed which has not yet been paid.

arrest /ə'rest/ *vt* **1** stop. **2** (of a policeman) seize and take to the police station (someone thought to be acting or to have acted unlawfully).

arrive /ə'raɪv/ *vi* get to a place. *n* **arrival** /ə'raɪvəl/ act of arriving; person who has just arrived.

arrogant /'ærəgənt/ *adj* claiming honour to which one has no right; very proud. *n* **arrogance** /'ærəgəns/.

arrow

arrow /'ærəʊ/ *n* stick pointed at one end, with feathers on the other end, shot from a BOW.

arrowroot /'ærəʊruːt/ *n* West Indian plant boiled with milk or water as a food for sick persons.

arsenal /'ɑːsənəl/ *n* place where governments make and store instruments and materials of war.

arsenic /'ɑːsənɪk/ *n* poisonous powder used sometimes as a medicine for the skin.

arson /'ɑːsən/ *n* unlawful act of setting fire to buildings or goods.

art /ɑːt/ *n* **1** human skill; work of man (not of natural forces). **2** knowledge and skill necessary for carrying out a certain kind of work, e.g. *The art of painting, The art of writing, The art of war.* *n* (*pl*) *:e* **arts** certain subjects of study, e.g. language, history etc., not the sciences. **3** cleverness; power of deceiving or of winning people over to one's opinion.

artefact, artifact /'ɑːtɪfækt/ *n* thing made by ancient man, not by nature.

artery /'ɑːtərɪ/ *n* blood vessel through which blood runs from the heart. *adj* **arterial** /ɑː'tɪərɪəl/.

artesian /ɑː'tiːzɪən/ *adj* (of a WELL) made by driving a pipe so deep that the water presses itself up it from below.

artful /'ɑːtfəl/ *adj* having great skill in deceiving.

arthritis /ɑː'θraɪtɪs/ *n* painful disease of the joints.

artichoke /'ɑːtɪtʃəʊk/ *n* plant with thick leaves, the lower ends of which are eaten. **Jerusalem artichoke** = a kind of white root used as a vegetable.

article /'ɑːtɪkəl/ *n* **1** thing; object. **2** written account of one subject, e.g. in a newspaper. **3** one part of a written agreement. **4** one of a small group of words used with a noun, e.g. in English, 'a' and 'the'. **the definite article** = the word "the". **articled clerk** = APPRENTICE in a law office.

articulate /ɑːˈtɪkjʊleɪt/ v join together; speak clearly. n **articulation** /ɑːˌtɪkjʊˈleɪʃən/ act of speaking, speaking clearly; act of joining, the way in which things (e.g. bones) are joined.

artifice /ˈɑːtɪfɪs/ n trick.

artificial /ˌɑːtɪˈfɪʃəl/ adj made by art, not by nature; pretended, not real.

artillery /ɑːˈtɪləri/ n big guns and the men in charge of them.

artisan /ˌɑːtɪˈzæn/ n skilled workman.

artist /ˈɑːtɪst/ n one who practises drawing, painting, music or the making of beautiful things; one who is specially clever in work of this kind. adj **artistic** /ɑːˈtɪstɪk/ having to do with the making of beautiful things; beautiful; loving beautiful things made by man. n **artistry** /ˈɑːtɪstrɪ/ skill and good taste of an artist.

artless /ˈɑːtləs/ adj simple and natural.

as /əz; strong æz/ prep in the manner of; like; in the position or part of. adv to an equal degree. **as ... as ...** = no less ... than ..., e.g. He's as tall as you. conj 1 when; while. 2 because. 3 in the manner in which.

asbestos /æsˈbestəs, æzˈbestəs/ n soft, white, wool-like material which cannot burn.

ascend /əˈsend/ v climb, go up. n **ascent** /əˈsent/ act of going up a hill; slope. **in the ascendant** = increasing in power and importance. n **ascendancy** /əˈsendənsɪ/ being at the top, having the power. n **ascension** /əˈsenʃən/ going up. **the Ascension** = going up of Christ into heaven.

ascertain /ˌæsəˈteɪn/ vt find out; make sure.

ascetic /əˈsetɪk/ n one who gives up all pleasures and controls his desires.

ascribe /əˈskraɪb/ vt point to (a person or thing) as the cause of (something).

ash[1] /æʃ/ n tree whose wood is used for making handles of spears, etc.

ash[2] /æʃ/ n fine dust left after something has been burnt.

ashamed /əˈʃeɪmd/ adj having a feeling of shame.

ashore /əˈʃɔː/ adv, adj on the shore.

aside /əˈsaɪd/ adv 1 on or to one side. 2 so as not to be heard by everyone.

ask /ɑːsk/ v 1 put or express (a question), e.g. He asked who I was. 2 politely tell (someone to do something), e.g. He asked me to open the window. **ask for** = try to get (someone) to find, give, or make known (something), e.g. You should ask for something if you want it. 3 invite, e.g. Ask a person to dinner.

askance /əˈskɑːns/ **to look askance** = look to one side, as if something were wrong or untrue.

askew /əˈskjuː/ adv, adj not straight; out of order.

asleep /əˈsliːp/ adj, adv sleeping; at rest. **fall asleep** = go into sleep.

asp /æsp/ n a kind of small poisonous snake.

asparagus /əˈspærəgəs/ n a kind of vegetable whose tops are eaten for food.

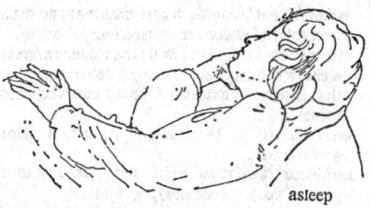

asleep

aspect /ˈæspekt/ n 1 appearance. 2 direction in which a thing faces. 3 way of considering or looking at a thing, e.g. To consider a question in all its aspects.

asperity /əˈsperətɪ/ n roughness, bitterness.

aspersion /əˈspɜːʃən/ n untrue report about a person's character, e.g. Cast aspersions on a person's character = say bad things about it.

asphalt /ˈæsfælt/ n hard black material used in making roads.

asphyxiate /əsˈfɪksɪeɪt/ vt cause (someone) to faint through lack of air. n **asphyxiation** /əsˌfɪksɪˈeɪʃən/.

aspic /ˈæspɪk/ n meat-jelly.

aspire /əˈspaɪə/ vi desire eagerly to reach some high aim. n **aspiration** /ˌæspɪˈreɪʃən/ hope. n **aspirant** /ˈæspɪrənt/ one who hopes.

aspirin /ˈæsprɪn/ n a kind of medicine used to drive away pain, e.g. pain in the head.

ass (1)

ass /æs/ n 1 donkey. 2 sl fool.

assail /əˈseɪl/ vt attack.

assassin /əˈsæsɪn/ n murderer of some important person. vt **assassinate** /əˈsæsɪneɪt/ to murder (some important person, such as a country's leader).

assault /əˈsɔːlt/ n sudden attack.

assay /əˈseɪ/ vt TEST whether (something) is pure.

assemble /əˈsembəl/ v come or bring together in a group. vt fit together (a machine). n **assembly** /əˈsemblɪ/ 1 group of people who have come together for some purpose. 2 the act of bringing the parts of a thing together. n **assembly-line** /ˈ... ˈ/ place where machines are assembled by groups of men, each man in the group adding a different part to the machine.

assent /ə'sent/ *vi* agree. *n* agreement; APPROVAL.

assert /ə'sɜːt/ *vt* declare. *n* **assertion** /ə'sɜːʃən/.

assess /ə'ses/ *vt* find out or fix the value. *n* **assessment** /ə'sesmənt/ act of fixing a value; the value that is fixed. *n* **assessor** /ə'sesəʳ/ one who fixes values.

asset /'æset/ *n* **1** something owned. **2** help; ADVANTAGE.

assiduous /ə'sɪdʒʊəs/ *adj* keeping steadily to a piece of work. *n* **assiduity** /ˌæsɪ'djuːəti/.

assign /ə'saɪn/ *vt* give. *n* **assignment** /ə'saɪnmənt/ something to be done by someone; lesson or part of a lesson for a learner to work on.

assimilate /ə'sɪməleɪt/ *vt* **1** make (one thing) like something else. **2** take in, e.g. food into the body, experience into the mind.

assist /ə'sɪst/ *vt* help. *n* **assistance** /ə'sɪstəns/ help. *n* **assistant** /ə'sɪstənt/ one whose work is to help (e.g. in a shop).

assizes /ə'saɪzɪz/ *n* sitting of a special court of law in country towns for the purpose of examining and judging people thought to be wrong-doers.

associate /ə'səʊʃɪeɪt/ *vi* join with a person, usually for a special purpose; join together ideas in the mind. *n* **associate** /ə'səʊʃɪət/ person joined with others. *n* **association** /əˌsəʊsɪ'eɪʃən/ group of persons acting together for some special purpose; joining of ideas in the mind; an idea so joined. **association football** = kind of football in which the ball may not be touched with the hands.

assorted /ə'sɔːtɪd/ *adj* various. *n* **assortment** /ə'sɔːtmənt/ group of things of various kinds.

assuage /ə'sweɪdʒ/ *vt* make less, e.g. pain, sorrow, etc.

assume /ə'sjuːm/ *vt* **1** take to oneself. **2** suppose, esp. suppose without good reason. *n* **assumption** /ə'sʌmpʃən/.

assure /ə'ʃʊəʳ/ *vt* make certain. **I assure you** = I say as a sure fact. *n* **assurance** /ə'ʃʊərəns/ belief in oneself. **life assurance** = life INSURANCE. *adj* **assured** /ə'ʃʊəd/ sure of oneself. *adv* **assuredly** /ə'ʃʊərɪdlɪ/ without doubt.

asterisk /'æstərɪsk/ *n* star (*) used in printing.

astern /ə'stɜːn/ *adv, adj* at or towards the back end of a ship.

asthma /'æsmə/ *n* disease which makes breathing noisy and difficult. *adj* **asthmatic** /æs'mætɪk/.

astigmatism /ə'stɪgmətɪzəm/ *n* fault in the eyes which causes one to see certain parts of a thing less clearly than the rest.

astonish /ə'stɒnɪʃ/ *vt* surprise.

astound /ə'staʊnd/ *vt* surprise greatly.

astray /ə'streɪ/ *adv* wandering out of the right way.

astride /ə'straɪd/ *adv* with the legs apart, as in horse-riding.

astringent /ə'strɪndʒənt/ *adj, n* tightening (substance), e.g. *An astringent liquid for the skin* = one which makes the skin tighter and harder.

astrology /ə'strɒlədʒɪ/ *n* study of the stars in order to learn the future.

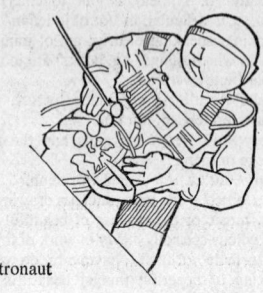

astronaut

astronaut /'æstrənɔːt/ *n* one who travels in space.

astronomy /ə'strɒnəmɪ/ *n* scientific study of space and the stars. *n* **astronomer** /ə'strɒnəməʳ/ one who studies astronomy. *adj* **astronomical** /ˌæstrə'nɒmɪkəl/ **1** having to do with astronomy. **2** (of numbers) very large.

astute /əs'tjuːt/ *adj* very clever, esp. at business.

asunder /ə'sʌndə/ʳ/ *adv* into pieces; apart.

asylum /ə'saɪləm/ *n* place where mad or helpless people are taken care of.

asymmetrical /ˌeɪsɪ'metrɪkəl/ *adj* having the two sides unequal or different.

at /ət; *strong* æt/ *prep* in or near (a place); (used before words for the place where something happened or the time when it happened).

atavism /'ætəvɪzəm/ *n* appearance in a child's body or character of something found in the family many years ago.

ate /et, eɪt/ *p.t.* of **eat**.

atheist /'eɪθɪ-ɪst/ *n* one who does not believe that there is a God.

athlete /'æθliːt/ *n* man who has a well-trained body, who is good at outdoor games. *adj* **athletic** /æθ'letɪk/ having to do with outdoor games.

atlas /'ætləs/ *n* book of maps.

atmosphere /'ætməsfɪəʳ/ *n* air round the earth; general feeling (in a room, etc.) *adj* **atmospheric** /ˌætməs'ferɪk/.

atoll /'ætɒl/ *n* CORAL island.

atom /'ætəm/ *n* part of matter so small that it cannot be divided; any very small amount. *adj* **atomic** /ə'tɒmɪk/. **atomic bomb** = exploding weapon in which the explosion is caused by the breaking up of atoms.

atomizer /'ætəmaɪzəʳ/ *n* instrument which blows out liquid in very small drops.

atone /ə'təʊn/ *vi* make repayment for wrong-doing.

atrocious /ə'trəʊʃəs/ *adj* very cruel or bad. *n* **atrocity** /ə'trɒsɪtɪ/ very cruel deed.

atrophy /'ætrəfɪ/ *vi* (of a part of the body) waste away because of lack of use or lack of blood supply.

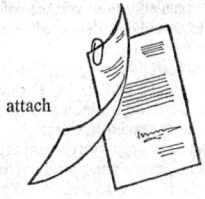

attach

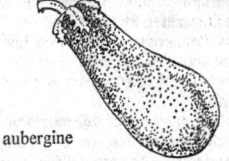

aubergine

aubergine /ˈəʊbəʒiːn/ *n* purple, egg-shaped vegetable.

auburn /ˈɔːbən/ *adj* red-brown.

auction /ˈɔːkʃən/ *n* public selling of goods by asking for offers and selling for the highest offer. *n* **auctioneer** /ˌɔːkʃəˈnɪə/ one who sells things in this way.

audacious /ɔːˈdeɪʃəs/ *adj* very daring. *n* **audacity** /ɔːˈdæsətɪ/.

audible /ˈɔːdəbəl/ *adj* loud enough to be heard.

audience /ˈɔːdɪəns/ *n* hearers; people in a meeting, theatre, etc.

audit /ˈɔːdɪt/ *n* examination of accounts. *vt* make such an examination of (accounts).

audition /ɔːˈdɪʃən/ *n* hearing of a singer, actor, etc., to discover whether he is good enough for employment.

auditorium /ˌɔːdɪˈtɔːrɪəm/ *n* large hall for meetings.

augment /ɔːɡˈment/ *vt* increase.

augur /ˈɔːɡə/ *n* one who in Roman times told the future; sign of the future. *vi* be a sign of the future, e.g. *This augurs no good.*

August /ˈɔːɡəst/ *n* the eighth month of the year.

august /ɔːˈɡʌst/ *adj* solemn; causing a feeling of fear and respect.

aunt /ɑːnt/ *n* father's or mother's sister; wife of one's uncle. **auntie** /ˈɑːntɪ/ *n* (child's word for) aunt.

aura /ˈɔːrə/ *n* faint smell or feeling around any object—like the smell round flowers.

auspices /ˈɔːspɪsɪz/ *n* (*pl*) signs of good fortune. **under the auspices of** = with the favour and help of. *adj* **auspicious** /ɔːˈspɪʃəs/ promising good fortune.

austere /ɔːˈstɪə/ *adj* very plain and simple in appearance; hard in character or manner. *n* **austerity** /ɔːˈsterətɪ/.

authentic /ɔːˈθentɪk/ *adj* real or true. *vt* **authenticate** /ɔːˈθentɪkeɪt/ show without doubt that (something) is real. *n* **authenticity** /ˌɔːθenˈtɪsətɪ/.

author /ˈɔːθə/ *n* first beginner of a new thing; writer of a book, story etc.

authority /ɔːˈθɒrətɪ/ *n* 1 right and power to give orders; person or group of persons having the right to govern. 2 person or book that may safely be believed on a certain subject, e.g. *He is a great authority on children's diseases. adj* **authoritative** /ɔːˈθɒrɪtətɪv/ said or written by a person who ought to be believed. *vt* **authorize** /ˈɔːθəraɪz/ give (someone) the right and power to act.

auto- /ˈɔːtə, ˈɔːtəʊ, ɔːˈtɒ/ self-, own-.

---

attach /əˈtætʃ/ *vt* join or fasten. *n* **attachment** /əˈtætʃmənt/ thing fixed on to something else; friendship.

attaché /əˈtæʃeɪ/ *n* man who goes with an AMBASSADOR.

attack /əˈtæk/ *v* go and fight against (someone or something); speak or write against. *n* act of attacking.

attain /əˈteɪn/ *vt* arrive at or reach. *n* **attainment** /əˈteɪnmənt/.

attempt /əˈtempt/ *vt* try. *n* act of trying to do something.

attend /əˈtend/ *vi* 1 fix the mind on; listen to, e.g. *Attend to the lesson.* 2 take care of, e.g. *Attend to one's children.* 3 wait upon, e.g. *To attend on the Queen. v* be present at (e.g. school). *n* **attendant** /əˈtendənt/ servant or nurse. *n* **attendance** /əˈtendəns/ act of attending; the persons present at (a meeting).

attention /əˈtenʃən/ *n* giving of the mind to a subject. **to attract attention** = cause oneself to be noticed. **to attention** = (of soldiers) standing upright with the feet together and the hands at the sides. **to pay attention** = attend. *adj* **attentive** /əˈtentɪv/ paying attention.

attenuate /əˈtenjʊeɪt/ *vt* make thin or less.

attest /əˈtest/ *vt* write one's name on a paper to show that (what is said in the paper) is true and correct; prove.

attic /ˈætɪk/ *n* room just under the roof of a house.

attire /əˈtaɪə/ *vt* dress. *n* clothing.

attitude /ˈætɪtjuːd/ *n* way in which one stands, etc.; way in which one feels or thinks about something.

attorney /əˈtɜːnɪ/ *n* lawyer. **power of attorney** = power to act for another person.

attract /əˈtrækt/ *vt* cause to come or remain near, e.g. *The earth attracts the moon. n* **attraction** /əˈtrækʃən/ something that attracts people. *adj* **attractive** /əˈtræktɪv/ having a pleasant appearance, manner, etc. *n* **attractions** things that draw crowds together, e.g. public shows, cheap things in the shops.

attribute /ˈætrɪbjuːt/ *n* quality; special part of the character of something, e.g. *Politeness is the attribute of a gentleman. vt* **attribute** /əˈtrɪbjuːt/ say that (something) is part of the character of; say that (something) is caused by e.g. *I attribute my success to hard work.*

autobiography /ˌɔːtəbaɪˈɒɡrəfɪ/ *n* story of a man's life written by himself.

autocrat /ˈɔːtəkræt/ *n* ruler who has complete and uncontrolled power.

autograph /ˈɔːtəɡrɑːf/ *n* person's name written by himself.

automatic /ˌɔːtəˈmætɪk/ *adj* moving or working by itself; not needing or not using thought. **automatic pistol** or **automatic** = hand-gun that puts a new shot in place after each shot has been fired.

automation /ˌɔːtəˈmeɪʃən/ *n* using machines that work by themselves instead of under the control of men.

automaton /ɔːˈtɒmətən/ *n* machine made to act like a man; man who works like a machine without thought.

automobile /ˈɔːtəməbiːl/ *n* car.

autonomy /ɔːˈtɒnəmɪ/ *n* power of self-government.

autopsy /ˈɔːtɒpsɪ/ *n* examining a body to find the cause of death.

autosuggestion /ˌɔːtəʊsəˈdʒestʃən/ *n* putting ideas into one's own mind, e.g. trying to make oneself well from illness by saying, "I am getting better".

autumn /ˈɔːtəm/ *n* season between summer and winter. *adj* **autumnal** /ɔːˈtʌmnəl/.

auxiliary /ɔːɡˈzɪlɪərɪ/ *adj* helping.

avail /əˈveɪl/ *vt* be of use or value to. **to avail oneself of** = make use of. **of** or **to no avail** = without any effect, in spite of trying. *adj* **available** /əˈveɪləbəl/ ready or able to be used.

avalanche /ˈævəlɑːnʃ/ *n* sudden slipping of a mass of snow down a mountain.

avarice /ˈævərɪs/ *n* great desire for wealth.

avenge /əˈvendʒ/ *vt* pay back (a hurt or wrong) by hurting the person who did the wrong.

avenue

avenue /ˈævənjuː/ *n* broad street; road with trees on both sides.

aver /əˈvɜː/ *vt* declare.

average /ˈævərɪdʒ/ *adj* like most others; common. *n* middle value of a set of numbers, e.g. the average of 3, 6, 9 is $\frac{18}{3} = 6$.

averse /əˈvɜːs/ *adj* very unwilling.

avert /əˈvɜːt/ *vt* turn away, e.g. one's eyes; prevent (some bad thing) from happening.

aviary /ˈeɪvɪərɪ/ *n* place for keeping birds.

aviation /ˌeɪvɪˈeɪʃən/ *n* science of flying by machines. *n* **aviator** /ˈeɪvɪeɪtə/ man skilled in using flying-machines.

avid /ˈævɪd/ *adj* hungry; eager.

avocation /ˌævəˈkeɪʃən/ *n* 1 one's regular business. 2 second business less important than one's chief or regular business.

avoid /əˈvɔɪd/ *vt* keep away from; escape.

avoirdupois /ˌævədəˈpɔɪz/ *n* way of measuring in pounds made up of 16 ounces.

avow /əˈvaʊ/ *vt* declare openly. *n* **avowal** /əˈvaʊəl/.

avuncular /əˈvʌŋkjʊlə/ *adj* having to do with an uncle.

await /əˈweɪt/ *vt* wait for.

awake /əˈweɪk/ *v* wake from sleep; excite to action. *adj* not sleeping; active in mind.

award /əˈwɔːd/ *vt* give by judgment of a court of law; give as a result of careful thought. *n* thing so given.

aware /əˈweə/ *adj* having knowledge.

awash /əˈwɒʃ/ *adv* level with the surface of the water.

away /əˈweɪ/ *adv, adj* not at home or in the usual place; apart; at or to a different place. **to throw away** = throw out as of no further use. **to pass away** = die. **to work away** = continue working. **to do away with** = destroy. **right away** or **straight away** = at once; now.

awe /ɔː/ *n* feeling of respect mixed with fear. *adj* **awesome** /ˈɔːsəm/ causing awe.

awful /ˈɔːfəl/ *adj* 1 causing great fear. 2 very bad, e.g. *An awful actor.* 3 (of something bad) great, e.g. *It's an awful shame.* *adv* **awfully** /ˈɔːfəlɪ/ 1 in an awful way. 2 *infml* very, e.g. *Awfully good, awfully bad.*

awhile /əˈwaɪl/ *adv* for a short time.

awkward /ˈɔːkwəd/ *adj* ungraceful; not clever in doing or making things; difficult to deal with.

awl /ɔːl/ *n* instrument for making holes.

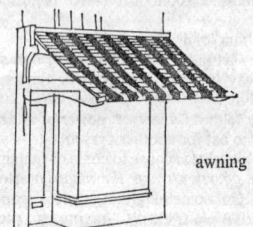

awning

awning /ˈɔːnɪŋ/ *n* covering to shade windows or doors of a house from the sun.

awoke /əˈwəʊk/ *p.t.* of **awake**.

awry /əˈraɪ/ *adj, adv* bent to one side, not straight.

axe /æks/ *n* heavy blade fixed to a handle used for cutting down trees, etc.

axiom /'æksɪəm/ *n* truth which everyone accepts as true without proof. *adj* **axiomatic** /ˌæksɪə'mætɪk/.

axis /'æksɪs/ *n* imaginary straight line round which a thing turns, e.g. *The axis of the earth.*

axle /'æksəl/ *n* bar on which a wheel turns.

ay, aye /aɪ/ *interj* yes.

azure /'æзə ^r, 'æзjʊə ^r/ *adj* sky-blue; light blue.

B

baa /bɑ:/ *n, interj* cry of a sheep.

babble /'bæbəl/ *vi* speak like a baby; talk foolishly; tell a secret; make a sound as of running water.

babel /'beɪbəl/ *n* disorder.

baboon /bə'bu:n/ *n* a kind of large monkey.

baby /'beɪbɪ/ *n* very young child.

baby-sitter /'. . ,. ./ *n* person who sits by the baby while the parents are out of the house.

bachelor /'bætʃələ ^r/ *n* unmarried man. **Bachelor of Arts** = person who has finished a course of study at a university.

bacillus /bə'sɪləs/ *n* very small living thing, often causing disease. (*pl*) **bacilli** /bə'sɪlaɪ/.

back /bæk/ *n* that part which is behind, e.g. part of the body, of the hand, of a chair, of a house, etc. *adv* towards the back; to the place in which it was first or to the person who had it first, e.g. *Give back; Go back.* *v* (also **back up**) **1** go or cause to go backwards. **2** give support to. **back down** = give up a claim or demand.

back-bencher /ˌ. '. ./ *n* member of PARLIAMENT who does not hold and has not held office in the government and therefore sits at the back.

backbite /'bækbaɪt/ *vi* speak unkindly of an absent person.

backbone /'bækbəʊn/ *n* **1** long row of bones in the middle of the back. **2** courage; strong will.

backfire /bæk'faɪə ^r/ *n* explosion inside a car engine which comes too soon and so does not drive the car forward. *vi* have a backfire.

backgammon /'bækgæmən/ *n* indoor game played with wooden pieces on a special board.

background /'bækgraʊnd/ *n* **1** more distant part of a view; that part of a picture against or upon which the chief figures are painted. **2** one's past experience, schooling, etc. **to keep in the background** = try not to be noticed.

backhand /'bækhænd/ *adv, adj* done with the back of the hand. **a backhanded compliment** = a saying which may be understood as either praise or blame.

backing /'bækɪŋ/ *n* support, e.g. in money matters.

backlog /'bæk-lɒg/ *n* work that was not done at the proper time and has grown into quite a heavy load to be dealt with now; orders for goods that the shop has not yet been able to send.

backside /bæk'saɪd/ *n* the part of the body on which one sits.

backward /'bækwəd/ *adj* **1** towards the back. **2** not DEVELOPED to the same degree as others of the same kind (e.g. other children; other countries). *adv* (also **backwards** /'bækwədz/) towards the back.

backwater /'bækˌwɔ:tə ^r/ *n* **1** small stream leading out of a river and fed by its water. **2** country area far from the towns.

backwoods /'bækwʊdz/ *n* distant uncleared forest land. *adj* (of people or their manners) rough.

bacon /'beɪkən/ *n* salted meat from the back and sides of a pig.

bacteria /bæk'tɪərɪə/ *n* (*pl*) microscopic living things that cause disease and decay.

bad /bæd/ *adj* not at all good; evil; unsatisfactory; poor.

badger /'bædʒə ^r/ *n* a kind of small night mammal that lives in a hole in the ground. *vt* trouble (someone) and make him angry, e.g. by continuing to ask questions.

baffle /'bæfəl/ *vt* make too difficult. *adj* **baffling** /'bæfəlɪŋ/ impossible to understand.

bag /bæg/ *n* container made of paper, cloth, leather, etc., in which things are carried. *vt* kill (birds, etc.); collect; obtain.

baggage

baggage /'bægɪdʒ/ *n* collection of bags, etc., of a traveller.

baggy /'bægɪ/ *adj* hanging down loosely like a bag.

bagpipes /'bægpaɪps/ *n* Scottish instrument of music.

bail[1] /beɪl/ *n* money given by a prisoner or his friends to a court of law so that the prisoner may be set free until he is judged (the money will be seized by the law if he does not come back when called). *vt* give such money for.

bail[2] /beɪl/, **bale** *vt* throw water out, e.g. from a boat. **bail out** = get out from an aeroplane when in the air; escape, or help (someone) escape, from a difficult state of affairs.

bail[3] /beɪl/ *n* small piece of wood laid on top of the upright pieces of wood used in the game of CRICKET.

bailiff /'beɪlɪf/ *n* officer of the law; man who looks after a farm or lands for the owner.

bait /beɪt/ *n* food put out in order to catch animals or fish; something which causes desire. **ground-bait** = food thrown into water to bring fish to that place. *vt* try to make (a person or animal) angry.

baize /beɪz/ *n* thick cloth made of wool.

bake /beɪk/ *v* cook by dry heat in a closed box. **half-baked** = imperfect; unfinished. *n* **baker** /'beɪkə/ one who makes bread. **baker's dozen** = 13. *n* **bakery** /'beɪkərɪ/ place where bread is made or sold.

balance /'bæləns/ *n* 1 instrument for measuring weight. 2 ability to remain upright when standing, walking, riding a bicycle, etc.; ability to control oneself and remain calm. *vt* weigh in a balance; weigh (one thing) against another; keep (one thing) equal to another. *vi* remain upright, esp. when this would be difficult. **to balance an account** = add up the two sides of an account and show the difference between them. **bank balance** = money a person still has in the bank. **a balance sheet** = paper showing money spent and received, owed by and owed to a business company.

balcony /'bælkənɪ/ *n* shelf-like place built out from the wall of a house for people to stand or sit on; upstairs seats in a theatre.

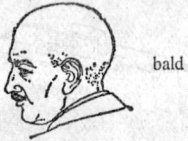

bald

bald /bɔːld/ *adj* having no hair—esp. on the head. **to speak baldly** = speak plainly, even cruelly.

bale[1] /beɪl/ *n* goods enclosed in cloth and tied with rope for sending by ship, train, or on the back of an animal.

bale[2] /beɪl/ see **bail**.

baleful /'beɪlfəl/ *adj* evil, full of desire to do harm.

balk, baulk /bɔːk/ *vt* prevent (someone) from doing what he wishes to do.

ball[1] /bɔːl/ *n* round object used in play; any round thing.

ball[2] /bɔːl/ *n* large number of people gathered for dancing. **have a ball** = enjoy oneself greatly.

ballad /'bæləd/ *n* short story told in the form of a poem; simple song.

ballast /'bæləst/ *n* heavy material put in the bottom of a ship to keep it steady; road material.

ball bearing /ˌ. '. ./ *n* one of the metal balls moving

in a ring round a bar in a machine so that the bar may turn more easily, with less rubbing.

ballerina /ˌbælə'riːnə/ *n* woman who dances in a BALLET.

ballet /'bæleɪ/ *n* a kind of theatrical dancing to specially written music in which the dancers' movements tell a story.

ballistics /bə'lɪstɪks/ *n* (*sing*) science of gun-fire.

balloon /bə'luːn/ *n* large bag filled with gas to make it lighter than air; a small coloured rubber bag filled with air, for children to play with.

ballot /'bælət/ *vi* elect secretly by writing names on pieces of paper, or putting a mark against printed names. *n* such an election.

balm /bɑːm/ *n* oily liquid obtained from a tree, used as a medicine, esp. to lessen pain.

balmy /'bɑːmɪ/ *adj* gentle; sweet-smelling.

balsam /'bɔːlsəm/ *n* 1 sweet-smelling material that comes from a tree. 2 a kind of tree. 3 a kind of flower.

balustrade /ˌbæləs'treɪd, 'bæləstreɪd/ *n* row of upright pieces of stone or wood with a bar along the top, guarding the outer edge of stairs or steps, or of any place from which people might fall.

bamboo /bæm'buː/ *n* tall hollow tree, formed like grass, found in hot countries.

ban /bæn/ *vt* forbid. *n* an order forbidding something.

banal /bə'nɑːl/ *adj* very common and uninteresting.

banana /bə'nɑːnə/ *n* common fruit, long and yellow, having a soft white centre.

band /bænd/ *n* 1 anything used for fastening things together; flat long piece of any material used for fastening, or forming part of a garment; long narrow line of colour different from that round it. 2 group of persons united for some special purpose. 3 group of persons playing musical instruments together.

bandage /'bændɪdʒ/ *n* long piece of cloth for tying up a wound. *vt* tie up in a bandage.

bandit /'bændɪt/ *n* armed thief.

bandolier /ˌbændə'lɪə/ *n* broad band with pockets for holding CARTRIDGES.

bandy /'bændɪ/ *vt* throw about, e.g *To bandy words* = talk and answer and talk again, quarrel.

bandy-legged

bandy-legged /ˌbændɪ ˈlegd/ adj having legs curved outwards at the knees.

bane /beɪn/ n 1 poison. 2 ruin, cause of ruin, e.g. *Disease is the bane of life.* adj **baneful** /ˈbeɪnfəl/ causing ruin.

bang /bæŋ/ n loud noise caused by a heavy blow, bursting, or exploding; shut with a loud noise. sl **It hit me bang in the eye** = exactly—.

bangle /ˈbæŋgəl/ n ring of metal worn on the arm or leg.

banish /ˈbænɪʃ/ vt drive away; send away to live in a foreign country.

banister /ˈbænɪstə/ n upright pieces of wood or metal with a bar along the top guarding the outer edge of stairs.

banjo /ˈbændʒəʊ, bænˈdʒəʊ/ n musical instrument with four strings and a body (main part) like a drum.

bank¹ /bæŋk/ n mass of earth raised up above the level of the ground; side of a river. v (in flying) make (an aeroplane) slope when turning.

bank² /bæŋk/ n place in which money is kept and paid out on demand. v pay (money) into a bank. **to bank on** = depend on. n **bank holiday** /ˌ ˈ.../ special day on which banks and all businesses are closed.

banknote /ˈbæŋknəʊt/ n piece of printed paper for which money is paid on demand at any bank.

bankrupt /ˈbæŋkrʌpt/ adj having failed in business; unable to pay one's debts. n **bankruptcy** /ˈbæŋkrʌptsɪ/.

banner /ˈbænə/ n flag with a special sign on it.

banns /bænz/ n notice of a marriage.

banquet /ˈbæŋkwɪt/ n feast.

bantam /ˈbæntəm/ n very small kind of cock or hen. **bantamweight** = a boxer weighing less than 116 pounds.

banter /ˈbæntə/ vt be merry and laugh at (someone).

Bantu /bænˈtuː/ adj belonging to a group of African languages or peoples.

banyan /ˈbænjən/ n tree whose branches go down into the ground and form many roots.

baobab /ˈbeɪəbæb/ n a kind of African tree.

baptize /bæpˈtaɪz/ vt put in the water, or put water on, as a sign of receiving as a Christian; give (someone) a name. n **baptism** /ˈbæptɪzəm/ practice of the Christian Church concerned with putting water on a child at the time of naming it.

bar /baː/ n 1 stiff long piece of wood, metal, etc. 2 long piece of wood or metal used to prevent people from passing, e.g. *A bar across the road.* 3 place where the prisoner stands in a court of law. **to join the bar** = become a lawyer. 4 place where wine and strong drink is sold. **bar of music** = a few notes of music marked off with downward lines. vt fix bars in (e.g. a window); keep (people) out. prep (also **barring**) except for.

barb /baːb/ n point of an arrow turned backwards to prevent it being pulled out of a

wound. adj **barbed** (of words) very cruel.

barbed wire = wire with sharp points on it intended to tear skin or clothes.

barbarian /baːˈbeərɪən/ n, adj (man) without laws, manners or good customs. adj **barbarous** /ˈbaːbərəs/ or **barbaric** /baːˈbærɪk/ of or like a barbarian, esp, in being cruel.

barbecue /ˈbaːbɪkjuː/ n 1 frame on which things are dried or cooked. 2 animal cooked whole; out-of-door feast.

barber /ˈbaːbə/ n one who cuts men's hair.

bare /beə/ adj 1 having no clothes or covering **to pick a bone bare** = get all the meat off. **to lay bare** = uncover; show what was hidden. 2 just enough; very slight. vt uncover; make bare. adv **barely** /ˈbeəlɪ/ hardly; only just.

barefaced /ˌbeəˈfeɪst/ adj without shame.

barefoot /ˈbeəfʊt/ adj, adv with no shoes on.

bargain /ˈbaːgən/ n 1 agreement about buying and selling. **into the bargain** = also. 2 something bought at a low price. vi talk about the price before buying. **I did not bargain for that** = did not expect.

barge /baːdʒ/ n large boat with a flat bottom. **to barge into** = run into. n **bargee** /baːˈdʒiː/ one who has charge of a barge.

baritone /ˈbærɪtəʊn/ n male voice not high or low but in the middle; singer with such a voice.

bark¹ /baːk/ n noise which a dog makes when excited. vi make such a noise.

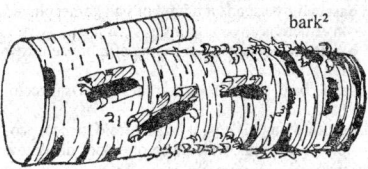

bark²

bark² /baːk/ n skin on the outside of a tree.

barley /ˈbaːlɪ/ n a kind of grain; plant which produces this.

barman /ˈbaːmən/ n man who serves drink in a BAR. n **barmaid** /ˈbaːmeɪd/ woman who serves drinks in a BAR.

barn /baːn/ n building used for storing things on a farm.

barnacle /ˈbaːnəkəl/ n kind of shellfish that fixes itself on to the bottom of ocean-going ships and rocks.

barometer /bəˈrɒmɪtə/ n instrument for telling how heavily the air is pressing down, and, from this, what the weather will be.

baron /ˈbærən/ n title of a nobleman. n **baroness** /ˈbærənəs/ wife of a baron; woman who has the title in her own right. adj **baronial** /bəˈrəʊnɪəl/ having to do with a baron, good enough for a baron, fine.

baronet /ˈbærənɪt/ n titled man next below a baron.

baroque /bə'rɒk, bə'rəʊk/ *n, adj* much ornamented (form of building, or art generally).

barracks /'bærəks/ *n* long buildings in which soldiers live.

barrage /'bærɑːʒ/ *n* **1** bar across a river. **2** line of falling shots from many guns.

barrel /'bærəl/ *n* **1** round wooden container with curved sides. **2** long round pipe of a gun through which the shot passes. **a barrel organ** = wind-instrument of music played by turning a handle round.

barren /'bærən/ *adj* having no fruit, children, or young; useless.

barricade /'bærɪkeɪd, ˌbærɪ'keɪd/ *n* quickly built wall of trees, earth, etc., used in fighting. *vt* make such walls for defending (a place).

barrier /'bærɪə ʳ/ *n* rough fence set across a path or road to prevent people from passing; anything which prevents people from passing.

barrister /'bærɪstə ʳ/ *n* lawyer who speaks in a law-court.

barter /'bɑːtə ʳ/ *v* to trade (things) without using money.

base[1] /beɪs/ *n* bottom—upon which other things are built up; most important part of a mixture, that into which other things are mixed; line from which a runner, an army, etc., starts. *vt* use as a base.

base[2] /beɪs/ *adj* not at all noble; shameful. **base coin** = money which is not made of real gold or silver.

baseball /'beɪsbɔːl/ *n* a kind of ball game, played in America.

basement /'beɪsmənt/ *n* rooms of a house below the ground.

bash /bæʃ/ *sl vt* hit with great force. *n* forceful blow.

bashful /'bæʃfəl/ *adj* (of a girl) afraid to meet people or to speak with those one does not know well.

basic /'beɪsɪk/ *adj* most important; main.

basin /'beɪsən/ *n* small open dish; bowl used for washing the face and hands in; hollow place containing water; valley of a river.

basis /'beɪsɪs/ *n* (*pl* **bases** /-siːz/) bottom; that upon which anything is built up; chief thing in a mixture, into which the other things are mixed.

bask /bɑːsk/ *vi* lie in the warm sun.

basket /'bɑːskɪt/ *n* container made of bent sticks used for carrying things.

basket-ball /'.. ./ *n* game in which each side tries to throw the ball up into a net on a high post.

bass[1] /beɪs/ *n* very low male voice; low notes in music.

bass[2] /bæs/ *n* a kind of fish.

bassoon /bə'suːn/ *n* instrument blown with the mouth which produces a very low note.

bastard /'bɑːstəd/ *n* **1** child whose parents were not married to each other. **2** unpleasant or unfortunate person. *adj* not real; not of the usual kind.

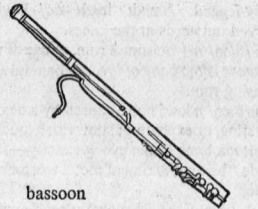

bassoon

baste /beɪst/ *vt* **1** join (cloth) together loosely when starting to make clothes. **2** pour melted fat over (meat) while it is cooking.

bastion /'bæstɪən/ *n* tower as part of a fort.

bat[1] /bæt/ *n* small flying mammal like a mouse with large wings.

bat[2] /bæt/ *n* stick used for hitting the ball in play.

batch /bætʃ/ *n* group of things of one kind; number of cakes or loaves of bread baked at one time.

bated /'beɪtɪd/ **with bated breath** = holding in the breath in great fear.

bath /bɑːθ/ *n* act of washing the body; large vessel in which one washes; water used in washing the body; building in which one has a bath, or in which one swims; container for liquid, e.g. the special liquids used in science. *v* have a bath or give a bath to.

bathe /beɪð/ *v* go or put into water; go for a swim in the sea.

bathos /'beɪθɒs/ *n* sudden change from very beautiful thoughts to very common or foolish thoughts.

batman /'bætmən/ *n* officer's servant.

baton /'bætən/ *n* stick used by policemen; stick used by leaders of music; also sign of high rank in the army.

batsman /'bætsmən/ *n* in some games, the man who hits a ball with a BAT.

battalion /bə'tæliən/ *n* group of about 1,000 soldiers.

batten /'bætn/ *vt* board; fix firmly with boards.

batter /'bætə ʳ/ *vt* hit hard and often. *n* mixture of eggs, milk and flour, used for cooking. *n* **battering-ram** /'bætərɪŋ-ræm/ large heavy log with an iron end used for breaking the doors and walls of towns and castles.

battery /'bætərɪ/ *n* **1** number of big guns together with the men and officers who serve them; set of guns mounted in a warship or in a fort. **2** box containing metal plates and acid used to produce or store electricity. **3** (in law) striking another person. **4** line of small boxes each containing one hen, arranged so that feeding them and collecting their eggs is easy.

battle /'bætl/ *n* fight between armies or between ships; any struggle, e.g. *The battle of life.* *vi* fight.

battlement /'bætlmənt/ *n* wall on top of a castle with openings for shooting out.

bauble /ˈbɔːbəl/ n pretty thing of no value.

baulk /bɔːk/ see **balk**.

bauxite /ˈbɔːksaɪt/ n earth from which aluminium is obtained.

bawdy /ˈbɔːdɪ/ adj amusing or intending to amuse by talk of sexual matters.

bawl /bɔːl/ vi shout very loud.

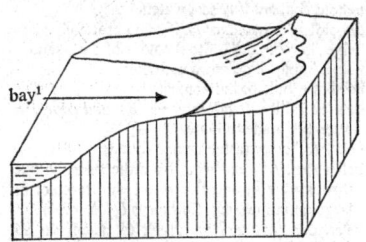

bay¹

bay¹ /beɪ/ n inward curve in the shore of a lake or sea. 2 part of a building; built-out part of a room. **bay window** = large window curving outwards from a room.

bay² /beɪ/ n tree whose leaves in old times were made into crowns for conquerors, successful poets and winners of races, and are now used in cooking.

bay³ /beɪ/ n low cry of a hunting dog. **to keep at bay** = keep (someone or something) at a safe distance away.

bayonet /ˈbeɪənɪt/ n blade fixed on the end of a gun.

bazaar /bəˈzɑː/ n 1 (in the East) part of the town where the shops are. 2 (in Europe, etc.) a shop where many kinds of useful things and playthings are sold; SALE of home-made things to get money for a church, school, etc.

be /bɪ; strong biː/ v have a certain quality or position; equal.

beach /biːtʃ/ n shore of a lake or sea.

beacon /ˈbiːkən/ n high hill or other object that can be seen from far away; light or fire on a high place to give warning.

bead /biːd/ n ball of glass or other material with a hole through it for a string, used for ornament.

beagle /ˈbiːgəl/ n dog used for hunting.

beak /biːk/ n horny mouth of a bird; any sharp point of this shape.

beaker /ˈbiːkə/ n wine cup; glass cup.

beam /biːm/ n 1 thick piece of wood, e.g. that holding up the roof of a house. 2 stream of light. vi shine; smile warmly.

bean /biːn/ n seed used for food. **full of beans** = very active; full of spirit. **French beans** = green seed-containers which are boiled and eaten as a vegetable.

bear¹ /beə/ n large wild mammal with long hair.

bear² /beə/ vt 1 carry. 2 suffer, e.g. *To bear pain.* **I can't bear him** = I dislike him greatly. 3 produce, e.g. *The tree bears good fruit; To bear children.*

beard /bɪəd/ n hair on the face below the mouth. adj **bearded** /ˈbɪədɪd/ having a beard.

bearing /ˈbeərɪŋ/ n 1 manner; way of behaving, e.g. *A proud bearing.* 2 meaning, e.g. *What you say has no bearing on the subject* = has nothing to do with. 3 direction.

beast /biːst/ n large animal; person who behaves like an animal. adj **beastly** /ˈbiːstlɪ/ like a beast; unpleasant.

beat /biːt/ vt 1 strike repeatedly. 2 conquer; win against. vi move regularly, e.g. *The heart beats.* n 1 regular movement of the heart; sound of a drum. 2 policeman's duty walk.

beauty /ˈbjuːtɪ/ n that quality which gives pleasure to the eye or ear; something or someone having this quality. adj **beautiful** /ˈbjuːtɪfəl/ having this quality.

beaver /ˈbiːvə/ n mammal with valuable fur, living on land and in the water, where it builds wonderful houses.

becalmed /bɪˈkɑːmd/ adj (of a ship) having no wind for movement.

became /bɪˈkeɪm/ p.t. of **become**.

because /bɪˈkɒz/ conj for the reason that; the cause being that. **because of** = caused by; as a result of.

beck /bek/ n 1 sign made to call someone. 2 small stream. **to be at a person's beck and call** = always ready to do everything they ask.

beckon

beckon /ˈbekən/ v make a silent sign with the finger to call (someone).

become /bɪˈkʌm/ v 1 to change from one state to another, e.g. *To become old.* 2 be suitable for. **become of** = happen to. adj **becoming** /bɪˈkʌmɪŋ/ suitable.

bed /bed/ n 1 thing on which one sleeps. 2 the course of a river or the hollow in which a sea lies. 3 part of garden used for growing flowers. n **bedclothes** /ˈbedkləʊðz/ coverings for a bed. n **bedding** /ˈbedɪŋ/ coverings for a bed; dry grass, etc., as a bed for an animal.

bedeck /bɪˈdek/ vt ornament.

bedlam /ˈbedləm/ n place for madmen; place of noise and disorder.

Bedouin /ˈbeduɪn/ n wandering Arab of the desert.

bedraggled /bɪˈdrægəld/ adj having the dress and hair in disorder.

bedridden /'bed,rıdn/ *adj* unable to get up from bed; ill, having to spend one's life in bed.

bedrock /'bed-rɒk/ *n* rock at the bottom.

bedroom /'bed-rʊm, -ru:m/ *n* room for sleeping.

bedspread /'bedspred/ *n* ornamental cloth spread over a bed.

bee /bi:/ *n* small flying insect that makes HONEY. **to have a bee in one's bonnet** = have some mad idea always in the mind.

beech /bi:tʃ/ *n* tree with hard wood and nuts that can be eaten.

beef /bi:f/ *n* meat of cattle.

beefsteak /'bi:fsteɪk/ *n* thick piece of BEEF.

beehive /'bi:haɪv/ *n* little hut made as a home for bees.

beeline /'bi:laɪn/ *n* straight line, the shortest way.

been /bi:n, bɪn/ p.p. of **be**.

beer /bɪə ʔ/ *n* bitter drink made from grain.

beet /bi:t/ *n* plant with a large, round root. *n* **beetroot** /'bi:t-ru:t/ the red root of a similar plant.

beetle

beetle /'bi:tl/ *n* one of several kinds of small hard-shelled insects.

beetling /'bi:tlɪŋ/ *adj* leaning out over the edge.

befall /bɪ'fɔ:l/ *v* happen (to).

befit /bɪ'fɪt/ *vt* be proper for.

before /bɪ'fɔ: ʔ *prep, adv* in front (of); earlier (than). *conj* earlier than when. *adv* **beforehand** /bɪ'fɔ:hænd/ earlier; already.

befriend /bɪ'frend/ *vt* help; treat in a friendly way.

beg /beg/ *vt* ask, ask as a kindness. **I beg your pardon** = 1 I ask you to forgive me. 2 kindly repeat what you said. *v* ask for food or money. **to beg the question** = take as true just that fact which is being questioned and reason from it as if it were accepted.

began /bɪ'gæn/ p.t. of **begin**.

beget /bɪ'get/ *vt* cause to be born; produce.

beggar /'begə ʔ *n* one who asks to be given money or food without working or paying for it. *adj* **beggarly** /'begəlɪ/ very poor; worthless.

begin /bɪ'gɪn/ *v* start. *n* **beginning** /bɪ'gɪnɪŋ/.

begotten /bɪ'gɒtn/ p.p. of **beget**.

begrudge /bɪ'grʌdʒ/ *vt* give unwillingly; be unwilling to let someone have something.

beguile /bɪ'gaɪl/ *vt* deceive; find some means of making time pass pleasantly, e.g. on a long journey.

begun /bɪ'gʌn/ p.p. of **begin**.

behalf /bɪ'hɑ:f/ **on behalf of** = for; in the place of.

behave /bɪ'heɪv/ *vt* act; act with good (or bad) manners. *n* **behaviour** /bɪ'heɪvjə ʔ way in which one acts. **to behave oneself** = behave well; act properly.

behead /bɪ'hed/ *vt* cut off the head of.

beheld /bɪ'held/ p.t. of **behold**.

behind /bɪ'haɪnd/ *prep, adv* at the back (of); in support of. *adv* **behindhand** /bɪ'haɪndhænd/ late.

behold /bɪ'həʊld/ *vt* see, watch.

beholden /bɪ'həʊldən/ *adj* feeling grateful.

beige /beɪʒ/ *n, adj* (of the) colour of dark sand.

being /'bi:ɪŋ/ *n* creature with life; life.

belabour /bɪ'leɪbə ʔ *vt* hit hard.

belated /bɪ'leɪtɪd/ *adj* late, e.g. *Belated efforts* = attempts made too late.

belay /bɪ'leɪ/ *vt* fasten a rope round.

belch /beltʃ/ *v* send wind from the stomach out through the throat; throw out with force or in large quantities, e.g. *Chimneys belch smoke.*

beleaguer /bɪ'li:gə ʔ *vt* attack (a place) on all sides.

belfry /'belfrɪ/ *n* part of a tower in which the bells hang.

belie /bɪ'laɪ/ *vt* show to be untrue.

belief /bɪ'li:f/ *n* act of regarding as true; thing regarded as true. *vt* **believe** /bɪ'li:v/ regard as true. **believe in** = have faith in.

belittle /bɪ'lɪtl/ *vt* cause to seem small or unimportant.

bell /bel/ *n* round, hollow, metal vessel, which makes a ringing sound when struck.

bellicose /'belɪkəʊs/ *adj* fierce; eager for war.

belligerent /bɪ'lɪdʒərənt/ *adj* making war; taking part in war.

bellow /'beləʊ/ *v* make a loud deep roar; shout loudly.

bellows /'beləʊz/ *n* instrument used for blowing air into a fire to make it burn quickly.

belly /'belɪ/ *n* that part of the body between the breast and legs that contains the stomach, etc. *vi* swell out, like a sail in the wind.

belong /bɪ'lɒŋ/ *vi* 1 be owned, e.g. *This book belongs to me.* 2 be a member of, e.g. *He belongs to that group.* 3 have as its proper place, e.g. *Put this back where it belongs.* *n* (*pl*) **belongings** /bɪ'lɒŋɪŋz/ those things which are one's own.

beloved /bɪ'lʌvd/ *adj* much loved. *adj, n* /bɪ'lʌvɪd/ much loved (person).

below /bɪ'ləʊ/ *adv, prep* under; lower (than).

belt /belt/ *n* band put around the waist; long piece of leather used to drive a machine.

bemoan /bɪ'məʊn/ *vt* be very sorry because of.

bemuse /bɪ'mju:z/ *vt* make unable to think properly.

bench /bentʃ/ *n* long seat; table at which a workman (e.g. shoemaker) works.

bend /bend/ *v* curve or become curved. *n* curve.

beneath /bɪ'ni:θ/ *prep* below; under.

benediction /,benɪ'dɪkʃən/ *n* blessing.

benefaction /,benɪ'fækʃən/ *n* doing good; giving money for some good purpose. *n* **benefactor**

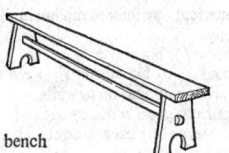

bench

/'benɪfæktə/ one who does good, who gives money for a good purpose.

beneficent /bɪ'nefɪsənt/ adj doing good; kind.

beneficial /ˌbenɪ'fɪʃəl/ adj helpful; useful.

beneficiary /ˌbenɪ'fɪʃərɪ/ n one who receives money, etc., at a person's death.

benefit /'benɪfɪt/ vt be good for; be of service to. n help; gift; ADVANTAGE.

benevolence /bɪ'nevələns/ n the desire to do good. adj **benevolent** /bɪ'nevələnt/.

benign /bɪ'nam/ adj of a kind or gentle nature; (of a disease) not dangerous.

beniseed /'benɪsiːd/ n a kind of seed grown esp. in West Africa, used to make an oil.

bent[1] /bent/ p.p. & p.t. of **bend**.

bent[2] /bent/ n special natural skill.

benumbed /bɪ'nʌmd/ adj having lost all feeling, e.g. because of cold.

bequeath /bɪ'kwiːð/ vt give or pass on (something) to others after death. n **bequest** /bɪ'kwest/ that which is given to others after death.

bereave /bɪ'riːv/ vt take away. adj **bereaved** having lost one's (wife, husband, etc.) n **bereavement** /bɪ'riːvmənt/ loss of a loved person by death.

bereft /bɪ'reft/ p.t. & p.p. of **bereave**.

beret /'bereɪ/ n flat cap.

beri-beri /ˌberɪ 'berɪ/ n disease caused by eating food, such as polished RICE, which lacks certain things necessary for health.

berry /'berɪ/ n small fruit.

berserk /bə'sɜːk/ adj mad; wild with anger.

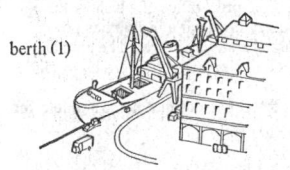

berth (1)

berth /bɜːθ/ n 1 place where a ship can stop and be tied up, e.g. in a harbour. 2 sleeping place in a ship or train.

beseech /bɪ'siːtʃ/ vt ask eagerly and anxiously (for).

beset /bɪ'set/ adj surrounded by (forces against one), e.g. *Beset with dangers.*

beside /bɪ'saɪd/ prep by; at the side of. **beside oneself** = almost mad with trouble or excitement. **beside the point** = having nothing to do with the subject.

besides /bɪ'saɪdz/ adv also, in addition to what has been said.

besiege /bɪ'siːdʒ/ vt attack on all sides.

besmirch /bɪ'smɜːtʃ/ vt make dirty.

besotted /bɪ'sɒtɪd/ adj foolish from drinking too much or from being in love.

besought /bɪ'sɔːt/ p.t. & p.p. of **beseech**.

best /best/ adj most good. adv most well. **best man** = friend who helps a man at his marriage.

bestial /'bestɪəl/ adj like an animal.

bestir /bɪ'stɜː/ vt cause to move quickly.

bestow /bɪ'stəʊ/ vt put. **to bestow upon** = give.

bet /bet/ v pay (money) which will be paid back, together with more money, if a certain event happens, but will be lost if it does not happen. n such an agreement; the money so paid. **I bet (that)** = I expect that; I feel certain that.

beta /'biːtə/ n second Greek letter, often used to mark work as being satisfactory though not very good.

betide /bɪ'taɪd/ **woe betide you** = may sorrow come to you.

betray /bɪ'treɪ/ vt sell one's country or a friend to the enemy; tell a secret. n **betrayal** /bɪ'treɪəl/.

betrothed /bɪ'trəʊðd/ adj promised in marriage.

better /'betə/ adj more good. adv more well. vt improve. **had better** = ought to; would be wise to, e.g. *We'd better go inside before it rains.*

between /bɪ'twiːn/ prep, adv in or into the space that separates or divides (two people, objects, or places). prep 1 in or during the time from one moment to another. 2 (indicating an action or relation from each to the other) e.g. *A fight between two friends.*

betwixt /bɪ'twɪkst/ archaic prep between.

bevel /'bevəl/ n sloping edge. **a bevel wheel, a bevel gear** = wheel that drives another wheel set corner-ways to it.

beverage /'bevərɪdʒ/ n drink, e.g. tea, wine, etc.

bevy /'bevɪ/ n group (of girls, birds, etc.).

bewail /bɪ'weɪl/ vt cry because of.

beware /bɪ'weə/ v be careful (of).

bewilder /bɪ'wɪldə/ vt make things difficult for (someone) to understand.

bewitch /bɪ'wɪtʃ/ vt have a magic effect on.

beyond /bɪ'jɒnd/ prep, adv on the farther side (of something); past; greater than; too difficult to be understood by.

bi- /baɪ/ twice, e.g. **bi-weekly** /ˌbaɪ 'wiːklɪ/ adv twice a week or once in two weeks.

bias /'baɪəs/ n 1 weight on one side of a ball which causes it to roll away from the straight course. 2 idea fixed in the mind causing one not to judge fairly. adj **biased** /'baɪəst/ having a bias.

bib /bɪb/ n cloth to keep a child clean when eating.

Bible /'baɪbəl/ n holy book of the Christian Church. adj **biblical** /'bɪblɪkəl/.

bibliography /ˌbɪblɪ'ɒgrəfɪ/ n list of books on some special subject.

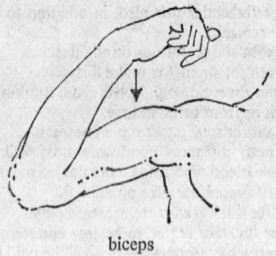

biceps

biceps /'baɪseps/ *n* large muscle on the front of the upper arm.

bicker /'bɪkə/ *vi* to quarrel about small matters.

bicycle /'baɪsɪkəl/ *n* two-wheeled machine that one drives along by turning a chain-wheel with the feet.

bid /bɪd/ *vt* **1** command; ask. **2** name a price at which one is prepared to buy something.

bide /baɪd/ **to bide one's time** = wait till a good chance comes.

biennial /baɪ'enɪəl/ *adj* happening every two years. *n* plant that lives for two years and then dies.

bier /bɪə/ *n* wooden carrier or table for a COFFIN.

big /bɪg/ *adj* large; great.

bigamy /'bɪgəmɪ/ *n* act of having two wives or husbands at the same time. *adj* **bigamous** /'bɪgəməs/.

bight /baɪt/ *n* bend in the shore; circle made in a rope.

bigot /'bɪgət/ *n* one who believes strongly in a thing and will not listen to reason. *n* **bigotry** /'bɪgətrɪ/ act of believing in a thing without reason.

bike /baɪk/ *infml n* bicycle.

bikini /bɪ'ki:nɪ/ *n* two-piece swimming suit.

bilateral /ˌbaɪ'lætərəl/ *adj* two-sided.

bile /baɪl/ *n* bitter, yellow-green liquid which changes fatty food in the body into a form in which it can be used by the body; bad temper.

bilge /bɪldʒ/ *n* **1** dirty water in the bottom of a ship; broad bottom of a ship. **2** *sl* foolish talk.

bilingual /ˌbaɪ'lɪŋgwəl/ *adj* speaking two languages.

bilious /'bɪlɪəs/ *adj* (of illness) caused by having too much BILE.

bill¹ /bɪl/ *n* **1** plan for a law, written down for elected members to consider. **2** list of things bought and the money owed or paid for them. **3** printed notice. **bill of exchange** = written order to pay money on a certain date.

bill² /bɪl/ *n* horny mouth of a bird.

billet /'bɪlɪt/ *n* lodging-house for a soldier. *vt* send (soldiers) to a lodging-house.

billiards /'bɪlɪədz/ *n* (*sing*) game played on a table with balls pushed with long sticks against each other or into pockets at the corners and sides.

billion /'bɪlɪən/ *n* one thousand million in France and America; one million million in Britain and Germany.

billow /'bɪləʊ/ *n* big wave.

bill-poster /'. ,. ./, **bill-sticker** /'. ,. ./ *n* man who sticks printed notices on to walls.

billy-goat /'bɪlɪ gəʊt/ *n* male goat.

bin /bɪn/ *n* large box used to contain bread, flour, coal, etc.; DUSTBIN.

bind /baɪnd/ *vt* tie; tie up.

binding /'baɪndɪŋ/ *n* cover of a book.

binoculars /bɪ'nɒkjʊləz/ *n* (*pl*) instrument used to see distant objects.

biography /baɪ'ɒgrəfɪ/ *n* written story of a person's life.

biology /baɪ'ɒlədʒɪ/ *n* science of living things.

biped /'baɪped/ *n* creature having two legs.

biplane

biplane /'baɪpleɪn/ *n* aeroplane with two wings, one above the other.

birch /bɜ:tʃ/ *n* a kind of tree; handful of sticks tied together used for punishing. *vt* hit with a birch, for punishment.

bird /bɜ:d/ *n* feathered creature which lays eggs. **bird's-eye view** /ˌ. . ./ = view seen from high up, general view of a subject.

birth /bɜ:θ/ *n* act of being born. *n* **birthday** /'bɜ:θdeɪ/ day of the year on which one was born. *n* **birthmark** /'bɜ:θmɑ:k/ mark on the body at birth. *n* **birth rate** /'. ,./ numbers of births for the numbers of people in a country. **birthright** /'bɜ:θraɪt/ *n* that which belongs to one because of one's birth (e.g. as a member of a certain nation).

biscuit /'bɪskɪt/ *n* small flat dry cake.

bisect /baɪ'sekt/ *vt* to cut into two equal parts.

bishop /'bɪʃəp/ *n* high officer in the Church. *n* **bishopric** /'bɪʃəprɪk/ office of a bishop, the part of the country in which a bishop has power.

bison /'baɪsən/ *n* large wild cow-like animal.

bit¹ /bɪt/ *n* small piece of anything. **a bit** = a little; slightly.

bit² /bɪt/ *n* metal bar put in a horse's mouth for riding or driving.

bit³ /bɪt/ *p.t.* of **bite**.

bitch /bɪtʃ/ *n* **1** female dog. **2** *sl* nasty woman.

bite /baɪt/ *v* to cut with the teeth. *adj* **biting** /'baɪtɪŋ/ cruel; causing pain.

bitten /'bɪtn/ *p.p.* of **bite**.

bitumen /'bɪtʃʊmən/ *n* hard black material, used in making roads.

bizarre /bɪ'zɑ:/ *adj* of peculiar appearance.

blab /blæb/ *sl vi* tell a secret.

black /blæk/ *adj, n* **1** (of the) darkest colour; without light. **2** (person) having a dark skin. *v* become or cause to become black. **black market** = unlawful sale of goods at high prices.

blacken /ˈblækən/ v become or cause to become black.

blackguard /ˈblægɑːd/ n very bad man.

blackhead /ˈblækhed/ n small swelling on the skin, usually having a black top.

blackleg /ˈblækleg/ n man who offers to work when all his fellow workers are refusing to work.

blackmail /ˈblækmeɪl/ vt demand money from (someone), saying that one will tell some bad thing about him if it is not paid.

blacksmith /ˈblæksmɪθ/ n man who works with iron and makes shoes for horses.

bladder /ˈblædə/ n that part of the body which contains waste liquid before it is passed out.

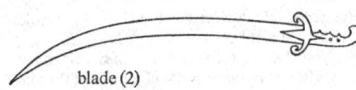

blade (2)

blade /bleɪd/ n 1 narrow leaf of a plant. 2 cutting part of a knife or sword; any narrow flat object.

blame /bleɪm/ vt say that (someone) is the cause of a certain trouble.

blanch /blɑːntʃ/ v make or become white.

blancmange /bləˈmɒnʒ, bləˈmɒndʒ/ n mixture of flour, sugar, milk and other materials which sets in stiff fancy shape when cold and ready to eat.

bland /blænd/ adj soft in speech; gentle.

blandishments /ˈblændɪʃmənts/ n arts of pleasing used to make a person agree—usually to a wrong act.

blank /blæŋk/ adj with no writing on it; empty, e.g. *A blank sheet of paper*. **to fire blank** = fire a gun with powder but no shot. **my mind was blank** = I had no ideas. **a blank look** = face showing no feeling or understanding. **to draw a blank** = be unsuccessful. **blank verse** = poetry without RHYMES.

blanket /ˈblæŋkɪt/ n thick woollen cloth, e.g. one used as a bed covering. vt cover with a blanket. adj not marking the differences between different things of roughly the same kind. **a wet blanket** = one who stops others from enjoying themselves.

blare /bleə/ n loud noise, as of a horn. vi make such a noise.

blasé /ˈblɑːzeɪ/ adj uninterested through having enjoyed too much of anything.

blaspheme /blæsˈfiːm/ vi say evil or foolish things about God. n **blasphemy** /ˈblæsfəmɪ/. adj **blasphemous** /ˈblæsfəməs/.

blast /blɑːst/ n strong rush of wind or hot air; explosion; sudden loud noise, e.g. *He blew a blast on his horn*. vt destroy with explosives; break (rock) with gunpowder; do great damage to, ruin. interj (a word expressing anger or DIS-APPOINTMENT). **blast you!** (= a cry of anger). **to blast off** = (of a ROCKET) leave the ground.

blatant /ˈbleɪtənt/ adj (of something bad) not hidden.

blaze /bleɪz/ vi burn brightly. n fierce fire.

blazer /ˈbleɪzə/ n woollen coat, usually of bright colour, worn at games.

blazon /ˈbleɪzən/ **to blazon abroad** = tell everywhere.

bleach /bliːtʃ/ v make or become white. n substance used to make things (esp. clothes) white.

bleak /bliːk/ adj cold and not cheerful.

bleary /ˈblɪərɪ/ adj having red, painful eyes; not seeing well.

bleat /bliːt/ n cry of a sheep. vi make this cry.

bleed /bliːd/ v lose or cause to lose blood.

blemish /ˈblemɪʃ/ n broken place or ugly mark on a beautiful thing.

blench /blentʃ/ vi move back in fear.

blend /blend/ v mix together; look well together, e.g. colours. n mixture.

bless /bles/ vt ask God to show favour to; express one's own favour to or good wishes for. **bless you!** (= said to someone who has just SNEEZED.) adj **blessed** /ˈblesɪd/ 1 holy, happy, having good fortune. 2 sl (used with other words to add colour to one's speech). n **blessing** /ˈblesɪŋ/ act of blessing; thing that brings happiness. **a blessing in disguise** = something that looked bad but was found to be very fortunate.

blew /bluː/ p.t. of **blow**.

blight /blaɪt/ n a disease of plants; any condition that destroys or is harmful.

blind[1] /blaɪnd/ adj unable to see. vt cause a person to be blind. n **blindness** /ˈblaɪndnəs/ state of being blind.

blind[2]

blind[2] /blaɪnd/ n cloth pulled down from a roller to cover a window.

blindfold /ˈblaɪndfəʊld/ vt cover the eyes of (someone) with a cloth. adj having the eyes so covered.

blink /blɪŋk/ v open and close (the eyes) quickly; (of lights) shine unsteadily.

blinkers /ˈblɪŋkəz/ n pieces of leather fixed at the sides of a horse's eyes.

bliss /blɪs/ n great happiness. adj **blissful** /ˈblɪsfəl/.

blister /ˈblɪstə/ n raised spot on the skin with clear liquid under it. vt cause to have blisters.

blitz /blɪts/ n very destructive attack, esp. from aeroplanes.

blizzard /ˈblɪzəd/ n storm with a strong, cold wind and snow.

bloated

bloated /'bləʊtɪd/ *adj* swollen up; unhealthily fat.

bloater /'bləʊtə/ *n* a kind of salted fish.

blob /blɒb/ *n* small round mass, e.g. of wax or paint.

bloc /blɒk/ *n* group (e.g. of countries) united by some common interest, e.g. the Sterling Bloc.

block /blɒk/ *n* **1** mass of wood, stone, etc. **2** an unbroken line of houses between two streets. *vt* prevent (something) passing. *n* **blockage** /'blɒkɪdʒ/ something that prevents what should pass through from doing so, e.g. *There is a blockage in the pipe.*

blockade /blɒ'keɪd/ *n* the shutting up of a place by warships or soldiers to prevent any persons or goods coming or going. *vt* shut up (a place) in this way.

blockhead /'blɒkhed/ *n* fool.

bloke /bləʊk/ *sl n* man.

blond(e) /blɒnd/ *adj* light brown, fair (hair, skin). *n* girl or woman with fair hair.

blood /blʌd/ *n* **1** red liquid that carries substances necessary for life to all parts of the body. **2** family, e.g. **he is of good blood** = comes of good family. **blue-blooded** = of noble family.

blood bank /'. ˌ./ *n* store of blood used for TRANSFUSION.

bloodhound /'blʌdhaʊnd/ *n* special kind of dog that can follow a smell for many hours.

bloodshed /'blʌdʃed/ *n* killing people.

bloodshot /'blʌdʃɒt/ *adj* (of the eyes) red with blood.

blood-vessel /'. ˌ. ./ *n* pipe through which blood flows in the body.

bloody /'blʌdɪ/ *adj* covered with blood; red like blood; *sl* (rude word) = very bad, much disliked.

bloom /bluːm/ *n* flower of a plant. *vi* (of a plant) have flowers on it. **in bloom** = blooming.

blossom /'blɒsəm/ *n* flower of a plant, esp. a tree.

blot /blɒt/ *n* mark, e.g. of ink on paper. **a blot on one's character** = fault. **to blot out** = take out words already written, destroy. *n* **blotting-paper** /'. . ˌ. ./ special kind of paper for drying ink.

blotch /blɒtʃ/ *n* ugly spot, e.g. on the skin.

blouse

blouse /blaʊz/ *n* loose outer garment worn by women on the upper half of the body.

blow¹ /bləʊ/ *v* **1** send forth (a stream of air). **2** play (a musical instrument) by blowing into it.

to blow out = cause (a flame) to go out by blowing. **to blow up** = **1** explode or cause to explode. **2** cause (something) to get bigger by blowing air into it.

blow² /bləʊ/ *n* sudden hard stroke. **come to blows** = begin fighting. **a terrible blow** = sudden and surprising misfortune or loss.

blower /'bləʊə/ *n* instrument for making a fire burn quickly by blowing air through the coals.

blowfly /'bləʊflaɪ/ *n* blue fly which lays eggs in meat.

blown /bləʊn/ *p.p.* of **blow**.

blowpipe /'bləʊpaɪp/ *n* pipe used to drive air through burning gas so as to get a very hot flame.

blubber /'blʌbə/ *n* fat of a WHALE. *vi* weep noisily.

bludgeon /'blʌdʒən/ *n* short thick stick. *vt* strike with such a stick.

blue /bluː/ *n, adj* (of the) colour of the clear sky. **once in a blue moon** = not often. **out of the blue** = as a surprise. **the blues** = a kind of American music, usually a rather slow song with sad words.

bluebell /'bluːbel/ *n* a kind of wild flower.

bluebottle /'bluːbɒtl/ *n* large blue fly, often seen near sweet things or meat.

blueprint /'bluːprɪnt/ *n* plan used in making a machine or building a house; any plan.

bluestocking /'bluːstɒkɪŋ/ *derog n* woman who is or pretends to be very learned.

bluff¹ /blʌf/ *n* cliff; steep place. *adj* having a rough and noisy manner.

bluff² /blʌf/ *vi* deceive by pretending to be very strong and sure of oneself.

blunder /'blʌndə/ *n* foolish mistake. *vi* make a foolish mistake, move in a rough and unskilful way.

blunt /blʌnt/ *adj* not having a sharp edge; rough and plain in speech, saying what one means without trying to be kind or polite to the hearer.

blur /blɜː/ *vt* make (a shape) unclear; make (something) hard to see or see through clearly.

blurb /blɜːb/ *n* short piece of writing telling what a book is about and how good it is.

blurt /blɜːt/ *vt* speak out suddenly; tell (a secret), e.g. *He blurted out everything we had tried to keep hidden.*

blush /blʌʃ/ *vi* become red in the face, e.g. as a sign of shame, happiness, surprise.

bluster /'blʌstə/ *vi* (of wind) blow hard; (of a person) try to get out of a difficulty by talking noisily.

boa /'bəʊə/ *n* long rope-shaped garment made of feathers worn by women about the neck.

boa-constrictor /'bəʊə kənˌstrɪktə/ *n* large South American snake.

boar /bɔː/ *n* wild pig; male pig.

board /bɔːd/ *n* **1** long flat piece of wood. **2** group of persons sitting round a table, controlling group, e.g. *Board of Governors* = group of persons who control a school. *v* get onto (a ship, aeroplane, etc.). **to board up** = cover (e.g. a window) with boards. **above board** = not secretly; lawful(ly). **board and lodging** = a place to stay, with meals provided. **on board** = ABOARD.

boarder /'bɔːdə ʳ/ n one who pays to live and have meals in another person's house, or lodging-house.

boarding house /'. . ./ n lodging-house that supplies meals.

boarding school /'. . ./ n school in which children live.

boast /bəʊst/ v speak proudly of (one's own qualities, past deeds, etc.); possess and feel proud of.

boat /bəʊt/ n thing moved by a sail, or a motor, or by rowing, used for travelling on water; any ship. **all in the same boat** = all in the same unfortunate position. **I've burnt my boats** = it is too late to turn back from this.

boater /'bəʊtə ʳ/ n hard hat for wear in summer, made of STRAW.

boatswain /'bəʊsən/ n chief seaman who calls the men to work.

bob /bɒb/ v **1** move quickly up and down. **2** cut short (the hair of a woman). **bob-tailed** /'bɒb teild / = having a short tail.

bobbin /'bɒbɪn/ n small roller holding many turns of cotton, silk or wool used in a machine for making cloth, also in a SEWING MACHINE.

bobby /'bɒbɪ/ sl n policeman.

bode /bəʊd/ vt be a sign of (what will happen, esp. of evil).

bodice /'bɒdɪs/ n upper part of a woman's dress.

body /'bɒdɪ/ n **1** the whole of a man or animal. **2** central part of a man or animal, without the limbs or head. **3** central part of anything, e.g. *The body of the hall* = large central part of the hall; *The body of a car* = that part of a motor-car in which one sits. **4** solid material part of a man, not the spirit. **5** mass, e.g. *Heavenly bodies* = the stars, etc. **6** group of persons, e.g. *The Governing Body of the school.*

bodyguard /'bɒdɪgɑːd/ n soldiers to guard (protect) a person.

bog /bɒg/ n soft, wet ground.

bogey /'bəʊgɪ/ n evil spirit; imagined fear.

bogus /'bəʊgəs/ adj pretending to be real.

bohemian /bəʊ'hiːmɪən/ n, adj (one, e.g. a painter or writer) who lives a free life not according to the usual customs of those around him.

boil¹ /bɔɪl/ n painful poisoned swelling on the body.

boil² /bɔɪl/ v **1** (esp. of liquids) make or become very hot. **2** cook in very hot water.

boiler /'bɔɪlə ʳ/ n iron container for holding hot water or water which is being turned into steam—e.g. as part of a steam-engine.

boisterous /'bɔɪstərəs/ adj wild, rough, noisy.

bold /bəʊld/ adj full of courage, fearless; clear and easily seen.

bole /bəʊl/ n thick stem of a tree.

boll

boll /bɒl/ n seed-container of the cotton plant.

bollard /'bɒləd/ n post on to which ships are tied.

bolster /'bəʊlstə ʳ/ n long soft CUSHION for putting under the head when sleeping. **to bolster up** = support.

bolt /bəʊlt/ n **1** short arrow. **bolt upright** = straight up. **a bolt from the blue** = great surprise. **2** bar used for fastening a door; sliding bar which closes one end of a gun before the shot is fired; iron pin used in holding together pieces of metal. vi suddenly run away. vt swallow (food) quickly.

bomb /bɒm/ n hollow metal container filled with explosive material which bursts after being thrown or dropped from the air. vt attack with bombs.

bombard /bɒm'bɑːd/ vt attack with guns; attack continuously.

bombast /'bɒmbæst/ n big words or big talk with little meaning. adj bombastic /bɒm'bæstɪk/.

bomber /'bɒmə ʳ/ n aeroplane from which bombs are dropped.

bombshell /'bɒmʃel/ n BOMB. **to drop a bombshell** = say something very surprising.

bona fide /ˌbəʊnə 'faɪdɪ/ adj, adv in good faith; real.

bond /bɒnd/ n **1** something that ties or holds firm. **2** written promise, esp. of a government, promising to pay money. **3** money given to a court of law to make sure that a prisoner will return when called.

bondage /'bɒndɪdʒ/ n state of being a slave.

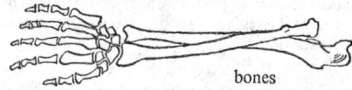

bones

bone /bəʊn/ n part of the hard frame of the body; the material of which this is made. **a bone of contention** = cause of quarrelling. **to have a bone to pick with** = have something to complain about to. **bone dry** = quite dry. **bone idle** = completely lazy. vt take the bones out of. adj **bony** /'bəʊnɪ/ like a bone; so thin that the bones can be seen.

bonfire /'bɒnfaɪə ʳ/ n large fire made out of doors for pleasure or to burn dead leaves in a garden.

bonnet /'bɒnɪt/ n **1** hat tied on the head with strings. **2** the covering over the engine of a car. **to have a bee in one's bonnet** = have some mad idea fixed in the mind.

bonny /'bɒnɪ/ adj pretty, gay and healthy.

bonus /'bəʊnəs/ *n* special payment above what is necessary.

boo /buː/ *interj* sound used to express dislike, or to drive away an animal.

booby /'buːbɪ/ *n* foolish person. *n* **booby prize** = something given to the last runner in a race or person who does worst in a game. *n* **booby trap** = foolish trick, e.g. placing a book above a door to fall on the head of a person entering.

book /bʊk/ *n* collection of sheets of paper fastened together as a thing to be read, or to be written in. **the books** = account books. *v* make earlier arrangements for (e.g. staying in a hotel, having a seat in the theatre).

bookcase /'bʊk-keɪs/ *n* set of shelves for books.

bookie /'bʊkɪ/ shortened form of **bookmaker.**

booking-clerk /'.../ *n* man who sells TICKETS.

bookish /'bʊkɪʃ/ *adj* liking books very much.

book-keeping /'. ͵ ./ *n* keeping of accounts of money.

booklet /'bʊklət/ *n* small book.

bookmaker /'bʊkmeɪkə/ *n* one who receives BETS from the public.

bookworm /'bʊkwɜːm/ *n* person who is always reading.

boom¹ /buːm/ *n, interj* deep sound, as of a large bell or big gun.

boom² /buːm/ *n* long pole on a ship used in loading; long pole to which a sail is fastened; chain fixed across a river to stop things, e.g. logs floating down.

boom³/buːm/ *n* time of quick money-making in business. *vi* (of a business, or business generally) be successful.

boomerang /'buːməræŋ/ *n* curved stick used by Australian natives which makes a circle and comes back when thrown, used to kill birds etc.

boon /buːn/ *n* a favour; a blessing, e.g. *A good book is a great boon on a long journey.*

boor /bʊə/ *n* uninteresting person, one with bad manners.

boost /buːst/ *vt* push upwards or forwards; increase the selling of goods; increase the value or power of.

booty /'buːtɪ/ *n* (*sing*) goods stolen by thieves.

booze /buːz/ *sl vi* drink ALCOHOL.

borax /'bɔːræks/ *n* white salt-like powder used for cleaning.

border /'bɔːdə/ *n* edge; line dividing two countries. *v* be on the edge or border (of a place). *adj* **borderline** /'bɔːdəlaɪn/ not clearly of one sort or the other.

bore¹ /bɔː/ *v* make (a hole). *vt* tire (someone) by talking to him in an uninteresting way; not to interest. *n* something or someone boring. *adj* **boring** /'bɔːrɪŋ/ uninteresting.

bore² /bɔː/ *n* very large wave caused by the TIDE.

bore³ /bɔː/ *n* measure across the inside of the barrel of a gun.

boredom /'bɔːdəm/ *n* state of being tired and not interested.

boric /'bɔːrɪk/ *adj* having to do with BORAX.

born /bɔːn/ **to be born** = start one's life; come into existence, e.g. *He was born in 1888.*

borne /bɔːn/ *p.p.* of **bear²**, e.g. *He had borne a heavy load; She had borne many children.*

borough /'bʌrə/ *n* town which has powers of self-government.

borrow /'bɒrəʊ/ *vt* obtain the use of a thing on the understanding that it will be given back.

bosom /'bʊzəm/ *n* human breast. **bosom friend** = close friend.

boss¹ /bɒs/ *n* round part which stands up from a flat surface, like the head of a very large nail.

boss² /bɒs/ *n* man in charge of workmen; head of any business. *vt* be head man (over); make oneself unpleasant by trying to control too much.

botany /'bɒtənɪ/ *n* science of plants.

botch /bɒtʃ/ *vt* do (work) badly; repair roughly.

both /bəʊθ/ *det* the two (of).

bother /'bɒðə/ *vt* be a trouble to; cause trouble. *vi* be anxious.

bottle /'bɒtl/ *n* container (usually of glass) for liquids. *vt* put (liquid or fruit) into a bottle. **to bottle up one's anger** = control, hide one's anger.

bottleneck /'bɒtlnek/ *n* narrow space in a road which slows down cars; part of a factory where production is slow, so slowing down the whole.

bottom /'bɒtəm/ *n* lowest part of anything; ground under the sea, a river, etc. *infml* the part of the body on which one sits.

boudoir /'buːdwɑː/ *n* lady's sitting-room.

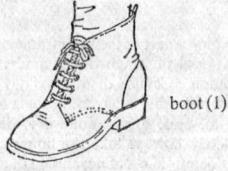

boot (1)

boot /buːt/ *n* **1** covering for the feet, usually made of leather or rubber, having an upper part covering part of the leg. **2** place, usually at the back of a car, for bags and boxes.

booth /buːð/ *n* hut; shop in a hut.

bootlegger /'buːtlegə/ *n* one who breaks the law by making or selling strong drink.

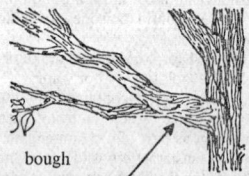

bough

bough /baʊ/ *n* branch of a tree.

bought /bɔːt/ *p.t. & p.p.* of **buy.**

boulder /'bəʊldə/ *n* large stone.

boulevard /'buːləvɑːd/ *n* broad street, usually having trees on each side.

bounce /baʊns/ *v* (of a ball) spring back again or cause to spring back from the floor, wall, etc.; (of a person) move in a rough and noisy way. *vi infml* (of a CHEQUE) not paid by the bank because the account concerned is empty. *n* act of bouncing.

bound¹ /baʊnd/ *vt* mark the edges of; keep within a certain space. *n* (*pl*) **bounds** edges so marked; edges beyond which one may not go.

bound² /baʊnd/ *vi* jump. *n* jump. **by leaps and bounds** = very quickly.

bound³ /baʊnd/ *p.p. & p.t.* of **bind**. **bound for** = going (e.g. sailing) towards. **bound to** = certain to.

boundary /'baʊndəri/ *n* fixed and agreed outside edge of a field, country; space within which a game is played.

bounteous /'baʊntɪəs/ *adj* generous.

bounty /'baʊnti/ *n* gift; act of being generous.

bouquet /bʊ'keɪ/ *n* **1** flowers tied together for holding in the hand. **2** smell of a wine.

bourgeois /'bʊəʒwɑː/ *adj* middle-class.

bout /baʊt/ *n* short time during which something happens.

bovine /'bəʊvaɪn/ *adj* having to do with cattle; slow and heavy like a cow.

bow¹

bow¹ /baʊ/ *v* bend, e.g. as a sign of respect.

bow² /bəʊ/ *n* **1** piece of wood held in a curve by a string, used for shooting arrows, also for rubbing strings to play music. **2** fancy knot such as is used for the shoes, also for a TIE.

bow³ /baʊ/ *n* front end of a ship.

bowel /'baʊəl/ *n* long pipe continuing from the stomach and leading the waste matter out of the body.

bowl¹ /bəʊl/ *n* round deep dish.

bowl² /bəʊl/ *n* large ball rolled along the ground in a game. *v* roll or throw (a ball) in any of several ball games.

bow-legged /bəʊ 'legd/ *adj* having the legs curving outwards at the knee.

bowler /'bəʊlə/ *n* man's round hard hat, usually black.

bowline /'bəʊlɪn/ *n* **1** rope running from the edge of a sail to the front part of a ship. **2** special sort of knot which does not slip.

bowls /bəʊlz/ *n* game in which one tries to roll large balls as near as possible to one small ball.

box¹ /bɒks/ *n* **1** case or container. **2** small room among the seats in a theatre.

box² /bɒks/ *v* fight with the FISTS.

Boxing day /'.. ./ *n* the day after Christmas day.

box-office /'. ,. ./ *n* place in a theatre at which seats for a play are sold.

boy /bɔɪ/ *n* male child; young man.

boycott /'bɔɪkɒt/ *vt* join together and refuse to buy from or sell to (someone) or do any business with him.

bra /brɑː/ see **brassière.**

brace¹ /breɪs/ *n* post or rope used to hold something firm. *vt* hold in place firmly **to brace oneself** = gather one's strength. **a pair of braces** = a pair of bands over the shoulders that hold up the trousers.

brace² /breɪs/ *n* pair; group of two.

bracelet /'breɪslət/ *n* band worn around the arm as an ornament.

bracing /'breɪsɪŋ/ *adj* making one feel strong and well.

bracken /'brækən/ *n* a kind of wild plant whose seeds are found on the under-side of the leaves.

bracket /'brækɪt/ *n* **1** piece of iron or wood put in or on a wall to support something. **2** either one of a pair of marks (e.g. the pair '(' and ')') between which a writer puts something that is not necessary to the main idea of the sentence. *vt* **1** join together with a bracket. **2** put in brackets.

brackish /'brækɪʃ/ *adj* salt-tasting.

bradawl /'brædɔːl/ *n* instrument used for making small holes.

brag /bræg/ *vi* express a very good opinion of one's own powers. *n* **braggart** /'brægət/ noisy fellow with a good opinion of himself.

Brahmin /'brɑːmɪn/ *n* member of the highest, priestly, class of Hindus in India.

braid /breɪd/ *n* narrow band of cloth used for making an edge to cloth and for binding things together. *vt* twist together into one string or band.

braille /breɪl/ *n* way of writing with raised dots so that BLIND people can read it with their fingers.

brain /breɪn/ *n* grey matter inside the head with which we think.

braise /breɪz/ *vt* cook (meat) very slowly in a closed pot.

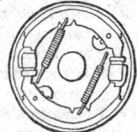

brake

brake /breɪk/ *n* block or band pressing upon a wheel which lessens or stops movement. *vi* (e.g. in a car) use the brake.

bramble /'bræmbəl/ *n* common wild prickly bush which bears a red fruit that later becomes black.

bran /bræn/ *n* skin of wheat and other grain separated from the flour.

branch /brɑːntʃ/ *n* limb of a tree growing out from the stem; *Branch of a river* = side stream; anything divided off from the chief part, e.g. *Branch road; Branch of a subject; Branches of a shop* = small shops controlled by one big shop. *vi* divide into branches.

brand /brænd/ *n* **1** piece of burning wood. **2** mark burned by such a piece of wood, or anything else, on animals, as a sign of ownership. **3** kind, e.g. *A brand of tea* = special kind shown by some mark or sign on the paper or box. **4** (in poetry) sword. *vt* mark. **to brand a man as a thief** = show that he is —.

brandish /'brændɪʃ/ *vt* wave (e.g. a sword) about.

brand new /ˌ. './ *adj* quite new.

brandy /'brændɪ/ *n* strong drink made from wine.

brash /bræʃ/ *adj* pushing oneself forward rudely.

brass /brɑːs/ *n* mixture of copper and ZINC. *adj* **1** made of brass. **2** having to do with musical instruments made of brass, e.g. *A brass band.*

brassière /'bræzɪə'/, **bra** *n* small tight undergarment worn by women over the breasts.

brat /bræt/ *n* bad-mannered child.

bravado /brə'vɑːdəʊ/ *n* show of courage.

brave /breɪv/ *adj* having courage in face of danger; able to suffer without complaint. *n* **bravery** /'breɪvərɪ/.

bravo! /brɑː'vəʊ/ *interj* (shout of joy because someone has done well).

brawl /brɔːl/ *vi,* quarrel with much noise; fight.

brawn /brɔːn/ *n* **1** strength. **2** pig-meat boiled and pressed into a pot.

bray /breɪ/ *n, vi* (make) the noise made by an ass.

brazen /'breɪzən/ *adj* **1** made of brass. **2** shameless.

brazier /'breɪzɪə/ *n* **1** one who works with brass. **2** pot used to contain burning coals.

breach /briːtʃ/ *n* act of breaking, e.g. the law, some agreement, or a promise.

bread /bred/ *n* common food made of flour. *n* **breadwinner** /'bredˌwɪnə'/ person who works to supply the family with food.

breadth /bretθ/ *n* distance across; broadness.

break /breɪk/ *v* **1** separate or cause to separate into pieces esp. by force. **2** (of a machine, piece of equipment, etc.) no longer work, or cause no longer to work properly. *vi* **1** have a short rest from what one is doing. **2** (of a boy's voice) take on the deeper notes of a man's voice. **to break a record** = run (etc.) faster than anyone before. **to break down** = be unable to continue (working, speaking, etc.). **break off** = **1** stop suddenly. **2** come off or cause to come off as a result of breaking. **break out** = **1** begin suddenly. **2** escape (from a prison, etc.). **break up** = **1** break into small pieces. **2** (of a school) end for the HOLIDAYS. *n* **1** breaking; place where something is broken; separation. **2** short rest from what one is doing. **3** *infml* a chance. **4** change of direction of a ball on hitting the ground.

breakdown /'breɪkdaʊn/ *n* event of something

(e.g. a car) breaking down. **a nervous breakdown** = disorder of the mind caused by too much work or other difficulties in life. **breakdown of figures** = rearrangement of figures so as to show how they are made up.

breaker /'breɪkə'/ *n* large wave rolling on the shore.

breakfast /'brekfəst/ *n* first meal of the day.

breakwater /'breɪkwɔːtə'/ *n* wall built to stop waves.

bream /briːm/ *n* a kind of fresh-water fish.

breast /brest/ *n* front part of the body between the neck and the stomach; that part of a woman's body that produces milk; place where the feelings are, e.g. *A troubled breast* = anxious mind.

breastwork /'brestwɔːk/ *n* low wall built as a defence in fighting.

breath /breθ/ *n* air let out or drawn into the body through the nose or mouth; act of letting out or drawing in such air. **under one's breath** = (spoken) very quietly so as not to be heard. **to take one's breath away** = surprise.

breathe /briːð/ *v* let (air or some other substance) out from or draw (such a substance) into the body through the nose or mouth.

bred /bred/ *p.p. & p.t.* of **breed.** *adj* **well bred** /ˌ. './ coming from a good family and having had careful training in manners, etc.

breech /briːtʃ/ *n* back part of a thing; end of a gun into which the shot is put.

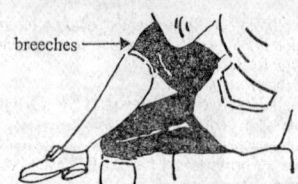

breeches

breeches /'brɪtʃɪz/ *n (pl)* garment covering a man's legs as far down as the knees.

breed /briːd/ *vi* (of an animal) produce young. *vt* arrange for (animals) to produce young. *n* group of related animals of the same kind.

breeze /briːz/ *n* light wind.

breeze block /'. ./ *n* light-weight grey block used in building, made from small pieces of burnt coal.

brethren /'breðrən/ *n (pl)* brothers.

breviary /'briːvɪərɪ/ *n* book of prayer.

brevity /'brevɪtɪ/ *n* shortness of speech or writing.

brew /bruː/ *v* **1** boil in water so that the taste is passed to the water. **2** make BEER. *n* act of so boiling; that which is boiled.

brewery /'bruːərɪ/ *n* place in which BEER is made.

briar /'braɪə'/ see **brier.**

bribe /braɪb/ *vt* offer money to (someone) to cause him to do what is wrong. *n* money thus offered. *n* **bribery** /'braɪbərɪ/ offering of such money.

bric-à-brac /ˈbrɪkəbræk/ n (sing) small ornaments in a house.

brick /brɪk/ n hard piece of baked earth or other material used for building houses. **to brick up =** cover or cover up with bricks.

bride /braɪd/ n woman about to be married, or newly married. adj **bridal** /ˈbraɪdl/. n **bridegroom** /ˈbraɪdgruːm, -grʊm/ man about to be married, or newly married. n **bridesmaid** /ˈbraɪdzmeɪd/ girl who attends on a woman who is being married.

bridge¹ /brɪdʒ/ n 1 thing built of wood, stone, iron, etc., carrying a road over a valley, river, etc. 2 that part of a ship where the captain stands.

bridge² /brɪdʒ/ n a kind of card game.

bridgehead /ˈbrɪdʒhed/ n strong place far forward in enemy country from which an attack will be made.

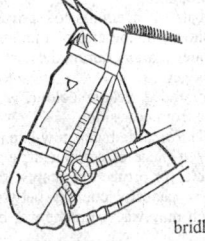

bridle

bridle /ˈbraɪdl/ n leather bands put on a horse's head. n **bridle path** /ˈ.. ./ narrow path just wide enough for a horse.

brief¹ /briːf/ adj short.

brief² /briːf/ n written notes used by a lawyer speaking in a court of law. **to brief an airman =** tell him necessary facts and what he has to do.

briefcase /ˈbriːfkeɪs/ n flat case for carrying papers.

brier /ˈbraɪə/ n a kind of small bush which pricks the skin; the root of this; a pipe for smoking made from this root.

brig /brɪg/ n ship with two MASTS and large square sails on both of them.

brigade /brɪˈgeɪd/ n part of an army, containing about 5000 soldiers. n **brigadier** /ˌbrɪgəˈdɪə/ officer in command of a brigade.

brigand /ˈbrɪgənd/ n thief, often one of a band of thieves living in mountains.

bright /braɪt/ adj 1 having light; having clear, easily seen colours. 2 quick at learning. v **brighten** /ˈbraɪtn/ make or become bright, or more cheerful.

brilliant /ˈbrɪlɪənt/ adj 1 shining very brightly. 2 very clever.

brim /brɪm/ n edge, e.g. of a cup, hat, etc. **brim full** /ˌ. ˈ./ adj full to the edge.

brimstone /ˈbrɪmstəʊn/ n SULPHUR.

brindled /ˈbrɪndəld/ adj marked with brown bands (e.g. a cow's skin).

brine /braɪn/ n salt water.

bring /brɪŋ/ vt 1 carry to the place where the speaker is; make or help (someone) come. 2 to cause. **to bring on, to bring about =** cause. **to bring off =** succeed in doing. **to bring up =** take care of and train (a child).

brink /brɪŋk/ n edge, e.g. of a cliff.

brisk /brɪsk/ adj quick, active.

brisket /ˈbrɪskɪt/ n meat from the breast of an animal.

bristle /ˈbrɪsəl/ n stiff hair. **to bristle with =** have many (sharp points, difficulties).

brittle /ˈbrɪtl/ adj hard and easily broken, like glass.

broach /brəʊtʃ/ vt open (a barrel of liquid); begin to talk about a subject.

broad /brɔːd/ adj wide; not narrow. adj **broadminded** /ˌbrɔːd ˈmaɪndɪd/ able to understand the opinions of others and their reasons for holding them, even if one does not agree.

broadcast /ˈbrɔːdkɑːst/ vt scatter in all directions; (also vi) send (words and music) through the air by electric waves. n something that is broadcast, e.g. on the radio.

broadside /ˈbrɔːdsaɪd/ n 1 the whole side of a ship; all the guns on one side of a warship fired at once. 2 sheet of paper printed on one side.

brocade /brəˈkeɪd/ n ornamental silk material often with gold and silver in it.

brochure /ˈbrəʊʃə, -ʃʊə/ n small book.

brogue /brəʊg/ n 1 kind of shoe. 2 the way in which the Irish speak English.

broil /brɔɪl/ vt cook (meat) by holding it close to the fire.

broke /brəʊk/ 1 p.t. of **break**. 2 sl adj having no money. **broken** /ˈbrəʊkən/ p.p. of **break**. adj **broken-hearted** /ˌbrəʊkən ˈhɑːtɪd/ very unhappy

broker /ˈbrəʊkə/ n one who does business for another, esp. in buying and selling foreign money or shares in business. n **brokerage** /ˈbrəʊkərɪdʒ/ money paid to a broker for buying and selling.

bromide /ˈbrəʊmaɪd/ n a kind of medicine used to produce a feeling of calm.

bronchitis /brɒŋˈkaɪtɪs/ n disease caught in cold wet weather which makes breathing difficult.

bronze /brɒnz/ n mixture of copper and TIN. adj, n (of the) colour of bronze; golden-brown. v make or become bronze in colour (esp. as a result of being in hot sun).

brooch /brəʊtʃ/ n ornamental pin worn on the clothes.

brood /bruːd/ n group of young animals. vi (of a bird) sit on (eggs). **to brood over =** think deeply about, e.g. To brood over one's troubles = continue to think angrily or sadly about—.

brook¹ /brʊk/ n small stream.

brook² /brʊk/ vt suffer, allow.

broom /bruːm/ n 1 a kind of plant with yellow flowers. 2 large brush used for cleaning the floor.

broth /brɒθ/ n liquid made by boiling meat, etc.

brook¹

bud

brother /'brʌðə⁷/ n another son of one's own parents; someone working in the same group as oneself. n **brotherhood** /'brʌðəhʊd/ group of men formed for some special purpose. n **brother-in-law** /'... ,/ brother of one's husband or wife; husband of one's sister.

brought /brɔːt/ p.p. & p.t. of **bring**.

brow /braʊ/ n front of the head above the eyes. **brow of a hill** = steep slope of a hill.

browbeat /'braʊbiːt/ vt shout at (someone) and treat him unkindly.

brown /braʊn/ adj, n (of the) colour of the earth. **in a brown study** = deep in thought. sl **browned off** = angry and tired; BORED.

browse /braʊz/ vi 1 feed on young plants. 2 read here and there in books.

bruise /bruːz/ n coloured place on the skin caused by a blow. vt cause (someone) to have a bruise.

brunette /bruː'net/ n woman with dark eyes and hair.

brunt /brʌnt/ **to bear the brunt** = suffer the heaviest part of the attack.

brush /brʌʃ/ n 1 instrument for cleaning or smoothing, made of sticks or stiff hair. 2 rough low bushes. 3 small fight or quarrel. vt clean or make smooth with a brush. **to brush aside** = not treat seriously. **to brush past a person** = push past him. **to brush up** = learn again. n **brushwood** /'brʌʃwʊd/ small sticks.

brusque /bruːsk/ adj quick and rough in manner.

brute /bruːt/ n animal; cruel man. adj **brutal** /'bruːtl/ cruel.

bubble /'bʌbəl/ n hollow ball of liquid containing air; ball of air in a liquid. vi (of a liquid) produce bubbles, as when boiling.

buccaneer /,bʌkə'nɪə⁷/ n sea ROBBER.

buck¹ /bʌk/ n male deer.

buck² /bʌk/ vi (of a horse) jump up with all four feet off the ground. sl **buck up** = be quick, be cheerful, work harder.

bucket /'bʌkɪt/ n container with a handle for carrying water. sl **kick the bucket** = die.

buckle /'bʌkəl/ n metal fastener used for joining the ends of two bands, or for ornament. **buckle to, buckle down to it** = set to work hard.

buckler /'bʌklə⁷/ n small shield.

buckskin /'bʌk,skɪn/ n, adj (made from) leather made of deer-skin.

buckwheat /'bʌk-wiːt/ n small black grain used as food for hens, and in America for making cakes.

bucolic /bjuː'kɒlɪk/ adj having to do with the country and countrymen.

bud /bʌd/ n young tightly rolled up flower before it opens. vi produce buds. **budding poet** = young poet who is just beginning to show his powers.

Buddha /'bʊdə/ n great religious teacher honoured by many people in China and the East. n **Buddhism** /'bʊdɪzəm/ the religion.

budge /bʌdʒ/ v move a little; cause to move. **he won't budge** = won't change his plans, or opinions.

budgerigar /'bʌdʒərɪgɑː⁷/ n a kind of small bright-coloured bird.

budget /'bʌdʒɪt/ n accounts of government money as shown at the end of the year with plans for money matters during the next year. vi prepare a budget.

buff /bʌf/ adj faded yellow colour. n yellow leather made from cow-skin.

buffalo /'bʌfələʊ/ n large black cow-like animal.

buffer /'bʌfə⁷/ n piece of equipment, e.g. on a railway engine, for protection against shock. **a buffer state** = peaceful country between two nations which may wish to make war on each other.

buffet¹ /'bʌfɪt/ n blow with the hand. vt hit.

buffet² /'bʊfeɪ/ n room or table where one can get food which one eats standing up.

buffoon /bʌ'fuːn/ n rough and noisy fool.

bug /bʌg/ n 1 dirty, wingless insect which drinks blood; any small insect. 2 sl hidden MICRO-PHONE. vt sl listen to (someone) using a bug.

bugbear /'bʌgbeə⁷/ n imagined cause of fear.

bugle /'bjuːgəl/ n metal horn used in the army to call soldiers.

build /bɪld/ v put together materials in order to make (something, e.g. a house). n shape or size of a person's body. n **building** /'bɪldɪŋ/ something built, e.g. a house. n **builder** /'bɪldə⁷/.

bulb /bʌlb/ n 1 round part of a plant, below the ground, from which the plant grows. 2 any object of this shape, esp. the glass part of an electric lamp from which the light shines.

bulge /bʌldʒ/ vi swell outward. n swelling.

bulk /bʌlk/ n large size.

bulkhead /'bʌlkhed/ n wall that divides a ship into separate parts, so that, if one part is damaged, water may not fill the whole ship.

bulky /'bʌlkɪ/ adj large and difficult to carry.

bull /bʊl/ n male of cattle; male form of any other such mammal, e.g. elephant.

bulldog /'bʊldɒg/ n a kind of large powerful dog.

bulldozer /'bʊldəʊzə⁷/ n big machine for moving earth.

bullet /'bʊlɪt/ n shot as fired from a gun.

bulletin /'bʊlətɪn/ *n* short printed or written report.

bullion /'bʊlɪən/ *n* quantity of gold or silver which has not been made into money.

bullock /'bʊlək/ *n* young BULL which cannot become a father.

bull's-eye /'bʊlz aɪ/ *n* centre of a TARGET.

bully /'bʊlɪ/ *n* one who uses his strength to hurt weaker persons. *v* use one's strength to hurt (someone weaker).

bulrush /'bʊlrʌʃ/ *n* tall, grass-like water plant with a brown or black woolly head.

bulwark /'bʊlwək/ *n* wall built to defend a place; side of a ship above the DECK.

bum /bʌm/ *sl n* back part of the body on which one sits.

bumblebee /'bʌmbəlbiː/ *n* large hairy bee which makes a loud noise when flying.

bump /bʌmp/ *n* **1** swelling caused by a blow. **2** dull noise made by one thing knocking into or falling onto another. *v* knock heavily into (something).

bumper¹ /'bʌmpə/ **a bumper crop** = very large crop.

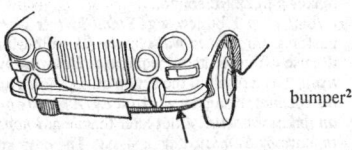

bumper²

bumper² /'bʌmpə/ *n* bar fixed on the front and back of a car to protect the car when it knocks against anything.

bumpkin /'bʌmpkɪn/ *n* foolish fellow from the country.

bumptious /'bʌmpʃəs/ *adj* pushing oneself forward; believing too much in one's own powers.

bun /bʌn/ *n* small round piece of sweetened bread.

bunch /bʌntʃ/ *n* group; number of things of the same kind fastened together.

bundle /'bʌndl/ *n* quantity of things tied together.

bung /bʌŋ/ *n* round piece of wood used to stop the hole in a barrel.

bungalow /'bʌŋgələʊ/ *n* low small house with no upper floor.

bungle /'bʌŋgl/ *v* do (a piece of work) badly.

bunion /'bʌnɪən/ *n* swelling on a joint of the foot.

bunk /bʌŋk/ *n* narrow bed fixed to the wall of a ship or car. *vi* sleep in such a bed.

bunker /'bʌŋkə/ *n* **1** place for storing coal. **2** place for sheltering from BOMBS. **3** a hollow with sand on a GOLF-course, set there to make play more difficult.

bunny /'bʌnɪ/ *n* child's word for rabbit.

bunsen burner /,bʌnsən 'bɜːnə/ *n* lamp which mixes air and gas to make a hot blue flame.

bunting /'bʌntɪŋ/ *n* kind of cloth used for making flags; flags and cloth-ornaments for buildings on some special day.

buoy

buoy /bɔɪ/ *n* floating object fastened to the bed of the sea to show ships where there are rocks. **to buoy up one's hopes** = keep up one's hopes.

buoyant /'bɔɪənt/ *adj* very light, which cannot sink; gay, full of hope and high spirits. *n* **buoyancy** /'bɔɪənsɪ/.

bur, burr /bɜː/ *n* seed-container of certain plants covered with prickles which make it hang on to the clothes; plant that has such seeds.

burden /'bɜːdn/ *n* heavy load. *vt* load heavily. **the burden of proof lies with you** = it is your duty to prove it.

bureau /'bjʊərəʊ/ *n* large writing-table with wooden cover which slides over the top to close it; a government office. *n* **bureaucracy** /bjʊ'rɒkrəsɪ/ government by the paid officers of government rather than by persons elected by the people. *n* **bureaucrat** /'bjʊərəkræt/ member of a bureaucracy; officer who tries to centre power in himself.

burglar /'bɜːglə/ *n* thief who breaks into houses, shops, etc.

burial /'berɪəl/ *n* act of putting a dead body into a grave.

burlesque /bɜː'lesk/ *n* speech or play in which a serious thing is made to seem foolish or a foolish thing is treated solemnly so as to make people laugh.

burly /'bɜːlɪ/ *adj* large, fat, strong.

burn /bɜːn/ *vt* set on fire. *vi* be in flames.

burnish /'bɜːnɪʃ/ *vt* make (a metal) bright by rubbing.

burnt /bɜːnt/ *p.t.* & *p.p.* of **burn.**

burr see **bur.**

burrow /'bʌrəʊ/ *n* hole in the ground made by rabbits, foxes, etc. *vi* make such a hole in the ground.

bursar /'bɜːsə/ *n* man in a university or school who has charge of the money.

burst /bɜːst/ *v* break or be broken open suddenly or by force coming from the inside. *n* sudden outbreak, e.g. *A burst of laughter.*

bury /'berɪ/ *vt* put (a dead body) into the grave; cover from sight; hide away.

bus /bʌs/ *n* large public vehicle which carries the public on payment of small amounts.

bush¹ /bʊʃ/ *n* small low tree. **the bush** = uncleared wild country in Australia or Africa.

bush² /bʊʃ/ *n* plate of soft metal put between two parts of a machine which rub against each other.

bushel /'bʊʃl/ *n* measure of grain, about 36½ litres.

bushy /'buʃɪ/ *adj* **1** (of country) having many bushes. **2** (of hair) growing thickly.

business /'bɪznəs/ *n* **1** one's work or employment; **2** trade and the getting of money; particular money-getting work, e.g. a shop. **3** duty, e.g. *It is a teacher's business to make boys learn.* **no business of yours** = nothing to do with you. **mind your own business** = look to your own matters and do not ask about mine. **4** matter; event, e.g. *I don't understand this business. n* **businessman** /'bɪznəsmən/ one engaged in trade, COMMERCE, etc.

businesslike /'bɪznəslaɪk/ *adj* doing things carefully and with common sense.

bust /bʌst/ *n* **1** head, shoulders and breast; (of a woman) the breasts. **2** person's head and shoulders cut in stone. *sl* **to go bust** = become BANKRUPT.

bustle /'bʌsl/ *n* noisy movement. *vi* be busy with much noise.

busy /'bɪzɪ/ *adj* working hard; having little time for play. **to busy oneself** = be busy doing.

busybody /'bɪzɪ bodɪ/ *n* one who interests himself too much in other people's concerns.

but /bət; *strong* bʌt/ *conj* and yet; although that is true it is also true that; even so. *prep* except.

butcher /'butʃə/ *n* one who (kills and) sells animals for food. *vt* murder cruelly.

butler /'bʌtlə/ *n* man-servant in a house in charge of the dining-room and wine.

butt¹ /bʌt/ *n* thick end (of something).

butt² /bʌt/ *vt* give a blow with the head; hit with the heavy end of. *sl* **to butt in** = to come when not wanted. *n* **1** blow with the head. **2** end of a used cigarette.

butter /'bʌtə/ *n* yellow fat made from milk, used on bread and in cooking. *vt* put butter on (e.g. bread). **to butter up** = praise (someone) in the hope of gaining some favour from him.

buttercup /'bʌtəkʌp/ *n* a kind of yellow wild flower.

butterfly /'bʌtəflaɪ/ *n* insect with large, beautifully coloured wings.

buttermilk /'bʌtəmɪlk/ *n* liquid which remains after butter is made from milk.

buttery /'bʌtərɪ/ *n* room from which food and drink are served.

buttock /'bʌtək/ *n* one side of that part of the body on which one sits.

butterfly

button /'bʌtn/ *n* **1** small round fastener on clothes. **2** any small round object used for pushing, e.g. to ring a bell. *n* **buttonhole** /'bʌtnhəʊl/ **1** hole for a button. **2** flower to put on the front of one's coat. *vt* catch (someone) and get him to listen.

buttress /'bʌtrəs/ *n* support for a wall. *vt* support.

buxom /'bʌksəm/ *adj* (of a woman) fat and healthy-looking.

buy /baɪ/ *vt* obtain by giving money. **to buy up** = buy all that can be obtained.

buzz /bʌz/ *n* noise that an insect makes when flying. *vi* make such a noise. *sl* **buzz off!** = go away!

buzzard /'bʌzəd/ *n* a kind of meat-eating bird.

buzzer /'bʌzə/ *n* electrical instrument which makes a BUZZING sound.

by /baɪ/ *prep* **1** beside, e.g. *Stand by this tree;* past, e.g *He used to walk by the house.* **2** with the use of; using as a means, e.g. *He came by train.* **3** as a result of the action of, e.g. *Killed by his enemies;* being the work of, e.g. *A picture by an unknown artist.* **4** not later than, e.g. *I hope to leave by Sunday. adv* past, e.g. *The days go by.*

by-, bye- /baɪ/ e.g. **by-product** = second thing produced in the course of producing some other important thing. **bypass** = new road built specially for cars to keep them away from towns.

bye-bye /ˌbaɪ 'baɪ, 'baɪ ˌbaɪ/ *interj* goodbye; (to children) time to go to bed; bed.

bygone /'baɪgɒn/ *adj* of the past.

by(e)-law /'. . ./ *n* special law or rule made, not by the government of the whole country, but by a town or railway, etc.

byre /'baɪə/ *n* cow-house.

byway /'baɪweɪ/ *n* small path leading away from the main path.

byword /'baɪwɜːd/ *n* common saying; person or thing to be laughed at, and thought little of.

C

C /siː/ Roman figure, 100.

cab /kæb/ *n* **1** TAXI. **2** that part of the engine of a train in which the driver stands.

cabaret /'kæbəreɪ/ *n* RESTAURANT where there is singing and dancing; show of dancing, etc., as given in such a place.

cabbage /'kæbɪdʒ/ *n* a kind of green vegetable of which the leaves are boiled for food

cabin /'kæbɪn/ *n* small house; room in a ship or aeroplane.

cabinet /'kæbɪnət, kæbnət/ *n* **1** small box; piece of furniture with glass windows used to contain ornaments and objects of interest. **2** special group of the chief men who control the government.

cable /'keɪbəl/ *n* **1** thick strong rope; strong wire laid under the sea or over the land for sending electric messages. **2** TELEGRAM. *v* send a telegram. *n* **cablegram** /'keɪbəlgræm/ TELEGRAM.

cache /kæʃ/ *n* secret place in which stores are hidden by travellers.

cackle /'kækəl/ *n* noise made by a hen; noisy talking.

cactus

cactus /'kæktəs/ *n* plant with thick leaves having on them many needle-like prickles.

cad /kæd/ *n* bad-mannered fellow.

cadaverous /kə'dævərəs/ *adj* like a dead body.

caddie /'kædɪ/ *n* boy or man who carries the instruments used in playing golf.

caddy /'kædɪ/ *n* small ornamental box, e.g. for tea.

cadence /'keɪdəns/ *n* rise and fall of the voice.

cadet /kə'det/ *n* youth learning to be an officer in the army etc.

cadge /kædʒ/ *infml v* ask (for money, etc.).

café /'kæfeɪ/ *n* place which sells meals and coffee. *n* **cafeteria** /ˌkæfɪ'tɪərɪə/ place for meals where those who eat serve themselves.

caffeine /'kæfiːn/ *n* substance obtained from coffee.

cage /keɪdʒ/ *n* **1** box with bars for holding birds and animals. **2** box used to take workers down into a MINE.

cagey /'keɪdʒɪ/ *infml adj* unwilling to answer questions.

cairn /keən/ *n* number of stones built up, wide at the bottom and pointed at the top.

cajole /kə'dʒəʊl/ *vt* get (someone) to do a thing by deceiving him with sweet speeches.

cake /keɪk/ *n* sweet bread made with eggs, butter, etc. **a cake of soap** = a piece of soap. **caked with dirt** = thickly covered with dirt.

calabash /'kæləbæʃ/ *n* bottle or container made of the hard shell of a GOURD.

calamity /kə'læmətɪ/ *n* any cause that produces great evil, e.g. war, fire, etc.

calcium /'kælsɪəm/ *n* pure material obtained from lime.

calculate /'kælkjʊleɪt/ *v* add, divide, etc., and work with numbers; examine and tell. *n* **calculation** /ˌkælkjʊ'leɪʃən/.

calculus /'kælkjʊləs/ *n* way of calculating the speed of growth, or speed of very small changes.

calendar /'kæləndə/ *n* list of days, weeks and months year by year.

calf[1] /kɑːf/ *n* young of a cow or of other animals. *n* **calfskin** /'kɑːf.skɪn/ leather made from the skin of the calf.

calf[1]

calf[2] /kɑːf/ *n* back of the leg between the knee and the foot.

calibrate /'kælɪbreɪt/ *vt* **1** measure the width of (e.g., the hole in the barrel of a gun). **2** make number marks on a measuring instrument so that it measures correctly.

calibre /'kælɪbə/ *n* **1** width of the hole in a gun. **2** (good) quality, esp. of a person.

calico /'kælɪkəʊ/ *n* a kind of cotton cloth.

caliph /'kælɪf, 'keɪlɪf/ *n* title given to descendants of Muhammad.

call /kɔːl/ *v* **1** cry out in a loud voice. **2** make a short visit at a person's house. **3** cause a person to come, e.g. *Call people together to a meeting.* **4** give a name to or use as a name of. **5** telephone. **to call for** = **1** ask for. **2** need, e.g. *This problem calls for thought.* **to call off** = CANCEL. **to call up** = order (someone) into service in the army. *n* **1** act of calling; shout. **2** short visit to someone's house. **3** act of telephoning. **a close call** = narrow escape.

calligraphy /kə'lɪgrəfɪ/ *n* good handwriting.

callipers /'kælɪpəz/ *n* (*pl*) instrument used for measuring round objects, objects of irregular shape and the insides of holes.

callous /'kæləs/ *adj* **1** (of skin) hardened. **2** without feeling for the sufferings of others.

callow /'kæləʊ/ *adj* young and inexperienced.

calm /kɑːm/ *adj* quiet; not rough. *v* make or become calm, e.g. *Try to calm him; Calm down.* *n* state of being calm.

calorie /'kælərɪ/ *n* measure of heat, esp. of the heat value of food.

calumniate /kə'lʌmnɪeɪt/ *vt* tell untrue stories about (someone) in order to do harm to his good name. *n* **calumny** /'kæləmnɪ/ untrue story.

calve /kɑːv/ *v* (of a cow) give birth to (young). **calves** *pl* of **calf**[1] and **calf**[2].

calyx /'keɪlɪks/ *n* circle of small leaves under a flower.

cam /kæm/ *n* part of a machine used for changing movement from circular to straight.

camber /'kæmbə/ *n* slightly arched shape (as of a road surface).

cambric /'keɪmbrɪk/ *n* thin white cloth.

came /keɪm/ *p.t.* of **come**.

camel /'kæməl/ *n* a kind of mammal having either one or two raised parts on its back.

cameo /'kæmɪəʊ/ *n* jewel with figures cut on it.

camera /'kæmərə/ *n* instrument used for taking photographs. **in camera** = in secret.

camouflage /'kæməflɑːʒ/ *vt* hide by making

(oneself or something else) the same colour as what is around one. *n* this way of hiding (oneself or something else).

camp /kæmp/ *n* open space with tents or huts in which soldiers or travellers live for a short time. *vi* form a camp; live, sleep etc. in a tent.

campaign /kæm'peɪn/ *n* movements and battles of an army in a war. **a campaign against** = making speeches, writing in the papers, etc., etc.

camphor /'kæmfə/ *n* white strong-smelling material used to keep insects out of clothes in store, and in medicine.

campus /'kæmpəs/ *n* grounds round a school or university.

can¹ /kən; *strong* kæn/ *v* be able to; have it in one's power to; know how to, e.g. *Can you speak French? He can fly an aeroplane; Nobody can jump as high as that.*

can² /kæn/ *n* small metal container, usually round, for holding foods. *vt* put into such containers, e.g. *Canned food* = food kept good by being shut up in tins.

canal /kə'næl/ *n* waterway dug by man. **alimentary canal** = path for food in the body from the mouth to the stomach and on through the bowel.

canary /kə'neərɪ/ *n* a yellow singing bird.

cancel /'kænsəl/ *vt* draw a line through a written word; undo what has been done, put an end to e.g. *To cancel a debt.*

cancer /'kænsə/ *n* painful illness caused by uncontrolled growth of some part of the body; any growing evil.

candid /'kændɪd/ *adj* honest, speaking the truth.

candidate /'kændɪdət, -deɪt/ *n* one who offers himself for an office; one who tries to be elected; one who sits for an examination.

candle /'kændl/ *n* round bar of wax with a string in the middle, used to give light.

candlestick /'kændl,stɪk/ *n* instrument used for holding a candle.

candour /'kændə/ *n* honesty; plain speaking.

candy /'kændɪ/ *n* sweets made from sugar. *vt* harden and preserve with sugar.

cane /keɪn/ *n* **1** easily bent stick; walking-stick. **2** sugar plant. *vt* hit with a cane.

canine /'keɪnaɪn/ *adj* having to do with dogs. **canine teeth** = pointed teeth third from the front in one's mouth.

canister /'kænɪstə/ *n* wooden or metal box, e.g. for tea.

canker /'kæŋkə/ *n* **1** painful place in the body of an animal where the skin is eaten away by disease; so also on a plant. **2** any evil which slowly grows and destroys.

cannibal /'kænɪbəl/ *n* person who eats human meat.

cannon /'kænən/ *n* **1** large gun. **2** striking one ball against another in the game of BILLIARDS.

cannonade /,kænə'neɪd/ *n* continued firing of large guns.

cannot /'kænɒt, 'kænət/ *v* (not + can); be unable

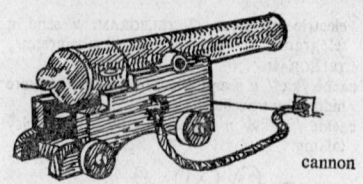

cannon

to; lack the power to, etc, e.g. *I cannot move it* = it is not the case that I can move it.

canny /'kænɪ/ *adj* careful; wise.

canoe /kə'nuː/ *n* narrow light boat moved by a stick with a broad, flat end. *vi* travel by canoe.

canon /'kænən/ *n* **1** rule of the Church. **2** officer of the Church. **3** list of books accepted as really written by a certain man. *adj* **canonical** /kə'nɒnɪkəl/ according to the rules of the Church; regular. **in full canonicals** = in full dress as a priest.

canopy /'kænəpɪ/ *n* **1** curtain hung above a THRONE or bed. **2** small roof over something, e.g. over a grave inside a building.

cant /kænt/ *n* **1** speaking in such a way as to make people believe that one is very good. **2** the special talk of any particular group of men, e.g. thieves.

can't /kɑːnt/ shortened form of **cannot**.

cantankerous /kæn'tæŋkərəs/ *adj* bad-tempered; eager to quarrel.

cantata /kæn'tɑːtə/ *n* piece of music in the form of a play which is sung but not acted.

canteen /kæn'tiːn/ *n* **1** drink shop in a soldiers' camp. **2** soldier's water bottle. **3** dining-room for workers in an office, factory, etc. **4** box of silver spoons, etc., as used at the table.

canter /'kæntə/ *vi* (of a horse) run slowly, moving the two front and back legs together.

canto /'kæntəʊ/ *n* part of a song or long poem.

canvas /'kænvəs/ *n* strong cloth used for ships' sails, tents, etc.

canvass /'kænvəs/ *vt* examine carefully. *vi* go from house to house asking people to buy, or to elect a person.

canyon /'kænjən/ *n* deep narrow valley with steep rocky sides.

cap /kæp/ *n* **1** hat with no edge standing out. **2** anything fitted on to the top or end of another object. **3** piece of paper containing a small amount of explosive material used in the guns children play with. *vt* put a cap onto (something).

capable /'keɪpəbəl/ *adj* clever; able (to do things well). *n* **capability** /,keɪpə'bɪlətɪ/.

capacious /kə'peɪʃəs/ *adj* able to contain a large amount.

capacity /kə'pæsətɪ/ *n* **1** power of doing things well. **2** amount that any container can hold.

cape¹ /keɪp/ *n* covering for the shoulders.

cape² /keɪp/ *n* point of land that goes out into the water.

caper¹ /'keɪpə/ *vi* jump and dance.

cape[1]

caper[2] /'keɪpə[?]/ n part of a plant specially treated to be used in making a SAUCE eaten with meat.

capillary /kə'pɪlərɪ/ adj having to do with the hair; very thin like a hair. **capillary attraction** = drawing-up of water through a hair-like pipe.

capital /'kæpɪtl/ n 1 chief city of a country (or of a part of a country). 2 money and equipment owned by a business or a person. adj 1 (of a letter) having the form used at the beginning of names, sentences, etc., e.g. 'A' not 'a', 'B' not 'b'. 2 (of a punishment) consisting in death.

capitalist /'kæpɪtəlɪst/ n one who controls large amounts of money. n **capitalism** /'kæpɪtəlɪzəm/ ownership of business by a small class of people rather than by everyone together.

capitulate /kə'pɪtʃʊleɪt/ vi yield to the enemy.

caprice /kə'priːs/ n sudden unreasonable idea or change of purpose. adj **capricious** /kə'prɪʃəs/.

capsize /kæp'saɪz/ v (of a boat) turn over in the water.

capstan /'kæpstən/ n upright iron roller, turned round by bars, used for winding in a rope.

capsule /'kæpsjuːl/ n small case, e.g. that containing seeds on a plant; case containing a measured amount of a medicine ready for swallowing.

captain /'kæptɪn/ n one who commands about 120 men in an army; master of a ship; leader of a group of players in a game. vt be the captain of.

caption /'kæpʃən/ n a few words telling the subject of what follows in a book, newspaper, or picture.

captious /'kæpʃəs/ adj eager to find fault.

captive /'kæptɪv/ n, adj (as a) prisoner. n **captivity** /kæp'tɪvətɪ/ state of being a prisoner.

captivate /'kæptɪveɪt/ vt hold as a prisoner by beauty or charm of manner.

captor /'kæptə[?]/ n one who seizes a prisoner.

capture /'kæptʃə[?]/ vt seize (a prisoner). n act of seizing as prisoner.

car /kɑː[?]/ n vehicle driven by an engine, usually with four wheels.

caramel /'kærəməl/ n sugar heated in such a way that it becomes very sticky but not hard; a sweet so made.

carat /'kærət/ n measure of weight used for precious stones and gold.

caravan /'kærəvæn/ n 1 company of travellers across the desert. 2 covered cart on wheels in which one can live.

carbide /'kɑːbaɪd/ n material which, mixed with water, gives off a gas that burns with a white flame.

carbine /'kɑːbaɪn/ n a kind of short gun.

carbolic acid /kɑːˌbɒlɪk 'æsɪd/ n brown liquid obtained from coal used for killing the seeds of disease.

carbon /'kɑːbən/ n material found in coal, wood, and the bodies of animals. n **carbon paper** /'..ˌ.ˌ./ black paper put between two sheets of white paper to get a second copy of writing.

carbuncle /'kɑːbʌŋkl/ n hard painful spot on the skin.

carburettor (-er) /ˌkɑːbjə'retə[?], -bə-, -bjʊ-/ n part of the engine of a car in which the liquid to be burnt is mixed with air.

carcass, carcase /'kɑːkəs/ n dead body of an animal.

card /kɑːd/ n 1 small stiff piece of paper; such a piece of paper folded in two having a picture on the outside and a message inside, e.g. *Christmas cards; Birthday cards.* 2 small stiff piece of paper with one's name on it. 3 one of a set of pieces of slightly stiff paper, each having different markings on, used for playing games. **a card game** = a game played with cards. **to play cards** = play such a game. **to put one's cards on the table** = make one's plans known.

cardboard /'kɑːdbɔːd/ n, adj (made of) very thick stiff paper-like material.

cardiac /'kɑːdɪæk/ adj having to do with the heart.

cardigan

cardigan /'kɑːdɪgən/ n short coat made of wool.

cardinal /'kɑːdɪnl, 'kɑːdənəl/ adj 1 chief; very important. 2 bright red in colour. n high officer in the Church of Rome.

care /keə[?]/ vi feel strongly, e.g. *I don't care* = it does not matter to me. **to care for** = love; take charge of and support. n anxious feeling watchfulness and serious thought. **to take care of** = look after, have charge of.

career /kə'rɪə[?]/ n one's way through life; what one works at in life. vi move quickly.

careful /'keəfəl/ adj taking trouble over a piece of work. adj **careless** /'keələs/ thoughtless; not careful.

caress /kəˈres/ *n* any act of touch expressing love.

caret /ˈkærət/ *n* the mark (∧) to show that something has been left out in writing.

caretaker /ˈkeəˌteɪkəʳ/ *n* one who remains in charge of an empty building; one who has charge of a building and keeps it clean, warm, etc.

cargo /ˈkɑːgəʊ/ *n* goods carried in a ship, aeroplane, etc.

caricature /ˌkærɪkəˈtʃʊəʳ, ˈkærɪkəˈtʃʊəʳ/ *n* picture drawn to make people laugh at the person shown in it. *vt* make such a picture of.

caries /ˈkeəriːz/ *n* decay in a tooth or bone.

carmine /ˈkɑːmɪn/ *n, adj* (of a) deep red colour.

carnage /ˈkɑːnɪdʒ/ *n* killing of many persons.

carnal /ˈkɑːnəl/ *adj* having to do with the body; sexual.

carnation /kɑːˈneɪʃən/ *n* white or coloured sweet-smelling flower.

carnival /ˈkɑːnɪvəl/ *n* joyful time of feasts and games.

carnivorous /kɑːˈnɪvərəs/ *adj* meat-eating.

carol /ˈkærəl/ *n* joyful song sung at Christmas.

carp¹ /kɑːp/ *n* a big fresh-water fish.

carp² /kɑːp/ *vi* find fault or blame without reason.

carpenter /ˈkɑːpɪntəʳ/ *n* one who works with wood. *n* **carpentry** /ˈkɑːpəntrɪ/ the work of a carpenter.

carpet /ˈkɑːpɪt/ *n* thick cloth covering for the floor. *vt* cover a floor with a carpet.

carriage /ˈkærɪdʒ/ *n* 1 act of carrying. 2 wheeled vehicle, e.g. one pulled by a horse or one of the parts into which a train is divided; the part of a train in which one sits.

carrion /ˈkærɪən/ *n* dead or decaying meat.

carrot /ˈkærət/ *n* a vegetable reddish-yellow root eaten as food.

carry /ˈkærɪ/ *vt* support the weight of a thing; support and move from one place to another. **to carry on** = continue. **to carry out** = do (what has been ordered, planned, etc.). *n* **carrier** /ˈkærɪəʳ/. *n* **carrier-bag** /ˈ. . ./ strong bag for carrying shopping in.

cart /kɑːt/ *n* thing with wheels for carrying goods, pulled by a horse. *vt* carry in a cart.

cartel /kɑːˈtel/ *n* union to keep cost of making a thing down and the price up.

cartilage /ˈkɑːtəlɪdʒ/ *n* strong bendable material found at the end of bones in the body.

carton /ˈkɑːtn/ *n* box made of strong card.

cartoon /kɑːˈtuːn/ *n* 1 drawing for the purpose of making people laugh or think—generally of a present event. 2 ANIMATION.

cartridge /ˈkɑːtrɪdʒ/ *n* small round box, holding powder and shot, put into a gun for firing; any similar container.

carve /kɑːv/ *v* 1 cut (a picture or figure) into or out of stone, wood, etc. 2 cut up (meat) for eating.

cascade /kæˈskeɪd/ *n* small water fall. *vi* fall as

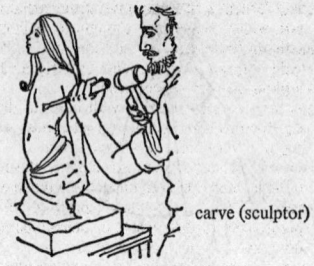

carve (sculptor)

water in a waterfall.

case¹ /keɪs/ *n* box, covering; SUITCASE.

case² /keɪs/ *n* 1 particular set of events, esp. one that demands action or thought, e.g. *A doctor's cases* = the sick persons whom he has to see. **a case in a law court** = claim made before a judge, or the trying of a wrong-doer. **that is not the case** = that is not true. **in your case** = in dealing with you. **in case** = to guard against the possibility that, e.g. *Take an umbrella in case it rains.* 2 form of a noun showing its relation to other words in the sentence.

casement /ˈkeɪsmənt/ *n* window which opens like a door.

cash /kæʃ/ *n* money in the form of COINS and banknotes. *vt* obtain cash for, e.g. *To cash a* CHEQUE *at the bank.* *sl* **to cash in on** = gain money as a result of.

cashier /kæˈʃɪəʳ/ *n* person in an office or shop who has charge of the money. *vt* send out of the army because of wrong-doing.

cashmere /ˈkæʃmɪəʳ/ *n* soft woollen cloth.

cash register /ˈ. ˌ. . ./ *n* machine in shops into which money is put.

casing /ˈkeɪsɪŋ/ *n* covering; frame.

casino /kəˈsiːnəʊ/ *n* hall for dancing and playing games (esp. games of chance) for money.

cask /kɑːsk/ *n* barrel for holding liquids.

casket /ˈkɑːskɪt/ *n* small box for precious stones, etc.

cassava /kəˈsɑːvə/ *n* plant from whose root a white flour is prepared; this flour used as food.

casserole /ˈkæsərəʊl/ *n* pot in which food is cooked and brought to the table; a meal so cooked.

cassock /ˈkæsək/ *n* long garment, usually black, worn in church, e.g. by a priest.

cast /kɑːst/ *vt* 1 throw; throw off. 2 pour (hot liquid metal or other liquid) into a shape in which it becomes solid. 3 give (an actor) a part to play in a film or play. *n* 1 that into which liquid is placed to be cast. 2 list of actors in a film or play. *n* **cast iron** /ˌ. ˈ. ./ hardened form of iron. *adj* **cast-iron** /ˈ. ˌ. ./ firm and unchangeable.

castaway /ˈkɑːstəweɪ/ *n* person who has come to land from a wrecked ship.

caste /kɑːst/ *n* in India, one of the social ranks into which people were thought to be born.

castigate /'kæstɪgeɪt/ *vt* beat; punish.

castle /'kɑːsəl/ *n* strong building; fort; fine house looking like an ancient castle.

castor[1] /'kɑːstə/ *n* bottle with holes in the top, e.g. for powdered sugar. *n* **castor** (also **caster**) **sugar** = very finely powdered sugar.

castor[2] /'kɑːstə/ *n* small wheel put on the bottom of beds, tables, etc., to make them move easily.

castor oil /ˌ.. './ *n* medicine produced from a plant, used to clear waste or poisonous matter downward through the bowels.

casual /'kæʒʊəl/ *adj* happening by accident; not planned; not regular; careless and rude in manner.

casualty /'kæʒʊəltɪ/ *n* one who is killed or wounded in war or in an accident, etc.

cat

cat /kæt/ *n* animal which lives in the house and catches mice; other wild animals of this class. **to let the cat out of the bag** = tell a secret. **to rain cats and dogs** = rain heavily.

cataclysm /'kætəklɪzəm/ *n* a sudden change that causes suffering, e.g. the overflow of a river, a war, etc.

catacomb /'kætəkuːm/ *n* underground caves in which dead bodies are put.

catalogue /'kætəlɒg/ *n* list of things to be shown, or for sale, of books, etc. *vt* make such a list of.

catalyst /'kætəlɪst/ *n* substance that is necessary for a change in other substances but which does not itself change.

catamaran /ˌkætəmə'ræn/ *n* boat made in two parts, like two boats fixed together by a bridge.

catapult /'kætəpʌlt/ *n* **1** weapon used for throwing stones. **2** Y-shaped stick on which a piece of rubber is tied, used by boys for shooting stones. *vt* throw or shoot (something) using a catapult.

cataract /'kætərækt/ *n* **1** large waterfall. **2** disease in which the glass-like part of the eye becomes white, causing loss of sight.

catarrh /kə'tɑː/ *n* illness of the nose and throat, with flowing of liquid from the nose and pain in the throat.

catastrophe /kə'tæstrəfɪ/ *n* event that causes great suffering or ruin.

catch /kætʃ/ *vt* **1** run after and seize. **2** seize and hold, e.g. *To catch a ball.* **3** meet and stop, e.g. *I caught him just as he was going out.* **4** receive the effect of some cause, e.g. *To catch an illness* = get an illness from another person. **5** dis-

catch (e.g., a ball)

cover, e.g. *To catch a person in the act* = just as he is doing wrong. **to catch a train** = be in time for. **to catch fire** = be made to burn. *sl* **to catch on** = come to understand. **to catch up** = come level with a person in walking, etc. *n* **1** act of catching. **2** fastener, e.g. *The catch of a window.* **3** thing caught (p.p. of **catch**). **a catch in it** = some trick. *sl* **no catch** = not worth anything.

catchword /'kætʃwɜːd/ *n* word that sticks in the mind and is often used without proper thought of its real meaning.

catchy /'kætʃɪ/ *adj* (music) such as pleases and is easily remembered.

catechism /'kætɪkɪzəm/ *n* set of questions, esp. about one's duty to God and the Church.

category /'kætɪgərɪ/ *n* class; sort or kind.

cater /'keɪtə/ *vi* provide food; supply what is wanted.

caterpillar /'kætəpɪlə/ *n* creature with many legs which later changes into a flying insect.

cathartic /kə'θɑːtɪk/ *adj* (of a medicine) for driving out waste or poisonous matter from the body.

cathedral /kə'θiːdrəl/ *n* church in which is the chair of a BISHOP.

catholic /'kæθəlɪk/ *adj* **1** found everywhere; very wide; having all kinds. **2** having to do with the Church of Rome. *n* member of this Church.

cattle /'kætl/ *n* (*pl*) cows and other animals of the same kind.

catty /'kætɪ/ *adj* (of a woman) saying unkind things about others.

caught /kɔːt/ p.t. & p.p. of **catch**.

cauldron /'kɔːldrən/ *n* large pot for boiling liquids.

cauliflower /'kɒlɪflaʊə/ *n* vegetable with large white head, boiled for food.

caulk /kɔːk/ *vt* press sticky, oily material into (the cracks of a ship) to keep out water.

cause /kɔːz/ *n* **1** that which produces an effect. **2** something believed in and fought for. *vt* produce (something) as an effect.

causeway /'kɔːzweɪ/ *n* road running along the top of a bank.

caustic /'kɔːstɪk/ *adj* having the power of slowly eating material away; burning.

cauterize /'kɔːtəraɪz/ *vt* burn away (skin).

caution /'kɔːʃən/ n sign or word that tells of danger; carefulness. vt warn. adj **cautious** /'kɔːʃəs/ careful; afraid of danger.

cavalcade /ˌkævəl'keɪd/ n long line of moving people, usually riding on horses.

cavalier /ˌkævə'lɪə/ n soldier on a horse; follower of King Charles I. adj gay; not caring.

cavalry /'kævəlrɪ/ n soldiers on horses.

cave /keɪv/ n large hollow place in a rock or hillside. **to cave in** = fall inwards like the falling roof of a cave; yield.

cavern /'kævən/ n large cave.

caviare, caviar /'kævɪɑː/ n eggs of certain fish used as food; something too good or costly for common use.

cavil /'kævl/ vi find fault without good reasons.

cavity /'kævɪtɪ/ n hole.

cavort /kə'vɔːt/ vi jump about in a noisy, uncontrolled way.

caw /kɔː/ n, interj rough sound made by some birds.

cayenne /keɪ'en/ n hot-tasting red powder eaten with food.

cease /siːs/ v stop.

cedar /'siːdə/ n tree that has sweet-smelling wood of which pencils, etc., are made.

cede /siːd/ vt give up.

ceiling /'siːlɪŋ/ n inside roof of a room; highest level of anything.

celebrate /'seləbreɪt/ v mark (an event) by a feast and rejoicings; perform a ceremony in honour of or in memory of. adj **celebrated** /'seləbreɪtɪd/ famous. n **celebrity** /sɪ'lebrətɪ/ fame; a famous person. n **celebration** /ˌselə'breɪʃən/ act of celebrating.

celerity /sɪ'lerətɪ/ n speed.

celery /'selərɪ/ n vegetable stem generally eaten uncooked, often with cheese.

celestial /sɪ'lestɪəl/ adj heavenly; of the sky.

celibacy /'selɪbəsɪ/ n state of being unmarried, usually for a religious reason. adj **celibate** /'selɪbət/ not married.

cell /sel/ n 1 small room, e.g. in a prison. 2 small container, e.g. those built by bees to hold HONEY. 3 small pieces of living matter of which the body is built up. 4 box containing metal plates and acid used to produce or store electricity.

cellar /'selə/ n room below the ground in a house.

cello

cello /'tʃeləʊ/ n musical instrument with four strings, giving deep notes when rubbed.

cellophane /'seləfeɪn/ n glass-like paper used for putting round food, etc.

cellular /'seljʊlə/ adj made up of CELLS.

celluloid /'seljʊlɔɪd/ n material which looks like glass, but can be bent and burns very easily.

cellulose /'seljʊləʊs/ n plant matter used to make paper, man-made FABRICS, etc.

cement /sɪ'mənt/ n any powder which, mixed with a liquid, becomes a solid mass after a time, e.g. that used in building, that used to fill holes in teeth, etc.; sticky liquid used to repair broken glass, etc. vt join firmly.

cemetery /'semətrɪ/ n piece of land (separate from a church) where there are many graves.

cenotaph /'senətɑːf/ n large stone put up in memory of a person or persons whose bodies lie in some other place.

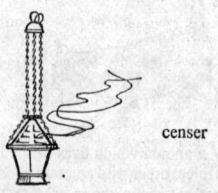

censer

censer /'sensə/ n container in which sweet-smelling powder is burned.

censor /'sensə/ n officer who examines books and pictures to prevent bad ones from being sold; in war, one who reads all letters and newspapers so that secret plans may not become known to the enemy. vt examine books, etc. thus. adj **censorious** /sen'sɔːrɪəs/ quick to find fault.

censure /'senʃə/ n, vt blame.

census /'sensəs/ n counting of the people in a country.

cent /sent/ n amount of money, in some countries, being one-hundredth part of some larger fixed amount. **per cent** = in each hundred.

centaur /'sentɔː/ n imaginary creature, half horse, half man.

centenarian /ˌsentɪ'neərɪən/ n person who is 100 years old.

centenary /sen'tiːnərɪ/ n hundredth year after an event; public ceremonies and feasting on this date. adj **centennial** /sen'tenɪəl/.

centimetre /'sentɪˌmiːtə/ n 1⁄100th of a metre.

centigrade /'sentɪgreɪd/ adj (of the level of heat) being measured by dividing up the distance between the freezing point and boiling point of water into one hundred equal parts.

centipede /'sentɪpiːd/ n insect-like creature with many (a hundred) legs.

centre /'sentə/ n the middle; person or thing in

the middle. *adj* central /'sentrəl/. *vt* **centralize** /'sentrəlaız/ bring to a centre; control (a business or the work of government) from the centre. *n* **centralization** /ˌsentrəlaı'zeıʃən/.

centrifugal /sen'trıfjʊgəl, ˌsentrı'fju:gəl/ *adj* (of a force) which makes things fly off from the middle of a quickly turning wheel, *adj* **centripetal** /sen'trıpıtl/ (of a force) pulling towards the centre.

centurion /sen'tjʊərıən/ *n* captain of a hundred men in the Roman army.

century /'sentʃərı/ *n* one hundred years.

ceramic /sı'ræmık/ *adj* having to do with POTTERY.

cereal /'sıərıəl/ *n* food made from grain, e.g. corn and other grain used as food.

ceremony /'serımənı/ *n* set of solemn acts as in a church or at a great public show; polite forms of behaviour. **to stand on ceremony** = behave in a stiff and solemn way. *n* **ceremonial** /ˌserı'məʊnıəl/ performing of a ceremony. *adj* **ceremonial** or **ceremonious** /ˌserı'məʊnıəs/.

certain /'sɜ:tn/ *adj* 1 sure, without doubt. 2 some particular; one; fixed. *adj* **certainly** without doubt.

certificate /sə'tıfıkət/ *n* writing declaring a certain fact, e.g. *A birth certificate*.

certify /'sɜ:tıfaı/ *vt* say or write that (a certain fact) is true.

certitude /'sɜ:tıtju:d/ *n* sureness.

cessation /se'seıʃən/ *n* act of stopping.

cession /'seʃən/ *n* agreement by law to give up something.

cesspit /'ses,pıt/ or **cesspool** /'ses-pu:l/ *n* deep hole for holding the dirty water that flows out of houses.

chafe /tʃeıf/ *vt* make hot by rubbing, make painful by rubbing.

chaff /tʃɑ:f/ *n* 1 covering separated from grain by beating. 2 worthless matter.

chagrin /'ʃægrın/ *n* feeling of anger and shame.

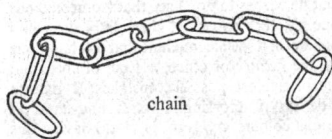

chain

chain /tʃeın/ *n* number of rings joined together to make one long piece. **a chain of mountains** = one long line of —.

chain store /'. ./ *n* one of a number of shops in different places all owned and controlled by one business company.

chair /tʃeə/ *n* 1 seat that can be moved, with a back. 2 post of the head of one of the subjects taught in a university. *vt infml* be in charge of (a meeting).

chairman /'tʃeəmən/ *n* one who has charge of a meeting.

chalet /'ʃæleı/ *n* wooden house as in Switzerland.

chalice /'tʃælıs/ *n* tall metal cup, used in a church.

chalk /tʃɔ:k/ *n* white material, used by teachers for writing on a blackboard.

challenge /'tʃæləndʒ/ *n* a call to fight. *vt* 1 call to fight or play a game. 2 show disbelief or distrust and demand proof from.

chamber /'tʃeımbə/ *n* 1 room. 2 group of persons who make laws. 3 hollow space, e.g. that part of a gun in which the powder and shot are put.

chamberlain /'tʃeımbəlın/ *n* officer in charge of the king's palace.

chambermaid /'tʃeımbəmeıd/ *n* woman who takes care of the sleeping rooms in a hotel or lodging-house.

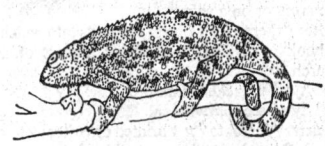

chameleon

chameleon /kə'mi:lıən/ *n* small reptile with four legs, which has the power of changing its colour.

chamois *n* 1 /'ʃæmwɑ:/ deer found on high mountains. 2 /'ʃæmı/ soft leather made from the skin of sheep, goats, etc.

champagne /ʃæm'peın/ *n* high-priced yellow wine which has gas in it.

champion /'tʃæmpıən/ *n* 1 one who defends or fights for some other person or for some good cause. 2 best of all players at a certain game. *vt* be a champion of (some cause).

chance /tʃɑ:ns/ *n* 1 event that happens by accident. **give me a chance** = make it possible for me to show that I can work well. *vi* happen by accident, do a thing unexpectedly and without purposing to do it, e.g. *I chanced to meet him.* **chance it** = take the risk.

chancel /'tʃɑ:nsəl/ *n* east end of a church.

chancellor /'tʃɑ:nsələ/ *n* chief man in the government; special officer who looks after the king's business; highest judge of law; head of a university.

chancery /'tʃɑ:nsərı/ *n* high court of law.

chandelier /ˌʃændə'lıə/ *n* frame with branches for holding many candles or other lights.

change /tʃeındʒ/ *v* make or become different. *vt* 1 take (one thing) instead of another. 2 obtain change for (money). *vi* put on different clothes. *n* 1 act of changing. 2 money equal in value to other money, e.g. foreign money for one's own or small COINS for paper money. **change for a pound** = 100 pence instead of —. **all change** = this train does not go any farther. *adj* **changeable** /'tʃeındʒəbəl/.

channel /'tʃænl/ *n* course in which a river flows; course a ship must follow in coming to harbour to keep clear of rocks, etc.; any course made for liquid; narrow piece of water joining two seas. *vt* direct.

chant /tʃɑːnt/ *n* slow song. *v* sing softly or slowly.

chaos /'keɪɒs/ *n* condition of no law or order; absence of any arrangement.

chap¹ /tʃæp/ *sl n* young fellow. **old chap** (= friendly form of address).

chap² /tʃæp/ *v* (of skin) make or become rough.

chapel /'tʃæpəl/ *n* small church; part of a larger church in which religious ceremonies can be held for a few people.

chaperon /'ʃæpərəʊn/ *n* older or married person in charge of young unmarried women.

chaplain /'tʃæplɪn/ *n* priest of a CHAPEL; priest in the army or on a ship.

chapter /'tʃæptə⁷/ *n* **1** one of the parts into which a book is divided. **2** group of officers of a church.

char¹ /tʃɑː⁷/ *v* blacken in the fire.

char² /tʃɑː⁷/ see **charwoman**.

character /'kærəktə⁷/ *n* **1** printed or written letter (A, B, C, etc.) or other mark. **2** one's nature as shown by one's acts; a person in a book or play. *n* **characteristic** /ˌkærəktə'rɪstɪk/ quality; some way in which a person is different from others. *adj* showing the nature of something or someone, e.g. *A characteristic action of his.*

charade /ʃə'rɑːd/ *n* game in which a word is acted part by part, then as a whole (e.g. car-pet, carpet), and those watching guess the word.

charcoal /'tʃɑːkəʊl/ *n* wood blackened by heating it without air, used for burning.

charge /tʃɑːdʒ/ *vt* **1** ask for money as payment from. **2** say that (someone) has done wrong. *v* rush at (someone) in order to attack. *n* **1** demand for payment. **2** claim that someone has done wrong. **3** act of rushing at (e.g. an enemy) in order to attack. **4** amount of explosive material used. **in charge of** = in control of.

charger /'tʃɑːdʒə⁷/ *n* officer's horse.

chariot /'tʃærɪət/ *n* car with two wheels used in war in ancient times. *n* **charioteer** /ˌtʃærɪə'tɪə⁷/ driver of a chariot.

charity /'tʃærɪtɪ/ *n* kindness; giving money to the poor. *adj* **charitable** /'tʃærətəbəl/ kind; generous.

charlatan /'ʃɑːlətən/ *n* dishonest person who pretends to have knowledge which he does not possess.

charm /tʃɑːm/ *n* **1** object or action (e.g. a song or dance) that has magic powers. **2** pleasant and likeable manner. *vt* work magic on; cause great pleasure to. *adj* **charming** /'tʃɑːmɪŋ/ having a pleasing, likeable manner.

chart /tʃɑːt/ *n* **1** map for the use of ships. **2** paper showing the increase or DECREASE of anything.

charter /'tʃɑːtə⁷/ *n* written paper from the government giving certain rights, or giving land to a person or group of persons. *vt* hire (a ship, aeroplane, etc.).

charwoman /'tʃɑːˌwʊmən/, **char** /tʃɑː⁷/ *n* servant who is employed by the hour or day to do house cleaning.

chary /'tʃeərɪ/ *adj* careful.

chase

chase /tʃeɪs/ *vt* run after; try to catch. *n* act of chasing.

chasm /'kæzəm/ *n* deep valley with steep sides.

chassis /'ʃæsɪ/ *n* wheels and frame on which the body of a car rests.

chaste /tʃeɪst/ *adj* without sexual experience. *n* **chasitity** /'tʃæstətɪ/.

chasten /'tʃeɪsn/ *vt* punish for the purpose of making better.

chastise /tʃæ'staɪz/ *vt* scold or beat as a punishment.

chat /tʃæt/ *n* friendly unimportant talk. *vi* have a chat.

château /'ʃætəʊ/ *n* French castle or large country house.

chattel /'tʃætl/ *n* one of the movable things in a house.

chatter /'tʃætə⁷/ *vi* talk quickly and foolishly. *n* quick and foolish talk. *n* **chatterbox** /'tʃætəbɒks/ one who chatters a lot.

chauffeur /'ʃəʊfə⁷/ *n* paid driver of a car.

chauvinist /'ʃəʊvɪnɪst/ *n* one who is too proud of something of his, having no respect for others.

cheap /tʃiːp/ *adj* **1** of low price. **2** of little value.

cheat /tʃiːt/ *v* deceive; get money (etc.) by a trick. *n* one who cheats.

check /tʃek/ *vt* **1** prevent (someone) from doing what he wishes to do. **2** see that (someone) has done his work correctly. **check in** = show in a book or on a special machine that one has come into the factory or office. *n* **1** act of checking; control against possible mistakes. **2** pattern made up of crossing squares and lines in various colours. *adj* (esp. of cloth) having this pattern.

checkmate /'tʃekmeɪt/ *n* winning position in CHESS. *vt* win against, in chess.

cheek /tʃiːk/ *n* **1** part of the face between the nose and ears. *sl adj* **cheeky** /'tʃiːkɪ/ rude and daring.

cheer /tʃɪə⁷/ *n* joy. *v* shout for joy or ENCOURAGEMENT (for). *adj* **cheerful** /'tʃɪəfəl/ happy. **to cheer up** = make or become less unhappy.

cheese /tʃiːz/ *n* milk made into a hard mass and kept so that it gets a pleasant strong taste.

cheesecloth /'tʃiːzklɒθ/ *n* very thin kind of cloth.

cheetah /'tʃiːtə/ *n* fierce, cat-like animal found in Africa and Southern Asia.

chef /ʃef/ *n* a male cook.

chemical /'kemɪkəl/ *n* matter in its pure form as used by scientists. *adj* having to do with CHEMISTRY.

chemist /'kemɪst/ *n* **1** one who studies CHEMISTRY. **2** one who keeps a shop for selling medicines.

chemistry /'kemɪstrɪ/ *n* that part of science which deals with the nature of various forms of matter and how these are made up, and of their action when mixed.

cheque /tʃek/ *n* an order to pay money.

chequered /'tʃekəd/ *adj* marked in squares of different colours. **a chequered career** = life in which there have been many changes of fortune, good and bad.

cherish /'tʃerɪʃ/ *vt* love; take care of or protect.

cherry /'tʃerɪ/ *n* small red fruit with a stone in it. *n, adj* (of a) clear light red colour.

cherub /'tʃerəb/ *n* spirit with wings, told of in the Bible; baby with wings, supposed to live in heaven.

chessmen

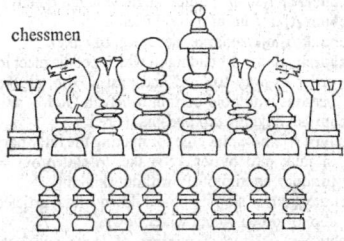

chess /tʃes/ *n* game played by moving small pieces according to rules across a board marked out in squares. *n* **chessmen** /'tʃesmen/ the pieces used in chess.

chest /tʃest/ *n* **1** strong box. **2** part of the body between the neck and the stomach.

chestnut /'tʃesnʌt/ *n* a kind of tree; the nut from this tree. *n, adj* (of) a warm reddish-brown colour.

chevron /'ʃevrən/ *n* V-shaped piece of cloth worn as a sign of rank in the army.

chew /tʃuː/ *v* break up (food) with the teeth.

chewing stick /'.. ./ *West African n* stick used for cleaning the teeth.

chic /ʃiːk/ *adj* charming and new in dress and appearance.

chicanery /ʃɪ'keɪnərɪ/ *n* dishonest reasoning; attempts to deceive.

chick /tʃɪk/ *n* newly-born hen.

chicken /'tʃɪkɪn/ *n* young hen; meat of the hen.

chicken-pox /'.. ./ *n* disease causing red spots on the body.

chicory /'tʃɪkərɪ/ *n* plant with bright blue flowers, eaten uncooked; the root dried and powdered is added to give a bitter taste to coffee.

chide /tʃaɪd/ *vt* blame for a fault.

chief /tʃiːf/ *n, adj* most important (leader). *n* chieftain /'tʃiːftən/ head man of a large group.

chiffon /'ʃɪfɒn/ *n* very thin kind of cloth used in women's clothes.

chilblain /'tʃɪlbleɪn/ *n* painful spot on the skin caused by cold.

child /tʃaɪld/ *n* young son or daughter; young or very young person.

childhood /'tʃaɪldhʊd/ *n* state of being a child.

childish /'tʃaɪldɪʃ/ *adj* like a child.

children /'tʃɪldrən/ *pl* of child.

chill /tʃɪl/ *n* coldness; illness caused by cold. *adj* chilly /'tʃɪlɪ/ (of the weather) rather cold.

chilli /'tʃɪlɪ/ *n* fruit (usually red) with a very hot taste.

chime /tʃaɪm/ *n* musical sound made by bells. *v* ring with a musical sound.

chimney /'tʃɪmnɪ/ *n* that through which the smoke goes up from the fire in a building; the tall round glass part of a lamp.

chimpanzee

chimpanzee /ˌtʃɪmpæn'ziː/ *n* large African monkey-like creature.

chin /tʃɪn/ *n* that part of the face below the mouth.

china /'tʃaɪnə/ *n* (*sing*) special white earth of which plates, cups, etc., are made; cups, plates, etc., made of such material.

chink[1] /tʃɪŋk/ *n* small crack.

chink[2] /tʃɪŋk/ *n* sound of pieces of money striking together.

chintz /tʃɪnts/ *n* cotton material used for curtains and chair covers.

chip /tʃɪp/ *n* **1** small piece of anything. **2** piece of potato cooked in hot fat. *vt* break off a small piece from. **to chip in** = suddenly to join in the talk of others.

chirp /tʃɜːp/ or chirrup /'tʃɪrəp/ *n, interj* cry of a small bird.

chisel /'tʃɪzəl/ *n* instrument with a sharp flat end used for cutting wood. *vt* cut with such an instrument.

chit /tʃɪt/ *n* short letter; written promise to pay.

chivalry /'ʃɪvəlrɪ/ *n* (*sing*) laws and customs of knights in ancient times; character of a noble person—courage, politeness, etc.

chlorine /'klɔːriːn/ *n* heavy gas which makes things lose their colour and become white.

chloroform /'klɒrəfɔːm/ *n* liquid used to make one lose all feeling, so that doctors may cut the body without causing pain.

chlorophyll /'klɒrəfil/ *n* green colouring matter of plants.

chock /tʃɒk/ *n* wooden block used to prevent things from rolling. **chock-full** /ˌ. './, **chock-a-block** /ˌ. . './ = very full; packed tight.

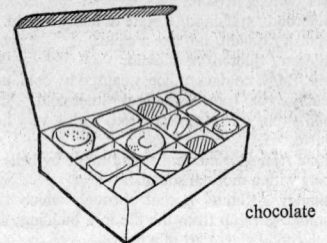

chocolate

chocolate /'tʃɒklət/ *n* brown sweet made from sugar and COCOA; hot drink made from these.

choice /tʃɔɪs/ *n* act of choosing; what is chosen. *adj* carefully chosen; specially good.

choir /'kwaɪə'/ *n* group of singers, e.g. in a church.

choke /tʃəʊk/ *v* be or cause to be unable to breathe, e.g. because a piece of food has gone into the WINDPIPE. *n* piece of equipment controlling the richness of FUEL in the engine of a car.

cholera /'kɒlərə/ *n* disease found in hot countries, causing sickness and continuous passing of waste matter from the body, often ending in death caused by loss of liquid.

choleric /'kɒlərɪk/ *adj* easily made angry.

choose /tʃuːz/ *v* show that one likes or wants (one person or thing) and not another.

chop /tʃɒp/ *vt* cut, e.g. with an axe. *n* piece of meat cut from the back or neck with its bone. *adj* **choppy** /'tʃɒpɪ/ (of the sea) rough; not calm.

chopsticks /'tʃɒpˌstɪks/ *n* sticks used by the Chinese in eating.

choral /'kɔːrəl/ *adj* having to do with singing in a CHOIR.

chord¹ /kɔːd/ *n* **1** straight line joining two points of a circle. **2** string of a musical instrument.

chord² /kɔːd/ *n* group of musical sounds which are pleasing when played together.

chore /tʃɔː'/ *n* small duty, e.g. in the house.

chorister /'kɒrɪstə'/ *n* member of a group of singers in a church.

chortle /'tʃɔːtl/ *vi* laugh by making a peculiar noise in the throat and through the nose.

chorus /'kɔːrəs/ *n* **1** group of singers. **2** part of a song which is repeated.

chose /tʃəʊz/ *p.t.* of **choose**.

chosen /'tʃəʊzən/ *p.p.* of **choose**.

christen /'krɪsən/ *vt* give a name to (a child).

Christendom /'krɪsəndəm/ *n* that part of the world which believes in Christ.

Christian /'krɪstɪən/ *adj, n* (one) believing in Christ. *adj* being the name chosen for one by one's parents; first (name).

Christmas /'krɪsməs/ *n* Dec. 25th, as a feast in honour of the birth of Christ.

chrome, chromium /'krəʊm(ɪəm)/ *n* strong grey-white metal, used in covering other metals, to protect them.

chromosome /'krəʊməsəʊm/ *n* one of the small bodies in the CELLS of living things, which fix the nature of the young plants or animals.

chronic /'krɒnɪk/ *adj* (of something bad) continuing a long time.

chronicle /'krɒnɪkl/ *n* account of events set down in order of time.

chronological /ˌkrɒnə'lɒdʒɪkəl/ *adj* having to do with past events in their order of time.

chronometer /krə'nɒmɪtə'/ *n* clock made to keep very exact time.

chrysalis /'krɪsəlɪs/ *n* shell-like form taken by a creeping insect before changing into a flying one.

chubby /'tʃʌbɪ/ *adj* fat.

chuck /tʃʌk/ *sl* **to chuck away** = throw away.

chuckle /'tʃʌkəl/ *n* quiet laugh. *vi* laugh quietly.

chum /tʃʌm/ *infml n* good friend.

chunk /tʃʌŋk/ *n* large piece (e.g. of cake).

church /tʃɜːtʃ/ *n* building in which people meet in order to pray to God and praise Him; all the persons who hold certain beliefs in God.

churlish /'tʃɜːlɪʃ/ *adj* bad-mannered.

churn /tʃɜːn/ *n* machine for making the fatty part of milk into butter. *vt* shake. **to churn out** = produce continuously without thinking.

chute /ʃuːt/ *n* sloping board down which articles slip, or down which water flows.

chutney /'tʃʌtnɪ/ *n* mixture of fruits and hot-tasting seeds eaten with food.

cicada

cicada /sɪ'kɑːdə/ *n* tree-insect which makes a loud noise.

cider /'saɪdə'/ *n* light drink made from apples.

cigar /sɪ'gɑː'/ *n* short thick roll of tobacco leaves closed at one end.

cigarette /ˌsɪgə'ret/ *n* finely cut tobacco rolled in paper.

cinch /sɪntʃ/ *n* band holding seat on a horse. *sl* **a cinch** = an easy and certain success.

cinder /'sɪndə'/ *n* hard burnt remains of coal.

cinema /'sɪnəmə/ *n* moving picture; building in which moving pictures are shown.

cinnamon /'sɪnəmən/ *n* brown powder made from the inner covering of a tree in India and Sri Lanka and used to give cakes a yellow colour and special taste.

cipher, cypher /'saɪfə/ *n* a piece of secret writing.

circa /'sɜːkə/ *Latin prep* about.

circle /'sɜːkəl/ *n* figure, every point on the edge of which is the same distance from the centre. **a circle of friends** = group of friends. *v* go round.

circuit /'sɜːkɪt/ *n* 1 path round; set of places through which a judge (or other officer) must travel. 2 path of electricity along a wire from where it is produced, through a lamp (machine, etc.) and back to the producer. *adj* **circuitous** /sɜː'kjuːɪtəs/ going a long way round.

circular /'sɜːkjʊlə/ *adj* 1 shaped like a circle; round. 2 (of a piece of reasoning) that does not lead to anything not already supposed to be true. *n* printed letter or notice sent to many people.

circulate /'sɜːkjʊleɪt/ *v* go round, pass from one person to another. *n* **circulation** /ˌsɜːkjʊ'leɪʃən/ act of going round and round, e.g. as the blood does in the body.

circumference /sɜː'kʌmfərəns/ *n* line round the outside; outside edge of a circle.

circumflex /'sɜːkəmfleks/ *n* mark over a letter to show the sound, e.g. ô.

circumlocution /ˌsɜːkəmlə'kjuːʃən/ *n* roundabout way of expressing some simple idea.

circumnavigate /ˌsɜːkəm'nævɪgeɪt/ *vt* sail round (esp. the world).

circumscribe /'sɜːkəmskraɪb/ *vt* keep within a certain space.

circumspect /'sɜːkəmspekt/ *adj* careful.

circumstance /'sɜːkəmstæns, -stəns/ *n* set of all the facts that are concerned with an act, e.g. place, time, events coming before; condition. *adj* **circumstantial** /ˌsɜːkəm'stænʃəl/.

circumvent /ˌsɜːkəm'vent/ *vt* by cleverness prevent or avoid.

circus /'sɜːkəs/ *n* show with men and animals which do clever things.

cirrus /'sɪrəs/ *n* very high white cloud.

cistern /'sɪstən/ *n* large container built to hold water.

citadel /'sɪtədəl/ *n* strong fort in a city.

cite /saɪt/ *vt* 1 call (someone) into a law court. 2 repeat words written by someone else, esp. as a proof of one's opinion. *n* **citation** /saɪ'teɪʃən/.

citizen /'sɪtɪzən/ *n* one who has rights in a country. *n* **citizenship** /'sɪtɪzənʃɪp/ these rights.

citron /'sɪtrən/ *n* a kind of sour yellow fruit.

citrus /'sɪtrəs/ (of a fruit) of the same kind as lemons, oranges, etc.

city /'sɪtɪ/ *n* large or important town.

civic /'sɪvɪk/ *adj* having to do with a city and its government.

civil /'sɪvəl/ *adj* 1 having to do with CITIZENS. 2 not having to do with soldiers or fighting. 3 polite. *n* **civil servant** /ˌ. . '. ./ person employed by the government not for purposes of war.

civilian /sɪ'vɪliən/ *n, adj* (of) any member of a country who is not a soldier.

civilize /'sɪvɪlaɪz/ *vt* change from being wild; teach good customs, manners, laws, science and art. *n* **civilization** /ˌsɪvɪlaɪ'zeɪʃən/ state of being civilized; group of people with a common CULTURE.

clad /klæd/ *adj* having clothes; covered.

claim /kleɪm/ *vt* 1 say or declare. 2 demand as one's right. *n* act of claiming; that which is claimed.

clairvoyant /kleə'vɔɪənt/ *n* person able to see distant or future events—usually by looking into a glass ball.

clam /klæm/ *n* large shellfish. **to clam up** = become silent; stop talking.

clamber /'klæmbə/ *vi* climb up with difficulty.

clammy /'klæmɪ/ *adj* wet, cold and sticky.

clamour /'klæmə/ *n* loud noise of people shouting.

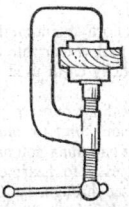

clamp

clamp /klæmp/ *n* instrument used for holding things very tightly. *vt* hold (one thing) to another tightly. **to clamp down** (on) = stop or prevent (something being done).

clan /klæn/ *n* family group.

clandestine /klæn'destɪn/ *adj* secret.

clang /klæŋ/ or **clank** /klæŋk/ *n, interj* sound made by striking metal against metal.

clap /klæp/ *v* make a noise by striking (the hands) together. *n* act of clapping; sound of bringing the hands together with force; any similar sudden sound.

claret /'klærət/ *n* a kind of red wine. *n, adj* (of a) dark red colour.

clarify /'klærɪfaɪ/ *vt* make clear.

clarinet /ˌklærɪ'net/ *n* a musical wind instrument.

clarion /'klærɪən/ *n* a small horn (music).

clarity /'klærətɪ/ *n* clearness.

clash /klæʃ/ *vi* come together with force; quarrel. *n* act of clashing.

clasp /klɑːsp/ *vt* join tightly together, e.g. hold one hand in the other. *n* metal instrument for joining things. *n* **clasp knife** /'. ./ a knife whose blade can be shut inside the handle.

class /klɑːs/ *n* 1 kind. 2 group of things or people all of the same kind. 3 group of learners, e.g. in a school. 4 social rank, e.g. *The upper classes* = lords, etc.; *The middle classes* = people who are not very rich or poor. **first class** = best.

classic /'klæsɪk/ *adj* having to do with the ancient learning of Greece and Rome. *n* work of art that will always be considered as good.

classify /'klæsɪfaɪ/ *vt* arrange (things) in classes.

clatter /'klætə/ n noise of falling things, of feet on a stone floor, or of many people talking. vi make such a noise.

clause /klɔːz/ n 1 group of words like a sentence, in the middle of a longer sentence. 2 one part of an agreement.

claustrophobia /ˌklɔːstrə'fəʊbɪə/ n fear of being shut in a small space.

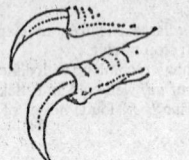

claw

claw /klɔː/ n sharp, horny point on the foot of a bird or beast (e.g. cat). vt tear with the claws.

clay /kleɪ/ n soft sticky earth used for making pots and bricks.

clean /kliːn/ adj not dirty; pure. vt (also cleanse /klenz/) make clean. infml to come clean = tell truthfully what bad thing you have done.

clear /klɪə/ adj 1 easy to hear; easy to understand; easy to see through, e.g. Clear glass; A clear sky = a sky without clouds. 2 easy or safe to pass along, e.g. The streets are clear. to keep clear of = keep at a safe distance from. v make or become clear. vt 1 avoid hitting or touching. 2 infml show (someone) not to have done wrong. to clear away = make a place TIDY by taking away. sl clear off! = go away! to clear up = set (things) in order; put right (a mistake or lack of understanding). n clearance /'klɪərəns/ 1 act of clearing, e.g. selling or throwing away things not needed. 2 cutting down trees to clear land. 3 distance between a moving object and some other thing, e.g. the side of a bridge. n clearing /'klɪərɪŋ/ piece of treeless land in a forest.

cleave¹ /kliːv/ vt divide by a heavy blow, e.g. with a sword. n cleavage /'kliːvɪdʒ/ separation; place where two things are divided. n cleaver /'kliːvə/ heavy knife.

cleave² /kliːv/ vi stick (to something or someone); keep near.

clef /klef/ n the sign 𝄞 or 𝄢 in music.

cleft /kleft/ p.t. & p.p. of cleave¹.

clemency /'klemənsɪ/ n forgiveness; mercy.

clench /klentʃ/ vt press together firmly, e.g. the fingers or hands; settle (an agreement).

clergy /'klɜːdʒɪ/ n priests of a Church.

clerical /'klerɪkəl/ adj having to do with one who writes or whose work consists mainly of paper work; having to do with CLERGY.

clerk /klɑːk/ n one who keeps accounts, writes letters, etc., in a business house or bank.

clever /'klevə/ adj quick in learning or understanding.

click /klɪk/ n, interj sudden slight noise.

client /'klaɪənt/ n one who gets service or advice, e.g. from a lawyer, etc. n clientèle /ˌkliːən'tel/ group of clients.

cliff /klɪf/ n tall steep bank.

climate /'klaɪmət/ n weather conditions of a country.

climax /'klaɪmæks/ n most exciting of a number of exciting events following each other.

climb /klaɪm/ v go up (a mountain, tree, etc.). infml to climb down = yield.

clinch /klɪntʃ/ vt drive in (a nail) and then knock the point sideways; fasten; settle once and for ever.

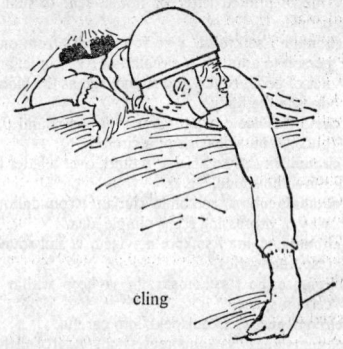

cling

cling /klɪŋ/ vi hold firmly.

clinic /'klɪnɪk/ n place in which doctors examine sick people and give advice. adj clinical /'klɪnɪkəl/ like the conditions in a hospital; to do with medicine.

clink /klɪŋk/ n, interj small sharp noise like that made by small pieces of metal or glass falling on a hard surface.

clinker /'klɪŋkə/ n mass of hard burnt brick or coal.

clip¹ /klɪp/ vt fasten together, e.g pieces of paper with bent pieces of metal. n small instrument for clipping one thing to another.

clip² /klɪp/ vt cut the edge off. n clipper /'klɪpə/ 1 instrument for clipping. 2 fast sailing-ship. n clipping /'klɪpɪŋ/ a piece of paper cut from a newspaper, etc.

clique /kliːk/ n small closely united group of persons who have the same interests, and who keep all others out of the group.

cloak /kləʊk/ n loose outer garment. vt cover, hide. n cloakroom /'kləʊkrʊm, -ruːm/ 1 place where one may leave one's coat, hat etc. (e.g. in a theatre or railway station). 2 LAVATORY.

clock /klɒk/ n instrument for showing the time in hours and minutes. adj, adv clockwise /'klɒkwaɪz/ moving round in the direction the hands move on the face of a clock. n clockwork /'klɒkwɜːk/ machine like that of a clock used for some other purpose, e.g. to move a child's plaything. **to clock in** = show on a special clock the time when one went into the factory or office.

clod /klɒd/ *n* hard piece or mass of earth.

clog /klɒg/ *vt* cause difficulty in moving or working, e.g. *The machine is clogged with thick oil. n* heavy wooden shoe.

cloister /ˈklɔɪstə/ *n* covered pathway joined to a church; place where men or women live lives of study and prayer apart from the world.

close¹ /kləʊz/ *v* shut; finish. *n* end; finish. **to close down** = cease or cause to cease (e.g. a shop) doing business. **to close up** = move or sit closer together. **closed shop** = factory in which all workers must belong to a TRADE UNION.

close² /kləʊs/ *adj* 1 lacking space. 2 near, e.g. *Close to the church; A close friend* = near and dear friend. 3 (of the weather) warm and damp, with no wind. *n* short road with houses on it which does not lead to another road. **a close call** = narrow escape. *n* **close-up** /ˈkləʊs ʌp/ photograph, esp. of a face, taken with the camera close to what is photographed.

closet /ˈklɒzɪt/ *n* very small room in which things are stored.

closure /ˈkləʊʒə/ *n* act of stopping; act of closing down.

clot /klɒt/ *vi* become thick as blood does in air. *n* solid piece of material in liquid.

cloth /klɒθ/ *n* material made of cotton, wool, silk, etc.

clothe /kləʊð/ *vt* put clothes on. *n (pl)* **clothes** /kləʊðz, kləʊz/ garments. *n (sing)* **clothing** /ˈkləʊðɪŋ/ garments.

cloud /klaʊd/ *n* mist floating high up in the air. **to cloud over** = become cloudy. *adj* **cloudy** /ˈklaʊdɪ/ (of the sky) having many clouds; (of a liquid) not clear.

clout /klaʊt/ *n* rough piece of cloth. *infml vt, n* hit.

clove¹ /kləʊv/ *n* dried flower of a certain tree used to give a special taste to cooked fruits, etc.

clove² /kləʊv/ p.t. of **cleave**.

cloven /ˈkləʊvən/ *adj* divided into two parts.

clover

clover /ˈkləʊvə/ *n* plant with leaves in sets of three, having sweet-smelling flowers, used for feeding cattle.

clown /klaʊn/ *n* man who amuses people by acting in a foolish way. *vi* act foolishly.

cloy /klɔɪ/ *v* cause dislike because of too much sweetness.

club¹ (2)

club¹ /klʌb/ *n* 1 heavy stick. 2 one of the four sets of playing cards in the pack. *vt* hit with a heavy stick.

club² /klʌb/ *n* number of people joined together for a common purpose, e.g. *A football club.*

cluck /klʌk/ *n, interj* noise made by a hen. *vi* make this noise.

clue /kluː/ *n* that which leads one to find the answer to a question.

clump /klʌmp/ *n* group (esp. of trees).

clumsy /ˈklʌmzɪ/ *adj* rough and unskilful in movement.

clung /klʌŋ/ p.t. & p.p. of **cling**.

cluster /ˈklʌstə/ *n* number of flowers or plants growing close together; any close group of things. *vi* group closely together.

clutch /klʌtʃ/ *vt* seize. *n* one of the controls in a car, which governs the way the engine drives the wheels.

clutter /ˈklʌtə/ *n* disorderly mass of things. **to clutter up** = make disorderly by putting too many things in the wrong places.

co- /kəʊ/ together, with each other, e.g. *n* **co-ownership** /ˌkəʊˈəʊnəʃɪp/ ownership of one thing by two or more people.

coach /kəʊtʃ/ *n* 1 large four-wheeled carriage; car or carriage in a train. 2 person who gives special training, e.g. to players for a game, to people for an examination. *vt* train or teach. *n* **coachman** /ˈkəʊtʃmən/ driver of a horse-carriage.

coagulate /kəʊˈægjʊleɪt/ *vi* become thick, as blood does in air.

coal /kəʊl/ *n* black material used for burning.

coalesce /ˌkəʊəˈles/ *vi* grow together; unite.

coalition /ˌkəʊəˈlɪʃən/ *n* joining of different or (till now) unfriendly groups.

coarse /kɔːs/ *adj* not fine; rough; not polite.

coast /kəʊst/ *n* edge of a country next to the sea. *vi* go down hill freely, e.g. on a bicycle. *n* **coastline** /ˈkəʊstlaɪn/ line of the coast.

coat /kəʊt/ *n* outer covering. **coat of arms** = figures painted on a shield as the sign of a certain person of a certain family.

coax /kəʊks/ *vt* beg sweetly—like a child.

cob /kɒb/ *n* 1 round piece, e.g of coal. 2 fruit of Indian corn. 3 strong, short-legged horse.

cobalt /ˈkəʊbɔːlt/ *n* blue metal. *n, adj* (of) a blue colour.

cobbler /ˈkɒblə/ *n* one who makes or repairs shoes.

cobblestone /'kɒblstəʊn/ *n* round stone used in road-making.

cobra /'kɒbrə, 'kəʊbrə/ *n* poisonous snake found in India.

cobweb /'kɒbweb/ *n* fine silk-like net made by a SPIDER.

cocaine /kə'keɪn/ *n* powerful medicine that takes away all feeling from the skin.

cock[1] /kɒk/ *n* male bird.

cock[2] /kɒk/ *n* L-shaped part in a gun which is made to come down with force in order to fire the gun. *vt* **1** raise this part of (a gun). **2** turn upwards and sideways, e.g. the ear of a dog.

cockade /kɒ'keɪd/ *n* ornament worn on the hat.

cockatoo

cockatoo /ˌkɒkə'tuː/ *n* brightly-coloured bird with feathers standing up on its head.

cockerel /'kɒkrəl/ *n* young COCK.

cockle /'kɒkəl/ *n* a kind of shellfish.

cockney /'kɒknɪ/ *n* special way of speaking English common in some parts of London; person born in one of these parts of London.

cockpit /'kɒk,pɪt/ *n* place in which the driver of an aeroplane sits.

cockroach /'kɒk-rəʊtʃ/ *n* large black or brown insect found in kitchens.

cocksure /ˌkɒk'ʃʊə/ *adj* always very sure of one's opinions.

cocktail /'kɒkteɪl/ *n* mixture of strong drinks and other liquids, taken before a meal.

cocoa /'kəʊkəʊ/ *n* fruit of a tree, powdered and boiled with milk and sugar to make a sweet hot drink.

coconut /'kəʊkənʌt/ *n* large round fruit in a hard shell, used as a food.

cocoon /kə'kuːn/ *n* silk covering which a creeping insect makes for itself before it changes into a flying insect.

cocoyam /'kəʊkəʊjæm/ *n* a kind of root grown for food, as in West Africa.

cod /kɒd/ *vt* large sea fish, used as food.

coddle /'kɒdl/ *vt* treat gently, as one would a baby.

code /kəʊd/ *n* **1** laws written down in a certain order. **2** form of secret writing; agreed arrangement by which certain signs are given a special meaning; numbers (for the area) used before telephone numbers.

coerce /kəʊ'ɜːs/ *vt* force (someone) to do something.

coffee /'kɒfɪ/ *n* small brown seeds of a bush powdered and boiled to make a rather bitter hot drink.

coffer /'kɒfə/ *n* large strong box used for keeping things of value.

coffin /'kɒfɪn/ *n* box in which a dead body is put.

cog

cog /kɒg/ *n* one of the teeth on a wheel enabling it to move another wheel.

cogent /'kəʊdʒənt/ *adj* (of a piece of reasoning) strong; making one agree.

cogitate /'kɒdʒəteɪt/ *vi* think.

cognac /'kɒnjæk/ *n* very strong drink made from wine.

cognate /'kɒgneɪt/ *adj* of the same group or family. **a cognate word** = word which is the same, or almost the same, in two languages.

cognition /kɒg'nɪʃən/ *n* act of knowing or noticing.

cognizance /'kɒgnɪzəns/ *n* having knowledge of, taking notice of.

cohere /kəʊ'hɪə/ *vi* stick together. *adj* **coherent** /kəʊ'hɪərənt/ reasoning well; well reasoned. *n* **cohesion** /kəʊ'hiːʒən/ condition or act of sticking together.

cohort /'kəʊhɔːt/ *n* company of soldiers in the Roman army.

coiffeur /kwɑː'fɜː/ *n* person who cuts, curls, etc., women's hair. *n* **coiffure** /kwɑː'fjʊə/ way of doing this.

coil /kɔɪl/ *vt* gather (a rope, etc.) up in circles. *n* set of circles so made.

coin /kɔɪn/ *n* any piece of money made of metal. *vt* **1** make (money) out of metal. **2** make up (a new word or group of words). *n* **coinage** /'kɔɪnɪdʒ/ money used in a country; a word or group of words newly made up.

coincide /ˌkəʊɪn'saɪd/ *vi* (of two spaces or drawings) fit exactly the one upon the other; (of events in time) happen at the same time; (of tastes or opinions) agree. *n* **coincidence** /kəʊ'ɪnsɪdəns/ something that happens, by accident, just at the same moment. *adj* **coincidental** /kəʊˌɪnsɪ'dentl/.

coke /kəʊk/ *n* coal from which the gas has been driven by heat.

colander /'kʌləndə/, **cullender** /'kʌləndə/ *n* metal pot with holes in it, used to get the water out of boiled vegetables, etc.

cold[1] /kəʊld/ *n* illness causing pain in the throat and running of liquid from the nose.

cold² /kəʊld/ *adj* opposite of hot; calm and without feelings; not showing love. **in cold blood** = when quite calm.

colic /'kɒlɪk/ *n* pain in the stomach or bowel.

collaborate /kə'læbəreɪt/ *vi* to work with another, esp. in writing books. *n* **collaboration** /kə,læbə'reɪʃən/.

collapse /kə'læps/ *vi* fall down; lose strength suddenly. *n* sudden fall or loss of strength.

collapsible /kə'læpsəbəl/ *adj* which can be folded into a small space, e.g. *A collapsible boat.*

collar /'kɒlə/ *n* band worn round the neck, e.g. of a dog. *vt* seize by the collar.

collate /kə'leɪt/ *vt* examine (two written papers) carefully side by side.

collateral /kə'lætərəl/ *adj* supporting or making sure.

colleague /'kɒliːg/ *n* one who works with another in an office, school, etc.

collect /kə'lekt/ *v* gather together. *n* **collection** /kə'lekʃən/ act of collecting things; set of things collected.

collective /kə'lektɪv/ *adj* of all, of all in the group, e.g. *Policy of collective ownership of land* = idea that land should be owned by the nation, not by single persons.

college /'kɒlɪdʒ/ *n* school; part of a university; place other than a university where one may study after leaving school. *adj* **collegiate** /kə'liːdʒɪət/.

collide

collide /kə'laɪd/ *vi* come together with great force by accident, e.g. *The trains collided.*

collier /'kɒlɪə/ *n* one who brings coal from the ground; a ship for carrying coal. *n* **colliery** /'kɒlɪərɪ/ place from which coal is obtained.

collision /kə'lɪʒən/ *n* act of COLLIDING.

collocation /,kɒlə'keɪʃən/ *n* setting together in order; things set together.

colloquial /kə'ləʊkwɪəl/ *adj* used in common speech.

collusion /kə'luːʒən/ *n* secret agreement for a wrong purpose.

colon¹ /'kəʊlən/ *n* the mark ':', used before giving lists, etc.

colon² /'kəʊlən/ *n* large lower part of the bowel.

colonel /'kɜːnəl/ *n* one who commands about 1,000 men in the army.

colonial /kə'ləʊnɪəl/ *adj* having to do with a COLONY (2nd below).

colonnade /,kɒlə'neɪd/ *n* row of pillars usually supporting arches.

colony /'kɒlənɪ/ *n* land settled in by people from another country; people who go settle; number of foreign persons living in a city, sometimes all in one part of the town. *vt* **colonize** /'kɒlənaɪz/ make into a colony; use as a colony.

colossus /kə'lɒsəs/ *n* very large figure cut in stone; very great man. *adj* **colossal** /kə'lɒsəl/ very large.

colour /'kʌlə/ *n* quality that makes the surface of an object either red, or green, or yellow, or blue etc.; material used, e.g. in painting, to give such a quality. *vt* give colour to, e.g. in painting.

colt /kəʊlt/ *n* young male horse.

column /'kɒləm/ *n* large round post; long line of anything.

coma /'kəʊmə/ *n* deep sleep in which all feeling is lost. *adj* **comatose** /'kəʊmətəʊs/ in a condition of coma.

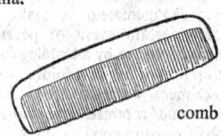

comb

comb /kəʊm/ *n* toothed instrument used for putting the hair in order. *vt* put (the hair) in order with a comb.

combat /'kɒmbæt/ *n, vt* fight. *n* **combatant** /'kɒmbətənt/ one who fights.

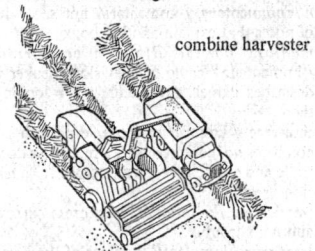

combine harvester

combination /,kɒmbɪ'neɪʃən/ *n* joining together; set of things joined together. **combine** /kəm'baɪn/ *v* join together. /'kɒmbaɪn/ *n* joining together and working together of several persons or business companies. *n* **combine harvester** /,.. '.../ machine as shown which cuts corn and takes out the seeds while moving round the field.

combustion /kəm'bʌstʃən/ *n* act of burning. *n, adj* **combustible** /kəm'bʌstəbəl/ (material) that burns easily.

come /kʌm/ *vi* move in the direction of the speaker; arrive. **come about** = happen. **come across** = meet or find by accident. **come by** = obtain.

comedian /kə'miːdɪən/ *n* one who is paid to amuse others, telling stories, etc.

comedy /'kɒmədɪ/ *n* amusing play.

comely /'kʌmlɪ/ *adj* pretty.

comet /'kɒmɪt/ *n* kind of heavenly body with a tail of light.

comfort /'kʌmfət/ *vt* care for the well-being of (someone); cheer when sad. *n* state of being comfortable. *adj* **comfortable** /'kʌmftəbəl/ pleasant and causing comfort.

comic /'kɒmɪk/ *adj* making people laugh. *n* 1 COMEDIAN. 2 children's paper with many coloured pictures in it.

comma /'kɒmə/ *n* the mark ',' used in writing where one would pause in speaking.

command /kə'mɑːnd/ *n, vt* order.

commandeer /ˌkɒmən'dɪə/ *vt* take for the use of the army, e.g. during war.

commandment /kə'mɑːndmənt/ *n* law or order.

commando /kə'mɑːndəʊ/ *n* one of a small party of specially trained soldiers used for very dangerous attacks into the enemy country.

commemorate /kə'meməreɪt/ *vt* make people remember (a certain event or person) by meetings, feasts, etc., or by a building (or other object) set up in memory of it (him).

commence /kə'mens/ *v* start.

commend /kə'mend/ *vt* praise. *adj* **commendable** /kə'mendəbəl/ worthy; good.

commensurate /kə'menʃʊrət/ *adj* of like measure or size.

comment /'kɒment/ *n* that which is said about a thing, usually to say how one feels about it or what one has noticed in it. *vi* make a comment. *n* **commentary** /'kɒməntərɪ/ notes, or book of notes that explain another book, e.g. *A commentary on the Bible*. *n* **commentator** /'kɒmənteɪtə/ radio or television speaker who describes games, races, etc., while looking at them.

commerce /'kɒmɜːs/ *n* trade, esp. with other countries *adj* **commercial** /kə'mɜːʃəl/ to do with trade and business. *n* ADVERTISEMENT on television or radio.

commiserate /kə'mɪzəreɪt/ *vi* express sorrow at another's trouble.

commissar /ˌkɒmɪ'sɑː/ *n* officer of the Russian government.

commissariat /ˌkɒmɪ'seərɪət/ *n* that part of an army which arranges the supply of the food.

commission /kə'mɪʃən/ *n* 1 duty; appointment to an office; paper of appointment, e.g. of an officer in the army. 2 payment for doing business for another. 3 group of persons given the duty of enquiring into some special matter and of making a report to the government. *n* **commissionaire** /kəˌmɪʃə'neə/ servant who stands at the door (shop, etc.). *n* **commissioner** /kə'mɪʃənə/ one appointed by the government to do certain work.

commit /kə'mɪt/ *vt* 1 do (something wrong). 2 say something so that (someone) is forced later to act in a certain way.

committee /kə'mɪtɪ/ *n* group of people appointed to consider some matter and report on it or make a decision.

commodious /kə'məʊdɪəs/ *adj* having plenty of room.

commodity /kə'mɒdətɪ/ *n* article of trade; anything in daily use.

commodore /'kɒmədɔː/ *n* officer in the NAVY higher than a captain.

common /'kɒmən/ *adj* 1 general; found everywhere. 2 shared. 3 not polite; rough in manner. *n* piece of public land, **common or garden** = very usual and well-known. **common sense** = good judgment. **House of Commons** = group of men elected to make the laws in Britain.

commoner /'kɒmənə/ *n* one who has no title or rank as a nobleman.

commonplace /'kɒmənpleɪs/ *adj* such as is often seen or heard. *n* uninteresting saying.

Commons, House of Commons = group of elected persons in the British PARLIAMENT.

commonwealth /'kɒmənwelθ/ *n* united group of self-governing countries.

commotion /kə'məʊʃən/ *n* great noise and much movement.

communal /'kɒmjʊnəl/ *adj* having to do with a way of living in which all things are owned in common by all.

commune /'kɒmjuːn/ *n* self-governing group in a country. *vi* **commune** /kə'mjuːn/ speak together as close friends.

communicate /kə'mjuːnɪkeɪt/ *v* pass something to another person, e.g. news, disease. *adj* **communicative** /kə'mjuːnɪkətɪv/ eager to talk; loving talking. *n* **communication** /kəˌmjuːnɪ'keɪʃən/.

communion /kə'mjuːnɪən/ *n* 1 sharing of thoughts and feelings. 2 religious ceremony held in the Christian Church in memory of Christ's last supper before His death.

communiqué /kə'mjuːnɪkeɪ/ *n* a piece of news given out by the government.

communism /'kɒmjʊnɪzəm/ *n* form of government, e.g. in Russia, in which all power is in the hands of the workers, and all land, buildings, etc., are owned by the public. *n* **communist** /'kɒmjʊnɪst/ one who believes this to be the best form of government.

community /kə'mjuːnətɪ/ *n* group of people living in one place or having the same interests.

commute /kə'mjuːt/ *vt* make (a punishment) less. *vi* travel regularly to and from work.

compact /kəm'pækt/ *adj* pressed closely together. *n* **compact** /'kɒmpækt/ box of face-powder carried in the bag by ladies.

companion /kəm'pænɪən/ *n* friend; one who goes with another.

companionway /kəm'pænjənweɪ/ *n* stairs on a ship.

company /'kʌmpənɪ/ *n* 1 group of people; number of invited guests. 2 group of 100–250 men in the army commanded by a captain. 3 group of persons united for purposes of business.

comparative /kəm'pærətɪv/ *adj* appearing by

COMPARISON to have a quality, e.g. *Leaving the battlefield behind, we returned to the comparative safety of the camp. n, adj* (form of an adjective) expressing COMPARISON, e.g. *'better' is the comparative of 'good'*.

compare /kəm'peə⁷/ *vt* look for and point out a likeness or difference. *adj* **comparable** /'kɒmpərəbəl/ of similar quality. *n* **comparison** /kəm'pærɪsən/ act of showing the likeness or difference.

compartment /kəm'pɑːtmənt/ *n* one of the small divided parts (rooms) in a carriage in a railway train; any part which has been divided and closed off.

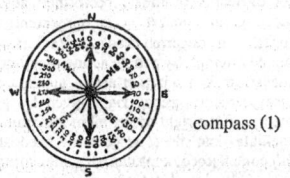

compass (1)

compass /'kʌmpəs/ *n* instrument with a bar of iron which always points north and south. **compasses** (also **pair of compasses**) = instrument for drawing circles.

compassion /kəm'pæʃən/ *n* feeling of pity for the sorrows of others. *adj* **compassionate** /kəm'pæʃənət/ having pity.

compatible /kəm'pætəbəl/ *adj* **1** agreeable; having the same character. **2** able to be true at the same time as something else.

compatriot /kəm'pætrɪət/ *n* native of the same country.

compel /kəm'pel/ *vt* force.

compendium /kəm'pendɪəm/ *n* short account of a book. *adj* **compendious** /kəm'pendɪəs/ containing much (knowledge) in a little space.

compensate /'kɒmpənseɪt/ *v* pay for; when one has done wrong or hurt someone, do something to make it right, or pay for damage. *n* **compensation** /ˌkɒmpən'seɪʃən/.

compete /kəm'piːt/ *vi* work, play or run with other persons and try to be best; try to win something desired by several other persons, e.g. trade.

competent /'kɒmpɪtənt/ *adj* able or fit for certain work; having the necessary power or right to do an act. *n* **competence** /'kɒmpɪtəns/.

competition /ˌkɒmpɪ'tɪʃən/ *n* act of COMPETING.

compile /kəm'paɪl/ *vt* collect and arrange in order.

complacent /kəm'pleɪsənt/ *adj* satisfied with oneself.

complain /kəm'pleɪn/ *vi* express dislike, pain, etc.; make one's difficulties or troubles known. *n* **complaint** /kəm'pleɪnt/ act of complaining; illness.

complaisant /kəm'pleɪzənt/ *adj* yielding to the wishes of others and eager to please.

complement /'kɒmplɪmənt/ *n* that thing or amount necessary to make up a whole; all the officers and men necessary for a ship. *vt* make up a complete whole when added to.

complete /kəm'pliːt/ *vt* finish; make whole. *adj* whole; finished. *n* **completion** /kəm'pliːʃən/.

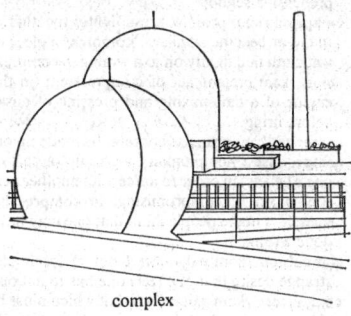

complex

complex /'kɒmpleks/ *adj* not simple; having many parts. *n* **1** set of ideas or desires which one does not know that one possesses, yet which have an effect upon one's behaviour. **2** group of buildings for some particular purpose.

complexion /kəm'plekʃən/ *n* condition of the skin on the face.

compliance /kəm'plaɪəns/ *n* agreement; yielding. *adj* **compliant** /kəm'plaɪənt/ ready to agree.

complicate /'kɒmplɪkeɪt/ *vt* make difficult or hard to understand. *n* **complication** /ˌkɒmplɪ'keɪʃən/.

complicity /kəm'plɪsəti/ *n* share in wrong-doing.

compliment /'kɒmplɪmənt/ *vt* express admiration for (someone). *n* expression of admiration.

comply /kəm'plaɪ/ *vi* yield; agree.

component /kəm'pəʊnənt/ *n* part of the whole.

compose /kəm'pəʊz/ *vt* put together; write (esp. music). *adj* **composed** calm.

composite /'kɒmpəzɪt/ *adj* made up of different parts.

composition /ˌkɒmpə'zɪʃən/ *n* act of putting together; something (e.g. a piece of music) written; arrangement of objects in a picture; way in which things are mixed to make something, e.g. a dish of food, earth for growing plants, a medicine, etc.

compositor /kəm'pɒzətə⁷/ *n* one who sets up TYPE for printing.

composure /kəm'pəʊʒə⁷/ *n* calmness.

compound¹ /kəm'paʊnd/ *vt* **1** mix together. **2** make worse (something already bad). *adj* **compound** /'kɒmpaʊnd/ made up of several different materials. *n* /'kɒmpaʊnd/ mixture; joining of two substances so that a new substance is produced.

compound² /'kɒmpaʊnd/ *n* group of buildings and the land around them, for men working in a certain place to live in.

comprehend /ˌkɒmprɪ'hend/ *vt* **1** take all into

53

consideration. **2** understand. *n* **comprehension** /ˌkɒmprɪ'henʃən/ understanding.

comprehensive /ˌkɒmprɪ'hensɪv/ *adj* **1** taking in everything, e.g. *A comprehensive report.* **2** (of a school) taking children of different levels of ability and teaching them together. *n* a comprehensive school.

compress /kəm'pres/ *vt* press tightly together. *v* make or become smaller. /'kɒmpres/ *n* piece of wet cloth tied tightly on to a wound. *n* **compression** /kəm'preʃən/ act of compressing; (in the engine of a car) mixing and pressing of gases before firing.

comprise /kəm'praɪz/ *vt* contain; be made up of.

compromise /'kɒmprəmaɪz/ *v* give up (a part of one's beliefs) in order to agree with another person. *n* act of compromising. **to compromise oneself** = make people think that one may have done wrong.

compulsion /kəm'pʌlʃən/ *n* **1** act of forcing. **2** strange desire that one feels one has to act on.

compulsory /kəm'pʌlsərɪ/ *adj* that which must be done; resulting from force.

compunction /kəm'pʌŋkʃən/ *n* pity; sorrow for a cruel act.

compute /kəm'pju:t/ *vt* find out the amount of; add, divide, etc. *n* **computer** /kəm'pju:tə'/.

comrade /'kɒmreɪd/ *n* friend, fellow-worker.

con¹ /kɒn/ *n* **the pros and cons** = the points for and against an idea.

con² /kɒn/ *sl vt* **1** deceive (esp. someone into parting with money). **2** learn by reading over and over.

concatenation /kənˌkætɪ'neɪʃən/ *n* chain of (events).

concave /'kɒŋkeɪv/ *adj* curved inwards.

conceal /kən'si:l/ *vt* hide; keep from being known.

concede /kən'si:d/ *v* give away; yield after disagreeing.

conceited /kən'si:tɪd/ *adj* having too good an opinion of oneself. *n* **conceit** /kən'si:t/ state of being conceited.

conceive /kən'si:v/ *v* **1** think of; imagine. **2** begin to produce (young).

concentrate /'kɒnsəntreɪt/ *vi* think hard about one thing. *vt* **1** bring together (e.g. soldiers) to one point. **2** increase the strength of a liquid by boiling it down. *n* **concentration** /ˌkɒnsən'treɪʃən/. **concentration camp** /ˌ.'ˌ. ./ = prison camp where prisoners are kept in crowded and very rough conditions.

concentric /kən'sentrɪk/ *adj* (of two circles) having the same centre.

concept /'kɒnsept/ *n* idea.

conception /kən'sepʃən/ *n* act of CONCEIVING; idea.

concern /kən'sɜːn/ *vt* have to do with; make anxious. *n* interest; something important to one, or which makes one anxious. **a going concern** = active business now really working. *adj* **concerned** /kən'sɜːnd/ feeling anxious.

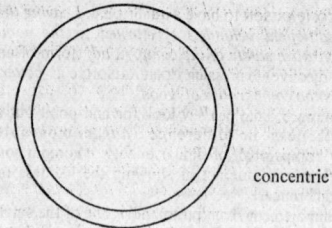

concentric

concert /'kɒnsət/ *n* meeting for hearing music; set of works of music performed at such a meeting. **in concert** = in agreement; acting together. **a concerted** /kən'sɜːtɪd/ **effort** = determined attempt, by people acting together.

concession /kən'seʃən/ *n* act of yielding after a disagreement; special right given by government, e.g. the right to get oil in a certain place.

conciliate /kən'sɪlɪeɪt/ *vt* gain the friendship of. *adj* **conciliatory** /kən'sɪlɪətərɪ/ conciliating.

concise /kən'saɪs/ *adj* short; putting a lot of meaning into a few words or small space.

conclude /kən'klu:d/ *vt* **1** bring to an end. **2** decide as a result of reasoning. *n* **conclusion** /kən'klu:ʒən/ **1** end. **2** result obtained after reasoning.

concoct /kən'kɒkt/ *vt* make by mixing. **concoct a story** = make up an untrue story.

concomitant /kən'kɒmɪtənt/ *adj, n* (that) which goes with something else, e.g. *Music is the usual concomitant of feasting.*

concord /'kɒŋkɔːd/ *n* agreement; peace.

concourse /'kɒŋkɔːs/ *n* meeting of many people.

concrete /'kɒŋkri:t/ *adj* formed into one mass; real; able to be touched and felt. *n, adj* (made of a) stone-like material used for roads, buildings, etc. **a concrete noun** = word which is the name of a real thing, not of a quality.

concur /kən'kɜː'/ *vi* meet at one point; agree.

concussion /kən'kʌʃən/ *n* shaking; loss of all the senses caused by a blow on the head.

condemn /kən'dem/ *vt* blame; declare (someone) to deserve punishment for wrong-doing; declare as not fit for use.

condense /kən'dens/ *vt* press together; express the meaning of (something) in fewer words.

condenser /kən'densə'/ *n* **1** part of a machine which makes gas into liquid. **2** instrument which stores electricity.

condescend /ˌkɒndɪ'send/ *vi* bring oneself down to the level of a person of less wisdom or importance, and make clear one's greatness in doing so. *n* **condescension** /ˌkɒndɪ'senʃən/.

condiment /'kɒndɪmənt/ *n* matter added to food to make it taste nicer.

condition /kən'dɪʃən/ *n* **1** state (of something). **2** something on which something else depends, e.g. *Fitness is a condition of entry into the army.* **on condition that** = only if.

condole /kənˈdəʊl/ vi express pity. n **condolence** /kənˈdəʊləns/.

condone /kənˈdəʊn/ vt forgive; not speak against (something wrong).

conduce /kənˈdjuːs/ vi help to produce something. adj **conducive** /kənˈdjuːsɪv/ helping to produce, e.g. *Late night quarrels are not conducive to good sleep.*

conduct /kənˈdʌkt/ vt **1** lead (someone) (e.g. to a seat). **2** allow to pass, e.g. *Metal conducts electricity.* **3** control and lead persons playing music. **4** carry on, e.g. *To conduct a business.* /ˈkɒndʌkt/ n behaviour. **to conduct oneself** = behave. n **conductor** /kənˈdʌktə/ **1** man controlling players of music. **2** man who collects money on a BUS from those wishing to travel on it.

conduit /ˈkɒndɪt/ n large pipe or underground way for water, etc.

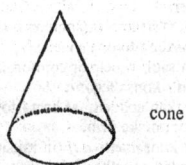

cone

cone /kəʊn/ n figure round at the bottom and pointed at the top; fruit of a certain kind of tree, e.g. FIR-trees.

confectionery /kənˈfekʃənərɪ/ n (*sing*) cakes and sweets. n **confectioner** /kənˈfekʃənə/ one who sells—

confederate /kənˈfedərət/ adj joined by agreement for a common purpose. n **confederation** /kənˌfedəˈreɪʃən/ group formed in this way.

confer /kənˈfɜː/ vt give (an honour) to. **to confer with** = talk to and get the ideas of. n **conference** /ˈkɒnfərəns/ meeting for talking about some business or for learning each other's ideas on some subject.

confess /kənˈfes/ v tell one's faults and wrongdoings; tell one's beliefs. n **confession** /kənˈfeʃən/ act of confessing; what is confessed. n **confessor** /kənˈfesə/ a priest who hears others confess.

confetti /kənˈfetɪ/ n small pieces of coloured paper which are thrown at newly-married people as they leave the church.

confide /kənˈfaɪd/ v have trust or faith (in); tell secrets to a trusted person.

confidence /ˈkɒnfɪdəns/ n **1** feeling of trust. **2** secret told to another person. **3** belief in oneself and one's abilities. **in confidence** = (told) as a secret. adj **confident** /ˈkɒnfɪdənt/ believing in oneself and one's abilities. adj **confidential** /ˌkɒnfɪˈdenʃəl/ told as a secret.

confine /kənˈfaɪn/ vt keep shut in. n **confinement** /kənˈfaɪnmənt/ **1** state of being shut in. **2** act of giving birth.

confirm /kənˈfɜːm/ vt make sure. n **confirmation** /ˌkɒnfəˈmeɪʃən/.

confiscate /ˈkɒnfɪskeɪt/ vt seize (a person's land or goods) as a punishment.

conflagration /ˌkɒnfləˈɡreɪʃən/ n great fire.

conflict /ˈkɒnflɪkt/ n fight; disagreement. /kənˈflɪkt/ vi disagree.

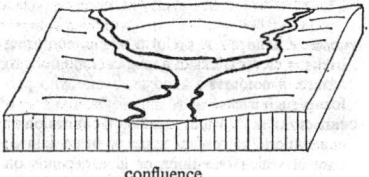

confluence

confluence /ˈkɒnfluəns/ n flowing together, e.g. of rivers into one stream.

conform /kənˈfɔːm/ vi act according to law or custom. n **conformity** /kənˈfɔːmətɪ/.

confound /kənˈfaʊnd/ vt mix together and cause disorder; make (someone) unable to understand.

confront /kənˈfrʌnt/ vt bring face to face with; meet face to face. n **confrontation** /ˌkɒnfrənˈteɪʃən/ coming together of two people or groups against each other.

confuse /kənˈfjuːz/ vt mix together; throw into disorder; mistake (one thing) for another. n **confusion** /kənˈfjuːʒən/.

congeal /kənˈdʒiːl/ v make or become thick, as blood does in air.

congenial /kənˈdʒiːnɪəl/ adj suiting one's likes and dislikes.

congenital /kənˈdʒenɪtl/ adj inborn, e.g. disease.

congest /kənˈdʒest/ vi collect into a mass. adj **congested** /kənˈdʒestɪd/ too full, e.g of people, of blood. n **congestion** /kənˈdʒestʃən/.

conglomerate /kənˈɡlɒməreɪt/ vt collect into a mass. n **conglomeration** /kənˌɡlɒməˈreɪʃən/.

congratulate /kənˈɡrætʃʊleɪt/ vt express pleasure at the good fortune of. n **congratulation** /kənˌɡrætʃʊˈleɪʃən/. interj **congratulations!** expression of pleasure at the good fortune of the person one is speaking to.

congregate /ˈkɒnɡrɪɡeɪt/ vi meet together. n **congregation** /ˌkɒnɡrɪˈɡeɪʃən/ large gathering of people, esp. in a church for prayer.

congress /ˈkɒnɡres/ n coming together of people; group of persons who make laws in America.

conical /ˈkɒnɪkəl/ adj shaped like a CONE.

conjecture /kənˈdʒektʃə/ n, v guess.

conjugal /ˈkɒndʒʊɡəl/ adj having to do with marriage, esp. the sexual side of marriage.

conjugate /ˈkɒndʒʊɡeɪt/ vt give the forms of a verb.

conjunction /kənˈdʒʌŋkʃən/ n **1** act of joining. **2** word which joins words or groups of words, e.g. 'And', 'But'.

conjurer

conjure /'kʌndʒə/ vi perform magic. **conjuring tricks** = clever tricks of a magical kind done to amuse. n **conjurer** /'kʌndʒərə/ one who performs such tricks.

connect /kə'nekt/ v join together. n **connexion** or **connection** /kə'nekʃən/ state of being joined; way in which one thing or idea depends on another: a person who belongs to one's family by marriage, not by blood.

connive /kə'naɪv/ vi help wrong-doers secretly; pretend not to see wrong-doing. n **connivance** /kə'naɪvəns/.

connoisseur /ˌkɒnə'sɜː/ n one who has special taste in, and knowledge of, objects of art and beauty.

connote /kə'nəʊt/ vt have (another meaning) besides the main or direct meaning. n **connotation** /ˌkɒnə'teɪʃən/.

conquer /'kɒŋkə/ vt take (a country) by force, e.g. by an army; win a victory over. n **conquest** /'kɒŋkwest/.

conscience /'kɒnʃəns/ n inner feeling which tells one about matters of right and wrong.

conscientious /ˌkɒnʃi'enʃəs/ adj careful to do one's duty properly; careful in one's work. a **conscientious objector** = one who refuses to fight for his country because he believes that war is wrong.

conscious /'kɒnʃəs/ adj awake and knowing; known to the thinking mind. n **consciousness** /'kɒnʃəsnəs/ power of the mind to feel and know. **to lose consciousness** = faint.

conscript /'kɒnskrɪpt/ n one who is forced by law to become a soldier. n **conscription** /kən'skrɪpʃən/ act, by a government, of forcing men to join the army.

consecrate /'kɒnsɪkreɪt/ vt make holy; give for the use of God and the Church. n **consecration** /ˌkɒnsɪ'kreɪʃən/.

consecutive /kən'sekjʊtɪv/ adj following in order.

consensus /kən'sensəs/ n general agreement.

consent /kən'sent/ vi agree; allow something; be willing. n permission.

consequence /'kɒnsɪkwəns/ n result. adj **consequent** /'kɒnsɪkwənt/ following as a result. adj **consequential** /ˌkɒnsɪ'kwenʃəl/ following as a result; having important effects.

conservation /ˌkɒnsə'veɪʃən/ n keeping from decay or from being destroyed.

conservative /kən'sɜːvətɪv/ adj wishing to keep things as they are. n one who does not want to make many or large changes in the laws.

conservatory /kən'sɜːvətrɪ/ n 1 glass house for flowers. 2 school of music or art.

conserve /kən'sɜːv/ vt keep safe; keep from decay; cook fruit with sugar so that it can be kept for a long time. n fruit so cooked.

consider /kən'sɪdə/ vt think about; hold a certain opinion; think of the feelings of.

considerable /kən'sɪdərəbəl/ adj worth considering; rather important; large.

considerate /kən'sɪdərət/ adj kind; thinking of other people's good. n **consideration** /kənˌsɪdə'reɪʃən/ 1 state of being considerate. 2 point to be considered.

consign /kən'saɪn/ vt send; put in charge of a person. n **consignment** /kən'saɪnmənt/ set of goods sent, e.g. to a trader for selling.

consist /kən'sɪst/ vi be made up of something.

consistency /kən'sɪstənsɪ/ n (of matter) thickness, solidity; (of a person) quality of being CONSISTENT.

consistent /kən'sɪstənt/ adj agreeing with oneself; acting according to one's ideas.

console /kən'səʊl/ vt help or comfort in sorrow. n **consolation** /ˌkɒnsə'leɪʃən/.

consolidate /kən'sɒlɪdeɪt/ vt bring together and make strong; make firm.

consonant /'kɒnsənənt/ adj (in music) pleasant when sounded together. n speech sound of a letter, other than a, e, i, o, u.

consort /'kɒnsɔːt/ n 1 husband or wife of a king or queen or ruler. 2 ship sailing under the protection of another. /kən'sɔːt/ vi go about in the company of someone, e.g. She used to consort with all sorts of people.

conspicuous /kən'spɪkjʊəs/ adj very noticeable.

conspiracy /kən'spɪrəsɪ/ n secret plan to do an unlawful act; secret plan to change the government by force. v **conspire** /kən'spaɪə/ make such plans.

constable /'kʌnstəbəl/ n policeman. n (sing) **constabulary** /kən'stæbjʊlərɪ/ all the police.

constant /'kɒnstənt/ adj remaining unchanged; faithful. n **constancy** /'kɒnstənsɪ/.

constellation /ˌkɒnstə'leɪʃən/ n group of stars.

consternation /ˌkɒnstə'neɪʃən/ n feeling of great surprise and fear.

constipated /'kɒnstɪpeɪtɪd/ adj having great difficulty in clearing waste matter from the body. n **constipation** /ˌkɒnstɪ'peɪʃən/.

constituency /kən'stɪtjʊənsɪ/ n group of people who elect a man to the government.

constituent /kən'stɪtjʊənt/ n, adj (forming) part of a whole.

constitute /'kɒnstɪtjuːt/ vt 1 set up; appoint a person or group and give power to act. 2 be what makes up; be, e.g. This constitutes an unfair practice.

constitution /ˌkɒnstɪ'tjuːʃən/ n 1 act of setting something up. 2 body of laws controlling the way a country is to be governed. 3 health of one's body.

constrain /kən'streɪn/ vt use force and make

(someone) do a certain act. *n* **constraint** /kən'streɪnt/.

constrict /kən'strɪkt/ *vt* press (together) tightly. *n* **constriction** /kən'strɪkʃən/.

construct /kən'strʌkt/ *vt* build; make. *n* **construction** /kən'strʌkʃən/ 1 anything built; the act or way of building. 2 group of words going together. *adj* **constructive** /kən'strʌktɪv/ which helps to build up rather than break down or destroy.

construe /kən'struː/ *vt* understand or regard (something) in a particular way, e.g. *His speech was construed as an attack on the government.*

consul /'kɒnsəl/ *n* elected judge or officer of government in ancient Rome; government officer living in a foreign city to help the trade and people of his country. *n* **consulate** /'kɒnsjʊlət/ house and office of a consul.

consult /kən'sʌlt/ *vt* seek the advice of another. *n* **consultant** /kən'sʌltənt/ one whose work is advising others; high-ranking hospital doctor in a special field of work. *n* **consultation** /ˌkɒnsəl'teɪʃən/.

consume /kən'sjuːm/ *vt* use up; take into the body (e.g. food or drink).

consummate /'kɒnsəmeɪt/ *vt* make perfect; finish. *adj* **consummate** /kən'sʌmət/ perfect; complete.

consumption /kən'sʌmpʃən/ *n* act of using up; amount used.

contact /'kɒntækt/ *n* act of touching; spot where something touches; joining place of two electric wires. *vt* get in touch with, talk to.

contagious /kən'teɪdʒəs/ *adj* (of a disease) able to be passed on by touch.

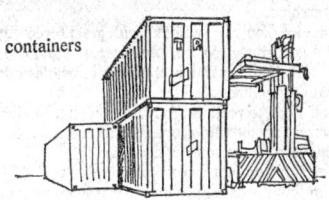

containers

contain /kən'teɪn/ *vt* hold within itself; hold in. *n* **container** /kən'teɪnə/ vessel used to contain anything.

contaminate /kən'tæmɪneɪt/ *vt* make dirty; have a bad effect on.

contemplate /'kɒntəmpleɪt/ *vt* look at and think about. *n* **contemplation** /ˌkɒntəm'pleɪʃən/.

contemporary /kən'tempərərɪ/ *n, adj* (one) living at the same time as another.

contempt /kən'tempt/ *n* feeling caused by something low, worthless and wholly bad; the act of showing this feeling. **contempt of court** = disobeying a judge. *adj* **contemptible** /kən'temptəbəl/ worthy of contempt.

contend /kən'tend/ *vi* struggle. *vt* claim.

content[1] /kən'tent/ *adj* satisfied; feeling easy in one's mind. *n* **contentment** /kən'tentmənt/.

content[2] /'kɒntent/ *n* what is contained (in a book, speech, etc.). *n* **contents** list at the beginning of a book showing what is in it.

contention /kən'tenʃən/ *n* opinion; quarrel or disagreement. *adj* **contentious** /kən'tenʃəs/ causing disagreement; eager to start a quarrel or disagreement.

contest /kən'test/ *vt* disagree with (an opinion). *vi* struggle or fight against others in order to gain something. /'kɒntest/ *n* struggle or fight. *n* **contestant** /kən'testənt/ one in a contest against others.

context /'kɒntekst/ *n* place in a book or speech in which a particular word or group of words is found.

contiguous /kən'tɪgjʊəs/ *adj* near; touching.

continent /'kɒntɪnənt/ *n* one of the six large bodies of land in the world.

contingent /kən'tɪndʒənt/ *adj* uncertain; which will happen if some other thing happens. *n* **contingency** /kən'tɪndʒənsɪ/.

continue /kən'tɪnjuː/ *v* go on without stopping; go on again after a pause. *adj* **continual** /kən'tɪnjʊəl/ lasting for ever; never ending. *n* **continuation** /kənˌtɪnjʊ'eɪʃən/ act of continuing; that which is added when work is continued.

continuous /kən'tɪnjʊəs/ *adj* without a break.

contort /kən'tɔːt/ *vt* bend out of natural shape. *n* **contortionist** /kən'tɔːʃənɪst/ one who bends his body into strange shapes to amuse people.

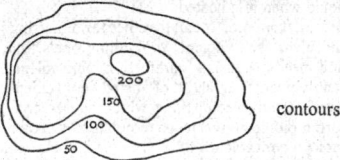

contours

contour /'kɒntʊə/ *n* shape, e.g. of land, mountains, etc.; line on a map showing all parts of the country which are of the same height.

contra- /'kɒntrə/ against; opposite.

contraband /'kɒntrəbænd/ *adj, n* (*sing*) (goods) which may not be brought into a country (or taken out), esp. in time of war; unlawful trade in such goods.

contraception /ˌkɒntrə'sepʃən/ *n* prevention of a child's life being started as a result of sexual relations between a man and a woman. *n, adj* **contraceptive** /ˌkɒntrə'septɪv/ (something) which will prevent a child's life being started.

contract[1] /kən'trækt/ *v* draw together and become smaller, as metal does when cold. **to contract an illness** = become ill.

contract[2] /'kɒntrækt/ *n* promise to do something, e.g. a written promise to supply goods or do work at a certain price.

contradict /ˌkɒntrə'dɪkt/ *vt* declare that (something said or written) is not true; say the opposite to (someone else).

contraption /kən'træpʃən/ *n* new and strange-looking machine or instrument.

contrary /'kɒntrərɪ/ *adj* opposite; unfavourable.

contrast /kən'trɑːst/ *vt* put side by side so as to show the difference. *vi* appear very different when set side by side. /'kɒntrɑːst/ *n* very noticeable difference.

contravene /ˌkɒntrə'viːn/ *vt* go against (e.g. a law). *n* **contravention** /ˌkɒntrə'venʃən/.

contribute /kən'trɪbjuːt/ *v* give with others for a common purpose, e.g. for some good cause. *n* **contribution** /ˌkɒntrɪ'bjuːʃən/.

contrite /'kɒntraɪt/ *adj* sorry for wrong-doing. *n* **contrition** /kən'trɪʃən/.

contrive /kən'traɪv/ *vt* think of a clever way of doing; cause an event to happen by some clever plan, or after some difficulty.

control /kən'trəʊl/ *vt* direct; guide; rule. *n* something that controls something else, e.g. one of the handles, SWITCHES, etc., used in an aeroplane to control its direction and speed.

controversy /'kɒntrəvɜːsɪ, kən'trɒvəsɪ/ *n* disagreement; quarrelling. *adj* **controversial** /ˌkɒntrə'vɜːʃəl/ difficult and causing controversy.

conundrum /kə'nʌndrəm/ *n* clever saying the meaning of which must be guessed; question to which there is an amusing answer.

convalesce /ˌkɒnvə'les/ *vi* get better by resting after an illness. *n* **convalescence** /ˌkɒnvə'lesəns/.

convection /kən'vekʃən/ *n* movement of gas or liquid when it is heated.

convene /kən'viːn/ *vt* call together for a meeting.

convenient /kən'viːnɪənt/ *adj* suiting one's time and needs; causing comfort. *n* **convenience** /kən'viːnɪəns/ quality of being convenient; comfort; any useful thing which causes comfort. **a public convenience** = public LAVATORY. **make a convenience of** = use to suit one's own purposes.

convent /'kɒnvənt/ *n* building in which religious women live apart from the world, giving their time to prayer, study and good works.

convention /kən'venʃən/ *n* **1** large meeting usually continuing for several days. **2** accepted custom or rule of behaviour. *adj* **conventional** /kən'venʃənəl/ usual; according to the general rules, manners or ideas.

converge /kən'vɜːdʒ/ *vi* come together at one point. *adj* **convergent** /kən'vɜːdʒənt/ converging.

conversant /kən'vɜːsənt/ *adj* having a knowledge of something, e.g. *Thoroughly conversant with their customs.*

conversation /ˌkɒnvə'seɪʃən/ *n* act of talking; friendly talk.

converse[1] /kən'vɜːs/ *vi* talk together in a friendly way.

converse[2] /'kɒnvɜːs/ *n, adj* opposite.

convert /kən'vɜːt/ *vt* **1** change from one state into another, e.g. *Convert the sitting-room into a bedroom.* **2** cause (someone) to change his beliefs about God. /'kɒnvɜːt/ *n* one who has changed his beliefs, esp. in coming to believe in God. *n* **conversion** /kən'vɜːʃən/.

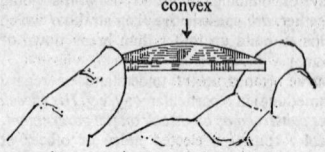
convex

convex /'kɒnveks/ *adj* curved outwards.

convey /kən'veɪ/ *vt* carry; take from one place to another; give ideas to another; give land or a house to another by a written paper according to law. *n* **conveyance** /kən'veɪəns/ carriage; act of conveying.

convict /kən'vɪkt/ *vt* prove that (someone) has done wrong in a court of law. /'kɒnvɪkt/ *n* one who is being punished in prison for breaking the law.

conviction /kən'vɪkʃən/ *n* **1** what one believes to be true or right. **2** act of proving wrong-doing in a court of law.

convince /kən'vɪns/ *vt* satisfy by showing proof; cause to believe.

convivial /kən'vɪvɪəl/ *adj* merry; being happy together.

convocation /ˌkɒnvə'keɪʃən/ *n* act of calling together a meeting; a meeting. *vt* **convoke** /kən'vəʊk/ call together.

convoy /'kɒnvɔɪ/ *vt* go with in order to protect. *n* ships sailing together and protected by warships.

convulse /kən'vʌls/ *vt* shake with great force, e.g. *He was convulsed with laughter. n* **convulsion** /kən'vʌlʃən/ shaking of the limbs or whole body caused by illness.

cook /kʊk/ *v* prepare (food) by boiling, baking, etc. *n* servant who prepares and cooks food. *n* **cookery** /'kʊkərɪ/ art of cooking.

cool /kuːl/ *adj* not warm; calm.

coop /kuːp/ *n* cage for animals, esp. hens. **to coop up** = enclose in a small space.

cooper /'kuːpə/ *n* one who makes barrels.

cooperate /kəʊ'ɒpəreɪt/ *vi* help another in a common aim. *adj* **cooperative** /kəʊ'ɒpərətɪv/ working together.

coordinate /kəʊ'ɔːdɪneɪt/ *vt* cause to work together for the same purpose.

coot /kuːt/ *n* water bird like a duck with a white spot on its head.

cop /kɒp/ *sl n* policeman.

cope /kəʊp/ *vi* deal successfully with a difficulty.

coping /'kəʊpɪŋ/ *n* sloping stones on the top of a wall to throw off the rain.

copious /'kəʊpɪəs/ *adj* plentiful, found in plenty.

copper /'kɒpə/ *n* a red metal; piece of money made of this metal.

coppice /ˈkɒpɪs/ n group of bushes or small trees.

copra /ˈkɒprə/ n dried inside of the COCONUT used to make soil rich.

copse /kɒps/ n group of bushes or small trees.

copy /ˈkɒpɪ/ n thing made exactly like something else. vt make a thing just like (another); write exactly (what is set down on another paper). vt **copyright** /ˈkɒpɪraɪt/ protect by law (something which one has written) so that others may not print it without asking and being allowed. n right of printing a work.

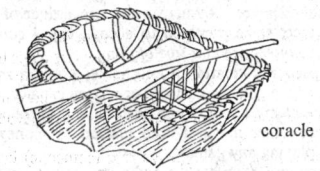

coracle

coracle /ˈkɒrəkəl/ n boat made of a large basket covered with leather.

coral /ˈkɒrəl/ n white or red stone-like material made by creatures in the ocean; red-brown colour.

cord /kɔːd/ n thick string; string-like part of the body.

cordial /ˈkɔːdɪəl/ adj friendly. n pleasant drink, e.g. made from fruit.

cordite /ˈkɔːdaɪt/ n (sing) yellow glass-like threads or plates made from cotton and certain acids and used in place of gunpowder.

cordon /ˈkɔːdən/ n line of soldiers, policemen, etc., set round as a guard.

corduroy /ˈkɔːdərɔɪ, ˈkɔːdʒʊrɔɪ/ n, adj (made out of) thick (cotton) material with raised lines on it.

core /kɔː/ n heart or centre of a thing; in fruit, part where the seeds are.

cork /kɔːk/ n outside covering of a tree, often made into round pieces used to close the hole in a bottle. vt put a cork in (a bottle). adj **corked** /kɔːkt/ (of wine) having a bad taste because of a bad cork. n **corkscrew** /ˈkɔːkskruː/ instrument for pulling corks from bottles.

cormorant /ˈkɔːmərənt/ n bird used by the Chinese to catch fish.

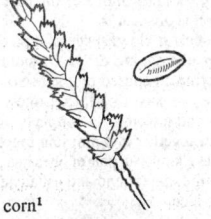

corn[1]

corn[1] /kɔːn/ n grain-bearing plant; grain of any such plant. n **corncob** /ˈkɔːnkɒb/ head of one such plant.

corn[2] /kɔːn/ n piece of hard thick skin on the foot caused by rubbing of the shoe.

cornea /ˈkɔːnɪə/ n thin glassy covering of the eye.

corner /ˈkɔːnə/ n that part of a room or anything else where two sides meet; bend in a road. vt drive (someone) into a difficult place from which he cannot get out.

cornerstone /ˈkɔːnəstəʊn/ n special stone put at a corner of a new building.

cornet /ˈkɔːnɪt/ n brass instrument of music—a kind of horn.

cornflour /ˈkɔːnflaʊə/ n flour made from MAIZE.

cornice /ˈkɔːnɪs/ n ornamental line of wood or stone, put at the top of a building or at the top of a wall in a room.

corollary /kəˈrɒlərɪ/ n result which follows naturally from proving something else.

coronation /ˌkɒrəˈneɪʃən/ n crowning of a king or queen.

coroner /ˈkɒrənə/ n officer of the law who inquires into the causes of sudden death, fires, etc.

coronet /ˈkɒrənet/ n small crown worn by a nobleman.

corporal[1] /ˈkɔːpərəl/ adj having to do with the body. **corporal punishment** = punishment by beating.

corporal[2] /ˈlɔːpərəl/ n one of the lower ranks in the army.

corporate /ˈkɔːpərət/ adj united in a group and given power by law to do business acting as one person; forming one group.

corporation /ˌkɔːpəˈreɪʃən/ n number of persons allowed by law to act as one, e.g. for purposes of business; group of persons who have charge of the public business of an English town.

corps /kɔː/ n large body of soldiers, officers of government or dancers.

corpse /kɔːps/ n human dead body.

corpulent /ˈkɔːpjʊlənt/ adj fat, esp. round the middle of the body.

corpuscle /ˈkɔːpʌsl, kɔːˈpʌsəl/ n very small piece of matter forming part of the blood.

corral /kəˈrɑːl/ n circular fence in which animals are kept.

correct /kəˈrekt/ adj right; according to rule or custom. vt set right; mark the mistakes in (written work). n **correction** /kəˈrekʃən/.

correlate /ˈkɒrəleɪt/ vt show how (two things) depend on each other. n **correlation** /ˌkɒrəˈleɪʃən/.

correspond /ˌkɒrɪˈspɒnd/ vi 1 write letters to and receive letters from a person. 2 be in agreement with, e.g. *His house corresponds to his wealth* = he has a big house because he is very rich. n **correspondence** /ˌkɒrɪˈspɒndəns/. n **correspondent** /ˌkɒrɪˈspɒndənt/ 1 one with whom one is in CORRESPONDENCE. 2 reporter for radio, a newspaper, etc., in a particular place or for a particular field.

corridor /'kɒrɪdɔː/ n narrow covered way joining two buildings, or two parts of one building; narrow piece of land.

corroborate /kə'rɒbəreɪt/ vt find further proof strengthening (proof obtained already).

corrode /kə'rəʊd/ vt eat away slowly as an acid acting on metal. n **corrosion** /kə'rəʊʒən/.

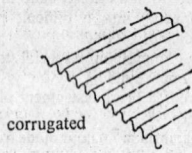

corrugated

corrugated /'kɒrəgeɪtɪd/ adj (of iron) pressed into many small waves.

corrupt /kə'rʌpt/ adj decayed; doing wrong for money. vt give money to (someone) to make him do wrong; make evil. n **corruption** /kə'rʌpʃən/.

corset /'kɔːsɪt/ n stiff under-garment worn by women to give a good shape to the body.

cosh /kɒʃ/ n instrument used for hitting a person on the head. vt hit with such an instrument.

cosmetics /kɒz'metɪks/ n liquids, powders, etc., used by women to make the skin, hair and face beautiful.

cosmic /'kɒzmɪk/ adj having to do with the UNI-VERSE. n **cosmic rays** /ˌ. . './ waves of force, like radio waves but much shorter, coming into the air around the earth from outside.

cosmopolitan /ˌkɒzmə'pɒlɪtən/ adj feeling at home in any country; (of a city) in which people of many nations live.

cosmos /'kɒzmɒs/ n (sing) all the stars and worlds in the sky considered as an ordered arrangement.

cost /kɒst/ n price to be paid; amount of money needed to produce an object or provide a service. vt have as its price, e.g. This book costs £5.

coster /'kɒstə/ or **costermonger**/ /'kɒstəmʌŋgə/ n one who sells fruit, plants, etc., on the street from a cart.

costly /'kɒstlɪ/ adj sold at a high price.

costume /'kɒstjuːm/ special dress, e.g. that of an actor.

cosy /'kəʊzɪ/ adj warm and comfortable. n cloth covering put over a teapot to keep it hot.

cot /kɒt/ n small bed, e.g. for a child.

cottage /'kɒtɪdʒ/ n small house.

cotton /'kɒtn/ n soft white material obtained from a plant; cloth made of this material; thread made from this material. **cotton wool** = cotton sold in its soft woolly state.

couch /kaʊtʃ/ n low bed; long low chair.

cough /kɒf/ vi force air from the throat suddenly and with noise, usually in trying to get some matter out of the throat. n act of coughing.

could /kʊd/ v 1 p.t. of **can**. 2 would be able to, e.g. If I had a car, we could drive there.

council /'kaʊnsəl/ n 1 meeting for making plans. 2 group of elected persons, or persons chosen to carry on some special business. n **councillor** /'kaʊnsələ/ member of such a group.

counsel /'kaʊnsəl/ n 1 advice. 2 adviser on matters of law, a lawyer who speaks in the law-courts.

count¹ /kaʊnt/ vi 1 say the numbers in order. 2 be important; matter. vt 1 add up or find the whole number of (a set of things). 2 take into one's counting, e.g. I did not count the baby. **to count on** = trust; depend on. n act of counting.

count² /kaʊnt/ n title of a foreign nobleman.

countenance /'kaʊntənəns/ n appearance of the face. vt be prepared to accept, e.g. I cannot countenance that sort of thing.

counter¹ /'kaʊntə/ n long table, e.g. in a shop, where goods are shown or money is paid.

counter² /'kaʊntə/ n small circular piece of bone or other material used instead of money in playing any game.

counter³ /'kaʊntə/ v make an opposite movement of any kind; strike back at.

counter-⁴ /'kaʊntə/ used to make meanings that have the idea of opposite, fighting against, e.g. **counteract** /ˌkaʊntə'rækt/ vt act against and bring to nothing.

counterfeit /'kaʊntəfɪt/ n, adj (bad money) made for a dishonest purpose.

counterfoil /'kaʊntəfɔɪl/ n part of a written piece of paper, e.g. receipt torn off and kept for making up accounts.

countermand /ˌkaʊntə'mɑːnd/ vt give a command to stop (another command).

counterpane /'kaʊntəpeɪn/ n outer covering on a bed.

counterpart /'kaʊntəpɑːt/ n that which is exactly like something else; thing which is like another but just opposite, e.g. the right and left hand.

countersign /'kaʊntəsaɪn/ vt write one's name as second name on (a paper).

countess /'kaʊntəs/ n title of the wife of an EARL or of a COUNT.

countless /'kaʊntləs/ adj very many in number.

countrified /'kʌntrɪfaɪd/ adj as of the country, without manners and customs of the city.

country /'kʌntrɪ/ n 1 land. 2 nation. 3 open land, not in the towns. n **countryman** /'kʌntrɪmən/ 1 one who is not of the town. 2 one who is from the same country or nation. n **countryside** /'kʌntrɪsaɪd/ open land, outside the towns.

county /'kaʊntɪ/ n one of the parts into which a nation is divided.

coup /kuː/ n blow; successful piece of business. **coup d'état** /ˌkuː deɪ'tɑː/ n sudden change of government caused by the use of force.

couple /'kʌpəl/ n pair, esp. one consisting of a man and a woman. **a couple of** = two or three. vt put together in pairs; join together.

couplet /'kʌplət/ n pair of lines in a poem that end with the same sound and usually contain a complete idea.

coupling /'kʌplɪŋ/ n **1** joining of two things. **2** instrument on the end of a railway carriage that joins it on to the next carriage.

coupon /'ku:pɒn/ n any small printed paper showing that one has a right to goods, a seat, payment, etc.

courage /'kʌrɪdʒ/ n quality of being brave. adj **courageous** /kə'reɪdʒəs/.

courier /'kʊrɪəʳ/ n **1** one who carries important messages. **2** one who goes with travellers to help them and show them the sights.

course /kɔːs/ n **1** onward movement e.g. The course of life. **in the course of** = during. **in due course** = at the proper time. **2** the path of movement, e.g. The course of a river; The course of a ship. **a course of action** = plan of action. **3** space specially marked out for a game or for races. **4** set of things which follow one after another, e.g. A course of lessons. **5** one of the parts, served in order, of which a meal consists. **of course** = naturally; certainly.

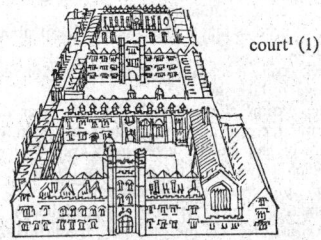

court¹ (1)

court¹ /kɔːt/ n **1** small open place with walls or buildings on all sides. **2** meeting of law officers to question and punish wrong-doers or to decide quarrels. **3** level place marked with lines for playing a game. **4** king, his family and officers in the palace.

court² /kɔːt/ v pay attention to (a girl or woman) with a view to winning her in marriage.

courteous /'kɜːtɪəs/ n very polite. n **courtesy** /'kɜːtəsɪ/ politeness.

courtier /'kɔːtɪəʳ/ n person who attends at a king's court.

courtly /'kɔːtlɪ/ adj very polite.

court-martial /ˌkɔːt 'mɑːʃəl/ n court of law in the army. vt try (a soldier) in such a court.

courtyard /'kɔːtjɑːd/ n space with walls or buildings on all sides.

cousin /'kʌzən/ n child of the brother or sister of either of one's parents. **second cousin** = child of one's parent's first cousin.

cove /kəʊv/ n small inlet in the coast.

covenant /'kʌvənənt/ n solemn promise or agreement.

cover /'kʌvəʳ/ vt **1** put one material over the surface of (another). **2** deal with, e.g. This law covers all such matters. **3** pass over, e.g. To cover the distance. **to cover up** = prevent from becoming known; hide. n anything that covers

or covers up something else. **under cover of** = hidden by. **to break cover** = run out of hiding.

coverlet /'kʌvələt/ n outer covering of a bed.

covert /'kʌvət/ adj covered, secret. n wood where birds and small animals take shelter.

covet /'kʌvɪt/ vt desire greatly (something) that belongs to another.

cow¹ /kaʊ/ n female of cattle.

cow² /kaʊ/ vt make (someone) spiritless and yielding by frightening him greatly.

coward /'kaʊəd/ n man of no courage. n **cowardice** /'kaʊədɪs/ state of being afraid when one ought to be brave.

cower /'kaʊəʳ/ vi lower the head and shoulders as from fear or shame.

cowl /kaʊl/ n **1** piece of clothing worn over the head by members of certain religious groups. **2** metal top for a chimney; metal cover, e.g. over a machine.

cowrie /'kaʊrɪ/ n small shell formerly used as money in parts of Asia and Africa.

cowslip /'kaʊˌslɪp/ n small yellow flower found in the fields of England.

cox /kɒks/ n shortened form of COXSWAIN.

coxswain /'kɒksən/ n person in command of and guiding a small boat.

coy /kɔɪ/ adj (of a woman) pretending to be afraid of men so as to draw them on.

crab /kræb/ n creature with a hard shell and ten legs found in water. **to walk crabwise** = walk sideways. vt **crab**, speak ill of, find fault with. adj **crabbed** /'kræbɪd/ bad-tempered.

crack (1)

crack /kræk/ v **1** break or cause to break without falling apart. **2** make a sudden sharp noise. n **1** line or point at which something has been cracked. **2** sudden sharp noise.

cracker /'krækəʳ/ n unsweetened BISCUIT. **a Christmas cracker** = ornamented pipe of paper containing a small gift—the two ends are pulled apart and break with a sharp noise.

crackle /'krækəl/ vi make a noise like walking on dry leaves.

cradle /'kreɪdl/ n small baby's bed which can be swung or rolled gently from side to side to put the child to sleep.

craft¹ /krɑːft/ n any kind of ship.

craft² /krɑːft/ n cleverness with the hands, e.g. in art; work, esp. in art; cleverness in deceiving. n **craftsman** /'krɑːftsmən/ one who practises an art. adj **crafty** /'krɑːftɪ/ deceiving.

crag /kræg/ n high, steep rock.

cram /kræm/ vt fill very full; press into a small space. infml vi learn a subject hastily for an examination.

cramp[1] /kræmp/ *vt* prevent movement or growth of; hold firm. *adj* **cramped** /kræmpt/ pressed into a small space.

cramp[2] /kræmp/ *n* painful uncontrolled hardening of the muscles.

crane /krein/ *n* **1** water bird with long legs and neck. **2** large machine used for raising heavy things. **to crane one's neck** = stretch out so as to see better.

cranium /'kreiniəm/ *n* bony container of the brain.

crank[1] /kræŋk/ *n* handle used for turning a wheel; part of a machine which changes an up and down movement into a circular movement, e.g. in a steam engine.

crank[2] /kræŋk/ *n* person with peculiar ideas, usually on one subject.

cranny /'kræni/ *n* small crack.

crape /kreip/ *n* black cloth worn at a funeral.

crash /kræʃ/ *vi* **1** fall heavily and break with great noise. **2** (of a business) fail. **3** have a road accident. *vt* cause (a vehicle) to be damaged or destroyed in a road accident. *n* **1** (noise of) something crashing. **2** ruin, failure (of a business). **3** road or aeroplane accident. **to crash into** = to hit with a crash. **crash helmet** = strong round hat worn by a rider to protect his head.

crass /kræs/ *adj* complete, e.g. *Crass foolishness.*

crate /kreit/ *n* box made of narrow boards which do not fit closely together.

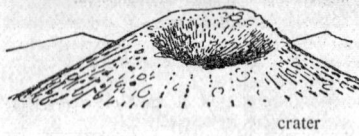

crater

crater /kreitə/ *n* hole in the top of a VOLCANO.

cravat /krə'væt/ *n* piece of cloth worn round the neck.

crave /kreiv/ *vt* ask eagerly for; have a great desire for. *n* **craving** /'kreiviŋ/.

crawl /krɔ:l/ *vi* move along the ground slowly. *n* **1** act of crawling. **2** way of swimming in which the arms are brought out of the water between strokes.

crayfish /'krei,fiʃ/ *n* fresh-water creature with a shell and ten legs.

crayon /'kreiən/ *n* coloured pencil.

craze /kreiz/ *vt* cause to become mad. *n* something everybody does for a short time. *adj* **crazy** /'kreizi/ mad.

creak /kri:k/ *n* sharp sound made by one thing rubbing on another. *vi* make such a sound.

cream /kri:m/ *n* **1** thick oily part of milk which comes to the top. **2** soft fat used as a medicine for the skin. *n, adj* (of a) yellow-white colour.

crease /kri:s/ *n* line made by folding. *vt* make such a line in.

create /kri'eit/ *vt* cause to be; make. *n* **creation** /kri'eiʃən/ act of creating; thing created; all things created by God. *adj* **creative** /kri'eitiv/ able to create (esp. beautiful) new things.

creature /'kri:tʃə/ *n* any living thing.

crêche /kreʃ/ *n* place where children are looked after while the mothers are at work.

credence /'kri:dəns/ *n* act of believing.

credentials /kri'denʃəlz/ *n* papers which prove that one may be trusted.

credible /'kredəbəl/ *adj* which can be believed.

credit /'kredit/ *n* **1** trust, esp. in someone's ability to pay what he owes. **to get goods on credit** = get goods promising to pay later. **2** money owed to one or owned by one, rather than money which one owes another, e.g. *The credit side of an account* = page showing money received by or owed to a business. **3** recognition, e.g. *Give him credit for his good sense.* **creditable** /'kreditəbəl/ *adj* worthy of praise. *n* **creditor** /'kreditə/ person to whom one owes money.

credulity /krə'dju:ləti/ *n* too great willingness to believe. *adj* **credulous** /'kredʒuləs/.

creed /kri:d/ *n* that which is believed, esp. about God.

creek /kri:k/ *n* small stream; narrow inlet on sea-coast or lake-shore.

creep /kri:p/ *vi* move with the body near the ground, e.g. as a legless creature moves; move slowly and quietly. *n* **creeper** /'kri:pə/ plant which grows along the ground or up the wall. *adj infml* **creepy** /'kri:pi/ causing fear.

cremate /kri'meit/ *vt* burn (a dead body). *n* **cremation** /kri'meiʃən/. *n* **crematorium** /,kremə'tɔ:riəm/ place where dead bodies are burnt.

creole /'kri:əul/ *n* **1** person born in the West Indies. **2** his language, or one which is like it in being a mixture of two languages.

creosote /'kri:əsəut/ *n* oily liquid obtained from coal, used for protecting things from decay.

crêpe /kreip/ *n* thin cloth or paper with many small folds or waves in it.

crept /krept/ *p.t.* of **creep.**

crescendo /kri'ʃendəu/ *adv* (in music) becoming louder.

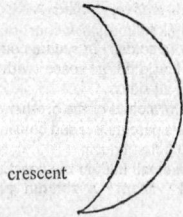

crescent

crescent /'kresənt/ *adj, n* (anything) shaped like a new moon.

cress /kres/ *n* a hot-tasting plant.

crest /krest/ *n* **1** top edge of a wave or hill. **2** top feathers on a bird's head. **3** sign which serves as the special mark of a family, e.g. one printed on a piece of letter-paper.

crestfallen /ˈkrestˌfɔːlən/ adj feeling sad and ashamed.

crevasse /krɪˈvæs/ n deep crack in a great mass of ice on a mountain side.

crevice /ˈkrevɪs/ n small crack.

crew[1] /kruː/ p.t. of **crow**[2].

crew[2] /kruː/ n group of men working together, esp. on a ship.

crib /krɪb/ n **1** part of a house for cattle in which one beast stands. **2** small room; hut or small house. **3** child's bed. v steal (ideas) and give them out as one's own; look secretly at a book or at another person's paper in an examination.

cribbage /ˈkrɪbɪdʒ/ n game played with cards and a board with many holes in it, a small stick being moved from one hole to another to count points won.

crick /krɪk/ n painful stiffness of the neck.

cricket[1] /ˈkrɪkɪt/ n game played by 22 men with a ball, a flat piece of wood and two sets of three upright sticks in the ground; one player tries to knock down the sticks with the ball while another tries to hit or stop the ball.

cricket[2] /ˈkrɪkɪt/ n small insect which makes a loud high sound.

cried /kraɪd/ p.t. of **cry**.

crime /kraɪm/ n act of breaking the law. n **criminal** /ˈkrɪmənəl/ law-breaker, adj against the law.

crimp /krɪmp/ vt put curves or curls into, e.g. hair.

crimson /ˈkrɪmzən/ n, adj (of a) deep red colour.

cringe /krɪndʒ/ vi bend low or go down on the knees because of fear or shame.

crinkle /ˈkrɪŋkəl/ vt bend into many small folds.

cripple /ˈkrɪpəl/ n one whose body is not perfect, e.g. with a useless arm or leg. vt hurt and make useless.

crisis /ˈkraɪsɪs/ n (pl **crises** /ˈkraɪsiːz/) turning-point in illness or in history; moment of great danger just before great changes.

crisp /krɪsp/ adj dry and easily broken. n very thin piece of potato cooked in fat.

criss-cross /ˈkrɪsˌkrɒs/ adj, adv crossing in different directions.

criterion /kraɪˈtɪərɪən/ n (pl **criteria** /kraɪˈtɪərɪə/) rule or example by which correct judgment can be made.

critic /ˈkrɪtɪk/ n one who judges works of art, or other work; one who points out faults. v **criticize** /ˈkrɪtɪsaɪz/ make unfavourable remarks about; complain. n **criticism** /ˈkrɪtɪsɪzəm/ **1** judgment of works of art. **2** unfavourable judgment about anything.

critical /ˈkrɪtɪkəl/ adj **1** very important. **2** having to do with judging writings or works of art. **3** eager to judge unfavourably, fault-finding.

critique /krɪˈtiːk/ n writing expressing an opinion of a work of art, book or play.

croak /krəʊk/ n, interj noise made by a FROG.

crochet /ˈkrəʊʃeɪ/ n way of making thread into garments by passing one ring or curl of thread through another. v make (a garment) in this way.

crock /krɒk/ n **1** earthen vessel. **2** old broken down animal, person, or vehicle.

crockery /ˈkrɒkərɪ/ n (sing) earthen dishes used in eating.

crocodile /ˈkrɒkədaɪl/ n large water reptile. **to shed crocodile tears** = pretend to be sorry.

crocus /ˈkrəʊkəs/ n a spring flower.

croft /krɒft/ n very small farm. n **crofter** /ˈkrɒftə/ owner of a croft.

crone /krəʊn/ n very old woman.

crony /ˈkrəʊnɪ/ n old friend, esp. one with the same interests.

crook (2)

crook /krʊk/ n **1** bend. **2** stick with a curve at one end. sl law-breaker; dishonest person. **by hook or by crook** = by some means or other. adj **crooked** /ˈkrʊkɪd/ **1** not straight. **2** sl not honest.

croon /kruːn/ vi sing softly.

crop[1] /krɒp/ n **1** pocket in the throat of birds in which the food is broken up. **2** stick with a piece of leather on the end, carried while riding horseback.

crop[2] /krɒp/ n fruits, grain, etc., produced by the earth in one year or season; collection of things all arising at the same time, e.g. A crop of spots on the face. **to crop up** = appear unexpectedly.

crop[3] /krɒp/ vt cut or bite off short, e.g. Sheep crop the grass.

cropper /ˈkrɒpə/ infml **to come a cropper** = fall, e.g. from a horse; fall badly.

croquet /ˈkrəʊkeɪ/ n game played by striking wooden balls and making them roll through HOOPS in the ground.

croquette /krəˈket/ n ball of something, e.g. meat, baked or cooked in fat.

cross[1] /krɒs/ n **1** mark made by drawing one line across another; anything of this shape **2** one piece of wood fastened across another. **the Cross** = wooden cross upon which Christ died.

cross[2] /krɒs/ vt lay across; go across. **to cross out** = strike out a word by drawing a line through it. **to cross (one plant or animal) with (another)** = produce a plant or animal of a mixed kind from them. n such a mixture; anything having some of the qualities of each of two other things.

cross[3] /krɒs/ adj angry.

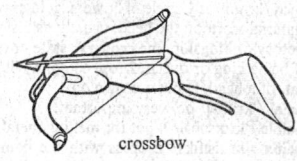

crossbow

crossbow /'krɒsbəʊ/ *n* curved piece of wood with a wire joining the two ends, fixed across a piece of wood shaped like a gun, used for shooting arrows and held as a gun is when aiming.

crossbreed /'krɒsbriːd/ *n* person, animal or plant come from parents of different races or kinds.

cross-examine /ˌ. .ˈ. ./ *vt* continue to question in order to prove or disprove the truth of what has already been said.

crossing /'krɒsɪŋ/ *n* **1** act of going across (e.g. a body of water). **2** place where one thing goes across another (e.g. where a road crosses a railway).

cross-purposes /ˌ. ˈ. . ./ *n* trying to work together but actually working with different aims and misunderstanding each other.

cross-question /ˌ. ˈ. ./ CROSS-EXAMINE.

crossroads /'krɒsrəʊdz/ *n* place where one road crosses another, or divides into two; any point at which one must make an important decision.

cross section /ˌ. ˈ. ./ picture of a thing as seen if cut across.

crossword (puzzle) /'krɒs-wɜːd/ *n* square to be filled in with letters to make words reading up and down as well as across, below which are given a few ideas to help one guess the words needed.

crotchet /'krɒtʃɪt/ *n* short note in music. *adj* **crotchety** /'krɒtʃɪtɪ/ bad-tempered.

crouch /kraʊtʃ/ *vi* bend down, as a cat does before jumping.

croupier /'kruːpɪə/ *n* man who takes in and pays out the money at a game played for money.

crow[1] /krəʊ/ *n* a kind of black bird.

crow[2] /krəʊ/ *vi* make a noise like a COCK.

crowbar

crowbar /'krəʊbɑː/ *n* long bar of iron used for breaking stone and moving heavy things.

crowd /kraʊd/ *n* large number of people; too many people in a small place. *v* come or cause to come together in large numbers.

crown /kraʊn/ *n* **1** circle of flowers, gold or other material worn on the head, usually as a sign of victory or kingship. **the crown** = state or office of being king or queen. **2** top, e.g. of a hill, of a hat, of a head. *vt* put a crown on.

crucial /'kruːʃəl/ *adj* very important.

crucible /'kruːsəbəl/ *n* pot for melting metals.

crucifix /'kruːsɪfɪks/ *n* cross with the figure of Christ on it. *vt* **crucify** /'kruːsɪfaɪ/ kill by nailing on a wooden cross. *n* **crucifixion** /ˌkruːsɪˈfɪkʃən/.

crude /kruːd/ *adj* rough and bitter to taste; in the natural state; (of work or speech) not well finished; not polished; bad-mannered.

cruel /'kruːəl/ *adj* taking pleasure in giving pain to others; heard-hearted; causing pain. *n* **cruelty** /'kruːəltɪ/.

cruet /'kruːɪt/ *n* set of small glass bottles for oil, VINEGAR, etc., used on the table at meals.

cruise /kruːz/ *n* journey by sea. *vi* travel by a ship. *n* **cruiser** /'kruːzə/ fast warship with big guns.

crumb /krʌm/ *n* very small piece of bread; very small piece of anything.

crumble /'krʌmbəl/ *v* break into small pieces; decay slowly.

crumpet /'krʌmpɪt/ *n* flat round bread-like cake eaten hot with butter.

crumple /'krʌmpəl/ *v* roll up and press in the hand, e.g. a sheet of paper; become bent into many folds. **to crumple up** = break or yield completely and suddenly.

crunch /krʌntʃ/ *n* sound made by biting hard food, or by walking on small stones. *v* bite making this sound.

crusade /kruːˈseɪd/ *n* war which the Christians fought to win back the Holy City, Jerusalem; fight against some evil or for some good cause. *vi* fight thus.

crush /krʌʃ/ *vt* press together and break with great force; press out of shape, press carelessly into folds (e.g. a dress) as is done by careless packing; force the liquid out of, e.g. fruit; make into powder; beat an enemy completely. *sl* **a crush** = crowded gathering of guests.

crust /krʌst/ *n* hard outer part, e.g. of bread.

crustacean /krʌˈsteɪʃən/ *n* hard-shelled water creature.

crusty /'krʌstɪ/ *adj* having a hard CRUST.

crutch /krʌtʃ/ *n* stick to help one walk when the legs are hurt or useless; anything on which one depends too greatly.

crux /krʌks/ *n* difficult point to decide; most important point on which some action or idea depends.

cry /kraɪ/ *vi* **1** speak in a loud voice; shout. **2** weep. **to cry off** = say that one will not fulfil (a promise). *n* shout or other short burst of sound, e.g. *Cries of pain.*

crypt /krɪpt/ *n* room under the main floor of a church, sometimes used for graves.

cryptic /'krɪptɪk/ *adj* secret; difficult to understand.

crystal /'krɪstl/ *n* hard clear stone; regular shape that salt and other materials take when they cease to be liquid and become solid. *adj* **crystalline** /'krɪstəlaɪn/. *v* **crystallize** /'krɪstəlaɪz/ make or become crystalline.

cub /kʌb/ *n* young of a meat-eating animal, e.g. lion.

cubbyhole /'kʌbɪhəʊl/ n small useful store-place or room.

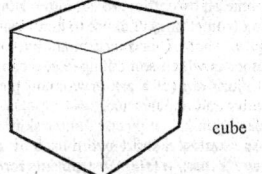

cube

cube /kju:b/ n square block. vt MULTIPLY (a number) by itself twice, e.g. *4 cubed* (also written *4³*) = *64* (since 4 × 4 = 16, and 16 × 4 = 64). adj **cubic** /'kju:bɪk/ **1** having the shape of a cube. **2** (of a measurement) giving VOLUME, e.g. 1 cubic foot is the volume of a cube each of whose sides measures 1 foot.

cubicle /'kju:bɪkəl/ n small room divided off from a larger place.

cuckoo /'kʊku:/ n bird which makes a sound like its name and lays its eggs in the nests of other birds.

cucumber /'kju:kʌmbə/ n creeping plant with a long green fruit.

cud /kʌd/ n food which some grass-eating animals bring back from the stomach and bite again and again.

cuddle /'kʌdl/ vt touch and hold (someone, e.g. a baby) in a loving manner.

cudgel /'kʌdʒəl/ n thick stick, e.g. one used as a weapon. **to take up the cudgels for** = defend.

cue /kju:/ n **1** long stick used to strike a ball with its point in any of several games played with balls on a table. **2** word or sign given to make an actor remember the following words, as in a play. vt give such a word or sign to.

cuff¹ /kʌf/ n band on clothing just above the hand.

cuff² /kʌf/ vt strike with the hand.

cuisine /kwɪ'zi:n/ n quality of cooking.

cul-de-sac /'kʌl də ˌsæk/ n street open only at one end.

culinary /'kʌlɪnərɪ/ adj having to do with cooking.

cull /kʌl/ vt pick out in order to destroy (unhealthy animals in a group from the healthier ones).

cullender see colander.

culminate /'kʌlmɪneɪt/ vi reach the highest and last point. n **culmination** /ˌkʌlmɪ'neɪʃən/.

culpable /'kʌlpəbəl/ adj deserving blame.

culprit /'kʌlprɪt/ adj wrongdoer.

cult /kʌlt/ n certain set of religious ceremonies and beliefs; love for a teacher or idea, e.g. *A cult of Browning.*

cultivate /'kʌltɪveɪt/ vt **1** prepare (land) for crops. **2** cause to grow, e.g. *To cultivate roses.* adj **cultivated** /'kʌltɪveɪtɪd/ having good manners and a knowledge of the arts. n **cultivation** /ˌkʌltɪ'veɪʃən/.

culture /'kʌltʃə/ n **1** manners and customs of a people. **2** growing of anything that needs special care. **3** making oneself better by study, esp. of the arts.

culvert /'kʌlvət/ n bridge built to allow water to run under the road.

cumbersome /'kʌmbəsəm/ adj large and difficult to move or deal with.

cummerbund /'kʌməbʌnd/ n broad band of silk worn round the waist.

cumulative /'kju:mjʊlətɪv/ adj slowly increasing by being added to.

cumulus /'kju:mjʊləs/ n a kind of cloud, round in shape with a flat bottom.

cuneiform /'kju:nɪfɔ:m/ n a form of ancient writing in Asia. adj shaped like an arrow-head.

cunning /'kʌnɪŋ/ adj clever; deceiving. n quality of being cunning.

cup /kʌp/ n small drinking vessel, usually with a handle; large silver or gold vessel given to the winner in games.

cupboard /'kʌbəd/ n piece of furniture with doors used for storing things. **cupboard love** = show of love (e.g. by a child or animal) in order to get sweets or food from the store cupboard.

cupidity /kju:'pɪdətɪ/ n strong desire, esp. for wealth.

cupola

cupola /'kju:pələ/ n small round top on a building.

cur /kɜ:/ n worthless dog.

curate /'kjʊərət/ n (usually younger) priest who helps another priest.

curator /kjʊ'reɪtə/ n one who has charge of—e.g. a building—where objects of interest are kept.

curb¹ /kɜ:b/ vt control. n metal band under a horse's mouth which helps to control it.

curb² /kɜ:b/ n see kerb.

curd /kɜ:d/ n thickened part of sour milk used to make cheese.

curdle /'kɜ:dl/ vt cause milk to thicken by making it sour. vi (of milk) thicken in this way.

cure /kjʊə/ vt **1** cause (someone) to return to health; cause (a disease) to disappear. **2** preserve (something) by making it hard, adding salt, etc. n act of curing (a person).

curfew /'kɜ:fju:/ n order to the people of a town, country, etc., to remain inside during certain hours.

curio /'kjʊərɪəʊ/ n strange and interesting object.

curious /'kjʊərɪəs/ adj **1** eager for knowledge. **2** strange. n **curiosity** /ˌkjʊərɪ'ɒsɪtɪ/ **1** eagerness for knowledge. **2** strange thing.

curl /kɜ:l/ *v* make into waves and circles, e.g. hair; bend up; turn in curves, as a plant growing round a stick. *n* wave, circle or bend. *adj* **curly** /'kɜ:lɪ/ (esp. of hair) having many curls.

curlew /'kɜ:lju:/ *n* water-bird with long legs and a long curved beak.

currant /'kʌrənt/ *n* small fruit of one of several bushes; this fruit dried for use in cakes.

currency /'kʌrənsɪ/ *n* money; that which is used for money.

current[1] /'kʌrənt/ *adj* in general use; in use now; present.

current[2] /'kʌrənt/ *n* stream; flow of electricity along a wire.

curriculum /kə'rɪkjʊləm/ *n* fixed course of study.

curry[1] /'kʌrɪ/ *vt* brush and clean a horse. **to curry favour** = try to gain favour by admiring or serving a person.

curry[2] /'kʌrɪ/ *n* meat (or fish, etc.) cooked in a hot-tasting yellow liquid.

curse /kɜ:s/ *vt* call down evil upon; SWEAR. *sl adj* **cursed** /'kɜ:sɪd/ hateful.

cursive /'kɜ:sɪv/ *adj* (of writing) in which the letters join on to one another.

cursory /'kɜ:sərɪ/ *adj* quick and careless, e.g. *A cursory glance* = a quick careless look.

curt /kɜ:t/ *adj* short in manner; too short to be polite.

curtail /kə'teɪl/ *vt* cut off part of (something) so as to shorten it.

curtain /'kɜ:tɪn/ *n* covering for a window; large piece of cloth hung up to hide or cover anything. **a curtain raiser** = short play given before the chief play in a theatre.

curtsey, curtsy /'kɜ:tsɪ/ *n* bending of the knees made by women as a sign of respect. *vi* bend the knees thus.

curvature /'kɜ:vətʃə/ *n* bending or curving, e.g. of the backbone.

curve /kɜ:v/ *n* line which is not straight; part of a circle. *v* bend into a circular shape; be so bent.

cushion /'kʊʃən/ *n* soft object for sitting on or putting behind the back; any soft thing that makes a shock less. *vt* lessen the effect of (a shock).

custard /'kʌstəd/ *n* yellow food made with milk, egg, sugar, etc.

custody /'kʌstədɪ/ *n* safe-keeping. **to take into custody** = put in prison.

custodian /kʌ'stəʊdɪən/ *n* keeper, e.g. of some public building.

custom /'kʌstəm/ *n* usual or common way of doing things; thing usually done, e.g. *It is the custom for Englishmen to drink tea.* *adj* **customary** /'kʌstəmərɪ/.

customer /'kʌstəmə/ *n* one who buys at a shop.

customs house /'.. ./ *n* office where money is paid on goods brought into a country.

customs (duty) *n* money paid on goods brought into a country.

cut /kʌt/ *vt* divide or break the surface of with a knife or other sharp edge. **to cut down** = **1** make

less, shorter. **2** cause to fall by cutting (e.g. trees). **to cut off** = **1** stop (e.g. supplies). **2** cause to come off by cutting. **to cut out** = **1** *infml* stop doing (something). **2** cause to come out by cutting. *n* **1** act of, or mark made by, cutting. **2** manner in which something (e.g. a coat) is cut.

cute /kju:t/ *adj* (of a girl or woman) pleasing in manner and appearance.

cuticle /'kju:tɪkəl/ *n* piece of outer skin.

cutlass /'kʌtləs/ *n* short sword used by seamen.

cutlery /'kʌtlərɪ/ *n* (*sing*) instruments for cutting.

cutlet /'kʌtlət/ *n* cooked meat from the neck of an animal.

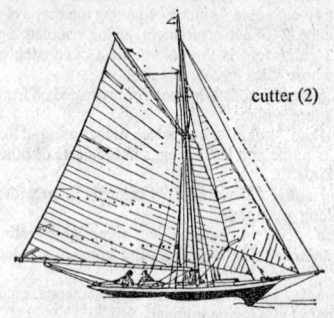

cutter (2)

cutter /'kʌtə/ *n* **1** one who cuts; person who cuts out (men's) clothes; instrument for cutting. **2** sailing boat.

cutting /'kʌtɪŋ/ *adj* cruel; causing pain. *n* piece cut out, e.g. *A newspaper cutting* = piece cut out from a newspaper; road cut through a hill.

cybernetics /ˌsaɪbə'netɪks/ *n* study of instruments used for controlling machines.

cycle /'saɪkəl/ *n* **1** set of events regularly repeated in a particular order, the last being followed by the first again. **2** bicycle. **in cycle** = in a circle. **a cycle of events** = things happening one after another as if in a circle. *n* **cyclist** /'saɪklɪst/ one who rides a bicycle.

cypress

cyclone /'saɪkləʊn/ n powerful wind blowing in a circle.

cygnet /'sɪgnɪt/ n young SWAN.

cylinder /'sɪlɪndə/ n roller-shaped object; round hollow box in which the steam or other gas pushes forward the bar which turns the wheel in an engine.

cymbal /'sɪmbəl/ n one of two brass plates struck together to make music.

cynical /'sɪnɪkəl/ adj not believing in the goodness of people; always pointing out the bad. n **cynic** /'sɪnɪk/.

cynosure /'sɪnəzjʊə, 'saɪn-, -ʒʊə/ n object at which everyone looks.

cypher /'saɪfə/ see **cipher**.

cypress /'saɪprəs/ n dark green tree often planted in graveyards.

cyst /sɪst/ n small bag-like growth in the body, usually containing liquid.

Czar /zɑː/ see **Tsar**.

D

D /diː/ roman figure, 500

dab /dæb/ vt touch gently as one does when washing a wound.

dabble /dæbəl/ vi play in the water. **to dabble in** = work at (something), but not seriously or continuously.

dachshund /'dækshʊnd/ n kind of dog with a long body and short legs.

dad /dæd/, **daddy** /'dædɪ/ infml (child's word for) father.

daddy-long-legs /,. .'. ./ n kind of small flying in-sect with six very long legs.

daffodil /'dæfədɪl/ n a yellow spring flower.

daft /dɑːft/ infml adj foolish; mad.

dagger /'dægə/ n pointed knife used as a weapon.

daily /'deɪlɪ/ adj happening or appearing every day. n daily newspaper.

dainty /'deɪntɪ/ adj beautiful and neat.

dairy /'deərɪ/ n place where cows are kept for producing milk; milk shop or milk business.

dais /'deɪ-ɪs/ n raised part of the floor.

daisy /'deɪzɪ/ n very common small flower, yellow in the centre and white round it.

dale /deɪl/ n valley.

dally /'dælɪ/ vi be slow or waste time. **to dally with** = play carelessly with, e.g. with love. n **dalliance** /'dælɪəns/ playing in a loving way.

dam¹ /dæm/ n wall or bank built to keep back water.

dam² /dæm/ n mother animal.

damage /'dæmɪdʒ/ vt break, hurt or destroy. n act of damaging; amount that something is damaged. n (pl) **damages** money paid to make good a loss (e.g. to pay for repairing).

damask /'dæməsk/ n 1 beautiful silk with raised figures worked into it. 2 fine steel made in Damascus. 3 light rose-colour.

dame /deɪm/ n title of honour given to women.

damn /dæm/ vt curse; send to everlasting punish-ment. interj damn! cry of anger.

damp /dæmp/ adj slightly wet. vt (also **dampen** /'dæmpən/) make damp; make quieter.

damper /'dæmpə/ n door in a chimney or fire-place used to make the fire burn more slowly.

damson /'dæmzən/ n small dark blue stone-fruit.

dance /dɑːns/ vi jump about; move to the time of music. n act of dancing; special manner of dan-cing; coming together of people in order to dance.

dance

dandelion /'dændɪlaɪən/ n small, yellow, wild flower.

dandle /'dændl/ vt move (a small child) up and down on the knee.

dandruff /'dændrʌf/ n (sing) small dry pieces of skin found among the hairs of the head.

dandy /'dændɪ/ n man who gives too much time and thought to his clothes.

dangerous /'deɪndʒərəs/ adj risky; which may cause harm. n **danger** /'deɪndʒə/.

dangle /'dæŋgəl/ v hang down and swing loosely.

dank /dæŋk/ adj cold and wet.

dapper /'dæpə/ adj (usually of a small person) neat and well dressed.

dappled /'dæpəld/ adj spotted.

dare /deə/ v be brave enough to (do something vt tell (someone) he is not brave enough to do something. n **daredevil** /'deə,devəl/ person who is not afraid of the greatest danger. adj **daring** /'deərɪŋ/ brave.

dark /dɑːk/ adj without light; secret or unknown; evil, brown or black (eyes, hair or skin); (of colour) deep, e.g. Dark red = deep red. v **darken** /'dɑːkən/ v make or become dark or darker. n **darkness** /'dɑːknəs/ state of being dark, esp. at night. **after dark** = at night.

darling /'dɑːlɪŋ/ n (form of address for) one who is greatly loved.

darn /dɑːn/ v repair (a hole in cloth) by passing threads through and across.

dart¹ /dɑːt/ *vi* run quickly.

dart² /dɑːt/ *n* sharp-pointed weapon thrown by hand. *n* (*sing*) **darts** a game played by throwing darts at a circular board.

dash /dæʃ/ *vi* make a sudden quick run. *vt* throw or be thrown with force; ruin. *n* **1** sudden quick run. **2** small amount of anything, esp. liquid.

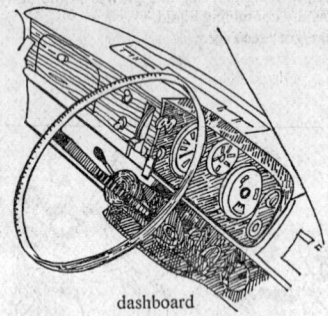

dashboard

dashboard /'dæʃbɔːd/ *n* instrument board in a car.

dashing /'dæʃɪŋ/ *adj* spirited; gay; active.

data /'deɪtə/ *n* (*sing* or *pl*) facts taken as true as the starting-point of a piece of reasoning.

date¹ /deɪt/ *n* time shown by the day, month and year; agreement to meet. *vt* write or show the date of, e.g. a letter. *vi* become out of date. **out of date** = not in present use; no longer suitable. *adj* **up-to-date** new; as now used.

date² /deɪt/ *n* a small brown sweet fruit with a long stone.

datum /'deɪtəm/ *n* a known fact.

daub /dɔːb/ *vt* make dirty marks on; paint badly.

daughter /'dɔːtə/ *n* female child of parent.

daunt /dɔːnt/ *vt* prevent a person from acting by fear; control by fear. *adj* **dauntless** /'dɔːntləs/ not afraid of anything.

davit /'dævɪt/ *n* one of two curved bars on the edge of a ship by means of which a boat is swung out and lowered.

dawdle /'dɔːdl/ *vi* waste time; stand about doing nothing.

dawn /dɔːn/ *n* coming of day. **it began to dawn on him** = he began to understand.

day /deɪ/ *n* **1** time from sunrise to sunset. **2** time lasting twenty-four hours. *n* **daybreak** /'deɪbreɪk/ sunrise. *vi* **daydream** /'deɪdriːm/ think pleasant but useless thoughts when awake. *n* **daylight** /'deɪlaɪt/ light from the sun during the day. *n* **daytime** /'deɪtaɪm/ time during the day.

daze /deɪz/ *vt* make foolish, e.g. by a sudden shock.

dazzle /'dæzəl/ *vt* make (someone) unable to see by shining a strong light in his eyes; cause to wonder by some act of great cleverness or power.

deacon /'diːkən/ *n* officer of the Church below a priest.

dead /ded/ *adj* lifeless; having ceased to live. *adv* complete, completely, e.g. *Dead tired; He is dead against that idea*. **dead centre** = in the exact middle point. *n* **deadline** /'dedlaɪn/ latest possible time at which something may be done. *adj* **deadpan** /'dedpæn/ (of a face) with no show of feeling in it. *n* **deadlock** /'dedlɒk/ disagreement that cannot be settled. **dead of night** = darkest part of the night. *vt* **deaden** /'dedn/ **1** lessen the ability of (the mind or the senses) to think or feel. **2** make (a sound) quieter. *adj* **deadly** /'dedlɪ/ **1** as if dead. **2** causing death, e.g. *Deadly poison*.

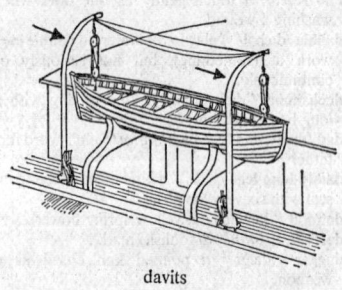

davits

deaf /def/ *adj* unable to hear. *vt* **deafen** /'defən/ make deaf, esp. for a short time as a result of a loud noise.

deal¹ /diːl/ *vt* **1** give, e.g. *To deal a blow*. **2** give each a share, e.g. *To deal cards*. *vi* **1** do business, e.g. *To deal in corn*. **2** make arrangements; do what is necessary, e.g. *To deal with a matter*. *n* **1** act of dealing, e.g. cards. **2** business arrangement. **a good deal; a great deal** = much; quite a lot, e.g. *He has caused me a good deal of trouble*.

deal² /diːl/ *n* a kind of soft white wood.

dealt /delt/ p.t. & p.p. of **deal¹**.

dean /diːn/ *n* **1** officer in the Church in charge of several priests. **2** the head of a part of a university, teaching a certain subject or group of subjects.

dear /dɪə/ *adj* **1** loved. **2** costly or precious. **Oh dear!, Dear me!, Dear, dear!** = cries of grief, wonder, surprise, etc.

dearth /dɜːθ/ *n* great lack.

death /deθ/ *n* **1** act of dying. **2** state of having died. *n* **death duties** share of a dead man's wealth taken by the government.

débâcle /deɪ'bɑːkəl/ *French n* sudden ruin, e.g. when an army runs away in disorder.

debar /dɪ'bɑː/ *vt* shut (someone) out from something.

debase /dɪ'beɪs/ *vt* make of less value. *n* **debasement** /dɪ'beɪsmənt/.

debate /dɪ'beɪt/ v consider and talk about (a question). n public meeting in which a question is talked over by two parties, each party taking one side. adj **debatable** /dɪ'beɪtəbəl/ able to be debated, there appearing to be reasons both for and against holding a particular view.

debauch /dɪ'bɔ:tʃ/ vt lead away from goodness or honesty. n **debauchery** /dɪ'bɔ:tʃərɪ/.

debenture /dɪ'bentʃə/ n written promise of a government or of a business company to pay a debt.

debilitate /dɪ'bɪləteɪt/ vt weaken. n **debility** /dɪ'bɪlətɪ/ weakness of the body, esp. because of illness.

debit /'debɪt/ vt write down as a debt, as money owed, in an account book. **the debit side of an account** = page showing payments and debts owed to others.

debonair /,debə'neə/ adj light-hearted, having nice manners.

debris, débris /'deɪbri:, 'deb-/ n (sing) broken, useless pieces.

debt /det/ n anything owed. n **debtor** /detə/ one who owes money to another.

debut /'deɪbju:, 'deb-/ n person's first performance or appearance.

deca- /'dekə/ having to do with ten.

decade /'dekeɪd, dɪ'keɪd/ n ten years.

decadent /'dekədənt/ adj decaying; becoming worse, esp. in behaviour.

decalogue /'dekəlɒg/ n the Ten Commandments in the Bible.

decamp /dɪ'kæmp/ vi run away secretly, e.g. with money.

decant /dɪ'kænt/ vt pour (liquid) carefully from one vessel into another. n **decanter** /dɪ'kæntə/ ornamental glass wine bottle.

decapitate /dɪ'kæpəteɪt/ vt cut off the head of.

decarbonize /di:'kɑ:bənaɪz/ vt take away the CARBON from—esp. from inside the engine of a car.

decay /dɪ'keɪ/ vi go bad; fall into ruin; become worse or less, e.g. *Man's powers decay in old age.*

decease /dɪ'si:s/ vi die. n death.

deceive /dɪsi:v/ vt cause (someone) to believe what is untrue; trick. n **deceit** /dɪ'si:t/. adj **deceitful** /dɪ'si:tfəl/ (of a person) not honest.

December /dɪ'sembə/ n the twelfth month of the year.

decent /'di:sənt/ adj fitting or right; good enough; not causing shame or shock to others. n **decency** /'di:sənsɪ/.

deception /dɪ'sepʃən/ n act of deceiving. adj **deceptive** /dɪ'septɪv/ deceiving; causing a wrong idea.

decide /dɪ'saɪd/ v judge and settle (a question). adv **decidedly** /dɪ'saɪdɪdlɪ/ clearly and undoubtedly.

deciduous /dɪ'sɪdʒʊəs/ adj (of a tree) whose leaves fall off in winter.

decimal /'desɪməl/ adj having to do with the

number "10", e.g. 1·3 (·3 is a decimal and means 3 tenths). n number in which tenths, hundredths, etc., are shown as figures after a point, e.g. 5·6 (= 5 and 6 tenths, i.e. 5⅗).

decimate /'desɪmeɪt/ vt kill a large number of.

decipher /dɪ'saɪfə/ vt discover the meaning of (difficult or secret writing).

decision /dɪ'sɪʒən/ n act of deciding; that which is decided. adj **decisive** /dɪ'saɪsɪv/ serving to settle a question completely.

deck¹ (1)

deck¹ /dek/ n 1 floor of a ship. 2 complete set of playing-cards.

deck² /dek/ vt dress in fine clothes; ornament, e.g. with flowers.

declaim /dɪ'kleɪm/ vi speak with strong feeling. n **declamation** /,deklə'meɪʃən/.

declare /dɪ'kleə/ vt say solemnly; make known to all. n **declaration** /,deklə'reɪʃən/.

declension /dɪ'klenʃən/ n giving the different forms of a noun or adjective.

decline /dɪ'klaɪn/ vi go or slope downwards; get worse (e.g. of health). v refuse (e.g. an offer). vt give the different forms of (a noun or adjective). n slow loss of strength or goodness.

declivity /dɪ'klɪvətɪ/ n slope, e.g. of a mountain side.

declutch /,di:'klʌtʃ/ vi loosen the CLUTCH of a car so that the engine goes on running but does not drive the wheels round.

decode /,di:'kəʊd/ vt change a (secret or shortened message) into common language.

decompose /,di:kəm'pəʊz/ v break up and separate into simple parts; decay. n **decomposition** /,di:kɒmpə'zɪʃən/.

decorate /'dekəreɪt/ vt add ornaments to; make beautiful; give a mark of honour to; paint and paper (a house). n **decoration** /,dekə'reɪʃən/.

decorous /'dekərəs/ adj fitting and pleasing in appearance.

decorum /dɪ'kɔ:rəm/ n correct dress and behaviour.

decoy /'di:kɔɪ, dɪ'kɔɪ/ n figure of a bird used to bring birds within range of guns; any similar trick. vt /dɪ'kɔɪ/ deceive (someone) into coming into danger.

decrease /dɪ'kri:s/ v make or become less or fewer. n /'di:kri:s/.

decree /dɪ'kri:/ n command of a king or government; judgment of a court of law.

decrepit /dɪ'krepɪt/ adj weak from old age. n **decrepitude** /dɪ'krepɪtju:d/.

decry /dɪ'kraɪ/ vt speak ill of; say bad things about.

decry

dedicate

dedicate /'dedɪkeɪt/ vt set apart for some good or holy purpose; give to God; set apart for some special purpose, e.g. *I dedicate all my spare time to writing.* n **dedication** /ˌdedɪ'keɪʃən/.

deduce /dɪ'djuːs/ vt reach (an idea) as a result of considering accepted facts or rules, e.g. *All insects have 6 legs; this creature has 8 legs; therefore I deduce that it is not an insect.*

deduct /dɪ'dʌkt/ vt take off, e.g. some amount from a bill.

deduction /dɪ'dʌkʃən/ n **1** act or result of DEDUCING; idea so reached; this sort of reasoning. **2** act or result of DEDUCTING.

deed /diːd/ n **1** act, e.g. *A brave deed.* **2** paper showing ownership of land; written agreement.

deem /diːm/ vt think.

deep /diːp/ adj **1** going far down, e.g. *Deep water.* **2** difficult to understand; having serious thoughts and feelings. **3** (of a colour) dark. **deep freeze** = box in which food is frozen hard and kept for a long time.

deer

deer /dɪə/ n beautiful wild animal (the males have wide branching horns).

deface /dɪ'feɪs/ vt destroy the surface of, e.g. of a picture by writing across it.

de facto /ˌdeɪ 'fæktəʊ/ *Latin adj* in actual fact, though not perhaps justly or according to law, e.g. *De facto owner.*

defame /dɪ'feɪm/ vt try to damage the good name of. n **defamation** /ˌdefə'meɪʃən/.

default /dɪ'fɔːlt/ vi fail to do a duty; fail to pay a debt. n such a failure. **a judgment in default** = judgment in a court of law when one fails to come and defend oneself.

defeat /dɪ'fiːt/ vt beat; win a battle against; cause to fail. n act of defeating or being defeated.

defect[1] /'diːfekt/ n fault. adj **defective** /dɪ'fektɪv/ having faults; not complete.

defect[2] /dɪ'fekt/ vi change one's loyalty from one's own country to another. n **defection** /dɪ'fekʃən/ deserting a leader; failing to do one's duty.

defend /dɪ'fend/ vt protect from harm; give reasons in support of (one's ideas). n **defence** /dɪ'fens/. adj **defensive** /dɪ'fensɪv/ serving to protect. **on the defensive** = protecting oneself, not attacking.

defer /dɪ'fɜː/ vt put off to a later time. vi yield to another's opinion. n **deference** /'defərəns/.

defiant /dɪ'faɪənt/ adj showing no fear or respect; fearlessly refusing to obey. n **defiance** /dɪ'faɪəns/.

deficient /dɪ'fɪʃənt/ adj not perfect; lacking something. n **deficiency** /dɪ'fɪʃənsɪ/. **deficiency disease** = illness caused by not having some substance (e.g. one contained in fresh fruit) which the body must have.

deficit /'defɪsɪt/ n amount of money owed beyond what one can pay.

defile[1] /dɪ'faɪl/ vt make unclean.

defile[2] /'diːfaɪl/ n narrow valley between mountains.

define /dɪ'faɪn/ vt **1** mark out the edges of. **2** explain the exact meaning of. adj **definite** /'defənɪt/ clear and exact in meaning; having clear or exact edges; not doubtful or uncertain. n **definition** /ˌdefə'nɪʃən/ **1** clearness; sharpness of line in a photograph. **2** act of defining; explanation of the meaning of a word. adj **definitive** /dɪ'fɪnətɪv/ which settles (a question) completely, without need of further change.

deflate /diː'fleɪt/ vt let the air or gas out of; cause paper money to have less value than that printed on it. n **deflation** /diː'fleɪʃən/.

deflect /dɪ'flekt/ vt turn (e.g. beam of light) away from a straight path. n **deflection** /dɪ'flekʃən/.

deform /dɪ'fɔːm/ vt make ugly or useless by changing from the natural form.

defraud /dɪ'frɔːd/ vt obtain money from (someone) by deceiving.

defray /dɪ'freɪ/ vt pay.

deft /deft/ adj skilful.

defunct /dɪ'fʌŋkt/ adj dead; no longer working.

defy /dɪ'faɪ/ vt be ready to fight against; show no fear of or respect for.

degenerate /dɪ'dʒenəreɪt/ vi become worse. adj, n **degenerate** /dɪ'dʒenərət/ (person) of very bad character.

degrade /dɪ'greɪd/ vt move down to a lower rank or class. n **degradation** /ˌdegrə'deɪʃən/.

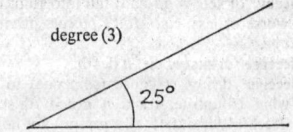

degree (3)

25°

degree /dɪ'griː/ n **1** step; **2** measure of heat. **3** measure of an angle. **4** title given for learning in a university.

dehydration /ˌdiːhaɪ'dreɪʃən/ n drying food so as to preserve it; loss of water from the body in great thirst.

deify /'diːɪfaɪ/ vt make a god of; regard as a god.

deign /deɪn/ v be not too proud (to).

deity /'diːətɪ/ n having the nature of God. **the Deity** = God.

dejected /dɪ'dʒektɪd/ adj having low spirits, sad. n **dejection** /dɪ'dʒekʃən/.

delay /dɪ'leɪ/ vt cause to be late. vi wait; act slowly on purpose.

delectable /dɪ'lektəbəl/ *adj* very pleasing; causing great enjoyment.

delegate /'delɪgeɪt/ *vt* give power to (someone) to carry out a certain piece of work. *n* /'delɪgət/ person sent (e.g. by government) to do a certain duty or to express its opinions on a certain subject. *n* **delegation** /ˌdelɪ'geɪʃən/ act of delegating; group of delegates.

delete /dɪ'liːt/ *vt* strike out (part of something written or printed). *n* **deletion** /dɪ'liːʃən/.

deliberate /dɪ'lɪbəreɪt/ *vi* consider a matter fully and seriously. *adj* **deliberate** /dɪ'lɪbərət/ done carefully and purposely.

delicate /'delɪkət/ *adj* tender, beautiful and easily harmed; pleasant and not easily known by the senses, e.g. a taste, a colour, a smell. *n* **delicacy** /'delɪkəsɪ/ **1** state of being delicate. **2** specially nice piece of food.

delicatessen /ˌdelɪkə'tesn/ *n* shop where certain nice-tasting foods are sold (esp. meats, fish, and cheese ready for eating).

delicious /dɪ'lɪʃəs/ *adj* (esp. of tastes and smells) very nice.

delight /dɪ'laɪt/ *n* great pleasure. *vt* cause great pleasure. *adj* **delightful** /dɪ'laɪtfəl/.

delimit /dɪ'lɪmɪt/ *vt* mark the outside or farthest edges of (something) so as to show how far it reaches.

delineate /dɪ'lɪnɪeɪt/ *vt* mark out with lines; draw a picture of.

delinquency /dɪ'lɪŋkwənsɪ/ *n* law-breaking. *n* **delinquent** /dɪ'lɪŋkwənt/ one who breaks the law.

delirious /dɪ'lɪərəs/ *adj* wandering in the mind and saying meaningless things because of serious illness. *n* **delirium** /dɪ'lɪərɪəm/.

deliver /dɪ'lɪvə ʲ/ *vt* **1** carry and give (e.g. a letter) to the owner. **2** give birth to (a child). **to deliver a speech** = make a speech.

dell /del/ *n* small valley with trees.

delta /'deltə/ *n* Greek letter Δ; anything of this shape, e.g. land at the mouth of a river.

delude /dɪ'luːd/ *vt* deceive.

deluge /'deljuːdʒ/ *n* heavy downpour of water; rush of words, questions, etc.

delusion /dɪ'luːʒən/ *n* untrue idea.

de luxe /dɪ 'lʌks/ *adj* specially good and intended for the wealthy.

delve /delv/ *vi* dig, esp. so as to find something.

demagogue /'deməgɒg/ *n* leader of the common people, who trusts to moving their feelings rather than to reason.

demand /dɪ'mɑːnd/ *vt* claim as a right; ask for. *n* act of demanding; that which is demanded. **in demand** = greatly wanted.

demarcate /'diːmɑːkeɪt/ *vt* mark and fix the exact outer edge of.

demean /dɪ'miːn/ *vt* lower the good name of.

demeanour /dɪ'miːnə ʲ/ *n* behaviour.

demented /dɪ'mentɪd/ *adj* mad.

demi- /'demɪ/ half, e.g. **demi-god.**

demise /dɪ'maɪz/ *n* **1** giving up land, money, etc.,

to somebody else. **2** death.

demobilize /diː'məʊbəlaɪz/ *vt* send (men) back from the army to peace-time work.

democracy /dɪ'mɒkrəsɪ/ *n* government in which the people elect those who govern; a country so governed. *n* **democrat** /'deməkræt/ one who believes in the right of the people to govern themselves. *adj* **democratic** /ˌdemə'krætɪk/.

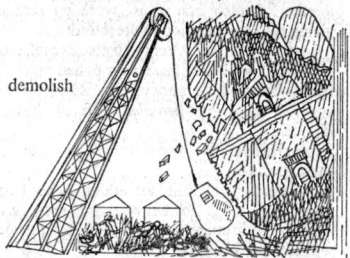

demolish

demolish /dɪ'mɒlɪʃ/ *vt* destroy (e.g. a building). *n* **demolition** /ˌdemə'lɪʃən/.

demon /'diːmən/ *n* devil; cruel person.

demonstrate /'demənstreɪt/ *vt* show; prove clearly. *vi* make a show of force or of public feeling. *n* **demonstration** /ˌdemən'streɪʃən/.

demoralize /dɪ'mɒrəlaɪz/ *vt* ruin the spirit and courage of.

demote /dɪ'məʊt/ *vt* move down into a lower class.

demur /dɪ'mɜː/ ʲ *vi* delay; draw back from an action and give reasons against doing it.

demur /dɪ'mɜː/ ʲ *vi* delay; draw back from an action and give reasons against doing it. *n* **manner.**

den /den/ *n* hole in which an animal lives; hiding-place, usually for thieves; small comfortable sitting-room.

denial /dɪ'naɪəl/ *n* act of saying that a thing is not true; act of refusing.

denier /'denɪə ʲ/ *n* measure of fineness of thread.

denizen /'denɪzən/ *n* one who lives in a place.

denomination /dɪˌnɒmɪ'neɪʃən/ *n* **1** name of a particular class or kind. **2** group of people holding certain special beliefs about God and religion. **3** set of pieces of money of a certain value.

denominator /dɪ'nɒmɪneɪtə ʲ/ *n* lower of the two figures in a FRACTION, e.g. *4 is the denominator of ¾.*

denote /dɪ'nəʊt/ *vt* be a sign of; mean. *n* **denotation** /ˌdiːnəʊ'teɪʃən/ act of denoting; meaning of a word.

dénouement /deɪ'nuːmɑ̃/ *French n* untying a knot; end of a story when everything comes out right or is explained.

denounce /dɪ'naʊns/ *vt* speak against.

dense /dens/ *adj* **1** crowded; thick. **2** *infml* slow of understanding *n* **density** /'densətɪ/ being dense; relation of weight to volume.

dent /dent/ *vt* cause a bend or hollow place in the surface of. *n* such a bend or hollow.

dental /'dentl/ *adj* having to do with the teeth. *n*

denude

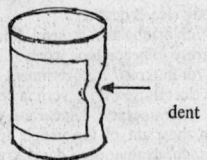

dent

dentist /'dentɪst/ one whose work consists in giving medical attention to the mouth and teeth. *n* **denture** /'dentʃə/ set of teeth made to take the place of those which have been pulled out.

denude /dɪ'nju:d/ *vt* uncover; cause to be uncovered, e.g. *A land denuded of trees* = having no trees.

denunciation /dɪˌnʌnsɪ'eɪʃən/ *n* act of DENOUNCING.

deny /dɪ'naɪ/ *vt* say that (something) is not true; refuse to give, e.g. *To deny oneself the pleasure.*

deodorant /di:'əʊdərənt/ *n* liquid or powder which takes away bad smells.

depart /dɪ'pɑ:t/ *vi* go away.

department /dɪ'pɑ:tmənt/ *n* branch of a business, shop, school, government, etc.; any part of a whole, e.g. one of the parts into which France is divided. **department store** = large shop selling many different kinds of goods.

departure /dɪ'pɑ:tʃə/ *n* act of going away.

depend /dɪ'pend/ *vi* be supported; trust to the support of something or someone; be partly caused or controlled, e.g. *Victory depends on strength and courage; Good temper depends largely on health.* **it all depends** = it is uncertain, until I know (certain other facts). *adj* **dependable** /dɪ'pendəbəl/ trustworthy. *n* **dependency** /dɪ'pendənsɪ/ country which is controlled by another country.

depict /dɪ'pɪkt/ *vt* show by a picture; describe carefully.

deplete /dɪ'pli:t/ *vt* empty; use until little or none is left. *n* **depletion** /dɪ'pli:ʃən/.

deplore /dɪ'plɔ:/ *vt* be sorry or angry that (something) happened. *adj* **deplorable** /dɪ'plɔ:rəbəl/ very bad and which should be deplored.

deploy /dɪ'plɔɪ/ *vt* spread out (an army) in line; arrange (things) for use in a fight or quarrel.

depopulate /di:'pɒpjʊleɪt/ *vt* take away the people from (a country or part of a country).

deport /dɪ'pɔ:t/ *vt* send (someone) out of a country as a punishment; send back (a foreigner) to his own country. **to deport oneself** = to behave. *n* **deportment** /dɪ'pɔ:tmənt/ graceful movement and behaviour.

depose /dɪ'pəʊz/ *vt* put down from some high office (e.g. a king).

deposit /dɪ'pɒzɪt/ *vt* **1** put down. **2** give for safe-keeping. *n* **1** solid matter that sinks to the bottom of a liquid. **2** money paid into a bank for safe-keeping. **3** part of the price of a thing paid at the time of giving the order to supply it.

depôt /'depəʊ/ *n* store-house for goods; place

where soldiers' stores are kept, and where new soldiers are trained.

deprave /dɪ'preɪv/ *vt* make bad in character. *n* **depravity** /dɪ'prævətɪ/.

deprecate /'deprəkeɪt/ *vt* ask that (something) be not done; speak against.

depreciate /dɪ'pri:ʃɪeɪt/ *v* make or become less in value.

depress /dɪ'pres/ *v* **1** make lower; push down. **2** make sad or low in spirits. *n* **depression** /dɪ'preʃən/ **1** sadness; loss of hope. **2** bad state of trade throughout a country.

deprive /dɪ'praɪv/ *vt* take away from; prevent from using *n* **deprivation** /ˌdeprɪ'veɪʃən/ condition of being without certain necessary things such as food, money, and good housing; act of depriving someone of something.

depth /depθ/ *n* quality of being deep; amount something is deep. **out of one's depth** = in water deeper than one's own height; in any condition that is too difficult for one, e.g. because one cannot understand something.

deputation /ˌdepjʊ'teɪʃən/ *n* giving of power to another to do one's business; small group which is given power to act or speak for a larger group. *vt* **depute** /dɪ'pju:t/ give such power. *n* **deputy** /'depjʊtɪ/ one who is given such power.

derail /di:'reɪl/ *vt* cause (a train) to go off the line.

derange /dɪ'reɪndʒ/ *vt* put out of order. *adj* **deranged** mad.

derelict /'derəlɪkt/ *adj* left to decay. *n* broken ship with no one on it.

deride /dɪ'raɪd/ *vt* laugh at as of no value. *n* **derision** /dɪ'rɪʒən/.

derive /dɪ'raɪv/ *vt* obtain from, e.g. *Deriving satisfaction from our misfortune.* *vi* have as its starting point, e.g. *The word 'absent' derives from Latin.* *n* **derivation** /ˌderɪ'veɪʃən/.

derogatory /dɪ'rɒgətərɪ/ *adj* causing loss of respect; showing dislike.

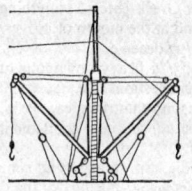

derrick

derrick /'derɪk/ *n* high frame with ropes and wheels for lifting heavy weights.

dervish /'dɜ:vɪʃ/ *n* follower of Muhammad who gives himself completely to the service of God.

descend /dɪ'send/ *vi* go down. **to be descended from** = have (someone) as an earlier member of one's family, e.g. a great-great-grandfather. *n* **descendant** /dɪ'sendənt/ one who is descended from someone, e.g. *The King's descendants will always rule.* *n* **descent** /dɪ'sent/ act of descending; chain by which one person is descended from another.

describe /dɪ'skraɪb/ *vt* tell what (something) is like. *n* **description** /dɪ'skrɪpʃən/.

descry /dɪ'skraɪ/ *vt* be able to see (something) a long way off.

desecrate /'desɪkreɪt/ *vt* use (something holy) for purposes which are not holy; put to a bad or improper use. *n* **desecration** /ˌdesɪ'kreɪʃən/.

desert[1] /dɪ'zɜ:t/ *v* leave; leave one's duty or one's leader; leave the army without being permitted.

desert[2] /'dezət/ *n* large sandy piece of land where nothing grows because there is no rain. *adj* without people.

desert[3] /dɪ'zɜ:t/ *n* something deserved.

deserve /dɪ'zɜ:v/ *vt* be worthy of.

desiccate /'desɪkeɪt/ *vt* make dry.

design /dɪ'zaɪn/ *vt* plan how (something) should be made, done, or built. *n* plan showing how something should be made, done or built.

designate /'dezɪgneɪt/ *vt* **1** appoint for special work. **2** point out or call by a special name. *n* **designation** /ˌdezɪg'neɪʃən/.

desire /dɪ'zaɪə/ *n, vt* want; wish. *adj* **desirable** /dɪ'zaɪərəbəl/ desired; pleasing.

desist /dɪ'zɪst/ *vi* cease doing something.

desk

desk /desk/ *n* table at which one reads, writes or does business.

desolate /'desələt/ *adj* (of a place) sad and without people in it; (of a person) sad and deserted by friends. *vt* **desolate** /'desəleɪt/ make like a desert.

despair /dɪ'speə/ *vi* be without hope. *n* state of being without hope.

despatch /dɪ'spætʃ/ *see* **dispatch.**

desperate /'despərət/ *adj* (of a person) ready for any wild act because of loss of hope; (of an action) wild or dangerous, done as a last attempt.

despise /dɪ'spaɪz/ *vt* look down on as low or worthless. *adj* **despicable** /dɪ'spɪkəbəl/ worthless.

despite /dɪ'spaɪt/ *prep* in spite of.

despoil /dɪ'spɔɪl/ *vt* steal, take away by force.

despondent /dɪ'spɒndənt/ *adj* having lost hope.

despot /'despɒt/ *n* one who has all the power of government and uses it unjustly or cruelly.

dessert /dɪ'zɜ:t/ *n* dish, usually sweet, served at the end of a meal.

destination /ˌdestɪ'neɪʃən/ *n* place to which one is going or to which a letter is being sent.

destined /'destɪnd/ *adj* fated; intended by God. *n* **destiny** /'destɪnɪ/ fate.

destitute /'destɪtjuːt/ *adj* without possessions or money.

destroy /dɪ'strɔɪ/ *vt* pull or break to pieces; ruin;

kill. *n* **destruction** /dɪ'strʌkʃən/. *adj* **destructive** /dɪ'strʌktɪv/ tending to destroy or damage.

desultory /'desəltərɪ/ *adj* passing from one piece of work to another without plan or purpose.

detach /dɪ'tætʃ/ *vt* take apart. *adj* **detached** /dɪ'tætʃt/ **1** separate, e.g. a house. **2** (of a person) not moved by other people's opinions.

detail /'diːteɪl/ *vt* **1** tell every smallest point about. **2** appoint for some special duty. *n* **1** small point, esp. if unimportant, in a story or description. **2** small number of soldiers for a special duty. *adj* **detailed** /'diːteɪld/ (of a story or description) containing all the details.

detain /dɪ'teɪn/ *vt* prevent (someone) from going away; delay.

detect /dɪ'tekt/ *vt* find out. *n* **detective** /dɪ'tektɪv/ special officer of the law who finds and catches thieves, murderers and other law-breakers. *n* **detector** /dɪ'tektə/ any instrument used for finding out the presence of a thing.

detention /dɪ'tenʃən/ *n* **1** act of DETAINING a person or state of being detained, e.g. while waiting to be tried in a court of law. **2** punishment for children by keeping them behind in school after school hours.

deter /dɪ'tɜ:/ *vt* keep from an act by fear, punishment, etc.

detergent /dɪ'tɜ:dʒənt/ *n* substance that cleans by destroying oily dirt.

deteriorate /dɪ'tɪərɪəreɪt/ *vi* become worse.

determine /dɪ'tɜ:mɪn/ *vt* fix; be the cause of; control, e.g *The quality of a man's clothes is determined by how much he can pay. adj* **determined** having an intention firmly fixed in one's mind. *n* **determination** /dɪˌtɜ:mɪ'neɪʃən/.

deterrent /dɪ'terənt/ *n, adj* (something, e.g. a weapon or possible punishment) that DETERS others from doing something (e.g. attacking one's country, or breaking the law).

detest /dɪ'test/ *vt* hate.

dethrone /diː'θrəʊn/ *vt* cause to cease being king or queen.

detonate /'detəneɪt/ *vt* cause to explode. *n* **detonation** /ˌdetə'neɪʃən/.

detour /'diːtʊə/ *n* way round.

detract /dɪ'trækt/ *vi* lessen the value of something.

detriment /'detrɪmənt/ *n* loss or harm. *adj* **detrimental** /ˌdetrɪ'mentl/.

deuce /djuːs/ *n* card of the value of two.

devastate /'devəsteɪt/ *vt* destroy everything in a country. *n* **devastation** /ˌdevə'steɪʃən/.

develop /dɪ'veləp/ *vi* **1** grow up, become larger or more complete, e.g. *A plant develops from a seed.* **2** cause to grow, e.g. *To develop a business.* **3** study or think out fully, e.g. *To develop an idea.* **4** make (a picture) appear on a film (used in photography). *n* **development** /dɪ'veləpmənt/ act or state of developing; way in which a state of affairs develops.

deviate /'diːvɪeɪt/ *vi* move away from the straight or correct path.

device

device /dɪ'vaɪs/ *n* **1** plan. **2** cleverly thought-out instrument, e.g. *A device for sharpening pencils.*

devil /'devəl/ *n* the spirit of evil; Satan.

devious /'diːvɪəs/ *adj* deceiving by indirectness; going round about.

devise /dɪ'vaɪz/ *vt* **1** make (a plan). **2** leave (money, land, etc.) to someone after death.

devitalize /diː'vaɪtəl-aɪz/ *vt* take away the life and power of.

devoid /dɪ'vɔɪd/ *adj* lacking, e.g. *Devoid of hope.*

devolve /dɪ'vɒlv/ *vt* pass on (work) to someone else to do.

devote /dɪ'vəʊt/ *vt* set apart for; give wholly (completely) to, e.g. *He devotes himself to his work. adj* **devoted** /dɪ'vəʊtɪd/ very loving, e.g. *A devoted husband. n* **devotee** /ˌdevəʊ'tiː/ person wholly given over to the service of God—or to other good work. *n* **devotion** /dɪ'vəʊʃən/.

devour /dɪ'vaʊə/ *vt* eat up quickly; read quickly.

devout /dɪ'vaʊt/ *adj* given to prayer and holy thoughts.

dew /djuː/ *n* water which forms on plants, etc., after the sun goes down.

dexterous /'dekstərəs/ *adj* clever with the hands. *n* **dexterity** /dek'sterətɪ/.

diabetes /ˌdaɪə'biːtiːz/ *n* disease causing too much sugar in the blood.

diabolic(al) /ˌdaɪə'bɒlɪk(əl)/ *adj* coming from the devil; evil; cruel.

diadem

diadem /'daɪədem/ *n* band of precious stones worn on the head.

diagnose /'daɪəgnəʊz/ *vt* find out the cause or nature of (a disease). *n* **diagnosis** /ˌdaɪəg'nəʊsɪs/.

diagonal /daɪ'ægənəl/ *adj* going across from corner to corner.

diagram /'daɪəgræm/ *n* figure drawn with lines to show or prove an idea.

dial /'daɪəl/ *n* face of a clock or any other instrument for measuring; numbered circle on a telephone, used in calling a person to speak on the telephone. *vt* call on the telephone.

dialect /'daɪəlekt/ *n* peculiar way of speaking a language used by those in some particular part of the country.

dialogue /'daɪəlɒg/ *n* talk between two or more people.

diameter /daɪ'æmɪtə/ *n* line going through the centre of a circle and touching the edges; length of this line.

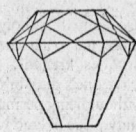

diamond

diamond /'daɪəmənd/ *n* **1** precious stone, usually colourless, of great value and hardness. **2** the shape of a four-sided figure, pointed at the top and bottom. **3** playing-card with this figure printed on it. **diamond wedding** = 60th year of being married. **a rough diamond** = person good at heart though rough in manner.

diaphanous /daɪ'æfənəs/ *adj* (of, e.g., cloth) so fine that it can be seen through.

diaphragm /'daɪəfræm/ *n* muscle which separates the LUNGS from the stomach; any thin plate (in various machines and instruments).

diarrhoea /ˌdaɪə'rɪə/ *n* illness, caused by eating wrong food, in which waste matter passes too often from the bowels.

diary /'daɪərɪ/ *n* book in which notes are written every day, e.g. of things done or of things to be done.

diatribe /'daɪətraɪb/ *n* fierce speech attacking a person or thing.

dice /daɪs/ *n* (*pl*) small six-sided pieces of bone or wood with one to six spots on each side, used for games of chance. *vt* cut into small squares for cooking.

dichotomy /daɪ'kɒtəmɪ/ *n* division into two parts.

dictate /dɪk'teɪt/ *v* **1** read or speak (something) while another person writes it down. **2** give (orders) and force people to obey. *n* **dictation** /dɪk'teɪʃən/. *n* **dictator** /dɪk'teɪtə/ ruler who has all the power of government in his own hands. *adj* **dictatorial** /ˌdɪktə'tɔːrɪəl/ behaving like a dictator; rude and commanding in manner.

diction /'dɪkʃən/ *n* way in which one uses words.

dictionary /'dɪkʃənərɪ/ *n* book containing a list of words in ALPHABETICAL order, with their meanings.

did /dɪd/ *p.t.* of **do**.

didactic /daɪ'dæktɪk/ *adj* teaching a lesson; in the manner of a teacher.

die¹ /daɪ/ *vi* cease to live. **diehard** /'daɪhɑːd/ *n* one who refuses to give up opinions formed a long time ago and now proved wrong.

dice (*npl*)

die² /daɪ/ *n* one of a pair of DICE. **the die is cast** = the matter is now decided.

direct

die³ /daɪ/ *n* metal block used for pressing metal, etc., into shape; an instrument used for cutting a screw on a bar.

diesel engine /'diːzəl ˌendʒɪn/ *n* engine that works by burning heavy oil.

diet¹ /'daɪət/ *n* **1** food and drink. **2** act of dieting; food and drink one may eat when dieting. *vi* eat only certain foods for reasons of health, or in order to become thinner. *n* **dietician** /daɪə'tɪʃən/ one who plans food so that the right amount of each kind is eaten.

diet² /'daɪət/ *n* group of persons who rule a country (e.g. Denmark); meeting of persons to decide certain questions.

differ /'dɪfə/ *vi* **1** be unlike something, e.g. *This plan hardly differs from that one.* **2** disagree.

difference /'dɪfərəns/ *n* **1** unlikeness; that which makes things unlike. **2** quarrel. *adj* **different** /'dɪfərənt/ unlike; various. *v* **differentiate** /ˌdɪfə'renʃɪeɪt/ show or see the difference between.

difficult /'dɪfɪkəlt/ *adj* **1** hard to do; not easy. **2** (of a person) hard to please. *n* **difficulty** /'dɪfɪkəltɪ/.

diffident /'dɪfɪdənt/ *adj* without belief in one's own powers.

diffuse /dɪ'fjuːs/ *adj* spread in every direction, e.g. a smell through air. *n* **diffusion** /dɪ'fjuːʒən/.

dig /dɪg/ *v* make a hole in the earth; turn up (earth) in doing so; search into books. *n* **digs** lodgings.

digest /dɪ'dʒest/ *vt* change (food) into a state in which it can be taken into the blood; take the meaning into the mind, e.g. *Digest a book.* *n* **digest** /'daɪdʒest/ short account of a book or other writing. *n* **digestion** /dɪ'dʒestʃən/. *adj* **digestive** /dɪ'dʒestɪv/.

digit /'dɪdʒɪt/ *n* **1** finger or TOE. **2** number, 0, 1, 2, 3, etc., up to 9.

dignify /'dɪgnɪfaɪ/ *vt* show honour to; cause to appear worthy of honour.

dignitary /'dɪgnətərɪ/ *n* person holding high office.

dignity /'dɪgnətɪ/ *n* calm and grand manner; noble quality of character.

digress /daɪ'gres/ *vi* wander from the subject in speaking or writing.

dike, dyke /daɪk/ *n* thick wall built to keep a river or sea from flowing on to low land.

dilapidated /dɪ'læpɪdeɪtɪd/ *adj* in a state of decay or ruin.

dilate /daɪ'leɪt/ *v* make or become wider.

dilemma /dɪ'lemə, daɪ-/ *n* choice of two answers or actions, both of which seem difficult or bad.

dilettante /ˌdɪlə'tæntɪ/ *n* one who studies a serious subject in a careless way.

diligent /'dɪlɪdʒənt/ *adj* working with care and not wasting time.

dilly-dally /ˌdɪlɪ 'dælɪ/ *vi* waste time.

dilute /daɪ'luːt/ *vt* weaken by mixing—usually with water. *n* **dilution** /daɪ'luːʃən/.

dim /dɪm/ *adj* not bright; (of an idea) not clear.

dimension /dɪ'menʃən, daɪ-/ *n* size; measure—of length, width, or height.

diminish /dɪ'mɪnɪʃ/ *v* make or become less. *n* **diminution** /ˌdɪmɪ'njuːʃən/.

diminutive /dɪ'mɪnjʊtɪv/ *adj* very small.

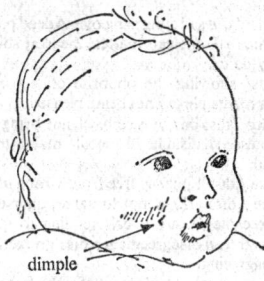

dimple

dimple /'dɪmpəl/ *n* little hollow in the skin, e.g. of the face.

din /dɪn/ *n* loud noise.

dine /daɪn/ *vi* eat dinner. *n* **diner** /'daɪnə/ **1** carriage on a train where meals are served. **2** one who eats dinner.

ding-dong /'dɪŋ dɒŋ/ *n. interj* noise made by a bell.

dinghy /'dɪŋgɪ/ *n* small boat.

dingy /'dɪndʒɪ/ *adj* dirty; faded.

dinner /'dɪnə/ *n* largest meal of the day, by some eaten in the middle of the day, by others in the evening.

dint /dɪnt/ *n* hollow mark in a surface caused by striking. **by dint of** = by means of.

diocese /'daɪəsɪs/ *n* part of the country in the charge of a BISHOP.

dip /dɪp/ *vt* let down into a liquid for a short time; lower for a short time. *n* short swim; quick bath.

diphtheria /dɪf'θɪərɪə/ *n* serious and easily spread disease of the throat.

diphthong /'dɪfθɒŋ/ *n* joining of two VOWELS and making one, e.g. bo-il = boil.

diploma /dɪ'pləʊmə/ *n* printed paper showing that one has successfully finished a course of study.

diplomacy /dɪ'pləʊməsɪ/ *n* making of agreements with foreign governments; cleverness in making such agreements. *n* **diplomat** /'dɪpləmæt/ one who acts for his government in such matters. *adj* **diplomatic** /ˌdɪplə'mætɪk/ clever in dealing with other people so as to get them to agree.

dire /daɪə/ *adj* fearful; very bad.

direct /dɪ'rekt, daɪ-/ *adj* straight; not going round about, e.g. *The direct road.* **direct current** = electricity flowing one way along a wire, not to and fro. *vt* **1** guide. **2** control, e.g. a business. **3** cause to turn, e.g. *Direct your eyes towards.* **4** aim at, or send to, e.g. *To direct a letter.* **5** tell a person the way to a place, e.g. *Please direct me to the post office.* **direction** /daɪ'rekʃən/ *n* course or line in which something moves or along which one would have to move to. get to

75

something. **directly** /dɪˈrektlɪ, daɪ-/ *adv* very soon. **director** /dɪˈrektəˈ, daɪ-/ *n* one controlling a business or other activity. **directory** /dɪˈrektərɪ, daɪ/ *n* list of names of people with their addresses, etc.

dirge /dɜːdʒ/ *n* sad song sung over a dead person.

dirt /dɜːt/ *n* **1** unclean matter. **2** earth; soil. *adj* **dirty** /ˈdɜːtɪ/.

dis- /dɪs/ showing the opposite of, e.g. *n* **displeasure** /dɪsˈpleʒəˈ/ not being pleased.

disability /ˌdɪsəˈbɪlətɪ/ *n* state of not being able; weakness. *vt* **disable** /dɪsˈeɪbəl/ make unable; wound.

disabuse /ˌdɪsəˈbjuːz/ *vt* free from wrong ideas.

disagree /ˌdɪsəˈgriː/ *vi* not to agree; quarrel. *adj* **disagreeable** /ˌdɪsəˈgriːəbəl/ tending to quarrel or disagree. *n* **disagreement** /ˌdɪsəˈgriːmənt/ act of disagreeing.

disappear /ˌdɪsəˈpɪəˈ/ *vi* go out of sight; be seen no more. *n* **disappearance** /ˌdɪsəˈpɪərəns/.

disappoint /ˌdɪsəˈpɔɪnt/ *vt* cause sorrow to (someone) because of failing to do what is expected. *adj* **disappointed** sad at not seeing one's hopes come true. *n* **disappointment** /ˌdɪsəˈpɔɪntmənt/.

disapprove /ˌdɪsəˈpruːv/ *vi* hold a bad opinion of something or someone. *n* **disapproval** /ˌdɪsəˈpruːvəl/.

disarm /dɪsˈɑːm/ *vi* give up arms, armies, warships, etc. *vt* take away arms from; drive away anger by friendliness.

disarrange /ˌdɪsəˈreɪndʒ/ *vt* put out of order.

disarray /ˌdɪsəˈreɪ/ *n* state of disorder.

disaster /dɪˈzɑːstəˈ/ *n* sudden great misfortune. *adj* **disastrous** /dɪˈzɑːstrəs/.

disavow /ˌdɪsəˈvaʊ/ *vt* say that one has no concern with or knows nothing of—.

disband /dɪsˈbænd/ *vt* break up (a group of people). *vi* (of a group) break up, the members going their separate ways.

disburse /dɪsˈbɜːs/ *vt* pay out (money).

disc

disc, disk /dɪsk/ *n* round flat object.

discard /dɪsˈkɑːd/ *vt* throw away as useless.

discern /dɪˈsɜːn/ *vt* see or feel—with some difficulty, e.g. a distant object, a fine difference, a faint smell.

discharge /dɪsˈtʃɑːdʒ/ *vt* **1** do (a duty). **2** send away (a person from employment). **3** unload (goods) from a ship. **4** fire (a gun). **5** pay (a debt) completely. /ˈdɪstʃɑːdʒ/ *n* act of discharging; poisonous matter that comes out of a wound.

disciple /dɪˈsaɪpəl/ *n* follower of a great teacher.

discipline /ˈdɪsəplɪn/ *n* training which produces OBEDIENCE; teaching which produces good qualities of mind or character. *vt* **1** control by discipline. **2** punish. **disciplinarian**

/ˌdɪsəplɪˈneərɪən/ *n* one who disciplines a group firmly. *adj* **disciplinary** /ˈdɪsəplɪnərɪ/.

disclaim /dɪsˈkleɪm/ *vt* say that one has nothing to do with, is not concerned with, does not own or make any claim upon.

disclose /dɪsˈkləʊz/ *vt* make known (what has been secret). *n* **disclosure** /dɪsˈkləʊʒəˈ/.

discolour /dɪsˈkʌləˈ/ *vt* change or destroy the natural or right colour of.

discomfit /dɪsˈkʌmfɪt/ *vt* cause a person's plans to fail; given an unpleasant shock.

disconcert /ˌdɪskənˈsɜːt/ *vt* give a shock to.

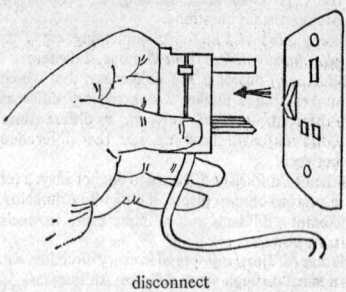

disconnect

disconnect /ˌdɪskəˈnekt/ *vt* cause to be joined no longer; separate.

disconsolate /dɪsˈkɒnsələt/ *adj* sad; hopeless.

discontented /ˌdɪskənˈtentɪd/ *adj* not satisfied; unhappy.

discontinue /ˌdɪskənˈtɪnjuː/ *vt* stop.

discord /ˈdɪskɔːd/ *n* **1** disagreement. **2** set of notes of music which do not sound well together.

discount /dɪsˈkaʊnt/ *vt* **1** take off (a certain amount) from the price or value. **2** not believe completely (e.g. a story); take no notice of. *n* /ˈdɪskaʊnt/ amount taken off the price of something.

discourage /dɪsˈkʌrɪdʒ/ *vt* cause (someone) to lose the courage or the desire to do something.

discourse /ˈdɪskɔːs/ *n* speech.

discourteous /dɪsˈkɜːtɪəs/ *adj* not polite.

discover /dɪˈskʌvəˈ/ *vt* find or ;nd out for the first time. *n* **discovery** /dɪˈskʌvərɪ/ act of discovering something; that which is discovered.

discredit /dɪsˈkredɪt/ *vt* cause a loss of belief in the goodness or truth of. *adj* **discreditable** /dɪsˈkredɪtəbəl/ causing harm to one's good name.

discreet /dɪsˈkriːt/ *adj* careful and showing good judgment.

discrepancy /dɪsˈkrepənsɪ/ *n* failing to agree; difference between two things said or written by a person which do not agree.

discretion /dɪsˈkreʃən/ *n* carefulness and good judgment.

discriminate /dɪˈskrɪmɪneɪt/ *vi* see the difference between two things; choose with judgment. **to**

discriminate against = treat unfairly. *n* **discrimination** /dɪˌskrɪmɪˈneɪʃən/.

discursive /dɪˈskɜːsɪv/ *adj* wandering; (of, e.g., a book or speech) without a fixed plan.

discuss /dɪˈskʌs/ *vt* talk about; reason together about. *n* **discussion** /dɪˈskʌʃən/.

disdain /dɪsˈdeɪn/ *vt* look down upon as not worthy of respect. *n* feeling of disrespect for.

disease /dɪˈziːz/ *n* illness.

disembark /ˌdɪsɪmˈbɑːk/ *vi* get off a boat.

disenchant /ˌdɪsɪnˈtʃɑːnt/ *vt* set free from the effects of magic; show (someone) that a thing loved or believed in is unworthy.

disentangle /ˌdɪsɪnˈtæŋgəl/ *vt* unite and straighten out a string which is knotted up; set in order and make clear a matter which is mixed up or in disorder.

disfigure /dɪsˈfɪgə/ *vt* harm the beauty or shape of.

disgorge /dɪsˈgɔːdʒ/ *vt* bring out from the throat (what has been eaten); give up (e.g. stolen goods).

disgrace /dɪsˈgreɪs/ *n* loss of respect because of wrong-doing. *vt* bring shame or dishonour upon.

disgruntled /dɪsˈgrʌntəld/ *adj* in a bad temper through not having got what was expected.

disguise /dɪsˈgaɪz/ *vt* change the appearance of (oneself or another) in order to deceive. *n* dress, paints, hair, etc., worn by an actor or dishonest person to hide the real appearance.

disgust /dɪsˈgʌst/ *n* strong feeling of dislike such as is caused by a very bad smell or unpleasant sight.

dish /dɪʃ/ *n* large flat plate, or bowl or other container, e.g. one used to contain food; food cooked and ready for serving. **to dish up** = put food in a dish and bring it to the table.

dishearten /dɪsˈhɑːtn/ *vt* cause to lose hope.

dispensary

dishevel /dɪˈʃevəl/ *vt* disarrange (clothes or hair).

dishonour /dɪsˈɒnə/ *vt* cause shame; treat rudely; refuse to pay.

disillusion /ˌdɪsɪˈluːʒən/ *vt* free (someone) from a wrong idea about the worth or goodness of something.

disinfect /ˌdɪsɪnˈfekt/ *vt* make clean and free from all seeds of disease. *n* **disinfectant** /ˌdɪsɪnˈfektənt/ substance that does this.

disinherit /ˌdɪsɪnˈherɪt/ *vt* say that (one's son or daughter) shall not have one's money, etc., after one's death.

disintegrate /dɪˈsɪntəgreɪt/ *vi* break into pieces; change slowly into a powder.

disinterested /dɪˈsɪntərəstɪd/ *adj* just and fair because not gaining anything for oneself.

disk see **disc. disk jockey** = one who plays RECORDS on the radio, at dances, etc.

dislocate /ˈdɪsləkeɪt/ *vt* put out of its proper place, e.g a bone in the body. *n* **dislocation** /ˌdɪsləˈkeɪʃən/.

dislodge /dɪsˈlɒdʒ/ *vt* move (something) from its place.

dismal /ˈdɪzməl/ *adj* cheerless; sorrowful.

dismantle /dɪsˈmæntl/ *vt* take apart (e.g. equipment).

dismay /dɪsˈmeɪ/ *n* loss of courage because of fear or great difficulty. *vt* cause this in (someone).

dismember /dɪsˈmembə/ *vt* cut the limbs off (a body); cut or take to pieces.

dismiss /dɪsˈmɪs/ *vt* send away; send away from employment. *n* **dismissal** /dɪsˈmɪsəl/.

dismount /dɪsˈmaʊnt/ *vi* get down from a horse, carriage, etc.

disorder /dɪsˈɔːdə/ *n* **1** absence of order; state of things not being arranged properly. **2** something wrong, e.g. with a person's mind or body. *adj* **disorderly** /dɪsˈɔːdəlɪ/ in a state of disorder.

disorganize /dɪsˈɔːgənaɪz/ *vt* put out of working order.

disown /dɪsˈəʊn/ *vt* refuse to accept as being one's own.

disparage /dɪˈspærɪdʒ/ *vt* speak ill against; say bad things about.

disparity /dɪˈspærətɪ/ *n* state of not being equal.

dispassionate /dɪˈspæʃənət/ *adj* free from strong feeling; just, because not feeling favour for either side.

dispatch, despatch /dɪˈspætʃ/ *vt* send off quickly. *n* message; government letter, e.g. to some foreign country.

dispel /dɪˈspel/ *vt* drive away, e.g. *The sun dispels the clouds.*

dispensary /dɪˈspensərɪ/ *n* place where medicines are mixed and given out.

dispensation /ˌdɪspənˈseɪʃən/ *n* **1** special act of God. **2** special act of allowing (something) that usually is not allowed.

dispense /dɪˈspens/ *vt* give out; measure out (medicine). **to dispense with** = do without.

disperse /dɪˈspɜːs/ *v* scatter.

dispirited /dɪˈspɪrɪtɪd/ *adj* sad and without hope.

displace /dɪˈspleɪs/ *vt* put out of place. *n* **displacement** /dɪˈspleɪsmənt/.

display

display /dɪ'spleɪ/ *vt* show. *n* arrangement of things displayed.

disport /dɪ'spɔːt/ **to disport oneself** = amuse oneself.

dispose /dɪ'spəʊz/ *vt* arrange; cause (someone) to feel in a certain way. **I am well disposed towards him** = I like him and am willing to help him. **to dispose of** = sell or give away. *n* **disposal** /dɪ'spəʊzəl/.

disposition /ˌdɪspə'zɪʃən/ *n* person's natural way of feeling and acting.

dispossess /ˌdɪspə'zes/ *vt* turn (someone) out of a place.

disproportionate /ˌdɪsprə'pɔːʃənət/ *adj* unequal; too much on one side and too little on the other.

dispute /dɪ'spjuːt/ *v* talk about and disagree; say that an opinion is not true *n* quarrel. *adj* **disputable** /dɪ'spjuːtəbəl/ not certain.

disqualify /dɪ'skwɒlɪfaɪ/ *vt* make unfit or unable to act.

disquiet /dɪs'kwaɪət/ *vt* make anxious. *n* state of feeling anxious.

disquisition /ˌdɪskwɪ'zɪʃən/ *n* long speech or written report about some subject.

disreputable /dɪs'repjʊtəbəl/ *adj* having a bad character or bad name.

disrobe /dɪs'rəʊb/ *v* take off (one's own or someone else's) clothes.

disrupt /dɪs'rʌpt/ *vt* break up (e.g. a meeting). *n* **disruption** /dɪs'rʌpʃən/.

dissect /dɪ'sekt/ *vt* cut up into pieces in order to examine, e.g. a dead body.

dissemble /dɪ'sembəl/ *vi* pretend not to be what one really is; hide one's feelings.

disseminate /dɪ'semɪneɪt/ *vt* scatter; spread around.

dissent /dɪ'sent/ *vi* disagree; quarrel. *n* **dissension** /dɪ'senʃən/ quarrelling.

dissertation /ˌdɪsə'teɪʃən/ *n* long report or speech.

disservice /dɪs'sɜːvɪs/ *n* harmful action.

dissimulate /dɪ'sɪmjʊleɪt/ *vi* hide one's feelings.

dissipate /'dɪsɪpeɪt/ *vt* scatter; waste by foolish spending. *n* **dissipation** /ˌdɪsɪ'peɪʃən/ waste of health and money by wild living.

dissociate /dɪ'səʊʃɪeɪt/ *vt* separate from; think of as separate. **to dissociate oneself from** = say that one has nothing to do with a person or idea.

dissolute /'dɪsəluːt/ *adj* living an evil life.

dissolve /dɪ'zɒlv/ *vt* make a solid or a gas liquid by putting it into liquid, e.g. *Sugar dissolves in water.* *vi* (of a solid or gas) become part of a liquid in this way.

dissuade /dɪ'sweɪd/ *vt* reason with (someone) to prevent him from taking a certain action.

distaff /'dɪstɑːf/ *n* stick from which the wool is pulled in making thread.

distance /'dɪstəns/ *n* amount of space between two points. **to keep one's distance** = not to go too near, not to be too friendly. *adj* **distant** /'dɪstənt/ far away; a long time ago.

distasteful /dɪs'teɪstfəl/ *adj* disliked; unpleasant.

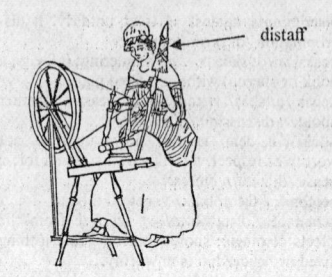

distaff

distemper /dɪ'stempə/ *n* **1** water-paint for walls. **2** disease of dogs.

distend /dɪ'stend/ *vt* cause to swell.

distil /dɪ'stɪl/ *vt* get the liquid from (a material) by heating it so that the liquid comes off in a gaseous form which is then cooled and becomes pure liquid. *vi* come drop by drop.

distillery /dɪ'stɪlərɪ/ *n* place where WHISKY or other such drinks are made.

distinct /dɪ'stɪŋkt/ *adj* separate; clear; with each part well marked *n* **distinction** /dɪ'stɪŋkʃən/ special mark of honour; difference. *adj* **distinctive** /dɪ'stɪŋktɪv/ serving to DISTINGUISH one thing from others.

distinguish /dɪ'stɪŋgwɪʃ/ *vt* notice carefully the difference between. **to distinguish oneself** = make oneself noticed by all, or famous.

distort /dɪ'stɔːt/ *vt* change the natural appearance of; turn from the true meaning. *n* **distortion** /dɪ'stɔːʃən/.

distract /dɪ'strækt/ *vt* cause (someone's) mind to wander in many directions. *n* **distraction** /dɪ'strækʃən/ state of being distracted; something distracting.

distraught /dɪ'strɔːt/ *adj* very anxious.

distress /dɪ'stres/ *n* pain or difficulty of any kind. *vt* cause distress to.

distribute /dɪ'strɪbjuːt/ *vt* give out, or scatter, among many people, or in different places. *n* **distribution** /ˌdɪstrɪ'bjuːʃən/.

district /'dɪstrɪkt/ *n* part of a country, etc.; part of a country marked out for some special purpose, e.g. government, school, etc.

distrust /dɪs'trʌst/ *vt* not to have faith in.

disturb /dɪ'stɜːb/ *v* change the usual or natural condition of, e.g. *A wind disturbed the surface of the water;* break in upon (someone) who is working; cause (someone) to become anxious.

disuse /dɪs'juːs/ *n* state of not being used. *adj* **disused** /dɪs'juːzd/.

ditch /dɪtʃ/ *n* water CHANNEL for carrying off water, e.g. at the side of a road. *vt sl* **1** bring down (an aeroplane) into the sea. **2** throw away; free oneself of.

ditto /'dɪtəʊ/ *n, interj* the same; a mark („ „ „) meaning that what is written above it is to be repeated.

ditty /'dɪtɪ/ *n* simple song.

78

divan /dɪˈvæn/ *n* long, low soft seat.

dive /daɪv/ *vi* jump head first into the water; go down quickly, as a rabbit into its hole. *n* **diver** /ˈdaɪvə/ man who works at the bottom of the sea in a special dress with a supply of air.

diverge /daɪˈvɜːdʒ/ *vi* go out in a different direction. *n* **divergence** /daɪˈvɜːdʒəns/. *adj* **divergent** /daɪˈvɜːdʒənt/.

diverse /daɪˈvɜːs/ *adj* different; various. **diversify** /daɪˈvɜːsɪfaɪ/ *vt* make (things) different from each other. **diversity** /daɪˈvɜːsətɪ/ *n* state of things being different from each other.

divert /daɪˈvɜːt/ *vt* turn from a regular course; amuse; cause to forget one's regular work. *n* **diversion** /daɪˈvɜːʃən/ act of turning from a regular course; any act which amuses and makes one forget one's regular work for a short time.

divest /daɪˈvest/ *vt* take off the clothes or coverings from.

divide /dɪˈvaɪd/ *v* **1** separate into parts. **2** see how many times greater (one number) is than another, e.g. *If one divides 18 by 3, one obtains the answer 6.*

dividend /ˈdɪvɪdend/ *n* share of the money which has been made by a business, divided among those who own the business.

divination /ˌdɪvɪˈneɪʃən/ *n* act of telling the unknown or the future.

divine[1] /dɪˈvaɪn/ *adj* **1** having to do with God. **2** *infml* very pleasing.

divine[2] /dɪˈvaɪn/ *vt* guess (what is hidden). **water-diviner** *n* one who finds underground streams with the help of a Y-shaped stick.

divinity /dɪˈvɪnətɪ/ *n* a god; study of the nature of God.

divisible /dɪˈvɪzəbəl/ *adj* which can be divided.

division /dɪˈvɪʒən/ *n* **1** act of dividing. **2** part divided off. **3** part of an army, about 20,000 men.

divorce /dɪˈvɔːs/ *n* act of separating a man and wife by a court of law. *vt* obtain such a separation from (one's husband or wife); separate.

divulge /daɪˈvʌldʒ/ *vt* tell (what has been secret).

dizziness /ˈdɪzɪnəs/ *n* unpleasant feeling in the head, e.g. after turning round many times. *adj* **dizzy** /ˈdɪzɪ/.

do /duː/ *vt* be active in; be the cause of; perform (an act). **to have to do with** = be concerned with. **to do away with** = kill; destroy; put an end to. *n infml* dance, party, etc.

docile /ˈdəʊsaɪl/ *adj* easily taught or led.

dock[1] /dɒk/ *n* place where ships stay while

dock

loading; place where ships are built or repaired. *vi* (of a ship) go into a dock.

dock[2] /dɒk/ *vt* cut off (a part).

dock[3] /dɒk/ *n* place in a court of law where the prisoner stands.

dockyard /ˈdɒk-jɑːd/ *n* yard where ships are built or repaired.

doctor /ˈdɒktə/ *n* **1** one who attends to people when they are ill. **2** highest title given by a university.

doctrinaire /ˌdɒktrɪˈneə/ *adj* having strong beliefs that one is always wishing to put into practice even in matters where they are unsuitable or impossible.

doctrine /ˈdɒktrɪn/ *n* what is taught, e.g. by the Church; set of beliefs.

document /ˈdɒkjʊmənt/ *n* written or printed paper. *n* **documentary** /ˌdɒkjʊˈmentərɪ/ film about real things or events.

dodder /ˈdɒdə/ *vi* shake and be unsteady like an old man.

dodge /dɒdʒ/ *v* move suddenly in order to escape (something); escape (one's duty) by a trick. *n* such a trick.

doe /dəʊ/ *n* female deer or rabbit.

does /dʌz/ *v* (3rd person singular of **do**).

dog

dog /dɒg/ *n* small mammal with four legs and a tail often kept by men in their houses. *adj* **dog-eared** /ˈdɒg-ɪəd/ (of a book) having the corners of the pages turned down.

dogged /ˈdɒgɪd/ *adj* having a character that refuses to yield or give up in the face of difficulty.

doggerel /ˈdɒgərəl/ *n* rough, foolish poetry.

dogma /ˈdɒgmə/ *n* fixed teaching accepted without reasoning. *adj* **dogmatic** /dɒgˈmætɪk/.

doily /ˈdɔɪlɪ/ *n* small ornamental cloth put under a dish or other vessel on the table.

doldrums /ˈdɒldrəmz/ *n* place on the ocean where sailing ships cannot move because there is no wind. **in the doldrums** = in a low and sad state of mind.

dole /dəʊl/ *n* share. *infml* **to dole out** = give out a part of (something) at a time.

doll /dɒl/ *n* small play-thing made like a human figure.

dollar /ˈdɒlə/ *n* name of an amount of money, the value of one bank-note in America and some other countries.

dolorous /ˈdɒlərəs/ *adj* sorrowful.

dolphin /ˈdɒlfɪn/ *n* sea animal, 6–8 feet long, which swims very quickly moving in and out of the water in curves.

dolt /dəʊlt/ *n* fool.

domain /dəˈmeɪn/ *n* land; right to rule over a

dome

dolphin

land. **the domain of science** = those studies which are dealt with by scientists.

dome /dəʊm/ n rounded top on a building; any rounded top or cover.

domestic /də'mestɪk/ adj having to do with the home; (of an animal) not wild. n servant in a home. vt **domesticate** /də'mestɪkeɪt/ make (a wild animal) no longer wild.

domicile /'dɒmɪsaɪl/ n home; country in which one's home is.

dominate /'dɒmɪneɪt/ v control or rule; be the most important. vt rise above, e.g. *This tall building dominates the city.* adj **dominant** /'dɒmɪnənt/. n **domination** /ˌdɒmɪ'neɪʃən/.

domineer /ˌdɒmɪ'nɪə / vi rule by force; force others to let one have one's own way.

dominion /də'mɪnɪən/ n right to rule; country ruled by one government.

domino /'dɒmɪnəʊ/ n flat piece of wood with white spots on it used for playing a game. n **dominoes** /'dɒmɪnəʊz/ game so played.

don[1] /dɒn/ n 1 teacher in a university. 2 title of a gentleman or nobleman in Spain.

don[2] /dɒn/ vt put on (clothes).

donate /dəʊ'neɪt/ vt give. n **donation** /dəʊ'neɪʃən/ act of giving, esp. to some good cause; thing so given.

done /dʌn/ p.p. of **do.**

donkey /'dɒŋkɪ/ n animal like a small horse with long ears, used for riding and as a load carrier.

donor /'dəʊnə / n one who gives something.

don't /dəʊnt/ infml do not.

doodle /'duːdl/ vi make meaningless marks on paper.

doom /duːm/ n fate; ruin. **to be doomed** = fated to fail, suffer, etc.

door /dɔː / n that through which one enters a house or room. **next door** = in the next house. **out of doors** = in the open air. n **doorway** /'dɔːweɪ/ a door; an opening.

dope /dəʊp/ n medicine not ordered by a doctor but taken because of a pleasant effect on the body. infml adj **doped** /dəʊpt/ having taken dope.

dormant /'dɔːmənt/ adj sleeping; not active.

dormitory /'dɔːmətərɪ/ n large sleeping-room for a number of persons.

dormouse /'dɔːmaʊs/ n small, mouse-like animal with a long furry tail.

dorsal /'dɔːsl/ adj having to do with the back.

dose /dəʊs/ n amount of medicine taken at one time; anything unpleasant that has to be taken.

dossier /'dɒsɪə / n collection of papers about a person.

dot /dɒt/ n any small round mark. infml **on the dot** = at the exact time.

dotage /'dəʊtɪdʒ/ n state of old age when one only remembers past events and does not notice present happenings.

dote /dəʊt/ vi love in a foolish way.

double /'dʌbəl/ adj, adv twice. adj meant for two persons, e.g. *A double bed.* v make or become double; fold a thing over on itself, e.g. a cloth.

double-cross /ˌ.. './ vt deceive.

double-dealing /ˌ.. '../ adj dishonest. n dishonesty.

double-entry /ˌ.. '. ./ adj (of way of keeping accounts) in which everything is written twice, once as an outgoing and once as an incoming amount.

doublet /'dʌblət/ n tight garment worn on the upper half of the body.

doubt /daʊt/ vt question the truth of; be uncertain of. adj **doubtful** /'daʊtfəl/ doubting; unsure.

dough /dəʊ/ n flour mixed with water ready for baking. n **doughnut** /'dəʊnʌt/ small soft round cake cooked in boiling fat.

dour /'dʊə / adj silent and unwilling to change an idea.

douse /daʊs/ vt put into water; throw water on; put out (a light).

dove

dove /dʌv/ n soft-voiced bird often used as a sign of peace. n **dovecot, dovecote** /'dʌvkɒt/ box or house built for doves to live in.

dovetail /'dʌvteɪl/ vt join (wood) together tightly in a special way.

dowry /'daʊrɪ/ n money, land, etc., which a woman brings when she is married.

doze /dəʊz/ vi be half asleep.

dozen /'dʌzən/ n group of twelve. **a baker's dozen** = thirteen.

drab /dræb/ adj without pleasant colours; uninteresting.

draft /drɑːft/ n 1 first rough writing of anything; rough plan. 2 written order to pay money, used in sending money to distant places. vt order (men) into the army as soldiers. **to draft** write or draw roughly; send soldiers. n **draftsman** /'drɑːftsmən/ man who draws plans, e.g. of machines or buildings, or draws up (writes) laws.

drag /dræg/ vt pull (a heavy object). vi be slow and uninteresting. n infml anything slow and uninteresting.

dragon /'drægən/ n imaginary fire-breathing animal in children's stories.

dragonfly /'drægənflaɪ/ n flying insect.

dragoon /drə'guːn/ n horse-soldier. vt treat (persons) fiercely and make them obey very quickly and exactly.

drill

drain /dreɪn/ *vt* make dry by running the water out of. *vi* (of liquid) flow. *n* pipe or CHANNEL for dirty water; continued loss, e.g. of blood, money, etc. *n* **drainage** /'dreɪnɪdʒ/ water or waste carried away; pipes, etc., which carry away waste water.

drake /dreɪk/ *n* male duck.

dram /dræm/ *n* small measure of weight; small amount of strong drink (e.g. whisky).

drama /'drɑːmə/ *n* play; set of exciting events like those in a play. *adj* **dramatic** /drə'mætɪk/ having to do with plays; sudden and surprising, as if it were an event in a play. *vt* **dramatize** /'dræmətaɪz/ **1** make into a play. **2** make more exciting or dramatic.

drape /dreɪp/ *vt* cover loosely with cloth.

draper /'dreɪpə/ *n* one who sells women's clothes, cloth, curtains, etc.

drastic /'dræstɪk/ *adj* serious and possibly producing harmful effects; done completely and with force.

draught /drɑːft/ *n* **1** stream of air blowing through a room. **2** plan or drawing. **3** amount taken at one time, e.g. *Draught of fishes* = number caught in the net; *Draught of wine* = one large mouthful.

draughts /drɑːfts/ *n* game played by two people, each with twelve round pieces on a board of sixty-four squares. *n* **draughtsman** /'drɑːftsmən/ **1** DRAFTSMAN. **2** piece used in the game of draughts.

draw /drɔː/ *vt* **1** pull, e.g. *A horse draws a load.* **2** receive; take out; take in, e.g. *To draw one's pay.* **3** sink to a certain depth, e.g. *The ship draws 30 feet.* **4** make (a line, figure etc.) on paper with pencil or pen. *v* finish (a game), neither side having won. *n* end of a game in which neither side wins. **to draw near** or **draw close** = come or go near. **to draw back** = come or go back. **to draw the line at** = be unwilling to go so far as. **to draw up** = **1** to stop. **2** to put into writing, to COMPOSE (a law, an agreement etc.).

drawback /'drɔːbæk/ *n* **1** difficulty; thing which causes trouble. **2** repayment of some of the money paid on foreign goods brought into a country.

drawbridge /'drɔːbrɪdʒ/ *n* bridge which can be pulled up, e.g. to let ships pass.

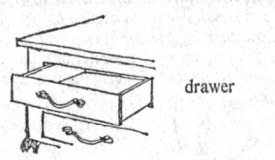

drawer

drawer /'drɔː/ *n* box-like container in a piece of furniture which can be pulled out or pushed in.

drawing /'drɔːɪŋ/ *n* picture drawn.

drawing-room /'.. ./ *n* sitting-room used in the afternoon and evening.

drawl /drɔːl/ *vi* speak slowly, making each word long. *n* such a way of speaking.

drawn /drɔːn/ p.p. of **draw**.

dray /dreɪ/ *n* heavy four-wheeled cart.

dread /dred/ *vt* fear greatly. *n* great fear. *adj* **dreadful** /'dredfəl/ **1** causing dread. **2** *infml* unpleasant; very bad.

dream /driːm/ *n* thoughts passing through the mind when asleep. *v* **1** have such thoughts; have it appear to one in a dream that. **2** have thoughts and hopes about the future, e.g. *I dream of having a boat of my own.* **I shouldn't dream of doing that** = will certainly not—.

dreary /'drɪərɪ/ *adj* cheerless; sad.

dredge[1] /dredʒ/ *vt* clear (a river, etc.) using a dredger. *n* **dredger** /'dredʒə/ boat with a machine for taking up mud from the bottom of a river or harbour.

dredge[2] /dredʒ/ *vt* scatter (sugar) over.

dregs /dregz/ *n* (*pl*) muddy matter at the bottom of a liquid, e.g. of wine.

drench /drentʃ/ *vt* make thoroughly wet.

dress /dres/ *v* put clothes on. *vt* wash and bind up (a wound). **to dress up** = put on special clothes as for a play. *n* **1** clothing. **2** a woman's outer garment. *n* **dressing table** /'.. ,. ./ piece of furniture at which one may sit while dressing, attending to the face, etc.

dress circle /,. '. ./ *n* raised seats in a theatre just above the lowest floor.

dresser /'dresə/ *n* piece of furniture in a kitchen with open shelves above and closed places below for pots, etc.

dressing /'dresɪŋ/ *n* **1** act of putting on clothes. **2** mixture of oil and other matter served with some foods. **3** material that is put on a wound.

dressing-gown /'.. ./ *n* long garment used when one is undressed.

drew /druː/ p.t. of **draw**.

dribble /'drɪbl/ *vi* let water from the mouth fall drop by drop. *v* give short quick kicks to (a ball) while running with it. *n* **driblet** /'drɪblət/ small amount, e.g. of liquid.

drift /drɪft/ *vi* float along slowly; go along having no plan or fixed idea. *n* **snowdrift** /'snəʊdrɪft/ snow blown by the wind to form a small hill. **the drift of a speech** = general meaning of the speech.

driftwood /'drɪftwʊd/ *n* wood blown on to the shore by wind.

drill[1] (n)

drill[1] /drɪl/ *v* make a hole (through or into). *n* machine or instrument used for making holes.

81

drill

drill² /drɪl/ vt plant (seeds) with a machine. n the machine used.

drill³ /drɪl/ vt train (soldiers) in correct movements; train by giving much practice. n correct movements as ordered.

drill⁴ /drɪl/ n heavy, cotton cloth.

drink /drɪŋk/ v take in (liquid) with the mouth. vi take wine, etc. n any liquid used for drinking, esp. strong drinks. **to take to drink** = begin to drink too much strong drink.

drip /drɪp/ n small drop of liquid. vi fall slowly in drops.

dripping /'drɪpɪŋ/ n fat used in cooking.

drive /draɪv/ vt force to go in a certain direction. v control (a moving vehicle, esp. a car); ride in a car. n **1** short car journey. **2** a road up to the door of a house.

drivel /'drɪvəl/ n foolish talk.

driven /'drɪvən/ p.p. of **drive**.

drizzle /'drɪzəl/ n fine rain. vi rain in small drops.

droll /drəʊl/ adj peculiar; causing laughter.

dromedary

dromedary /'drɒmədərɪ/ n CAMEL with one raised place on its back.

drone /drəʊn/ n **1** male bee. **2** lazy person. **3** low sound as of bees. vi **1** make this sound. **2** infml talk in an uninteresting way for a long time.

droop /druːp/ vi bend downwards like a half-dead plant; lose one's spirits.

drop /drɒp/ v fall or cause or allow to fall. n **1** act of falling; distance fallen. **2** small amount of liquid falling or about to fall; any small amount of liquid. **to drop in** (on) = pay a short visit (to). **to drop off** = fall asleep.

droppings /'drɒpɪŋz/ n (pl) waste matter left by animals or birds.

dross /drɒs/ n worthless matter taken off the surface when metal is melted.

drought /draʊt/ n lack of rain.

drove¹ /drəʊv/ p.t. of **drive**.

drove² /drəʊv/ n number of animals, e.g. sheep, being driven along together.

drover /'drəʊvə/ n one who drives cattle.

drown /draʊn/ vi die by being under water for a long time. vt **1** kill in this way. **2** make so much noise that (a sound) cannot be heard.

drowsy /'draʊzɪ/ adj sleepy.

drudge /drʌdʒ/ n one who does hard unpleasant work for little pay.

drug /drʌg/ n **1** medicine, or material of which medicines are mixed. **2** medicine which takes away feeling and causes sleep, or causes unusual feelings. vt give drugs to. n **druggist** /'drʌgɪst/ one who sells medicines.

drum

drum /drʌm/ n musical instrument with a tight skin over a round, hollow box, beaten with sticks to make a loud sound. vi play (music) on a drum.

drunk /drʌŋk/ p.p. of **drink**. adj not able to think and act properly because of having taken too much wine, etc. n **drunkard** /'drʌŋkəd/ one who often drinks too much strong drink. adj **drunken** /'drʌŋkən/ p.p. of **drunk**.

dry /draɪ/ adj not wet; not interesting, e.g. A dry book. v make or become dry. **to dry up** = stop talking because of not being able to think what to say.

dry dock /ˌ. './ n a place in which a ship is taken out of the water for repair.

dry rot /ˌ. './ n diseased growth in wood (e.g. wooden floors) which turns wood into powder.

dual /'djuːəl/ adj having to do with two; DOUBLE.

dub¹ /dʌb/ vt **1** make (someone) a knight by touching him on the shoulder with a sword. **2** name.

dub² /dʌb/ vt put English speech on to (a French-speaking film) or French, etc. on to English, etc.

dubious /'djuːbɪəs/ adj doubtful.

ducal /'djuːkəl/ adj having to do with a DUKE.

duchess /'dʌtʃəs/ n wife of a DUKE.

duchy /'dʌtʃɪ/ n part of a country controlled by a DUKE.

duck¹ /dʌk/ n **1** a common water-bird. **like water off a duck's back** = having no effect. **2** infml in CRICKET, absence of runs.

duck² /dʌk/ vt push under water. vi move the body down quickly so as to save the head from a blow.

duckling /'dʌklɪŋ/ n young duck.

duct /dʌkt/ n any pipe, e.g. in the body.

dud /dʌd/ n, adj useless (person or thing).

due /djuː/ adj **1** owed, e.g. The debt is due on April 15th = it should be paid on April 15th. **2** proper, e.g. With due respect. **due to** = caused by, e.g. Death due to an accident.

duel /'djuːəl/ n fight between two people because of a quarrel, esp. over a matter of honour.

duet /djuː'et/ n piece of music performed by two people.

duffel coat

82

duffel coat /'dʌfəl kəʊt/ *n* coat as shown, with wooden fasteners.

dug /dʌg/ p.p. of **dig** *n* (in animals) point where the young gets milk from the mother.

dugout /'dagaʊt/ *n* **1** boat made by hollowing out a tree. **2** an underground room used as a shelter in war-time.

duke /dju:k/ *n* highest rank for an English nobleman below a prince.

dulcet /'dʌlsɪt/ *adj* soft and pleasant sounding.

dull /dʌl/ *adj* **1** slow in understanding. **2** uninteresting. **3** not keen (of sight or other senses). **4** not bright or clear (of light, sounds, pain). **5** not sharp, e.g. a knife. **6** not active, e.g. trade. *vt* make dull.

dullard /'dʌləd/ *n* one who is slow of understanding.

dumb /dʌm/ *adj* **1** unable to speak. **2** *sl* foolish.

dumbfound /dʌm'faʊnd/ *vt* cause one to lose the power of speech, e.g. because of surprise.

dummy /'dʌmɪ/ *n* **1** object made to look like and take the place of a real thing; human figure made of wood or wax used to show off clothes. **2** rubber thing put in a baby's mouth to keep it quiet. **3** the set of cards on the table in playing BRIDGE.

dump /dʌmp/ *n* place in the open for storing goods, esp. in war; place for throwing unwanted matter. **to be down in the dumps** = to be sad and spiritless. *vt* throw down in mass; set down carelessly.

dumpling /'dʌmplɪŋ/ *n* round mass of boiled food made of flour, fat, etc., sometimes with meat or fruit in the middle.

dumpy /'dʌmpɪ/ *adj* short and thick.

dunce /dʌns/ *n* slow learner.

dune /dju:n/ *n* hill consisting of sand.

dung /dʌŋ/ *n* waste matter passed from the bodies of animals, often mixed with soil to make the soil produce more plants.

dungarees /ˌdʌŋgə'ri:z/ *n* outer garments worn by men who look after trains, engines, etc., to protect their clothes.

dungeon /'dʌndʒən/ *n* dark, underground prison.

dunk /dʌŋk/ *vt* dip (e.g. bread) in a liquid, e.g. coffee, before eating it.

dupe /dju:p/ *n* one who is deceived; one who is unknowingly used by another for a wrong purpose. *vt* deceive.

duplicate /'dju:plɪkeɪt/ *vt* make an exact copy of. *n* **duplicate** /'dju:plɪkət/ exact copy. *n* **duplicator** /'dju:plɪkeɪtə/ machine used for making many copies of a letter.

duplicity /dju:'plɪsɪtɪ/ *n* act of being dishonest.

durable /'djʊərəbəl/ *adj* lasting a long time, e.g. *Durable shoes, cloth.*

duration /djʊ'reɪʃən/ *n* time during which anything continues.

duress /djʊ'res/ *n* state of being in prison or of acting under force.

during /'djʊərɪŋ/ *prep* while (something) is going on; at or for the time of.

dusk /dʌsk/ *n* time when daylight is fading. *adj* **dusky** /'dʌskɪ/ rather dark.

dust /dʌst/ *n* powder made up of very small pieces of waste matter; finely powdered earth. **to bite the dust** = to die. *vt* **1** cover with, e.g. *Dust with sugar.* **2** take the dust off, e.g. *Dust a room.*

duster /'dʌstə/ *n* cloth used to clean away dust.

dutiful /'dju:tɪfəl/ *adj* obeying regularly and willingly.

duty /'dju:tɪ/ *n* **1** that which one ought to do. **2** money which must be paid to the government before goods can come into the country. *adj* **dutiable** /'dju:tɪəbəl/ (of goods) on which one must pay duty.

dwarf /dwɔ:f/ *n* man who is very much smaller than the natural size; anything unusually small. *vt* cause to appear small.

dwell /dwel/ *vi* live in a place. **to dwell on** = think or talk much about. *n* **dwelling** /'dwelɪŋ/ a house.

dwelt /dwelt/ p.t. of **dwell**.

dwindle /'dwɪndl/ *vi* become less and less.

dye /daɪ/ *vt* cause (e.g. cloth) to become of a certain colour. *n* material used to make colour.

dying /'daɪ-ɪŋ/ *adj* nearing death; becoming useless.

dyke /daɪk/ see **dike**.

dynamic /daɪ'næmɪk/ *adj* having to do with or producing force or power; (of a person) having great strength of character or great ENERGY.

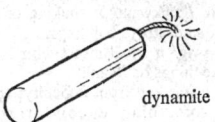

dynamite

dynamite /'daɪnəmaɪt/ *n* powerful explosive, used to break up rocks. *vt* destroy with dynamite.

dynamo /'daɪnəməʊ/ *n* machine that produces electric power.

dynasty /'dɪnəstɪ/ *n* line of kings all of the same family; time during which a number of kings of the same family rule a country.

dysentery /'dɪsəntrɪ/ *n* a disease of the bowel.

dyspepsia /dɪs'pepsɪə/ *n* difficulty in changing food in the stomach into a form in which it can be built into the body.

E

each /iːtʃ/ *det* every.

eager /ˈiːgə/ *adj* full of desire; very anxious to do something.

eagle /ˈiːgəl/ *n* a large meat-eating bird.

ear¹ /ɪə/ *n* that part of the body with which we hear. **an ear for music** = power of hearing music clearly and enjoying it.

ear² /ɪə/ *n* head of a grain-producing plant.

ear-drum /ˈ. ./ *n* tight thin skin in the ear which causes one to hear the sound waves that beat against it.

earl /ɜːl/ *n* title of an English nobleman, 3rd below prince.

early /ˈɜːlɪ/ *adj, adv* **1** near the beginning of (the day, etc.). **2** arriving or starting before the time arranged.

earmark /ˈɪəmɑːk/ *n* mark made on the ear of a sheep, pig, etc., so that its owner may know it; any special mark by which a thing may be known. *vt* set (e.g. money) on one side for a special purpose.

earn /ɜːn/ *vt* obtain as payment for work; be worthy of.

earnest /ˈɜːnɪst/ *adj* eager and serious.

earring /ˈɪərɪŋ/ *n* ring or ornament worn on the ear.

earshot /ˈɪəʃɒt/ **within earshot** = near enough to hear.

earth /ɜːθ/ *n* **1** world on which we live. **how on earth—?** = in what possible way? **2** the surface of the ground. **3** wire leading to the earth from electrical equipment. *vt* provide (a piece of electrical equipment) with such a wire.

earthenware /ˈɜːθənweə/ *n* (*sing*) dishes made of baked earth.

earthquake /ˈɜːθkweɪk/ *n* shaking of the earth which often destroys buildings.

earwig /ˈɪəwɪg/ *n* small insect with two curved tooth-like things on its tail.

ease /iːz/ *n* freedom from difficulty; comfort. *vt* make (something uncomfortable) less uncomfortable.

easel /ˈiːzəl/ *n* frame for holding a picture while it

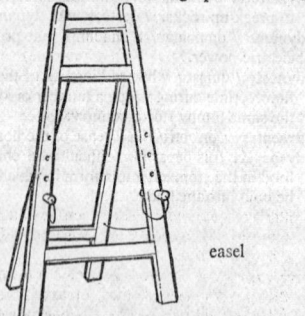

easel

is being painted.

east /iːst/ *n* direction in which the sun rises. **the Middle East** = the countries of Turkey, Syria, Jordan and neighbouring countries. **the Far East** = China, Japan, etc.

Easter /ˈiːstə/ *n* feast-day in memory of Christ's rising from the dead.

eastern /ˈiːstən/ *adj* towards the east or having to do with the east. *adj* **easterly** /ˈiːstəlɪ/ in or coming from the east. *adj, adv* **eastward(s)** /ˈiːstwəd(z)/ towards the east.

easy /ˈiːzɪ/ *adj* not difficult; free from care or pain; comfortable. *adj* **easy-going** /ˌ. . ˈ. ./ (of a person) who does not trouble himself or other people. **easy money** = money obtained for little work. *n* **easy chair** /ˈ. . ./ large comfortable chair.

eat /iːt/ *v* take in (food) through the mouth. **to eat into** = destroy part of.

eaves /iːvz/ *n* (*pl*) edge of a roof that comes out beyond the wall.

eavesdrop /ˈiːvzdrɒp/ *vi* listen secretly to other people talking.

ebb /eb/ *vi* flow back; become lower and lower slowly. *n* **ebb tide** flow of the sea back from the shore.

ebony /ˈebənɪ/ *n, adj* (made of) very hard heavy wood.

ebullient /ɪˈbʌlɪənt/ *adj* full of high spirits and excitement; in a state of boiling.

eccentric /ɪkˈsentrɪk/ *adj* **1** not moving in a regular circle. **2** (of behaviour) unusual, peculiar; (of a person) rather mad. *n* **eccentricity** /ˌeksənˈtrɪsətɪ/.

ecclesiastic /ɪˌkliːzɪˈæstɪk/ *adj* having to do with government of the Church. *n* officer of the Church.

echo /ˈekəʊ/ *n* the same sound coming back again, as when one shouts in a large hall. *vi* (of a sound) to come back in this way.

eclectic /ɪˈklektɪk/ *adj* not following one opinion but choosing ideas here and there.

eclipse /ɪˈklɪps/ *n* shutting off the sun's light by the moon coming between the sun and the earth (or of the moon's light by the earth).

ecology /ɪˈkɒlədʒɪ/ *n* study of living things in their surroundings.

economics /ˌiːkəˈnɒmɪks/ *n* scientific study of the laws which govern the production of wealth. *adj* **economic** having to do with economics. *adj* **economical** /ˌiːkəˈnɒmɪkəl/ not using much money. *n* **economist** /iːˈkɒnəmɪst/ one who studies economics. *vi* **economize** /iːˈkɒnəmaɪz/ spend less money.

economy /iːˈkɒnəmɪ/ *n* **1** careful saving of money or materials. **2** state of production, trade, wealth, etc., in a country.

ecstasy /ˈekstəsɪ/ *n* wild happiness. *adj* **ecstatic** /ɪkˈstætɪk/.

eczema /'eksɪmə/ *n* a disease of the skin.

eddy /'edɪ/ *n* movement of water or air in a circle.

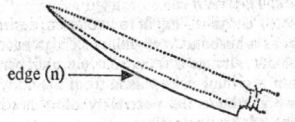

edge (n)

edge /edʒ/ *n* thin sharp cutting part of a knife; border of anything. *vi* move sideways in such a way as not to be noticed. *adv* **edgeways** /'edʒweɪz/ in the direction of the edge. **can't get a word in edgeways** = have no chance to speak.

edible /'edəbəl/ *adj* fit to be eaten.

edict /'iːdɪkt/ *n* order, e.g. of the king or government.

edifice /'edɪfɪs/ *n* building.

edify /'edɪfaɪ/ *vt* improve the mind or faith of. *n* **edification** /ˌedɪfɪ'keɪʃən/.

edit /'edɪt/ *vt* prepare matter for printing. *n* **edition** /ɪ'dɪʃən/ one printing of a book, paper, etc.; form in which a book is printed. *n* **editor** /'edɪtə/ one who prepares books, papers, etc., for printing. *n* **editorial** /ˌedɪ'tɔːrɪəl/ part of a newspaper written by the editor giving an opinion on some question of the day.

educate /'edʒʊkeɪt/ teach; cause to have knowledge, good character and manners, and power to make a living. *n* **education** /ˌedʒʊ'keɪʃən/.

eel /iːl/ fish shaped like a snake.

eerie, eery /'ɪərɪ/ *adj* strange and fearful.

efface /ɪ'feɪs/ *vt* rub (writing) off the surface. **to efface the memory of** = cause to forget.

effect /ɪ'fekt/ *n* result of a cause; result produced on the mind. **my effects** = my goods, things belonging to me. *adj* **effective** /ɪ'fektɪv/, **effectual** /ɪ'fektʃʊəl/.

effeminate /ɪ'femɪnət/ *adj* (of a man) behaving like a woman.

effervesce /ˌefə'ves/ *vi* (of a liquid) give off gas; (of a person) be gay, in high spirits. *adj* **effervescent** /ˌefə'vesənt/.

effete /ɪ'fiːt/ *adj* worn out; useless.

efficacious /ˌefɪ'keɪʃəs/ *adj* having power to produce a desired result. *n* **efficacy** /'efɪkəsɪ/.

efficient /ɪ'fɪʃənt/ *adj* performing a duty well; producing a desired result. *n* **efficiency** /ɪ'fɪʃənsɪ/.

effigy /'efɪdʒɪ/ *n* shape of a person cut in wood or stone, or painted. **to be burnt in effigy** = having some figure of oneself (e.g. of wood dressed in old clothes) burnt by people as a sign of anger and hatred.

effluent /'efluənt/ *adj* flowing out. *n* liquid waste from FACTORIES etc. flowing into rivers, the sea, etc.

effort /'efət/ *n* use of strength, e.g. *Make an effort.*

effrontery /ɪ'frʌntərɪ/ *n* daring rudeness, without sense of shame.

effusion /ɪ'fjuːʒən/ *n* act of pouring out or sending out; outburst of excited writing.

effusive /ɪ'fjuːsɪv/ *adj* expressing feeling very freely.

egg /eg/ *n* rounded object containing new life, laid by female birds, fishes, snakes, etc.; seed of life in a mother animal. **to put all one's eggs in one basket** = risk all in one attempt, put all one's money into shares in one company. **to egg on** = urge on.

ego /'iːgəʊ, 'egəʊ/ *n* **1** the self. **2** respect for oneself. *n* **egoism** /'iːgəʊɪzəm, 'eg-/ thinking too much about oneself. *n* **egoist** /'iːgəʊɪst, 'eg-/ one who thinks always about himself. *n* **egotism** /'iːgətɪzəm, 'eg-/ talking too much about oneself. *n* **egotist** /'iːgətɪst, 'eg-/ one who talks too much about himself. *adj* **egoistic (al)**.

egress /'iːgres/ *n* act or power of going out; way out.

egret /'iːgret/ *n* white bird with a long white tail and back feathers.

eiderdown /'aɪdədaʊn/ *n* thick covering for a bed filled with the fine feathers of a duck.

eight /eɪt/ *det, n* number following seven, often written **8**.

eighteen /eɪ'tiːn/ *det, n* number got by adding eight to ten, often written **18**.

eighty /'eɪtɪ/ *det, n* number often written **80**, being eight times ten.

either /'aɪðə/ *det, pron* one or the other of two. *adv* **he will not go, and I shall not either** = I also shall not. *conj* (used with **or**) e.g. *Either you have lost it or she has.*

ejaculate /ɪ'dʒækjʊleɪt/ *v* cry out suddenly; throw out (liquid) with force.

eject /ɪ'dʒekt/ *vt* throw out with force.

eke /iːk/ *vt* cause a small supply to last a long time by being careful, or by obtaining small amounts to add to it, e.g. *Eking out the little that remained.*

elaborate /ɪ'læbərət/ *adj* worked out with great care; having many different parts, e.g. *An elaborate machine.* *vi* **elaborate** /ɪ'læbəreɪt/ do more work and improve on something. *n* **elaboration** /ɪˌlæbə'reɪʃən/.

elapse /ɪ'læps/ *vi* (of time) pass.

elastic /ɪ'læstɪk/ *adj* **1** (of a material) springing back after being stretched. **2** (of, e.g. rules) not fixed too firmly. *n* an elastic material, esp. rubber covered with silk or cotton.

elated /ɪ'leɪtɪd/ *adj* full of joy.

elbow /'elbəʊ/ *n* place where the arm bends; anything L-shaped, e.g bend in a pipe. *vt* push with the elbow.

elder /'eldə/ *n, adj* older (person). *n* officer in the Church having years and wisdom. *adj* **eldest** /'eldɪst/ oldest.

elect /ɪ'lekt/ *vt* choose, e.g. choose a member for the government of the country. *n* **election** /ɪ'lekʃən/ act by a group of people of electing a

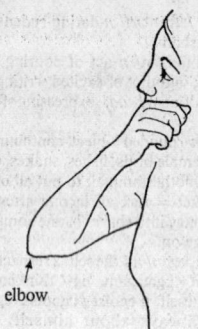

elbow

leader, etc. *n* **electioneering** /ɪˌlekʃəˈnɪərɪŋ/ working to get someone elected by the people. *n* (*sing*) **electorate** /ɪˈlektərət/ all those persons who have the right to join in electing a person.

electricity /ɪˌlekˈtrɪsəɪ/ *n* power used to produce heat, light, etc. *adj* **electric** /ɪˈlektrɪk/, **electrical** /ɪˈlektrɪkəl/. *n* **electrician** /ɪˌlekˈtrɪʃən/ man who makes or repairs electrical equipment. *vt* **electrify** /ɪˈlektrɪfaɪ/ put electricity into; surprise greatly. *vt* **electrocute** /ɪˈlektrəkjuːt/ kill by electricity.

electrolysis /ɪˌlekˈtrɒləsɪs/ *n* breaking up chemical substances by means of electricity.

electromagnet /eˈlektrəʊˌmægnət/ *n* MAGNET made by passing electricity round a soft iron bar.

electron /ɪˈlektrɒn/ *n* one of the parts of an ATOM.

electronics /ɪˌlekˈtrɒnɪks, ˌeləkˈtrɒnɪks/ *n* the study of instruments in which electrons move, e.g. radio, television, radar. *adj* **electronic**.

elegant /ˈelɪɡənt/ *adj* graceful; neat and beautiful.

elegy /ˈelɪdʒɪ/ *n* poem expressing sorrow for the dead. *adj* **elegiac** /ˌelɪˈdʒaɪək/.

element /ˈelɪmənt/ *n* **1** simple thing of which other things are made up. **2** material that scientists cannot break up or separate into other materials different from itself. *adj* **elementary** /ˌelɪˈmentərɪ/ suitable for beginners.

elephant /ˈelɪfənt/ *n* very large mammal with a long nose which hangs down and two TUSKS. **a white elephant** = useless possession of which one would gladly be free, e.g. a very large piece of furniture.

elevate /ˈelɪveɪt/ *vt* lift up to a higher level or rank. *adj* **elevated** /ˈelɪveɪtɪd/ (of thoughts, writing, etc.) fine; noble. *n* **elevation** /ˌelɪˈveɪʃən/ **1** act of lifting up. **2** hill. **3** plan showing one side of a building. *n* **elevator** /ˈelɪveɪtə/ machine for lifting people or goods from one floor of a house to another; **a grain elevator** = machine used for loading corn (wheat) or other grain on to ships, or for unloading it from ships.

eleven /ɪˈlevən/ *n, det* number following ten, often written **11.**

elf /elf/ *n* small fairy. *adj* **elfin** /ˈelfɪn/.

elicit /ɪˈlɪsɪt/ *vt* draw out, e.g. *A teacher elicits knowledge from a child by questioning.*

elide /ɪˈlaɪd/ *vt* leave out a letter or sound, e.g. *He's, They're.* *n* **elision** /ɪˈlɪʒən/.

eligible /ˈelɪdʒəbəl/ *adj* fit to be chosen; desirable, e.g. as a husband. *n* **eligibility** /ˌelɪdʒəˈbɪlətɪ/.

eliminate /ɪˈlɪmɪneɪt/ *vt* take out, e.g. unfit persons from a group; pass poison from the body. **we may eliminate the possibility of** = need not think of that as possible.

elite /ɪˈliːt/ *n* (*sing*) most powerful, or best people in any group.

elixir /ɪˈlɪksə/ *n* imaginary liquid able to turn metals into gold—or to make life last for ever.

elk

elk /elk/ *n* large deer with broad flat horns.

ellipse /ɪˈlɪps/ *n* curve seen when you look at a circle sideways.

elm /elm/ *n* a kind of large tree.

elocution /ˌeləˈkjuːʃən/ *n* art of public speaking—esp. the proper use of the voice.

elongate /ˈiːlɒŋɡeɪt/ *vt* make longer.

elope /ɪˈləʊp/ *vi* run away from home and marry secretly.

eloquent /ˈeləkwənt/ *adj* (of a speaker or his words) expressing oneself well. *n* **eloquence** /ˈeləkwəns/.

else /els/ *adv* (form of 'other' used after 'some', 'no', 'every', and 'any') e.g. *No one else* = no other person. **or else** = or otherwise. *adv* **elsewhere** /ˌelsˈweə/ in some other place.

elucidate /ɪˈluːsɪdeɪt/ *vt* make the meaning of (something) clear.

elude /ɪˈluːd/ *vt* escape—esp. by means of a trick. *adj* **elusive** /ɪˈluːsɪv/ such as escapes, e.g. *An elusive person* = one who is difficult to catch; *An elusive word* = word which escapes the memory or is difficult to remember.

emaciated /ɪˈmeɪsɪeɪtɪd/ *adj* very thin because of poor health or lack of food. *n* **emaciation** /ɪˌmeɪsɪˈeɪʃən/.

emanate /ˈeməneɪt/ *vi* come from; be made or caused by, e.g. *This offer emanates from Mr. X* = comes from, was made by; (of gas, light, etc.) to come out from.

emancipate /ɪˈmænsɪpeɪt/ *vt* make free (e.g. slaves). *n* **emancipation** /ɪˌmænsɪˈpeɪʃən/.

emasculate /ɪˈmæskjʊleɪt/ vt take away the strength of; take away the power of becoming a father from.

embalm /ɪmˈbɑːm/ vt preserve (a dead body) so that it does not decay.

embankment /ɪmˈbæŋkmənt/ n wide wall of stones and earth, e.g. one built to keep a river in its course.

embargo /ɪmˈbɑːgəʊ/ n order forbidding movement of ships or trade; any order forbidding an action.

embark /ɪmˈbɑːk/ vi go on to a ship. **to embark upon** = start doing (something).

embarrass /ɪmˈbærəs/ vt make (someone) feel uncomfortable about himself. n **embarrassment** /ɪmˈbærəsmənt/.

embassy /ˈembəsɪ/ n building for officers sent by a government to do its business with the government of another country.

embed /ɪmˈbed/ vt put into, as in a bed; set firmly in, e.g. *Precious stones embedded in rocks.*

embellish /ɪmˈbelɪʃ/ vt make beautiful with ornaments.

ember /ˈembə/ n red-hot piece of wood or coal.

embezzle /ɪmˈbezəl/ vt use for oneself (money) entrusted to one for some other purpose. n **embezzlement** /ɪmˈbezəlmənt/.

embittered /ɪmˈbɪtəd/ adj sad and angry because of some past event.

emblem /ˈembləm/ object that is a sign of something, e.g. *A crown is the emblem of the King.* adj **emblematic** /ˌembləˈmætɪk/.

embody /ɪmˈbɒdɪ/ vt give form to, e.g. *Words embody thought;* to collect together, e.g. *This book embodies all the rules of chess.* n **embodiment** /ɪmˈbɒdɪmənt/.

emboss /ɪmˈbɒs/ vt make (raised figures, letters, etc.) on metal or other material by pressing this material up from the back.

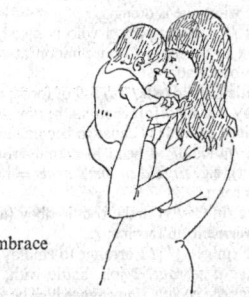

embrace

embrace /ɪmˈbreɪs/ vt hold (someone) in the arms.

embrasure /ɪmˈbreɪʒə/ n opening in a wall of a fort through which the defenders may shoot.

embroider /ɪmˈbrɔɪdə/ vt ornament (cloth) with a needle and thread; improve (a story) by adding

something from the imagination. n **embroidery** /ɪmˈbrɔɪdərɪ/ art of embroidering cloth; embroidered cloth.

embryo /ˈembrɪəʊ/ n young of any creature in its first state before birth. adj **embryonic** /ˌembrɪˈɒnɪk/ adj anything in a very early stage of growth.

emend /ɪˈmend/ vt correct; improve and make free from faults. n **emendation** /ˌiːmenˈdeɪʃən/.

emerald /ˈemərəld/ n a green precious stone. n, adj (of a) bright green colour.

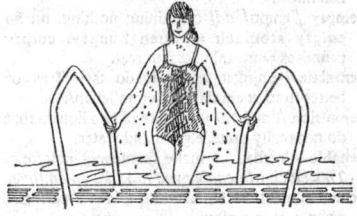

emerge

emerge /ɪˈmɜːdʒ/ vi (of a person) come out, e.g. from water, from a hiding-place; (of things) become known as a result of inquiry.

emergency /ɪˈmɜːdʒənsɪ/ n sudden happening which makes it necessary to act without delay.

emery /ˈemərɪ/ n very hard material, often made into powder and stuck on paper, used for smoothing wood, metals, etc. **emery wheel** = wheel made of emery used for sharpening knives and other cutting instruments.

emetic /ɪˈmetɪk/ n any medicine given to cause one to throw up the contents of the stomach.

emigrate /ˈemɪgreɪt/ vi leave one's own country and go to live in another country. n **emigrant** /ˈemɪgrənt/ one emigrating. n **emigration** /ˌemɪˈgreɪʃən/ act of emigrating.

eminent /ˈemɪnənt/ adj high in rank or fame. n **eminence** /ˈemɪnəns/.

emir /eˈmɪə/ n in Northern Africa or the Middle East, a prince or chief.

emissary /ˈemɪsərɪ/ n one who is sent to carry a message or do some special piece of work.

emission /ɪˈmɪʃən/ n act of sending out; matter sent out, e.g. smoke from a gun.

emit /ɪˈmɪt/ vt send out, e.g. a smell, light from the sun.

emolument /ɪˈmɒljʊmənt/ n money received by one who holds an office.

emotion /ɪˈməʊʃən/ n deep feeling. adj **emotional** /ɪˈməʊʃənəl/ expressing or having to do with emotion; (of a person) tending to have strong feelings and to become easily excited by them.

emperor /ˈempərə/ n ruler of an empire.

emphasis /ˈemfəsɪs/ n special force given to certain words or ideas in speaking or writing so that they will be noticed and remembered. vt **emphasize** /ˈemfəsaɪz/ give emphasis to. adj **emphatic** /ɪmˈfætɪk/.

empire /'empaɪə/ n number of different countries ruled by one chief government.

empirical /ɪm'pɪrɪkəl/ adj guided by experience rather than by ideas.

emplacement /ɪm'pleɪsmənt/ n special place built for guns.

employ /ɪm'plɔɪ/ vt 1 use. 2 use the services of; take on as a paid worker. n **employee** /ɪm'plɔɪ-iː, ˌemplɔɪ'iː/ person employed. n **employment** /ɪm'plɔɪmənt/ paid work.

empress /'emprəs/ n wife of an EMPEROR; female EMPEROR.

empty /'emptɪ/ adj containing nothing. **on an empty stomach** = when hungry. **empty promises** = meaningless, unreal.

emulate /'emjʊleɪt/ vt try to do as well as, or better than. n **emulation** /ˌemjʊ'leɪʃən/.

emulsion /ɪ'mʌlʃən/ n mixture of two liquids that do not really unite, e.g. oil and water.

enable /ɪ'neɪbəl/ vt make (someone) able, e.g. *This clock will enable you to wake up on time.*

enact /ɪ'nækt/ vt 1 make into a law. 2 perform, e.g. a part in a play.

enamel /ɪ'næməl/ n 1 glassy material melted at great heat and put on metals as an ornament. 2 paint which has a shining appearance when it dries. 3 hard outer covering of the teeth.

enamoured /ɪ'næməd/ **to be enamoured of** = be in love with.

encamp /ɪn'kæmp/ v make a camp; be in a camp.

encase /ɪn'keɪs/ vt put in a case; shut up within some material, e.g. *Encased in gold.*

enchant /ɪn'tʃɑːnt/ vt put a magic charm on; please greatly. n **enchantment** /ɪn'tʃɑːntmənt/.

encircle /ɪn'sɜːkəl/ vt form a circle around.

enclose /ɪn'kləʊz/ vt close in and shut off from things outside; put (something) inside a letter.

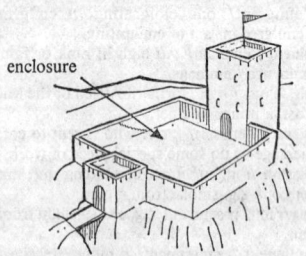

enclosure

enclosure /ɪn'kləʊʒə/ n thing enclosed, e.g. piece of ground with a fence round; thing put in with a letter.

encompass /ɪn'kʌmpəs/ vt encircle; contain.

encore /'ɒŋkɔː/ interj word said by listeners who are pleased by a song or other performance to get the performer(s) to sing or play again. n short performance made to satisfy the listeners' desire to hear more.

encounter /ɪn'kaʊntə/ vt meet with, e.g. an enemy or a great difficulty.

encourage /ɪn'kʌrɪdʒ/ vt give courage to; urge on; help on. n **encouragement** /ɪn'kʌrɪdʒmənt/.

encroach /ɪn'krəʊtʃ/ vi go beyond one's own land and take part of the land of another person.

encrusted /ɪn'krʌstɪd/ adj covered with a thin hard outer covering.

encumber /ɪn'kʌmbə/ vt make it difficult for (someone) to act freely, e.g. *Encumbered with boxes.* n **encumbrance** /ɪn'kʌmbrəns/ thing that prevents free action.

encyclical /en'sɪklɪkəl/ n letter sent round by the POPE to all his churches.

encyclopaedia /ɪnˌsaɪklə'piːdɪə/ n book or set of books in which all branches of knowledge are dealt with in order from A to Z.

end /end/ n 1 farthest or last point. **at a loose end** = having nothing to do. **to make both ends meet** = get just enough money for one's needs. **odds and ends** = small useless pieces. **to put an end to, make an end of** = stop, destroy. 2 purpose, e.g. *To gain one's ends.* **the end justifies the means** = wrong-doing may be allowed if the purpose is good. v finish.

endear /ɪn'dɪə/ vt cause to be loved. n **endearment** /ɪn'dɪəmənt/ loving word or act.

endeavour /ɪn'devə/ n, v try.

endemic /en'demɪk/ adj (of a disease) always present in certain people or places.

endorse /ɪn'dɔːs/ vt 1 agree with (what has been said or done). 2 write one's name on the back of (a written or printed paper). n **endorsement** /ɪn'dɔːsmənt/.

endow /ɪn'daʊ/ vt give (e.g. to a school) a large amount of money which brings in a yearly amount for use. **well endowed by nature** = clever, beautiful (etc.) by birth. n **endowment** /ɪn'daʊmənt/.

endure /ɪn'djʊə/ vt suffer bravely and without complaining. vi last. n **endurance** /ɪn'djʊərəns/ ability to endure pain, tiredness, etc., and continue what one is doing.

enemy /'enəmɪ/ n person who is hated, who is trying to do harm to one; nation at war with one's own nation.

energetic /ˌenə'dʒetɪk/ adj full of force; active. n **energy** /'enədʒɪ/ force; strength; power.

enervate /'enəveɪt/ vt cause to become weak.

enfold /ɪn'fəʊld/ vt bend something round (an object), e.g. *Enfold in one's arms* = put one's arms round.

enforce /ɪn'fɔːs/ vt make people obey (a law). n **enforcement** /ɪn'fɔːsmənt/.

engage /ɪn'geɪdʒ/ vt 1 arrange to employ, e.g. *To engage a servant.* 2 join battle with, e.g. *To engage the enemy.* vi to **engage in** = be active in. adj **engaged** /ɪn'geɪdʒd/ 1 busy. 2 having promised to get married. 3 (e.g. of a telephone) already in use. n **engagement** /ɪn'geɪdʒmənt/ 1 promise to marry. 2 promise to meet or go out with a person.

engender /ɪn'dʒendə/ vt produce; be the cause of.

engine /'endʒɪn/ *n* machine that produces power; any machine.

engineer /ˌendʒɪ'nɪə/ *n* one who makes or has charge of engines; one who understands the building of roads, bridges, etc. *vt* arrange (esp. something secret).

engrave /ɪn'greɪv/ *vt* cut names, pictures, etc., on (metal or stone or wood).

engross /ɪn'grəʊs/ *vt* fill (someone)'s time; fill (someone)'s mind.

engulf /ɪn'gʌlf/ *vt* swallow up, e.g. *The waves engulfed the ship.*

enhance /ɪn'hɑːns/ *vt* increase the value, beauty, etc., of.

enigma /ɪ'nɪgmə/ *n* something difficult to understand. *adj* **enigmatic** /ˌenɪg'mætɪk/.

enjoin /ɪn'dʒɔɪn/ *vt* command.

enjoy /ɪn'dʒɔɪ/ *vt* 1 have delight in. 2 possess or have the use of. *n* **enjoyment** /ɪn'dʒɔɪmənt/.

enlarge /ɪn'lɑːdʒ/ *vt* make larger. *n* **enlargement** /ɪn'lɑːdʒmənt/ larger copy of a small picture.

enlighten /ɪn'laɪtn/ *vt* cause to understand. *n* **enlightenment** /ɪn'laɪtənmənt/.

enlist /ɪn'lɪst/ *v* join or cause (someone) to join the army.

enliven /ɪn'laɪvən/ *vt* make bright and full of action.

en masse /ˌɒn 'mæs/ *French adv* in a mass; in a crowd.

enmesh /ɪn'meʃ/ *vt* catch in a net.

enmity /'enmɪti/ *n* state or feeling of being an enemy.

enormity /ɪ'nɔːmɪti/ *n* something very large or very bad; state of being ENORMOUS.

enormous /ɪ'nɔːməs/ *adj* very large.

enough /ɪ'nʌf/ *adv, det* as much as is needed.

enquire /ɪn'kwaɪə/ *v* see **inquire.**

enrage /ɪn'reɪdʒ/ *vt* make very angry.

enrapture /ɪn'ræptʃə/ *vt* delight greatly.

enrol(l) /ɪn'rəʊl/ *vt* write on a list; make (someone) a member of a group.

en route /ˌɒn 'ruːt/ *French adv* on the way.

enshrine /ɪn'ʃraɪn/ *vt* put in a holy place.

ensign /'ensaɪn/ *n* flag, serving as a special sign on a ship.

ensnare /ɪn'sneə/ *vt* trap.

ensue /ɪn'sjuː/ *vi* come as a result.

ensure /ɪn'ʃʊə/ *vt* make certain.

entail /ɪn'teɪl/ *vt* make necessary, e.g. *Writing this book has entailed a lot of work.*

entangle /ɪn'tæŋgəl/ *vt* get (someone) tied up as in a net; put into difficulties. *n* **entanglement** /ɪn'tæŋgəlmənt/.

enter /'entə/ *v* 1 go into (a place), e.g. *To enter the room.* 2 become a member of, e.g. *Enter the army.* 3 put (someone)'s name on to a list, e.g. *Enter a boy for an examination*; write down in a book, e.g. *Enter this amount in the account book.*

enterprise /'entəpraɪz/ *n* daring plan; carrying out of a daring plan. **a business enterprise =** an attempt to start a new business. *adj* **enterprising**

/'entəpraɪzɪŋ/ willing to do daring things.

entertain /ˌentə'teɪn/ *vt* 1 receive as a guest; give food and drink to. 2 amuse. *adj* **entertaining** /ˌentə'teɪnɪŋ/ amusing. *n* **entertainment** /ˌentə'teɪnmənt/ an amusement, e.g. a play, singing, etc.

enthral(l) /ɪn'θrɔːl/ *vt* hold by magic charm and have power over. *adj* **enthralling** /ɪn'θrɔːlɪŋ/ very interesting.

enthrone /ɪn'θrəʊn/ *vt* make (someone) king.

enthusiasm /ɪn'θjuːzɪæzəm/ *n* excited desire to do something. *n* **enthusiast** /ɪn'θjuːzɪæst/ one who is very eager and interested in some idea. *adj* **enthusiastic** /ɪnˌθjuːzɪ'æstɪk/.

entice /ɪn'taɪs/ *vt* draw away, usually for evil purposes; draw over to one's side by an offer of some desirable thing.

entire /ɪn'taɪə/ *adj* whole; complete; unbroken; undamaged.

entitle /ɪn'taɪtl/ *vt* give a right to.

entity /'entɪti/ *n* any real thing.

entomology /ˌentə'mɒlədʒi/ *n* study of insects.

entrails /'entreɪlz/ *n* (*pl*) inside parts of an animal.

entrance[1] /'entrəns/ *n* acts, power or means of entering; large front door of a building.

entrance[2] /ɪn'trɑːns/ *vt* cause to be in a state of great wonder and delight.

entrant /'entrənt/ *n* one who goes in; one who takes part in a race, examination, etc.

entreat /ɪn'triːt/ *vt* pray; beg. *n* **entreaty** /ɪn'triːti/.

entrench /ɪn'trentʃ/ *vt* protect a place or army with TRENCHES. *adj* **entrenched** /ɪn'trentʃt/ (of an opinion, person's position, etc.) firmly fixed and not likely to be given up or able to be attacked with success.

entrust /ɪn'trʌst/ *vt* give into another's care; give a person (a duty) to do.

entry /'entri/ *n* 1 act of coming in. 2 something written down, e.g. in an account of money.

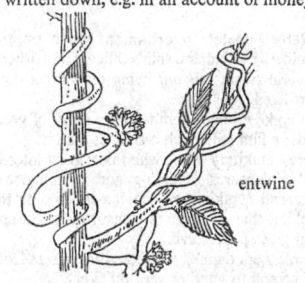

entwine

entwine /ɪn'twaɪn/ *v* twist round and round; grow round and round, e.g. a plant round a tree.

enumerate /ɪ'njuːməreɪt/ *vt* count; name one by one.

enunciate /ɪ'nʌnsɪeɪt/ *vt* say solemnly or clearly; form (one's words) clearly in speaking.

envelop /ɪn'veləp/ *vt* bind round or cover, e.g. in a garment. in flames, in clouds.

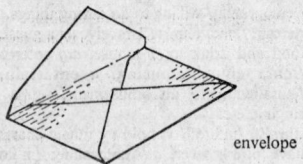

envelope

envelope /'envələʊp/ n cover for a letter; any covering that contains something.

enviable, envious see envy.

environment /ɪn'vaɪərənmənt/ n all the conditions that have an effect on growth and character; place where something lives, is found, etc.

envisage /ɪn'vɪzɪdʒ/ vt imagine.

envoy /'envɔɪ/ n person of high rank sent from one government to another to carry messages.

envy /'envɪ/ n feeling of hate or ill-will caused by the sight of another's success or wealth. vt desire (something owned by another) and hate the owner for possessing it. adj **enviable** /'envɪəbəl/ worth having for oneself. adj **envious** /'envɪəs/ (of a person) tending to envy others.

enzyme /'enzaɪm/ n substance produced by living matter that causes chemical changes, e.g. *Our bodies produce an enzyme that changes* STARCH *into sugar.*

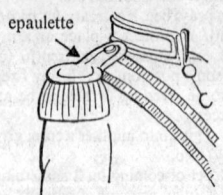

epaulette

epaulette /'epəlet/ n ornament worn on the shoulders by soldiers, ship's officers and others.

ephemeral /ɪ'femərəl/ adj living only for a day; short-lived.

epic /'epɪk/ n long poem telling a story of great deeds; a film with such a subject matter.

epicure /'epɪkjʊə'/ n one who takes great interest in the pleasures of eating and drinking. adj **epicurean** /ˌepɪkjʊ'riːən/ having to do with the teaching that what gives pleasure is good and what gives pain is evil.

epidemic /ˌepɪ'demɪk/ n disease that passes from one person to another very quickly.

epigram /'epɪgræm/ n a few words expressing a clever or amusing thought. adj **epigrammatic** /ˌepɪgrə'mætɪk/.

epilepsy /'epɪlepsɪ/ n disease causing one to fall down because of sudden loss of thought and feeling. adj **epileptic** /ˌepɪ'leptɪk/ having to do with, or caused by, epilepsy. n one suffering from this disease.

epilogue /'epɪlɒg/ n short speech given at the end of a play; end or finishing-off of a speech or book.

episcopal /ɪ'pɪskəpəl/ adj having to do with BISHOPS.

episode /'epɪsəʊd/ n account of one separate set of events in a play or book; one separate event (usually important) in a set of events. adj **episodic** /ˌepɪ'sɒdɪk/.

epistle /ɪ'pɪsəl/ n letter, usually long and important. adj **epistolary** /ɪ'pɪstələrɪ/.

epitaph /'epɪtɑːf/ n that which is written on a stone above a grave.

epithet /'epɪθet/ n word expressing some quality of a thing.

epitome /ɪ'pɪtəmɪ/ n very good example of something.

epoch /'iːpɒk/ n certain length of time during which a set of important events happened, such as would all be told together in one part of a history book, e.g. *The Great War begins a new epoch in history.* adj **epoch-making** /'iːpɒk ˌmeɪkɪŋ/ very important.

equable /'ekwəbəl/ adj steady; not changing suddenly; (of the weather in some place) never very hot nor very cold.

equal /'iːkwəl/ adj same in value, weight, size, etc. n person who is neither better nor worse than oneself. vt be equal to. n **equality** /ɪ'kwɒlɪtɪ/.

equanimity /ˌiːkwə'nɪmətɪ/ n calmness of mind.

equate /ɪ'kweɪt/ vt make equal; say that (two things) are of the same kind.

equation /ɪ'kweɪʒən/ n expression showing that two quantities are equal e.g. $x + 3y = 7$.

equator /ɪ'kweɪtɔ'/ n imaginary line round the middle of the earth, dividing the north half from the south half. adj **equatorial** /ˌekwə'tɔːrɪəl/.

equestrian /ɪ'kwestrɪən/ adj having to do with riding horses.

equilateral /ˌiːkwɪ'lætərəl/ adj (of a figure) having all sides equal.

equilibrium /ˌiːkwɪ'lɪbrɪəm/ n state in which a thing is held level or steady because there is equal weight on each side.

equine /'ekwaɪn/ adj having to do with horses.

equinox /'iːkwɪnɒks/ n either of those times in each year (about March 21st and September 22nd) when day and night are of equal length.

equip /ɪ'kwɪp/ vt supply with the necessary knowledge or instruments for doing certain special work. n **equipment** /ɪ'kwɪpmənt/ instruments or machinery needed for something.

equitable /'ekwɪtəbəl/ adj just; fair. n **equity** /'ekwətɪ/ justice; fairness. **equity shares** = ordinary shares in a business.

equivalent /ɪ'kwɪvələnt/ adj equal in value to. n **equivalence**.

equivocal /ɪ'kwɪvəkəl/ adj 1 of doubtful meaning. 2 (of a person) of doubtful character. vt **equivocate** /ɪ'kwɪvəkeɪt/ avoid expressing a clear meaning, so as to deceive another.

era /'ɪərə/ *n* time in history usually begun from some important event, e.g. the *Christian era* began with the birth of Christ.

eradicate /ɪ'rædɪkeɪt/ *vt* take out from the roots; destroy completely.

erase /ɪ'reɪz/ *vt* rub out, e.g. pencil marks. *n* **erasure** /ɪ'reɪʒə/ word rubbed out.

erect /ɪ'rekt/ *adj* upright; standing up on end. *vt* set up on end; build. *n* **erection** /ɪ'rekʃən/ **1** act of making or becoming erect; (of parts of the body) state of being erect. **2** building.

ermine /'ɜːmɪn/ *n* small animal which has thick white fur in winter, with a black end to its tail; fur of this animal.

erode /ɪ'rəʊd/ *v* wear away slowly, e.g. *The sea is eroding the land*. *n* **erosion** /ɪ'rəʊʒən/.

erotic /ɪ'rotɪk/ *adj* having to do with love or sex.

err /ɜː/ *vi* make a mistake; do what is wrong.

errand /'erənd/ *n* journey made to carry a message or to bring back something.

erratic /ɪ'rætɪk/ *adj* not regular in movement or behaviour.

erratum /e'rɑːtəm/ *n* mistake in printing or writing. (*pl*) **errata** /e'rɑːtə/.

erroneous /ɪ'rəʊnɪəs/ *adj* mistaken; not correct.

error /'erə/ *n* mistake; wrong idea.

erudite /'erʊdaɪt/ *adj* full of learning. *n* **erudition** /ˌerʊ'dɪʃən/.

erupt /ɪ'rʌpt/ *vi* break out or through, e.g. teeth through the skin inside the mouth, or fire and smoke from a mountain. *n* **eruption** /ɪ'rʌpʃən/.

escalator /'eskəleɪtə/ *n* set of stairs moved by a machine to save the trouble of walking up or down.

escapade /'eskəpeɪd/ *n* wild and exciting act; daring disobeying of rules.

escape /ɪ'skeɪp/ *v* get free from prison or from anything that takes away or threatens to take away one's freedom; avoid (something unpleasant). *n* act of escaping. **to escape one's notice** = not be noticed by one.

escapement /ɪ'skeɪpmənt/ *n* that part of a clock which keeps the clock running true to time.

escapist /ɪ'skeɪpɪst/ *n* person who tries not to face reality.

escarpment

escarpment /ɪ'skɑːpmənt/ *n* steep slope just below the wall of a fort.

eschew /ɪ'stʃuː/ *vt* keep away from something thought to be wrong.

escort /ɪ'skɔːt/ *vt* take (a woman) out; go along with to protect or in order to show the way. *n* /'eskɔːt/ **1** one who escorts another. **2** group of armed men or of warships protecting the journey of an unarmed group or ship.

escutcheon /ɪ'skʌtʃən/ *n* shield on which the signs of families are painted.

esoteric /ˌesə'terɪk/ *adj* having deep or secret meanings that can only be understood by some special group of persons.

especial /ɪ'speʃəl/ *adj* worthy of particular notice; particular.

espionage /'espɪənɑːʒ/ *n* secret work aimed at finding out about the war-plans, armies, etc., of foreign governments.

espouse /ɪ'spaʊz/ *vt* **1** marry. **2** decide to support (some idea or work).

espy /ɪ'spaɪ/ *vt* see, usually from a distance—or something hidden.

esquire /ɪ'skwaɪə/ *n* **1** one who looks after a knight. **2** polite way of addressing a man on a letter, e.g. *G. Smith, Esq*.

essay /'eseɪ/ *n* **1** an attempt. **2** short piece of writing on one subject. *vt* **essay** /e'seɪ/ make an attempt.

essence /'esəns/ *n* that which contains or shows the real nature of a thing; best of a thing with all the unnecessary parts taken away. *adj* **essential** /ɪ'senʃəl/ having to do with the real nature of; very necessary.

establish /ɪ'stæblɪʃ/ *vt* make firm; build up; prove. *n* **establishment** /ɪ'stæblɪʃmənt/ set of persons kept together for a certain purpose; building where they work.

estate /ɪ'steɪt/ *n* **1** all the money, goods, etc., that a man owns. **2** large country house and the land it stands in. *n* **estate agent** /.'. ,.. / man who arranges the buying and selling of houses.

housing estate = group of similar houses and the roads joining them.

esteem /ɪ'stiːm/ *vt* set a high value on; have a high opinion of.

estimable /'estɪməbəl/ *adj* worthy of respect.

estimate /'estɪmeɪt/ *vt* form an opinion about the value, cost, size of, etc. *n* **estimate** /'estɪmət/ account of the probable cost of doing a certain piece of work. *n* **estimation** /ˌestɪ'meɪʃən/ *In my estimation* = in my opinion.

estrange /ɪ'streɪndʒ/ *vt* cause to become unfriendly.

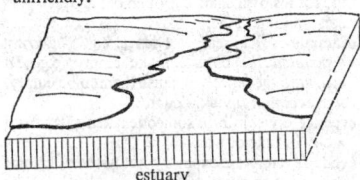

estuary

estuary /'estʃʊərɪ/ *n* broad mouth of a river into which the sea flows.

etcetera /ɪt'setərə/ *Latin* and the rest, and other things of the same kind.

etch /etʃ/ *vt* cut (a picture) with the help of acid into the surface of a metal plate so as to print from it. *n* **etching** picture so printed.

eternal /ɪ'tɜːnəl/ adj without beginning or end; lasting for ever. n eternity /ɪ'tɜːnɪtɪ/ time without end; life after death.

ether /'iːθə/ n gas used in medicine to make people sleep and lose all feeling.

ethereal /ɪ'θɪərɪəl/ adj very light, like air; like a spirit or fairy.

ethics /'eθɪks/ n study of right and wrong in human behaviour. adj ethical /'eθɪkəl/.

ethnic /'eθnɪk/ adj having to do with a race of people. n ethnology /eθ'nɒlədʒɪ/ study of the races of man.

etiquette /'etɪket/ n (sing) rule of good behaviour.

etymology /ˌetɪ'mɒlədʒɪ/ n study of the history of words; history of a particular word.

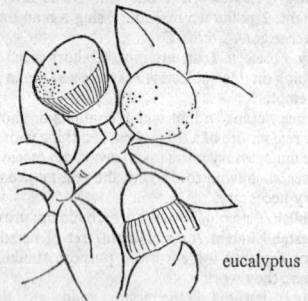

eucalyptus

eucalyptus /ˌjuːkə'lɪptəs/ n tree that produces a strong-smelling oil used in medicine.

eugenics /juː'dʒenɪks/ n improvement of the human race or the quality of animals by care in choosing the fathers and mothers.

eulogy /'juːlədʒɪ/ n speech or writing praising some person or thing.

eunuch /'juːnək/ n man so treated that he cannot become a father.

euphemism /'juːfəmɪzəm/ n pleasant way of saying an unpleasant truth, e.g. 'He is rather excited'—meaning that he has drunk too much. adj euphemistic /ˌjuːfə'mɪstɪk/.

euthanasia /ˌjuːθə'neɪzɪə/ n taking of someone's life for his own sake, e.g. of an old and sick person wanting to die.

evacuate /ɪ'vækjʊeɪt/ vt 1 leave, e.g. The army evacuated the city. 2 make empty, e.g. To evacuate the bowels = cause them to be empty. n evacuation /ɪˌvækjʊ'eɪʃən/.

evacuee /ɪˌvækjʊ'iː/ n someone taken away from a city in time of war.

evade /ɪ'veɪd/ vt escape; try not to meet; try not to answer (a question).

evanescent /ˌiːvə'nesənt/ adj quickly disappearing.

evangelist /ɪ'vændʒəlɪst/ n 1 one who takes the Christian religion to non-Christians. 2 writer of one of the four books of the Bible which tell the life of Christ. adj evangelical /ˌiːvæn'dʒelɪkəl/ having to do with the books of the Bible telling of Christ's life; basing one's religious beliefs closely on what is contained in those books.

evaporate /ɪ'væpəreɪt/ vt change (a liquid) into a gas. vi (of a liquid) turn into gas. n evaporation /ɪˌvæpə'reɪʃən/.

evasion /ɪ'veɪʒən/ n act of EVADING. adj evasive /ɪ'veɪsɪv/.

eve /iːv/ n 1 evening. 2 day before something, e.g. Christmas Eve; time just before an important event, e.g. On the eve of a great discovery.

even¹ /'iːvən/ adj 1 not rough, e.g. An even surface. 2 regular; not changing, e.g. Even-tempered = calm, not easily made angry. 3 (of a number) that can be divided by 2.

even² /'iːvən/ adv though one might not have expected as much, e.g. I even gave him my own shoes. even if = although.

evening /'iːvnɪŋ/ n first few hours of darkness.

event /ɪ'vent/ n anything that happens; important happening. in the event of (his death) = if (he dies). at all events = whatever happens.

eventual /ɪ'ventʃʊəl/ adj happening as a result; last.

ever /'evə/ 1 at any time. 2 Ever gives force to a word or group of words, e.g. Ever so much = very much; What ever do you mean? = I cannot imagine what you mean.

evergreen /'evəgriːn/ adj, n (tree or plant) that does not lose its leaves in winter.

every /'evrɪ/ det each. every now and again = from time to time. pron everybody /'evrɪbɒdɪ/, everyone /'evrɪwʌn/ every person. adj everyday /'evrɪdeɪ/ not for special occasions; found or used every day. pron everything /'evrɪθɪŋ/ every thing. adv. everywhere /'evrɪweə/ in all places.

evict /ɪ'vɪkt/ vt make (someone) go out of a house (or off land) by using the power of the law. n eviction /ɪ'vɪkʃən/.

evidence /'evɪdəns/ n anything that helps to prove a fact.

evident /'evɪdənt/ adj plain and clear to the mind.

evil /'iːvəl/ adj bad; harmful.

evince /ɪ'vɪns/ vt show (feeling).

evoke /ɪ'vəʊk/ vt call forth; produce.

evolution /ˌiːvə'luːʃən/ n way in which simple forms of life, by slow changes, grow into other higher forms of life, e.g. man is said to have evolved from a kind of monkey; any similar set of changes resulting in the improvement of something.

evolve /ɪ'vɒlv/ vi change by EVOLUTION.

ewe /juː/ n female sheep.

ewer /'jʊə/ n large water-pot with a handle.

ex- /eks/ formerly but not now, e.g. Ex-king = one who has ceased to be a king.

exacerbate /ɪg'zæsəbeɪt/ vt make worse or more bitter.

exact /ɪg'zækt/ adj correct. vt make someone pay (money). adj exacting /ɪg'zæktɪŋ/ demanding much work or care. exactly = that is just what I think. n exactitude /ɪg'zæktɪtjuːd/ great care in being correct.

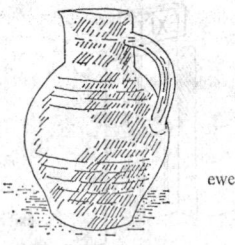

ewer

exaggerate /ɪg'zædʒəreɪt/ v say that (something) is larger (better, etc.) than it is; add to the true facts. n **exaggeration** /ɪg,zædʒə'reɪʃən/.

exalt /ɪg'zɔːlt/ vt raise in rank; praise. n **exaltation** /,egzɔːl'teɪʃən/ state of great excitement and of pleasure at one's own skill, cleverness or good fortune. adj **exalted** /ɪg'zɔːltɪd/ high; noble.

examine /ɪg'zæmɪn/ vt 1 look at and consider carefully. 2 question (e.g. a school-child). 3 question a man in a court of law. n **examination** /ɪg,zæmɪ'neɪʃən/ 1 act of examining someone or something. 2 school question papers. n **examinee** /ɪg,zæmɪ'niː/ person being examined, e.g. in a school or university.

example /ɪg'zɑːmpəl/ n 1 particular event or thing that shows the meaning of some general rule. 2 one thing that shows what others are like, e.g. An example of his painting. 3 thing to be copied, e.g. To set a good example = behave so well that others may perhaps do the same.

exasperate /ɪg'zæspəreɪt/ vt excite anger in (someone).

excavate /'ekskəveɪt/ v dig; uncover what has been covered by earth, e.g. an ancient city. n **excavation** /,ekskə'veɪʃən/.

exceed /ɪk'siːd/ vt go beyond (what is necessary or allowed); be greater, faster, or better than. adv **exceedingly** /ɪk'siːdɪŋlɪ/ very greatly.

excel /ɪk'sel/ vi be better than others; have the highest qualities. n **excellence** /'eksələns/ state of being very good. **Your Excellency**, form of address to high officers of government, e.g. the Governor. adj **excellent** /'eksələnt/ very good.

except /ɪk'sept/ vt leave out. prep not including. n **exception** /ɪk'sepʃən/ act of not counting something; a thing that is not counted or not covered by the rule. **to take exception to** = disagree with; be angry at. adj **exceptional** /ɪk'sepʃənəl/ unusual; better than usual.

excerpt /'eksɜːpt/ n short piece of writing taken out of a book.

excess /ɪk'ses/ n the amount beyond what is right or necessary, e.g. Excess baggage = that weight of bags, boxes, etc., beyond what is allowed free to a traveller by train, etc., on which he has to pay. adj **excessive** /ɪk'sesɪv/ too great, e.g. Excessive caution.

exchange /ɪks'tʃeɪndʒ/ vt give (something) and receive something else for it. **stock exchange** =

place where money, shares in businesses, companies, etc., are bought and sold. **telephone exchange** = central place where all the telephone wires are joined so that people may speak to each other.

exchequer /ɪks'tʃekə/ n that part of the government which deals with public money.

excise /'eksaɪz/ n money that must be paid to the government on certain goods produced in the country, e.g. wine and strong drink.

excite /ɪk'saɪt/ vt make active; cause strong feeling in. n **excitement** /ɪk'saɪtmənt/.

exclaim /ɪks'kleɪm/ vt cry out suddenly; speak with strong feelings. n **exclamation** /,eksklə'meɪʃən/ act of crying out; word or words spoken suddenly with strong feeling, e.g. "Oh, how terrible!" adj **exclamatory** /ɪks'klæmətərɪ/.

exclude /ɪks'kluːd/ vt not include; shut out. n **exclusion** /ɪk'skluːʒən/. adj **exclusive** /ɪks'kluːsɪv/ shutting out; kept for a special class, e.g. An exclusive school = one that takes in only the children of well-known or rich people.

excommunicate /,ekskə'mjuːnɪkeɪt/ vt take away the special rights of (a member of the Christian Church).

excrement /'ekskrəmənt/ n waste matter passed out of the body.

excrescence /ɪks'kresəns/ n out-growth; unnatural growth on the surface.

excrete /ɪks'kriːt/ vt separate and pass out, e.g. The body excretes waste matter.

excruciating /ɪks'kruːʃieɪtɪŋ/ adj (of pain) very great.

exculpate /'ekskʌlpeɪt/ vt free from blame.

excursion /ɪks'kɜːʃən/ n short journey made for pleasure.

excuse /ɪks'kjuːz/ vt free from blame or duty; forgive. n /ɪks'kjuːs/ reason given when asking to be forgiven.

execrable /'eksɪkrəbəl/ adj very bad; worthy of being cursed. vt **execrate** /'eksɪkreɪt/ curse.

execute /'eksɪkjuːt/ vt 1 carry out (e.g. orders, a plan). 2 put to death by order of the law. n **execution** /,eksɪ'kjuːʃən/ 1 way in which work is carried out. 2 act of putting to death. n **executioner** /,eksɪ'kjuːʃənə/ man who kills people by order of the law. adj **executive** /ɪg'zekjʊtɪv/ carrying into effect. n man who has charge of a business. n **executor** /ɪg'zekjʊtə/ person appointed to carry out a dead person's last wishes.

exemplary /ɪg'zemplərɪ/ adj worthy of being copied.

exemplify /ɪg'zemplɪfaɪ/ vt show by example.

exempt /ɪg'zempt/ vt make free from, e.g. To exempt someone from service in the army. n **exemption** /ɪg'zempʃən/.

exercise /'eksəsaɪz/ n 1 use of any part of the body in order to strengthen it, e.g. Voice exercises; also such use of the mind, e.g. An exercise

exercise (n1)

exit

in clear thinking. **2** piece of work set to a learner or school-child, e.g. *A French exercise. v* use; make stronger or better by use; move (parts of the body) quickly or against PRESSURE etc., so as to strengthen them or make one fit.

exert /ɪg'zɜːt/ *vt* use (strength or force). **to exert oneself** = try hard. *n* **exertion** /ɪg'zɜːʃən/.

exhale /ɪks'heɪl/ *v* breathe out. *n* **exhalation** /ˌekshə'leɪʃən/ act of breathing out; air breathed out; mist or steam.

exhaust /ɪg'zɔːst/ *vt* **1** use up completely; finish. **2** make very tired or weak. *n* burnt gas that is passed out of an engine. *n* **exhaustion** /ɪg'zɔːstʃən/. *adj* **exhaustive** /ɪg'zɔːstɪv/ complete, leaving no part unfinished.

exhibit /ɪg'zɪbɪt/ *vt* show; put in a public place for people to look at. *n* **exhibition** /ˌeksɪ'bɪʃən/ act of exhibiting something; thing exhibited. **to make an exhibition of oneself** = to make oneself appear very foolish. *n* **exhibitionist** /ˌeksɪ'bɪʃənɪst/ person who tries to make other people look at him (her), e.g. by showy or strange dress or behaviour.

exhilarate /ɪg'zɪləreɪt/ *vt* cause (someone) to have joyful feelings; make (someone) feel fresh and strong. *n* **exhilaration** /ɪgˌzɪlə'reɪʃən/.

exhort /ɪg'zɔːt/ *vt* urge; advise strongly, e.g. to do good. *n* **exhortation** /ˌegzɔː'teɪʃən/.

exhume /ɪks'hjuːm/ *vt* take (a body) out of a grave.

exigency /ek'sɪdʒənsɪ/ *n* **1** such a state of things as demands that some action be taken at once, e.g. some great danger. **2** state of being very poor.

exile /'eksaɪl/ *vt* send (someone) out of his own country as a punishment. *n* this form of punishment; person so punished.

exist /ɪg'zɪst/ *vi* be; have life. *n* **existence** /ɪg'zɪstəns/.

exit /'eksɪt, 'egzɪt/ *n* door for going out; act of going out.

exodus /'eksədəs/ *n* outward march of many people, e.g. of the Jews from Egypt.

exonerate /ɪg'zɒnəreɪt/ *vt* free from blame.

exorbitant /ɪg'zɔːbɪtənt/ *adj* (of a price, demand, etc.) far too great.

exorcize /'eksɔːsaɪz/ *vt* drive out evil spirits from.

exotic /ɪg'zɒtɪk/ *adj* strange, foreign.

expand /ɪk'spænd/ *v* make or become larger. *n* **expanse** /ɪk'spæns/ wide stretch of land, water,

etc. *n* **expansion** /ɪk'spænʃən/. *adj* **expansive** /ɪk'spænsɪv/ large; (of a person) expressing his thoughts and feelings freely.

expatiate /ɪk'speɪʃɪeɪt/ *vi* speak or write at length about something.

expatriate /ɪks'pætrɪət/ *n, adj* (person) driven from his own country.

expect /ɪk'spekt/ *vt* **1** think that (something) will probably happen. **2** wait for a visit from (someone). *adj* **expectant** /ɪk'spektənt/ **1** expecting something. **2** soon to give birth to a child. *n* **expectation** /ˌekspek'teɪʃən/.

expedient /ɪk'spiːdɪənt/ *adj* (of an action) well fitted to a certain state of things, or wise at a certain time; not right, but useful. *n* **expediency** /ɪk'spiːdɪənsɪ/ thinking of what is useful or helpful, rather than of what is right.

expedite /'ekspɪdaɪt/ *vt* make go faster; send quickly.

expedition /ˌekspɪ'dɪʃən/ *n* march of a body of soldiers to make war in some place; journey for the purpose of discovery, etc.; quickness. *adj* **expeditious** /ˌekspɪ'dɪʃəs/ quick.

expel /ɪk'spel/ *vt* drive out, e.g. *To expel from a school* = make (a pupil) leave a school because of bad behaviour.

expletive /ɪk'spliːtɪv/ *n* meaningless word, often thought to be rude, spoken in anger.

explicit /ɪk'splɪsɪt/ *adj* clearly and fully expressed.

explode /ɪk'spləʊd/ *v* burst or cause to burst with a loud noise.

exploit /'eksplɔɪt/ *n* great deed. /ɪk'splɔɪt/ *vt* **1** make full use of, e.g. *To exploit the coal and iron fields.* **2** make unfair use of, e.g. *To exploit the poor and helpless by making them work for very low pay. n* **exploitation** /ˌeksplɔɪ'teɪʃən/.

explore /ɪk'splɔː/ *v* to search into; to travel through a strange country and learn about it. *n* **exploration** /ˌeksplə'reɪʃən/. *adj* **exploratory** /ɪk'splɒrətərɪ/.

explosion /ɪk'spləʊʒən/ *n* act of exploding. *n* **explosive** /ɪk'spləʊsɪv/ substance used to cause explosions.

exponent /ek'spəʊnənt/ *n* one who explains the meaning; example.

export /ɪk'spɔːt/ *v* send (goods) to other countries. /'ekspɔːt/ *n* something exported.

expend /ɪk'spend/ *vt* spend time, money, etc.; use

up (e.g. one's strength) in doing something. *n*
expenditure /ɪk'spendɪtʃə/ spending of money,
money spent.

expense /ɪk'spens/ *n* money spent; cost. **at the
expense of** = with the loss of, causing the loss
of. *adj* **expensive** /ɪk'spensɪv/ costing a lot of
money.

experience /ɪk'spɪərɪəns/ *n* **1** knowledge or skill
gained by practice or by living; events which
have given one such knowledge or skill. **2**
knowledge gained through the senses. *vt* feel,
see, or hear, etc.

experiment /ɪk'sperɪmənt/ *n* scientific work to see
if an idea is correct. *vi* do such work.

expert /'ekspɜːt/ *n* one who has special
knowledge or power obtained by practice; *adj*
skilful, practised.

expertise /ˌekspə'tiːz/ *n* special knowledge and
judgment about a certain subject.

expiate /'ekspɪeɪt/ *vt* pay for (a wrong act) by
suffering the full punishment.

expire /ɪk'spaɪə/ *vi* die; come to an end.

explain /ɪk'spleɪn/ *vt* tell the meaning of; give
reasons for. *n* **explanation** /ˌeksplə'neɪʃən/. *adj*
explanatory /ɪk'splænətərɪ/.

expose /ɪk'spəʊz/ *vt* uncover; lay open to the
effects of, e.g *To expose one's skin to the
sunlight*; show the true character of.

exposé /ek'spəʊzeɪ/ *n* piece of writing, film, etc.,
making known a secret wrongdoing.

exposition /ˌekspə'zɪʃən/ *n* **1** explaining of a
thing. **2** act of putting goods out for the public
to see; collection of things so shown.

expostulate /ɪk'spɒstʃʊleɪt/ *vi* reason with a person and urge a different idea.

exposure /ɪk'spəʊʒə/ *n* state of being exposed,
esp. state of the body's being exposed for a long
time to cold air, as a cause of suffering or death.

expound /ɪk'spaʊnd/ *vt* explain clearly.

express /ɪk'spres/ *vt* say or show clearly. *adj* **1**
clearly said, e.g. *He did it for this express purpose* = he did it for this reason, and he said
clearly that this was the reason. **2** fast, e.g. *An
express train*. *n* **expression** /ɪk'spreʃən/ **1** particular set of words, e.g. *He used some very rude
expressions*. **2** use of the voice in showing
feelings, e.g. *She sang with great expression* =
she sang showing great feeling in her voice. **3**
appearance or look of the face as showing
feelings. *adj* **expressive** /ɪk'spresɪv/.

expropriate /eks'prəʊprɪeɪt/ *vt* take away (a thing
possessed).

expulsion /ɪk'spʌlʃən/ *n* act of driving out, e.g. a
bad child from school.

expunge /ek'spʌndʒ/ *vt* rub out (a word).

expurgate /'ekspəgeɪt/ *vt* take out what is thought
to be bad or dirty from (a book) so as to make
the book fit for children.

exquisite /ɪk'skwɪzɪt, 'ekskwɪzɪt/ *adj* carefully
chosen; very fine and beautiful.

extant /ek'stænt/ *adj* still standing; still living;
not destroyed.

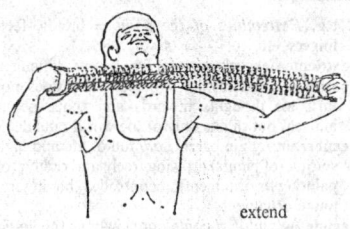

extend

extend /ɪk'stend/ *v* stretch out; make longer or
larger. *n* **extension** /ɪk'stenʃən/ act of extending
something; part built on to a house. *adj* **exten-
sive** /ɪk'stensɪv/ stretching a long way; wide. *n*
extent /ɪk'stent/ size; distance a thing stretches.

extenuate /ɪk'stenjʊeɪt/ *vt* weaken; make (a fault)
seem less bad.

exterior /ɪk'stɪərɪə/ *n, adj* outside.

exterminate /ɪk'stɜːmɪneɪt/ *vt* destroy (all, e.g.
animals of a certain kind).

external /ɪk'stɜːnəl/ *adj* having to do with the outside; foreign.

extinct /ɪk'stɪŋkt/ *adj* dead; no longer found
alive, e.g. *Extinct animals* = animals of ancient
times. *n* **extinction** /ɪk'stɪŋkʃən/.

extinguish /ɪk'stɪŋgwɪʃ/ *vt* put out (e.g. fire with
water). **fire extinguisher** = instrument for putting out fire.

extol /ɪk'stəʊl/ *vt* praise very highly.

extort /ɪk'stɔːt/ *vt* obtain unjustly or by force, e.g.
*He extorted a promise from me; The king
extorted money from his people*. *adj* **extor-
tionate** /ɪk'stɔːʃənət/ demanding too much
(money).

extra /'ekstrə/ *n* something added. *adv* more than
usual.

extra- /'ekstrə/ outside, e.g. *Extra-mural* = outside the walls.

extract /ɪk'strækt/ *vt* pull or draw out; take out
(part of a book) as an example of what the book
contains. *n* **extract** /'ekstrækt/ part taken out;
the purest form of anything, e.g. *Extract of
meat* = best part of meat obtained by boiling it
down to a liquid.

extradite /'ekstrədaɪt/ *vt* send (someone) back to
his own country.

extraneous /ɪk'streɪnɪəs/ *adj* foreign; not
belonging to the special group being studied,
spoken of, etc.

extraordinary /ɪk'strɔːdənrɪ/ *adj* unusual;
causing wonder because greater (better, etc.)
than usual.

extravagant /ɪk'strævəgənt/ *adj* wasteful; spending money foolishly. *n* **extravagance**
/ɪk'strævəgəns/.

extreme /ɪk'striːm/ *n* the very end of anything,
e.g. farthest, lowest, best, worst, least, etc. *adj* of
the extreme; very great. *n* **extremist**
/ɪk'striːmɪst/ one who holds extreme opinions. *n*
extremity /ɪk'stremətɪ/ last or farthest point,

e.g. *Extremities of the body* = hands, feet, fingers, etc.

extricate /'ekstrɪkeɪt/ vt set free from a difficulty.

extrovert /'ekstrəvɜːt/ n person who does not turn his thoughts inwards and think about himself, but thinks only of the world outside.

exuberant /ɪg'zjuːbərənt/ adj full of life and high spirits; (of plants) growing freely and richly; (of painting or ornament) uncontrolled, having too much ornament.

exude /ɪg'zjuːd/ vi come out slowly as the liquid through the skin when one is hot.

exult /ɪg'zʌlt/ vi show great joy; feel proud of having done something. adj **exultant** /ɪg'zʌltənt/.

eye /aɪ/ n 1 that part of the body with which we see. 2 any small hole. 3 power of knowing the value of, e.g. *An eye for beauty.* 4 spot, e.g. on some vegetable roots. **to see eye to eye** = agree on all points. **to make eyes at** = look lovingly at. vt look at angrily or with desire. n **eyebrow** /'aɪbraʊ/ the hair above the eye. n **eyelash** /'aɪlæʃ/ hair on the edge of the EYELID.

eyelet /'aɪlət/ n hole with a metal ring round it, e.g. in a shoe; any small hole, e.g. in cloth.

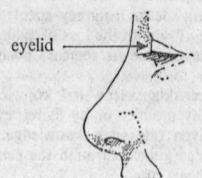

eyelid

eyelid /'aɪlɪd/ n cover that comes down over the eye.

eye-opener /'. ,. ./ n anything that causes great surprise.

eyesight /'aɪsaɪt/ n power of seeing. **within eyesight** = near enough to be seen.

eyesore /'aɪsɔː/ n any very ugly or unpleasant thing.

eye-witness /'. ,. ./ n one who himself saw an event happen.

F

fable /'feɪbəl/ n story teaching about good behaviour; fanciful story of something that could not happen, e.g. fairy-story.

fabric /'fæbrɪk/ n material made into cloth; material used for making or building things.

fabricate /'fæbrɪkeɪt/ vt make up or put together, e.g. *To fabricate an untrue story.* n **fabrication** /ˌfæbrɪ'keɪʃən/.

fabulous /'fæbjʊləs/ adj 1 concerned with FABLES; impossible to believe. 2 *infml* very good; very pleasant.

façade (1)

façade /fə'sɑːd/ n 1 outside face of a building. 2 deceiving appearance.

face /feɪs/ n 1 front of the head containing eyes, mouth, etc. 2 front of anything. **on the face of it** = judging by outward appearances only. **make a face** or **pull a face** = cause one's face to become ugly by moving the mouth, eyes, etc. **to save (one's) face** = pretend that one has succeeded when one has failed. vt look towards; stand opposite to; stand bravely against. **face up to** = accept (an unpleasant fact), not pretend that it is not so. n **face value** /ˌ. '. ./ value marked on a piece of money, stamp, etc., not always its real value.

facet /'fæsɪt/ n 1 small flat side, e.g. on a precious stone. 2 part of a subject or way of looking at something, e.g. *Another facet of the same problem.*

facetious /fə'siːʃəs/ adj trying to be amusing.

facial /'feɪʃəl/ adj of the face.

facile /'fæsaɪl/ adj too easily done; careless; lacking thought or real understanding.

facilitate /fə'sɪləteɪt/ vt make (work) easier to do.

facility /fə'sɪlətɪ/ n 1 easiness; special skill. 2 (often pl) something provided for one to use, e.g. necessary equipment for work.

facsimile /fæk'sɪmɪlɪ/ n exact copy.

fact /fækt/ n something done, e.g. *Before or after the fact;* something that has really happened, or that is really true. **in fact** or **in point of fact** = really. **as a matter of fact** = to tell you the truth.

faction /'fækʃən/ n group that quarrels with, and will not work with, others. adj **factious** /'fækʃəs/.

factor /'fæktə/ n 1 that which helps to produce a result, e.g. *Rain and heat are factors in growing food.* 2 a number that divides into another number exactly, e.g. *2 and 3 are factors of 6.*

factory /'fæktərɪ/ n building in which things are made, usually by machines.

factual /'fæktʃʊəl/ adj concerned with facts; using only the facts.

faculty /'fækəltɪ/ n 1 power of doing anything, e.g. *A person's faculties* = powers of hearing, seeing, thinking, etc. 2 part of a university, e.g. *The Faculty of Medicine* = those teachers in a university who teach medicine.

fad /fæd/ n custom or interest that lasts only a short time; foolish or unreasonable practice.

fade /feɪd/ v lose or cause to lose colour, brightness, or strength.

fag /fæg/ sl vt make tired. n 1 anything one does not want to do because it is tiring or uninteresting. 2 cigarette.

faggot /'fægət/ n 1 number of small sticks tied together for burning. 2 a kind of RISSOLE.

Fahrenheit /'færənhaɪt/ adj way of measuring heat in which the freezing point of water is 32 degrees and the boiling point is 212 degrees.

fail /feɪl/ v not to succeed; lose power or health; lose all one's money in business. **do not fail me** = keep your promise to me, do not deceive me. n **failing** /'feɪlɪŋ/ weakness, e.g. A failing for drink = desire to drink too much. n **failure** /'feɪljə/ act of not succeeding, e.g. Failure to report = not reporting when one ought.

faint /feɪnt/ adj lacking in strength; not bright; difficult to hear, see, etc. vi experience a sudden loss of all feeling caused by illness or shock. n this experience. adj **faint-hearted** /ˌfeɪnt'hɑːtɪd/ having little courage.

fair[1] /feə/ adj 1 beautiful. 2 clean, e.g. A fair copy. 3 just. **fair play** = honest behaviour. 4 good, but not very good, e.g. A fair chance of success. **a fair amount** = some but not a lot. 5 fine; calm, e.g. Fair weather. 6 light coloured, e.g. Fair hair. adv **fairly** /'feəlɪ/ e.g. Fairly well = well, but not very well.

fair[2] /feə/ n gathering of people at a special time and place to buy and sell or to see strange things and amuse themselves.

fairy /'feərɪ/ n imaginary small beautiful creature supposed to have more than human powers.

faith /feɪθ/ n belief based on trust; religious belief. adj **faithful** /'feɪθfəl/ 1 loyal, e.g. to one's wife or to a group one is part of. 2 having faith in something.

fake /feɪk/ vt change a thing so as to make it look like the real thing. n, adj (something) pretending to be what it is not.

falcon

falcon /'fɔːlkən/ n meat-eating bird used to catch other birds for a hunter. n **falconry** /'fɔːlkənrɪ/ hunting birds with falcons.

fall /fɔːl/ vi 1 to drop from a higher to a lower place. 2 become less, e.g. Prices are falling. 3 yield, e.g. The Greeks attacked Troy and the city fell. n act of falling; distance fallen. infml to **fall for** = 1 be charmed by and yield. 2 fall in love with. **to fall out (with)** = have a quarrel (with). **to fall through** = (e.g. of a plan) to fail.

fallacy /'fæləsɪ/ n untrue idea; that which deceives the eye or mind. adj **fallacious** /fə'leɪʃəs/.

fallen /'fɔːlən/ p.p. of **fall**.

fallible /'fæləbəl/ adj likely to make mistakes.

fallow /'fæləʊ/ adj 1 light brown. 2 (of land) which has been prepared for seed and left for a year. **to lie fallow** = to rest.

false /fɔːls/ adj wrong; not true; not faithful or loyal. n **falsehood** /'fɔːlshʊd/ untruth.

falsetto /fɔːl'setəʊ/ n, adv (in a) high voice such as a man uses when trying to sing like a woman.

falsify /'fɔːlsɪfaɪ/ vt 1 show to be or make untrue. 2 change (e.g. a story) to make it untrue. n **falsification** /ˌfɔːlsɪfɪ'keɪʃən/.

falter /'fɔːltə/ vi speak unsteadily, as if afraid; walk unsteadily.

fame /feɪm/ n good name; state of being known by all.

familiar /fə'mɪlɪə/ adj well-known; seen often; friendly. vt **familiarize** /fə'mɪlɪəraɪz/ make (someone) familiar with something.

family /'fæməlɪ/ n father, mother and children; children of two parents; group of people having a common parent in the past; any group of similar or related things (e.g. plants).

famine /'fæmɪn/ n state of many people having no food.

famished /'fæmɪʃt/ adj very hungry.

famous /'feɪməs/ adj well known, e.g. because of having done great things.

fan /fæn/ n 1 instrument for moving the air, or for sending a stream of air in a certain direction. 2 admirer of an actor, singer, etc. vt drive air towards.

fanatic /fə'nætɪk/ n one who has a fierce belief in some opinion, and is unable to understand reason or common sense on that subject. adj **fanatical** /fə'nætɪkəl/.

fancy /'fænsɪ/ n imagination; something imagined. vt feel like; want; like. adj ornamented; intended to be specially pretty. **fancy dress** = clothing worn to dress up as something special that one is not, e.g. a fairy princess, for amusement at parties, etc. infml **to fancy oneself** = have a high opinion of oneself. adj **fanciful** /'fænsɪfəl/.

fanfare /'fænfeə/ n noise of blowing TRUMPETS, e.g. when an important person arrives; piece of music intended to have a similar effect.

fang /fæŋ/ n long sharp pointed tooth.

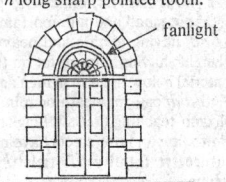

fanlight

fanlight /'fænlaɪt/ n window shaped like a FAN, usually above a door.

fantastic

fantastic /fæn'tæstɪk/ *adj* **1** strange; unreal and impossible. **2** *infml* very good.

fantasy /'fæntəsɪ/ *n* strange idea; strange and unusual piece of writing or music.

far /fɑː/ *adv* **1** not near; at a distance. **2** very much (better, etc.), e.g. *Far stronger* = much stronger. **far and away the best** = easily the best. **few and far between** = not often found. *adj* distant.

farce /fɑːs/ *n* play meant only to make people laugh; anything very foolish causing laughter. *adj* **farcical** /'fɑːsɪkəl/.

fare /feə/ *vi archaic* go, e.g. *He fared forth* = went out. **it fared ill with him** = he was unsuccessful. *n* **1** cost of a journey. **2** food. **a bill of fare** = list of foods in a hotel.

farewell /ˌfeə'wel/ *n, interj* good-bye.

far-fetched /ˌfɑː'fetʃt/ *adj* unreasonable; foolish.

farinaceous /ˌfærɪ'neɪʃəs/ *adj* (of food) made of flour.

farm /fɑːm/ *n* piece of land used for growing corn, vegetables, feeding cattle, etc. *v* keep and use (land) as a farm. **to farm out the work** = give it to several people to do. **farmer** /'fɑːmə/ *n* one who owns or works a farm. **farmstead** /'fɑːmsted/ *n* farmhouse and buildings near it. **far-seeing** /ˌ. '. ./, **far-sighted** *adj* wise and thinking of the future.

farther /'fɑːðə/ *adj, adv* more distant.

fascinate /'fæsɪneɪt/ *vt* charm; hold the interest of. *n* **fascination** /ˌfæsɪ'neɪʃən/.

fascist /'fæʃɪst/ *n* member of a group that does not believe in government by elected persons, but wants the country to be ruled by one leader.

fashion /'fæʃən/ *n* **1** way in which a thing is made; manner. **after a fashion** = not very well. **after the fashion of** = like. **2** that way of dressing or behaving which is considered the best at a certain time, e.g. *Short skirts were the fashion in 1969. vt* shape, make. *adj* **fashionable** /'fæʃənəbəl/ according to the present fashion (esp. of clothes).

fast[1] /fɑːst/ *adj, adv* **1** quick(ly). **2** (of clock) showing a time later than the actual time.

fast[2] /fɑːst/ *vi* eat no food.

fast[3] /fɑːst/ *adj* firmly fixed; (of a colour) not fading. **fast asleep** = in a deep sleep.

fasten /'fɑːsən/ *v* make firm; fix on to. *n* **fastening** act of making firm; thing that makes firm, that holds things firmly together.

fastidious /fæ'stɪdɪəs/ *adj* difficult to please; too careful about small and unimportant things.

fat /fæt/ *adj* having a wide and heavy body for one's height; having a lot of fat on the body. *n* oily material below the skin in men and animals.

fatal /'feɪtl/ *adj* causing death or ruin. *n* **fatalism** /'feɪtəlɪzəm/ teaching that all things happen according to fate and one's acts have no effect on the future. *n* **fatality** /fə'tælətɪ/ death; a misfortune.

fate /feɪt/ *n* imaginary power which has settled everything that is to happen; future events so settled. *adj* **fateful** /'feɪtfəl/ full of the possibility of good or evil; very important.

father /'fɑːðə/ *n* **1** male parent. **2** (title of respect for a) priest. *vt* be the father of. *n* **father-in-law** /'. . . ./ father of one's wife (or husband).

fathom /'fæðəm/ *n* measure of six feet in length used in measuring depth of water. *vt* find out and understand.

fatigue /fə'tiːg/ *n* tiredness; tiring piece of work.

fatuity /fə'tjuːətɪ/ *n* foolishness. *adj* **fatuous** /'fætʃʊəs/.

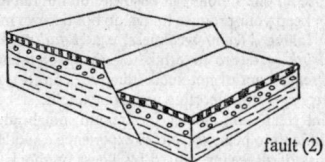

fault (2)

fault /fɔːlt/ *n* **1** mistake or failing; bad part in any material; weak place in one's character. **it's my fault** = I am to be blamed. **2** crack along which rock has moved up or down. *adj* **faulty** /'fɔːltɪ/ having faults.

faun /fɔːn/ *n* spirit of the woods, with the body of a man and the feet of a goat.

fauna /'fɔːnə/ *n* all the animals found in a certain place.

favour /'feɪvə/ *n* **1** feeling of kindness towards. **2** small act of kindness. *vt* **1** show kindness to. **2** show special kindness to one person of a group who should all be treated equally. **to be in favour of** = want; agree with. *adj* **favourable** /'feɪvərəbəl/ helpful; according to one's wishes. *adj, n* **favourite** /'feɪvərɪt/ (person or thing) that is especially loved.

fawn /fɔːn/ *n* young deer. *adj, n* (of a) yellow-brown colour.

fear /fɪə/ *n* feeling that one has when in danger; state of being very anxious. *vt* be afraid (of, or that something is the case). *adj* **fearful** /'fɪəfəl/ **1** afraid. **2** causing fear. *adj* **fearsome** /'fɪəsəm/ causing fear.

feasible /'fiːzəbəl/ *adj* able to be done.

feast /fiːst/ *n* day of special joy in honour of some past event; specially large meal. *vi* eat a feast. **to feast one's eyes on** = enjoy looking at.

feat /fiːt/ *n* act worthy of notice because of special difficulty, courage, etc.

feather

feather /'feðə/ *n* one of the light coverings that grow on a bird's body; any very light object like those on a bird's wing. **birds of a feather** = people of the same kind. **to feather one's nest** = get enough money to make oneself comfortable, get money dishonestly.

feature /'fi:tʃə/ *n* 1 one part of the face, e.g. nose, mouth, etc.; important or noticeable part of anything. 2 long piece written on a subject in a newspaper, etc. *vt* give an important place to. **feature film** = the long important film in a cinema show.

February /'febrʊərɪ/ *n* the second month of the year.

fed /fed/ *p.t.* and *p.p.* of **feed**. **fed up (with)** = tired (of) and angry (with).

federation /ˌfedə'reɪʃən/ *n* joining together of separate parts of a country to form one government, each state keeping control of some matters; similar joining together of business companies. *adj* **federal** /'fedərəl/.

fee /fi:/ *n* payment made for special services of any kind, e.g. *A doctor's fee.*

feeble /'fi:bəl/ *adj* having no strength.

feed /fi:d/ *vt* give food to. *vi* (esp. of animals) eat, e.g. *Cows feed on grass.* *n* food for animals.

feel /fi:l/ *vt* 1 have an experience of, e.g. *To feel cold.* 2 touch. 3 suffer, e.g. *I feel the cold* = I suffer from the cold weather. 4 understand or be moved by e.g. *I feel the beauty of his poem.* 5 have an opinion, e.g. *I feel that you are right.* **to feel like** = want. *n* **feelers** /'fi:ləz/ long thread-like things on the front of an insect's head. *n* **feeling** /'fi:lɪŋ/ something felt, e.g. anger, sorrow, love, etc.

feet /fi:t/ *pl* of **foot**.

feign /feɪn/ *vt* pretend.

feint /feɪnt/ *n* pretended blow or attack.

felicitate /fə'lɪsɪteɪt/ *vt* wish happiness to; show that one is pleased by another's good fortune.

felicitous /fə'lɪsɪtəs/ *adj* well expressed and suited to that special time.

felicity /fə'lɪsɪtɪ/ *n* state of being happy. **he expresses himself with great felicity** = using just the right words.

feline /'fi:laɪn/ *adj* like a cat; of cats.

fell[1] /fel/ *p.t.* of **fall**.

fell[2] /fel/ *vt* cut down (a tree); knock down (a man or animal).

fellah /'felə/ *n* worker on the land in Egypt or Syria. *pl* **fellahin** /ˌfelə'hi:n/.

fellow /'feləʊ/ *n* 1 *infml* man. 2 one who works, plays or studies (etc.) with another; an equal; member of any special group. **our fellow workers** = those who work with us.

felony /'felənɪ/ *n* serious breaking of the law, e.g. murder, burning a house, etc. *n* **felon** /'felən/ one who does such an act.

felt[1] /felt/ *p.t.* & *p.p.* of **feel**.

felt[2] /felt/ *n* material like thick cloth, made by pressing and sticking hair together, used to make hats.

female /'fi:meɪl/ *n* woman; a human, animal or bird which is able to produce eggs or young.

feminine /'femənɪn/ *adj* belonging to women; like a woman.

feminist /'femənɪst/ *n, adj* (someone) believing in equal rights for women and men.

fen /fen/ *n* flat low wet land.

fence[1] /fens/ *vi* practise fighting with swords; try not to give a straight answer to a question, turn a question aside.

fence[2] /fens/ *n* light wall of wood, or of wire stretched between poles, used to keep men and animals in (or out of) a field. *vt* put up a fence round.

fend /fend/ *vi* **to fend for** = care for; protect. **to fend off** = protect oneself from.

fender /'fendə/ *n* anything used to prevent damage caused by striking against another thing, e.g. mass of rope or wood put between a ship and the wall of the harbour; guard round the fireplace in a room.

ferment /fə'ment/ *vt* change the liquid of (fruits) into wine. *vi* (of this liquid) change into wine. *n* **ferment** /'fɜ:ment/ material which causes this change. **in a ferment** = very excited.

fern

fern /fɜ:n/ *n* flowerless green plant with leaves, with its seeds found on the backs of the leaves.

ferocious /fə'rəʊʃəs/ *adj* fierce; cruel.

ferret /'ferɪt/ *n* cat-like mammal used to hunt rabbits by going into their holes and driving them out. **to ferret out** = make a careful search into hidden or secret things.

ferrous /'ferəs/ *adj* containing or having to do with iron.

ferry /'ferɪ/ *n* boat that carries people across a river or other stretch of water. *vt* take across a river in a boat.

fertile /'fɜ:taɪl/ *adj* 1 (of land) producing much; fruitful. 2 able to bear children. *n* **fertility** /fə'tɪlətɪ/.

fertilize /'fɜ:tɪlaɪz/ *vt* cause to bear fruit. *n* **fertilizer** /'fɜ:tɪlaɪzə/ any material scattered on the earth in order to make it produce larger crops.

fervent /'fɜ:vənt/ *adj* eager; (of feeling) strong, e.g. *Fervent desire.*

fervid /'fɜ:vɪd/ *adj* burning; (of a person's mind) very keen. *n* **fervour** /'fɜ:və/.

festal /'festl/ *adj* having to do with a feast; gay.

fester /'festə/ *vi* (of a wound) become poisoned, decay; (of the feelings) become bitter and angry from a continued sense of wrong.

festival /'festɪvəl/ *n* feast-day; day of rejoicing. *adj* **festive** /'festɪv/.

festoon /fe'stu:n/ *n* ornament fixed at both ends and hanging in a curve, e.g. a paper chain or string of flags hung from one side of a room to the other. *vt* hang with festoons.

fetch /fetʃ/ *vt* go to another place and bring a thing from it. *adj* **fetching** /'fetʃɪŋ/ pleasing.

fête /feɪt/ *n* outdoor gathering for amusement, often where money is raised in various ways for a special purpose.

fetid /'fetɪd, 'fiːtɪd/ *adj* having a very bad smell.

fetish /'fetɪʃ/ *n* charm having magical powers; any object loved, or regarded as holy or as sexually exciting, in a foolish or unnatural manner.

fetter /'fetəʳ/ *n* chain for the feet, used on prisoners; anything that takes away one's freedom.

fettle /'fetl/ **in fine fettle** = in very good spirits.

feud /fju:d/ *n* long-continued quarrel between persons, families, or groups, usually resulting in killing.

feudal /'fju:dl/ *adj* (of a social system) in which social ranks are clearly separated, esp. one in which people hold land in return for services to the landowner (e.g. fighting in time of war).

fever /'fi:vəʳ/ *n* great heat in the body caused by disease; state of excitement. *adj* **feverish** /'fi:vərɪʃ/.

few /fju:/ *det, pron* not many. **a few** = some.

fez /fez/ *n* red cap with black threads hanging from the top as worn by many Muslims.

fiancé /fɪ'ɒnseɪ/ *n* man who is promised in marriage. *n* **fiancée** /fɪ'ɒnseɪ/ woman who is promised in marriage.

fiasco /fɪ'æskəʊ/ *n* foolish laughable failure.

fib /fɪb/ *n, vi infml* LIE, esp. if unimportant.

fibre /'faɪbəʳ/ *n* thread-like part of anything, e.g. wood, muscles, etc. *adj* **fibrous** /'faɪbrəs/.

fickle /'fɪkəl/ *adj* changeable; having no quality of faithfulness.

fiction /'fɪkʃən/ *n* anything that is only imagined, not a fact; story; art of writing stories. *adj* **fictitious** /fɪk'tɪʃəs/ made up; not real.

fiddle /'fɪdl/ *n* VIOLIN. **fit as a fiddle** = in perfect condition. *vi* play the fiddle; waste time doing useless things; play with any small object without thinking. *vt* cheat over (something).

fidelity /fɪ'delətɪ/ *n* faithfulness; (of a copy) exactness.

fidget /'fɪdʒɪt/ *vi* move restlessly because unable to sit or stand still. *n* one who fidgets.

field /fi:ld/ *n* **1** open country, e.g. *Beasts of the field.* **2** any large open space, esp. if covered by grass or grain etc. **3** part of a subject, e.g. *His interests lie in a different field.*

field day /'. ./ *n* day on which soldiers go into the country and practise fighting; any time of great activity.

field glasses /'. ,. ./ *n* (*pl*) instrument put to both eyes for seeing distant things.

field marshal /,. '. ./ *n* the highest officer in the army.

fiend /fi:nd/ *n* very evil or cruel person.

fierce /fɪəs/ *adj* cruel; wild; uncontrolled.

fiery /'faɪərɪ/ *adj* hot; quick-tempered.

fife /faɪf/ *n* small musical instrument for blowing.

fifteen /fɪf'ti:n/ *det, n* number following fourteen, often written **15**. *det, n* fifty /'fɪftɪ/ number often written **50**, being five times ten.

fifth /fɪfθ/ *adj* coming after the first four, e.g. *E is the fifth letter of the alphabet.*

fig

fig /fɪg/ *n* small fruit with many very small seeds in it.

fight /faɪt/ *v* struggle (against). *n* struggle.

figment /'fɪgmənt/ *n* something imagined or pretended.

figurative /'fɪgjʊrətɪv/ *adj* **1** (of a word or saying) not to be understood in its exact meaning, e.g. "He's as big as a house" = he is very big; "She's murdering that music" = playing it very badly. **2** having in it many such figures of speech.

figure /'fɪgəʳ/ *n* **1** form of the human body, esp. female, e.g. *She has a beautiful figure.* **2** stone, wood or metal cut into the shape of a man or animal. **3** picture or drawing, e.g. *A curtain ornamented with beautiful figures.* **a figure of speech** = a FIGURATIVE way of speaking. **4** a shape, e.g. one drawn for ornament in a book. **5** fixed set of steps in a dance. **6** written number, e.g. 1, 2, 3. *vi* appear; be important. **to figure out** = work out the answer to a question of figures; to add.

figurehead /'fɪgəhed/ *n* one whose name is used in a business, government, etc. but who has no real power.

filament /'fɪləmənt/ *n* very thin thread; thin metal thread used in an electric light.

filch /fɪltʃ/ *vt* steal.

file[1] /faɪl/ *vt* **1** arrange in order (e.g. letters, papers, etc.). *vi* walk in a straight line, one man behind another. *n* **1** box or other container in which letters, papers, etc. are kept in order. **2** a straight line of anything, e.g. soldiers. **single file** = one line of men walking one behind another. **the rank and file** = common soldiers; lower ranks in anything.

file[2] /faɪl/ *n* metal instrument with rough points on it used for making metals or wood smooth by rubbing. *vt* wear away by rubbing.

filial /'fɪlɪəl/ *adj* having to do with sons or daughters.

filigree /'fɪlɪgriː/ *n* ornamental work made of fine

gold or silver wire; any fine work that is open, so that one can see through it.

filings /'failıŋz/ n (pl) fine dust made when rubbing or cutting a piece of metal.

fill /fıl/ vt put into (a container) all that it will hold; make full; satisfy. **to fill out** = become fat. **to fill in** or **fill out** = write what is necessary in all the empty spaces in (a printed paper).

fillet /'fılıt/ n **1** thin band worn round the hair; thin band of wood or metal used as an ornament or to give strength. **2** thin piece of meat or fish without any bones in it. vt take the bones out of (fish or meat).

filly /'fılı/ n young female horse.

film /fılm/ n **1** thin skin or covering of any kind. **2** thin band used for making photographs. **3** long band of pictures used in a cinema show.

filter /'fıltə/ n instrument used to take all solid or impure matter out of liquids. vt take out (such matter) from liquid. vi flow in or out very slowly, e.g. *New ideas filter into people's minds.*

filth /fılθ/ n dirty matter. adj **filthy** /'fılθı/.

filtrate /'fıltreıt/ n liquid obtained by FILTERING.

fins

fin /fın/ n wing-like part on the backs and sides of sea animals, fish, etc., with which they swim.

final /'faınəl/ adj last; settling a question. n **finale** /fı'naːlı/ ending of a play, piece of music, etc. n **finality** /faı'nælıtı/ state of being settled and complete.

finance /'faınæns, fı'næns/ n science of controlling money, e.g. public money. vt provide the money for (a plan). adj **financial** /faı'nænʃəl, fı-/ having to do with money matters. n **financier** faı'nænsıə ͬ, fı-/ one who understands money matters; one who controls a large amount of money.

find /faınd/ vt **1** discover, e.g. *He found gold in Australia.* **2** get back a thing lost, e.g. *I found my pen in the bedroom.* **3** provide, e.g. *Find the money for starting a new school.* **4** decide or judge, e.g. *The court found the prisoner guilty.* **to find out** = learn or discover. n **finding** /'faındıŋ/ judgment, e.g. of a court.

fine¹ /faın/ n amount of money paid to a court of law as a punishment for breaking the law. vt demand such money of (someone).

fine² /faın/ adj **1** good; beautiful, e.g. *A fine day* = good weather. **2** thin, e.g. *A fine line; Fine dust; Fine cloth.*

finery /'faınərı/ n (sing) beautiful clothes and ornaments.

finesse /fı'nes/ n clever way of dealing with a difficult matter so that the purpose is gained without making anyone angry.

finger /'fıŋgə ͬ/ n one of the five end parts of either hand; anything similar in shape to this, or with a similar use, e.g. for pointing. vt. touch and rub with the fingers. n **fingerprint** /'fıŋgəˌprınt/ system of markings on the skin at the end of the finger.

finical /'fınıkəl/, **finicking** /'fınıkıŋ/, **finicky** /'fınıkı/ adj taking too much trouble about small unimportant matters; (of a thing) having many small parts, troublesome and difficult to use.

finish /'fınıʃ/ v come or bring to an end; make perfect. n end; something that completes a piece of work. **the table has a good finish** = it is well polished.

finite /'faınaıt/ adj having a beginning and an end; able to be counted, measured, etc.

fiord, fjord /fjɔːd/ n long opening from the sea with hills on each side.

fir /fɜː ͬ/ n a kind of tree that has needle-like leaves and long hard egg-shaped containers for seeds.

fire /faıə ͬ/ n **1** burning flames. **2** form of heating equipment, esp. by gas or electricity. vt **1** shoot (a gun). **2** *infml* end the services of (someone) working for one. **on fire** = burning.

firearm /'faıərɑːm/ n any gun that can be carried.

fire brigade /'. ˌ./ n special group of men, having necessary machines, who put out unwanted fires (e.g. burning houses) in a city.

fire engine /'. ˌ./ n machine for forcing water through a pipe to throw it on a burning building.

firefly /'faıəflaı/ n insect that gives out light from its body.

fireplace

fireplace /'faıəpleıs/ n part of a room in a house where coal or wood is burnt for warmth.

fireproof /'faıəpruːf/ adj that cannot be burned.

firework /'faıəwɜːk/ n stick made from gunpowder and other materials, which burns with beautiful colours, or bursts with a loud noise—or does both.

firm¹ /fɜːm/ adj solid; strong; steady. **to be firm with children** = make them obey.

firm² /fɜːm/ n business company.

firmament /'fɜːməmənt/ n sky.

first /fɜːst/ adj, adv (coming) before all others; earliest; most important. **from the first** = from the beginning. n **first aid** /ˌ. './ help given to one who is wounded, before the doctor arrives. adj **first-class** /ˌ. './ of the best quality. adj **first-hand** /ˌ. './ (of knowledge) that one has obtained by one's own ears, eyes, etc., not by being told by someone else. adj **first-rate** /ˌ. './ of the best kind.

firth /fɜːθ/ n mouth of a river.

fiscal

fiscal /'fɪskəl/ adj having to do with money, esp. the money paid to governments.

fish /fɪʃ/ n cold-blooded creature that lives in water. v catch (fish). **to fish for** = try to make a person give (something) without actually asking for it. n **fisherman** /'fɪʃəmən/ one who catches fish for a living. n **fishmonger** /'fɪʃˌmʌŋgə/ seller of fish. adj **fishy** /'fɪʃɪ/ **1** having to do with fish, esp. their smell. **2** infml of doubtful honesty.

fission /'fɪʃən/ n breaking into two parts.

fissure /'fɪʃə/ n crack.

fist /fɪst/ n hand when closed tight. **close-fisted, tight-fisted** /ˌ. '. ./ = very unwilling to spend money.

fit¹ /fɪt/ n sudden uncontrollable set of body movements, e.g. as caused by some illnesses; any state of uncontrolled movement, feeling, etc. **by fits and starts** = starting and stopping.

fit² /fɪt/ adj **1** proper; suitable. **2** healthy. vt be right for; be large enough, not too large (or small) for. adj **fitting** right; proper. n thing fitted on to another thing, e.g. *The inside fittings of a car.*

fitful /'fɪtfəl/ adj not regular: unsteady.

five /faɪv/ n, det number following four, often written 5.

fix /fɪks/ vt **1** make firm; prevent from being moved or changed; settle; join firmly on to. **2** repair.

fixture /'fɪkstʃə/ n one of the things that are fixed into a house and are not taken away when one leaves the house. **a football fixture** = game arranged on a certain future date. **I'm a fixture here** = I shall not leave this place.

fizz /fɪz/ vi make a noise of gas coming out of liquid.

fizzle /'fɪzəl/ vi make a noise like water on the fire. infml **to fizzle out** = come to a foolish end.

flabbergast /'flæbəgɑːst/ vt greatly surprise or shock.

flabby /'flæbɪ/ adj soft; not firm; lacking in strength of character.

flaccid /'flæksɪd/ adj weak; soft.

flag¹ /flæg/ n piece of coloured cloth, usually with special marks on it, used as the sign of some group or nation.

flag² /flæg/ vi become tired; lose strength.

flagon /'flægən/ n vessel with a narrow opening used for containing liquids.

flagrant /'fleɪgrənt/ adj clearly wrong, e.g. *A flagrant wrongdoer* = one who does wrong openly and without shame.

flagstone /'flægstəʊn/ n large flat stone used in making a path or floor.

flail /fleɪl/ n wooden instrument used for beating the grain out of a plant.

flair /fleə/ n natural liking for a thing; natural power of doing anything.

flake /fleɪk/ n small thin piece of anything. vi come off in flakes.

flamboyant /flæm'bɔɪənt/ adj highly coloured; richly ornamented.

flame /fleɪm/ n mass of burning gas rising from a fire. vi burn brightly; be bright.

flamingo /flə'mɪŋgəʊ/ n water-bird having long legs and red wings.

flan /flæn/ n flat open pastry container filled with fruit.

flange /flændʒ/ n edge of a wheel so made as to keep it from running off the line.

flank /flæŋk/ n side of the body; the right or left side of an army.

flannel /'flænəl/ n soft woollen cloth.

flap¹ /flæp/ v **1** move up and down, as a bird moves its wings. **2** (of any wide flat object) to move, e.g. *A flag flaps in the wind.* sl **in a flap** = excited. vi become unnecessarily excited. n state of unnecessarily great excitement.

flap² /flæp/ n piece of cloth, leather, etc., fixed at one edge and hanging down over an opening, e.g. *The flap of a pocket*; any flat part made to hang down, e.g. *The flap of a folding table.*

flare /fleə/ vi burn; shine; burn with a sudden unsteady light. **to flare up** = suddenly burst into flame; suddenly become very angry. n **1** bright light used as a sign of, e.g. a boat or ship's being in danger and needing help. **2** lower part of skirts, dresses, or trousers when this spreads out to make a slight bell shape.

flash /flæʃ/ v appear with sudden brightness; move very quickly. n sudden bright light. **a flash in the pan** = something which has a great effect for a short time, but soon fails. n **flash-back** going back in a story or film to tell something which had happened earlier.

flashlight /'flæʃlaɪt/ n small electric handlamp.

flashy /'flæʃɪ/ adj looking very bright and good but really worthless, e.g. cheap clothes or jewelled ornaments which are not real.

flask /flɑːsk/ n flat bottle.

flat /flæt/ adj **1** smooth; even; without interest. **2** (in music) below the true note. **3** (of a TYRE) having no air in it. n set of rooms, usually all on one floor of a building, used as a home for one person or family.

flatter /'flætə/ vt please by praising greatly without being careful to say only what is true.

flatulence /'flætʃʊləns/ n gas in the stomach.

flaunt /flɔːnt/ vt wave (something) about proudly

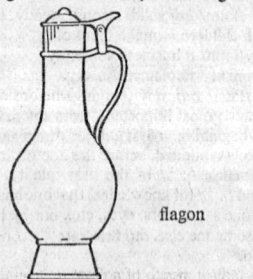

flagon

and more than is necessary; make a great show of (something) of which one is very proud.

flavour /ˈfleɪvə/ *n* taste. *vt* give a taste to (e.g. food).

flaw /flɔː/ *n* crack; imperfect part in anything, likely to cause it to break or fail.

flax /flæks/ *n* plant used for making fine cloth; the thread made from this. *adj* **flaxen** /ˈflæksən/ **1** having to do with flax. **2** light yellow.

flay /fleɪ/ *vt* take the skin off, esp. with a WHIP; say very strong words to (a wrongdoer) so as to make him feel ashamed.

flea /fliː/ *n* very small jumping insect that bites animals in order to get blood.

fleck /flek/ *n* spot of colour. *vt* mark with spots.

fled /fled/ *p.t.* of **flee**.

fledge /fledʒ/ *vi* grow feathers. *n* **fledgeling, fledgling** /ˈfledʒlɪŋ/ young bird with just enough feathers to fly. **a newly-fledged doctor** = one who has just obtained the right to practise. **fully fledged** = having full powers, full right, e.g. to act as a doctor.

flee /fliː/ *v* run away from, e.g. danger.

fleece

fleece /fliːs/ *n* the woolly covering of a sheep's body; any soft warm material that feels like wool.

fleet[1] /fliːt/ *adj* fast. *adj* **fleet-footed** /ˌfliːt ˈfʊtɪd/ able to run very fast.

fleet[2] /fliːt/ *n* number of ships together; large group of warships under one commander.

fleeting /ˈfliːtɪŋ/ *adj* moving quickly and silently away.

flesh /fleʃ/ *n* meat on a body. **one's own flesh and blood** = members of one's family.

flew /fluː/ *p.t.* of **fly**.

flex /fleks/ *v* bend or cause to bend. *n* easily bent electric wire. *adj* **flexible** /ˈfleksəbəl/ able to be bent; easily made to obey. *n* **flexibility** /ˌfleksəˈbɪlətɪ/.

flick /flɪk/ *vt* strike lightly with a quick small movement.

flicker /ˈflɪkə/ *vi* burn unsteadily; give an unsteady light—as a lamp about to go out.

flight[1] /flaɪt/ *n* **1** act of flying through the air; distance flown. **2** one of the feathers on an arrow. **a flight of stairs** = set of steps, e.g. *Two flights up* = up two sets of stairs.

flight[2] /flaɪt/ *n* act of running away. **to put to flight** = cause to run away.

flighty /ˈflaɪtɪ/ *adj* unsteady in character; changeable.

flimsy /ˈflɪmzɪ/ *adj* thin; weak; easily destroyed.

flinch /flɪntʃ/ *vi* Draw back in pain or fear.

fling /flɪŋ/ *vt* throw with great force; throw hurriedly, e.g. *To fling one's clothes on* = dress quickly. *n* **1** chance; attempt. **2** a Scottish dance.

flint /flɪnt/ *n* **1** very hard stone which can be struck to make fire. **2** small bar of metal rubbed by a wheel in a cigarette-lighter.

flip /flɪp/ *vt* strike with a light quick blow of the first finger pressed outward from the inner side of the thumb.

flippant /ˈflɪpənt/ *adj* speaking lightly about serious matters.

flipper /ˈflɪpə/ *n* limb of a water-creature (other than a fish) used in swimming.

flirt /flɜːt/ *vi* play at love-making. *n* one (esp. a woman) who plays at love-making. *n* **flirtation** /flɜːˈteɪʃən/. *adj* **flirtatious** /flɜːˈteɪʃəs/.

flit /flɪt/ *vi* move quickly from place to place as a small bird from tree to tree.

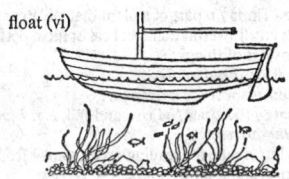
float (vi)

float /fləʊt/ *vi* rest on the surface of a liquid, e.g. *Wood floats in water*; move easily, e.g. *Clouds float across the sky*. *n* thing that floats, e.g. piece of wood from which a fishing hook or net hangs.

flock /flɒk/ *n* group of animals or birds. *vi* come together in a crowd.

floe /fləʊ/ *n* large piece of floating ice.

flog /flɒg/ *vt* **1** punish by beating. **to flog a dead horse** = go on with a thing after everyone has lost interest in it. **2** *sl* sell.

flood /flʌd/ *n* great amount of water covering land that is usually dry; sudden rush of anything, e.g. tears. *v* (e.g. of a river) overflow with water so as to cause a flood in (a place). *n* **floodlight** /ˈflʌdlaɪt/ very powerful lamp used to light up the outside of a beautiful building at night. *n* **flood tide** /ˈ ˌ ˌ/ highest point of the TIDE.

floor /flɔː/ *n* bottom part of a room on which one walks; any smooth flat bottom; lowest level of anything, e.g. prices.

flop /flɒp/ *vi* fall heavily; (esp. of a play) fail completely. *n* play which fails completely; unsuccessful person.

flora /ˈflɔːrə/ *n* plant life of a place, country, etc. *adj* **floral** /ˈflɔːrəl/ of flowers.

florid /ˈflɒrɪd/ *adj* flowery; richly ornamental.

florist /ˈflɒrɪst/ *n* grower or seller of flowers.

floss /flɒs/ *n* short threads of natural silk.

flotilla /flə'tɪlə/ n group of warships, usually all of the same kind.

flotsam /'flɒtsəm/ n (sing) goods floating on the water, e.g. from a wreck. **flotsam and jetsam** = goods floating on the water, or thrown up on the shore.

flounce /flaʊns/ n ornamental piece joined to the lower edge of a woman's dress. **to flounce out of a room** = go out quickly and angrily.

flounder /'flaʊndə/ vi make strong but useless movements, as in trying to get out of water; roll about helplessly; become mixed up in speaking, and talk foolishly. n a flat sea-fish.

flour /'flaʊə/ n fine white powder made from grain and used to make bread.

flourish /'flʌrɪʃ/ vi grow in a healthy way. vt wave (something) so that others can see it. n short burst of music.

flout /flaʊt/ vt treat with great lack of respect; laugh at.

flow /fləʊ/ vi run or spread like water. n act or way of flowing.

flower /'flaʊə/ n part of a plant that will produce seed; any flower-like shape; best or most perfect of any set of things.

flown /fləʊn/ p.p. of **fly**.

flu /fluː/ n short for **influenza**.

fluctuate /'flʌktʃʊeɪt/ vi rise and fall, e.g. *Fluctuating prices*.

flue /fluː/ n pipe for leading away smoke from a fire or leading air to a fire.

fluent /'fluːənt/ adj having a ready flow of words and ideas. n fluency /'fluːənsɪ/.

fluff /flʌf/ n fine soft feathery material. vi forget one's words when acting in the theatre. **to fluff out** = shake out, make loose, e.g. as a bird fluffs out its feathers.

fluid /'fluːɪd/ n, adj (substance) able to flow like water; not settled and firm.

fluke /fluːk/ n unexpected fortune.

flummox /'flʌməks/ vt make (someone) unable to speak or answer.

flung /flʌŋ/ p.t. & p.p. of **fling**.

fluorescent /flʊə'resənt/ adj giving a bright and even white light.

flurry /'flʌrɪ/ n sudden light fall of snow or rain with high wind; state of great excitement.

flush /flʌʃ/ vt wash clean with a flow of water. v flow or cause to flow quickly. vi become red because of a rush of blood to the face. adj level, e.g. *Flush with the edge of the table*.

fluster /'flʌstə/ vt excite; make a person too excited or anxious to be able to work or act.

flute /fluːt/ n musical instrument which is blown.

fluting /'fluːtɪŋ/ n long narrow hollows cut up and down on the surface of a pillar, as ornament.

flutter /'flʌtə/ v move (the wings) quickly, as a bird does; move about quickly in excitement. n act of fluttering; state of excitement.

flux /flʌks/ n state of flowing; state of continued movement and change.

fly[1] /flaɪ/ n 1 small flying insect. 2 small object made to look like this insect for catching fish. 3 (also **flies** n (pl)) opening at the front of a pair of trousers fastened by a ZIP, etc.

fly[2] /flaɪ/ vi 1 move through the air like a bird. **as the crow flies** = in a straight line across country. 2 move quickly.

flyblown /'flaɪbləʊn/ adj covered with dirt and eggs of flies.

flyleaf /'flaɪliːf/ n unprinted page at the beginning or end of a book.

flywheel /'flaɪwiːl/ n heavy wheel which, by its weight, keeps a machine running at a regular speed.

foal /fəʊl/ n very young horse. vi give birth to a horse.

foam /fəʊm/ n mass of BUBBLES. vi (e.g. of a liquid) send out foam. **to foam at the mouth** = be very angry.

fob /fɒb/ n ornamental chain put on a watch; small pocket for a watch. **to fob (someone) off with** = deceive into taking (some worthless thing).

focus /'fəʊkəs/ n point where lines, e.g. of light, come together; any central point. vi of lines (e.g. of light) come together at a point. vt get (e.g. a CAMERA) to take or to show a clear picture. adj focal /'fəʊkəl/.

fodder /'fɒdə/ n food for cattle.

foe /fəʊ/ n enemy.

fog /fɒg/ n thick cloud-like condition of the air which makes it impossible to see clearly. adj foggy /'fɒgɪ/.

fogey /'fəʊgɪ/ **an old fogey** = person with old ideas which he is unwilling to change.

foible /'fɔɪbəl/ n weak or foolish point in one's character.

foil[1] /fɔɪl/ vt cause (an enemy) to fail in an attempt.

foil[2] /fɔɪl/ n metal rolled into very thin sheets.

foil[3] /fɔɪl/ n thin sword without any point, used for practice.

foist /fɔɪst/ vt secretly or by a trick to cause a person to accept (something bad), e.g. *To foist off bad money on a person*.

fold[1] /fəʊld/ vt bend and press one part of a thing on another. n line along which something has been folded. n folder /'fəʊldə/ anything that folds or is used for folding; stiff sheet of paper bent in two and used for holding letters, papers, etc.

fold[2] /fəʊld/ n place where sheep are kept; group of sheep. **to return to the fold** = come home.

flute

foliage /ˈfəʊlɪ-ɪdʒ/ n (sing) leaves (of a tree).

folio /ˈfəʊlɪəʊ/ n sheet of paper folded over to make two pages; large book.

folk /fəʊk/ n (pl) people. n **folk-dance** /ˈ. ‿./ one of the ancient dances of the country people. n **folklore** /ˈfəʊk-lɔː/ study of the stories, beliefs and customs of people in early times.

follicle /ˈfɒlɪkəl/ n 1 small hole in the skin out of which the hair grows. 2 (in a plant) little bag containing a seed.

follow /ˈfɒləʊ/ v 1 go or come after; be next in rank or importance. 2 understand, e.g. *Do you follow me?* 3 take a continuing interest in, e.g. *To follow the business of the law-courts.* 4 mean necessarily, e.g. *He is good, but it does not follow that he is wise.* **the following** = those things named in the list below.

folly /ˈfɒlɪ/ n foolishness.

foment /fəʊˈment/ vt put hot cloth or hot medicines onto (part of the body) in order to bring blood to one place, so as to get poison out or to lessen pain; cause excitement or trouble.

fomentation /ˌfəʊmenˈteɪʃən/ n hot material put on a diseased part.

fond /fɒnd/ adj loving.

fondle /ˈfɒndl/ vt touch in a loving way.

font

font /fɒnt/ n large stone container for the water that is put on a child when he is BAPTIZED.

food /fuːd/ n anything eaten.

foofoo /ˈfuːfuː/ *West African* n food made from boiled and beaten roots such as YAMS, CASSAVA, etc.

fool /fuːl/ n person without good sense. vt deceive. **to fool around, fool about** = play or act foolishly. n **foolscap** /ˈfuːlskæp/ large size of paper, 13 × 8 inches. n **foolery** /ˈfuːlərɪ/ amusing play. adj **foolhardy** /ˈfuːlhɑːdɪ/ going into unnecessary danger. adj **foolish** /ˈfuːlɪʃ/ without the necessary thought; silly. adj **foolproof** /ˈfuːlpruːf/ so simple and easy that no one can make a mistake.

foot¹ /fʊt/ n length of 12 inches (30·479 cm).

foot² /fʊt/ n 1 lowest part of the leg on which one walks; lowest part of anything. n pl **feet** /fiːt/ group of sounds in a line of poetry. 2 **to foot the bill** = pay the cost. **to put one's foot down** = give clear and firm orders that a certain thing is to be stopped. **to put one's foot in it** = make a serious or amusing mistake. n **football** /ˈfʊtbɔːl/ 1 game in which a ball is kicked between two sides. 2 ball used in this game. n **footfall** /ˈfʊtfɔːl/ sound of a step. n **foothill** /ˈfʊt-hɪl/ one of the low hills at the bottom of high mountains. n **foothold** /ˈfʊthəʊld/ place for the foot in climbing; a beginning from which one may go on. n **footing** /ˈfʊtɪŋ/ firm place, e.g. *To get a footing in a group of persons* = be accepted as a member. n **footlights** /ˈfʊtlaɪts/ lights on the floor of the theatre STAGE. n **footman** /ˈfʊtmən/ manservant. n **footnote** /ˈfʊtnəʊt/ note at the bottom of a page. n **footpath** /ˈfʊtpɑːθ/ path along which one may walk, esp. in the country.

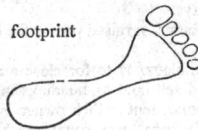

footprint

n **footprint** /ˈfʊtprɪnt/ the mark made by a foot, e.g. in sand. n **footstep** /ˈfʊtstep/ sound or mark made when walking.

fop /fɒp/ n man who has too great a love for fine clothes.

for /fə; *strong*, fɔː/ prep 1 so as to help, e.g. *I did it for John.* 2 so as to gain or obtain; receiving in exchange, e.g. *I did it for money.* 3 intended to be used as or used by, e.g. *This knife is for cutting bread.* 4 instead of. 5 in spite of, e.g. *For all our efforts, the plan failed.* 6 on account of, e.g. *For what reason?* 7 during; lasting, e.g. *In hospital for a month.* 8 considering one's being, e.g. *She's very strong for a young girl.* conj because; after all.

forage /ˈfɒrɪdʒ/ n food for cattle. vi go out and seek food.

foray /ˈfɒreɪ/ n sudden attack made in order to take away goods or cattle by force.

forbade /fəˈbæd/ p.t. of **forbid**.

forbear /fɔːˈbeə/ vi keep oneself from doing, e.g. *To forbear from hitting an enemy.*

forbid /fəˈbɪd/ vt order (someone) not to do something. (p.p. **forbidden** /fəˈbɪdn/.)

forbore /fɔːˈbɔː/ p.t. of **forbear**.

force /fɔːs/ n 1 strength; power. 2 group of men doing the same work. vt use force to get (someone) to do something or (something) to happen. **a forced laugh** = laugh when one is really not pleased or amused. n **forcemeat** /ˈfɔːs-miːt/ meat and pleasant-tasting vegetables cut small and mixed.

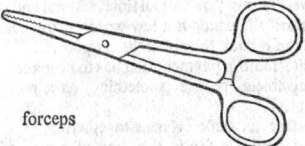

forceps

forceps /ˈfɔːseps/ n (pl) instrument used by doctors for getting a tight hold, e.g. on a tooth.

forcible /ˈfɔːsəbəl/ adj using force.

ford

ford /fɔːd/ *n* part of a river where the water is not deep, used as a crossing.

fore- /fɔː/ before; in the front part. **fore and aft** = in front and behind, from the front to the back of a ship.

forearm¹ /ˈfɔːrɑːm/ *n* lower part of the arm.

forearm² /fɔːˈrɑːm/ *vt* prepare for an attack.

forebode /fɔːˈbəʊd/ *vt* tell or be a sign of (some future event).

forecast /ˈfɔːkɑːst/ *vt* tell (future events). *n* act of forecasting, e.g *The weather forecast* = account of the weather that is to be expected during the next few days.

forecastle /ˈfəʊksl/ *n* raised part at the front of a ship.

foreclose /fɔːˈkləʊz/ *vt* **to foreclose a mortgage** = seize and sell land or buildings in order to get back money lent to their owner.

forefather /ˈfɔːˌfɑːðə/ *n* person from whom one is descended.

forefront /ˈfɔːfrʌnt/ **in the forefront** = right in the front.

foregoing /fɔːˈɡəʊɪŋ/ *adj* earlier. *adj* **foregone** /fɔːˈɡɒn/ **foregone conclusion** = result that was never in doubt.

foreground /ˈfɔːɡraʊnd/ *n* front part of a picture.

forehead /ˈfɒrɪd, ˈfɔːhed/ *n* front part of the head above the eyes.

foreign /ˈfɒrən/ *adj* not belonging to one's own country. **foreign matter** = matter out of proper place, e.g. a grain of sand in the eye. **foreign to** = not usual for. *n* **foreigner** /ˈfɒrənə/ foreign person.

foreman /ˈfɔːmən/ *n* man in charge of a number of workmen.

foremost /ˈfɔːməʊst/ *adj* first in time, place, rank, or importance.

forensic /fəˈrensɪk/ *adj* having to do with the law.

foresee /fɔːˈsiː/ *vt* see (what will happen) in the future.

foreshadow /fɔːˈʃædəʊ/ *vt* be a sign of (future events).

foreshore /ˈfɔːʃɔː/ *n* that part of the shore near the water.

foresight /ˈfɔːsaɪt/ *n* power to see the future and care in preparing for it.

forest /ˈfɒrɪst/ *n* large piece of land covered with trees.

forestall /fɔːˈstɔːl/ *vt* prevent (someone) from doing something by doing it first.

forestry /ˈfɒrɪstrɪ/ *n* art of taking care of forests.

forever /fəˈrevə/ *adv* for all time; without end.

foreword /ˈfɔːwɜːd/ *n* a few words at the beginning of a book to explain its purpose.

forfeit /ˈfɔːfɪt/ *n* payment that has to be made as a punishment. *vt* lose (something) as a punishment.

forgather /fɔːˈɡæðə/ *vi* meet together.

forge¹ /fɔːdʒ/ *n* fire in the shop of a man who works with iron. *vt* make or shape (an iron instrument) in a fire. **to forge ahead** = push forward through difficulties.

forge² /fɔːdʒ/ *vt* make or change (a written paper) in order to deceive. *n* **forgery** /ˈfɔːdʒərɪ/.

forget /fəˈɡet/ *v* fail to remember. *adj* **forgetful** /fəˈɡetfəl/ tending to forget things.

forgive /fəˈɡɪv/ *vt* forget (a wrong); decide not to punish (someone) for a wrong.

forgo /fɔːˈɡəʊ/ *vt* do without; give up.

forgot /fəˈɡɒt/ p.t. of **forget**.

forgotten /fəˈɡɒtn/ p.p. of **forget**.

fork /fɔːk/ *n* instrument with a handle and two or more points used for picking up food, for loosening or turning over soil; anything of this shape—Y-shaped, e.g. *A fork in the road* = place where the road divides into two roads. *vt* put a fork through. *vi* divide into two (e.g. as a road does). *n* **tuning-fork** /ˈ.. ./ instrument that gives a true note in music.

forlorn /fəˈlɔːn/ *adj* cheerless; deserted.

form¹ /fɔːm/ *n* class in a school.

form² /fɔːm/ *n* **1** appearance; shape. **2** sort, kind, e.g. *A form of slavery*. **3** piece of paper on which the answers to questions must be given in order to obtain something. *vt* give shape to; make. *vi* take shape.

formal /ˈfɔːməl/ *adj* according to all the correct rules and customs. *n* **formality** /fɔːˈmælɪtɪ/.

formation /fɔːˈmeɪʃən/ *n* act or state of being shaped or planned; manner in which anything, e.g. an army, is set in order.

former /ˈfɔːmə/ *adj* earlier in time; no longer being, e.g. *The former Prime Minister*. *adj, n* the person or thing first spoken of.

formidable /ˈfɔːmɪdəbəl/ *adj* great; causing fear.

formula /ˈfɔːmjʊlə/ *n* fixed form of words to be used at the proper time and place; any truth that has been written out in a short form. *vt* **formulate** /ˈfɔːmjʊleɪt/ set out in a short and clear form.

forsake /fəˈseɪk/ *vt* give up; leave, e.g. one's old friends, a former way of living; p.t. **forsook** /fəˈsʊk/, p.p. **forsaken** /fəˈseɪkən/.

forswear /fɔːˈsweə/ *vt* promise not to use any more. p.p. **forsworn** /fɔːˈswɔːn/.

fort

fort /fɔːt/ *n* castle or strong place that may be defended against an enemy.

forth /fɔːθ/ *archaic adv* forward; out. *adj* **forthcoming** /fɔːθˈkʌmɪŋ/ that will soon come.

forthright /ˈfɔːθraɪt/ *adj* honest; saying what is in one's mind.

forthwith /ˌfɔːθˈwɪθ, -ˈwɪð/ *adv* at once.

fortify /ˈfɔːtɪfaɪ/ *vt* make a place strong against the attack of an enemy.

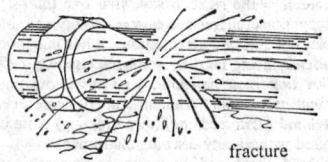

fox (1)

fortitude /ˈfɔːtɪtjuːd/ *n* courage and self-control.

fortnight /ˈfɔːtnaɪt/ *n* two weeks.

fortress /ˈfɔːtrəs/ *n* large fort.

fortuitous /fɔːˈtjuːɪtəs/ *adj* happening by chance.

fortunate /ˈfɔːtʃənət/ *adj* succeeding by chance.

fortune /ˈfɔːtʃuːn/ *n* 1 chance. 2 the good and evil that happen to a man. 3 great wealth. **to tell fortunes** = tell what one's future will be.

forty /ˈfɔːtɪ/ *det, n* number often written **40,** being four times ten.

forum /ˈfɔːrəm/ *n* market-place in a Roman town; any place in which questions of public interest are talked about.

forward /ˈfɔːwəd/ *adj* too eager; not polite. *vt* send on. *adv* **forward(s)** /ˈfɔːwəd(z)/ towards the front; onwards. **to look forward to** = expect with feelings of pleasure.

fossil /ˈfɒsəl/ *n* ancient plant or animal changed to stone and found in rocks or in the earth. **an old fossil** = old man who will not change his ideas.

foster /ˈfɒstə/ *vt* bring up; nurse. **a foster mother** = woman who nurses and brings up a child instead of the real mother. **foster brother, sister** = one of two children brought up as above.

fought /fɔːt/ *p.p. & p.t. of* **fight.**

foul /faʊl/ *adj* dirty; unpleasant. *n* (in a game) act that is against the rules. **fall foul of** = quarrel with.

found[1] /faʊnd/ *p.t. and p.p. of* **find.**

found[2] /faʊnd/ *vt* 1 begin the building of a house. 2 set up or start, e.g. *To found a school. n* **foundation** /faʊnˈdeɪʃən/ 1 that part of a building below the ground on which the walls stand. 2 strongest or most necessary part of anything. 3 amount of money given for the support, e.g., of a school.

founder /ˈfaʊndə/ *vi* 1 fill with water and sink, e.g. a ship at sea. 2 be unable to go on running.

foundling /ˈfaʊndlɪŋ/ *n* child left by its parents and found by other persons.

foundry /ˈfaʊndrɪ/ *n* place where metals, etc., are melted and made into things.

fount[1] /faʊnt/ *n* water coming up out of the ground; cause or beginning of anything.

fount[2] /fɒnt, faʊnt/ *n* all the letters of one size used in printing books.

fountain /ˈfaʊntɪn/ *n* water coming up out of the ground; water thrown high into the air from a pipe. **fountain pen** = pen containing a supply of ink, which can be filled again when empty.

four /fɔː/ *n, det* number following three, often written **4.**

foursome /ˈfɔːsəm/ *n* game between two pairs of players.

fourteen /fɔːˈtiːn/ *n, det* number following thirteen, often written **14.**

fowl /faʊl/ *n* any bird that is eaten.

fox /fɒks/ *n* **1** a small wild dog-like animal—usually red, with a bushy tail. 2 clever, dishonest person.

foxtrot /ˈfɒkstrɒt/ *n* kind of dance.

foxy /ˈfɒksɪ/ *adj* 1 clever and deceiving. 2 (e.g. of a smell) like a fox.

foyer /ˈfɔɪeɪ/ *n* large room at the entrance of a hotel or theatre.

fracas /ˈfrækɑː/ *n* noisy quarrel or fight.

fraction /ˈfrækʃən/ *n* 1 part, esp. a small part of anything. 2 pair of figures, one above the other (e.g. ½ ¾), the lower one showing how many parts the whole is divided into and the upper one how many of these parts make up the amount in question.

fractious /ˈfrækʃəs/ *adj* in a bad temper, e.g. *A fractious child.*

fracture

fracture /ˈfræktʃə/ *v, n* break, esp. of a limb.

fragile /ˈfrædʒaɪl/ *adj* very fine and easily broken; easily harmed.

fragment /ˈfrægmənt/ *n* small part broken off. *adj* **fragmentary** /ˈfrægməntərɪ/.

fragrance /ˈfreɪgrəns/ *n* pleasant smell. *adj* **fragrant** /ˈfreɪgrənt/.

frail /freɪl/ *adj* weak; easily broken; easily led to do wrong. *n* **frailty** /ˈfreɪltɪ/ state of being frail.

frame /freɪm/ *n* 1 most important bars or poles, posts, etc., on which the rest of a thing is built, e.g. *The frame of a house.* **he has a strong frame** = he has a strong body. 2 any form made up of bars with the spaces not filled in; open square (or other shape) of metal or wood into which a picture is put; box with a glass top used to grow plants quickly. *vt* 1 to put together, make, e.g. *To frame a plan.* 2 set in a frame, e.g. *To frame a picture.* 3 *sl* make it appear that (someone) has done some wrong act. **frame of mind** = state of mind. *n* **framework** /ˈfreɪmwɜːk/ frame on which, or round which, something will be made.

franc /fræŋk/ *n* piece of French money.

franchise /ˈfræntʃaɪz/ *n* right to elect people to the government.

frank /fræŋk/ *adj* freely saying one's real thoughts; honest.

frankincense /ˈfræŋkɪnsens/ *n* matter obtained from a tree, burned to give a sweet-smelling smoke.

frantic /'fræntɪk/ *adj* wildly excited or uncontrolled with joy, fear, pain, etc.

fraternal /frə'tɜːnəl/ *adj* having to do with brothers; like a brother.

fraternity /frə'tɜːnɪtɪ/ *n* **1** state of being brothers. **2** group united for a certain purpose.

fraternize /'frætənaɪz/ *vi* meet together in a friendly way.

fraud /frɔːd/ *n* trick; dishonesty. **he is a fraud** = not what he pretends to be. *adj* **fraudulent** /'frɔːdʒʊlənt/.

fraught /frɔːt/ **fraught with danger(s)** = very dangerous.

fray[1] /freɪ/ *n* fight.

fray[2] /freɪ/ *v* wear or pull the edge of cloth into loose threads.

freak /friːk/ *n* peculiar and unusual act or thing (e.g. a sheep with five legs).

freckle /'frekəl/ *n* light brown spot on the skin. *vt* mark with spots.

free /friː/ *adj* **1** able to do what one wishes; not tied; not in prison; not controlled by rules. **free speech** = the right to say what one thinks. **2** easy; graceful. **free and easy** = friendly and simple, not stiff and ceremonious. **3** not busy; not already being used by someone else, e.g. *I am free tomorrow morning.* **4** given without payment. *n* **freedom** /'friːdəm/ state of being free.

freehand /'friːhænd/ *adj* (of a drawing) done by hand without any drawing instrument.

freehold /'friːhəʊld/ *n* complete ownership of land.

freelance /'friːlɑːns/ *adj* (of a writer) who belongs to no one newspaper but writes, as he pleases, for any.

freemason /'friːmeɪsən/ *n* member of an ancient group that holds secret meetings and has secret signs by which the members may know each other.

freethinker /ˌfriː'θɪŋkə/ *n* one who forms his own ideas about God without following the teaching of others.

freeze /friːz/ *v* **1** become or cause to become solid because of cold; make or be very cold. **2** (of an animal or soldier) suddenly to keep quite still so as not to be seen. **to freeze prices** = cause prices to stay the same. *n* time during which prices may not increase.

freight /freɪt/ *n* load of any kind; money paid for carrying goods. *n* **freighter** /'freɪtə/ ship that carries goods only.

frenetic /frə'netɪk/ *adj* FRANTIC.

frenzy /'frenzɪ/ *n* state of wild feeling; madness.

frequency /'friːkwənsɪ/ *n* number of times anything happens. *adj* **frequent** /'friːkwənt/ happening very often.

fresco /'freskəʊ/ *n* painting on a wall, e.g. of a church.

fresh /freʃ/ *adj* **1** newly grown, newly made, e.g. *Fresh green grass; Fresh milk.* **2** smelling, tasting or looking clean and new, e.g. *Fresh air; Fresh paint.* **3** not experienced. **4** not seen or

heard before, e.g. *Have you any fresh news?* **5** not tired. **6** (of water) not salt. **7** *infml* not showing proper respect, esp. of a man's behaviour towards a woman.

fret /fret/ *vi* be anxious. *v* wear away by rubbing.

fretsaw /'fretsɔː/ *n* very narrow blade with teeth used for cutting out pieces from a thin piece of wood so as to make an ornament. *n* **fretwork** /'fretwɜːk/ art of making wooden ornaments in this way.

friar /'fraɪə/ *n* member of a religious group.

friction /'frɪkʃən/ *n* rubbing; waste of power caused by rubbing together of parts of a machine; quarrelling.

Friday /'fraɪdɪ/ *n* the sixth day of the week.

fridge /frɪdʒ/ *n* short for **refrigerator.**

friend /frend/ *n* one who likes another person. *adj* **friendly** /'frendlɪ/ of or like a friend. *n* **friendship** /'frendʃɪp/ state of being friends.

frieze /friːz/ *n* ornamented band along the top of a wall just below the roof.

frigate /'frɪgət/ *n* fast warship.

fright /fraɪt/ *n* state of being greatly afraid. *vt* **frighten** /'fraɪtn/ make afraid. *adj* **frightful** /'fraɪtfəl/ **1** causing great fear. **2** *infml* very bad; ugly. *adv* **frightfully** *infml* very.

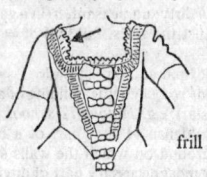

frill

frill /frɪl/ *n* loose ornamental edge on a garment; ring of long feathers or hairs growing on a bird or animal; unnecessary ornament of any kind.

fringe /frɪndʒ/ *n* ornamental edge of loose threads; edge of the hair when this hangs down over part of the face; any outside edge or unimportant part of anything.

frisk /frɪsk/ *vi* to jump and run about; behave in a joyful way. *adj* **frisky** /'frɪskɪ/ playful.

fritter[1] /'frɪtə/ *n* piece of fruit or meat enclosed in a mixture of egg and flour, cooked in hot fat.

fritter[2] /'frɪtə/ *vt* cut or break into small pieces. **to fritter away one's time** = waste time.

frivolous /'frɪvələs/ *adj* not serious; foolish; too interested in light and amusing things. *n* **frivolity** /frɪ'vɒlɪtɪ/.

fro /frəʊ/ **to and fro** = forward and back again.

frock /frɒk/ *n* long outer garment; woman's dress.

frog /frɒg/ *n* green and brown jumping creature which lives both on land and in the water. **a frog in one's throat** = uncomfortable feeling in the throat that causes difficulty in speaking. *vt* **frogmarch** carry (someone) face downwards, one man holding each of his limbs.

frogman /'frɒgmən/ *n* man specially dressed and equipped to swim for a long time under water.

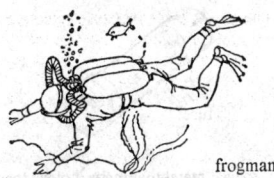
frogman

frolic /'frɒlɪk/ *vi* play happily.

from /frəm; *strong* frɒm/ *prep* **1** out of; leaving at. **2** beginning at. **3** because of.

frond /frɒnd/ *n* long leaf-like part of a plant.

front /frʌnt/ *n* **1** the face; the forward part. **in front of** = before. **2** place where the two armies are fighting in a war.

frontage /'frʌntɪdʒ/ *n* **1** front of a building. **2** that part of a piece of land which is on the edge of a street, river, etc.

frontier /'frʌntɪə/ *n* farthest edge of a country; border.

frontispiece /'frʌntɪspiːs/ *n* picture in the front of a book.

frost /frɒst/ *n* act or state of freezing. *n* **frostbite** /'frɒstbaɪt/ damage caused by cold to a part of the body.

froth /frɒθ/ *n* mass of small BUBBLES.

frown /fraʊn/ *vi* draw the skin above the eyes into folds as when displeased, or when thinking deeply.

frowzy /'fraʊzɪ/ *adj* smelling unpleasant because unwashed.

froze /frəʊz/ *p.t.* of freeze.

frozen /'frəʊzən/ *p.p.* of freeze.

frugal /'fruːgəl/ *adj* careful not to waste, e.g. money, food.

fruit /fruːt/ *n* **1** anything produced from the earth, e.g. grain, apples, eatable leaves, etc. **2** sweet eatable part of a plant that contains the seed. **3** anything produced, e.g. *The fruit of his labours.* *n* **fruiterer** /'fruːtərə/ one who sells fruit. *n* **fruition** /fruː'ɪʃən/ enjoyment of the fruit or result. *adj* **fruitless** /'fruːtləs/ without result; unsuccessful. **fruity** /'fruːtɪ/ *adj* like fruit, having a strong taste or smell.

frustrate /frʌ'streɪt/ *vt* bring (someone)'s plans to nothing; prevent from doing. *n* **frustration** /frʌ'streɪʃən/.

fry[1] /fraɪ/ *v* cook in hot fat. *n* **frying-pan** /'.. ./ flat cooking vessel for frying in.

fry[2] /fraɪ/ *n* small young fish. **small fry** = unimportant people or things.

fuddled /'fʌdld/ *adj* not able to think clearly because one has drunk too much.

fudge /fʌdʒ/ *n* kind of soft sweet.

fuel /'fjuːəl/ *n* material for burning, e.g. wood, coal, oil.

fug /fʌg/ *infml* *n* hot air that is not fresh. *adj* **fuggy.**

fugitive /'fjuːdʒətɪv/ *n* one who is running away from the law. *adj* escaping; not lasting very long.

fugue /fjuːg/ *n* piece of music in which the TUNE is repeated on higher or lower notes while it continues.

fulcrum /'fʌlkrəm/ *n* support on which a LEVER moves.

fulfil /fʊl'fɪl/ *vt* complete, e.g. a promise. **to fulfil his expectations** = be as good as he hoped.

full /fʊl/ *adj* having in it as much as it will contain; complete.

fulminate /'fʌlmɪneɪt/ *vi* speak loudly and angrily against someone or something.

fumble /'fʌmbəl/ *vi* lack skill in using one's hands; fail in doing something.

fume /fjuːm/ *n* smoke or gas coming from burning material or from a strong acid. *vi* give off fumes; show signs of anger.

fumigate /'fjuːmɪgeɪt/ *vt* make (a room) free from disease by burning a substance that gives off a heavy smoke.

fun /fʌn/ *n* amusement; play; pleasure. **to poke fun at** = cause others to laugh at.

function /'fʌŋkʃən/ *n* **1** any natural action, e.g. *The function of the eye is to see.* **2** special work or duty, e.g. *The function of a judge is to decide questions of law.* **a social function** = meeting of people for pleasure or in honour of some great person. *vi* work; have as its function. *n* **functionary** /'fʌŋkʃənərɪ/ officer with certain special duties to perform.

fund /fʌnd/ *n* amount of money set apart for some special purpose; a supply.

fundamental /ˌfʌndə'mentəl/ *adj* at the bottom of, as that upon which all else is built up; of first importance; most necessary.

funeral /'fjuːnərəl/ *n* all those customs and acts that have to do with putting a dead person in the grave. *adj* **funereal** /fjuː'nɪərɪəl/.

fungus /'fʌŋgəs/, *pl* **fungi** /'fʌŋgaɪ/ *n* kind of plant that has no green leaves but gets its food from decayed vegetable matter.

funnel /'fʌnəl/ *n* **1** vessel round at the top and becoming small at the bottom, used in pouring liquids into a small opening. **2** smoke-pipe of a steamship.

funny /'fʌnɪ/ *adj* **1** amusing. **2** strange *n* **funnybone** /'.. ./ pointed bone at the outside of the bend of the arm.

fur /fɜː/ *n* thick soft hair on some animals, e.g. cats; skin of an animal with the hair still on, e.g. used as a garment.

furbish /'fɜːbɪʃ/ *vt* cause to shine and look like new.

furious /'fjʊərɪəs/ *adj* (of any feeling or force) strong and uncontrolled; very angry.

furl /fɜːl/ *vt* roll up (e.g. a sail).

furlong /'fɜːlɒŋ/ *n* ⅛ of one mile (201 metres).

furlough /'fɜːləʊ/ *n* time of rest from one's work, e.g. such as is given to a man working in a foreign country so that he may return home.

furnace /'fɜːnəs/ *n* large enclosed fire, e.g. as part of a steam-engine.

furnish /'fɜːnɪʃ/ *vt* supply, esp. the things of daily

use in a home, e.g. chairs, tables, curtains, etc. *n* (*sing*) **furniture** /'fɜːnɪtʃə/ things of daily use in a home, e.g. tables, chairs, etc.

furrow (n)

furrow /'fʌrəʊ/ *n* long line cut in the earth by a PLOUGH. *vt* make furrows or lines in.

furry /'fɜːrɪ/ *adj* like fur or having fur.

further /'fɜːðə/ *adj, adv* more forward; more, e.g. *I have no further orders*. *vt* help to go further; help to succeed. *n* **furtherance** /'fɜːðərəns/ act of helping a plan or work.

furtive /'fɜːtɪv/ *adj* done secretly.

fury /'fjʊərɪ/ *n* great anger; great uncontrolled force.

furze /fɜːz/ *n* low-growing evergreen bush.

fuse[1] /fjuːz/ *v* melt; change into liquid by heat; join two metals by heating them together. *n*

fuse[1]

piece of special metal that melts if more than a certain amount of electricity flows through it, thus preventing possible damage by fire.

fuse[2] /fjuːz/ *n* instrument for starting large explosions at a fixed time.

fuselage /'fjuːzəlɑːʒ/ *n* frame of the body of an aeroplane.

fusion /'fjuːʒən/ *n* **1** act of melting by heat. **2** act of mixing materials together when melted.

fuss /fʌs/ *n* excited and anxious state of mind. *vi* be excited and anxious. *n* **fusspot** /'fʌs-pɒt/ person who often makes a fuss.

fusty /'fʌstɪ/ *adj* having a bad, not fresh, smell.

futile /'fjuːtaɪl/ *adj* worthless; having no effect. *n* **futility** /fjuː'tɪlətɪ/.

future /'fjuːtʃə/ *n, adj* (that) which is going to come or happen.

fuzzy /'fʌzɪ/ *adj* **1** (of hair) very curly. **2** not clear in shape.

G

gab /gæb/ **the gift of the gab** = power of speaking well—or much.

gabble /'gæbəl/ *vi* talk quickly and foolishly.

gable /'geɪbəl/ *n* pointed part of a wall between the two sloping sides of a roof; small roof over a window.

gad /gæd/ *vi* wander without purpose; go from place to place looking for amusement. *n* **gadabout** /'gædəbaʊt/ person (usually a woman) who loves to go visiting rather than work at home.

gadfly /'gædflaɪ/ *n* a kind of fly that bites cattle.

gadget /'gædʒɪt/ *n* any useful instrument.

gaffe /gæf/ *n* mistake; action or words that may accidentally hurt others' feelings.

gaffer /'gæfə/ *infml n* **1** old man. **2** man in charge.

gag /gæg/ *vt* stop the mouth of (someone) by force. *n* **1** something put in the mouth to keep it open and prevent speech. **2** *infml* JOKE.

gaiety /'geɪətɪ/ *n* state of being very happy and light-hearted. *adv* **gaily** happily. **gaily dressed** = in bright colours.

gain /geɪn/ *vt* get by working; obtain.

gainsay /geɪn'seɪ/ *vt* say that (something) is wrong or untrue.

gait /geɪt/ *n* manner of walking.

gaiter /'geɪtə/ *n* covering (usually of leather) for the lower part of the leg.

gable

gala /'gɑːlə/ *n* time of feasting and general happiness.

galaxy /'gæləksɪ/ *n* very large group of stars.

gale /geɪl/ *n* strong wind.

gall[1] /gɔːl/ *n* swelling on plants caused by an insect; painful place on the skin of an animal caused by rubbing. *vt* **1** rub something until it is sore. **2** hurt the feelings of; anger.

gall[2] /gɔːl/ *n* **1** bitter liquid which mixes with food after it leaves the stomach and changes the fats into liquids that can be built into the body. **2** feeling of bitterness or hatred. **3** shameless boldness.

gallant /'gælənt/ *adj* brave; (also /gə'lænt/) attending ladies in a polite way.

galleon /'gælɪən/ *n* large sailing-ship of former times, e.g. about AD 1600.

gallery /'gælərɪ/ *n* **1** long narrow hall, e.g. one in which pictures are hung. **2** upper floor at the back of a large hall or theatre in which people sit to see a show or hear music. **to play to the gallery** = seek the praise of the common people.

galley /'gælɪ/ *n* ancient warship. *n* **galley-slave** /'.../ one sent to be a slave on a warship; *n* **galley proofs** /'.../ long pieces of paper containing the first printing of a book to be corrected.

gallivant /'gælɪvænt/ *vi* go about seeking pleasure.

gallon /'gælən/ *n* measure for liquids or grain = 4½ litres.

gallop /'gæləp/ *vi* ride a horse at its fastest speed; (of a horse) run its fastest.

gallows /'gæləʊz/ *n* wooden framework for killing wrongdoers by hanging by the neck.

galore /gə'lɔː/ *adv* in plenty.

galoshes /gə'lɒʃɪz/ *n* rubber overshoes to keep the feet dry.

galvanize /'gælvənaɪz/ *vt* **1** put a coat of metal onto (something) using electricity. **2** cause sudden action.

gambit /'gæmbɪt/ *n* move made in a game, esp. in CHESS, in which although a piece is lost, a better position later comes about; any similar clever trick.

gamble /'gæmbəl/ *vi* play cards or other games for money. *v* risk (money) on a future event or possible happening.

gambol /'gæmbəl/ *n* playful jumping about. *vi* jump about playfully.

game /geɪm/ *n* **1** any form of play; certain form of play with special rules, e.g. football. **2** wild birds or animals that may be shot or hunted. *n* **gamekeeper** /'geɪmˌkiːpə/ one who prevents outsiders from shooting birds and animals, e.g. on the lands of a lord. *n* **gamesmaster** /'geɪmzˌmɑːstə/ one who teaches games in a school. *n* **gamester** /'geɪmstə/ one who plays cards or other games for money.

gammon /'gæmən/ *n* **1** part of a pig salted and prepared for food. **2** a trick to deceive.

gamut /'gæmət/ *n* full range of a musical instrument, from the lowest note to the highest; full range of anything.

gander /'gændə/ *n* male GOOSE.

gang /gæŋ/ *n* **1** number of men working together. **2** group of law-breakers. **3** *infml* group of friends.

gangplank /'gæŋplæŋk/ *n* movable bridge between a ship and the shore.

gangrene /'gæŋgriːn/ *n* decay of a part of the body caused by lack of blood-supply or damage.

gangster /'gæŋstə/ *n* member of a group of law-breakers.

gangway /'gæŋweɪ/ *n* **1** path between rows of seats. **2** movable bridge from a ship to the shore.

gaol, jail /dʒeɪl/ *n* prison. *n* **gaol-bird**/'. ./ person who is often in prison. *n* **gaoler** /'dʒeɪlə/ prison guard.

gap /gæp/ *n* space between two things; hole, e.g. in a wall; deep valley.

gape /geɪp/ *v* look (at) in a foolish way without understanding, esp. with the mouth open wide.

garage /'gærɑːʒ/ *n* **1** building in which a car is stored. **2** shop in which things needed for cars are sold and cars are repaired.

garb /gɑːb/ *n* (*sing*) clothes.

garbage /'gɑːbɪdʒ/ *n* waste food, etc., thrown outside the house.

garble /'gɑːbəl/ *vt* change (a story) so as to cause it to be untrue, e.g. *A garbled report of a meeting.*

garden /'gɑːdn/ *n* place for growing vegetables or flowers; any place, e.g. in a city, for the public to walk in, where grass, flowers, trees etc. grow. *v* look after (a garden).

gargantuan /gɑː'gæntʃʊən/ *adj* very large; eating a great deal of food.

gargle /'gɑːgəl/ *vi* wash the throat by holding the head back and singing with liquid medicine in the mouth. *n* liquid medicine for gargling.

gargoyle /'gɑːgɔɪl/ *n* stone figure of a man, animal or strange creature, cut hollow and built on the walls and corners of a building, e.g. a church, to carry off water from the roof.

gari /'gærɪ/ *West African n* flour made from CASSAVA.

garish /'geərɪʃ/ *adj* bright; showy.

garland /'gɑːlənd/ *n* circle of leaves or flowers, often used as a sign of victory.

garlic /'gɑːlɪk/ *n* very strong-smelling vegetable, used to flavour other dishes.

garment /'gɑːmənt/ *n* any article of dress.

garner /'gɑːnə/ *vt* gather in. *n* store-house.

garnish /'gɑːnɪʃ/ *vt* add ornaments to.

garret /'gærət/ *n* small room just under the roof of a house.

garrison /'gærɪsən/ *n* soldiers who live in and guard a town.

garrulous /'gærʊləs/ *adj* talking a lot about unimportant matters.

garter /'gɑːtə/ *n* band worn round the leg. **Knight of the Garter** = a knight of the highest rank in England.

gas /'gæs/ *n* air-like substance, lighter than solids and liquids. *adj* **gaseous** /'gæsɪəs/.

gash /gæʃ/ *n* deep cut in the body. *vt* cut deeply.

gasket /'gæskɪt/ *n* rope for fastening a sail; any thin material put between metal surfaces in an engine to prevent oil from running out, or to make the joint tight.

gasolene, -ine /'gæsəliːn/ *n* light easily burnt oil used for driving cars.

gasometer /gæ'sɒmɪtə/ *n* large container in which gas is stored for the use of a city.

gasp /gɑːsp/ *vi* struggle for breath; take short

111

gastric

garter

quick breaths, e.g. when very surprised. *n* act of gasping.

gastric /ˈɡæstrɪk/ *adj* having to do with the stomach. *n* **gastronomy** /ɡæˈstrɒnəmɪ/ art of cooking and choosing food. *adj* **gastronomic** /ˌɡæstrəˈnɒmɪk/.

gate /ɡeɪt/ *n* entrance in a wall, fence, etc. *n* **gate-crasher** /ˈ.ˌ.ˈ./ uninvited guest.

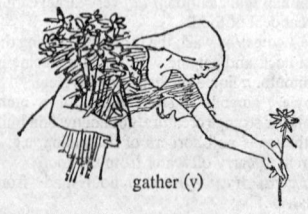

gather (v)

gather /ˈɡæðə^r/ *v* bring or come together; pick (flowers). *vt* be led to understand, e.g. *I gather he is ill*. *n* **gathering** /ˈɡæðərɪŋ/ meeting of people.

gauche /ɡəʊʃ/ *adj* unable to behave gracefully or politely in company.

gaudy /ˈɡɔːdɪ/ *adj* (e.g. of ornaments) worthless and showy.

gauge /ɡeɪdʒ/ *vt* measure the size, power, value etc. *n* instrument for measuring, e.g. *A wind-gauge*.

gaunt /ɡɔːnt/ *adj* thin, looking ill or death-like.

gauntlet /ˈɡɔːntlət/ *n* metal or leather covering for the hand. **to throw down the gauntlet** = show that one is ready to fight. **to run the gauntlet** = to pass between two rows of people who strike as one passes or through other dangers.

gauze /ɡɔːz/ *n* fine cloth through which one can see.

gave /ɡeɪv/ p.t. of **give**.

gay /ɡeɪ/ *adj* **1** merry; (of colours) bright. **2** *sl* having sexual feelings for members of the same sex.

gaze /ɡeɪz/ *vi* look at, usually for a long time, e.g. with wonder or desire.

gazelle /ɡəˈzel/ *n* graceful deer-like animal.

gazette /ɡəˈzet/ *n* newspaper, esp. one printed by the government or a university giving notices of public matters. *n* **gazetteer** /ˌɡæzəˈtɪə^r/ list of

place-names showing where they are to be found on a map.

gear /ɡɪə^r/ *n* **1** equipment. **2** one of the toothed wheels that make a machine go faster or slower while the engine runs at the same speed. **3** one of the arrangements of such wheels in a car chosen by the driver to suit his speed, road conditions, etc.

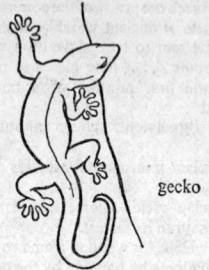

gecko

gecko /ˈɡekəʊ/ *n* small reptile with a long tail, often found in houses in warm countries.

geese /ɡiːs/ *pl* of **goose**.

gelatin /ˈdʒelətɪn/, **gelatine** /ˈdʒelətiːn/ *n* clear material that melts in hot water and thickens to a jelly when cold. *adj* **gelatinous** /dʒɪˈlætɪnəs/ like gelatine; jelly-like.

gelding /ˈɡeldɪŋ/ *n* male horse that cannot become a father.

gem /dʒem/ *n* jewel.

gender /ˈdʒendə^r/ *n* **1** sex. **2** grouping of nouns in a language according to the sex of what they describe.

gene /dʒiːn/ *n* very small body that fixes the appearance, etc., of the young of plants and animals.

genealogy /ˌdʒiːnɪˈælədʒɪ/ *n* plan or history of the descendants of a family. *adj* **genealogical** /ˌdʒiːnɪəˈlɒdʒɪkəl/.

general /ˈdʒenərəl/ *adj* having to do with all or the whole; common. *n* high officer of the army. *n* **generality** /ˌdʒenəˈrælɪtɪ/. *adv* **generally** /ˈdʒenərəlɪ/ **1** in a general way. **2** usually. *vt* **generalize** /ˈdʒenərəlaɪz/ say something of all persons or things. *n* **generalization** /ˌdʒenərəlaɪˈzeɪʃən/.

generate /ˈdʒenəreɪt/ *vt* produce esp. power, heat, etc.; cause to happen, e.g *Unhappiness generates wrongdoing*. *n* **generation** /ˌdʒenəˈreɪʃən/ **1** act of producing. **2** all the people of the same time or age in a family. *n* **generator** /ˈdʒenəreɪtə^r/ machine for producing electricity, gas, etc.

generic /dʒɪˈnerɪk/ *adj* having to do with a class as a whole.

generous /ˈdʒenərəs/ *adj* giving freely; kind, noble-minded. *n* **generosity** /ˌdʒenəˈrɒsɪtɪ/.

genesis /ˈdʒenəsɪs/ *n* the beginning; act of producing. *n* **Genesis** book of the Bible telling how the earth and man were first made.

genetic /dʒɪ'netɪk/ adj 1 having to do with GENES. 2 having to do with the producing or beginning of anything.

genial /'dʒiːnɪəl/ adj pleasant and cheerful in manner.

genie /'dʒiːnɪ/ n good or evil spirit in Eastern stories.

genital /'dʒenɪtəl/ adj having to do with the producing of young. n **genitals** sexual parts of the male or female body.

genitive /'dʒenətɪv/ n word or sign showing ownership.

genius /'dʒiːnɪəs/ n 1 person of great power and skill. 2 great skill in a person.

genocide /'dʒenəsaɪd/ n killing off a whole race of people.

gent /dʒent/ infml gentleman.

genteel /dʒen'tiːl/ adj too polite.

gentile /'dʒentaɪl/ n not a Jew.

gentility /dʒen'tɪlətɪ/ n state of having good manners or of being well-born.

gentle /'dʒentl/ adj kind; not rough; slow and soft.

gentleman /'dʒentlmən/ n 1 man. 2 man born of a good family, having good manners.

gentry /'dʒentrɪ/ n people of high social rank below the titled people.

genuflection /ˌdʒenjʊ'flekʃən/ n act of bending the knee as a sign of respect.

genuine /'dʒenjʊɪn/ adj real; true.

genus /'dʒenəs/ n group of living things that are related.

geography /dʒɪ'ɒgrəfɪ/ n study of the earth, its peoples, seas and mountains, weather, etc. adj **geographical** /dʒɪə'græfɪkəl/.

geology /dʒɪ'ɒlədʒɪ/ n study of rocks and the surface of the earth so as to learn its history and how it was formed. n **geologist** /dʒɪ'ɒlədʒɪst/ one who studies geology. adj **geological** /dʒɪə'lɒdʒɪkəl/.

geometry /dʒɪ'ɒmɪtrɪ/ n science of lines and figures. adj **geometrical** /dʒɪə'metrɪkəl/.

geriatrics /ˌdʒerɪ'ætrɪks/ n medical treatment of old people.

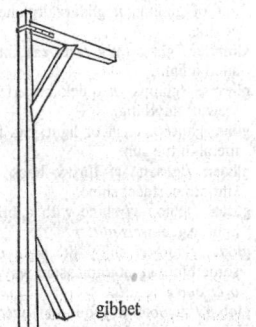

gibbet

germ /dʒɜːm/ n 1 very small animal that causes disease. 2 very small piece of living matter from which a plant or animal grows.

germicide /'dʒɜːmɪsaɪd/ n any cleaning material that kills the seeds of disease.

germinate /'dʒɜːmɪneɪt/ v cause or start to grow.

gestation /dʒe'steɪʃən/ n act or condition of producing young in the body.

gesticulate /dʒe'stɪkjʊleɪt/ vi express ideas or feelings by movements of the hands and face.

gesture /'dʒestʃə/ n deed, or movement of the face, hands, etc., used to express feelings. vi make a gesture.

get /get/ v 1 obtain; bring; buy. 2 cause to be done, e.g. *I got my hair cut* = caused it to be cut. 3 arrive, e.g. *We cannot get home tonight.* 4 become, e.g. *The days are getting warmer.* 5 go, e.g. *Get out!* = go out of the room. **to get away** = escape. **to get up** = rise (e.g. in the morning).

geyser (1)

geyser /'giːzə/ n 1 natural spring of hot water which shoots up into the air. 2 an instrument for heating water quickly by running it over plates heated by gas.

ghastly /'gɑːstlɪ/ adj terrible.

gherkin /'gɜːkɪn/ n small, long, and round green vegetable.

ghetto /'getəʊ/ n part of a city where poor people live in crowded conditions.

ghost /gəʊst/ n spirit of a dead person appearing to the living; shadowy likeness of a thing. **ghost writer** = person who writes a book for a well-known man and lets the other pretend that he has written it.

ghoul /guːl/ n evil spirit that feeds on the dead; person who delights in terrible things.

giant /'dʒaɪənt/ n, adj (person) of more than ordinary, or human, size; very large powerful person in fairy stories.

gibber /'dʒɪbə/ vi make quick meaningless word-like noises. n (sing) **gibberish** /'dʒɪbərɪʃ/ such noises.

gibbet /'dʒɪbɪt/ n wooden frame used for hanging law-breakers.

gibbon /'gɪbən/ n man-like monkey.

gibe /dʒaɪb/ vi laugh at someone, intending to hurt his feelings.

giblets /'dʒɪbləts/ n those inside parts of a bird that can be cooked and eaten.

giddy /'gɪdɪ/ *adj* feeling as if the head were turning round; not steady or serious in character.

gift /gɪft/ *n* **1** that which is given. **2** natural inborn power, e.g. *A gift for poetry.*

gig /gɪg/ *n* **1** light two-wheeled carriage. **2** small boat.

gigantic /dʒaɪ'gæntɪk/ *adj* very large.

giggle /'gɪgəl/ *vi* laugh in a silly way but not loudly. *n* such a laugh.

gild /gɪld/ *vt* cover thinly with gold. **to gild the pill** = make an unpleasant thing seem pleasant.

gill /gɪl/ *n* that part of a fish's body with which it breathes.

gilt /gɪlt/ *adj* covered with gold or gold paint.

gimlet /'gɪmlət/ *n* small T-shaped instrument used for making holes in wood.

gin[1] /dʒɪn/ *n* colourless strong drink.

gin[2] /dʒɪn/ *n* **1** instrument used for pulling up heavy weights. **2** machine for cleaning cotton. **3** instrument for catching animals.

ginger /'dʒɪndʒə/ *n* hot-tasting root of a plant. *n, adj* (of a) red-brown colour. *n* **gingerbread** /'dʒɪndʒəbred/ cake with ginger in it.

gipsy, gypsy /'dʒɪpsɪ/ *n* member of a wandering race which lives in covered carts and is always moving about.

giraffe /dʒɪ'rɑːf/ *n* an African horse-like mammal with a very long neck.

gird /gɜːd/ *vt* tie on firmly, e.g. a sword. **to gird up one's loins** = get ready, e.g. for battle.

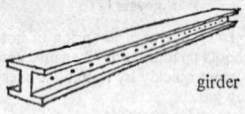

girder

girder /'gɜːdə/ *n* large support, usually made of iron, used in building bridges and roofs.

girdle /'gɜːdl/ *n* garment worn by a woman under her clothes to keep her body in a certain shape.

girl /gɜːl/ *n* female child; young female; young female servant.

girt /gɜːt/ *p.t.* and *p.p.* of **gird**.

girth /gɜːθ/ *n* **1** distance round the middle. **2** band round the middle of a horse to keep the SADDLE in place.

gist /dʒɪst/ *n* most necessary or most important part, e.g. of a story.

give /gɪv/ *vt* **1** cause to have without payment. **2** allow (someone) to have the use of. **3** to cause or produce. **to give out news** = to make the news public. **his voice gave him away** = showed what he wished to keep secret. **4** yield or stretch, e.g. *A soft chair gives when one sits in it.* **to give up** = stop trying, believing, etc. **to give in** = yield. *n* **give** power of yielding, state of not being quite stiff. **given** /'gɪvən/ **1** *p.p.* of give. **2** *adj* already fixed or agreed upon, e.g. *Within a given time.*

gizzard /'gɪzəd/ *n* second stomach of a bird in which the food is broken into very small pieces.

glacier /'glæsɪə/ *n* very large slow-moving river or mass of ice. *adj* **glacial** /'gleɪʃəl, 'gleɪsɪəl/ having to do with glaciers; like ice.

glad /glæd/ *adj* happy.

glade /gleɪd/ *n* open space between trees.

gladiator /'glædɪeɪtə/ *n* trained fighter of ancient Rome who fought with men or wild animals for public amusement.

glamour /'glæmə/ *n* such charm or beauty as deceives one and causes things to appear different from what they really are. *adj* **glamorous** /'glæmərəs/.

glance /glɑːns/ *vi* give a quick look. *n* quick look. **to glance off** = (of a blow, knife, etc.) hit and slip off a hard surface.

gland /glænd/ *n* small part of the body which produces a liquid which, in the bloodstream, produces certain effects on the body. *adj* **glandular** /'glændʒʊlə/.

glare /gleə/ *vi* **1** shine with a very bright light. **2** look angrily. *adj* **glaring** /'gleərɪŋ/ (of a fault or mistake) easily noticed.

glass /glɑːs/ *n* **1** hard clear material that lets light in through windows. **2** drinking vessel. *n* (*pl*) **glasses** pieces of specially shaped glass held in a frame in front of the eyes to correct weak eyesight. *n* **glasspaper** /'glɑːsˌpeɪpə/ paper covered with powdered glass, used for making a surface smooth.

glaze /gleɪz/ *n* any paint-like liquid used to give a glassy surface. *vt* cover with a shining surface like glass. *n* **glazier** /'gleɪzɪə/ one who fixes glass into windows.

gleam /gliːm/ *vi* send out light. *n* narrow beam of light.

glean /gliːn/ *v* gather (what is left when the grain has been cut and taken away); gather slowly.

glee /gliː/ *n* state of being very happy or merry.

glen /glen/ *n* narrow valley.

glib /glɪb/ *adj* easy-flowing (in speech), but having no deep thought, or not speaking the truth.

glide /glaɪd/ *vi* **1** move gently and quietly over a smooth surface or through the air. **2** pass from one note of music to another without a stop. *n* act of gliding. *n* **glider** airplane that has no engine.

glimmer /'glɪmə/ *vi* give a weak, unsteady light. *n* such a light.

glimpse /glɪmps/ *n* quick imperfect or passing view of anything.

glint /glɪnt/ *n* flash of light, e.g. from polished metal in the sun.

glisten /'glɪsən/ *vi* throw back light from a smooth surface; shine.

glitter /'glɪtə/ *vi* shine with a bright unsteady light, e.g. *Jewels glitter.*

gloat /gləʊt/ *vi* enjoy the sight or thought of something, in an unpleasant way, e.g. *To gloat over one's wealth.*

global /'gləʊbəl/ *adj* found all over the earth.

globe /gləʊb/ *n* **1** anything shaped like a ball. **2**

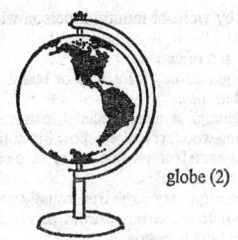

globe (2)

the earth; a ball on which the earth is mapped. *n* **globe-trotter** /'. ,. ./ one who is always travelling to foreign countries. *n* **globule** /'globjuːl/ very small ball of matter; drop of liquid.

gloom /gluːm/ *n* darkness; low spirits. *adj* **gloomy** /'gluːmɪ/.

glorify /'gloːrɪfaɪ/ *vt* **1** praise highly. **2** make (something) appear or sound better than it is.

glorious /'gloːrɪəs/ *adj* beautiful, heavenly; very fine.

glory /'gloːrɪ/ *n* praise; fame and honour.

gloss /glɒs/ *n* **1** brightness; bright shining surface. **2** note explaining the meaning of a piece of writing. *vt* provide such a note for. **to gloss over** = cover over (a mistake). *adj* **glossy** /'glɒsɪ/ shining brightly.

glossary /'glɒsərɪ/ *n* list of difficult words with notes explaining them.

glove /glʌv/ *n* covering for the hand.

glow /gləʊ/ *vi* give out heat without fire; feel warm and comfortable, e.g. after exercise. *n* state of glowing.

glower /'glaʊə/ *vi* give a fierce, angry look.

glucose /'gluːkəʊs/ *n* natural sugar found in fruits and plants.

glue /gluː/ *n* material used for sticking things together.

glum /glʌm/ *adj* silent and low in spirits.

glut /glʌt/ *vt* fill too full; supply too much. *n* too great a supply.

glutinous /'gluːtɪnəs/ *adj* sticky, like GLUE.

glutton /'glʌtn/ *n* one who eats too much.

glycerine /'glɪsərɪn, -riːn/ *n* sweet clear liquid obtained from animal and plant fats, used for medicine and in science.

gnarled /naːld/ *adj* having a rough surface like that of an old tree.

gnash /næʃ/ *vt* strike or press (the teeth) together in anger.

gnat /næt/ *n* small flying insect which bites and draws blood.

gnaw /noː/ *vt* keep in the mouth and continue to bite, esp. with the back teeth, e.g. *A dog gnaws a bone.*

gnome /nəʊm/ *n* small ugly fairy supposed to guard hidden gold and jewels.

gnu /nuː/ *n* an African deer.

go /gəʊ/ *vi* **1** move from place to place, e.g. *To go*

to France. **2** leave or pass away, e.g. *It is time to go.* **3** become, e.g. *To go black in the face (with anger).* **4** have a special place, e.g. *The shoes go in this box.* *n* move in a game. **to go about something** = do it, e.g. *I don't know how to go about it.* **to go along with** = agree with. **to go for** = **1** attack. **2** like. **to go in for** = like and give time to, e.g. *He goes in for stamp collecting.* **to go off** = **1** (of food) become bad through age. **2** (of people) cease to like or want. **3** explode; (of a gun) be fired. **to go on** = continue, e.g. *Don't go on talking.* **to go out** = leave the house. **to go with** = be suitable with (e.g. of one colour with another), e.g. *Her dress does not go with her hair* = the colour of the dress is wrong for the hair. **a going concern** = successful business.

goad /gəʊd/ *n* pointed stick used to drive cattle. *vt* drive; urge.

goal /gəʊl/ *n* place or effect aimed at; that which marks the end of a race. **to score a goal in football** = get one point by kicking the ball between the two posts guarded by other players. *n* **goalkeeper** /'gəʊl,kiːpə/ player who guards the goal.

goat /gəʊt/ *n* animal like a sheep, having long hair and horns.

gobble /'gɒbəl/ *v* swallow (food) in a hasty bad-mannered way.

go-between /'. ,. ./ *n* one who makes arrangements for matters between people who do not meet.

goblet /'gɒblət/ *n* drinking vessel.

goblin /'gɒblɪn/ *n* fairy that plays tricks on people.

go-cart /'. ./ *n* small carriage for a baby, pushed by hand.

god /gɒd/ *n* one of a number of beings believed to have power over man. *n* **goddess** /'gɒdəs/ female god. *n* **God** a single being thought of as having measureless power; the ruler of heaven *n* **godchild** /'gɒd-tʃaɪld/ a friend's child whom one has promised to help with religious teaching. *n* **godfather** /'gɒd,faːðə/ man who has made such a promise. *n* **godmother** /'gɒd,mʌðə/ woman who has made such a promise. *n* **godsend** /'gɒdsend/ any great help that comes unexpectedly.

goggle /'gɒgəl/ *vi* open the eyes very wide. *n* **goggles** glasses to protect the eyes from dust.

goitre /'gɔɪtə/ *n* swelling in the neck caused by disease.

gold /gəʊld/ *n* precious yellow metal. *adj* **golden** /'gəʊldn/ made of gold; like gold. *n, adj* (of the) colour of gold. *n* **gold leaf** /,. './ very thin sheet of gold used for ornamenting things, e.g. the edges of books. *n* **goldsmith** /'gəʊld,smɪθ/ one who makes things of gold.

golf /gɒlf/ *n* game in which a small ball is hit into each of 18 holes arranged in a large open piece of land, the winner being the one who takes fewest strokes to put his ball into all the holes.

gondola /'gɒndələ/ *n* long narrow boat with high

ends used in Venice. *n* **gondolier** /ˌgɒndəˈlɪəʳ/ one who rows a gondola.

gone /gɒn/ p.p. of **go**.

gong /gɒŋ/ *n* flat metal instrument that makes a bell-like sound when struck.

good /gʊd/ *adj* of fine quality. *n, interj* **goodbye** /gʊdˈbaɪ/ expression used when going away. *adj* **goodly** /ˈgʊdlɪ/ good, e.g. *A goodly share* = large share. *n* **goods** /gʊdz/ any materials, articles, etc.

goose

goose /guːs/ *n* large duck-like bird, used for food.

gooseberry /ˈgʊzbərɪ/ *n* 1 small round fruit which grows on a bush. 2 *infml* unwanted third person walking or sitting with two lovers.

gore[1] /gɔːʳ/ *n* blood.

gore[2] /gɔːʳ/ *vt* wound with the horns, as a cow does.

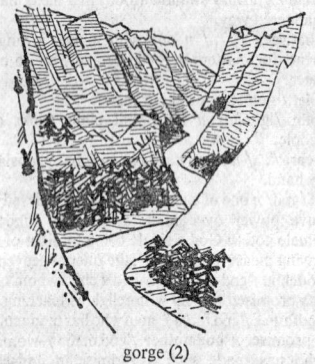

gorge (2)

gorge /gɔːdʒ/ *n* 1 food-passage to the stomach. 2 deep narrow passage between hills. *v* eat too quickly and more than is necessary.

gorgeous /ˈgɔːdʒəs/ *adj* very fine and beautiful.

gorilla /gəˈrɪlə/ *n* large African monkey-like creature.

gorse /gɔːs/ *n* low bush with sharp points on its branches and sweet-smelling yellow flowers.

gosling /ˈgɒzlɪŋ/ *n* young GOOSE.

gospel /ˈgɒspəl/ *n* one of the four books of the Bible telling of the life and teachings of Christ. **gospel truth** = pure truth.

gossamer /ˈgɒsəməʳ/ *n* material of fine silky threads.

gossip /ˈgɒsɪp/ *n* 1 worthless talk, usually about the faults and mistakes of others; news that is

spread by word of mouth. 2 person who talks thus.

got /gɒt/ p.t. of **get**.

Gothic /ˈgɒθɪk/ *adj* (of a way of building) with pointed arches.

gouge /gaʊdʒ/ *n* curved sharp instrument for hollowing wood. *vt* make hollow by cutting out.

goulash /ˈguːlæʃ/ *n* hot-tasting mixture of boiled meat and vegetables.

gourd /gʊəd/ *n* very large fruit usually grown on the ground; vessel made from this fruit when dried and made hollow.

gourmand /ˈgʊəmənd/ *n* one who eats too much.

gourmet /ˈgʊəmeɪ/ *n* one who takes great interest in food and chooses his food very carefully.

gout /gaʊt/ *n* disease caused by too much acid in the blood, resulting in swelling and pain in the joints, e.g. knee, foot, fingers.

govern /ˈgʌvən/ *vt* direct or control or rule. *n* **government** /ˈgʌvənmənt, ˈgʌvəmənt/ that body of people which rules a country. *n* **governor** /ˈgʌvənəʳ/ 1 man appointed by a government to rule any part of a country. 2 instrument in an engine that controls the speed.

governess /ˈgʌvənəs/ *n* woman who teaches and takes charge of young children.

gown /gaʊn/ *n* 1 long indoor garment. 2 woman's dress. 2 long black garment worn by teachers in a college.

grab /græb/ *vt* seize quickly, take by force, e.g. the land of another country.

grace /greɪs/ *n* 1 beauty. 2 pleasant way of moving, of writing. 3 kindness. 4 the kindness of God. **a state of grace** = state in which one is doing God's will. 5 short prayer of thanks to God before or after a meal. *vt* give beauty to; make pleasant. **your Grace** = way of addressing a high officer of the Church or a nobleman. *adj* **graceful** /ˈgreɪsfəl/ having grace, esp. in movement.

gracious /ˈgreɪʃəs/ *adj* pleasant in manner; kind; gentle. **good gracious!**—a cry of surprise.

gradate /grəˈdeɪt/ *vt* arrange in order so that the difference between one thing and the next is not very noticeable. *n* **gradation** /grəˈdeɪʃən/.

grade /greɪd/ *n* 1 step; class. 2 slope. *infml* **to make the grade** = be good enough. *vt* to arrange in groups according to size or kind, etc. *n* **gradient** /ˈgreɪdɪənt/ steepness of a road.

gradual /ˈgrædʒʊəl/ *adj* going step by step; slowly.

graduate /ˈgrædʒʊət/ *n, adj* (one) who has finished a course of study at a university. *vi* /ˈgrædʒʊeɪt/ finish successfully such a course.

graduated /ˈgrædʒʊeɪtɪd/ *adj* marked with lines for measuring, e.g. *A graduated glass.*

graft[1] /grɑːft/ *v* take (a piece of living material) from one place and get it to grow in another part of the same plant or animal, or on another plant or animal. *n* piece of living material grafted.

graft[2] /grɑːft/ *vi* get money secretly and dishonestly, usually from the government. *n* such dishonesty; money got dishonestly.

grain /greɪn/ *n* **1** any small piece of matter. **2** single seed of wheat, corn, etc.; mass of corn, etc., spoken of generally. **3** arrangement of lines of growth in wood.

grammar /ˈɡræmə/ *n* (study of the) arrangement of words in the sentences of a language. *n* **grammar school** /ˈ.. ˌ./ school for children aged 11 to 18, often leading to a university or learned employment. *adj* **grammatical** /ɡrəˈmætɪkəl/ **1** having to do with grammar. **2** (of a sentence) properly formed.

gramme, gram /græm/ *n* measure of weight = 0.035 ounce.

gramophone /ˈɡræməfəʊn/ *n* machine that produces music from a flat black plate.

granary /ˈɡrænərɪ/ *n* store-house for grain.

grand¹ /grænd/ *adj* **1** very fine and noble, e.g. *A grand sight; A grand character.* **2** large and fine-looking, e.g. *A grand house.* **3** (of persons) proud, thinking oneself very important, e.g. *He is too grand to speak to us.* **4** largest, most important, e.g. *The grand stairway.*

grand-² /grænd/, **grandfather** /ˈɡræn(d)ˌfɑːðə/ one's father's or mother's father. *n* **grandmother** /ˈɡræn(d)ˌmʌðə/ one's father's or mother's mother. *n* **grandson** /ˈɡræn(d)sʌn/ one's son's son; one's daughter's son.

grandee /grænˈdiː/ *n* nobleman of high rank.

grandeur /ˈɡrændʒə/ *n* state of being great or beautiful in appearance, character, etc.

grandiloquent /ɡrænˈdɪləkwənt/ *adj* using high-sounding long words.

grandiose /ˈɡrændɪəʊs/ *adj* pretending to be grand, but not really so.

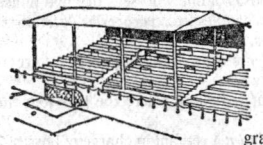

grandstand

grandstand /ˈɡrændstænd/ *n* long rows of seats built up one above the other for people to sit and watch a game or horse-races.

grange /greɪndʒ/ *n* farm-house with all the small outside buildings.

granite /ˈɡrænɪt/ *n* a very hard rock.

granny /ˈɡrænɪ/ *infml n* **1** old woman. **2** (child's word for) grandmother.

grant /grɑːnt/ *vt* give; allow. *n* amount of money given for a purpose. **to take for granted** = to accept as true without reason or proof being given.

granule /ˈɡrænjuːl/ *n* small grain of matter. *vt* **granulate** /ˈɡrænjʊleɪt/ make into small grains.

grape /greɪp/ *n* fruit from which wine is made. **sour grapes** = that which one says is worthless because one cannot obtain it.

grapefruit /ˈɡreɪpfruːt/ *n* a rather sour fruit like a very large light-coloured orange.

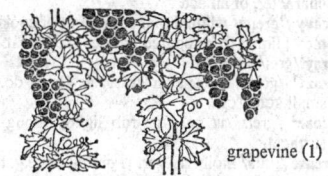

grapevine (1)

grapevine /ˈɡreɪpvaɪn/ *n* **1** plant on which grapes grow. **2** *infml* secret spreading of news in a country.

graph /grɑːf/ *n* straight line or curve drawn on squared paper to show the relation between two changing quantities, e.g. my age and height.

graphic /ˈɡræfɪk/ *adj* **1** written. **2** very clear and like the real thing, e.g. *A graphic account of a fight.* **the graphic arts** = drawing, painting, printing.

graphite /ˈɡræfaɪt/ *n* black material used inside pencils.

grapnel /ˈɡræpnəl/ *n* hooked instrument used for holding an enemy's ship during a fight, or for holding a small boat from being carried away.

grapple /ˈɡræpəl/ *vt* seize and hold. *vi* hold and fight with an enemy.

grasp /grɑːsp/ *vt* **1** seize and hold with the hand. **2** understand (an idea). *adj* **grasping** not generous.

grass /grɑːs/ *n* that green or light brown very common low-growing plant which covers fields, hills, etc. *n* **grasshopper** /ˈɡrɑːsˌhɒpə/ a jumping insect that lives among grass.

grate¹ /greɪt/ *n* iron frame used to hold wood or coal in a fireplace.

grate² /greɪt/ *vt* break in pieces by rubbing on a rough, hard surface. *vi* make a hard unpleasant noise.

grateful /ˈɡreɪtfəl/ *adj* **1** thankful. **2** pleasing.

gratify /ˈɡrætɪfaɪ/ *vt* please or satisfy.

grating /ˈɡreɪtɪŋ/ *n* frame with small openings.

gratis /ˈɡrætɪs, ˈɡreɪtɪs, ˈɡrɑːtɪs/ *adv* free; without payment of money.

gratitude /ˈɡrætɪtjuːd/ *n* thankfulness.

gratuitous /ɡrəˈtjuːɪtəs/ *adj* **1** free, without payment. **2** not asked for; unwanted; unnecessary.

gratuity /ɡrəˈtjuːətɪ/ *n* small gift of money to a servant.

grave¹ /greɪv/ *n* hole in the earth in which a dead body is put.

grave² /greɪv/ *adj* serious, important.

gravel /ˈɡrævəl/ *n* **1** mixture of earth and small stones used for roads and paths. **2** small solid pieces formed in the body and passed out with the waste water of the body.

graven /ˈɡreɪvən/ *adj* cut, as a figure in stone.

gravitate /ˈɡrævəteɪt/ *vi* move in any direction as if pulled by some force; feel a desire to go, e.g. *In summer people gravitate to the seaside.*

gravity /ˈgrævəti/ n 1 force that pulls objects to the ground. 2 seriousness of manner or character, of an act.

gravy /ˈgreɪvɪ/ n liquid that comes out of cooked meat; liquid to be poured over cooked meat.

gray /greɪ/ see **grey**.

graze¹ /greɪz/ vi feed on grass, as sheep do. n small SCRATCH.

graze² /greɪz/ vt pass or rub lightly along (a surface).

grease /griːs/ n oily matter. vt put oil on (e.g. the parts of a machine).

great¹ /greɪt/ adj 1 big; extending far and wide. 2 very good; important, e.g. *A great writer*.

great-² /greɪt/ e.g. **great-grandmother** /ˌ. ˈ. ../ n grandmother of either of one's parents.

greed /griːd/ n great desire to get for oneself only; too great an interest in food. adj **greedy** /ˈgriːdɪ/.

green /griːn/ n, adj (of the) colour of fresh leaves and grass. adj (of fruit) not ready to be eaten. adj without experience or training. n open piece of grass-land in the middle of a village. (pl) **greens** green vegetables.

greengage /ˈgriːngeɪdʒ/ n small green fruit with a large stone in it.

greengrocer /ˈgriːnˌgrəʊsə/ n one who sells fruit and vegetables.

greenhouse /ˈgriːnhaʊs/ n house, made of glass, in which plants are grown.

greet /griːt/ vt express welcome or pleasure at meeting (a person). n **greeting** /ˈgriːtɪŋ/ such a welcome.

gregarious /grɪˈgeərɪəs/ adj living in large groups; liking to live in a group.

grenade /grɪˈneɪd/ n iron shell filled with powder which explodes when it strikes anything—or after a "xed time. n **grenadier** /ˌɡrenəˈdɪə/ soldier in the Grenadier Guards.

grew /gruː/ p.t. of **grow**.

grey, gray /greɪ/ n, adj (of the) colour obtained by mixing black and white. **grey matter** /ˈ. ˈ. ./ = part of the brain. n **greyhound** /ˈgreɪhaʊnd/ large fast-running dog.

grid /grɪd/ n iron framework; frame of fine wires in an electrical instrument.

griddle /ˈgrɪdl/ n round iron plate for cooking cakes.

gridiron /ˈgrɪdaɪən/ n framework of iron bars used in cooking; any arrangement of things in lines like a gridiron.

grief /griːf/ n great sorrow. **to come to grief** = fail; have an accident.

grievance /ˈgriːvəns/ n cause for complaint.

grieve /griːv/ vi feel sorrow. vt cause sorrow to.

grill /grɪl/ v cook over a hot fire on iron bars. n 1 eating-house where food is so cooked. 2 meat or fish so cooked.

grille /grɪl/ n iron bars across an opening in a wall.

grim /grɪm/ adj having a cruel, unpleasant and unyielding appearance.

grimace /grɪˈmeɪs/ n strange or ugly look on the face. vi give such a look.

grime /graɪm/ n dirt, specially that collected on the skin.

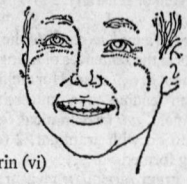

grin (vi)

grin /grɪn/ n wide smile. vi smile broadly.

grind /graɪnd/ vt rub into a powder; rub on a hard stone, e.g. to make a knife sharp. n **grindstone** /ˈgraɪndstəʊn/ hard stone used for sharpening knives and other instruments. **to keep one's nose to the grindstone** = force oneself to work very hard. n **grinder** /ˈgraɪndə/.

grip /grɪp/ vt seize or hold firmly in the hand. n act or way of seizing or holding. adj **gripping** /ˈgrɪpɪŋ/ (e.g. of a story) very interesting.

grisly /ˈgrɪzlɪ/ adj causing terror; unpleasant.

grist /grɪst/ n corn which is to be made into flour.

gristle /ˈgrɪsl/ n soft bone-like material in meat.

grit /grɪt/ n small hard pieces of matter, e.g. fine sand. **to grit the teeth** = press them firmly together, e.g. when doing something difficult or painful.

grizzly (bear) /ˈgrɪzlɪ/ n large fierce bear in Canada and U.S.

grizzled /ˈgrɪzəld/ adj grey.

groan /grəʊn/ vi make a low sound, as in pain. n such a sound.

grocer /ˈgrəʊsə/ n one who sells dry and tinned food, soap, candles, etc. n **groceries** /ˈgrəʊsərɪz/ such goods.

grog /grɒg/ n strong drink. adj **groggy** /ˈgrɒgɪ/ unsteady, weak.

groin /grɔɪn/ n hollow where the legs join the body.

groom /gruːm/ n 1 servant in charge of horses. 2 man just about to be married. vt brush and clean (e.g. a horse). **well groomed** = (of a man) looking neat and clean.

groove /gruːv/ n long narrow hollow cut in wood or other material. vt cut a groove in.

grope /grəʊp/ vi feel for something with out-stretched hands, e.g. when looking for something in the dark.

gross¹ /grəʊs/ adj 1 too big; fat. 2 not fine or polite. 3 (of an amount) including everything.

gross² /grəʊs/ n group of 144 things.

grotesque /grəʊˈtesk/ adj so strange as to appear unpleasant or foolish.

grotto /ˈgrɒtəʊ/ n small cave.

ground¹ /graʊnd/ p.t. & p.p. of **grind**.

ground² /graʊnd/ n 1 bottom or lowest part of anything. 2 solid surface of the earth. 3 reason for having an opinion. vt 1 place on the ground.

2 make firm. *vi* (of a ship) run onto the ground. *adj* **groundless** /'graʊndləs/ (e.g. of hopes, fears) without reason or real cause.

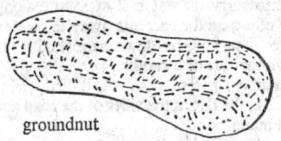

groundnut

groundnut /'graʊndnʌt/ *n* an oily seed one inch long with a thin white cover and yellow inside skin, which grows under the ground and may be eaten.

grounds /graʊndz/ *n* 1 small bits left at the bottom of a cup or pot of liquid. 2 garden or land round a house.

group /gruːp/ *n* number of persons or objects in one place, or gathered for a special purpose; class or kind. *v* come or bring together in a group.

grouse /graʊs/ *n* small wild bird shot for food.

grove /grəʊv/ *n* small group of trees.

grovel /'grɒvəl/ *vi* lie on the ground face down, as a prisoner begging for mercy.

grow /grəʊ/ *vi* (of plants) live, e.g. *Roses grow in England.* *v* 1 become or cause to become larger. 2 become, e.g *His hair has grown grey.* **to grow on** = start to be liked by. **to grow up** = (of a person or animal) become older.

growl /graʊl/ *vi* make a low sound in the throat as wild animals do when angry. *n* such a sound.

grown /grəʊn/ p.p. of **grow**; of full growth, not children. *infml* **grown-up** /'grəʊn ʌp, ˌgrəʊn 'ʌp/, *adj* /grəʊn 'ʌp/ person who is no longer a child.

growth /grəʊθ/ *n* act or amount of growing; that which is produced. **a growth in the body** = diseased mass growing in the body.

grub¹ /grʌb/ *vi* search in the earth for food. **to grub up** = dig up out of the ground. *sl* food.

grub² /grʌb/ *n* form of an insect before it changes into its winged form.

grubby /'grʌbɪ/ *adj* dirty.

grudge /grʌdʒ/ *vt* 1 give or allow unwillingly. 2 hate (someone) because he has something which one has not got. *n* angry feeling against a person for something he has done in the past.

gruel /'gruːəl/ *n* thick liquid food made from powdered grain.

gruelling /'gruːəlɪŋ/ *adj* very tiring; causing suffering; cruel.

gruesome /'gruːsəm/ *adj* very unpleasant; terrible.

gruff /grʌf/ *adj* rough and unpleasant in voice or manner.

grumble /'grʌmbəl/ *vi* 1 complain. 2 make a low noise like distant thunder.

grumpy /'grʌmpɪ/ *adj* bad-tempered.

grunt /grʌnt/ *vi* make a noise like that of a pig. *n* such a noise.

guano /'gwɑːnəʊ/ *n* waste matter dropped by sea-birds and used to make plants grow better.

guarantee /ˌgærən'tiː/ *n* promise to see that another person fulfils his promise; promise by one who makes or sells something that it will work properly for a certain time. *vt* make such a promise about (something).

guard /gɑːd/ *v* watch against danger or surprise; defend against attack. *n* 1 person who watches or defends; soldier of the home army. 2 thing which prevents damage, e.g. *A fire-guard* = iron frame used to keep children out of the fire. *n* **guardian** /'gɑːdɪən/ one who guards; one who has charge of, e.g., children.

guava /'gwɑːvə/ *n* (tree with a) bitter fruit which grows in hot countries.

guer(r)illa /gə'rɪlə/ *n* member of a group of men who are not regular soldiers and who fight in small bands, usually against the government of their own countries.

guess /ges/ *v* form (an idea) without real proof or reason; try to get the correct answer to a question by chance, when one does not really know. *n* idea so formed.

guest /gest/ *n* visitor; one who stays for meals or sleeps in the house; any invited person.

guffaw /gə'fɔː, 'gʌfɔː/ *n* loud laugh. *vi* laugh loudly.

guide /gaɪd/ *vt* lead or direct in the right way. *n* one who leads or shows the way.

guild /gɪld/ *n* group joined together for trade or other purposes.

guile /gaɪl/ *n* cleverness in deceiving.

guillotine /'gɪlətiːn/ *n* 1 machine used for cutting off the heads of law-breakers in France. 2 for cutting off the edges of the pages in a book.

guilt /gɪlt/ *n* fact of having done wrong. *adj* **guilty** /'gɪltɪ/ having done wrong.

guinea-fowl /'gɪnɪ faʊl/ *n* large spotted bird used for food.

guinea-pig /'gɪnɪ ˌpɪg/ *n* 1 small animal rather like a rabbit. 2 person used, e.g. to try out a medicine.

guise /gaɪz/ *n* general appearance; deceiving appearance.

guitar

guitar /gɪ'tɑː/ *n* musical instrument having six strings which are moved by the fingers to make the sounds.

gulf /gʌlf/ *n* narrow part of the sea with land on all sides except one; deep hole in the earth.

gull¹ /gʌl/ *n* large sea-bird.

gull² /gʌl/ *n* easily deceived person. *vt* deceive.

gullet /'gʌlɪt/ *n* that part of the throat down which food passes when swallowed.

gullible /'gʌləbəl/ *adj* easily deceived.

gully /'gʌli/ *n* small valley worn by running water.

gulp /gʌlp/ *v* swallow quickly in large amounts; make a movement of the throat as if swallowing. *n* such a movement or the sound of gulping.

gum¹ /gʌm/ *n* red part of the mouth in which the teeth are set.

gum² /gʌm/ *n* sticky liquid obtained from trees; a form of rubber. *n* **chewing-gum** /'. . ./ sweet-tasting wax-like substance kept in the mouth and bitten—as a form of pleasure.

gumboil /'gʌmbɔɪl/ *n* painful swelling inside the mouth.

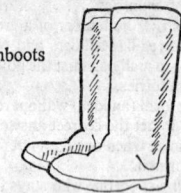

gumboots

gumboots /'gʌmbuːts/ *n* high boots made of rubber.

gun /gʌn/ *n* instrument used for shooting. *n* **guncotton** /'. ,./ explosive made from cotton and acids. *n* **gunpowder** /'gʌn,paʊdə/ an explosive substance. *n* **gunrunning** /'gʌn,rʌnɪŋ/ taking guns into a country when it is against the law. *n* **gunsmith** /'gʌn,smɪθ/ one who makes or repairs guns.

gunwale, gunnel /'gʌnəl/ *n* upper edge of the side of a boat.

gurgle /'gɜːgəl/ *vt* make a sound like running water.

guru /'gʊruː/ *n* religious teacher in India.

gush /gʌʃ/ *vi* flow out quickly. *adj* **gushing** /'gʌʃɪŋ/ giving expression to one's feelings too freely and pretending to feel more than one really does.

gusset /'gʌsɪt/ *n* piece of cloth put into a garment to make it larger.

gust /gʌst/ *n* sudden rush of wind.

gusto /'gʌstəʊ/ *n* enjoyment.

gut /gʌt/ *n* **1** pipe-like part of the body which leads from the stomach and takes away the waste matter. **2** strong string made from the bowel of a sheep and used in musical in-

struments. **3** narrow water-course or path. *n* **guts** *infml* courage.

gutter¹ /'gʌtə/ *n* **1** hollow pipe along the edge of a roof to carry off water. **2** CHANNEL along the side of a road for carrying away the water.

gutter² /'gʌtə/ *vi* run down as melted wax runs down the side of a candle.

guttersnipe /'gʌtəsnaɪp/ *n* small dirty child who plays in the dirt at the sides of the road and has bad manners.

guttural /'gʌtərəl/ *adj* (of a sound) formed in the throat.

guy¹ /gaɪ/ *n* rope used to fasten something and keep it steady.

guy² /gaɪ/ *n* **1** figure made to look like a man dressed in old clothes and burned on November 5th. **2** *infml* man.

guzzle /'gʌzəl/ *v* eat and drink quickly, usually with bad manners.

gymkhana /dʒɪmˈkɑːnə/ *n* show of games, running, of men and horses, etc.

gymnasts

gymnasium /dʒɪmˈneɪzɪəm/ *n* **1** large room in which gymnastics are done. **2** High School in Germany, Holland, etc. *n* **gymnast** /'dʒɪmnæst/ one who is good at gymnastics. *n* **gymnastics** /dʒɪmˈnæstɪks/ exercises for making the body strong and graceful.

gynaecology /,gaɪnəˈkɒlədʒɪ/ *n* study of the diseases of women.

gypsum /'dʒɪpsəm/ *n* chalk-like material used to make soil better and for other purposes.

gypsy /'dʒɪpsɪ/ see **gipsy.**

gyrate /dʒaɪˈreɪt/ *vi* turn round and round.

gyroscope /'dʒaɪərəskəʊp/ *n* a heavy wheel, usually in a frame, which, when turning quickly, will stay just as it is put, used to keep ships and aeroplanes steady. *adj* **gyroscopic** /,dʒaɪərəˈskɒpɪk/.

H

ha! /hɑː/ *interj* expression of surprise or sudden feeling.

habeas corpus /,heɪbɪəs ˈkɔːpəs/ *n* paper ordering that a prisoner be brought before a judge to decide whether his imprisonment is according to law.

haberdasher /'hæbədæʃə/ *n* one who sells thread, pins, needles, small ornaments for clothes, hats, etc. *n* **haberdashery** /,hæbəˈdæʃərɪ/ place where such things are sold; the goods themselves.

habit /'hæbɪt/ *n* **1** custom; fixed way of doing

things. **2** special clothing, e.g. for riding horses in.

habitable /'hæbɪtəbəl/ *adj* fit to live in. *n* **habitation** /ˌhæbɪ'teɪʃən/ place in which one lives.

habitat /'hæbɪtæt/ *n* natural place of growth of a plant or animal.

habitual /hə'bɪtʃʊəl/ *adj* fixed by HABIT.

hack¹ /hæk/ *vt* cut to pieces.

hack² /hæk/ *n* **1** horse which may be hired; horse used for all kinds of work. **2** person employed to do uninteresting work, e.g. writing the less important parts of a book.

hackneyed /'hæknɪd/ *adj* (of an expression) lacking meaning through having been used too often.

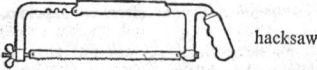

hacksaw

hacksaw /'hæksɔː/ *n* narrow blade with teeth on the edge used for cutting metal.

had /həd, əd; *strong* hæd/ p.t. of **have**. **to be had up** = be brought before a judge. *sl* **you've been had** = you've been deceived.

haddock /'hædək/ *n* kind of sea fish used for food.

haemorrhage, hemorrhage /'hemərɪdʒ/ *n* sudden and serious loss of blood.

haemorrhoids, hemorrhoids /'hemərɔɪdz/ *n* painful places at the lower end of the bowel.

hag /hæg/ *n* ugly old woman.

haggard /'hægəd/ *adj* having a worn and tired look.

haggis /'hægɪs/ *n* meat cut into small pieces, mixed with grain, etc., and boiled in a sheep's stomach—eaten in Scotland.

haggle /'hægəl/ *vi* talk about the price of an article, trying to make it less.

hail¹ /heɪl/ *n* frozen rain falling as little balls of ice. *n* **hailstone** /'heɪlstəʊn/ one of these balls of ice.

hail² /heɪl/ *vt* shout an expression of welcome to.

hair /heə/ *n* fine thread-like growth on the skin of men and animals.

hairdresser /'heəˌdresə/ *n* one who cuts and curls hair.

halcyon /'hælsɪən/ **halcyon days** = days of peace and happiness.

hale /heɪl/ *adj* healthy.

half /hɑːf/ *n* one of the two equal parts of a thing.

half-blood /'. ./ *adj* (of relations) having the same mother but a different father (or same father but a different mother).

half-breed /'. ./, **half-caste** /'. ./ *n* a person whose parents are of different races, e.g. of a white and a coloured race.

half-mast /ˌ. './ *n* position of a flag halfway down the pole it is on, as a sign of respect at the death of a great man.

halfway /ˌhɑːf'weɪ/ *adv* half of the way, e.g. *Halfway to America.*

half-witted /ˌhɑːf'wɪtɪd/ *adj* half mad.

halibut /'hælɪbət/ *n* large flat sea fish.

hall /hɔːl/ *n* **1** large room, e.g. *A dining-hall* = room for eating. **2** part of a house just inside the entrance. **3** large building, e.g. the home of a lord. **4** a building used for meetings or amusements. **the city hall** = house in which government of the city is carried on. *n* **hallmark** /'hɔːlmɑːk/ special mark placed on articles to show that they are made of real silver or gold.

hallelujah /ˌhælɪ'luːjə/ *interj* expression of praise.

hallo /hə'ləʊ/ *interj* expression used in greeting or to get a person's attention.

hallow /'hæləʊ/ *vt* make holy.

hallucination /həˌluːsɪ'neɪʃən/ *n* thinking that one sees things, although they are not really there.

halo /'heɪləʊ/ *n* circle of light, e.g. round the head of a holy person in a picture.

halt¹ /hɔːlt/ *v, n* stop.

halt² /hɔːlt/ *vi* walking with difficulty because one leg is damaged. **halting speech** = speaking in a difficult and uncertain way.

halter /'hɔːltə/ *n* **1** arrangement of bands put round a horse's head for holding or leading it. **2** rope used for hanging a bad man.

halve /hɑːv/ *vt* divide into two equal parts.

halyard /'hæljəd/ *n* rope used for pulling up a sail or flag on a ship.

ham /hæm/ *n* **1** upper part of the back leg of a pig salted and ready for cooking. **2** *infml* bad actor. *adj* **ham-fisted** /ˌ. '. ./ unskilful with his hands.

hamburger /'hæmbɜːgə/ *n* hot cooked meat cut small and put between two halves of a roll.

hamlet /'hæmlət/ *n* small village.

hammer /'hæmə/ *n* instrument for driving in nails. *v* drive in (nails) with such an instrument; make any similar noise. **to hammer out** = produce as a result of hard work.

hammock /'hæmək/ *n* hanging bed made of thick cloth or string network.

hamper¹ /'hæmpə/ *n* large closed basket usually shaped like a box—often used to contain food.

hamper² /'hæmpə/ *vt* cause difficulty to; prevent natural movement.

hamstring /'hæmˌstrɪŋ/ *n* thick string-like part at the back of the knee.

hand /hænd/ *n* **1** end of the arm which has the power of holding things. **2** pointer of a clock. **3** worker. **at hand** = near. *vt* pass (something) by hand. **to hand out** = give out (something) to each of a group of people. **to hand over** = give or pass (something one is unwilling to part with) by hand. *n* **hand-out** /'. ./ something handed out, esp. a piece of paper telling people about something.

handbill /'hændˌbɪl/ *n* printed paper given out in the street.

handbook /'hændbʊk/ *n* small book of useful facts or notes.

handcuff /'hændkʌf/ *n* one of a pair of iron bands for fastening the hands of a prisoner. *vt* put handcuffs on.

handful /'hændfʊl/ *n* amount as much as the

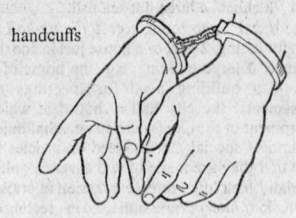

handcuffs

hand can contain. **he's a handful** = difficult to control.

handicap /'hændɪkæp/ *n* 1 way of making a game equal, by giving a number of points (or other help) to the weaker player, or by making the game more difficult for the stronger player. 2 anything which makes it difficult for one to succeed, esp. something wrong with one's body or mind. *vt* be a handicap to; give a handicap to.

handicraft /'hændɪkrɑːft/ *n* skilled work done with the hands, e.g. making pots, cloth, ornaments, etc.

handiwork /'hændɪwɜːk/ *n* work done with the hands.

handkerchief /'hæŋkətʃɪf/ *n* cloth used for keeping the nose clean.

handle /'hændl/ *vt* 1 touch or feel with the hands. 2 deal with or control. *n* the name of anything which is made to be held by the hands, e.g. for opening a door or holding a cooking-pot with. *n* **handlebar(s)** /'hændlbɑː(z)/ bar for guiding a bicycle.

handrail /'hændreɪl/ *n* upright framework to hold, e.g. when going upstairs.

handsome /'hænsəm/ *adj* 1 (of a man) good-looking. 2 generous.

handy /'hændɪ/ *adj* 1 clever with one's hands. 2 near; easy to reach.

handyman /'hændɪmæn/ *n* man who can do any sort of work with his hands; man who does small repairs and other work in the house.

hang¹ /hæŋ/ *v* support or be supported from some point above; fix one end leaving the other end free to swing. **to hang one's head** = allow the head to fall forward on the breast as a sign of shame. **to hang back** = hold back or delay. **to hang on** = wait. **to hang together** = support each other. **his story does not hang together** = can be shown to be untrue. **to hang up** = on the telephone, to put the receiver down. *infml n* **hang-up** subject that causes a person special anxiety. **to get the hang of** = understand the general idea of.

hang² /hæŋ/ *v* kill (a law-breaker) by means of a rope around his neck. *vi* die in this way.

hangar /'hæŋgə/ *n* building in which aeroplanes are kept.

hangdog /'hæŋdɒg/ *adj* (of a look) expressing shame.

hanger-on /ˌ.. './ *n* one who depends on another, who joins himself to another person in hope of gain.

hangman /'hæŋmən/ *n* the man who kills law-breakers by hanging them.

hangover /'hæŋəʊvə/ *n* feeling of illness on the morning after drinking too much.

hank /hæŋk/ *n* 1 amount of silk or woollen thread. 2 iron ring for fastening rope to a pole.

hanker /'hæŋkə/ *v* **to hanker after, hanker for** = desire.

haphazard /hæp'hæzəd/ *adj* happening by chance.

hapless /'hæpləs/ *adj* unfortunate.

happen /'hæpən/ *vi* (of an event) be, take place; take place by chance. **to happen on** = find by chance.

happy /'hæpɪ/ *adj* glad; merry. *n* **happiness** /'hæpɪnəs/.

happy-go-lucky /ˌ.. '../ *adj* not anxious; careless or thoughtless.

harangue /hə'ræŋ/ *n* loud angry speech, esp. to a crowd. *v* make such a speech (to).

harass /'hærəs/ *vt* cause difficulties for; make anxious.

harbinger /'hɑːbɪndʒə/ *n* that which goes before and tells or shows what will happen, e.g. *Birds are harbingers of spring.*

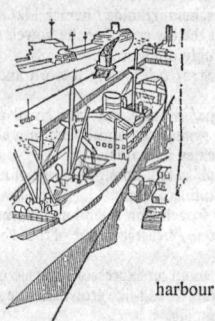

harbour

harbour /'hɑːbə/ *n* place of safety in which ships take shelter. *vt* keep safe. **to harbour evil thoughts** = allow them to remain in the mind.

hard /hɑːd/ *adj* 1 difficult. 2 not soft. 3 unkind, cruel or unjust. **hard water** = water with a lot of lime in it. **hard of hearing** = not able to hear clearly. *infml* **hard up** = having no money. **to try hard** = really try. **to work hard** = really work, with all one's ability *v* **harden** /'hɑːdn/ make or become hard or harder.

hard-headed /ˌ. '../ *adj* keen and clever in making money; without the gentler feelings.

hardly /'hɑːdlɪ/ *adv* not quite.

hardware /'hɑːdweə/ *n* (*sing*) articles made of metal used in the house.

hardy /'hɑːdɪ/ *adj* bold; strong; difficult to kill.

hare /heə/ *n* a rabbit-like animal. *adj* hare-

brained /ˈ. ./ foolish; thoughtless. *n* **hare lip** /ˌ. ˈ./ lip divided below the nose.

harem /ˈheərəm, hɑːˈriːm/ *n* women's part of the house in the East; women in a harem.

haricot /ˈhærɪkəʊ/ **haricot bean** = large seed boiled for food.

hark /hɑːk/ *vi* listen. **to hark back** = return to what one was saying.

harlequin /ˈhɑːləkwɪn/ *n* fool in a play, usually wearing bright clothes of many colours.

harm /hɑːm/ *n, vt* damage. *adj* **harmful** /ˈhɑːmfəl/. **harmless** /ˈhɑːmləs/ *adj* not causing harm: safe.

harmattan /ˈhɑːmətæn/ *n* (in West Africa) a dry wind which blows from the desert towards the coast in some seasons.

harmonic /hɑːˈmɒnɪk/ *adj* producing a right and pleasing mixture of musical sounds. *adj* **harmonious** /hɑːˈməʊnɪəs/ producing pleasant sounds; friendly and agreeing with each other. *n* **harmony** /ˈhɑːmənɪ/ agreement; proper arrangement of musical notes. *v* **harmonize** /ˈhɑːmənaɪz/ be.in or bring into harmony or agreement.

harmonium /hɑːˈməʊnɪəm/ *n* musical instrument played by pressing down keys with the fingers, while the feet are.used to force air through small holes covered with thin metal blades.

harness /ˈhɑːnɪs/ *n* (*sing*) bands, ropes, etc., used to tie a horse to what it is pulling; any similar equipment. *vt* put a harness on; control and use (some great force).

harp /hɑːp/ *n* musical instrument having many strings played by touching the strings with the fingers. **harping on the same string** = saying the same thing again and again. **to harp on, keep harping on** = keep talking about or returning to the subject of.

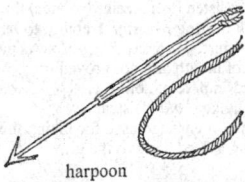

harpoon

harpoon /hɑːˈpuːn/ *n* long spear used for killing large sea animals.

harpsichord /ˈhɑːpsɪkɔːd/ *n* large musical instrument of earlier times, played by striking keys with the fingers.

harpy /ˈhɑːpɪ/ *n* **1** creature, half bird, half woman, told of in ancient Greek stories. **2** person who tries to get everything for herself; woman of bad character.

harrow /ˈhærəʊ/ *n* instrument with many sharp points pulled over the soil to break up the surface and make it even. *adj* **harrowing** /ˈhærəʊɪŋ/ causing great anxiety or suffering.

harry /ˈhærɪ/ *vt* steal by force; destroy (enemy cities).

harsh /hɑːʃ/ *adj* rough; unpleasant to feel or taste; cruel.

hart /hɑːt/ *n* male deer.

harvest /ˈhɑːvɪst/ *n* time for gathering in the crops; that which is produced by the earth; results of work or of one's behaviour. *vt* gather in (crops at harvest).

harvester /ˈhɑːvɪstə/ *n* **1** man who gathers the crops. **2** machine for cutting and gathering grain (e.g. corn, wheat, etc.). **3** small biting insect.

has /həz, əz; *strong* hæz/ (present t. form of **have** used after 'he', 'she', 'it' and singular nouns).

hash /hæʃ/ *n* dish of meat cut small and heated up again. **to make a hash of** = do (work) badly.

hashish /ˈhæʃɪʃ/ *n* preparation made from an Indian plant that has an effect on the mind when smoked.

hasp /hɑːsp/ *n* fastener for a door.

hassock /ˈhæsək/ *n* small square cushion on the floor used when kneeling in church.

haste /heɪst/ *n* hurry. *v* **hasten** /ˈheɪsən/ hurry. *adj* **hasty** /ˈheɪstɪ/ done without thought.

hat /hæt/ *n* covering for the head.

hatch[1] /hætʃ/ *n* opening, e.g. in the wall of a room for passing food through from the kitchen.

hatch[2] /hætʃ/ *vt* cause (young ones) to come out of eggs. *vi* (of the young of e.g. birds) come out from eggs.

hatchery /ˈhætʃərɪ/ *n* place where young fish are produced from eggs.

hatchet /ˈhætʃɪt/ *n* small axe. **to bury the hatchet** = make peace.

hatchway /ˈhætʃweɪ/ *n* opening in the DECK of a ship.

hate /heɪt/ *vt, n* (have a) very strong feeling of dislike for. *n* **hatred** /ˈheɪtrɪd/.

haughty /ˈhɔːtɪ/ *adj* having or expressing a high opinion of oneself and often a low opinion of others.

haul /hɔːl/ *vt* pull by force. *n* amount taken, e.g. by a thief or a fisherman. **to haul over the coals** = to scold.

haunch /hɔːntʃ/ *n* thick part of the body and leg where they join together.

haunt /hɔːnt/ *vt* **1** (of a GHOST) visit regularly (a person or place). **2** visit often. **3** keep coming back to the mind, e.g. a picture, music.

have /həv, əv; *strong* hæv/ *vt* **1** own; keep. **2** suffer, e.g. *To have an illness.* **3** be forced to, e.g. *I have to go to school* = I must—; **4** cause to be done, e.g. *To have a house built.* **5** take, e.g. *To have breakfast, have a swim.* **to have a baby** = give birth. **to have to do with** = be concerned with.

haven /ˈheɪvən/ *n* harbour; any place of shelter or rest.

haversack /ˈhævəsæk/ *n* bag tied on the back, used by soldiers and travellers.

havoc /ˈhævək/ *n* widespread waste or destruction.

haversack

headdress

haw /hɔ:/ *n* fruit of a HAWTHORN.

hawk¹ /hɔ:k/ *n* a meat-eating bird. *adj* **hawk-eyed** /ˌ. './ having very good eyesight.

hawk² /hɔ:k/ *v* carry (things) about the streets on a cart to sell them. *n* **hawker** street-seller.

hawser /'hɔ:zə/ *n* thick strong rope.

hawthorn /'hɔ:θɔ:n/ *n* tree which has small white or red rose-like flowers and a small dark red fruit, often grown round the edges of fields in England.

hay /heɪ/ *n* grass cut and dried for use as food for cattle.

hay fever /'. ˌ. ./ *n* running of liquid from the nose, pain in the throat, etc., caused by POLLEN from flowers or plants getting into the throat and nose.

hayrick /'heɪˌrɪk/, **haystack** /'heɪstæk/ *n* store of hay built up in the shape of a hut.

haywire /'heɪwaɪə/ *infml adj* mad.

hazard /'hæzəd/ *n* risk; danger. *vt* risk. *adj* **hazardous** /'hæzədəs/.

haze /heɪz/ *n* mist; lack of clearness in the air.

hazel /'heɪzəl/ *n* bush which has eatable nuts. *n, adj* (of a) light brown colour.

hazy /'heɪzɪ/ *adj* not clear; misty.

he /hi,ɪ; *strong* hi:/ *pron* (used in speaking of a man or boy) e.g. *Harry is a kind man; he is also very clever.*

head /hed/ *n* **1** that part of the body above the neck. **to lose one's head** = become too excited or afraid to think clearly. **to keep one's head** = remain calm. **2** chief or most important part of, e.g. *Head of the business.* **3** top. **a head** = for each person, e.g. *£5 a head. vt* **1** strike (e.g. a ball) with the head. **2** be in control of (a group). **to head for** = go in the direction of.

headache /'hedeɪk/ *n* **1** pain in the head. **3** *infml* something that causes difficulties or anxieties.

headdress /'hed-dres/ *n* any ornamental covering for the head.

heading /'hedɪŋ/ *n* words at the top of a piece of printed matter showing the subject of what follows.

headland /'hedlənd/ *n* high piece of land reaching out into the sea.

headlight /'hedlaɪt/ *n* one of the big lamps at the front of a car.

headline /'hedlaɪn/ *n* line of large print at the top of the news in a newspaper.

headlong /'hedlɒŋ/ **to fall headlong** = head first. **to rush headlong** = run with the head down, not looking where one is going.

headmaster /hed'mɑ:stə/ *n* man in charge of the teachers and children at a school.

headmistress /hed'mɪstrəs/ *n* woman in charge of the teachers and children at a school.

headquarters /'hedˌkwɔ:təz/ *n* chief place of business; in the army, the place where the commanding officer is.

headstrong /'hedstrɒŋ/ *adj* determined to have one's own will.

headtie /'hedtaɪ/ *n* piece of cloth worn by women in West Africa as a covering for the head.

headway /'hedweɪ/ *n* **1** forward movement. **2** clear space over one's head, e.g. in a doorway.

heady /'hedɪ/ *adj* ungovernable; exciting.

heal /hi:l/ *vt* cause to become well or healthy. *vi* (of a wound) become well.

health /helθ/ *n* state of being well. *adj* **healthy** /'helθɪ/ well.

heap /hi:p/ *n* amount or number of things put together one on top of the other; put things in this way. **heaps of** = much; many.

hear /hɪə/ *v* listen (to); receive (sounds) through the ear. *n* **hearing** /'hɪərɪŋ/ **1** ability to hear. **2** trial in a court. *n* **hearsay** /'hɪəseɪ/ news passed by word of mouth and not proved true.

heard /hɜ:d/ *p.p. & p.t.* of **hear**.

hearken /'hɑ:kən/ *old vi* listen.

hearse /hɜ:s/ *n* carriage used for taking the box containing a dead body to the grave.

heart (2)

heart /hɑ:t/ *n* **1** that part of the body which sends the blood through the body. **2** anything of the supposed shape of a heart. **3** the centre of the kindly tender feelings. **by heart** = by memory. **take to heart** = consider (something) seriously;

be greatly grieved by. **to have one's heart in one's mouth** = feel great fear. **to lose heart** = feel that what one is doing is worthless. **a change of heart** = change from being bad to good.

heartache /'hɑːt-eɪk/ *n* sorrow; unsatisfied desire.

heartbeat /'hɑːtbiːt/ *n* movement of the heart.

heartbreak /'hɑːtbreɪk/ *n* great sorrow; that which causes great sorrow. *adj* **heartbroken** /'hɑːtˌbrəʊkən/ suffering great sorrow.

heartburn /'hɑːtbɜːn/ *n* discomfort in the stomach after a meal.

hearten /'hɑːtn/ *vt* give courage and hope to.

heartfelt /'hɑːtfelt/ *adj* deeply felt.

hearth /hɑːθ/ *n* large flat stone before an open fireplace.

heartless /'hɑːtləs/ *adj* cruel; without tender feelings.

heartrending /'hɑːt-rendɪŋ/ *adj* causing sorrow or pain in the mind.

hearty /'hɑːtɪ/ *adj* high-spirited; healthy; full of deep true feeling. **to have a hearty meal** = eat a lot with great enjoyment.

heat /hiːt/ *n* **1** state of being hot. **2** one game or race in a set to determine who will play or run in later games or races. **3** season of sexual excitement in female animals, e.g. dogs. *v* become or cause to become hot. *adj* **heated** /'hiːtɪd/ angry.

heath /hiːθ/ *n* stretch of waste land.

heathen /'hiːðən/ *adj, n* (person) having no true knowledge of God.

heather /'heðə'/ *n* rough wild plant with very small red-blue flowers found on waste land, mountain sides, etc.

heave /hiːv/ *v* lift or move (any heavy object); pull hard at a rope. *vi* breathe deeply; move up and down like waves. **to heave to** = (of a ship) stop. **to heave a sigh** = give out a deep breath.

heaven /'hevən/ *n* place of complete happiness after death. **the heavens** = sky.

heavy /'hevɪ/ *adj* having great weight; difficult to lift; serious.

heckle /'hekəl/ *v* shout out rudely at (a public speaker).

hectic /'hektɪk/ *adj* very active or excited.

hecto- /'hektəʊ, 'hektə/ one hundred, e.g. **hectogram** /'hektəgræm/ = 100 grams (= a measure of weight).

hedge

hedge /hedʒ/ *n* row of bushes used as a wall or fence. *vt* protect as with a hedge; shelter. *vi* not to give a straight answer to a question.

hedgehog /'hedʒhɒg/ *n* small mammal covered with long prickles which protect it from enemies.

hedgerow /'hedʒrəʊ/ *n* HEDGE.

hedonist /'hiːdənɪst/ *n* one who believes that pleasure is the chief good.

heed /hiːd/ *vt* give attention to; take notice of. *adj* **heedless** /'hiːdləs/ careless.

heel[1] /hiːl/ *n* **1** the back part of the foot. **2** *sl* low-down, dishonest person. **3** part of a shoe under the heel of the foot. *vt* **1** strike with the heel. **2** put a heel onto (a shoe).

heel[2] /hiːl/ *vi* lean over to one side.

hefty /'heftɪ/ *adj* heavy; strong.

hegemony /hɪ'gemənɪ, 'hedʒɪmənɪ/ *n* leadership among a group of nations.

heifer /'hefə'/ *n* young cow which has not yet produced a young one.

height /haɪt/ *n* state of being high; distance from the top to the bottom; high place. **at the height of his power** = when he had greatest power.

heinous /'heɪnəs/ *adj* very bad.

heir /eə'/ *n* person who will get certain money, lands, or power when another person dies. *n* **heirloom** /'eəluːm/ any valuable thing that is passed on to an heir and may not be sold out of the family.

held /held/ p.t. and p.p. of **hold**.

helical /'helɪkəl/ *adj* screw-shaped.

helicopter /'helɪkɒptə'/ *n* flying-machine able to go straight up from the ground, stay still in the air, or move forward.

helio- /'hiːlɪəʊ/ having to do with the sun, e.g. *n* **heliograph** /'hiːlɪəgrɑːf/ instrument used for sending messages by means of sunlight.

helium /'hiːlɪəm/ *n* very light gas that will not burn.

hell /hel/ *n* place where the souls of wrongdoers are punished after death; any very unpleasant place or condition.

hello /he'ləʊ/ *interj* HALLO.

helm /helm/ *n* (in a boat) handle of the **rudder**.

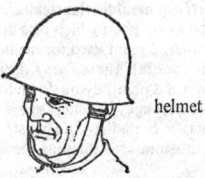

helmet

helmet /'helmɪt/ *n* iron covering to protect the head when fighting.

help /help/ *v* do part of another person's work; do something for (another person); save from difficulty or danger. **he helped me to some vegetables** = put some vegetables on my plate at the table. **help yourself** = take what you want. **I can't help it** = I can do nothing to prevent it. *n* act of helping; servant. *adj* **helpful** /'helpfəl/ giving help; useful. *n* **helping** /'helpɪŋ/ food put on one's plate. *adj* **helpless** /'helpləs/ without help; unable to help oneself.

helter-skelter /ˌheltə 'skeltə/ *adj, adv* in a hurry; in disorder.

hem /hem/ *n* edge of cloth folded over and fastened down at the end of a garment. *vt* put a hem onto (material). **to hem in** = enclose (someone) so that he is not free to move.

hemi- /'hemɪ/ half, e.g. *n* **hemisphere** /'hemɪsfɪə/ half of a ball. **the northern hemisphere** = northern half of the earth.

hemlock /'hemlɒk/ *n* poisonous plant.

hemorrhage /'hemərɪdʒ/, **hemorrhoids** /'hemərɔɪdz/ see **haem-**.

hemp /hemp/ *n* plant used for making rope and heavy cloth; threads prepared from the plant of which rope, etc., is made.

hemstitch /'hem,stɪtʃ/ *n* ornamental work done with needle and thread, usually at the edge of cloth.

hen /hen/ *n* a bird used as food and for laying eggs; any female bird.

hence /hens/ *adv* **1** from here, e.g. *A year hence* = a year from now. **2** for this reason.

henceforth /hens'fɔːθ/, **henceforward** /hens'fɔːwəd/ *adv*. from now on.

henchman /'hentʃmən/ *n* supporter; servant.

henna /'henə/ *n* red-brown colouring matter made from the leaves of a plant, used to colour finger-nails and hair.

henpecked /'henpekt/ *adj* (of a married man) ruled by his wife.

her /hɜː/ *pron* (from of she used after verbs and prepositions). *det* belonging to her. *pron* **hers** /hɜːz/ something belonging to her.

herald /'herəld/ *n* one who declares important news to the public, e.g. war; any person or thing which acts as a sign of some future event, e.g. *Birds are heralds of spring*. *vt* be a sign of (some future event).

heraldry /'herəldrɪ/ *n* study of the special signs painted on shields, etc., as the family sign of noble persons. *adj* **heraldic** /he'rældɪk/.

herb /hɜːb/ *n* **1** any plant which dies down to the roots in winter. **2** plant used for medicine or for giving a special taste. *adj* **herbaceous** /hɜː'beɪʃəs/ (of a plant) dying down to the roots in winter. *n* **herbage** /'hɜːbɪdʒ/ grass and other field plants. *n* **herbalist** /'hɜːbəlɪst/ one who studies plants and uses them as medicines. *adj* **herbal**.

herculean /ˌhɜːkjʊ'liːən/ *adj* (of a piece of work) that needs more than human strength.

herd /hɜːd/ *n* number of beasts together; all the cattle of one kind on a farm. *vt* collect together; be in charge of (a herd). *n* **herdsman** /'hɜːdzmən/ man who takes care of, is in charge of, cattle.

here /hɪə/ *adv* to or in this place.

hereabouts /'hɪərəbaʊts/ *adv* near here.

hereafter /hɪə'rɑːftə/ *adv* after now; from now on.

hereditary /hɪ'redɪtərɪ/ *adj* that is passed down from parents to children. *n* **heredity** /hə'redɪtɪ/ the passing on of powers and character from parents to their children.

heresy /'herəsɪ/ *n* any teaching which is not according to what has been settled as true by the Church; teaching not in agreement with what is believed by most people. *n* **heretic** /'herətɪk/ one who teaches heresy.

hereupon /ˌhɪərə'pɒn/ on this; straight after this.

heritage /'herɪtɪdʒ/ *n* that which is passed on to a person by his or her parents.

hermetic /hɜː'metɪk/ *adj* fitting so closely as to keep out all air.

hermit /'hɜːmɪt/ *n* man who lives apart from all people, e.g. in order to live a holy life.

hernia /'hɜːnɪə/ *n* breaking or separating of the covering muscles in front of the body, allowing part of the bowel to come through or move from its natural place.

hero /'hɪərəʊ/ *n* **1** great man in the early history of any people. **2** very brave person. **3** chief person in a play, poem, etc. *adj* **heroic** /hɪ'rəʊɪk/. **heroics** loud and foolish talk, as when pretending to be very brave. *n* **heroism** /'herəʊɪzəm/ great courage.

heroin /'herəʊɪn/ *n* medicine which stops the feeling of pain and causes one to sleep.

heroine /'herəʊɪn/ *n* female HERO.

heron

heron /'herən/ *n* large bird with very long legs and neck.

herring /'herɪŋ/ *n* small fish used for food. **a red herring** = something talked about although it has nothing to do with the real subject. *adj* **herringbone** /'herɪŋbəʊn/ (of any ornamental work) shaped like the backbone of a fish.

hesitate /'hezəteɪt/ *vi* pause because on is undecided. *adj* **hesitant** /'hezɪtənt/. *n* **hesitation** /ˌhezə'teɪʃən/.

hessian /'hesɪən/ *n* rough stiff cloth.

hetero- /'hetərəʊ, 'hetərə/ different. *adj* **heterodox** /'hetərədɒks/ not according to the opinion held by other people. *adj* **heterogeneous** /ˌhetərəʊ'dʒiːnɪəs/ of many different kinds.

heterosexual /ˌhetərəʊ'sekʃʊəl/ *n, adj* (one) who enjoys sexual relations with members of the opposite sex.

hew /hjuː/ *vt* cut with heavy blows.

hexa- /'heksə/ having to do with six, e.g. *n* **hexagon** /'heksəgən/ six-sided figure.

hey /heɪ/ *interj* expression of surprise or questioning.

heyday /'heɪdeɪ/ *n* time of greatest strength, high spirits and joy of living.

hiatus /haɪ'eɪtəs/ *n* break in a written paper where some words are lost; two open sounds coming together, e.g. India Office.

hibernate /'haɪbəneɪt/ *vi* go into a state of sleep for the winter.

hiccup /'hɪkʌp/ *n, vi* (experience a) sudden catching of the breath—sometimes caused by eating or drinking too much or too quickly.

hickory /'hɪkərɪ/ *n* American tree with very hard wood.

hid /hɪd/ *p.t.* of hide.

hide[1] /haɪd/ *v* cover up; keep out of sight or keep secret.

hide[2] /haɪd/ *n* the skin of an animal. *n* hiding beating.

hidebound /'haɪdbaʊnd/ *adj* very narrow-minded; unable to receive a new idea.

hideous /'hɪdɪəs/ *adj* very ugly; very unpleasant.

hierarchy /'haɪərɑːkɪ/ *n* order of ranks of priests or holy persons; any order of rank one above another. *adj* hierarchical /ˌhaɪə'rɑːkɪkəl/.

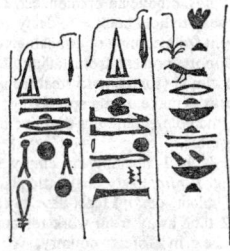

hieroglyphs

hieroglyph /'haɪərəglɪf/ *n* piece of picture-writing as in ancient Egypt. *adj* hieroglyphic /ˌhaɪərə'glɪfɪk/.

higgledy-piggledy /ˌhɪgəldɪ 'pɪgəldɪ/ *adj* in complete disorder.

high /haɪ/ *adj* 1 near the top; raised up. 2 *sl* excited or feeling happy because of some substance one has taken into the body, e.g. strong drink. it is high time you were gone = you are late in going. high school = school for children aged 12 or 13 upwards.

highbrow /'haɪbraʊ/ *adj* putting on an appearance of great learning; (of music, etc.) too difficult to be understood by the general public.

highfalutin /ˌhaɪfə'luːtɪn/ *adj* full of high-sounding words but really foolish.

high-flown /ˌ. '.' / *adj* (of language) sounding fine but meaning little.

high-handed /ˌ. '.' / *adj* using one's powers in a way which hurts other people's feelings. feelings.

highland(s) /'haɪlənd(z)/ *n* mountainous country.

highlight /'haɪlaɪt/ *n* most striking part of anything.

high-minded /ˌ. '.' / *adj* very good and honest.

highness /'haɪnəs/ **Your Highness** = way of addressing princes and members of the king's family.

high(ly)-strung /ˌ. (.) '.' / *adj* easily excited.

highway /'haɪweɪ/ *n* main road.

highwayman /'haɪweɪmən/ *n* thief who uses a gun and steals from travellers.

hike /haɪk/ *n* long walk taken for amusement. *vi* go on a hike.

hilarious /hɪ'leərɪəs/ *adj* very amusing. *n* hilarity /hɪ'lærətɪ/.

hill /hɪl/ *n* small mountain. *n* hillock /'hɪlək/ small hill.

hilt /hɪlt/ *n* handle of a sword. up to the hilt = completely.

him /ɪm; *strong* hɪm/ *pron* (form of he used after verbs and prepositions).

hind[1] /haɪnd/ *n* female deer.

hind[2] /haɪnd/ **hind legs** = legs at the back of an animal. *adj* hindmost /'haɪndməʊst/ farthest back.

hinder /'hɪndə/ *vt* try to stop (someone) doing what he wants to. *n* hindrance /'hɪndrəns/ anything that causes trouble or difficulty.

Hinduism /'hɪnduːɪzəm/ *n* Indian religion. *n, adj* Hindu /hɪn'duː/ (one) of this religion.

hinge /hɪndʒ/ *n* instrument for joining two parts so that one of them can move (e.g. a door and its door-post, or a box and its top). to hinge upon = depend on.

hint /hɪnt/ *v* say (something) indirectly. *n* 1 something so said. 2 slight appearance.

hinterland /'hɪntəlænd/ *n* inner part of a country a long way from the coast or from a large river or cities.

hip[1] /hɪp/ *n* upper part of the leg where it joins the body.

hip[2] /hɪp/ *n* seed-container of the wild rose.

hip[3] /hɪp/ **hip! hip! hurrah!** = shout of joy.

hippodrome /'hɪpədrəʊm/ *n* place for racing; public place of amusement.

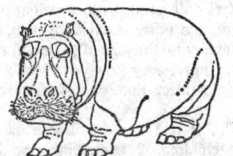

hippopotamus

hippopotamus /ˌhɪpə'pɒtəməs/ *n* very large wild animal found in Africa.

hire /'haɪə/ *vt* pay money for the use of (a thing or a person's services). *n* such payment; act of hiring. to hire out = allow people the use of (something). hireling /'haɪəlɪŋ/ *n* one who gives service for money. *n* hire purchase /ˌ. '.' / buying a thing by small payments made while using it.

hirsute /'hɜːsjuːt/ *adj* hairy.

his /ɪz; strong hɪz/ det, pron (something) belonging to him.

hiss /hɪs/ vi make a sound like the letter "s"—e.g. as an expression of great dislike.

history /'hɪstərɪ/ n study and story of past events, conditions, or thought. adj historical /hɪ'stɒrɪkəl/ having to do with the past or with history. adj historic /hɪ'stɒrɪk/ historically important. n historian /hɪ'stɔːrɪən/ one who studies or writes history.

histrionic /ˌhɪstrɪ'ɒnɪk/ adj having to do with acting plays; like an actor; not real or honest.

hit /hɪt/ vt strike. to hit upon = find by chance. n act of hitting. n, adj success(ful).

hitch¹ /hɪtʃ/ vt pull up; fasten. sl adj hitched /hɪtʃt/ married. vi hitch-hike /'. ./ travel by asking for rides from passing cars, etc.

hitch² /hɪtʃ/ n 1 simple knot. 2 difficulty or cause of delay, e.g. A hitch in one's plans.

hither /'hɪðə/ adv in this direction. adv hitherto /ˌhɪðə'tuː/ up to this time.

hives

hive /haɪv/ n hut-shaped container in which bees live. a hive of industry = place of busy work.

hoary /'hɔːrɪ/ adj grey or white from age; very old.

hoard /hɔːd/ n store of hidden money. vt store up secretly for one's own use.

hoarding /'hɔːdɪŋ/ n wooden frame or wall on which are stuck public notices, etc.

hoarse /hɔːs/ adj (of the voice) rough-sounding, e.g. after shouting too much.

hoax /həʊks/ vt deceive (someone) in order to be able to laugh at him. n trick of this kind.

hob /hɒb/ n shelf at the side of a fire on which pots are kept warm.

hobble /'hɒbəl/ vi walk putting more weight on one leg than on the other because of pain, a damaged leg, etc. vt tie the legs of (a horse) so that he can only move very slowly.

hobby /'hɒbɪ/ n subject that one studies for amusement.

hobby-horse /'. . ./ n 1 wooden horse as a plaything for children. 2 something one is specially interested in and may talk about even when others are not interested.

hobgoblin /hɒb'gɒblɪn/ n fairy which does harmful tricks.

hobnail /'hɒbneɪl/ n short nail with a large head fixed in the bottoms of shoes.

hobnob /'hɒbnɒb/ vi be friendly with someone.

hobo /'həʊbəʊ/ n unemployed person who wanders from place to place.

hock /hɒk/ n 1 joint in the middle of the back legs of a horse. 2 light white wine.

hockey /'hɒkɪ/ n game played on grass or ice, using curved sticks and a ball or round object which must be pushed or hit between two upright posts.

hocus-pocus /ˌhəʊkəs 'pəʊkəs/ n talk or action for the purpose of deceiving.

hod /hɒd/ n container used for carrying bricks, coal, etc.

hoe /həʊ/ n instrument used in the garden for loosening the soil and getting unwanted plants out. v go over (ground) with a hoe.

hog /hɒg/ n pig; dirty person. vt seize (e.g. food) in an eager and rude way. to go the whole hog = do something completely and thoroughly.

hoist /hɔɪst/ vt lift up to a higher position. hoist with his own petard = caught by his own trick. n machine used for lifting up goods.

hold¹ /həʊld/ n place in a ship that contains the goods.

hold² /həʊld/ vt 1 keep in the hand. 2 support, as a post holds up a roof; arrange and have charge of (e.g. a meeting). 3 contain e.g. This box holds four pounds. 4 have an opinion, e.g. I hold him to be a fool. to hold back = to delay. to hold off = prevent from coming or attacking. to hold up = 1 support; prevent from falling. 2 delay. 3 point a gun at (someone to steal from him). to hold forth = make a long speech.

holding /'həʊldɪŋ/ n amount that one owns, e.g. in a business.

hole /həʊl/ n 1 opening or empty space in anything. 2 infml nasty dirty little place.

holiday /'hɒlədɪ, -deɪ/ n 1 feast-day; day free from work. 2 time away from work for amusement and rest, e.g. in a foreign country.

hollow /'hɒləʊ/ adj having an empty space inside. n hole that is wide but not deep; small valley.

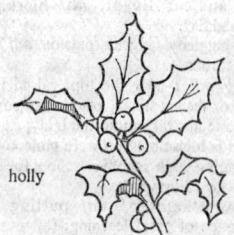

holly

holly /'hɒlɪ/ n an evergreen tree with a small red fruit and leaves that have sharp points.

holocaust /'hɒləkɔːst/ n any terrible event that completely destroys something, e.g. the burning of many houses.

holster /'həʊlstə/ n leather case for carrying a gun.

holy /'həʊlɪ/ adj having to do with God; respected as being very good and pure.

homage /'hɒmɪdʒ/ n act of showing great respect or readiness to serve.

home /haʊm/ *n* place where one lives; one's native place or country. *adv* to or at one's home. *adj* **homesick** /'haʊm‚sɪk/ having a great desire to return home.

homely /'haʊmlɪ/ *adj* homelike or causing one to remember home; simple.

homestead /'haʊmsted/ *n* farm or home with the land round it.

homicide /'hɒmɪsaɪd/ *n* act of killing another person.

homily /'hɒmɪlɪ/ *n* speech about God, being good, etc.; long uninteresting speech about goodness.

homogeneous /‚hɒmə'dʒiːnɪəs/ *adj* of the same nature in all parts.

homonym /'hɒmə‚nɪm/ one of two or more words having the same sound but different meaning, e.g. spring.

homosexual /‚haʊmə'sekʃʊəl/ *adj, n* (one) who enjoys sexual relations with persons of the same sex.

hone /haʊn/ *n* small smooth stone used for giving a sharp edge to cutting instruments.

honest /'ɒnɪst/ *adj* true; free from anything that deceives; fair. *n* **honesty** /'ɒnɪstɪ/.

honey /'hʌnɪ/ *n* sweet liquid made by bees. *n* **honeycomb** /'hʌntkaʊm/ six-sided wax framework made by bees for storing their honey.

honeymoon /'hʌnɪmuːn/ *n* time between marriage and settling in a new home, often spent in travel.

honeysuckle /'hʌnɪsʌkəl/ *n* sweet-smelling flower.

honk /hɒŋk/ *n* noise made by the horn of a motor-car.

honorary /'ɒnərərɪ/ *adj* working without pay, e.g. *Honorary Magistrate* = judge having the rank and title, but not the pay.

honorarium /‚ɒnə'reərɪəm/ *n* money given for services for which it is not usual to fix a price.

honour /'ɒnə/ *n* **1** good name; self-respect. **2** something increasing one's good name or self-respect. **birthday honours** = list of high ranks and titles declared on the birthday of the king or queen. **your Honour** = a way of speaking to a judge. *vt* do honour to; respect. *adj* **honourable** /'ɒnərəbəl/ honest; respected.

hood /hʊd/ *n* **1** covering for the head, neck and shoulders. **2** top of a car which can be folded back.

hoodlum /'huːdləm/ *n* rough, dishonest or bad-mannered fellow.

hoodwink /'hʊd‚wɪŋk/ *vt* cover the eyes of (an animal); deceive (a person).

hoof /huːf/ *n* solid part of some animals' feet, e.g. horses.

hook /hʊk/ *n* piece of metal bent in the shape of a J, used, e.g., in catching fish. *v* fasten or be fastened with a hook. *sl* **do it on my own hook** = alone, without help.

hookup /'hʊkʌp/ *n* joining together radio-

stations so that many hear the same thing.

hookworm /'hʊkwɜːm/ *n* small creature which enters the body, hooks on to the inside of the bowel, and sucks blood, so causing illness and loss of strength.

hooligan /'huːlɪgən/ *n* rough person who fights and makes a noise in the streets. *n* **hooliganism** /'huːlɪgənɪzəm/.

hoop /huːp/ *n* ring of thin metal, wire or wood.

hoot /huːt/ *n* shout showing anger or dislike; noise made by an OWL. *vi* make a hoot. *n* **hooter** /'huːtə/ instrument which makes a deep sound.

hop[1] /hɒp/ *vi* move by short jumps; jump on one leg. *sl* **hop it!** = go away. *n* short jump; small dance.

hop[2] /hɒp/ *n* tall, climbing plant, the fruit of which is used in making BEER.

hope /haʊp/ *vt* desire and expect. *n* feeling of hope; thing hoped for. *adj* **hopeful** /'haʊpfəl/ having hope; (of something hoped for) still possible. *adj* **hopeless** /'haʊpləs/ without hope; beyond help.

hopper /'hɒpə/ *n* **1** box with a wide opening in the top, sloping sides, and a small hole in the bottom through which material is poured into a machine. **2** any small insect that jumps.

horde /hɔːd/ *n* large disorderly crowd.

horizon /hə'raɪzən/ *n* **1** line where the earth and sky appear to meet. **2** width of one's ideas or experiences.

horizontal /‚hɒrɪ'zɒntl/ *adj* level or flat.

hormone /'hɔːmaʊn/ *n* material carried by the blood to different parts of the body which excites those parts to increased action.

horn /hɔːn/ *n* **1** hard bone-like material that covers the upper ends of the fingers, and the feet of some animals. **2** long pointed objects on the head of a cow, deer, etc. **take the bull by the horns** = deal with a danger or difficulty in a fearless way. **3** musical instrument played by blowing. **4** instrument on a motor-car that makes warning sounds.

hornet

hornet /'hɔːnɪt/ *n* large bee-like insect.

hornpipe /'hɔːnpaɪp/ *n* dance usually performed by seamen.

horoscope /'hɒrəskaʊp/ *n* plan of the stars at the moment of a person's birth (or other time) and an account of future events said to be made probable by the stars.

horrible /'hɒrəbəl/ *adj* causing great fear or dislike.

horrid /'hɒrɪd/ *adj* very unpleasant.

horrify /'hɒrɪfaɪ/ *vt* cause HORROR to.

horror /'hɒrə/ *n* great fear and dislike. *adj* (of stories, films, etc.) containing material intended to make one afraid.

hors d'oeuvre

hors d'oeuvre /ˌɔː ˈdɜːv/ *n* collection of various strong-tasting foods served at the beginning of a dinner.

horse /hɔːs/ *n* **1** four-footed mammal used for riding. **2** any frame shaped like a horse. **horse sense** = good common sense. *n* **horse-play** /ˈ. ./ rough noisy play.

horseman /ˈhɔːsmən/ *n* man riding a horse; horse soldier.

horsepower /ˈhɔːspaʊə/ *n* measure of power, equal to that which is necessary to lift 550 pounds to a height of one foot in one second.

horseradish /ˈhɔːsˌrædɪʃ/ *n* plant with a white hot-tasting root eaten with meat.

horseshoe /ˈhɔːʃ-ʃuː/ *n* piece of metal fixed to the bottom of a horse's foot for protection.

horticulture /ˈhɔːtɪˌkʌltʃə/ *n* gardening.

hose[1]

hose[1] /həʊz/ *n* pipe (usually made of rubber) used for throwing a stream of water, e.g. on a fire, garden, etc.

hose[2] /həʊz/ *n* coverings for the legs, made of silk, wool, or cotton. *n* **hosiery** /ˈhəʊzɪərɪ/ **1** hose. **2** men's underclothes. *n* **hosier** /ˈhəʊzɪə/ seller of men's underclothes.

hospice /ˈhɒspɪs/ *n* house of rest for travellers.

hospitable /həˈspɪtəbəl/ *adj* friendly and kind to guests.

hospital /ˈhɒspɪtl/ *n* building used for the care of sick people.

hospitality /ˌhɒspɪˈtælətɪ/ *n* act of serving guests.

host[1] /həʊst/ *n* man who receives guests. *n* **hostess** /ˈhəʊstəs/ woman acting as host; the wife of one's host.

host[2] /həʊst/ *n* great crowd; army. **a (whole) host of** = a great many.

host[3] /həʊst/ *n* holy bread in that ceremony of the Church which calls to memory the last supper of Jesus Christ.

hostage /ˈhɒstɪdʒ/ *n* person held prisoner until some promise has been fulfilled.

hostel /ˈhɒstəl/ *n* place of rest for travellers; living-house for persons studying at a school or university away from home.

hostile /ˈhɒstaɪl/ *adj* acting like an enemy. *n* **hostility** /hɒˈstɪlətɪ/.

hot /hɒt/ *adj* **1** giving out or causing much heat. **2** feeling great heat. **3** having a strong burning taste. **hot air** = talk which doesn't mean anything. *n* **hot dog** /ˈ. ./ hot SAUSAGE between pieces of bread.

hotbed /ˈhɒtbed/ *n* place where plants are kept warm and grow quickly. **a hotbed of crime** = place that produces much wrongdoing.

hotchpotch /ˈhɒtʃpɒtʃ/ *n* disorderly mixture.

hotel /həʊˈtel/ *n* place where travellers may find rooms and food.

hot-headed /ˌ. ˈ. ./ *adj* easily made angry; easily moved to unthoughtful action.

hothouse /ˈhɒthaʊs/ *n* glasshouse for growing plants out of the proper season.

hound /haʊnd/ *n* large hunting dog. **to hound out** = drive out.

hour /ˈaʊə/ *n* measure of time, ¹⁄₂₄ of a day. *adj* **hourly** /ˈaʊəlɪ/ happening every hour.

hourglass /ˈaʊəɡlɑːs/ *n* glass containing sand used for measuring hours of time.

house /haʊs/ *n* **1** building made to live in. **2** one of the divisions of a school. **3** place of business. **to keep house** = stay at home, to have charge of the work in a home. **House of God** = church. **a full house** = full theatre. /haʊz/ *vt* give room in a house to.

housebreaker /ˈhaʊsˌbreɪkə/ *n* **1** thief who breaks into houses in the daytime. **2** man employed to pull down useless houses.

household /ˈhaʊshəʊld/ *n* family; all those living in one house. **a household word** = something known and talked of by everybody.

housekeeping /ˈhaʊsˌkiːpɪŋ/ *n* art of taking care of a house and the things in it.

housewarming /ˈhaʊsˌwɔːmɪŋ/ *n* feast given after entering a new house.

housewife /ˈhaʊs-waɪf/ *n* lady in charge of a house.

hove /həʊv/ *p.t.* of heave.

hovel /ˈhɒvəl/ *n* poor dirty home.

hover /ˈhɒvə/ *vi* (of a bird) remain in one place in the air; (of a person) wait about near a person or thing in an uncertain manner.

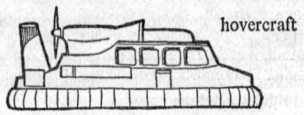

hovercraft

hovercraft /ˈhɒvəkrɑːft/ *n* vehicle that travels over land or water on a thin bed of air.

how /haʊ/ *adv* **1** in what way, e.g. *How did it happen?* **2** so much, e.g. *How foolish!*

however /haʊˈevə/ *adv* no matter how, e.g. *I shall gain, however the war ends*. *conj* on the other hand; but.

howitzer /ˈhaʊɪtsə/ *n* short gun used for dropping heavy shells straight down on the enemy.

howl /haʊl/ *n* cry of dogs and such animals. *vi* make this, or any similar, sound. *n* **howler** very laughable mistake.

hub /hʌb/ *n* centre of a wheel.

hubbub /ˈhʌbʌb/ *n* great noise.

huddle /ˈhʌdl/ *vi* crowd together, e.g. when cold, or in fear.

hue /hjuː/ *n* colour; darkness or lightness of colour; particular kind of a colour.

huff /hʌf/ *vi* show anger; act in a sour way. *adj* **huffy** /ˈhʌfɪ/ easily made angry.

hug /hʌɡ/ *vt* press close to the body with one's arms, as a mother does a child. *n* act of hugging.

huge /hjuːdʒ/ *adj* very large.

hulk /hʌlk/ *n* body of an old ship no longer in use; any large ungraceful person or thing difficult to move. *adj* **hulking** /'hʌlkɪŋ/ large and ungraceful.

hull[1] /hʌl/ *n* outer covering of a grain.

hull[2] /hʌl/ *n* body of a ship.

hullabaloo /ˌhʌləbə'luː/ *n* great noise.

hullo /hʌ'ləʊ/ *interj* expression of greeting or surprise.

hum /hʌm/ *vi* make a noise like a bee. *v* sing (something) with the lips closed.

human /'hjuːmən/ *adj* having to do with man; having the qualities of man. **human being** = person; man or woman.

humane /hjʊ'meɪn/ *adj* kind and gentle.

humanism /'hjuːmənɪzəm/ *n* form of thought which regards man as the most important object of study—not God or nature.

humanitarian /hjʊˌmænə'teərɪən/ *adj, n* (one) having kindness and mercy; trying to make pain and suffering less.

humanity /hjʊ'mænətɪ/ *n* the whole human race. **the humanities** = study of languages, history, etc.

humble /'hʌmbəl/ *adj* not proud; not trying to bring oneself to the notice of others. **of humble birth** = born of common, poor people.

humbug /'hʌmbʌg/ *n* act done for the purpose of deceiving; dishonest or untrue talk.

humdrum /'hʌmdrʌm/ *adj* uninteresting; unchanging.

humid /'hjuːmɪd/ *adj* (esp. of the air) slightly wet. *n* **humidity** /hjʊ'mɪdətɪ/ wetness; amount of water in the air.

humiliate /hjuː'mɪlɪeɪt/ *vt* make ashamed. *n* **humiliation** /hjuːˌmɪlɪ'eɪʃən/.

humility /hjuː'mɪlɪtɪ/ *n* HUMBLE state of mind.

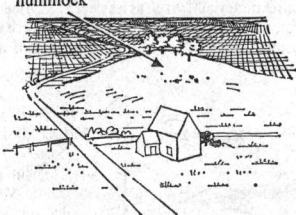

hummock

hummock /'hʌmək/ *n* little hill.

humour /'hjuːmə/ *n* **1** quality of mind which causes one to see and tell the amusing side of things, e.g. *He has a sense of humour.* **2** state of feeling, e.g. *Good-humoured* = kind, pleased, never angry. **to humour a child** = make him happy by giving all he wants. *adj* **humorous** /'hjuːmərəs/ amusing. *n* **humorist** /'hjuːmərɪst/ one who speaks or writes in an intentionally humorous way.

hump /hʌmp/ *n* rounded raised-up part, e.g. on a person's or animal's back.

humus /'hjuːməs/ *n* earth made by decayed leaves.

hunch /hʌntʃ/ *n* rounded raised-up part. *vt* curve (the back) as a cat does when angry. *n,* **hunchback** /'hʌntʃbæk/ (one) having the back so curved. *infml* **to have a hunch that** = believe (though without reason) that.

hundred /'hʌndrəd/ *n* number often written **100**, being ten times ten.

hung /hʌŋ/ p.t. of **hang**[1].

hunger /'hʌŋgə/ *n* desire for food; any strong desire. **to go on a hunger strike** = to refuse to eat when in prison. *adj* **hungry** /'hʌŋgrɪ/.

hunk /hʌŋk/ *n* large piece.

hunt /hʌnt/ *v* go after (wild animals) and try to catch or kill them; look for (that which is lost). *n* **hunter** /'hʌntə/ man who hunts animals.

hurdle /'hɜːdl/ *n* movable frame over which men or horses jump.

hurl /hɜːl/ *vt* throw with great force.

hurly-burly /ˌhɜːlɪ'bɜːlɪ/ *n* great noise and action.

hurrah /hʊ'rɑː/, **hurray** /hʊ'reɪ/ *interj* shout of joy.

hurricane /'hʌrɪkən/ *n* very strong wind blowing in a circle; any strong wind. *n* **hurricane lamp** /'... ˌ./ special kind of lamp that is not blown out by the wind.

hurry /'hʌrɪ/ *v* (cause to) move or act quickly; increase speed.

hurt /hɜːt/ *v* cause pain of body or mind; damage or destroy.

hurtle /'hɜːtl/ *vi* rush with great force or speed.

husband /'hʌzbənd/ *n* man to whom a woman is married.

husbandman /'hʌzbəndmən/ *n* farmer. *n* **husbandry** /'hʌzbəndrɪ/ work of farming.

hush /hʌʃ/ *vt* make silent. **Hush!** = be silent. **to hush up the affair** = keep secret, prevent talk about. *n* **hush-money** = money paid to one who knows of wrongdoing so that he may be silent.

husk /hʌsk/ *n* dry outer covering of a grain.

husky /'hʌskɪ/ *adj* (of the voice) rough, not clear—because the throat is dry or tired.

hussar /hʊ'zɑː/ *n* horse-soldier.

hussy /'hʌzɪ/ *n* troublesome girl.

hustle /'hʌsəl/ *v* **1** to hurry; push roughly against. **2** *sl* obtain money by doubtful means.

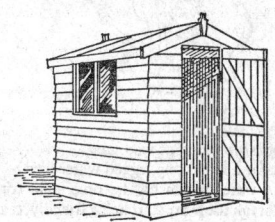

hut

hut /hʌt/ *n* small roughly-built house.

hutch /hʌtʃ/ *n* box with bars across the front used for keeping rabbits or other small animals.

hyacinth /'haɪəsɪnθ/ n a sweet-smelling spring flower.

hyaena /haɪ'iːnə/ see **hyena**.

hybrid /'haɪbrɪd/ adj having parents of different kinds.

hydrant /'haɪdrənt/ n large pipe in the street from which water may be drawn, e.g. to put out the fire in a burning house.

hydraulic /haɪ'drɔːlɪk/ adj worked by water-power.

hydro- /'haɪdrəʊ, 'haɪdrə/ having to do with water, e.g. **hydroelectric** /ˌhaɪdrəʊɪ'lektrɪk/ adj making electricity by water-power.

hydrogen /'haɪdrədʒən/ n lightest known gas.

hydrophobia /ˌhaɪdrə'fəʊbɪə/ n disease caused by the bite of a mad dog.

hydroplane /'haɪdrəpleɪn/ n motor-boat that travels at great speed on the surface of water

hyena /haɪ'iːnə/ n wild animal, something like a dog, said to have a cry like laughter.

hygiene /'haɪdʒiːn/ n science of keeping people healthy in body and mind. adj **hygienic** /haɪ'dʒiːnɪk/.

hymn /hɪm/ n song of praise, usually used in church. n **hymnal** /'hɪmnəl/ book of hymns.

hyper- /'haɪpə/ prefix over, above, too much. (e.g. **hypercritical**).

hyperbola /haɪ'pɜːbələ/ n a kind of curve.

hyperbole /haɪ'pɜːbəlɪ/ n way of speaking that says more than the truth, e.g. to say that the boys in the class are all asleep when only half are asleep.

hypertrophy /haɪ'pɜːtrəfɪ/ n too great growth of some part of the body.

hyphen /'haɪfən/ n mark (-) used to join or separate words, e.g. "self-praise". vt **hyphenate** /'haɪfəneɪt/ write (a word) with a hyphen.

hypnotism /'hɪpnətɪzəm/ n art of producing a state of sleep during which a person will do whatever is ordered. vt **hypnotize** /'hɪpnətaɪz/ cause (someone) to fall into this state. n **hypnosis** /hɪp'nəʊsɪs/ the state itself. adj **hypnotic** /hɪp'nɒtɪk/.

hypochondria /ˌhaɪpə'kɒndrɪə/ n state of being too anxious about one's health. n **hypochondriac** /ˌhaɪpə'kɒndrɪæk/ one in this state.

hypocrisy /hɪ'pɒkrəsɪ/ n act of pretending to have goodness and strength of character which one does not possess. **hypocrite** /'hɪpəkrɪt/ n one who does this. adj **hypocritical** /ˌhɪpə'krɪtɪkəl/.

hypodermic /ˌhaɪpə'dɜːmɪk/ adj having to do with parts just under the skin. n **1** medicine put just under the skin by a needle. **2** needle used for this purpose.

hypotenuse /haɪ'pɒtənjuːz/ n longest side in a right-angled (90°) TRIANGLE.

hypothesis /haɪ'pɒθəsɪs/ n that which is supposed in order to explain certain facts. adj hypothetical /ˌhaɪpə'θetɪkəl/.

hysteria /hɪ'stɪərɪə/, **hysterics** /hɪ'sterɪks/ n disorder of the feelings, causing one to cry or laugh without cause; state in which one's feelings cannot be controlled; uncontrolled excitement. adj **hysterical** /hɪ'sterɪkəl/.

I

I /aɪ/ pron (used in speaking of oneself) e.g. I can't run as fast as he can.

floating in the sea. n **ice cream** /ˌ. './ CREAM with other materials frozen as a sweet food. n **ice-pack** /'. ./ **1** mass of broken ice in the far north or far south. **2** bag of ice laid on the head of a sick person.

ibex

icicle

ibex /'aɪbeks/ n a kind of wild goat.
ibis /'aɪbɪs/ n a large long-legged water-bird.
ice /aɪs/ n water which has become solid with cold. **to break the ice** = start being friendly, take the first step in a difficult matter. **to cut no ice** = be of no importance or have no effect. vt **1** make (food) cold. **2** to cover with sugar, e.g. To ice a cake. n **iceberg** /'aɪsbɜːg/ mountain of ice

icicle /'aɪsɪkəl/ n long hanging piece of ice caused by the freezing of water which is dropping slowly, e.g. from a roof.
icing /'aɪsɪŋ/ n covering of sugar on cakes.
icon /'aɪkɒn/ n holy object, e.g picture of a holy person.
iconoclast /aɪ'kɒnəklæst/ n breaker of holy

objects; one who tries to destroy old beliefs or customs.

icy /'aɪsɪ/ *adj* covered with ice; like ice; very cold.

idea /aɪ'dɪə/ *n* thought or picture in the mind.

ideal /aɪ'dɪəl/ *adj* 1 perfect; according to one's highest idea; which is an idea only, not real. 2 *n* idea of how things should be. *n* **idealism** /aɪ'dɪəlɪzəm/ (in character) forming high ideals. *v* **idealize** /aɪ'dɪəlaɪz/ form ideals; think of (a person or thing) as perfect not noticing the faults.

identical /aɪ'dentɪkəl/ the same; exactly alike.

identify /aɪ'dentɪfaɪ/ *vt* show or prove to be the same, e.g. *To identify a thief* = recognize a certain person as the thief. *n* **identification** /aɪˌdentɪfɪ'keɪʃən/ *n* **identity** /aɪ'dentətɪ/ who one is.

ideology /ˌaɪdɪ'ɒlədʒɪ/ *n* set of ideas, esp. about how nations should be governed.

idiocy /'ɪdɪəsɪ/ *n* complete lack of understanding; great foolishness.

idiom /'ɪdɪəm/ *n* group of words which have a special meaning when used together, e.g. "to cut no ice" = produce no result. *adj* **idiomatic** /ˌɪdɪə'mætɪk/.

idiosyncrasy /ˌɪdɪə'sɪŋkrəsɪ/ *n* way of feeling or behaving that is peculiar to one person.

idiot /'ɪdɪət/ *n* person having no power of mind. *adj* **idiotic** /ˌɪdɪ'ɒtɪk/.

idle /'aɪdl/ *adj* 1 doing no work; be not in use, e.g. *The machines are lying idle.* **I have not an idle moment** = I am always busy. 2 lazy. 3 of no use or effect. *n* **idleness** /'aɪdlnəs/.

idol /'aɪdəl/ *n* 1 holy object made in the form of a man or animal. 2 person or thing which is greatly admired or respected. *n* **idolater** /aɪ'dɒlətə/ one who believes in idols. *vt* **idolize** /'aɪdəl-aɪz/ regard as holy, admire greatly. *n* **idolatry** /aɪ'dɒlətrɪ/ belief in idols.

idyll /'ɪdɪl/ *n* short poem describing simple country life. *adj* **idyllic** /ɪ'dɪlɪk/ of an idyll; very delightful and charming.

if /ɪf/ *conj* on condition that; provided that.

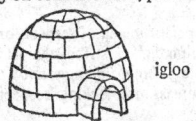

igloo

igloo /'ɪɡlu:/ *n* hut made of ice.

igneous /'ɪɡnɪəs/ *adj* having to do with fire; (of rocks) formed by great heat.

ignite /ɪɡ'naɪt/ *vt* set fire to. *vi* start to burn. **ignition** /ɪɡ'nɪʃən/ *n* 1 act of igniting. 2 setting fire to the gas in a car to make it go.

ignoble /ɪɡ'nəʊbəl/ *adj* of low birth; of low character.

ignominious /ˌɪɡnə'mɪnɪəs/ *adj* shameful. **ignominy** /'ɪɡnəmɪnɪ/ *n* dishonour.

ignoramus /ˌɪɡnə'reɪməs/ *n* one who knows nothing.

ignorant /'ɪɡnərənt/ *adj* having no knowledge;

not having been told of something. *n* **ignorance** /'ɪɡnərəns/.

ignore /ɪɡ'nɔ:/ *vt* take no notice of; refuse to know.

ill /ɪl/ *adj* 1 in bad health. 2 harmful. **illness** /'ɪlnəs/ *n* disease.

ill-advised /ˌ. .'./ *adj* unwise.

ill-bred /ˌ. .'./ *adj* not polite.

ill-disposed /ˌ. .'./ *adj* wishing to do harm; not in favour of.

illegal /ɪ'li:ɡəl/ *adj* not according to law.

illegible /ɪ'ledʒəbəl/ *adj* not clear enough to be read.

ill-favoured /ˌ. '. ./ *adj* ugly, unpleasant.

illegitimate /ˌɪlɪ'dʒɪtɪmət/ *adj* 1 unlawful. 2 (of a child) whose parents were not married.

illicit /ɪ'lɪsɪt/ *adj* not lawful.

illiteracy /ɪ'lɪtərəsɪ/ *n* state of not being able to read or write. *adj* **illiterate** /ɪ'lɪtərət/.

ill-natured /ˌ. '. ./ *adj* having a bad temper.

illogical /ɪ'lɒdʒɪkəl/ *adj* not according to reason.

illuminate /ɪ'lu:mɪneɪt/ *vt* 1 give light to. 2 make clear to the mind. 3 cause the mind to have noble thoughts. 4 make the page of a book beautiful with coloured letters and pictures. *n* **illumination** /ɪˌlu:mɪ'neɪʃən/.

illumine /ɪ'lu:mɪn/ *vt* give light to.

illusion /ɪ'lu:ʒən/ *n* belief which is not according to facts; seeing what is really not there. *adj* **illusive** /ɪ'lu:sɪv/, **illusory** /ɪ'lu:sərɪ/ deceiving the senses or mind.

illustrate /'ɪləstreɪt/ *vt* 1 make clear by means of an example. 2 add pictures to (a book). *n* **illustration** /ˌɪlə'streɪʃən/ picture, example. *adj* **illustrative** /'ɪləstrətɪv/ serving as an example. *adj* **illustrious** /ɪ'lʌstrɪəs/ famous.

image /'ɪmɪdʒ/ *n* 1 likeness or copy of anything, made of wood, metal, etc. 2 picture in the mind. 3 public idea of what a person is like.

imagery /'ɪmɪdʒərɪ/ *n* 1 figures of men, animals, etc., made of stone or metal. 2 (in writing or speech) use of words which cause pictures to come into the mind.

imagine /ɪ'mædʒɪn/ *vt* form a picture of (something) in the mind; believe without proof. *adj* **imaginary** /ɪ'mædʒɪnərɪ/ imagined, not real. *n* **imagination** /ɪˌmædʒɪ'neɪʃən/ power of imagining or thinking up new things. *adj* **imaginative** /ɪ'mædʒɪnətɪv/ having or sharing a good imagination; one who thinks of many new ideas—or of ideas which are of no use in practice.

imam /ɪ'mɑ:m/ *n* leader of prayer among Muslims.

imbecile /'ɪmbəsi:l/ *n* one of weak mind. *n* **imbecility** /ˌɪmbə'sɪlətɪ/.

imbed /ɪm'bed/ *vt* fix firmly in any matter, e.g. *Plants imbedded in the earth.*

imbibe /ɪm'baɪb/ *vt* drink in; take in as if drinking, e.g. ideas.

imbue /ɪm'bju:/ *vt* wet completely; fill right through; colour all through.

imitate /'ımıteıt/ *vt* copy; act or behave in the same way as. *n* **imitation** /ˌımı'teıʃən/.

immaculate /ı'mækjʊlət/ *adj* pure; without fault.

immanent /'ımənənt/ *adj* remaining within; present everywhere.

immaterial /ˌımə'tıərıəl/ *adj* 1 not solid; not real. 2 of no importance.

immediate /ı'mi:dıət/ *adj* 1 close; very near. 2 (in time) following at once.

immemorial /ˌımə'mɔ:rıəl/ *adj* beyond the reach of memory; very old.

immense /ı'mens/ *adj* very large.

immerse /ı'mɜ:s/ *vt* put into liquid. **immersed in a book** = deeply interested in reading. *n* **immersion** /ı'mɜ:ʃən/.

immigrant /'ımıgrənt/ *n* one who comes to a country to settle and live there. **immigrate** /'ımıgreıt/ *vi* come to a country as an immigrant. *n* **immigration** /ˌımı'greıʃən/.

imminent /'ımınənt/ *adj* very near; which will probably happen very soon.

immoral /ı'mɒrəl/ *adj* wrong; evil; of bad character. *n* **immorality** /ˌımə'rælətı/.

immortal /ı'mɔ:tl/ *adj* which will never die; famous for all time. *n* **immortality** /ˌımɔ:'tælətı/.

immune /ı'mju:n/ *adj* free from; not able to be attacked by, e.g. *I have had that disease and so I am now immune. n* **immunity** /ı'mju:nətı/.

immutable /ı'mju:təbəl/ *adj* which cannot be changed.

imp /ımp/ *n* small devil; evil spirit; troublesome child.

impact /'ımpækt/ *n* striking together of two objects.

impair /ım'peə/ *vt* harm or make less useful.

impale

impale /ım'peıl/ *vt* push a sharp-pointed instrument through.

impalpable /ım'pælpəbəl/ *adj* not able to be felt because so fine; not easily understood.

impart /ım'pɑ:t/ *vt* give.

impartial /ım'pɑ:ʃəl/ *adj* not favouring one side; just.

impasse /'æmpɑ:s/ *n* place from which one cannot escape; great difficulty; point in a talk at which the two sides or persons are quite unable to agree.

impassioned /ım'pæʃənd/ *adj* full of strong feeling.

impassive /ım'pæsıv/ *adj* showing no sign of feeling.

impatient /ım'peıʃənt/ *adj* unable to suffer delay; eager to go or act. *n* **impatience** /ım'peıʃəns/.

impeach /ım'pi:tʃ/ *vt* say that someone has been dishonest or disloyal; bring a person (e.g. a member of the government) before a court of law for this reason.

impeccable /ım'pekəbəl/ *adj* faultless; unable to do wrong.

impecunious /ˌımpı'kju:nıəs/ *adj* having no money.

impede /ım'pi:d/ *vt* delay or prevent from moving.

impediment /ım'pedımənt/ *n* thing which stops or delays an action from going on; difficulty in speaking caused by the muscles of the throat and tongue.

impel /ım'pel/ *vt* push on or urge.

impending /ım'pendıŋ/ *adj* very near; (of some feared event) which will happen soon.

impenetrable /ım'penıtrəbəl/ *adj* not able to be passed through.

imperative /ım'perətıv/ *n* (of a word or form of a verb) used in commanding. *adj* very necessary.

imperial /ım'pıərıəl/ *adj* having to do with an empire or the ruler of an empire.

imperil /ım'perıl/ *vt* cause to be in danger.

imperious /ım'pıərıəs/ *adj* loving to command or use power.

impersonate /ım'pɜ:səneıt/ *vt* pretend to be (another person). *n* **impersonation** /ımˌpɜ:sə'neıʃən/.

impertinent /ım'pɜ:tınənt/ *adj* not polite; not showing proper respect.

imperturbable /ˌımpə'tɜ:bəbəl/ *adj* calm; not easily made angry or excited.

impervious /ım'pɜ:vıəs/ *vt* not allowing to pass through, e.g. *Rubber is impervious to liquid.*

impetuous /ım'petʃʊəs/ *adj* acting hastily without thinking first. *n* **impetuosity** /ımˌpetʃʊ'ɒsıtı/.

impetus /'ımpətəs/ *n* force which moves or drives anything.

impiety /ım'paıətı/ *n* lack of respect for God.

impinge /ım'pındʒ/ *vi* strike against or upon something, e.g. *Light impinges upon the eye.*

impious /'ımpıəs/ *adj* lacking respect, esp. fo God.

implacable /ım'plækəbəl/ *adj* feeling anger or hate which cannot be changed or softened; unforgiving.

implant /ım'plɑ:nt/ *vt* set deeply into, e.g. *To implant ideas in the mind.*

implement /'ımplımənt/ *n* any instrument. *vt* **implement** /'ımplıment/ put (e.g. a plan) into action.

implicate /'ımplıkeıt/ *vt* show that someone has a share in, e.g. *He was implicated in the murder. n* **implication** /ˌımplı'keıʃən/ 1 state of being implicated in some matter. 2 act of IMPLYING something; thing IMPLIED.

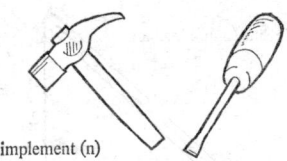

implement (n)

implicit /ɪmˈplɪsɪt/ *adj* understood but not expressed; unquestioning, e.g. *Implicit faith.*

implore /ɪmˈplɔː/ *vt* beg or pray (someone) to do something.

imply /ɪmˈplaɪ/ *vt* mean without saying directly, e.g. *You do not say that you were present, but your words imply that you were.*

imponderable /ɪmˈpɒndərəbəl/ *adj* unable to be weighed or measured.

import /ɪmˈpɔːt/ *vt* bring (goods) into a country. *n* **import** /ˈɪmpɔːt/ **1** meaning. **2** (often *pl*) (a load of) goods brought into a country.

important /ɪmˈpɔːtənt/ *adj* serious; of great value; which will probably produce a great effect; (of a person) having power. *n* **importance** /ɪmˈpɔːtəns/.

importunate /ɪmˈpɔːtʃʊnət/ *adj* continuing always and at all times to ask or claim, so that the hearer is made angry. *n* **importunity** /ˌɪmpɔːˈtʃuːnətɪ/.

impose /ɪmˈpəʊz/ *v* lay (a load or unpleasant duty) upon a person.

imposing /ɪmˈpəʊzɪŋ/ *adj* fine; causing one to admire.

imposition /ˌɪmpəˈzɪʃən/ *n* **1** act of putting on; laying of a load or unpleasant duty or punishment upon. **2** unpleasant duty; unreasonable demand for money; school-child's punishment, e.g. to copy out a poem.

impostor /ɪmˈpɒstə/ *n* person who pretends to be something which he is not; deceiver. *n* **imposture** /ɪmˈpɒstʃə/ act of pretending; a trick.

impotent /ˈɪmpətənt/ *adj* **1** having no powers; unable to act. **2** (of a man) unable to have sexual relations.

impound /ɪmˈpaʊnd/ *vt* **1** shut in. **2** seize by power of the law.

impoverish /ɪmˈpɒvərɪʃ/ *vt* cause to become poor.

impracticable /ɪmˈpræktɪkəbəl/ *adj* not able to be done or used.

imprecate /ˈɪmprɪkeɪt/ *vt* curse or call down evil upon.

impregnable /ɪmˈpregnəbəl/ *adj* able to be defended against all attacks.

impregnate /ˈɪmpregneɪt/ *vt* **1** cause to be full of or filled with, e.g. the smell or taste, of something. **2** cause to bear fruit.

impresario /ˌɪmprɪˈsɑːrɪəʊ/ *n* one who has charge of the business matters of a play, of a famous singer, or other performer.

impress /ɪmˈpres/ *vt* **1** mark by pressing. **2** press upon the mind, cause to remember, e.g. *He impressed on me the need of hard work* = told me that I must work hard. **3** cause (someone) to

think highly of one. **impression** /ɪmˈpreʃən/ *n* **1** act of pressing; mark left by pressing; number of copies of a book printed at one time. **2** effect produced in the mind; general idea, e.g. *I have an impression that* = I think but am not sure. **impressionable** /ɪmˈpreʃənəbəl/ *adj* whose feelings or opinions are easily changed by other persons or by experience.

impressionist /ɪmˈpreʃənɪst/ *n* painter who paints, not the real scene, but the effect produced by the scene in his mind.

impressive /ɪmˈpresɪv/ *adj* grand; solemn.

imprint /ˈɪmˌprɪnt/ *n* mark made by pressing; effect produced on the mind or character; printer's name in a book.

imprison /ɪmˈprɪzən/ *vt* put into prison. *n* **imprisonment** /ɪmˈprɪzənmənt/.

impromptu /ɪmˈprɒmptʃuː/ *adj, adv* without preparation, e.g. *To speak impromptu.*

improve /ɪmˈpruːv/ *v* make or become better. *n* **improvement** /ɪmˈpruːvmənt/ act of improving; what makes something better than it was.

improvident /ɪmˈprɒvɪdənt/ *adj* not looking to the future, e.g. not laying aside money for future needs.

improvise /ˈɪmprəvaɪz/ *v* do (something) which one has not prepared before, e.g. play music. **to improvise a bed (meal, etc.)** = make hastily and without having the proper material. *n* **improvisation** /ˌɪmprəvaɪˈzeɪʃən/.

impudent /ˈɪmpjʊdənt/ *adj* rude; not showing proper respect. *n* **impudence** /ˈɪmpjʊdəns/.

impugn /ɪmˈpjuːn/ *vt* question with the idea of proving untrue.

impulse /ˈɪmpʌls/ *n* sudden desire to act, usually without careful thought. *adj* **impulsive** /ɪmˈpʌlsɪv/ acting without first planning what to do.

impunity /ɪmˈpjuːnətɪ/ *n* freedom from the possibility of punishment. **with impunity** = without fear of being punished.

impute /ɪmˈpjuːt/ *vt* consider as belonging to, e.g. *To impute evil to* = say that a person is bad or did wrong. *n* **imputation** /ˌɪmpjʊˈteɪʃən/.

in[1] /ɪn/ *prep* **1** contained by; inside. **2** before the end of. **3** during; at some time during.

in-[2] /ɪn/ not, e.g. **inability** /ˌɪnəˈbɪlətɪ/ *n* state of not being able.

inadvertence /ˌɪnədˈvɜːtəns/ *n* lack of care or attention. *adj* **inadvertent** /ˌɪnədˈvɜːtənt/.

inalienable /ɪˈneɪlɪənəbəl/ *adj* not able to be separated or taken away, e.g. *An inalienable right.*

inane /ɪˈneɪn/ *adj* very foolish or silly.

inapt /ɪˈnæpt/ *adj* **1** not skilful. **2** not concerned with the matter which is being talked about.

inarticulate /ˌɪnɑːˈtɪkjʊlət/ *adj* unable to express one's thoughts or feelings.

inasmuch /ˌɪnəzˈmʌtʃ/ because. **inasmuch as** = considering that.

inaugurate /ɪˈnɔːgjʊreɪt/ *vt* begin in a solemn way and with ceremony (e.g. a show).

135

inborn

inborn /ˌɪnˈbɔːn/ *adj* which one has at birth.

inbred /ˌɪnˈbred/ *adj* which is born in one; natural.

inbreeding /ˈɪnˌbriːdɪŋ/ *n* (of animals) always having as parents two from the same family.

incalculable /ɪnˈkælkjʊləbəl/ *adj* so great that it cannot be measured or counted.

incandescent /ˌɪnkænˈdesənt/ *adj* able to become white with heat without burning, e.g. electric lamps.

incantation /ˌɪnkænˈteɪʃən/ *n* something sung or spoken in order to produce a magic effect.

incapable /ɪnˈkeɪpəbəl/ *adj* helpless; unable; unfit for one's work.

incapacitate /ˌɪnkəˈpæsəteɪt/ *vt* make unfit or useless.

incarcerate /ɪnˈkɑːsəreɪt/ *vt* put in prison.

incarnate /ɪnˈkɑːnət/ *adj* appearing in a body, in human shape. /ɪnˈkɑːneɪt/ *vt* give human form to. *n* **incarnation** /ˌɪnkɑːˈneɪʃən/ *act* of taking on a body.

incendiary /ɪnˈsendɪərɪ/ *adj* intentionally setting fire to buildings.

incense[1] /ɪnˈsens/ *vt* cause to become angry.

incense[2] /ˈɪnsens/ *n* material burned to make a sweet-smelling smoke.

incentive /ɪnˈsentɪv/ *n* that which gives one a desire to act, to work hard, etc.

inception /ɪnˈsepʃən/ *n* beginning.

incessant /ɪnˈsesənt/ *adj* continuing without stopping.

incest /ˈɪnsest/ *n* sexual relations between members of the same family, e.g. between father and daughter.

inch /ɪntʃ/ *n* measurement of length = 2.54 CENTIMETRES.

incidence /ˈɪnsɪdəns/ *n* direction of falling or way of having an effect, e.g. *The incidence of a disease* = number, or kind, of people who catch the disease.

incident /ˈɪnsɪdənt/ *n* a happening; unimportant event. *adj* **incidental** /ˌɪnsɪˈdentəl/ small, unimportant; happening without any special purpose or meaning. **incidental to** = which are a necessary but less important part of.

incinerator /ɪnˈsɪnəreɪtə/ *n* large enclosed fire for burning waste matter.

incipient /ɪnˈsɪpɪənt/ *adj* just beginning.

incise /ɪnˈsaɪz/ *vt* cut into. *n* **incision** /ɪnˈsɪʒən/ *act* of cutting in; a cut. *adj* **incisive** /ɪnˈsaɪsɪv/ (of words) sharp; cruel.

incite /ɪnˈsaɪt/ *vt* urge on.

inclement /ɪnˈklemənt/ *adj* (esp. of weather) rough; bad.

incline /ɪnˈklaɪn/ *v* lean or cause to lean towards, or away from; slope; cause to turn, bend towards. **to be inclined to** = have a slight desire or tendency to *n* **incline** /ˈɪnklaɪn/ slope, e.g. *An incline of 1 in 4* = hill rising one foot in every four feet of distance. *n* **inclination** /ˌɪnklɪˈneɪʃən/.

include /ɪnˈkluːd/ *vt* contain; consider as

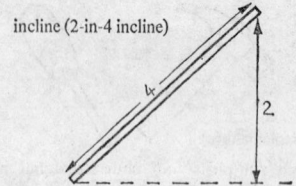

incline (2-in-4 incline)

belonging to a group, e.g. *I include him among my friends*. *n* **inclusion** /ɪnˈkluːʒən/. *adj* **inclusive** /ɪnˈkluːsɪv/ containing or counting all, e.g. *From May 10th to 18th inclusive*, i.e. counting both the 10th and 18th.

incognito /ˌɪnkɒgˈniːtəʊ/ *adj, adv* using a different name in order to escape notice, e.g. *The Prince arrived incognito*.

incoherent /ˌɪnkəʊˈhɪərənt/ *adj* (of the expression of ideas) in bad order, not well arranged; (of a person) unable to express his ideas clearly.

income /ˈɪnkʌm/ *n* money coming in; amount of money that one receives each year.

incommensurate /ˌɪnkəˈmenʃərət/ *adj* not equal; not enough.

incommode /ˌɪnkəˈməʊd/ *vt* give trouble to; make uncomfortable.

incomparable /ɪnˈkɒmpərəbəl/ *adj* which cannot be COMPARED; better than all others.

incompatible /ˌɪnkəmˈpætəbəl/ *adj* having opposite or disagreeing natures, e.g. fire and water.

incompetent /ɪnˈkɒmpɪtənt/ *adj* unskilful; unable to do one's work properly.

incongruous /ɪnˈkɒŋgrʊəs/ *adj* not suitable.

inconsequential /ˌɪnˌkɒnsɪˈkwenʃəl/ *adj* not following the natural order; not making sense, e.g. to say "I am ill but it is raining."

inconsiderable /ˌɪnkənˈsɪdərəbəl/ *adj* small; not worth noticing.

inconvenient /ˌɪnkənˈviːnɪənt/ *adj* causing trouble or difficulty.

incorporate /ɪnˈkɔːpəreɪt/ *vt* 1 take into one's own group or body, e.g. *The English language sometimes incorporates foreign words*. 2 form (a business company) according to law.

incorrigible /ɪnˈkɒrɪdʒəbəl/ *adj* not able to be set right or made to behave well; hopelessly bad.

increase /ɪnˈkriːs/ *v* make or become greater in size, number, value, etc. *n* **increase** /ˈɪnkriːs/ *act* of increasing; amount by which something has increased.

incredible /ɪnˈkredəbəl/ *adj* unbelievable. *adj* **incredulous** /ɪnˈkredʊləs/ disbelieving, not willing to believe.

increment /ˈɪnkrɪmənt/ *n* increase; amount of an increase, esp. a regular yearly increase in pay.

incriminate /ɪnˈkrɪmɪneɪt/ *vt* show that (someone) had something to do with a wrong act.

incubate /ˈɪŋkjʊbeɪt/ *vt* bring the young out of (eggs) by keeping them warm; form a plan in

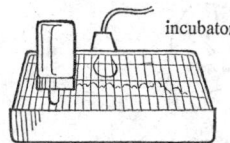

incubator

(the mind). *n* **incubator** /'ɪŋkjʊbeɪtə/ piece of equipment for incubating eggs; piece of equipment for keeping babies born too early warm and safe from disease.

inculcate /'ɪnkʌlkeɪt/ *vt* fix firmly in the mind of another person.

inculpate /'ɪnkʌlpeɪt/ *vt* say that (another) has done wrong as well as oneself.

incumbent /ɪn'kʌmbənt/ *adj* lying on or pressing on. **it is incumbent upon me to** = it is my duty to. *n* person who holds an office, e.g. as a priest.

incur /ɪn'kɜː/ *vt* run into, e.g. *To incur debt* = get into debt, to owe money; *I incurred his anger* = I caused him to be angry with me.

incursion /ɪn'kɜːʃən/ *n* sudden quick bursting in, e.g. attack by enemy soldiers, unexpected visit from a large number of unwelcome guests.

indebted /ɪn'detɪd/ *adj* owing money; owing thanks.

indecent /ɪn'diːsənt/ *adj* not proper; shocking.

indecision /ˌɪndɪ'sɪʒən/ *n* state of being unable to decide.

indeed /ɪn'diːd/ *adv* in fact; in truth. **indeed!** (expression of surprise or doubt).

indefatigable /ˌɪndɪ'fætɪgəbəl/ *adj* untiring; not resting until one has gained one's purpose.

indelible /ɪn'deləbəl/ *adj* not able to be rubbed out or cleaned off, e.g. *Indelible pencil.*

indelicate /ɪn'delɪkət/ *adj* not polite.

indemnify /ɪn'demnɪfaɪ/ *vt* repay for loss or damage. **indemnity** /ɪn'demnətɪ/ *n* such payment.

indent /ɪn'dent/ *vt* **1** make a small hollow in. **2** start (the first line of a block of printing) further in than the others. *n* **indent** /'ɪndent/ an order for goods. *n* **indenture** /ɪn'dentʃə/ agreement between a master and a learner of a trade; any agreement of which two copies are made.

independent /ˌɪndɪ'pendənt/ *adj* not controlled by or depending on another; self-governing; free to live one's own life and think one's own thoughts; having enough money to live without working. *n* **independence** /ˌɪndɪ'pendəns/.

indeterminate /ˌɪndɪ'tɜːmɪnət/ *adj* uncertain; not fixed in time, place or meaning.

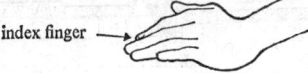

index finger

index /'ɪndeks/ *n* **1** that which points out or guides. **2** list of names or subjects at the back of a book. **index finger** = finger with which one points.

indicate /'ɪndɪkeɪt/ *vt* show signs of; point out;

induction

cause to see. *n* **indication** /ˌɪndɪ'keɪʃən/. *adj* **indicative** /ɪn'dɪkətɪv/ acting as a sign of. *n* that part of a verb which tells an action or a fact.

indices /'ɪndɪsiːz/ *pl* of **index.**

indict /ɪn'daɪt/ *vt* say that (someone) has broken the law. **indictable offence** = serious wrongdoing for which one can be tried in a court of law. *n* **indictment** /ɪn'daɪtmənt/.

indifferent /ɪn'dɪfərənt/ *adj* **1** not interested in or not caring for. **2** without any very good or bad qualities. *n* **indifference** /ɪn'dɪfərəns/.

indigenous /ɪn'dɪdʒɪnəs/ *adj* born or produced in the country; not foreign.

indigent /'ɪndɪdʒənt/ *adj* very poor.

indigestion /ˌɪndɪ'dʒestʃən/ *n* illness or pain caused by the stomach being unable to deal with the food which has been eaten.

indignant /ɪn'dɪgnənt/ *adj* angry because one thinks one has been wronged. *n* **indignation** /ˌɪndɪg'neɪʃən/.

indignity /ɪn'dɪgnətɪ/ *n* very rude treatment of a person, causing him shame and loss of self-respect.

indigo /'ɪndɪgəʊ/ *n* plant from which a blue colouring matter is obtained. *n, adj* (of a) deep blue colour.

indiscretion /ˌɪndɪ'skreʃən/ *n* any act done without good judgment or thought of possible results.

indiscriminate /ˌɪndɪ'skrɪmɪnət/ *adj* not choosing carefully.

indispensable /ˌɪndɪ'spensəbəl/ *adj* without which a certain action or piece of work cannot be done, e.g. *Air is indispensable for (to) life.*

indisposed /ˌɪndɪ'spəʊzd/ *adj* unwilling; ill and unfit for work. *n* **indisposition** /ˌɪndɪspə'zɪʃən/ illness which is not serious.

individual /ˌɪndɪ'vɪdʒʊəl/ *n* single person or thing. *adj* alone, single or being apart from everything else; having to do with a single person. *n* **individualism** /ˌɪndɪ'vɪdʒʊəlɪzəm/ teaching that the rights of each person are more important than the rights of the group; unwillingness to work with others. **individuality** /ˌɪndɪvɪdʒʊ'ælətɪ/ *n* special character different from others.

indoctrinate /ɪn'dɒktrɪneɪt/ *vt* force one's ideas to be accepted by.

indolent /'ɪndələnt/ *adj* lazy.

indomitable /ɪn'dɒmɪtəbəl/ *adj* unyieldingly courageous.

indoor /'ɪndɔː/ *adj* in the house, not in the open air. *adv* **indoors** /ɪn'dɔːz/.

indubitable /ɪn'djuːbɪtəbəl/ *adj* certain.

induce /ɪn'djuːs/ *vt* **1** cause; lead (someone) to act by giving reasons or causing desire. **2** cause (electricity) to flow along an inner wire by sending electricity through a wire twisted round it, but not touching it. *n* **inducement.**

induction /ɪn'dʌkʃən/ *n* way of reasoning from many known facts to one general law. *adj* **inductive** /ɪn'dʌktɪv/.

137

indulge /ɪn'dʌldʒ/ *vi* yield to and please the tastes or desires; give pleasure to. *n* **indulgence** /ɪn'dʌldʒəns/ **1** the act of satisfying one's desires. **2** (in religion) freedom given by a priest from the punishment for wrongdoing. *adj* **indulgent** /ɪn'dʌldʒənt/.

industrial /ɪn'dʌstrɪəl/ *adj* having to do with the making of goods for trade.

industry /'ɪndəstrɪ/ *n* **1** quality of working hard. **2** making of goods in large numbers with the help of machines. *adj* **industrious** /ɪn'dʌstrɪəs/ working hard.

industrialist /ɪn'dʌstrɪəlɪst/ *n* owner of a large mill or workshop where things are made.

inebriated /ɪ'niːbrɪeɪtɪd/ *adj* having lost all reason because of taking too much wine.

ineffable /ɪ'nefəbəl/ *adj* which cannot be expressed or described, because it is too beautiful or too good.

ineffectual /ˌɪnɪ'fektʃʊəl/ *adj* unable to produce the desired result.

inept /ɪ'nept/ *adj* silly; out of place. *n* **ineptitude** /ɪ'neptɪtjuːd/.

ineradicable /ˌɪnɪ'rædɪkəbəl/ *adj* deeply rooted; difficult to change.

inert /ɪ'nɜːt/ *adj* **1** lifeless and soft, as when asleep. **2** (of a substance) not able to mix with other substances. **inertia** /ɪ'nɜːʃə/ *n* **1** state of being powerless, too lazy to move. **2** that force which prevents a thing from being moved when it is standing still, and keeps it moving when it is moving.

inestimable /ɪ'nestɪməbəl/ *adj* not able to be measured or valued; of very great value.

inevitable /ɪ'nevɪtəbəl/ *adj* which must happen; allowing no escape.

inexorable /ɪ'neksərəbəl/ *adj* which cannot be changed or prevented; working regularly and without pity, e.g. *The inexorable laws of nature.*

inexperience /ˌɪnɪk'spɪərɪəns/ *n* lack of experience.

inextricable /ˌɪnɪk'strɪkəbəl/ *adj* which cannot be untied or set in order.

infallible /ɪn'fæləbəl/ *adj* unable to fail or be mistaken.

infamous /'ɪnfəməs/ *adj* having a very bad character; very evil. *n* **infamy** /'ɪnfəmɪ/ dishonour; very bad behaviour.

infant /'ɪnfənt/ *n* very young child. *n* **infancy** /'ɪnfənsɪ/ state or time of being very young. *adj* **infantile** /'ɪnfəntaɪl/ as of an infant. *n* **infanticide** /ɪn'fæntɪsaɪd/ killing of an infant.

infantry /'ɪnfəntrɪ/ *n* foot-soldiers.

infatuate /ɪn'fætʃʊeɪt/ *vt* cause one to admire or love so completely as to lose judgment or reason. *n* **infatuation** /ɪnˌfætʃʊ'eɪʃən/.

infect /ɪn'fekt/ *vt* pass on disease to; cause to have wrong ideas. *n* **infection** /ɪn'fekʃən/. *adj* **infectious** /ɪn'fekʃəs/ (of, e.g. a disease) able to be passed on from one person to another.

infer /ɪn'fɜː/ *vt* reach an idea by reasoning. *n* **inference** /'ɪnfərəns/.

infant

inferior /ɪn'fɪərɪə/ *adj*, *n* (one who is) lower in value, importance, place, rank. *n* /ɪnˌfɪərɪ'ɒrətɪ/.

infernal /ɪn'fɜːnəl/ *adj* having to do with HELL; very unpleasant.

inferno /ɪn'fɜːnəʊ/ *n* HELL; any very hot place, e.g. *The burning house became an inferno.*

infest /ɪn'fest/ *vt* be in great numbers around.

infidel /'ɪnfɪdl/ *n* one who does not believe in certain teachings about God.

infidelity /ˌɪnfɪ'delətɪ/ *n* act or state of being disloyal or unfaithful, esp. to the person whom one has married.

infiltrate /'ɪnfɪltreɪt/ *v* pass through and into, as liquids pass through sand; (of ideas) get into people's minds.

infinite /'ɪnfɪnɪt/ *adj* without end(s); not able to be measured or counted. *n* **infinity** /ɪn'fɪnətɪ/ infinite amount or size.

infinitesimal /ˌɪnfɪnɪ'tesɪməl/ *adj* so small that it cannot be measured.

infinitive /ɪn'fɪnətɪv/ *n* form of the verb expressing state or action without the subject, in English usually named with 'to', e.g. 'to look'.

infirmary

infirm /ɪn'fɜːm/ *adj* weak in body or mind. *n* **infirmary** /ɪn'fɜːmərɪ/ place for sick people. *n* **infirmity** /ɪn'fɜːmətɪ/ weakness of body; disease.

inflame /ɪn'fleɪm/ *vt* set on fire; excite; make or become red and swollen. *adj* **inflammable**

/ɪnˈflæməbəl/ easily set on fire. *n* **inflammation** /ˌɪnfləˈmeɪʃən/ painful swollen place on the body. *adj* **inflammatory** /ɪnˈflæmətərɪ/ (e.g. of a speech) exciting to anger.

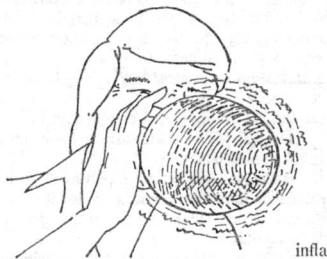

inflate

inflate /ɪnˈfleɪt/ *v* swell or cause to swell with air or gas.

inflation /ɪnˈfleɪʃən/ *n* **1** swelling, esp. caused by filling with air or gas. **2** increase in the amount of money, but the money can buy less, so prices are higher.

inflect /ɪnˈflekt/ *vt* **1** raise or lower the voice while speaking. **2** change the form of a word to show person and number, e.g. I do, he does. *n* **inflexion** /ɪnˈflekʃən/.

inflexible /ɪnˈfleksəbəl/ *adj* that which cannot be bent; (of purpose) unchangeable.

inflict /ɪnˈflɪkt/ *vt* cause to suffer (pain or a wrong, etc.) *n* **infliction** /ɪnˈflɪkʃən/.

influence /ˈɪnfluəns/ *vt* have an effect on; *n* an effect, cause of an effect, e.g. *He is an influence for good. adj* **influential** /ˌɪnfluˈenʃəl/ having influence, important.

influenza /ˌɪnfluˈenzə/ *n* fever with liquid flowing from the nose, pain in the throat, etc.

influx /ˈɪnflʌks/ *n* flowing in, esp. in great amounts.

inform /ɪnˈfɔːm/ *vt* tell. **well informed** = having knowledge about many subjects. *n* **information** /ˌɪnfəˈmeɪʃən/ facts, knowledge. *adj* **informative** /ɪnˈfɔːmətɪv/ giving much information.

informal /ɪnˈfɔːməl/ *adj* without ceremony or ceremonial dress; not formal.

infraction /ɪnˈfrækʃən/ *n* act of breaking, e.g. a law or rule.

infringe /ɪnˈfrɪndʒ/ *vt* break (a law or rule). *n* **infringement** /ɪnˈfrɪndʒmənt/.

infuriate /ɪnˈfjʊərɪeɪt/ *vt* make very angry.

infuse /ɪnˈfjuːz/ *v* pour into; put into boiling water, e.g. tea leaves. *n* **infusion** /ɪnˈfjuːʒən/ liquid in which a vegetable has been boiled so as to get out its special taste or medicinal quality.

ingenious /ɪnˈdʒiːnɪəs/ *adj* clever, skilful; (of a thing) cleverly planned and skilfully made. *n* **ingenuity** /ˌɪndʒɪˈnjuːətɪ/.

ingenuous /ɪnˈdʒenjʊəs/ *adj* simple and inexperienced.

ingot /ˈɪŋɡɒt/ *n* short thick bar of metal.

ingot

ingrained /ɪnˈɡreɪnd/ *adj* fixed deeply in the nature or character.

ingratiate /ɪnˈɡreɪʃɪeɪt/ *vt* get (oneself) into the favour of a person.

ingredient /ɪnˈɡriːdɪənt/ *n* part of a mixture.

inhabit /ɪnˈhæbɪt/ *vt* live in (a country). *n* **inhabitant** /ɪnˈhæbɪtənt/ one who lives in (a city, country).

inhale /ɪnˈheɪl/ *v* draw in the breath; breathe in.

inhere /ɪnˈhɪə/ *vi* be a necessary part; belong as a quality. *adj* **inherent** /ɪnˈhɪərənt/.

inherit /ɪnˈherɪt/ *vt* receive (money, a title, etc.) as the descendant of a person at his death; receive (qualities of character) from the persons from whom one is descended. *n* **inheritance** /ɪnˈherɪtəns/ anything so received.

inhibit /ɪnˈhɪbɪt/ *vt* prevent from doing. *n* **inhibition** /ˌɪnhɪˈbɪʃən/ **1** act of inhibiting. **2** stopping oneself from expressing a desire, e.g. because it does not seem right.

inhuman /ɪnˈhjuːmən/ *adj* not human; cruel; evil.

inimical /ɪˈnɪmɪkəl/ *adj* not friendly; unfavourable.

inimitable /ɪˈnɪmɪtəbəl/ *adj* which cannot be copied; very good; very unusual.

iniquitous /ɪˈnɪkwətəs/ *adj* very evil.

initial /ɪˈnɪʃəl/ *adj* first; beginning. *n* one of first letters of a person's names, e.g. *The initials of John Smith are J.S.*

initiate /ɪˈnɪʃɪeɪt/ *vt* **1** begin; set going. **2** take (someone) in as a new member of a group. *n* **initiation** /ɪˌnɪʃɪˈeɪʃən/.

initiative /ɪˈnɪʃətɪv/ *n* quality or power of starting new courses of action, e.g. *He did it on his own initiative* = he did it by himself, not because he was ordered to do it. **to have the initiative** = have the power or right to make the first move; **to take the initiative** = begin, make the first move (e.g. in a battle).

inject /ɪnˈdʒekt/ *vt* force liquid or gas into; put medicine into the body through a hollow needle. *n* **injection** /ɪnˈdʒekʃən/.

injunction /ɪnˈdʒʌŋkʃən/ *n* command; written order from a court of law saying something shall be done.

injure /ˈɪndʒə/ *vt* do harm to. *adj* **injurious** /ɪnˈdʒʊərɪəs/ *n* **injury** /ˈɪndʒərɪ/ wound; damage to the body.

ink /ɪŋk/ *n* coloured liquid used for writing and printing books.

inkling /ˈɪŋklɪŋ/ *n* slight idea or sign of.

inland /ɪnˈlænd/ *adv* away from the coast. *adj* /ˈɪnlənd/.

in-laws /ˈɪn lɔːz/ *n* (*pl*) relatives by marriage. **mother-in-law** /ˈ . . . ˌ/ = wife's (or husband's) mother; **brother-in-law** = wife's (or husband's) brother. **son-in-law** = the man who has married one's daughter.

inlay /ɪn'leɪ/ vt cut a hollow place in a surface and fill it with (ornamental material such as gold, silver, bone, etc.). /'ɪnleɪ/ n inlaid material.

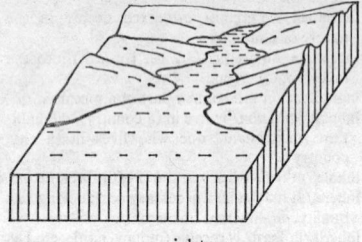

inlet

inlet /'ɪnlet/ n small arm of the sea; entrance.

inmate /'ɪnmeɪt/ n one who is kept in a place, e.g. *The inmates of a prison* = prisoners.

inn /ɪn/ n house in which travellers may eat, drink and sleep.

innate /ɪ'neɪt/ adj born in one; natural.

inner /'ɪnə/ adj inside; having to do with the inside.

innings /'ɪnɪŋz/ n time of being in; (in CRICKET) the time during which each player in turn has a chance of hitting the ball; one's chance of showing one's skill or power.

innocent /'ɪnəsənt/ adj knowing or doing or having done no evil. n **innocence** /'ɪnəsəns/.

innocuous /ɪ'nɒkjʊəs/ adj causing no harm.

innovate /'ɪnəveɪt/ vt start something new. n **innovation** /ˌɪnə'veɪʃən/.

innuendo /ˌɪnjʊ'endəʊ/ n words having a hidden meaning.

inoculate /ɪ'nɒkjʊleɪt/ vt put the dead or harmless GERMS of a disease into the body of a person so that the person may become free from the danger of the disease. n **inoculation** /ɪˌnɒkjʊ'leɪʃən/.

inoperable /ɪ'nɒpərəbəl/ adj not able to be treated by SURGERY, e.g. *An inoperable growth in the body*.

inordinate /ɪ'nɔːdɪnət/ adj uncontrolled; too great.

inorganic /ˌɪnɔː'gænɪk/ adj (of matter) which is not part of the body of any living thing.

inquest /'ɪnkwest/ n examination to find the reason for a person's death or to decide the lawful owner of valuable things, e.g. money found hidden in the ground.

inquire /ɪn'kwaɪə/ vi ask; examine into some important matter. n **inquiry** /ɪn'kwaɪərɪ/.

inquisition /ˌɪnkwɪ'zɪʃən/ n act of questioning, usually with the idea of punishing those who do not believe in certain teachings.

inquisitive /ɪn'kwɪzətɪv/ adj eager to know other people's business.

inroad /'ɪnrəʊd/ n sudden attack made into the enemy's country.

insane /ɪn'seɪn/ adj mad. n **insanity** /ɪn'sænətɪ/.

insatiable /ɪn'seɪʃəbəl/ adj not able to be satisfied.

inscribe /ɪn'skraɪb/ vt write in or on. n **inscription** /ɪn'skrɪpʃən/ that which is written in or on something, e.g. the words cut on a stone in memory of a dead person.

inscrutable /ɪn'skruːtəbəl/ adj not able to be understood.

insect /'ɪnsekt/ n any small creature having six legs. n **insecticide** /ɪn'sektɪsaɪd/ substance used for killing insects.

insemination /ɪnˌsemɪ'neɪʃən/ n putting seeds in. **artificial insemination** = putting male substance into (e.g. a cow) with an instrument so as to produce young.

insensate /ɪn'senseɪt/ adj without sense; without feelings of right and wrong.

insensible /ɪn'sensəbəl/ adj having no feelings; not knowing about, e.g. *Insensible of any danger*.

insert /ɪn'sɜːt/ vt put into or add to. n **insertion** /ɪn'sɜːʃən/.

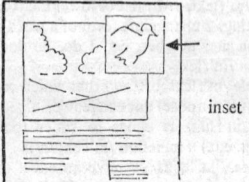

inset

inset /'ɪnset/ n thing set in, e.g. a small picture inside a larger one.

inside /'ɪnsaɪd, ɪn'saɪd/ n inner part; part contained within. *prep* to or on the inside of. *adv, adj* to or on the inside; INDOORS.

insidious /ɪn'sɪdɪəs/ adj doing harm secretly.

insight /'ɪnsaɪt/ n power of seeing into the real meaning; knowledge gained by careful thought and study.

insignia /ɪn'sɪgnɪə/ n (pl) signs of rank or honour.

insignificant /ˌɪnsɪg'nɪfɪkənt/ adj unimportant.

insinuate /ɪn'sɪnjʊeɪt/ vt say (something) unkind or harmful indirectly. n **insinuation** /ɪnˌsɪnjʊ'eɪʃən/.

insipid /ɪn'sɪpɪd/ adj possessing no taste or interest.

insist /ɪn'sɪst/ vi declare with force, e.g. *He insisted on having the money*. adj **insistent** /ɪn'sɪstənt/.

insolent /'ɪnsələnt/ adj very rude; esp. to elders or persons of higher rank. n **insolence** /'ɪnsələns/.

insoluble /ɪn'sɒljʊbəl/ adj which cannot be made liquid; impossible to understand or explain.

insolvent /ɪn'sɒlvənt/ adj unable to pay one's debts.

insomnia /ɪn'sɒmnɪə/ n state of being unable to sleep.

inspect /ɪnˈspekt/ vt look carefully at; examine carefully. n **inspection** /ɪnˈspekʃən/. n **inspector** /ɪnˈspektə/ one whose work is inspecting e.g. other people's work.

inspire /ɪnˈspaɪə/ vt **1** breathe in air. **2** cause an increase of fine feelings or great thoughts in the mind. adj **inspired** receiving thoughts from God; filled with great thoughts. n **inspiration** /ˌɪnspəˈreɪʃən/.

instability /ˌɪnstəˈbɪlətɪ/ n lacking steadiness, esp. of character.

install /ɪnˈstɔːl/ vt put (someone) into an office; fix (machines) into a place. n **installation** /ˌɪnstəˈleɪʃən/.

instalment /ɪnˈstɔːlmənt/ n part payment of a debt; piece of anything supplied part by part at different times, e.g. one part of a story printed part by part each week.

instance /ˈɪnstəns/ n example. **for instance** = as an example. **in the first instance** = at the beginning.

instant /ˈɪnstənt/ n very short time. adj readily prepared; not delaying; not stopping. adj **instantaneous** /ˌɪnstənˈteɪnɪəs/ happening at once and without delay.

instead /ɪnˈsted/ adv in (its, his, my, etc.) place. **instead of** = in place of.

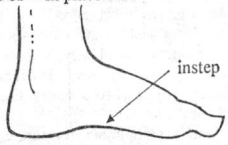

instep

instep /ˈɪnstep/ n curved inner part of the middle of the foot.

instigate /ˈɪnstɪgeɪt/ vt cause (an act).

instil /ɪnˈstɪl/ vt pour in slowly. **to instil knowledge** = teach.

instinct /ˈɪnstɪŋkt/ n natural desire or inborn skill which causes animals to act in a certain way without teaching or experience. adj **instinctive** /ɪnˈstɪŋktɪv/.

institute /ˈɪnstɪtjuːt/ vt set up, e.g. To institute a new custom. n group of men working for some common purpose; group formed for some special purpose; building in which its work is carried on. n **institution** /ˌɪnstɪˈtjuːʃən/ something that has been set up, e.g. a custom, law; group of persons which supplies some public need, or the buildings used for this purpose, e.g. A university is an institution of learning.

instruct /ɪnˈstrʌkt/ vt **1** teach. **2** order. n **instruction** /ɪnˈstrʌkʃən/. adj **instructive** /ɪnˈstrʌktɪv/ teaching one much.

instrument /ˈɪnstrəmənt/ n thing by means of which something is done. adj **instrumental** /ˌɪnstrəˈmentəl/ **1** helping or causing something to happen. **2** (of music) produced by means of instruments, not by the human voice.

insubordinate /ˌɪnsəˈbɔːdɪnət/ adj not obeying higher officers. n **insubordination** /ˌɪnsəbɔːdɪˈneɪʃən/.

insular /ˈɪnsjʊlə/ adj of an island. **insular ideas** = narrow, not thinking of other nations. n **insularity** /ˌɪnsjʊˈlærətɪ/.

insulate /ˈɪnsjʊleɪt/ vt separate from everything around; cover (wire) with material which will not allow electricity to pass away. n **insulation** /ˌɪnsjʊˈleɪʃən/.

insult /ɪnˈsʌlt/ vt be rude to. n /ˈɪnsʌlt/ piece of insulting language or behaviour.

insuperable /ɪnˈsjuːpərəbəl/ adj (e.g. of a difficulty) with which one cannot deal.

insupportable /ˌɪnsəˈpɔːtəbəl/ adj which cannot, or should not, be suffered.

insurance /ɪnˈʃʊərəns/ n act or business of INSURING.

insure /ɪnˈʃʊə/ vt pay money each year so that an agreed sum may be paid in the event of loss of, death of, or harm to.

insurgent /ɪnˈsɜːdʒənt/ adj rising up to fight against the government. n **insurrection** /ˌɪnsəˈrekʃən/.

intact /ɪnˈtækt/ adj unharmed; whole and complete.

intake /ˈɪnteɪk/ n taking in, e.g. Intake of men into the army. **intake pipe** = pipe through which (air, etc.) is taken.

intangible /ɪnˈtændʒəbəl/ adj not able to be felt by touch; so slight that it cannot be noticed.

integer /ˈɪntɪdʒə/ n whole number. adj **integral** /ˈɪntɪgrəl/ having to do with the whole; whole and complete.

integrate /ˈɪntɪgreɪt/ vt bring all parts of (something) together to make a whole.

integrity /ɪnˈtegrətɪ/ n **1** condition of being complete. **2** honesty.

intellect /ˈɪntɪlekt/ n power of mind by which we think and know. adj **intellectual** /ˌɪntɪˈlektʃʊəl/ using or showing great intellect. n one whose interests are intellectual.

intelligence /ɪnˈtelɪdʒəns/ n **1** ability to reason well, think clearly etc. **2** group of men whose duty is to collect news secretly about the plans of the enemy. adj **intelligent** /ɪnˈtelɪdʒənt/ having intelligence. n **intelligentsia** /ɪnˌtelɪˈdʒentsɪə/ n learned people in a country. adj **intelligible** /ɪnˈtelɪdʒəbəl/ able to be understood.

intend /ɪnˈtend/ vt have the purpose of.

intense /ɪnˈtens/ adj very great or very strong; (of a person) very serious about everything. adj **intensive** /ɪnˈtensɪv/ using all one's powers; thorough; complete.

intent /ɪnˈtent/ n purpose. **intent on** = attending carefully to.

intention /ɪnˈtenʃən/ n purpose or plan. adj **intentional** /ɪnˈtenʃənəl/ done on purpose.

inter /ɪnˈtɜː/ vt to put in the grave.

inter- /ˈɪntə/ between or among.

interact /ˌɪntəˈrækt/ vi have an effect upon each other.

141

intercede /ˌɪntəˈsiːd/ vi ask for a favour for someone, e.g. that his punishment be lighter.

intercept /ˌɪntəˈsept/ vt catch or stop on the way; prevent from going farther; stop (messages) passing from one place to another.

intercession /ˌɪntəˈseʃən/ n act of INTERCEDING.

interchange /ˌɪntəˈtʃeɪndʒ/ vt 1 give and receive. 2 put each in place of the other. n /ˈɪntətʃeɪndʒ/.

intercom /ˈɪntəkɒm/ n telephone system inside an aeroplane, office building, etc.

intercourse /ˈɪntəkɔːs/ n dealing with, e.g. *Social intercourse* = meeting other people at dinners, dances and other gatherings. **sexual intercourse** = act of sexual union between a man and a woman.

interest /ˈɪntərəst/ n 1 a share or right, e.g. in a business. **to look after one's own interests** = one's own gain or chances of gain. **in your interest** = for your good. 2 eager attention, e.g. *The book aroused great interest.* 3 thing to which one gives eager attention, e.g. *Music is one of his interests.* 4 money paid for the use of money lent to one. vt cause (someone) to have interest; gain the attention or help of. adj **interesting** /ˈɪntərəstɪŋ/.

interfere /ˌɪntəˈfɪə ʳ/ vi come between; push oneself into a matter which does not concern one; prevent a person from carrying out his plans. n **interference** /ˌɪntəˈfɪərəns/.

interim /ˈɪntərɪm/ n time between two events. adj meant to serve for the present, e.g. *An interim report* = given before the real long report is ready.

interior

interior /ɪnˈtɪərɪə ʳ/ n, adj inside.

interject /ˌɪntəˈdʒekt/ vt throw in (e.g. a word). n **interjection** /ˌɪntəˈdʒekʃən/ word expressing sudden feeling, e.g. *Oh!*

interlock /ˌɪntəˈlɒk/ vi lock together firmly.

interloper /ˈɪntələʊpə ʳ/ n one who forces himself in where he has no right to be.

interlude /ˈɪntəluːd/ n pause or rest, e.g. in a play.

intermediary /ˌɪntəˈmiːdɪərɪ/ n, adj (one) acting between two people or groups, etc.

intermediate /ˌɪntəˈmiːdɪət/ adj having a middle place; between a high level and a low level (e.g. of teaching).

interment /ɪnˈtɜːmənt/ n act of putting into the grave.

interminable /ɪnˈtɜːmɪnəbəl/ adj unending, too long.

intermission /ˌɪntəˈmɪʃən/ n time between acts in the theatre.

intermittent /ˌɪntəˈmɪtənt/ adj happening, then stopping, then beginning again ...; not continuous.

intern /ɪnˈtɜːn/ vt keep a person as a prisoner in order to prevent him from doing harm. /ˈɪntɜːn/ n young doctor who lives in a hospital.

internal /ɪnˈtɜːnəl/ adj having to do with the inside of a thing; obtained from inside.

international /ˌɪntəˈnæʃənəl/ adj between nations; having to do with different nations.

interplay /ˈɪntəpleɪ/ n action between parts (of a machine), or between persons in a group.

interpolate /ɪnˈtɜːpəleɪt/ vt put into a book, speech, etc., (parts) which were not written in it at first.

interpose /ˌɪntəˈpəʊz/ v put between or come between.

interpret /ɪnˈtɜːprɪt/ vt explain the meaning of (e.g. of a foreign language). n **interpreter** /ɪnˈtɜːprɪtə/ one who puts into the language of the hearer things spoken in a foreign language. n **interpretation** /ɪn,tɜːprɪˈteɪʃən/.

interrogate /ɪnˈterəgeɪt/ vt question (someone) in a thorough and forceful way. n **interrogation** /ɪn,terəˈgeɪʃən/. n, adj **interrogative** /ˌɪntəˈrɒgətɪv/ (of a) word or expression used in asking a question.

interrupt /ˌɪntəˈrʌpt/ v break in upon, e.g. speak to a person who is speaking; to get in the way of or cause to stop. e.g. *To interrupt the flow of electricity.* n **interruption** /ˌɪntəˈrʌpʃən/.

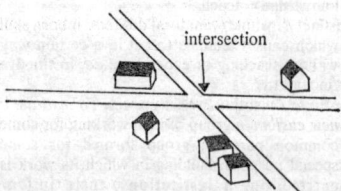

intersection

intersect /ˌɪntəˈsekt/ vt cut across. n **intersection** /ˌɪntəˈsekʃən/ act of crossing or the place of crossing.

intersperse /ˌɪntəˈspɜːs/ vt set here and there among other things, e.g. *Flowers interspersed among the corn.*

interval /ˈɪntəvəl/ n time or space between.

intervene /ˌɪntəˈviːn/ vi come in between, e.g. as a third person between two who are fighting; come between (in time). n **intervention** /ˌɪntəˈvenʃən/.

interview /ˈɪntəvjuː/ n meeting for the purpose of getting a person's opinion for doing business, or for finding out whether he is suitable for certain work. *vt* hold an interview with.

intestate /ɪn'testeɪt/ *adj* dying without having made a WILL.

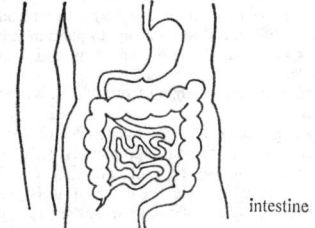

intestine

intestine /ɪn'testɪn/ *n* bowel; pipe in the body leading from the stomach.

intimate /'ɪntɪmət/ *adj* inside; secret, e.g. *One's intimate thoughts.* **an intimate friend** = a very close friend. *vt* /'ɪntɪmeɪt/ tell in an indirect way.

intimidate /ɪn'tɪmɪdeɪt/ *vt* cause to be afraid. *n* **intimidation** /ɪn,tɪmɪ'deɪʃən/.

into /'ɪntə; *strong* 'ɪntʊ/ *prep* to or towards a position inside.

intolerable /ɪn'tɒlərəbəl/ *adj* which cannot or should not be suffered.

intolerant /ɪn'tɒlərənt/ *adj* unwilling to allow other people to think or act differently from oneself.

intone /ɪn'təʊn/ *vt* say in a singing voice. *n* **intonation** /,ɪntə'neɪʃən/ the PITCH changes that are used in speaking.

intoxicate /ɪn'tɒksɪkeɪt/ *vt* cause loss of control or great excitement, e.g. by the use of wine. *n* **intoxicant** /ɪn'tɒksɪkənt/ wine and other strong drinks. *n* **intoxication** /ɪn,tɒksɪ'keɪʃən/.

intra- /'ɪntrə/ in, inside, within.

intractable /ɪn'træktəbəl/ *adj* not easily controlled; unwilling to obey.

intransigent /ɪn'trænsɪdʒənt/ *adj* not willing to come to an agreement.

intrepid /ɪn'trepɪd/ *adj* fearless.

intricate /'ɪntrɪkət/ *adj* having a great many small parts, difficult to understand.

intrigue /ɪn'triːg/ *vi* make a secret plan. *vt* interest greatly. /'ɪntriːg/ *n* secret planning.

intrinsic /ɪn'trɪnsɪk/ *adj* having to do with the real nature of a thing.

introduce /,ɪntrə'djuːs/ *vt* **1** lead in; bring in; put in, e.g. *To introduce a new law.* **2** make (one person) known to another in a meeting. *n* **introduction** /,ɪntrə'dʌkʃən/ **1** act of introducing. **2** piece of writing at the beginning of a book introducing the reader to the subject.

introspect /,ɪntrə'spekt/ *vi* look into one's own mind and feelings. *adj* **introspective** /,ɪntrə'spektɪv/.

introvert /'ɪntrəvɜːt/ *n* one who is always looking into his own mind to examine his thoughts and feelings.

intrude /ɪn'truːd/ *vi* enter without being invited or welcome. *n* **intrusion** /ɪn'truːʒən/. *adj* **intrusive** /ɪn'truːsɪv/.

intuition /,ɪntjʊ'ɪʃən/ *n* knowledge obtained without reasoning; the power of knowing things in this way, e.g. *A woman's intuition as to the feelings of a man. adj* **intuitive** /ɪn'tjuːɪtɪv/.

inundate /'ɪnʌndeɪt/ *vt* flow over and cover with water. **inundated with letters** = receiving a large number of —. *n* **inundation** /,ɪnʌn'deɪʃən/.

inure /ɪ'njʊə/ *vt* harden and make used to, e.g. *Soldiers are inured to cold and hunger.*

invade /ɪn'veɪd/ *vt* go into (another's country) as an act of war; rush into.

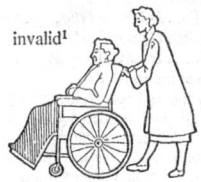

invalid¹

invalid¹ /'ɪnvəlɪd/ *n* person in weak health.

invalid² /ɪn'vælɪd/ *adj* of no force. *vt* **invalidate** /ɪn'vælɪdeɪt/.

invaluable /ɪn'væljʊəbəl/ *adj* of the greatest possible value.

invariable /ɪn'veərɪəbəl/ *adj* not changeable.

invasion /ɪn'veɪʒən/ *n* rushing into and attacking.

invective /ɪn'vektɪv/ *n* strongly expressed blame; cursing.

inveigh /ɪn'veɪ/ *vi* attack someone with words.

inveigle /ɪn'viːgəl/ *vt* use dishonest means to lead a person to do something.

invent /ɪn'vent/ *vt* think out and make (something new, e.g. a new machine or instrument.) *n* **invention** /ɪn'venʃən/ new thing or idea thought out. *adj* **inventive** /ɪn'ventɪv/.

inventory /'ɪnvəntərɪ/ *n* list of things.

inverse /ɪn'vɜːs/ *adj* opposite. *n* **inversion** /ɪn'vɜːʃən/ state of being in the wrong or opposite order.

invert /ɪn'vɜːt/ *vt* turn (something) over.

invest /ɪn'vest/ *vt* put upon (someone) clothes which are a sign of rank or office. *v* lend (money) or put (money) into a business so that one may get more money by means of it.

investigate /ɪn'vestɪgeɪt/ *v* inquire into (a matter) and examine. *n* **investigation** /ɪn,vestɪ'geɪʃən/.

investiture /ɪn'vestɪtʃə/ *n* solemn act of giving rank or office to a person.

investment /ɪn'vestmənt/ *n* act of INVESTING money; money invested.

inveterate /ɪn'vetərət/ *adj* firmly fixed by custom.

invidious /ɪn'vɪdɪəs/ *adj* causing ill-feeling or dislike.

invigilate /ɪn'vɪdʒɪleɪt/ *vt* watch over, e.g. watch persons writing an examination paper in order to prevent dishonesty.

143

invigorate /ɪn'vɪgəreɪt/ *vt* make (someone) feel strong.

invincible /ɪn'vɪnsəbəl/ *adj* unconquerable.

inviolate /ɪn'vaɪələt/ *adj* unharmed; kept holy. *adj* **inviolable** /ɪn'vaɪələbəl/ that which may not or cannot be harmed.

invisible /ɪn'vɪzəbəl/ *adj* which cannot be seen.

invite /ɪn'vaɪt/ *vt* **1** ask politely, e.g. *He invited her to sing.* **2** ask (a guest) to a meal or gathering, or to stay at one's house. *n* **invitation** /ˌɪnvɪ'teɪʃən/.

invocation /ˌɪnvə'keɪʃən/ *n* calling upon God; prayer.

invoice /'ɪnvɔɪs/ *n* list of goods sent and their prices.

invoke /ɪn'vəʊk/ *vt* call upon (God); ask for solemnly, e.g. *He invoked the power of the law.*

involuntary /ɪn'vɒləntərɪ/ *adj* not under control of the will. *adv* **involuntarily** /ɪn'vɒləntərɪlɪ/ without meaning to do it.

involve /ɪn'vɒlv/ *vt* **1** roll up in; mix up with, as a person gets tied up in a net, e.g. *Involved in debt.* **2** bring with it as a necessary result, e.g. *Living in a hot country always involves some loss of health. adj* **involved** mixed up and difficult to understand, e.g. *His reasoning is very involved.*

invulnerable /ɪn'vʌlnərəbəl/ *adj* not able to be wounded.

inward /'ɪnwəd/ *adj* inside; moving or turned towards the inside. *adv* **inward(s)** /'ɪnwəd(z)/ towards the inside.

iodine /'aɪədiːn/ *n* salt-like material from which a brown liquid is obtained, used to put on cuts and wounds.

iota /aɪ'əʊtə/ *n* small amount.

I.O.U. /ˌaɪ əʊ 'juː/ *n* written promise to pay money.

irascible /ɪ'ræsəbəl/ *adj* easily made angry.

irate /aɪ'reɪt/ *adj* angry.

iridescence /ˌɪrɪ'desəns/ *n* quality of a surface which breaks up light and shows many changing colours. *adj* **iridescent** /ˌɪrɪ'desənt/.

iris (1)

iris /'aɪərɪs/ *n* **1** a beautiful flower. **2** coloured part of the eye.

irk /ɜːk/ *vt* make tired; cause trouble to. *adj* **irksome** /'ɜːksəm/ tiring and uninteresting.

iroko /ɪ'rəʊkəʊ/ *n* a kind of large tree found in West Africa.

iron /'aɪən/ *n* **1** very common hard metal. **2** instrument for pressing clothes, sheets, etc., flat. *adj* **1** made of iron. **2** very hard; very firm. *vt* press (clothes, etc.) with an iron. **to iron out** = make smooth and flat (parts of a piece of clothing, etc. which are not flat) with an iron; cause (difficulties) to go away. **to put a man in irons** = fasten the arms and legs with iron bands.

ironmonger /'aɪənˌmʌŋgə/ *n* one who sells metal goods.

irony /'aɪərənɪ/ *n* **1** use of words which are opposite to one's meaning, usually with an amusing purpose, e.g. *This is lovely weather*—when one means that it is bad weather. **2** course of events which has the opposite result from what is expected, appearing to be directed by a spirit of evil, e.g. *The irony of fate. adj* **ironic(al)** /aɪ'rɒnɪk(əl)/.

irrelevant /ɪ'reləvənt/ *adj* having nothing to do with the subject.

irreparable /ɪ'repərəbəl/ *adj* not able to be repaired.

irreproachable /ˌɪrɪ'prəʊtʃəbəl/ *adj* without fault of any kind.

irrespective /ˌɪrɪ'spektɪv/ *adj* without thinking of or troubling about. **irrespective of** = in spite of.

irresponsible /ˌɪrɪ'spɒnsəbəl/ *adj* not caring about the results of one's acts; not to be trusted to do work carefully.

irrevocable /ɪ'revəkəbəl/ *adj* not able to be changed, e.g. *An irrevocable decision.*

irrigate /'ɪrɪgeɪt/ *vt* bring water to (dry land) by CANALS; pour water on to *n* **irrigation** /ˌɪrɪ'geɪʃən/.

irritate /'ɪrɪteɪt/ *vt* cause pain or discomfort in (a part of the body), e.g. by rubbing or by a strong medicine; make angry. *adj* **irritable** /'ɪrɪtəbəl/ easily made angry. *n* **irritation** /ˌɪrɪ'teɪʃən/.

is /z, s; *strong* ɪz/ *v* (present t. form of **be** used after 'he', 'she', 'it' and singular nouns).

island /'aɪlənd/ *n* piece of land with water all round it; raised place of safety in the middle of a wide street. *n* **isle** /aɪl/ island. *n* **islet** /'aɪlət/ small island.

iso- /'aɪsəʊ, 'aɪsə/ equal in value, e.g. **isobar** /'aɪsəbɑː/ *n* line on themap joining places where the air PRESSURE is the same.

isolate /'aɪsəleɪt/ *vt* put apart or alone; separate from others of the same kind. *n* **isolation** /ˌaɪsə'leɪʃən/.

isosceles /aɪ'sɒsəliːz/ *adj* (of a TRIANGLE) having two sides equal.

issue /'ɪʃuː, 'ɪsjuː/ *v* come out; give or send out. *n* **1** something issued; act of issuing. **2** copy, e.g. of a newspaper. **3** matter; subject, esp. one on which a decision must be reached.

isthmus /'ɪsməs/ *n* narrow neck of land joining two large bodies of land.

it /ɪt/ *pron* (used in speaking of a non-living thing or most animals). *det, pron* **its** /ɪts/ (something) belonging to it.

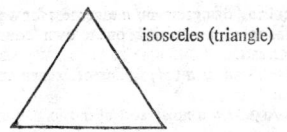

isosceles (triangle)

italic /ɪ'tælɪk/ sloping kind of *printing*.
itch /ɪtʃ/ *n, vi* (have a) feeling on the skin which gives one a desire to rub or SCRATCH.

item /'aɪtəm/ *n* one separate thing written in a list; one part of a whole; a piece of news. *vt*
itemize /'aɪtəmaɪz/ set out (things) one by one.
itinerant /aɪ'tɪnərənt/ *adj* travelling round from place to place. *n* **itinerary** /aɪ'tɪnərərɪ/ course followed or to be followed on a journey.
ivory /'aɪvərɪ/ *n* valuable white bone obtained from the long teeth of an elephant.
ivy /'aɪvɪ/ *n* plant with large green leaves which grows on walls and sides of buildings.

J

jab /dʒæb/ *vt* hit or push roughly, e.g. with the finger. *n* act of jabbing.
jabber /'dʒæbə/ *vi* talk quickly and in a way that is difficult to understand.
jack /dʒæk/ *n* **1** one of a set of playing-cards. **2** machine for raising heavy weights. **3** flag. **Jack of all trades** = man skilled in all kinds of work.
to jack up = raise up with the use of a jack.
jackass /'dʒækæs/ *n* **1** male donkey. **2** fool. **3** an Australian bird.
jackal /'dʒækəl/ *n* a wild animal like a dog.
jackboot /'dʒækbuːt/ *n* large high boot.
jackdaw /'dʒækdɔː/ *n* noisy bird which steals small bright objects.
jacket /'dʒækɪt/ *n* **1** short coat. **2** any covering, e.g. of a hot-water pipe.

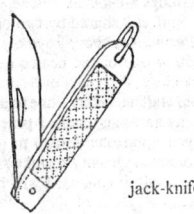

jack-knife

jack-knife /'. ₁./ *n* large knife with a blade which folds over into the handle.
jackpot /'dʒækpɒt/ *n* the biggest prize in a game (e.g. card-game) played for money.
jade /dʒeɪd/ *n* precious green stone.
jaded /'dʒeɪdɪd/ *adj* tired and ill.
jagged /'dʒægɪd/ *adj* rough, having sharp points, e.g. a jagged tooth.
jaguar /'dʒægjʊə/ *n* a large wild cat found in South America.
jail /dʒeɪl/ *see* gaol.
jam¹ /dʒæm/ *vt* press into a small space. *vi* become fixed, e.g. *The door is jammed and will not open*. **radio jamming** = stopping radio from being heard by sending out other radio waves. *infml* **in a jam** = in a difficulty and not knowing how to get out of it.
jam² /dʒæm/ *n* fruit boiled in sugar.
jamb /dʒæm/ *n* side post of a door or window.

jamboree /ˌdʒæmbə'riː/ *n* joyful gathering, e.g. of Boy Scouts.
jangle /'dʒæŋgəl/ *v* make an unpleasant sound as of many bells ringing at once.
janitor /'dʒænɪtə/ *n* door-keeper; man who takes care of a building.
January /'dʒænjʊərɪ/ *n* the first month of the year.
jar¹ /dʒɑː/ *n* bottle with a short neck and large opening.
jar² /dʒɑː/ *n* **1** unpleasant sound. **2** shock or shaking caused when two things run into each other or are struck together. *vi* **1** make an unpleasant sound. **2** cause shock or shaking. **to jar on** = displease.
jargon /'dʒɑːgən/ *n* special language of some group which cannot be understood by others.
jasmin(e) /'dʒæsmɪn, dʒæz-/ *n* sweet-smelling bush.
jaundice /'dʒɔːndɪs/ *n* yellowness of the skin caused by illness. *adj* **jaundiced 1** having jaundice. **2** bitter; full of spite or hatred.
jaunt /dʒɔːnt/ *n* short journey taken for pleasure.
jaunty /'dʒɔːntɪ/ *adj* feeling self-satisfied and pleased with life.
javelin /'dʒævəlɪn/ *n* light spear for throwing.
jaw /dʒɔː/ *n* one of the bones in which the teeth are set.
jay /dʒeɪ/ *n* noisy bright-coloured bird.
jaywalker /'dʒeɪˌwɔːkə/ *n* person who crosses the street in a careless and dangerous way.
jazz /dʒæz/ *n* sort of music to which people dance, usually having a strong RHYTHM. *adj*
jazzy /'dʒæzɪ/ **1** (of music) like jazz. **2** having a bright mixture of colours.
jealous /'dʒeləs/ *adj* **1** guarding carefully, e.g. *Jealous of one's good name*. **2** wanting something which another possesses; fearing that another will take what one has, and therefore hating him. *n* jealousy /'dʒeləsɪ/.
jeep /dʒiːp/ *n* a kind of car used for very rough work and across rough country.
jeer /dʒɪə/ *v* laugh rudely (at). *n* act of jeering.
jelly /'dʒelɪ/ *n* soft clear material made by boiling bones; such material given a sweet taste (e.g. of fruit) and served for food; any material, neither liquid nor solid but between the two states.

jellyfish /'dʒelɪ,fɪʃ/ *n* sea-creature with a body like jelly.

jemmy /'dʒemɪ/ *n* bar used by a thief for breaking open doors, etc.

jeopardy /'dʒepədɪ/ *n* danger. *vt* **jeopardize** /'dʒepədaɪz/ put in danger.

jerk /dʒɜːk/ *n* **1** sudden movement. **2** *sl* useless or unpleasant man. *v* move or pull suddenly.

jerkin /'dʒɜːkɪn/ *n* tight coat, usually of leather.

jerry-built /'dʒerɪ ,bɪlt/ *adj* badly built.

jersey /'dʒɜːzɪ/ *n* tight KNITTED covering for the upper part of the body, usually made of wool.

jest /dʒest/ *n* something said to produce a laugh. *vi* make a jest. *n* **jester** /'dʒestə ⁷/ paid fool in a king's court.

jet[1] /dʒet/ *n* hard black material used for ornament on dresses. *adj* **jet-black** /ˌ. '.'/ quite black.

jet[2] /dʒet/ *n* **1** stream of liquid coming out of a small hole. **2** small hole from which liquid comes out with force. **3** aeroplane driven by jet propulsion. **jet propulsion** = causing an aeroplane to go forward by drawing in air in front, mixing it with oil and sending out hot burning gases at the back.

jetsam /'dʒetsəm/ *n* goods thrown out to make a ship lighter.

jettison /'dʒetɪsən/ *vt* throw (goods) out of a ship to make it lighter.

jetty

jetty /'dʒetɪ/ *n* place where one gets on to a ship, or gets down on to land from a ship.

jewel /'dʒuːəl/ *n* precious stone; ornament made with precious stones; any very precious thing. *n* **jeweller** /'dʒuːələ ⁷/ one who sells jewels. *n* **jewelry, jewellery** /'dʒuːəlrɪ/ things made of precious metals and stones.

jib /dʒɪb/ *n* **1** small sail. **2** the long bar which stands out at an angle from a CRANE. *vi* stop and refuse to go on.

jibe, gibe /dʒaɪb/ *v* laugh disrespectfully (at).

jiffy /'dʒɪfɪ/ *infml n* moment.

jig[1] /dʒɪg/ *n* a kind of quick dance; music for it. *vt* dance up and down quickly.

jig[2] /dʒɪg/ *n* instrument used to guide a cutting tool.

jigsaw puzzle /'.. ,..'/ *n* a picture stuck on wood or CARDBOARD and cut up into many small pieces to be fitted together as a game.

jilt /dʒɪlt/ *vt* send away (a lover) after pretending to love him or her. *n* one who does this.

jingle /'dʒɪŋgəl/ *vi* make a sound like that of small bells. *n* **1** such a sound. **2** simple short song e.g. used on the radio trying to get people to buy a product.

jingoism /'dʒɪŋgəʊɪzəm/ *n* eagerness for war as a means of protecting one's own country's interests.

jitters /'dʒɪtəz/ *n* (*pl*) feeling of excitement and fear.

jive /dʒaɪv/ *n* a noisy sort of music. *vi* dance to such music.

job /dʒɒb/ *n* **1** piece of work. **2** employment. *n* **jobbery** /'dʒɒbərɪ/ dishonest use of one's power as an officer of government.

jockey /'dʒɒkɪ/ *n* one who rides horses in races.

jocose /dʒə'kəʊs/, **jocular** /'dʒɒkjʊlə ⁷/ *adj* merry and trying to make people laugh.

jocund /'dʒɒkənd/ *adj* merry.

jog /dʒɒg/ *n* push (someone) suddenly so as to get attention. **to jog a person's memory** = try to make him remember. *vi* go at a slow steady run. **jog-trot** /'. ./ *n* slow steady run.

join /dʒɔɪn/ *v* come or put together; fix together. *n* **joiner** /'dʒɔɪnə ⁷/ *n* wood-worker. *n* **joinery** /'dʒɔɪnərɪ/ wood-work.

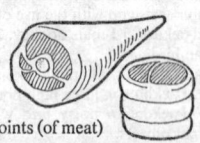

joints (of meat)

joint /dʒɔɪnt/ *n* **1** place of joining; arrangement by which things are joined. **2** bone, with meat to be eaten on it. *adj* shared by two or more people, e.g. *Our joint opinion; To take joint action.*

joist /dʒɔɪst/ *n* one of the beams on which the floor is fixed.

joke /dʒəʊk/ *n* thing said or done to make people laugh. *vi* say amusing things. **a practical joke** = trick played upon one person to give amusement to others. *n* **joker** /'dʒəʊkə ⁷/ **1** one who jokes. **2** special playing-card which may have any value.

jolly /'dʒɒlɪ/ *adj* happy; merry. *adv infml* very, e.g. *Jolly nice. n* **jollification** /ˌdʒɒlɪfɪ'keɪʃən/ merry-making.

jolt /dʒəʊlt/ *n* sudden movement throwing one up from one's seat in a car or carriage; unpleasant surprise. *v* move with a jolt.

jostle /'dʒɒsəl/ *vi* knock or push (against).

jot[1] /dʒɒt/ *vt* write a short note, e.g. *Jot down his name.*

jot[2] /dʒɒt/ **not a jot** = none at all.

journal /'dʒɜːnəl/ *n* **1** report written every day; daily newspaper. **2** that part of a turning bar in a machine which rests upon a support.

journalese /ˌdʒɜːnə'liːz/ *n* kind of writing found in newspapers. *n* **journalism** /'dʒɜːnəlɪzəm/ *n* writing and preparing newspapers, story papers, etc. *n* **journalist** /'dʒɜːnəlɪst/ *n* person who works at journalism.

journey /'dʒɜːnɪ/ *n* act of travelling; distance travelled.

joust /'dʒaʊst/ *n* fight with spears between men in armour. *vi* have such a fight.

jovial /'dʒəʊvɪəl/ *adj* merry. *n* **joviality** /ˌdʒəʊvɪ'ælɪtɪ/.

jowl /dʒaʊl/ *n* lower part of the face. **cheek by jowl** = very close together.

joy /dʒɔɪ/ *n* gladness. *adj* **joyful** /'dʒɔɪfəl/ happy.

jubilant /'dʒuːbɪlənt/ *adj* rejoicing. *n* **jubilation** /ˌdʒuːbɪ'leɪʃən/.

jubilee /'dʒuːbɪliː/ *n* fiftieth year after an event; rejoicing for this reason. **silver jubilee** = 25th year. **diamond jubilee** = 60th year.

judge /dʒʌdʒ/ *n* one who decides questions and tries prisoners in a court of law: person chosen to decide any question. *vt* give an opinion on. *n* **judgment** /'dʒʌdʒmənt/ **1** opinion; ability to form correct opinions, e.g. of people. **2** act of judging (e.g. in a court).

judicature /'dʒuːdɪkətʃə ʸ/ *n* all the judges and law-officers of a country; their work.

judicial /dʒuː'dɪʃəl/ *adj* having to do with a judge; able to decide wisely.

judiciary /dʒuː'dɪʃərɪ/ *adj* having to do with a court of law. *n* all the judges.

judicious /dʒuː'dɪʃəs/ *adj* wise; having good judgment.

judo /'dʒuːdəʊ/ *n* Japanese art of fighting without weapons.

jug /dʒʌg/ *n* pot for liquids, with a handle. *vt* boil (meat) in a closed pot.

juggle /'dʒʌgəl/ *vi* do clever tricks with the hands for amusement. **to juggle with facts** = choose facts to show what is not really true.

jugular /'dʒʌgjʊlə ʸ/ *adj* having to do with the neck.

juice /dʒuːs/ *n* liquid part of a plant, or of food.

jukebox /'dʒuːkbɒks/ *n* machine that plays music when money is put into it.

July /dʒuː'laɪ/ *n* the seventh month of the year.

jumble /'dʒʌmbəl/ *vt* mix in disorder. *n* disorderly mixture. **jumble sale** /ˈ . . ./ = the selling cheap of various used things to help some good work with the money so obtained.

jump /dʒʌmp/ *vi* spring off the ground; move suddenly. *n* act of jumping; sudden increase.

jumper /'dʒʌmpə ʸ/ *n* short covering for the upper part of the body, put on over the head.

jumpy /'dʒʌmpɪ/ *adj* in an excited and easily frightened state of mind.

junction /'dʒʌŋkʃən/ *n* joining; place of joining; railway station where two or more lines join.

juncture /'dʒʌŋktʃə ʸ/ *n* place of joining; point in

jump

time. **at this juncture** = just at the moment when things were in this state.

June /dʒuːn/ *n* the sixth month of the year.

jungle /'dʒʌŋgəl/ *n* land covered with wild bushes, plants and trees.

junior /'dʒuːnɪə ʸ/ *adj* younger; lower in position, e.g. in a firm.

juniper /'dʒuːnɪpə ʸ/ *n* bush whose oil is used for its pleasant smell.

junk[1] /dʒʌŋk/ *n* (*sing*) old things of little value.

junk[2] /dʒʌŋk/ *n* a Chinese sailing-ship.

junket /'dʒʌŋkɪt/ *n* milk made solid, with sugar added. *vi* to feast.

juridical /dʒʊ'rɪdɪkəl/ *adj* having to do with the law.

jurisdiction /ˌdʒʊərɪs'dɪkʃən/ *n* **1** giving of law. **2** land or country over which a law-court, judge, or officer has power.

jurisprudence /ˌdʒʊərɪs'pruːdəns/ *n* art and science of law-giving.

jurist /'dʒʊərɪst/ *n* one skilled in the law.

juror /'dʒʊərə ʸ/ *n* member of a JURY.

jury /'dʒʊərɪ/ *n* group of twelve persons chosen to decide questions of fact in a law-court, having solemnly promised to give an honest opinion.

just[1] /dʒʌst/ *adj* fair; right; true.

just[2] /dʒʌst/ *adv* **1** exactly. **just now** = a very short time ago. **just perfect** = quite perfect. **2** only, e.g. *He was just sixteen.*

justice /'dʒʌstɪs/ *n* **1** fairness; justness. **2** action of the law. **3** a judge, e.g. *Justice of the Peace.*

justify /'dʒʌstɪfaɪ/ *vt* show to be right, true, or blameless. *adj* **justifiable** /'dʒʌstɪfaɪəbəl/ able to be proved just. *n* **justification** /ˌdʒʌstɪfɪ'keɪʃən/ action of justifying; that which justifies.

jut /dʒʌt/ *vi* stand out from the main mass, e.g. *A rock jutting out into the sea.*

jute /dʒuːt/ *n* plant whose skin is used for making rope and rough cloth.

juvenile /'dʒuːvənaɪl/ *adj* young.

juxtapose /ˌdʒʌkstə'pəʊz/ *vt* set side by side. *n* **juxtaposition** /ˌdʒʌkstəpə'zɪʃən/.

K

kaleidoscope /kə'laɪdəskəʊp/ *n* instrument in which one may see many different colours and shapes changing quickly, for amusement. *adj* **kaleidoscopic** /kəˌlaɪdə'skɒpɪk/.

kangaroo /ˌkæŋgə'ruː/ *n* Australian mammal which jumps along on its large back legs.

kaolin /'keɪəlɪn/ *n* fine white earth used for making cups, plates, etc.

kapok /'keɪpɒk/ *n* kind of cotton used for filling CUSHIONS.

kayak /'kaɪæk/ *n* small boat used in the far north.

keel /kiːl/ *n* the long bar along the bottom of a

keen

boat from which the whole frame is built up. **to keel over** = turn over on one side.

keen /ki:n/ *adj* **1** having a sharp edge; (of sound or light) strong; (of the senses) good, e.g. *Keen hearing; A keen sense of smell.* **2** eager; quick of understanding. **keen on** = very much interested in; in love with.

keep[1] /ki:p/ *vt* **1** hold, continue to possess. **2** protect; have charge of, e.g. *To keep a shop.* **3** support or pay for, e.g. *To keep a family; To keep a horse.* **4** remain, e.g. *Keep calm.* **to keep (someone) from** = prevent. **keep oneself to oneself** = not make friends. **keep up** = support; continue.

keep[2] /ki:p/ *n* great tower of a castle.

keeper /'ki:pə/ *n* guard, person in charge of.

keepsake /'ki:pseik/ *n* thing kept as a memory of a person.

keg

keg /keg/ *n* small barrel.

ken /ken/ **beyond (someone's) ken** = beyond (his) knowledge.

kennel /'kenəl/ *n* small wooden hut for a dog; place in which dogs are kept.

kept /kept/ *p.p. & p.t.* of **keep.**

kerb /kɜ:b/ *n* line of raised stones separating the footpath (for walkers) from the road.

kerchief /'kɜ:tʃif/ *n* cloth covering for the head.

kernel /'kɜ:nəl/ *n* soft centre part of a nut; centre, esp. if small, of anything.

kerosene /'kerəsi:n/ *n* kind of oil for heating and lighting.

kestrel /'kestrəl/ *n* red-brown bird which feeds on mice, insects and small birds.

ketch /ketʃ/ *n* small sailing-ship.

ketchup /'ketʃəp/ *n* liquid used to give a pleasant taste to meat.

kettle /'ketl/ *n* pot with a handle and a pipe from which liquid is poured, used for boiling water.

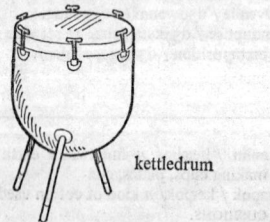

kettledrum

kettledrum /'ketldrʌm/ *n* large drum with a round curved-up bottom.

key /ki:/ *n* **1** instrument used to open a lock. **2** anything pressed by the finger in a TYPEWRITER, musical instrument, etc. **3** that which explains a matter; explanation of signs used in a map. **4** set of musical notes which can be arranged in a regular way, starting from one note. *adj* most important; serving to explain the whole matter. *n* **keyboard** /'ki:bɔ:d/ part of a musical instrument containing the keys. *n* **keynote** /'ki:nəʊt/ starting note of a key; chief idea in a speech or book. *n* **keystone** /'ki:stəʊn/ *n* middle stone in the top of an arch; most important part of something, on which the rest depends. **keyed up** = excited.

khaki /'kɑːki/ *n* yellow-brown cloth worn by soldiers. *n, adj* (of) this colour.

kick /kik/ *vt* strike with the foot. *n* act of kicking. **to kick the bucket** = die. **to kick out** = send away rudely. **to kick up** = make trouble.

kid /kid/ *n* **1** young goat. **2** leather of goat-skin. **3** *infml* child. *vt* deceive.

kidnap /'kidnæp/ *vt* take away (e.g. a child) so as to ask money for returning him (her).

kidney /'kidni/ *n* part of the body which takes poisons out of the blood and passes them out of the body in the water.

kill /kil/ *vt* cause the death of; destroy. *n* act of killing. *n* **kill-joy** = one who ruins the pleasure of a party of friends. **to kill time** = make time pass easily, while waiting for something.

kiln /kiln/ *n* large closed fireplace, e.g. in which bricks are made.

kilo- /'kilə/ one thousand, e.g. **kilometre** /'kiləmi:tə, ki'lɒmitə/ = 1,000 metres (about 6/10ths of a mile).

kilt /kilt/ *n* short skirt worn by Scotsmen.

kimono /ki'məʊnəʊ/ *n* long coat as worn in Japan.

kin /kin/ *n* members of one's family, relations by blood.

kind[1] /kaind/ *n* sort; class.

kind[2] /kaind/ *adj* gentle; good; loving.

kindergarten /'kindəgɑ:tn/ *n* school for very young children.

kindle /'kindl/ *vt* light (a fire); help (a fire) to burn. *n* **kindling** /'kindliŋ/ dry wood used for lighting a fire.

kindly /'kaindli/ *adj* pleasant, gentle.

kindred /'kindrəd/ *adj, n* (state of) being of the same family; similar(ity).

king /kiŋ/ *n* male ruler of a country, because of being the son of an earlier ruler. *n* **kingdom** /'kiŋdəm/ *n* country ruled by a king.

kingfisher /'kiŋˌfiʃə/ *n* small brightly-coloured bird which catches fish.

kingpin /'kiŋˌpin/ *n* **1** pin which holds the wheel of a car in place. **2** most important person or thing on whom everything depends.

kink /kiŋk/ *n* **1** backward turn or twist in a rope or chain. **2** peculiarity of the mind. *adj* **kinky** /'kiŋki/.

kinship /'kinʃip/ *n* relationship; likeness.

kiosk /'kiːɒsk/ *n* small open hut, e.g. one used for selling newspapers.

kipper /'kɪpə / *n* dried fish (HERRING) salted.

kiss /kɪs/ *vt* touch with the lips as a greeting or sign of love. *n* act of kissing.

kit /kɪt/ *n* **1** equipment, esp. if carried about with one. **2** one's clothing. **3** set of parts which are sold in a pack to be put together by the buyer e.g. to make a chair.

kitchen /'kɪtʃɪn/ *n* room used for cooking. **kitchen-garden** /ˌ. '../ *n* garden where vegetables are grown for food.

kite[1] /kaɪt/ *n* a bird which catches and eats other birds, etc.

kite[2] /kaɪt/ *n* light frame covered with paper which is made to fly up in the air by children.

kith /kɪθ/ **kith and kin** = friends and members of one's family.

kitten /'kɪtn/ *n* young cat.

kitty /'kɪtɪ/ *n* all the money to be gained at one time in a game of chance.

kleptomania /ˌkleptəˈmeɪnɪə/ *n* uncontrollable desire to steal things. *n* **kleptomaniac** /ˌkleptəˈmeɪnɪæk/ one who has such a desire.

knack /næk/ *n* special skill in some one kind of work.

knapsack /'næpsæk/ *n* bag carried on the back by a traveller or soldier.

knave

knave /neɪv/ *n* tricky dishonest fellow; playing-card as shown. *adj* **knavish** /'neɪvɪʃ/ as of a knave.

knead /niːd/ *vt* press and mix (flour, water, etc.) with the hands so as to make bread.

knee /niː/ *n* middle joint of the leg, where the leg bends.

kneel /niːl/ *vi* go down on the knees.

knell /nel/ *n* sound of a bell rung at someone's death.

knelt /nelt/ *p.t.* of **kneel.**

knew /njuː/ *p.t.* of **know.**

knickerbockers /'nɪkəbɒkəz/ *n* loose garment covering the body from the waist down to just below the knees. *n* **knickers** /'nɪkəz/ women's underclothing covering the body from the waist to the tops of the legs.

knick-knack /'nɪk næk/ *n* any small object used as an ornament for the house or dress.

knife /naɪf/ *n* blade fixed in a handle used for cutting. *vt* drive a knife into (someone).

kiosk

knight /naɪt/ *n* **1** (in the past) soldier of noble rank. **2** man of rank allowed to put "Sir" before his name.

knit /nɪt/ *v* join together a thread of wool or cotton in a close network so as to form (a garment); join closely, e.g. *He knit his fingers together.*

knives /naɪvz/ *pl* of **knife.**

knob /nɒb/ *n* round mass used as a handle, e.g. on the end of a stick, as handle of a door, etc.

knock /nɒk/ *vt* strike with a hard blow. *vi* strike the door of a building as a sign of desire to enter. *n* hard blow. **to knock down** = strike and cause to fall. **knock out** = strike so as to make senseless. **to knock together** = make quickly. **knock-kneed** /ˌ. './ having the legs bent inwards. *n* **knocker** /'nɒkə / a metal instrument used by visitors for knocking at a door.

knoll /nəʊl/ *n* small round hill.

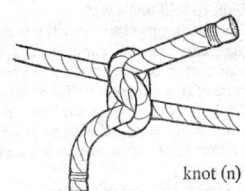
knot (n)

knot[1] /nɒt/ *vt* join (two pieces of string) together. *n* **1** joining of string or rope. **2** hard mass in wood where a branch has come out of the main stem of a tree.

knot[2] /nɒt/ *n* measure of the speed of a ship, about 6,080 feet (1·852 km) in one hour.

know /nəʊ/ *v* believe correctly; have facts in the mind; understand; remember; recognize. *vt* have met (someone); be acquainted with (someone).

knowing /'nəʊɪŋ/ *adj* clever. *adv* **knowingly** = knowing that one is doing it, e.g. *To steal knowingly.*

knowledge /'nɒlɪdʒ/ *n* things known; **not to my knowledge,** = not so far as I know. *adj* **knowledgeable** /'nɒlɪdʒəbəl/ *adj* knowing a lot.

known /nəʊn/ *p.p.* of **know.**

knuckle

knuckle /'nʌkəl/ *n* bone where a finger joins on to the hand. **to knuckle down to** = yield to.

kolanut /'kəʊlənʌt/ *n* seed eaten, as in West Africa, that has an effect upon the senses.

kosher /'kəʊʃə⁊/ *n, adj* (of) food, especially meat, which it is lawful for the Jews to eat.

kraal /krɑːl/ *n* native village in South Africa with a fence round it.

kudos /'kjuːdɒs/ *n* praise; honour.

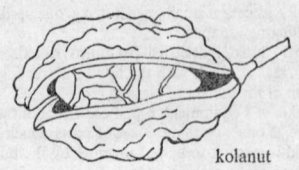

kolanut

L

L /el/ Roman figure, 50.

label /'leɪbəl/ *n* **1** piece of paper fixed to a thing, e.g. to a book showing its number, to a box showing the address to which it is to be sent. **2** name for a class of similar things. *vt* **1** put a label on. **2** give a label to.

labial /'leɪbɪəl/ *adj* of the lips.

laboratory /lə'bɒrətrɪ/ *n* place in which scientists work.

laborious /lə'bɔːrɪəs/ *adj* working hard.

labour /'leɪbə⁊/ *n* **1** work. **hard labour** = work given to prisoners as part of their punishment. **2** group of all those persons who work for others. **3** pains of a woman in giving birth to a child. *vi* work; have difficulty in doing something. *vt* work too hard on; spend too long on, e.g. *To labour the point* = explain a matter with unnecessary care.

labyrinth /'læbərɪnθ/ *n* arrangement of a number of paths with walls on each side through which it is difficult to find one's way.

lace /leɪs/ *n* **1** string used to draw the edges of a thing together, e.g. *A shoe-lace*. **2** fancy network of cotton or silk used as an ornament for dresses. *vt* draw together with a string. **red laced with blue** = having lines of blue in it. **tea laced with brandy** = mixed with BRANDY.

lacerate /'læsəreɪt/ *vt* wound. *n* **laceration** /ˌlæsə'reɪʃən/.

lachrymal /'lækrɪməl/ *adj* of tears.

lachrymose /'lækrɪməʊs/ *adj* tearful, easily made to weep.

lack /læk/ *n* want of, absence of. *vt* be without. **money was lacking** = there was no —.

lackadaisical /ˌlækə'deɪzɪkəl/ *adj* behaving in a weak, lazy and unnatural way.

lackey /'lækɪ/ *n* manservant; person who behaves like a servant.

lacklustre /'læklʌstə⁊/ *adj* having no brightness.

laconic /lə'kɒnɪk/ *adj* expressed in few words.

lacquer /'lækə⁊/ *n* hard paint; hard coating.

lactation /læk'teɪʃən/ *n* production of milk in the breast. *adj* **lactic** /'læktɪk/ having to do with milk.

lad /læd/ *n* boy.

ladder /'lædə⁊/ *n* two long bars (or ropes) with short bars across as steps, used for climbing up.

laden /'leɪdn/ *adj* loaded down.

lading /'leɪdɪŋ/ *n* goods loaded onto, e.g. a ship.

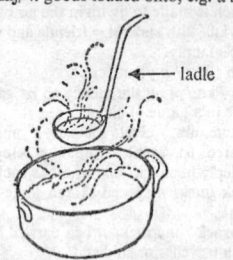

ladle

ladle /'leɪdl/ *n* spoon with a long handle used for liquids.

lady /'leɪdɪ/ *n* woman of good class; polite word for woman. **lady** (title of a woman of rank), e.g. *Lady Smith*, wife of Sir John Smith.

ladybird /'leɪdɪbɜːd/ *n* small red or yellow insect with black spots.

ladykiller /'leɪdɪˌkɪlə⁊/ *n* one who thinks himself very pleasing to the ladies.

ladyship /'leɪdɪʃɪp/ **her Ladyship** = 'she', in speaking of a lady of high rank.

lag[1] /læg/ *n* one who has been often in prison.

lag[2] /læg/ *vi* be slow and fall behind.

lager /'lɑːgə⁊/ *n* light BEER.

laggard /'lægəd/ *n* one who is slow in action.

lagoon /lə'guːn/ *n* salt-water lake cut off from the sea.

lain /leɪn/ p.p. of **lie**.

lair /leə⁊/ *n* home of a wild animal.

laird /leəd/ *n* a Scottish landowner.

laissez-faire /ˌleɪseɪ 'feə⁊/ *n* idea that the government should not make too many laws but allow things to go on in their own way.

laity /'leɪtɪ/ *n* general public other than those with some special skill or work.

lake /leɪk/ *n* large sheet of water with land all round it.

lamb /læm/ *n* young of a sheep; sheep used as meat.

lame /leɪm/ *adj* having a bad leg and not able to walk properly. **a lame duck** = person who cannot help himself.

lament /lə'ment/ *v* show great grief (at). *adj* **lamentable** /'læməntəbəl/ very sad; so bad as to cause grief or anger. *n* **lamentation** /ˌlæmən'teɪʃən/.

laminated /'læmɪneɪtɪd/ *adj* made up of very thin plates or sheets of material.

lamp /læmp/ *n* instrument used to give light.

lampoon /læm'puːn/ *vt, n* (make a) written attack upon (a person).

lamprey /'læmprɪ/ *n* fish-like creature with a long body, like a snake, about 16 inches (40 cm) long.

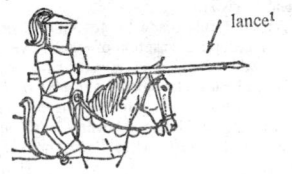

lance¹

lance¹ /lɑːns/ *n* spear used by horse-soldiers. **lancer** /lɑːnsə/ *n* horse-soldier who uses a lance.

lance² /lɑːns/ *vt* to cut with a LANCET.

lance corporal /ˌ. '. ./ *n* rank in the British army, just above the common soldier.

lancet /'lɑːnsɪt/ *n* small knife used by doctors.

land /lænd/ *n* 1 ground. 2 country. *vi* 1 go off a ship on to the land. 2 (of an aeroplane) come down to earth. *vt* bring (an aeroplane) down. *n* **landing** /'lændɪŋ/ 1 act of bringing or coming to land. 2 flat place between two sets of stairs.

landlady /'lændˌleɪdɪ/ *n* 1 woman who rents furnished rooms. 2 woman in charge of a hotel, inn, etc.

landlocked /'lændlɒkt/ *adj* (of a piece of water) shut in by land.

landlord /'lændlɔːd/ *n* 1 man who rents rooms or houses for others to live in. 2 man in charge of a hotel, inn, etc.

landmark /'lændmɑːk/ *n* mark showing the edge of one's land; any clearly seen object used in telling or finding the way to a place.

landscape /'lændskeɪp/ *n* beautiful natural scene; painting of such a scene.

landslip, /'lændˌslɪp/, **landslide** /'lændslaɪd/ *n* fall of earth, e.g. from the face of a cliff.

lane /leɪn/ *n* narrow road.

language /'læŋgwɪdʒ/ *n* 1 system of sounds for expressing thoughts. 2 speech, writing, or the use of words in general.

languid /'læŋgwɪd/ *adj* weak, without interest.

languish /'læŋgwɪʃ/ *vi* become weak. **to languish in prison** = live very unhappily in prison. *n* **languor** /'læŋgə/ weakness.

lank /læŋk/ *adj* hanging loosely.

lanky /'læŋkɪ/ *adj* thin and tall; having long arms and legs.

lanolin /'lænəlɪn/ *n* fat of wool made pure and used as a medicine for the skin.

lantern /'læntən/ *n* 1 glass case for a lamp or candle 2 top of a building or small tower with windows on all sides.

lanyard /'lænjəd/ *n* string worn round the shoulder or neck with a knife or whistle, etc., on the other end.

lap¹ /læp/ *n* (sing) person's knees and upper part of legs used as a seat for a child. *n* **lapdog** /'læpdɒg/ small dog.

lap² /læp/ *n* turn or twist of string round (a stick, etc.); (in a race) going once round the course.

lap³ /læp/ *vt* drink with the tongue as a cat does. **waves lapped the shore** = touched the shore with a sound as of lapping.

lapel /lə'pel/ *n* that part of the front of a coat which is turned back towards the shoulders.

lapse /læps/ *n* mistake; a fall from goodness; passing of time. *vi* 1 fall away from, e.g. *He has lapsed back into his old bad ways*. 2 (of land or goods) pass from one person to another because some rule or law has not been fulfilled; (of a claim) come to an end, be of no more use or effect.

larceny /'lɑːsənɪ/ *n* stealing.

larch /lɑːtʃ/ *n* tall straight tree whose wood is used for making posts.

lard /lɑːd/ *n* pig's fat.

larder /'lɑːdə/ *n* store-room for food.

large /lɑːdʒ/ *adj* taking up much space; able to contain a great amount; big. **at large** = not in prison. **the world at large** = all people. *adv* **largely** /'lɑːdʒlɪ/ in great amount, chiefly.

largess(e) /lɑː'dʒes/ *n* money scattered by a king or lord to the people.

lariat /'lærɪət/ *n* rope for tying up horses.

lark¹ /lɑːk/ *n* singing bird.

lark² /lɑːk/ *vi* be merry; play in a merry way. **for a lark** = to amuse, not meaning it seriously.

larva /'lɑːvə/ *pl* **larvae** /'lɑːviː/ *n* form in which an insect first lives after it leaves the egg.

larynx /'lærɪŋks/ *n* upper part of the throat in which the voice is produced. *n* **laryngitis** /ˌlærɪn'dʒaɪtɪs/ pain and redness in the larynx.

lascivious /lə'sɪvɪəs/ *adj* full of improper sexual desire.

lash /læʃ/ *vt* 1 hit with a WHIP. 2 tie or fasten with rope. *n* 1 single stroke of a whip; sound of such a stroke. 2 EYELASH.

lass /læs/ *n* girl.

lassitude /'læsɪtjuːd/ *n* tiredness.

lasso /læ'suː, 'læsəʊ/ *n* rope made of leather used for catching cattle in America.

last¹ /lɑːst/ *n* wooden or iron shape of a foot on which shoes are made. **to stick to one's last** = do one's own work, not other people's.

last² /lɑːst/ *adj, adv* after all others, coming at the end.

last³ /lɑːst/ *vi* continue; stay alive or in use.

latch /lætʃ/ *n* simple lock for a door, made of a short falling bar which is pulled up with a string from outside, or pressed up with a short handle. *n* **latchkey** /'lætʃkɪ/ key of the front door of a house.

late /leɪt/ *adj, adv* 1 after the proper time. 2 far on in time. 3 who has just died; who has just left

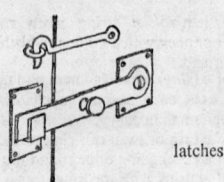

latches

office, e.g. *The late headmaster* = the headmaster before the present one or the headmaster who is just dead. *adv* **lately** /'leɪtlɪ/ not long ago. **of late** = lately.

latent /'leɪtənt/ *adj* lying hidden.

lateral /'lætərəl/ *adj* at the side; of the side.

latest /'leɪtɪst/ *adj* most late; newest. **the latest** = what has just happened, the newest story.

latex /'leɪteks/ *n* white liquid that comes out of plants, e.g. out of the rubber-tree.

lath /lɑːθ/ *n* long thin piece of wood.

lathe /leɪð/ *n* machine which turns a piece of wood or metal round while it is cut or shaped.

lather /lɑːðə/ *n* white mass made by rubbing up soap and water.

Latin /'lætɪn/ *adj* having to do with the ancient Romans. *n* the language of ancient Rome.

latitude /'lætɪtjuːd/ *n* 1 freedom—esp. of opinion or choice. 2 one of the imaginary lines drawn round the world or drawn on a map of the world by means of which one tells how far north or south a place is.

latrine /lə'triːn/ *n* camp LAVATORY.

latter /'lætə/ *adj* later. *adj, n* second of two people or things just spoken about.

lattice /'lætɪs/ *n* network made of wood, e.g. one on which climbing plants grow upwards.

lattice window /ˌ. '. ./ *n* window in which the glass is fixed in cross-pieces of metal.

laud /lɔːd/ *vt* praise. *adj* **laudable** /'lɔːdəbəl/ worthy of praise. *adj* **laudatory** /'lɔːdətrɪ/ praising.

laugh /lɑːf/ *vi* make sounds showing pleasure or amusement. *n* single act of laughing. **to laugh at** = be amused at; show disrespect to. **to laugh off** = try to show one is not really anxious at (something) by laughing. *adj* **laughable** /'lɑːfəbəl/ causing persons to laugh. *n* **laughing stock** /'. . ./ person (or thing) at whom all laugh; something very foolish. *n* **laughter** /'lɑːftə/ (sound of) laughing.

launch /lɔːntʃ/ *n* small boat driven by a motor. *vt* send (a newly built ship) into the water; start (anything new). **to launch out on** = begin (new work). **to launch out** = spend much money.

launder /'lɔːndə/ *vt* wash (clothes). *n* **laundress** /'lɔːndrəs/ woman who washes others' clothes. *n* **laundry** /'lɔːndrɪ/ place where clothes are washed; clothes to be washed. *n* **launderette** /ˌlɔːn'dret/ place where one may pay to wash one's clothes in a machine.

laureate /'lɒrɪət/ *adj* crowned with LAUREL, e.g.

a poet. **Poet Laureate** = title of honour given for life to a poet specially appointed by the king.

laurel /'lɒrəl/ *n* bush with bright green leaves.

lava /'lɑːvə/ *n* liquid thrown out by a VOLCANO which afterwards becomes hard rock.

lavatory /'lævətrɪ/ *n* place where one leaves the waste matter of the body.

lavender /'lævɪndə/ *n* plant with small blue-red flowers with a pleasant smell.

lavish /'lævɪʃ/ *adj* giving freely, generous. *vt* spend or give freely.

law /lɔː/ *n* 1 rule made by government or the king. 2 general description of regular events of nature which happen as expected by scientists. *adj* **law-abiding** /'lɔːˌnˌbaɪdɪŋ/ keeping the laws. *n* **law court** /'. ˌ./ *n* place where a judge settles matters of law. *adj* **lawful** /'lɔːfəl/ according to the law. *adj* **lawless** /'lɔːləs/ not keeping the laws.

lawn[1] /lɔːn/ *n* fine white cloth.

lawn tennis

lawn[2] /lɔːn/ *n* piece of carefully kept grass near a house. *n* **lawnmower** /'lɔːnˌməʊə/ machine for cutting grass. **lawn tennis** /ˌ. '. ./ *n* game in which a ball is hit over a net on a piece of open ground 78 feet (23 m) long, 36 feet (11 m) wide.

lawsuit /'lɔːsuːt/ *n* making of a claim in a law-court before a judge.

lawyer /'lɔːjə/ *n* person who has studied the law and has the right to give advice on matters of law.

lax /læks/ *adj* loose; careless. *n* **laxity** /'læksətɪ/

laxative /'læksətɪv/ *n* medicine which clears out waste matter from the body.

lay[1] /leɪ/ *vt* 1 place; put down; cause to lie. 2 put things needed for a meal, such as knives, forks, etc. on to (a table). 3 (of a bird) produce (eggs).

lay[2] /leɪ/ *n* song.

lay[3] /leɪ/ *adj* of the general public, not the members of a specially trained group.

lay[4] /leɪ/ *p.t.* of **lie.**

lay-by /'. ./ *n* place at the side of a road where cars may stop for a time without getting in the way of cars on the road.

layer /'leɪə/ *n* thin covering spread over, e.g. sugar on a cake; part of something all at the same level, e.g. *A layer of hard rock below the soil.*

layout /'leɪaʊt/ *n* (of a printed page, etc.) arrangement.

lazy /'leɪzɪ/ *adj* not liking work. *n* **lazy-bones**

/'leɪzɪbəʊnz/ lazy person. *vi* laze /leɪz/ lie around or rest; be lazy. *n* laziness /'leɪzɪnəs/.

lea /liː/ *n* field of grass.

lead[1] /led/ *n* **1** a soft heavy metal. **2** black material in a pencil. *adj* **leaden** /'ledn/ made of lead; heavy.

lead[2] /liːd/ *v* **1** guide; direct. **2** get (someone) to follow; get (someone) to do something, e.g. *He led me to believe that you were out.* **3** act as chief; be in charge of, e.g. *To lead an army.* **4** serve as a path to, e.g. *This road leads to the church.* **5** pass or spend (time), e.g. *To lead a happy life.* **6** go in front; play first in a card-game. *n* **1** act of leading. **2** the right to play first. **3** chief part in a play. **4** string used for leading a dog. *n* **leader** /'liːdə/ guide; one who leads a group. **leading article** /ˌ.. '../ part of a newspaper in which the opinions of the chief or head of the newspaper are expressed.

leaf /liːf/ *n* **1** green blade of a plant. **2** both sides of a page in a book. **3** part of the top of a table which can be taken out so as to make the table smaller. **4** anything thin and flat like a leaf. **to leaf through** = turn the pages of (a book). **turn over a new leaf** = decide to behave better in future.

leaflet /'liːflət/ *n* **1** small leaf of a plant; printed paper folded but not sewn. **2** small book.

league[1] /liːg/ *n* group whose members join together to help each other in some common purpose.

league[2] /liːg/ *n* measure of distance, about 3 miles or 5 kilometres.

leak /liːk/ *n* small hole through which liquid escapes or breaks in. *vi* enter or escape through a small hole. *n* **leakage** /'liːkɪdʒ/ a leaking. *adj* **leaky** /'liːkɪ/ leaking.

lean[1] /liːn/ *adj* thin; of bad quality; small in amount. **lean years** = years when crops are small.

lean[2] /liːn/ *v* bend towards; rest against. *n* **leaning** /'liːnɪŋ/ tendency e.g. *He has a leaning towards* = has a liking for, will probably become interested in.

leap frog

leap /liːp/ *vi, n* jump. *n* **leap-frog** /ˈ. ./ game in which children jump over each other's backs. **leap year** = year in which there are 366 days.

learn /lɜːn/ *v* come to know; gain knowledge; practise doing something. *adj* **learned** /'lɜːnɪd/ having much knowledge.

lease /liːs/ *n, vt* (make an) agreement to give the use of (a house or land) for a number of years on payment of certain money as rent. **a new lease of life** = chance of living longer or more happily owing to some trouble or disease ending. *n* **leasehold** /'liːshəʊld/ land or a house held by lease.

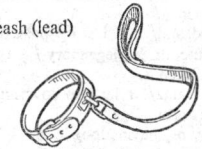

leash (lead)

leash /liːʃ/ *n* string for holding a dog.

least /liːst/ *adj, adv* smallest, in the smallest amount.

leather /'leðə/ *n* skin of an animal prepared for use.

leave[1] /liːv/ *n* permission, esp. permission to go or stay away from work. **to take French leave** = go without asking to be allowed to go.

leave[2] /liːv/ *vt* **1** allow to remain. **2** give (money) to a person at one's death. **3** trust a person to, e.g. *Leave it to me* = trust me to do it. *v* go away (from); go out (of). *infml* **to leave off** = stop (doing something). **to leave out** = not to include; miss.

leaven /'levən/ *n* soft grey-white material used to make bread light.

lectern /'lektɜːn/ *n* sloping table on which the Bible is put in a church.

lecture /'lektʃə/ *v, n* (make a) speech given to teach a class. *n* **lectureship** /'lektʃəʃɪp/ employment as a lecturer.

led /led/ p.t. and p.p. of **lead**.

ledge /ledʒ/ *n* narrow flat place in a wall or cliff, e.g. one on which one can put one's feet; flat rock under the sea.

ledger /'ledʒə/ *n* book in which accounts of money are written.

lee /liː/ **in the lee of** = in the shelter of. *adj* **leeward** /'liːwəd/ on the side away from the wind. *n* **leeway** /'liːweɪ/ movement off the right course caused by wind; loss of time in doing work, e.g. *I have a lot of leeway to make up.*

leech /liːtʃ/ *n* small water creature which fixes itself on the skin and drinks blood.

leek /liːk/ *n* strong-smelling vegetable which is cooked for food.

leer /lɪə/ *vi* look at someone in an evil and unpleasant way. *n* such a look.

lees /liːz/ *n* thick liquid at the bottom of a bottle or barrel of wine.

left[1] /left/ p.t. and p.p. of **leave**.

left[2] /left/ *n, adj, adv* (on or to) that side of the body on which the heart is. *adj* **left-wing** /ˌ. '../ favouring systems of government in which the working classes have greater control.

leg /leg/ *n* **1** one of the limbs used for walking. **2** a support, e.g. *The leg of a table.* **3** that part of a garment which covers the leg.

legacy /'legəsɪ/ *n* money or other things passed on to another at death.

legal /'li:gəl/ *adj* **1** according to law. **2** having to do with the law. *n* **legal tender** /,. . '. ./ money such as must be accepted according to law.

legalize /'li:gəlaɪz/ *vt* make lawful. *n* **legalization** /,li:gəlaɪ'zeɪʃən/.

legend /'ledʒənd/ *n* old story passed down by word of mouth. *adj* **legendary** /'ledʒəndərɪ/ as told of in legends.

leggings /'legɪŋz/ *n* leather coverings for the lower part of the legs.

leggy /'legɪ/ *adj* having long legs.

legible /'ledʒəbəl/ *adj* easily read.

legion /'li:dʒən/ *n* company of soldiers in the Roman army.

legislate /'ledʒɪsleɪt/ *vi* make laws. *n* **legislation** /,ledʒɪs'leɪʃən/. *adj* **legislative** /'ledʒɪslətɪv/.

legislator /'ledʒɪsleɪtə/ *n* maker of laws. *n* **legislature** /'ledʒɪslətʃə/ men who make laws.

legitimate /lɪ'dʒɪtɪmət/ *adj* **1** according to law; allowable. **2** (of a child) born in marriage. *vt* **legitimize** /lɪ'dʒɪtɪmaɪz/ make legitimate.

leisure /'leʒə/ *n* time not given to work. *adj* **leisurely** /'leʒəlɪ/ slowly; not in a hurry. *adj* **leisured** /'leʒəd/ having plenty of free time.

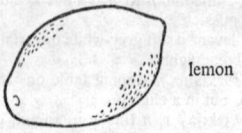

lemon

lemon /'lemən/ *n* yellow, very sour fruit; tree bearing this fruit. *n, adj* (of the) colour of this fruit. *n* **lemonade** /lemə'neɪd/ **lemon squash** /,. . '. ./ drink made from lemons.

lemur /'li:mə/ *n* kind of monkey with a hairy tail.

lend /lend/ *vt* give the use of (something) on the understanding that it will be given back.

length /leŋθ/ *n* distance from one end of a thing to the other. **at length** = after a long time. *v* **lengthen** /'leŋθən/ make or become longer. *adj* **lengthwise** /'leŋθwaɪz/ along the length. *adj* **lengthy** /'leŋθɪ/ lasting a long time.

lenient /'li:nɪənt/ *adj* gentle and forgiving.

lens /lenz/ *n* piece of glass which collects light into one beam.

Lent /lent/ *n* time of year when some Christians eat simple food and give up things they like.

lent /lent/ *p.p. & p.t.* of **lend.**

lentil /'lentl/ *n* yellow seed of a kind of bean-plant.

leopard /'lepəd/ *n* a large meat-eating mammal, of the cat family, yellow with black spots, found in the forests of India and Africa.

leper /'lepə/ *n* one suffering from LEPROSY.

leprosy /'leprəsɪ/ *n* disease which slowly eats the body away. *adj* **leprous** /'leprəs/.

lesbian /'lezbɪən/ *n, adj* (woman) who enjoys sexual relations with other women.

lesion /'li:ʒən/ *n* wound.

less /les/ *det, adv* not so much; taken from. *v* **lessen** /'lesən/ make or become less. *adj* **lesser** /'lesə/ smaller.

lessee /le'si:/ *n* person who rents a house.

lesson /'lesən/ *n* thing to be learnt; amount of teaching given at one time.

lest /lest/ *conj* for fear that.

let[1] /let/ *vt* allow; leave. **to let down** = disappoint. **to let off** = forgive.

let[2] /let/ *vt* give the use of (a house) for rent.

lethal /'li:θəl/ *adj* causing death.

lethargy /'leθədʒɪ/ *n* sleepiness; lack of spirit or interest. *adj* **lethargic** /lɪ'θɑ:dʒɪk/.

letter /'letə/ *n* **1** one of the characters used in writing, e.g. A, B, C, etc. **2** written message, a note. **a man of letters** = man who writes books or studies good writings.

letterpress /'letəpres/ *n* printed matter.

lettuce /'letɪs/ *n* vegetable with green leaves eaten uncooked, often with cold meat.

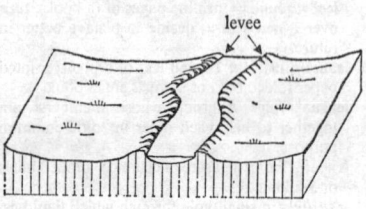

levee

levee /'levɪ/ *n* bank to prevent a river from flowing over the land.

level /'levəl/ *adj* flat; not hilly. *n* flat place; set of places at the same height. **on the level** = honest. *vt* make flat. *n* **level crossing** /,. . '. ./ place where road and rail cross without a bridge. *adj* **level-headed** /,hedɪd/ not easily excited.

lever /'li:və/ *n* bar with a fixed support at one point, used for lifting things. *n* **leverage** /'li:vərɪdʒ/ power of a lever.

leviathan /lɪ'vaɪəθən/ *n* very large sea-creature; any very large thing.

levitate /'levəteɪt/ *v* lift or be lifted up from the ground as if by magic.

levity /'levɪtɪ/ *n* state of mind in which solemn things are treated lightly and disrespectfully.

levy /'levɪ/ *vt* collect (money) from the people, e.g. for government; raise an army. *n* collection of money or soldiers.

lewd /lu:d/ *adj* sexually improper or rude.

lexicon /'leksɪkən/ *n* book giving the meanings of words. *n* **lexicographer** /,leksɪ'kɒgrəfə/ writer of books in which the meanings of words are given.

liable /'laɪəbəl/ *adj* **1** bound by law. **I am liable for his debts** = I shall have to pay if he does not. **2** open to attack, e.g. *Liable to illness* = open to attacks of illness. **3** probably going to. *n* **liability** /ˌlaɪə'bɪlətɪ/ debt.

liaison /lɪ'eizən/ *n* **1** relationship between lovers, friends, or those working together. **2** joining of the last sound of one word with the first sound of the next.

liar /'laɪə/ *n* one who does not speak the truth.

libation /laɪ'beɪʃən/ *n* wine poured out as an offering to a god.

libel /'laɪbəl/ *n* something printed or written which is damaging to a person's good name. *adj* **libellous** /'laɪbələs/.

liberal /'lɪbərəl/ *adj* **1** free; generous; plentiful. **2** believing that men should be free to do as they want provided others are not harmed by their actions; favouring freedom of speech, etc.

liberate /'lɪbəreɪt/ *vt* set free (e.g. a country from foreign rulers). *n* **liberation** /ˌlɪbə'reɪʃən/.

libertine /'lɪbətiːn/ *n* pleasure-seeker of loose character.

liberty /'lɪbətɪ/ *n* freedom. **to take liberties** = do acts which one has no real right to do.

library /'laɪbrərɪ/ *n* **1** collection of books or reading-room in a house. **2** place where books are kept to be lent to the public. *n* **librarian** /laɪ'breərɪən/ one who is in charge of a library.

libretto /lɪ'bretəʊ/ *n* book of words of a musical play.

lice /laɪs/ *pl* of **louse**.

licence /'laɪsəns/ *n* **1** leave; permission. **2** piece of paper proving one is permitted to do something, e.g. drive a car, keep a pet, use one's own television, carry a gun, etc. **3** too great freedom.

license, licence /'laɪsəns/ *vt* **1** permit; give PERMISSION **2** give a license to; get a licence for (e.g. a car). *n* **licensee** /ˌlaɪsən'siː/ holder of a licence.

licentious /laɪ'senʃəs/ *adj* rough and badly behaved.

lichen /'laɪkən, 'lɪtʃən/ *n* very small plant which covers rocks.

lick /lɪk/ *vt* **1** pass the tongue over. **2** *infml* beat. *n* **licking** /'lɪkɪŋ/ beating.

lid /lɪd/ *n* cover, e.g. of a box.

lido /'liːdəʊ/ *n* place in the open air where people can swim and lie out in the sunshine.

lie[1] /laɪ/ *vi* remain flat on; be at rest on; be kept in. **to lie in** = stay in bed late in the morning.

lie[2] /laɪ/ *vi* intentionally say what is not true. *n* act of lying.

lien /'liːən/ **to have a lien on** = have the right to keep something until a debt is paid.

lieu /luː/ **in lieu of** = instead of.

lieutenant /lef'tenənt/ *n* officer of low rank in the army or on a ship.

life /laɪf/ *n* **1** power of living. **2** living creatures. **3** time between birth and death.

lifebelt /'laɪfbelt/ *n* thing put round the waist so as to prevent one sinking in water.

lifeboat /'laɪfbəʊt/ *n* boat used to save men from a wreck.

lifebuoy /'laɪfbɔɪ/ *n* floating thing to which men hold when in water.

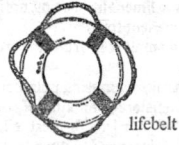
lifebelt

lifeless /'laɪfləs/ *adj* dead; appearing to be without movement or life.

lifelong /'laɪflɒŋ/ *adj* lasting the whole of life.

lift /lɪft/ *vt* raise up. *n* **1** machine that raises goods or people up in a building. **2** being taken in someone else's car.

ligament /'lɪgəmənt/ *n* band joining two bones in the body, or holding some part of the body in its place.

ligature /'lɪgətʃə/ *n* string used for tying up the end of a blood-vessel.

light[1] /laɪt/ *n* **1** that which comes from the sun (etc.) by which we see. **2** lamp. **3** flame for a smoker. *vt* **1** give light to. **2** set fire to. *n* **lighter** /'laɪtə/ small instrument for lighting cigarettes.

light[2] /laɪt/ *adj* not dark in colour, e.g. *Light blue*.

light[3] /laɪt/ *adj* not heavy; not serious or painful, e.g. *A light attack of illness; A light punishment; Light reading* = amusing books, etc., not difficult to understand.

light[4] /laɪt/ **to light upon** = find when not expecting to do so.

lighten /'laɪtn/ *v* **1** make or become light or lighter in weight. **2** make or become light or lighter in colour.

lighter /'laɪtə/ *n* flat-bottomed boat used for unloading ships.

lighthouse /'laɪthaʊs/ *n* tower with a lamp in it to warn ships of rocks.

lightning /'laɪtnɪŋ/ *n* flashing of light seen in the sky during a storm.

lights /laɪts/ *n* LUNGS of an animal, used for food.

lignite /'lɪgnaɪt/ *n* a sort of coal.

like[1] /laɪk/ *adj, prep* not different (from); similar (to).

like[2] /laɪk/ *vt* enjoy; find pleasant.

likely /'laɪklɪ/ *adj* probable; probably suitable. **most likely** = quite probably. *n* **likelihood** /'laɪklɪhʊd/ probability.

likeness /'laɪknəs/ *n* similarity, esp. of a picture to what is painted in the picture.

likewise /'laɪkwaɪz/ *adv* in the same way; also.

lilac /'laɪlək/ *n* bush with a blue-red or white flower.

lilt /lɪlt/ *n* regular beat of music.

lily /'lɪlɪ/ *n* a kind of beautiful flower.

limb /lɪm/ *n* arm or leg or wing; branch of a tree.

limber /'lɪmbə/ *adj* easily bent; active. **to limber up** = do movement exercises to get the body fit for something.

lime[1] /laɪm/ *n* **1** white powder mixed with sand to make a material used to join bricks in building. **2** sticky material used for catching birds. *n* **limelight** /'laɪmlaɪt/ powerful light used in the

lime

theatre. **in the limelight** = being noticed, important at the present time.

lime² /laɪm/ n small sour fruit; the tree on which this grows.

limerick /'lɪmərɪk/ n amusing poem of five lines.

limestone /'laɪmstəʊn/ n a kind of rock.

limit /'lɪmɪt/ n border; farthest edge. vt keep within a certain space, within certain rules. n

limitation /ˌlɪmɪ'teɪʃən/ act of limiting; state of being limited.

limousine /'lɪməziːn/ n large car with a separate place for the driver.

limp¹ /lɪmp/ adj not stiff.

limp² /lɪmp/ vi walk as if with a wounded leg.

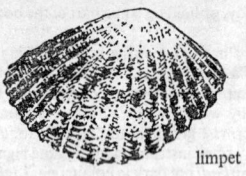
limpet

limpet /'lɪmpɪt/ n shell-fish which holds tightly on to rocks.

limpid /'lɪmpɪd/ adj clear.

linchpin /'lɪntʃˌpɪn/ n pin which prevents a wheel falling off a cart.

line¹ /laɪn/ n 1 string, e.g. *A fishing line.* 2 thin mark. 3 row, e.g. of soldiers, of words on a page, etc. 4 set of ships or aeroplanes giving regular service, e.g. *The Cunard Line.* 5 set of ideas. 6 business, e.g. *What line is he in* = what things does he sell or make or do? v set in line; stand in line.

line² /laɪn/ vt cover the inside of (something) with cloth or other material.

lineage /'lɪnɪ-ɪdʒ/ n line of persons from whom one is descended. adj **lineal** /'lɪnɪəl/ in the direct line of father—son—grandson, etc.

lineament /'lɪnɪəmənt/ n part of the face which gives it its special character, is most easily recognized.

linen /'lɪnɪn/ n 1 a kind of cloth. 2 clothes and cloths used in the house.

liner /'laɪnə ʳ/ n large ship which carries people across the ocean.

linger /'lɪŋɡə ʳ/ vi stay a long time; stay behind.

lingerie /'lænʒərɪ, lɛ̃ʒərɪ/ n (sing) women's undergarments.

lingo /'lɪŋɡəʊ/ sl n language.

lingua franca /ˌlɪŋɡwə 'fræŋkə/ n mixed language serving as a common language for several peoples.

lingual /'lɪŋɡwəl/ adj of the tongue.

linguist /'lɪŋɡwɪst/ n 1 one who speaks many languages. 2 one who studies language(s). adj **linguistic** /lɪŋ'ɡwɪstɪk/ having to do with languages. n **linguistics** scientific study of language.

liniment /'lɪnɪmənt/ n medical oil rubbed into the skin.

lining /'laɪnɪŋ/ n covering of the inside (e.g. of a coat).

link /lɪŋk/ n ring of a chain. v join together, join with a link. **to link arms** = join arms.

links /lɪŋks/ n grassy sandhills; place where GOLF is played.

linoleum /lɪ'nəʊlɪəm/ (shortened to **lino** /'laɪnəʊ/) n floor covering made of cloth covered with a mixture of CORK and hardened oil.

linseed /'lɪnsiːd/ n seed of FLAX from which oil is obtained, used in making paint, etc.

lint /lɪnt/ n soft cotton material used for covering wounds.

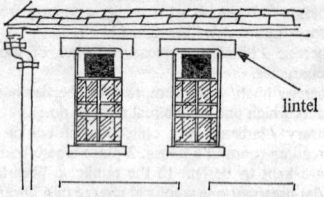
lintel

lintel /'lɪntl/ n top beam or bar of a door or window.

lion /'laɪən/ n large meat-eating mammal of the cat family found in Africa. vt **lionize** /'laɪənaɪz/ treat (someone) as if he were important. n **lioness** /'laɪənəs/ female lion.

lip /lɪp/ n edge of the mouth; edge of a thing. **lip service** = saying that one will serve a person but not meaning to do so. n **lipstick** /'lɪpˌstɪk/ pencil used by women to colour the lips.

liqueur /lɪ'kjʊə ʳ/ n sweet strong drink taken in a very small glass, usually after dinner.

liquid /'lɪkwɪd/ n, adj (of) matter in a form which can be poured like water. adj (in business) easily sold or changed for money. v **liquefy** /'lɪkwɪfaɪ/ make or become liquid. n **liquefaction** /ˌlɪkwɪ'fækʃən/ causing to become a liquid.

liquidate /'lɪkwɪdeɪt/ v pay off debts; break up a (business company). vt *infml* destroy. n **liquidation** /ˌlɪkwɪ'deɪʃən/.

liquor /'lɪkə ʳ/ n 1 a liquid. 2 strong drink (e.g. WHISKY).

liquorice /'lɪkərɪs/ n black material used in medicine, also eaten as a sweet.

lisp /lɪsp/ vi speak saying the s sound as th. n such a way of speaking.

lissom /'lɪsəm/ adj graceful and active.

list¹ /lɪst/ vt, n (write down) a line of names of (things), e.g. of things to be bought at a shop.

list² /lɪst/ vi (of a ship) lean to one side.

listen /'lɪsən/ v hear and attend to.

listless /'lɪstləs/ adj weak and uninterested.

lit /lɪt/ p.t. and p.p. of **light.**

litany /'lɪtənɪ/ n form of prayer to God to forgive our wrongdoing and bless all men.

literacy /'lɪtərəsɪ/ n ability to read and write.

literal /ˈlɪtərəl/ *adj* exact as to words; according to the actual meaning of the words.

literary /ˈlɪtərərɪ/ *adj* having to do with writing books.

literate /ˈlɪtərət/ *adj* able to read and write.

literature /ˈlɪtərətʃəʔ/ *n* books and writings of poets and good writers.

lithe /laɪð/ *adj* easily bent or turned, e.g. *Lithe as a snake.*

lithograph /ˈlɪθəgrɑːf/ *n* something printed from a drawing made on a special kind of stone or prepared surface.

litigate /ˈlɪtɪgeɪt/ *vi* go to law; make a claim in a law-court. *n* **litigation** /ˌlɪtɪˈgeɪʃən/. *adj* **litigious** /lɪˈtɪdʒəs/ who is always going to law.

litmus /ˈlɪtməs/ *n* blue colouring matter which is turned red by an acid.

litre /ˈliːtəʔ/ *n* measure of liquid, equal to 1¾ PINTS.

litter[1] /ˈlɪtəʔ/ *n* bed used for carrying people about, e.g. for carrying wounded.

litter[2] /ˈlɪtəʔ/ *n* waste paper and useless bits of things lying about. *v* drop or leave litter around (a place).

litter[3] /ˈlɪtəʔ/ *n* the young of an animal at birth, e.g. *A litter of puppies* = the young of a dog.

little /ˈlɪtl/ *adj* small; short; young. *adv, det* not much. **a little** = 1 rather, e.g. *A little anxious.* 2 small amount.

littoral /ˈlɪtərəl/ *adj* lying along the sea-shore.

liturgy /ˈlɪtədʒɪ/ *n* form of public prayer to God.

live[1] /lɪv/ *vi* 1 be alive. 2 have one's home, e.g. *Where do you live?* **to live up to** = be as good as (someone's expectation of one).

live[2] /laɪv/ *adj* 1 living; not dead. 2 (e.g. of coals) still burning. 3 with real BULLETS. 4 (of a wire) carrying electricity. *adv, adj* (of radio and television) sent out as it happens.

livelihood /ˈlaɪvlɪhʊd/ *n* means by which one gets money to live.

lively /ˈlaɪvlɪ/ *adj* quick; full of life and action.

liver /ˈlɪvəʔ/ *n* large (inside) part of the body which takes poisons out of the blood and stores up sugar.

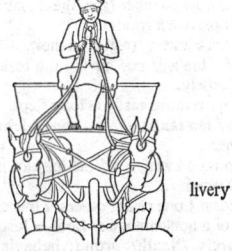

livery

livery /ˈlɪvərɪ/ *n* special dress worn by the servants of a nobleman or rich man, or of an ancient City Company in London.

livestock /ˈlaɪvstɒk/ *n* horses, cows, sheep, etc., on a farm.

livid /ˈlɪvɪd/ *adj* 1 blue-white, bloodless because of illness or fear. 2 *infml* very angry.

living /ˈlɪvɪŋ/ **to make one's living** = get enough money to live. **good living** = good food and comfort. **living-room** = room for general use in the day.

lizard /ˈlɪzəd/ *n* reptile with skin like a snake but with four legs.

llama /ˈlɑːmə/ *n* mammal like a sheep with a long neck and long hair, found in South America.

load /ləʊd/ *vt* 1 put on a ship (horse, cart, etc. the goods which it is to carry). 2 add weight to, e.g. *A loaded stick* = one with heavy metal at one end. 3 put powder and shot into (a gun). *n* goods loaded; weight. **loaded** *infml adj* 1 drunk. 2 very rich. *infml* **a load of** or **loads of** = a lot of.

loadstone /ˈləʊdstəʊn/ see **lodestone**.

loaf[1] /ləʊf/ *n* 1 mass of bread as baked. 2 large block of sugar.

loaf[2] /ləʊf/ *vi* waste time doing no work.

loam /ləʊm/ *n* good soil.

loan /ləʊn/ *n* thing lent. *vt* lend.

loath, loth /ləʊθ/ *adj* unwilling.

loathe /ləʊð/ *vt* hate. *adj* **loathsome** /ˈləʊðsəm/ hateful; very nasty.

lob /lɒb/ *n* ball sent high in the air. *vt* throw (e.g. a ball) high up.

lobby /ˈlɒbɪ/ *n* hall in a house. *vt* try to get (e.g. a government) to accept one's ideas about what should be done.

lobe /ləʊb/ *n* soft hanging part, esp. of the ear.

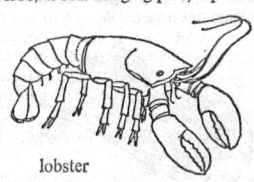

lobster

lobster /ˈlɒbstəʔ/ *n* a shell-fish with a long tail.

local /ˈləʊkəl/ *adj* found in or having to do with a certain place. *n* **locality** /ləʊˈkælətɪ/ a place. *vt* **localize** /ˈləʊkəlaɪz/ keep to a certain place.

locate /ləʊˈkeɪt/ *vt* find the place of. *n* **location** /ləʊˈkeɪʃən/ place.

loch /lɒk/ *n* lake in Scotland; narrow arm of the sea.

lock[1] /lɒk/ **a lock of hair** = a curl of hair; number of hairs hanging down together.

lock[2] /lɒk/ *n* enclosed place in a CANAL or river, used for moving boats to the upper or lower part of the stream.

lock[3] /lɒk/ *n* 1 instrument for fastening a door. 2 part of a gun. *vt* Fasten (something, e.g. a door) with a lock. *vi* become fixed or fastened, as with a lock. **to lock up** = 1 put (someone) into a locked room, as in a prison. 2 lock the door of (a house). 3 become fixed or united. **to lock up capital in** = put money into a business in such a way that one cannot get it back when one may need it. *n* **lockjaw** /'lɒkdʒɔ:/ disease in which the body becomes stiff and the mouth cannot be opened.

locker /'lɒkə/ *n* small box with a lock, fixed to the wall.

locket /'lɒkɪt/ *n* small box made of precious metal, worn round the neck, containing a picture or the hair of a loved one.

lockout /'lɒkaʊt/ *n* act of keeping workmen out of their place of work in a disagreement.

locksmith /'lɒksmɪθ/ *n* one who makes locks.

locomotive /ˌləʊkə'məʊtɪv/ *adj* having the power of moving from place to place. *n* engine of a train.

locum tenens /ˌləʊkəm 'ti:nənz/ *n* priest or doctor who during another's absence does his work.

locust /'ləʊkəst/ *n* a winged insect.

lode /ləʊd/ *n* line of natural metal in a rock.

lodestar /'ləʊdstɑ:/ *n* star by which a ship is guided. *n* **lodestone** /'ləʊdstəʊn/ stone which acts like a compass needle.

lodge /lɒdʒ/ *n* house for a shooting or hunting party; small house used by the gate-keeper of a great house. *vt* 1 put in a place. 2 take a person into one's house. *vi* 1 live in another's house on payment. 2 become fixed after being thrown. **to lodge a complaint** = make a complaint before a judge or officer. *n* **lodger** /'lɒdʒə/ paying guest. *n* **lodgings** /'lɒdʒɪŋz/ rooms for paying guests.

loft /lɒft/ *n* room at the top of a house.

lofty /'lɒftɪ/ *adj* 1 very high. 2 showing a very high opinion of oneself.

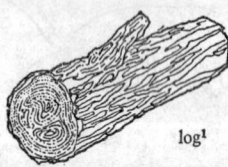

log[1]

log[1] /lɒg/ *n* rough unprepared piece of a tree.

log[2] /lɒg/ *n* instrument for measuring the speed of a boat.

logbook /'lɒgbʊk/ *n* book in which the events of a sea journey are written down each day by the captain.

logarithm /'lɒgərɪθəm/ *n* power to which a number must be raised in order to give another number.

loggerheads /'lɒgəhedz/ **at loggerheads (with)** = quarrelling (with).

logic /'lɒdʒɪk/ *n* art of reasoning. *adj* **logical** /'lɒdʒɪkəl/ 1 having to do with logic. 2 according to reason; able to reason well. *n* **logician** /lə'dʒɪʃən/ one who teaches logic.

logistics /lə'dʒɪstɪks/ *n* art of moving armies in war.

loin /lɔɪn/ *n* part of the body on either side just above the top of the legs.

loiter /'lɔɪtə/ *vi* waste time going to a place; stand about.

loll /lɒl/ *vi* sit or lie lazily.

lone /ləʊn/ *adj* alone; by oneself. *adj* **lonely** /'ləʊnlɪ/ feeling sad because alone. *n* **loneliness** /'ləʊnlɪnəs/.

long[1] /lɒŋ/ *adj* having length. *adv* greatly, e.g. *Long before that happens.*

long[2] /lɒŋ/ *vi* feel great desire. *n* **longing** /'lɒŋɪŋ/.

longevity /lɒn'dʒevətɪ/ *n* length of life.

longhand /'lɒŋhænd/ *n* the usual kind of handwriting (not SHORTHAND).

longitude /'lɒndʒɪtjuːd, 'lɒŋgɪ-/ *n* one of the imaginary lines drawn on the world (or lines drawn on a map) by means of which one can tell how far east or west a place is. *adj* **longitudinal** /ˌlɒndʒɪ'tjuːdməl/.

longshoreman /'lɒŋʃɔːmən/ *n* man who works on the shore.

long-suffering /ˌ. '. '. . ./ *adj* suffering without complaining.

long-winded /ˌlɒŋ 'wɪndɪd/ *adj* talking much, without expressing many ideas.

look /lʊk/ *vi* 1 turn the eyes towards something, e.g. *Look at that.* 2 seem in appearance to be, e.g. *It looked rather dull.* **to look after** = take care of. **to look down on** = have a low opinion of. **look forward to** = expect with pleasure. **to look for** = try to find. **to look in on** = visit. **to look into** = examine. **look out!** = be careful. *n* act of looking; appearance of the face.

looking-glass /'. . ,./ *n* mirror.

lookout /'lʊkaʊt/ *n* 1 place from which one watches. 2 watchman.

loom[1] /luːm/ *n* machine for making cloth.

loom[2] /luːm/ *vi* appear in an unclear form and larger than the real thing.

loop /luːp/ *n* line curved back upon itself; string so curved. *v* form or be formed in a loop.

loophole /'luːphəʊl/ *n* 1 narrow hole in a wall through which men shoot. 2 way of escaping e.g. the intended effects of a tax.

loose /luːs/ *adj* 1 free; uncontrolled. 2 not tight. 3 not controlled by rule or law. **at a loose end** = having nothing to do. *v* **loosen** /'luːsən/ make or become loose.

loot /luːt/ *n* goods taken from the enemy in time of war. *v* take (such goods).

lop /lɒp/ *vt* cut away (e.g. branches).

lopeared /ˌlɒp'ɪəd/ *adj* having the ears hanging down loosely.

lope /ləʊp/ *vi* move easily in long steps.

lopsided /ˌlɒp'saɪdɪd/ *adj* with one side lower than the other.

loquacious /lə'kweɪʃəs/ *adj* talking a lot. *n* **loquacity** /lə'kwæsətɪ/.

lord /lɔːd/ *n* 1 one ruling others. 2 owner. 3 God. 4 title of a nobleman. **our Lord** = Jesus Christ. *adj* **lordly** /'lɔːdlɪ/ proud; behaving like a lord. *n* **lordship** /'lɔːdʃɪp/ power or rule of a lord; state of being a lord. **your Lordship** = form of address for a lord.

lore /lɔː/ *n* learning; set of facts, esp. facts handed down by word of mouth.

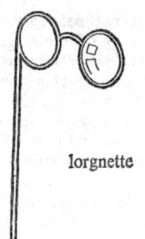

lorgnette

lounge suit

lorgnette /lɔːˈnjet/ *n* pair of eye-glasses with a handle.

lorry /ˈlɒrɪ/ *n* large motor vehicle used for carrying goods.

lose /luːz/ *vt* fail to keep; be unable to find. *v* not to win in (a game or fight).

loss /lɒs/ *n* act of losing; thing lost. **I am at a loss** = do not know what to do.

lost /lɒst/ p.t. and p.p. of **lose**.

lot[1] /lɒt/ *n* collection of things; large amount of.

lot[2] /lɒt/ *n* one of a set of objects used to decide something by chance. **to cast lots** = to decide by chance. **my lot** = my fate.

loth /ləʊθ/ see **loath**.

lotion /ˈləʊʃən/ *n* liquid for putting on the skin, on wounds, etc.

lottery /ˈlɒtərɪ/ *n* game of chance in which part of the money paid for TICKETS is given to the owner of one ticket chosen by chance.

lotus /ˈləʊtəs/ *n* plant (told of in stories) supposed, when eaten, to cause one to forget everything; a water-lily.

loud /laʊd/ *adj* making a lot of noise; easily heard; (of colours) bright; (of behaviour) noisy and rude. *n* **loudspeaker** /ˌlaʊdˈspiːkə/, ˈlaʊdˌspiːkə/ electrical instrument used to make sounds louder.

lounge /laʊndʒ/ *n* sitting-room with large comfortable chairs in it. *n* **lounge suit** /ˈ. ./ suit of clothes as usually worn by Europeans in the day.

lour, lower /ˈlaʊə/ *vi* look at a person as if one hated him.

louse /laʊs/ *pl* **lice** /laɪs/ *n* small insect which lives on the body or in the hair. *adj* **lousy** /ˈlaʊzɪ/ **1** having lice. **2** *infml* bad; worthless.

lout /laʊt/ *n* ungraceful fellow with bad manners.

love[1] /lʌv/ *n* feeling of great friendliness for; feeling of desire for. *vt* have such feelings for. **to fall in love** = begin to love a person.

love[2] /lʌv/ *n* (in a game) absence of points, e.g. *A is leading 2-love* = A has two points, B has none.

lovely /ˈlʌvlɪ/ *adj* beautiful; very nice; very good.

low[1] /ləʊ/ *adj* **1** not high. **2** (in music) deep. **3** sad.

low[2] /ləʊ/ *n, vi* (make) the noise of a cow.

lower[1] /ˈləʊə/ *vt* make less high; cause to descend. **to lower oneself** = behave in an unworthy way or without pride.

lower[2] /ˈlaʊə/ see **lour**.

lowland /ˈləʊlənd/ *n* area of flat country.

lowly /ˈləʊlɪ/ *adj* **1** not proud. **2** not of high birth.

loyal /ˈlɔɪəl/ *adj* faithful (e.g. to one's king). *n* **loyalty**.

lozenge /ˈlɒzɪndʒ/ *n* **1** four-sided figure. **2** medicine for the throat made in the form of a sweet.

lubricate /ˈluːbrɪkeɪt/ *vt* put oil onto (something) to make the movements of its parts better; to oil a machine. *n* **lubricant** /ˈluːbrɪkənt/ oil. *n* **lubrication** /ˌluːbrɪˈkeɪʃən/.

lucid /ˈluːsɪd/ *adj* clear; easily understood. *n* **lucidity** /luːˈsɪdətɪ/.

luck /lʌk/ *n* fortune, good or bad. *adj* **lucky** /ˈlʌkɪ/ having good luck. *adj* **luckless** /ˈlʌkləs/ having bad luck.

lucrative /ˈluːkrətɪv/ *adj* bringing in money or gain.

ludicrous /ˈluːdɪkrəs/ *adj* silly; making people laugh.

lug /lʌg/ *vt* pull along with difficulty.

luggage /ˈlʌgɪdʒ/ *n* boxes and bags of a traveller.

lugger /ˈlʌgə/ *n* small sailing-boat.

lugubrious /luːˈguːbrɪəs/ *adj* sad.

lukewarm /ˌluːkˈwɔːm/ *adj* slightly warm; not eager.

lull /lʌl/ *vt* calm with sounds; sing to sleep; make quiet. *n* short time of quiet in a storm or in pain.

lullaby /ˈlʌləbaɪ/ *n* song for sending a child to sleep.

lumbago /lʌmˈbeɪgəʊ/ *n* illness causing pain in the lower back.

lumbar /ˈlʌmbə/ *adj* having to do with the part of the body just above the top of the legs.

lumber[1] /ˈlʌmbə/ *vi* move heavily *n* (*sing*) useless things. **to lumber up** = fill with useless things.

lumber[2] /ˈlʌmbə/ *vi* cut down trees and prepare them for selling. *n* (*sing*) wood and trees so cut and prepared. *n* **lumberjack** /ˈlʌmbədʒæk/ man employed in this work.

luminary /ˈluːmɪnərɪ/ *n* **1** star. **2** person wellknown for learning.

luminous /ˈluːmɪnəs/ *adj* bright; giving light. *n* **luminosity** /ˌluːmɪˈnɒsətɪ/.

lump /lʌmp/ *n* shapeless mass; swelling. **a lump sum** = one amount of money to pay for various small things. **to lump together** = put (things) together in one mass or in one class.

lunar /ˈluːnə/ *adj* having to do with the moon.

lunatic /'lu:nətɪk/ n madman. n **lunacy** /'lu:nəsɪ/ madness.

lunch /lʌntʃ/, **luncheon** /'lʌntʃən/ n meal taken in the middle of the day.

lung /lʌŋ/ n one of the two parts of the body into which the air is drawn when we breathe.

lunge /lʌndʒ/ vi move forward as if pushing.

lurch[1] /lɜːtʃ/ **to leave in the lurch** = leave in difficulties.

lurch[2] /lɜːtʃ/ n sudden roll to one side. vi roll suddenly.

lure /lʊə/ vt draw a person on by promising gain or pleasure. n such a promised gain.

lurid /'lʊərɪd/ adj 1 looking like flames seen through smoke, white-yellow. 2 (e.g. of a story) unpleasant and frightening.

lurk /lɜːk/ vi lie in wait; lie hidden.

luscious /'lʌʃəs/ adj very sweet and pleasant to the taste; too sweet.

lush /lʌʃ/ adj (e.g. of grass) growing freely and very green.

lust /lʌst/ n strong desire, esp. sexual desire. vi feel such desire.

lustre /'lʌstə/ n brightness; glory.

lusty /'lʌstɪ/ adj young and strong.

lute /lu:t/ n musical instrument.

luxury /'lʌkʃərɪ/ n 1 possession and enjoyment of beautiful and costly things. 2 something enjoyable but not necessary. adj **luxurious** /lʌg'ʒʊərɪəs/ very comfortable. adj **luxuriant** /lʌg'ʒʊərɪənt/ (of plants) growing very freely.

lymph /lɪmf/ n colourless liquid in the body, like blood without any red material in it.

lynch /lɪntʃ/ vt (usually of a crowd) put a man to death without a lawful trial. n **lynch law** /'. ./ punishment by a crowd or group not according to the law.

lynx /lɪŋks/ n wild cat-like animal which has keen sight.

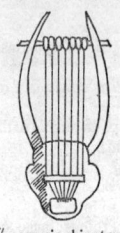

lyre

lyre /'laɪə/ n musical instrument with strings held in a D-shaped frame.

lyric /'lɪrɪk/ n words of a song. poem meant to be sung; short poem telling the poet's own thoughts and feelings. adj **lyrical** /'lɪrɪkəl/ adj (of a poem) short and personal.

M

M /em/ Roman figure, 1,000

ma'am /mɑːm/ shortened form of **madam**.

macadam /mə'kædəm/ n material made of broken stones which are rolled very flat, used for covering roads. adj **macadamized** /mə'kædəmaɪzd/ (of a road) covered with this material; road so made.

macaroni /ˌmækə'rəʊnɪ/ n dried flour and water formed into small pipes, made in Italy and other countries, boiled for food.

macaroon /ˌmækə'ruːn/ n small sweet cake made of eggs, sugar, and powdered nuts.

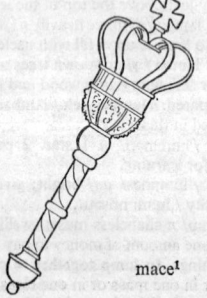

mace[1]

mace[1] /meɪs/ n stick with a metal head, formerly used as a weapon, now carried by an officer as a sign of his office.

mace[2] /meɪs/ n dried outer covering of NUTMEG, used for giving a pleasant taste to food.

machination /ˌmækɪ'neɪʃən/ n making of plans to do evil.

machine /mə'ʃiːn/ n instrument made up of several parts used to do work or to move itself or other things about. vt make or prepare with the help of a machine. n (sing) **machinery** /mə'ʃiːnərɪ/ parts of a machine; a set of machines. n **machinist** /mə'ʃiːnɪst/ n one who makes or works machines. n **machine-gun** /.'. ./ gun which shoots one shot after another without being loaded each time.

mackerel /'mækərəl/ n a sea fish with a blue and silver skin.

mackintosh /'mækɪntɒʃ/ n coat which keeps out the rain.

macro- /'mækrəʊ, 'mækrə/ large, long. n **macrocosm** /'mækrəkɒzəm/ = the great world—all the stars and heavenly bodies in the sky.

mad /mæd/ adj 1 having a disordered mind; very unwise. 2 very angry. n **madness** /'mædnəs/.

madam /'mædəm/ n form of address used by servants and shopkeepers in speaking to a lady.

madden /'mædn/ vt make very angry.

made /meɪd/ p.p. & p.t. of **make.**

mademoiselle /ˌmædəmwəˈzel/ n French title for an unmarried woman.

Madonna /məˈdɒnə/ n Mary, the Mother of Christ.

madrigal /ˈmædrɪɡəl/ n **1** short love-poem or song. **2** song for three or more voices.

maelstrom /ˈmeɪlstrəʊm/ n **1** part of the sea near Norway where the water turns round and round very quickly and draws ships down into it. **2** any great disorder, e.g. of the mind.

magazine[1] /ˌmæɡəˈziːn/ n storehouse for gun-powder and things used by soldiers; box-like part of a gun in which CARTRIDGES are kept ready for firing.

magazine[2] /ˌmæɡəˈziːn/ n book of stories, articles, etc., by different writers sold usually every month or every week.

magenta /məˈdʒentə/ n blue-red colouring matter obtained from coal. *adj, n* (of) this colour.

maggot /ˈmæɡət/ n small creature without legs, e.g. found in bad meat or food.

magic /ˈmædʒɪk/ n art of causing things to happen with the help of spirits and strange powers. *adj* **magical** /ˈmædʒɪkəl/ of magic; wonderful; done as if by magic. n **magician** /məˈdʒɪʃən/ one who works with magic.

magistrate /ˈmædʒɪstreɪt/ n judge; officer of government. *adj* **magisterial** /ˌmædʒɪˈstɪərɪəl/.

magnanimous /mæɡˈnænɪməs/ *adj* having a great soul, generous and high-thinking. n **magnanimity** /ˌmæɡnəˈnɪmətɪ/.

magnate /ˈmæɡneɪt/ n person who has much money and power.

magnesium /mæɡˈniːzɪəm/ n white metal which burns with a bright light. n **magnesia** /mæɡˈniːzɪə/ white powder made from magnesium, used as a medicine for the stomach.

magnet /ˈmæɡnɪt/ n piece of iron which draws to it other pieces of iron and, if hung up, always points north and south. *adj* **magnetic** /mæɡˈnetɪk/ acting as a magnet. n **magnetism** /ˈmæɡnɪtɪzəm/ power of a magnet; study of magnets; (in a person) charm and power of making others do what one wishes.

magneto /mæɡˈniːtəʊ/ n electric machine which sets fire to the gas in a car engine.

magnificent /mæɡˈnɪfɪsənt/ *adj* very fine; very good.

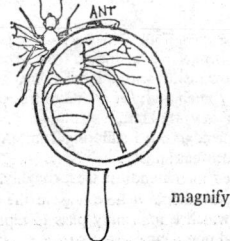

magnify

magnify /ˈmæɡnɪfaɪ/ *vt* make something seem larger, e.g. by looking at it through a curved glass. n **magnification** /ˌmæɡnɪfɪˈkeɪʃən/.

magniloquent /mæɡˈnɪləkwənt/ *adj* speaking in a foolishly solemn way.

magnitude /ˈmæɡnɪtjuːd/ n size; importance.

magpie /ˈmæɡpaɪ/ n a black and white bird which makes a lot of noise and steals small objects.

maharaja /ˌmɑːhəˈrɑːdʒə/ n great prince or king in India.

mahogany /məˈhɒɡənɪ/ n a red-brown wood.

maid /meɪd/ n **1** young unmarried woman. **2** woman servant. n **old maid** /ˌ. ˈ./ old unmarried woman.

maiden /ˈmeɪdn/ n young unmarried woman. n **maiden name** /ˈ.. ˌ./ woman's name before she was married. n **maiden voyage** /ˌ.. ˈ. ./ first journey made by a new ship.

mail[1] /meɪl/ n armour.

mail[2] /meɪl/ n letters, the general post. *vt* post (a letter).

maim /meɪm/ *vt* cause (someone) to lose the use of a limb.

main /meɪn/ *adj* chief; most important. n **mainland** /ˈmeɪnlənd/ large piece of land, not small islands near it. *adv* **mainly** /ˈmeɪnlɪ/ chiefly. n **mainspring** /ˈmeɪnˌsprɪŋ/ chief spring, e.g. of a clock; most important cause of an event or reason for action.

mainstay /ˈmeɪnsteɪ/ n chief support, e.g. of a family.

maintain /meɪnˈteɪn/ *vt* **1** support; pay the costs of. **2** hold (an opinion). n **maintenance** /ˈmeɪntənəns/ payment of the costs of.

maisonette /ˌmeɪzəˈnet/ n small house or part of a house used as a home for one family.

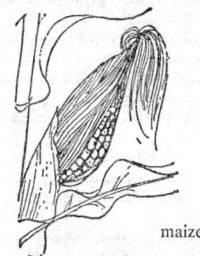

maize

maize /meɪz/ n Indian corn.

majesty /ˈmædʒəstɪ/ n honour and glory. **Your Majesty** = form of address for a king or queen. *adj* **majestic** /məˈdʒestɪk/ very fine and glorious.

major[1] /ˈmeɪdʒə/ *adj* most important; greater.

major[2] /ˈmeɪdʒə/ n rank in the army next above that of captain.

majority /məˈdʒɒrətɪ/ n the greater number; amount greater than a half.

make /meɪk/ *vt* **1** produce; build; lead to; create, e.g. *Making shoes; Make a noise.* **2** cause; cause to become, e.g. *He made me go; He made me unhappy.* **3** arrange the sheets etc. of (a bed) so that it is ready to sleep in. **to make for** = go towards. **to make off** = run away. **to make up** = **1** INVENT (e.g. a story). **2** put powder, etc., on (one's face). *n* kind (e.g. of car) made by one company. *n, adj* **make-believe** /'. .,./ (something) pretended. *v* /,. .'./ pretend. *n* **makeshift** /'meɪk,ʃɪft/ means or instrument used because the right one is not obtainable. *n* **make-up** /'meɪk ʌp/ powder and paint put on a woman's or actor's face. *n* **makeweight** /'meɪk-weɪt/ a little added to make something seem stronger or better.

mal- /mæl/ bad; badly, e.g. *adj* **malformed** /mæl'fɔːmd/ badly formed. *n, adj* **malcontent** /'mælkəntent/ not contented, discontented.

malachite /'mæləkaɪt/ *n* green stone used for ornament.

maladjusted /,mælə'dʒʌstɪd/ *adj* fitting badly.

malady /'mælədɪ/ *n* illness.

malaria /mə'leərɪə/ *n* illness caused by the bite of a MOSQUITO.

male /meɪl/ *adj, n* of the sex of a man; animal (which can become a father); (in a plant) having that power which makes seeds able to grow.

malediction /,mælɪ'dɪkʃən/ *n* speaking evil against a person.

malefactor /'mælɪfæktə/ *n* wrongdoer.

malevolence /mə'levələns/ *n* desire to do harm to others. *adj* **malevolent** /mə'levələnt/.

malformation /,mælfɔː'meɪʃən/ *n* bad shape of a part of the body.

malice /'mælɪs/ *n* desire to do harm to others. *adj* **malicious** /mə'lɪʃəs/ desiring to ——.

malign /mə'laɪn/ *vt* speak evil of. *adj* evil.

malignant /mə'lɪgnənt/ *adj* **1** feeling great hatred against. **2** (of a disease) getting worse, probably going to lead to death.

malinger /mə'lɪŋgə/ *vi* pretend to be ill.

mallard /'mæləd/ *n* a kind of wild duck.

malleable /'mælɪəbəl/ *adj* able to be shaped or beaten into a thin sheet.

mallet /'mælɪt/ *n* small hammer usually made of wood.

malnutrition /,mælnju:'trɪʃən/ *n* not getting enough (of the right) food.

malodorous /mæ'ləʊdərəs/ *adj* having a nasty smell.

malt /mɔːlt/ *n* grain which has begun to grow in water and is then dried and used for making strong drink.

maltreat /mæl'tri:t/ *vt* treat badly. *n* **maltreatment** /mæl'tri:tmənt/.

mammal /'mæməl/ *n* animal of the kind that feeds its young with its milk.

mammon /'mæmən/ *n* wealth—esp. as an evil.

mammoth /'mæməθ/ *n* animal like an elephant, but hairy, which lived many thousands of years ago. *adj* very large.

mammy-wagon /'mæmɪ ,wægən/ *West African n* LORRY with a roof, seats and open sides, used to carry people.

man /mæn/ *n* **1** human being. **2** male human being. **3** grown man, not a boy. **man of the world** = experienced person. **man in the street** = any man who has no special knowledge of the subject spoken of. **4** small piece of bone or wood used in a game. *vt* supply (e.g. guns, a ship) with men.

manacle /'mænəkəl/ *n, vt* (put on) iron bands and a chain for the hands of a prisoner.

manage /'mænɪdʒ/ *vt* **1** control; direct, e.g. *Manage a business.* **2** do successfully. *adj* **manageable** /'mænɪdʒəbəl/ able to be dealt with; not too difficult or too large. *n* **management** /'mænɪdʒmənt/ group of persons controlling a business. *n* **manager** /'mænɪdʒə/ man controlling a business. *n* **manageress** /,mænɪdʒə'res/ woman controlling a business. *adj* **managerial** /,mænɪ'dʒɪərɪəl/.

mandarin /'mændərɪn/ *n* **1** officer of the government in ancient China. **2** small orange.

mandate /'mændeɪt/ *n* **1** command. **2** power to act for another.

mandolin /'mændəlɪn, ,mændə'lɪn/ *n* musical instrument with strings.

mane /meɪn/ *n* long hair at the back of the neck of a horse or lion, etc.

manful /'mænfəl/ *adj* brave.

manganese /'mæŋgəni:z/ *n* a grey metal.

mange /meɪndʒ/ *n* skin disease, esp. of dogs and cats.

manger /'meɪndʒə/ *n* container, fixed to the wall, in which a horse's food is put.

mangle[1] /'mæŋgəl/ *n* machine used for pressing washed clothes to dry them. *vt* put through a mangle.

mangle[2] /'mæŋgəl/ *vt* cut and make useless.

mango

mango /'mæŋgəʊ/ *n* an Indian fruit, green outside, yellow inside, with a large stone.

mangrove /'mæŋgrəʊv/ *n* a kind of tree or bush found on very wet land.

mangy /'meɪndʒɪ/ *adj* **1** suffering from MANGE. **2** *infml* bad; weak; nasty.

manhandle /'mænhændl/ *vt* treat roughly.

manhole /'mænhəʊl/ *n* hole (e.g. in the street) through which a man may pass to repair underground pipes, etc.

mania /'meɪnɪə/ n 1 mental disorder in which there is great uncontrolled excitement. 2 great interest, e.g. *She has a mania for the theatre.* n **maniac** /'meɪnɪæk/ madman, esp. if dangerous. *adj* **maniacal** /mə'naɪəkəl/.

manicure /'mænɪkjʊə/ n treatment of the finger-nails and hands to make them beautiful.

manifest /'mænɪfest/ vt show or express clearly. *adj* clearly shown. n list of goods carried on a ship. n **manifestation** /ˌmænɪfe'steɪʃən/ n showing, e.g. *A manifestation of feeling.*

manifesto /ˌmænɪ'festəʊ/ n declaration of future plans made by a group of men, a ruler, etc.

manifold /'mænɪfəʊld/ adj many and various.

manilla /mə'nɪlə/ n 1 material of which rope is made. 2 strong brown paper.

manipulate /mə'nɪpjʊleɪt/ vt handle; deal with cleverly or dishonestly.

mankind /mæn'kaɪnd/ n race of man.

manly /'mænlɪ/ adj brave and noble.

manna /'mænə/ n food given by God to the people of Israel in the desert.

mannequin /'mænɪkɪn/ n 1 figure made of wax used to show clothes in a shop. 2 woman in a shop who puts on dresses to show a possible buyer what they look like when being worn.

manner /'mænə/ n 1 way in which a thing happens or is done. 2 way of speaking and behaving in public. **good manners** = polite behaviour. **to have no manners** = be impolite.

mannerism /'mænərɪzəm/ n action used too often by a person in his behaviour, speech, writing, etc.

mannish /'mænɪʃ/ adj like a man, e.g. *A very mannish woman.*

manoeuvre /mə'nuːvə/ v 1 move armies or ships of war. 2 arrange matters to suit one's own purposes. n **manoeuvres** movements of warships or armies for practice; tricks to obtain one's aims.

manor /'mænə/ n house and a certain amount of farm land held by an important landowner.

manse /mæns/ n house of a Scottish priest.

mansion /'mænʃən/ n large house, e.g. of a rich man.

manslaughter /'mænslɔːtə/ n unlawful killing of a person without meaning to kill him (or her).

mantelpiece /'mæntlpiːs/ n ornamental square built round and above the fire-place in a room. n **mantelshelf** /'mæntlʃelf/ flat place on top of the mantelpiece on which a clock and ornaments may be put.

mantle /'mæntl/ n loose outer garment; any covering. vt cover; spread over.

manual /'mænjʊəl/ adj done with the hands. n 1 short book on a special subject. 2 that part of an ORGAN which is played by the hands.

manufacture /ˌmænjʊ'fæktʃə/ vt make things in a factory.

manure /mə'njʊə/ n matter spread on the soil so as to give food to plants.

manuscript /'mænjʊskrɪpt/ n article or book written by hand and ready for printing.

many /'menɪ/ det, adj large number of.

map /mæp/ n flat plan of a country or of the world. vt make a map of.

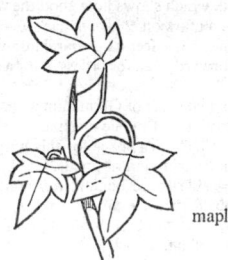

maple

maple /'meɪpəl/ n a kind of tree.

mar /mɑː/ vt make useless; ruin.

marathon /'mærəθən/ n a very long race (for men, not horses), e.g. 41·8 kilometres (26 miles).

maraud /mə'rɔːd/ vi make an attack so as to carry away money and goods. n **marauder** /mə'rɔːdə/.

marble /'mɑːbəl/ n 1 hard stone which is polished and used for buildings, graves, etc. 2 small stone or glass ball used by children in playing.

march /mɑːtʃ/ vi walk like a soldier. vt cause to march. n 1 act of marching; distance marched. 2 piece of music to which soldiers march.

March /mɑːtʃ/ n the third month of the year.

marchioness /'mɑːʃənəs/ n wife of a MARQUIS.

mare /meə/ n female horse. n **mare's nest** /ˌ. './ n wonderful discovery imagined, not real.

margarine /ˌmɑːdʒə'riːn, ˌmɑːgə'riːn/ n fat obtained from plants or animals and made to look and taste like butter.

margin /'mɑːdʒɪn/ n 1 border. 2 white part round a printed page. 3 further amount allowed beyond what is necessary.

marginal /'mɑːdʒɪnəl/ adj not important.

marijuana, marihuana /ˌmærɪ'hwɑːnə/ n plant sometimes put in cigarettes, which causes excitement and dreams.

marine /mə'riːn/ adj of the sea. n soldier serving on a ship. n **mariner** /'mærɪnə/ seaman.

marionette

marionette /ˌmærɪə'net/ n wooden figure moved by strings in a theatre.

marital /'mærɪtl/ adj having to do with a husband or marriage.

163

maritime /ˈmærɪtaɪm/ *adj* bordering on the sea.

mark[1] /mɑːk/ *n* **1** any sign or line made on a clean surface. **2** number on a piece of work, e.g. done by a child, which shows how good the work is. *vt* **1** make a mark on. **2** give a mark to. **to mark time** = move the feet as if marching, without moving forward; wait for orders or for a chance to act.

mark[2] /mɑːk/ *n* piece of German money.

market /ˈmɑːkɪt/ *n* **1** public meeting of people to buy and sell. **2** open space for this purpose. **3** trade in a certain kind of goods. *vt* sell. **on the market** = able to be bought. *adj* **marketable** /ˈmɑːkɪtəbəl/ such as can be sold. *n* **market-garden** /ˌ. . ˈ. ./ garden in which vegetables are grown for selling.

marksman /ˈmɑːksmən/ *n* man who shoots well.

marmalade /ˈmɑːməleɪd/ *n* (*sing*) oranges cut up and boiled in sugar.

maroon[1] /məˈruːn/ *n, adj* (of a) brown-red colour.

maroon[2] /məˈruːn/ *vt* leave (someone) on a desert island.

marquee /mɑːˈkiː/ *n* large tent, e.g. one in which tea is served at a public gathering in the open air.

marquis /ˈmɑːkwɪs/ *n* title of a nobleman, second below a prince.

marrow /ˈmærəʊ/ *n* **1** fat inside a bone. **2** large fruit which grows on the ground and is cooked for food.

marry /ˈmærɪ/ *vt* join as husband and wife. *v* take (someone) as husband or wife. *n* **marriage** /ˈmærɪdʒ/.

marsh /mɑːʃ/ *n* low-lying wet land.

marshal /ˈmɑːʃəl/ *n* high officer in the court of a king. *vt* **1** arrange in order. **2** lead solemnly.

marsupial /mɑːˈsuːpɪəl/ *n* animal which carries its young in a pocket, e.g. the KANGAROO.

mart /mɑːt/ *n* market-place.

martial /ˈmɑːʃəl/ *adj* having to do with war; warlike.

martin /ˈmɑːtɪn/ *n* a small bird.

martyr /ˈmɑːtə/ *n* one who is put to death for refusing to give up his faith; one who is in continuous suffering. *n* **martyrdom** /ˈmɑːtədəm/ *n* state of being a martyr.

marvel /ˈmɑːvəl/ *n* wonderful thing. *vi* wonder; find something surprising and worth admiring. *adj* **marvellous** /ˈmɑːvələs/ surprisingly good; wonderful.

marzipan /ˈmɑːzɪpæn/ *n* mixture of powdered nut, sugar and egg, often put on the top of a cake.

mascara /mæˈskɑːrə/ *n* dark paint used round the eyes to make them beautiful.

mascot /ˈmæskət/ *n* thing, person, or animal supposed to bring good fortune.

masculine /ˈmæskjʊlɪn/ *adj* **1** having to do with men, not women; strong. **2** (in language) of a word used for men.

mash /mæʃ/ *n* warm food for horses; any soft food. *vt* make into a soft wet mass.

mask /mɑːsk/ *n* small piece of cloth used to cover the upper half of the face; painted shape of an animal's face or strange human face used to hide one's real face; any covering or protection for the face. *vt* cover with a mask; hide.

masochism /ˈmæsəkɪzəm/ *n* taking pleasure (esp. sexual pleasure) in suffering pain.

mason /ˈmeɪsən/ *n* man who works with stone. *n* **masonry** /ˈmeɪsənrɪ/ stonework.

masquerade /ˌmæskəˈreɪd/ *n* dance at which MASKS are worn. *vi* pretend to be some other person; make a false appearance.

Mass /mæs/ *n* religious ceremony in the Church of Rome in which Christ's Last Supper is remembered.

mass /mæs/ *n* quantity of matter; number of separate things pressed together to make one solid body; large quantity. **the masses** = the common people.

massacre /ˈmæsəkə/ *n* a general killing of men, women and children. *vt* kill (someone) in a massacre.

massage /ˈmæsɑːʒ/ *n* rubbing of the body as a means of lessening pain or bringing back health to a certain part. *vt* give massage to. *n* **masseur** /mæˈsɜː/ man skilled in that art. *n* **masseuse** /mæˈsɜːz/ woman masseur.

massive /ˈmæsɪv/ *adj* having great size and weight.

mass production /ˌ. .ˈ. ./ *n* making very large numbers of things so that they may be produced cheaply.

mast

mast /mɑːst/ *n* upright pole in a ship to which the sails are fixed.

master /ˈmɑːstə/ *n* one who employs another; head of a house; owner; chief or leader; teacher; writer or painter of great fame. *vt* conquer; learn thoroughly. *adj* **masterful** /ˈmɑːstəfəl/ having a strong will; not listening to others.

master key /ˈ. . ./ *n* key which opens several locks.

masterly /ˈmɑːstəlɪ/ *adj* very cleverly done.

masterpiece /ˈmɑːstəpiːs/ *n* best piece of work done by a writer, painter, etc.

mastery /ˈmɑːstərɪ/ *n* thorough learning of a subject.

masticate /ˈmæstɪkeɪt/ *vt* bite thoroughly.

mastiff /ˈmæstɪf/ *n* a kind of large dog.

mat¹ /mæt/ *n* small floor covering; small piece of cloth or other material put under a flower-pot or plate.

mat², **matt** /mæt/ *adj* having a surface which is not shining.

matador /ˈmætədɔː/ʔ *n* man who kills the BULL in a bull-fight in Spain.

match¹ /mætʃ/ *n* small stick with a head used for making fire. *n (sing)* **matchwood** /ˈmætʃwʊd/ small sticks.

match² /mætʃ/ *n* **1** person or thing exactly like another. **2** one's equal in a game. **3** a game played between two persons or groups. **4** marriage. *v* look exactly like (something else); be suitable in appearance to go with (something else). *vt* get something like (something else) in appearance. *adj* **matchless** /ˈmætʃləs/ very good; without an equal.

matchet /ˈmætʃɪt/ *n* large heavy knife with a broad blade, used (e.g. in West Africa) for cutting plants and as a weapon.

matchmaker /ˈmætʃmeɪkə/ʔ *n* woman who interests herself in arranging marriages.

mate /meɪt/ *n* **1** fellow-worker. **2** husband or wife. **3** officer in rank next below the captain on a ship. *v* **1** marry. **2** (of animals) have sexual relations.

material /məˈtɪərɪəl/ *adj* **1** of matter, not of the spirit. **2** very important matter from which anything is made. **3** cloth. *n* **materialist** /məˈtɪərɪəlɪst/ **1** one who enjoys only material things. **2** one who believes that there is nothing except matter, no soul or spirit. *v* **materialize** /məˈtɪərɪəlaɪz/ make or become real. *adv* **materially** /məˈtɪərɪəlɪ/ actually; very much.

maternal /məˈtɜːnəl/ *adj* like or having to do with a mother. *n* **maternity** /məˈtɜːnətɪ/ having to do with being a mother.

mathematics /ˌmæθəˈmætɪks/ *n* science of space and numbers. *adj* **mathematical** /ˌmæθəˈmætɪkəl/. *n* **mathematician** /ˌmæθəməˈtɪʃən/ one who studies mathematics.

matinee /ˈmætɪneɪ/ *n* morning or afternoon show in a theatre.

matricide /ˈmætrɪsaɪd/ *n* **1** one who kills his mother. **2** act of killing one's mother.

matriculate /məˈtrɪkjʊleɪt/ *vi* enter into a university; pass an examination. *n* **matriculation** /məˌtrɪkjʊˈleɪʃən/.

matrimony /ˈmætrɪmənɪ/ *n* marriage. *adj* **matrimonial** /ˌmætrɪˈməʊnɪəl/.

matrix /ˈmeɪtrɪks/ *n (pl* **matrices** /ˈmeɪtrɪsiːz/) shape into which hot metal is poured.

matron /ˈmeɪtrən/ *n* **1** woman in charge of the food and housework in a school. **2** woman in charge of the nurses and nursing in a hospital.

matted /ˈmætɪd/ *adj* twisted together, e.g. *Matted hair* = disordered hair twisted together into a mass.

matter /ˈmætə/ʔ *vi* be important. *n* **1** that of which all things are made. **2** subject being talked about; ideas of a book or speech. **as a matter of**

fact = actually. **a matter of course** = something expected; a natural result. **what's the matter?** = what is troubling you? **printed matter** = printed books and papers. *adj* **matter-of-fact** /ˌ. . . ˈ./ keeping to real things; not imagining things.

matting /ˈmætɪŋ/ *n* floor-covering made of dried stems of plants or other rough vegetable material.

mattock /ˈmætək/ *n* instrument used for breaking up ground.

mattress /ˈmætrəs/ *n* large flat bag of hair or other soft material laid on a bed.

mature /məˈtʃʊə/ʔ *adj* fully grown; made perfect; ready for use; carefully thought out. *v* make or become mature.

maudlin /ˈmɔːdlɪn/ *adj* full of weak and silly feeling.

maul /mɔːl/ *vt* beat; treat roughly.

mausoleum /ˌmɔːzəˈlɪəm/ *n* beautiful building used as a grave.

mauve /məʊv/ *n, adj* (of a) light red-blue colour.

mawkish /ˈmɔːkɪʃ/ *adj* having a nasty rather sweet taste; (of a book, play, etc.) full of weak and silly feeling.

maxim /ˈmæksɪm/ *n* short saying expressing a general truth; rule of behaviour.

maximum /ˈmæksɪməm/ *n, adj* greatest possible size, number, quality, etc. *vt* **maximize** /ˈmæksɪmaɪz/ make (something) as great as possible.

may /meɪ/ *v* **1** be permitted to, e.g. *May we walk on the grass?* **2** might, e.g. *He may have already arrived* = It is possible that he has already arrived.

May /meɪ/ *n* the fifth month of the year.

maybe /ˈmeɪbiː/ *adv* possibly; perhaps.

mayonnaise /ˌmeɪəˈneɪz/ *n* thick yellow liquid put on fish and uncooked green vegetables.

mayor /meə/ʔ *n* chief officer of a town or city.

maypole /ˈmeɪpəʊl/ *n* high post ornamented with flowers round which people dance.

maze /meɪz/ *n* LABYRINTH.

me /miː/ *pron* (form of I used after verbs and prepositions).

mead¹ /miːd/ *n* strong drink made from HONEY.

mead² /miːd/, **meadow** /ˈmedəʊ/ grassy field.

meagre /ˈmiːgə/ʔ *adj* thin; not enough.

meal¹ /miːl/ *n* powdered grain used for food.

meal² /miːl/ *n* time when food is taken; food taken.

mean¹ /miːn/ *adj* low, bad, unkind, or dishonest in small ways; too careful with money.

mean² /miːn/ *n* amount or state just half-way between two quantities or qualities, neither very great nor small, good nor bad.

mean³ /miːn/ *vt* **1** intend, e.g. *I didn't mean to do that.* **2** have an aim or purpose in mind. **3** (of a word or group of words) express a certain idea, e.g. *The Latin word "homo" means "a man".* **4** be important, e.g. *This work means a lot to me.* *n* **meaning** /ˈmiːnɪŋ/ **1** idea expressed by a word or group of words. **2** purpose, reason.

meander

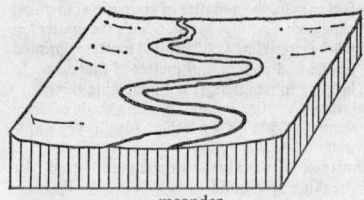

meander

meander /mɪˈændə/ *vi* (of a river) flow along a very wandering course.

means /miːnz/ *n* (*sing* or *pl*) **1** that by which something is done. **2** money; being able to pay, e.g. *To live within one's means* = not spend more money than one has. **a man of means** = a rich man. **means test** = asking how much money a person is getting before giving help (money, a cheap house, etc.) from the government.

meantime /ˈmiːntaɪm/, **meanwhile** /ˈmiːnwaɪl/ in the time between two events; at the same time.

measles /ˈmiːzəlz/ *n* disease which spreads from one person to another, causing red spots on the skin and liquid running from the eyes and nose.

measly /ˈmiːzlɪ/ *adj* poor and of no value.

measure /ˈmeʒə/ *n* **1** size, weight, or amount expressed as metres/feet, grams/pounds, etc. **2** instrument used for measuring; way of measuring, e.g. *An inch is a measure of length.* **3** regular beat of poetry or music. **4** the plan of a law being considered by the government. **5** action, e.g. *To take measures against wrongdoers* = do something to stop wrongdoing. *vt* judge the amount, size, weight, etc., of. *adj* **measured** /ˈmeʒəd/ slow and steady. *adj* **measureless** /ˈmeʒələs/ so large or great that it cannot be measured. *n* **measurement** /ˈmeʒəmənt/ act of measuring; amount measured.

meat /miːt/ *n* part of the body of an animal used as food.

mechanic /mɪˈkænɪk/ *n* one employed in working machines *adj* **mechanical** /mɪˈkænɪkəl/ having to do with machines, done by machines; behaving like a machine, acting in the same way again and again without thought. *n* **mechanism** /ˈmekənɪzəm/ piece of machinery. *vt* **mechanize** /ˈmekənaɪz/ make mechanical. *n* **mechanization** /ˌmekənaɪˈzeɪʃən/.

medal /ˈmedl/ *n* piece of metal with a picture and writing cut or pressed upon it, given as an honour, e.g. to a soldier. *n* **medallion** /mɪˈdælɪən/ round piece of stone or metal with a picture on it.

meddle /ˈmedl/ *vi* busy oneself with the concerns of other people. *adj* **meddlesome** /ˈmedlsəm/ always concerning oneself with other people's business.

media /ˈmiːdɪə/ *pl* of **medium. the media** = means of giving information, e.g. newspapers, radio, television.

mediate /ˈmiːdɪeɪt/ *vi* make peace between two people; settle a quarrel. *n* **mediation** /ˌmiːdɪˈeɪʃən/.

medical /ˈmedɪkəl/ *adj* having to do with the treatment of the sick, the work of doctors, etc.

medicated /ˈmedɪkeɪtɪd/ *adj* having medicine added, e.g. *Medicated wool.* *n* **medicament** /mɪˈdɪkəmənt/ form of medicine.

medicine /ˈmedsən/ *n* **1** science and art of bringing sick persons back to health. **2** substance used for this purpose. **a medicine man** = one who does magic. *adj* **medicinal** /mɪˈdɪsɪnəl/.

medieval, mediaeval /ˌmedɪˈiːvəl/ *adj* having to do with the MIDDLE AGES.

mediocre /ˌmiːdɪˈəʊkə/ *adj* not very good. *n* **mediocrity** /ˌmiːdɪˈɒkrətɪ/.

meditate /ˈmedɪteɪt/ *vi* think deeply. *n* **meditation** /ˌmedɪˈteɪʃən/.

medium /ˈmiːdɪəm/ *adj* at a level in between the highest and the lowest; middle. *n* **1** means by which a thing is done. **2** person supposed to be able to receive messages from the spirits of the dead. **3** that place in which a creature can live, e.g. *Fish live in a watery medium.* **4** material used in painting or drawing.

medley /ˈmedlɪ/ *n* mixture; mixed piece of music.

meek /miːk/ *adj* gentle; not proud.

meet /miːt/ *v* **1** come together from opposite directions; come face to face (with). **2** pay a debt. **to make both ends meet** = make one's cost of living no greater than the money one has. **to meet with trouble** = suffer. *n* gathering of dogs and men for a hunt. *n* **meeting** /ˈmiːtɪŋ/ coming together of persons for some special purpose.

megalomania /ˌmegələˈmeɪnɪə/ *n* mad desire for greatness; mad idea that one is great.

megaphone /ˈmegəfəʊn/ *n* metal horn used to make the voice louder.

melancholy /ˈmelənkəlɪ/ *n, adj* (experiencing) a long-lasting feeling of sadness.

mêlée /ˈmeleɪ/ *n* mixed-up fight, in which all seem to be fighting against each other.

mellifluous /mɪˈlɪflʊəs/ *adj* smooth and sweet.

mellow /ˈmeləʊ/ *adj* made soft, sweet or gentle by time.

melodious /mɪˈləʊdɪəs/ *adj* sweet sounding.

melodrama /ˈmelədrɑːmə/ *n* play, full of exciting events, which ends happily. *adj* **melodramatic** /ˌmelədrəˈmætɪk/.

melody /ˈmelədɪ/ *n* set of notes, one after another, which makes a pleasing piece of music.

melon

melon /ˈmelən/ *n* large sweet fruit which grows on the ground and has a very watery inside.

melt /melt/ v make or become liquid by heat. **to melt away** = disappear.

member /'membə / n 1 limb. 2 one of a group. n **membership** /'membəʃɪp/.

membrane /'membreɪn/ n thin covering of skin inside the body; any thin film.

memento /mə'mentəʊ/ n that which helps one to remember an event.

memo /'meməʊ/ n note to help the memory.

memoir /'memwɑ: / n written account of events. n (pl) **memoirs** story of interesting events and experiences remembered in one's life.

memorable /'memərəbəl/ adj worth remembering; easily remembered.

memorandum /ˌmemə'rændəm/ n note to help the memory; report.

memorial /mə'mɔːrɪəl/ n thing used to cause persons to remember, e.g. stone put up in honour of the dead.

memorize /'meməraɪz/ vt fix in the memory.

memory /'memərɪ/ n 1 power of remembering. 2 something remembered. **in memory of** = intended to cause people to remember.

menace /'menɪs/ n probable danger. vt say that one will do harm to (someone).

menagerie /mə'nædʒərɪ/ n collection of wild animals kept for show.

mend /mend/ vt repair; put right. vi become better in health.

mendacious /men'deɪʃəs/ adj untruthful.

mendicant /'mendɪkənt/ n person who begs for money.

menial /'miːnɪəl/ adj having to do with a servant in a house; (work) such as a servant does.

menopause /'menəpɔːz/ n time of bodily changes in a woman after which she can no longer have children.

menstruation /ˌmenstrʊ'eɪʃən/ n monthly loss of blood from a woman's WOMB. adj **menstrual** /'menstrʊəl/.

mensuration /ˌmensjʊ'reɪʃən/ n science and art of measuring or of calculating length and size.

mental /'mentl/ adj having to do with the mind. n **mentality** /men'tæləti/ n kind of mind, e.g. A soldier's mentality.

mention /'menʃən/ vt speak of. n act of mentioning.

mentor /'mentɔː / n trusted adviser.

menu /'menjuː/ n list of foods which will be served at a meal.

mercantile /'mɜːkəntaɪl/ adj having to do with trade; employed in trade.

mercenary /'mɜːsənərɪ/ adj eager for money; working only for money, not for honour, or loyalty. n hired soldier.

merchandise /'mɜːtʃəndaɪz/ n (sing) goods bought and sold.

merchant /'mɜːtʃənt/ n one who carries on trade in a large way. **the merchant service** = ships that carry travellers and goods. n **merchantman** /'mɜːtʃəntmən/ ship which carries goods and sometimes travellers.

merciful /'mɜːsɪfəl/ adj showing mercy.

merciless /'mɜːsɪləs/ adj showing no mercy.

mercurial /mɜː'kjʊərɪəl/ adj quickly changing in mind and feelings.

mercury /'mɜːkjʊrɪ/ n a liquid white metal.

mercy /'mɜːsɪ/ n gentleness; pity; forgiveness. **at the mercy of** = in the power of.

mere /mɪə / adj being only; not more than, e.g. A mere child. adv **merely** only.

meretricious /ˌmerə'trɪʃəs/ adj making an outward but unreal show of beauty or goodness.

merge /mɜːdʒ/ v join completely. n **merger** /'mɜːdʒə / n uniting of several business companies.

meridian /mə'rɪdɪən/ n 1 imaginary line drawn on the earth from north to south; such a line on a map. 2 twelve o'clock, or the middle of the day. 3 highest point reached by a star; time of greatest power or success.

meringue /mə'ræŋ/ n mixture of egg and sugar baked into a light cake.

merino /mə'riːnəʊ/ n a kind of sheep; soft cloth made from its wool.

merit /'merɪt/ vt be worthy of. n that of which one is worthy. adj **meritorious** /ˌmerɪ'tɔːrɪəs/ good; worthy.

mermaid

mermaid /'mɜːmeɪd/ n imaginary sea creature, half woman and half fish. n **merman** /'mɜːmən/ half man and half fish.

merry /'merɪ/ adj full of happiness; gay. n **merriment** /'merɪmənt/.

merry-go-round /'. . . ˌ./ n machine having seats made in the shape of animals, on which people are carried round in a circle as an amusement.

mesh /meʃ/ n one of the open spaces of a net; vi (of a wheel) fit with another wheel so as to move it.

mess[1] /mes/ n state of dirt and disorder. vt make dirty. infml **to mess about** = move about in a lazy way, not doing any real work. **to mess up** = ruin; make a mess in. **to make a mess of** = do (something) very unsuccessfully. adj **messy** /'mesɪ/.

mess[2] /mes/ n meals served to a group of soldiers.

message /'mesɪdʒ/ n news or orders sent by letter or word of mouth. n **messenger** /'mesəndʒə / one who carries a message.

Messiah /mə'saɪə/ n expected deliverer of the Jews; Jesus Christ; any hoped-for deliverer.

Messrs /'mesəz/ *pl* of **Mr**, e.g. *Messrs Smith and Jones* = Mr Smith and Mr Jones.

met /met/ *p.p. & p.t.* of **meet**.

metabolism /mɪ'tæbəlɪzəm/ *n* complete change, e.g. building up of food into the body.

metal /'metl/ *n, adj* (made of) a certain kind of substance, such as gold, iron, etc. *adj* **metallic** /mɪ'tælɪk/.

metallurgy /mɪ'tælədʒɪ/ *n* art of making metals pure.

metamorphosis /ˌmetə'mɔːfəsɪs, ˌmetəmɔː'fəʊsɪs/ *n* change of shape or character.

metaphor /'metəfə/ *n* way of stretching the meaning of a word and using it to express an idea different from its own usual meaning, e.g. The sea—A sea of troubles. *adj* **metaphorical** /ˌmetə'forɪkəl/.

metaphysics /ˌmetə'fɪzɪks/ *n* study of the beginning of everything, of the character and cause of life, the nature of God etc. *adj* **metaphysical** /ˌmetə'fɪzɪkəl/.

mete /miːt/ *vt* measure out, e.g. *To mete out punishment*.

meteor /'miːtɪə/ *n* shining mass which appears for a short time in the sky.

meteorology /ˌmiːtɪə'rolədʒɪ/ *n* scientific study of the weather, and telling what future weather will be. *adj* **meteorological** /ˌmiːtɪərə'lɒdʒɪkəl/.

meter

meter /'miːtə/ *n* instrument for measuring, e.g. electricity.

method /'meθəd/ *n* way of doing something; regular arrangement. *adj* **methodical** /mɪ'θɒdɪkəl/ careful in arranging things properly.

Methodist /'meθədɪst/ *n* member of a group of Christian people following the teaching and practice of John Wesley.

methylated spirits /ˌmeθəleɪtɪd 'spɪrɪts/ *n* ALCOHOL made unfit for drinking, used for burning in lamps to produce heat.

meticulous /mə'tɪkjʊləs/ *adj* very careful about small things.

metre¹ /'miːtə/ *n* regular arrangement of sounds in poetry. *adj* **metrical** /'metrɪkəl/.

metre² /'miːtə/ *n* measure = 39.37 inches. *adj* **metric** /'metrɪk/.

metropolis /mə'trɒpəlɪs/ *n* chief city of a country. *adj* **metropolitan** /ˌmetrə'pɒlɪtən/.

mettle /'metl/ *n* courage; high spirits.

mew /mjuː/ *vi* cry like a cat.

mews /mjuːz/ *n* line of small houses for horses and carriages; such a line of houses changed so that people may live in them.

miaow /mɪ'aʊ/ *n, interj* cry of a cat.

miasma /mɪ'æzmə/ *n* harmful mist.

mica /'maɪkə/ *n* material found in the ground which looks like glass, easily broken into very thin leaves or sheets.

mice /maɪs/ *pl* of **mouse**.

micro-/'maɪkrəʊ, 'maɪkrə/ small.

microbe /'maɪkrəʊb/ *n* very small living thing, esp. one causing disease.

microcosm /'maɪkrəkɒzəm/ *n* a small world which shows the arrangement and nature of a large world, e.g. an ant-hill—of a city.

micrometer /maɪ'krɒmɪtə/ *n* instrument used for measuring very small distances.

microphone

microphone /'maɪkrəfəʊn/ *n* instrument used for changing sound-waves into electric waves, or for making sounds louder.

microscope /'maɪkrəskəʊp/ *n* instrument by which very small things can be seen. *adj* **microscopic** /ˌmaɪkrə'skɒpɪk/ very small.

mid- /mɪd/ the middle of, e.g. *Midday*.

middle /'mɪdl/ *n* centre; equal distance between two points. **middle age** = middle part of life, age 40 to 60. **the Middle Ages** = A.D. 500 to A.D. 1500. **middle class** = not noblemen, not common working men, but those in between, e.g. shopkeepers, doctors, teachers, etc.

middleman /'mɪdlmæn/ *n* trader who buys goods in large quantities from the maker, and sells in smaller quantities to shops.

middling /'mɪdlɪŋ/ *adj* **1** of middle size. **2** not good, nor bad.

midge /mɪdʒ/ *n* a very small winged insect which bites.

midget /'mɪdʒɪt/ *n* very small person.

midnight /'mɪdnaɪt/ *n* twelve o'clock in the middle of the night.

midriff /'mɪdrɪf/ *n* wall of muscle separating the stomach from the LUNGS.

midshipman /'mɪdʃɪpmən/ *n* young man learning to be a ship's officer in the NAVY.

midst /'mɪdst/ *n* middle.

midwife /'mɪdwaɪf/ *n* woman who helps women in childbirth.

mien /miːn/ *n* person's appearance and behaviour.

might¹ /maɪt/ *v* could possibly, e.g. *I might be late* = It is possible that I shall be late.

might² /maɪt/ *n* power, strength.

migraine /'mi:grein/ *n* very bad pain in the head.
migrate /mai'greit/ *vi* move from one place to another, e.g. to leave one's own country and go to live in another—as birds do in winter. *n* **migrant** /'maigrənt/ one who migrates. *n* **migration** /mai'greiʃən/.
mike /maik/ *infml* short for **microphone.**
mild /maild/ *adj* gentle; calm; not strong.
mildew /'mildju:/ *n* sort of plant which grows on wet things, e.g. on leather, books, clothes.
mile /mail/ *n* measure of length, 1760 yards or 1·609 kilometres.
mileage /'mailidʒ/ *n* number of miles travelled.
milestone /'mailstəun/ *n* **1** stone by the side of the road showing how far away a place is. **2** important event.
militant /'militənt/ *adj* using force; fighting. *n* **militarist** /'militərist/ one who believes in war. *adj* **military** /'militəri/ having to do with soldiers and war. *vi* **militate** /'militeit/ act (against); be a reason (against). *n* **militia** /mi'liʃə/ members of a nation who are trained as soldiers to be called on when needed to defend their country.
milk /milk/ *n* white liquid on which animals feed their young. *v* get milk from (an animal). *adj* **milky** /'milki/. *n* **milkman** /'milkmən/ man who brings milk round to houses for people to buy.
milktooth /'milktu:θ/ *n* one of the first set of teeth of a child.
Milky Way /ˌ. '. './ *n* broad band of light across the sky made up of countless stars.
mill /mil/ *n* machinery for making grain into flour; building containing this; machines used in making goods; building in which goods are made. *v* cut lines, e.g. on the edge of a coin.
millennium /mi'leniəm/ *n* **1** one thousand years. **2** the thousand years during which Christians thought that Christ would rule on earth; a time of great happiness.
millepede, millipede /'milipi:d/ *n* small creature with many legs.
miller /'milə / *n* one who owns or works in a flour mill.
millet /'milit/ *n* a grain-bearing grass.
milli- /'mili/ one thousandth part of, e.g. *n* **milligram(me)** /'miligræm/ = 1/1000th part of a gram.
milliner /'milinə / *n* one who makes or sells women's hats and other small articles of women's dress. *n* **millinery** /'milinri/ things sold by a milliner.
million /'miliən/ *n* number often written 1,000,000, being a thousand times a thousand. *n* **millionaire** /ˌmiliə'neə / one who has a million pounds or dollars; a very rich man.
millstone /'milstəun/ *n* round stone used for pressing grain into flour.
mime /maim/ *n, vi* (act in a) kind of play, acted by dancing, with little or no speaking.
mimic /'mimik/ *vt* copy another person's behaviour or voice in order that he may be

laughed at. *n* one who does this. *n* **mimicry** /'mimikri/.
mimosa /mi'məuzə/ *n* tree with sweet-smelling flowers which grows in warm countries.

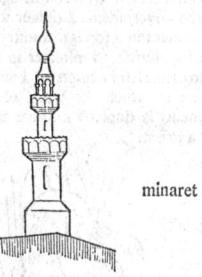

minaret

minaret /ˌminə'ret/ *n* tower of a MOSQUE.
mince /mins/ *vt* cut (esp. meat) into very small pieces. *vi* **1** speak in a silly unnatural way. **2** walk with short steps in a foolish manner. *n* **mincemeat** /'minsmi:t/ mixture of dried fruits, fat, sugar, flour, etc. *n* **mince-pie** /ˌ. './ pastry container with mincemeat in it.
mind¹ /maind/ *n* **1** memory. **to call to mind** = remember. **2** thought, not matter; power of thinking. **to be out of one's mind** = mad. **have something on one's mind** = be anxious about something. **presence of mind** = power of deciding quickly when one is in danger. **to make up one's mind** = decide.
mind² /maind/ *vt* **1** attend to, e.g. *Mind your own business* = do not try to take part in matters that do not concern you; *Mind the step* = be careful not to fall over the step; *Mind one's ps and qs* = be careful of what one says. **2** dislike, e.g. *Do you mind my smoking?* = will it displease you if I smoke? **3** take care of, be in charge of, e.g. *Mind the children*. *infml* **mind out!** = be careful. **never mind** = it does not matter. *adj* **mindful** /'maindfəl/ careful. *adj* **mindless** /'maindləs/ foolish.
mine¹ /main/ *pron* something belonging to me.
mine² /main/ *n* deep hole from which coal, metals, etc., are obtained. *vt* dig for (something) in a mine. *n* **miner** /'mainə / one who works in a mine.
mine³ /main/ *n* box of explosive material placed in the sea or under the ground in order to destroy an enemy.
mineral /'minərəl/ *n* non-living material found in the body of the earth, such as copper, gold, etc. *n* **mineral water** /'... ˌ. ./ sweet drink bottled with gas.
mingle /'miŋgəl/ *vi* mix.
mini /'mini/ *adj, n* very small (thing).
miniature /'minitʃə / *n* very small picture of a person; any very small thing.
minimize /'minimaiz/ *vt* make a thing unimportant; make seem small.

minimum /'mɪnɪməm/ *n, adj* smallest possible size or quantity. *adj* **minimal** /'mɪnɪməl/.

minion /'mɪnɪən/ *n* one who serves another like a slave and is treated with great favour.

minister /'mɪnɪstə/ *n* **1** person in charge of one part of the government. **2** officer who acts for his government in a foreign country. **3** priest in charge of a church. **to minister to** = serve; be helpful to. *n* **ministry** /'mɪnɪstrɪ/ **1** act of serving. **2** building in which the work of a minister (government) is done. **3** number of priests. **4** work of a priest.

mink

mink /mɪŋk/ *n* animal valued for its fur.

minnow /'mɪnəʊ/ *n* very small freshwater fish.

minor /'maɪnə/ *adj* not important; smaller. *n* someone under the age of 18 (or 21). *n* **minority** /maɪ'nɒrətɪ, mɪ-/ smaller number in a group or meeting, holding opinions different from those of the rest.

minster /'mɪnstə/ *n* large and important church used, or formerly used, by religious men living apart, giving their lives to God.

minstrel /'mɪnstrəl/ *n* wandering singer in ancient days.

mint[1] /mɪnt/ *n* place where money is made from metal. *vt* make (money) out of metal.

mint[2] /mɪnt/ *n* a plant whose leaves are used to give a pleasant taste to sweets and food.

minuet /ˌmɪnjʊ'et/ *n* slow, graceful dance; music for this.

minus /'maɪnəs/ *prep* less, e.g. *3 minus 1 = 2.*

minute[1] /'mɪnɪt/ *n* 1/60 of an hour. *n (pl)* **minutes** written account of opinions expressed and things decided in a meeting.

minute[2] /maɪ'njuːt/ *adj* very small.

minx /mɪŋks/ *n* rather rude and daring girl.

miracle /'mɪrəkəl/ *n* wonderful event not according to the laws of nature. *adj* **miraculous** /mɪ'rækjʊləs/.

mirage /'mɪrɑːʒ/ *n* false appearance of trees, lakes, etc., seen in the sky over a hot desert.

mire /maɪə/ *n* wet ground; mud.

mirror /'mɪrə/ *n* glass in which one can see one's face.

mirth /mɜːθ/ *n* joy and laughing.

mis- /mɪs/ wrongly, badly, unfortunately.

misadventure /ˌmɪsəd'ventʃə/ *n* unfortunate event.

misanthrope /'mɪzənθrəʊp/ *n* one who hates all men. *adj* **misanthropic** /ˌmɪzən'θrɒpɪk/.

misbehave /ˌmɪsbɪ'heɪv/ *vi* behave badly.

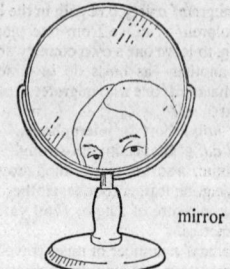

mirror

miscarriage /'mɪskærɪdʒ/ *n* **1** failure to complete successfully. **2** birth of a baby before it is old enough to live outside the mother. **a miscarriage of justice** = wrong judgment.

miscarry /mɪs'kærɪ/ *vi* **1** go wrong. **2** (of a woman) have a MISCARRIAGE.

miscellaneous /ˌmɪsə'leɪnɪəs/ *adj* of various kinds mixed together.

mischief /'mɪstʃɪf/ *n* damage; harm done on purpose, not by accident. **the children are up to mischief** = they are planning some wrongdoing. *adj* **mischievous** /'mɪstʃɪvəs/ causing trouble; trying to cause trouble; (of children) playful.

misconceive /ˌmɪskən'siːv/ *vt* judge wrongly. *n* **misconception** /ˌmɪskən'sepʃən/.

misconstrue /ˌmɪskən'struː/ *vt* understand wrongly.

miscreant /'mɪskrɪənt/ *n* evil-doer.

misdeal /mɪs'diːl/ *vt* give out (playing-cards) wrongly so that one player gets less or more than the proper number.

misdemeanour /ˌmɪsdɪ'miːnə/ *n* unlawful act of a not very serious nature.

miser /'maɪzə/ *n* one who saves and loves money.

miserable /'mɪzərəbəl/ *adj* **1** very unhappy. **2** pitiable; bad. *n* **misery** /'mɪzərɪ/ one who is miserable; state of great unhappiness.

misfire /mɪs'faɪə/ *vi* **1** (of a gun) fail to shoot. **2** (of a plan) go wrong.

misfit /'mɪs.fɪt/ *n* one who cannot fit in socially with others.

misfortune /mɪs'fɔːtʃən/ *n* (piece of) bad fortune.

misgiving /mɪs'gɪvɪŋ/ *n* feeling of doubt and fear.

misguided /mɪs'gaɪdɪd/ *adj* led by others into wrong.

mishap /'mɪshæp/ *n* unfortunate event.

mislay /mɪs'leɪ/ *vt* put in a wrong place and be unable to find.

mislead /mɪs'liːd/ *vt* give (someone) a wrong idea.

misnomer /mɪs'nəʊmə/ *n* name which is not suitable.

misplace /mɪs'pleɪs/ *vt* **1** put (something) in the wrong place. **2** lose.

misprint /'mɪs.prɪnt/ *n* mistake in printing.

miss[1] /mɪs/ *v* fail to hit; fail to catch a ball; fail to get what one wants. **it just missed being a great success** = was nearly but not quite. **I was sorry**

to miss you = sorry that I did not meet you. **to miss out a word** = not say, not write. **we shall miss you very much** = feel sad at your absence. *sl* **to give a person a miss** = try not to meet, escape from.

miss² /mɪs/ *n* form of address for an unmarried woman or girl.

missile /'mɪsaɪl/ *n* **1** thing which is thrown in order to wound or do damage. **2** ROCKET which explodes when it hits something, used as a weapon.

mission /'mɪʃən/ *n* **1** sending or being sent on some service. **2** group of persons so sent. **3** group of persons teaching about God in a foreign land. *n* **missionary** /'mɪʃənrɪ/ person sent to teach about God in a foreign land.

missive /'mɪsɪv/ *n* letter or message.

misspent /mɪs'spent/ *adj* wasted.

mist /mɪst/ *n* cloud close to the ground; rain in very small drops.

mistake /mɪ'steɪk/ *n* wrong idea; failure to understand; unwise action. *vt* take (one person or thing) for someone or something else.

mistletoe /'mɪsəltəʊ/ *n* plant with a small white fruit which grows on various trees and is used to ornament houses at Christmas-time.

mistress /'mɪstrəs/ *n* woman who employs other persons; woman teacher.

mistrust /mɪs'trʌst/ *vt* not to trust. *n* absence of trust.

misunderstand /ˌmɪsʌndə'stænd/ *v* understand wrongly. *n* **misunderstanding** /ˌmɪsʌndə-'stændɪŋ/ **1** failure to understand properly. **2** small quarrel.

misuse /mɪs'juːz/ *vt* use or treat wrongly. *n* **misuse** /mɪs'juːs/.

mite /maɪt/ *n* **1** very small insect. **2** very small child.

mitigate /'mɪtɪgeɪt/ *vt* make less serious. *n* **mitigation** /ˌmɪtɪ'geɪʃən/.

mitre /'maɪtə/ *n* **1** kind of crown worn by high officers of the Church. **2** way of fitting two pieces of wood to each other; instrument for doing this.

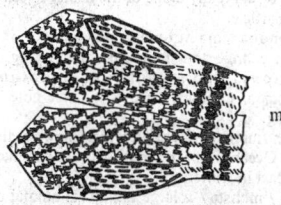

mittens (2)

mitten /'mɪtn/ *n* **1** covering for the hand that leaves the ends of fingers free and uncovered. **2** covering for the hand which does not have separate parts for the fingers.

mix /mɪks/ *vt* put (things) together to form one mass. *vi* **1** join together in a mass, e.g. *Oil and water do not mix.* **2** come together socially. *n*

mixture /'mɪkstʃə/ something formed by putting two or more things together.

mnemonic /nɪ'mɒnɪk/ *n, adj* (something) helping the memory.

moan /məʊn/ *vi, n* (make a) low sound in pain or grief.

moat /məʊt/ *n* ring of deep water round the walls of a town or castle.

mob /mɒb/ *n* disorderly crowd of people. *vt* attack in a crowd.

mobile /'məʊbaɪl/ *adj* easily moved. *n* ornament which hangs in the air, with light parts which are easily moved.

mobilize /'məʊbɪlaɪz/ *vt* (call up) soldiers for war. *n* **mobilization** /ˌməʊbɪlaɪ'zeɪʃən/.

moccasin /'mɒkəsɪn/ *n* soft shoe, made of deerskin, used in North America.

mock /mɒk/ *vt* cause people to laugh disrespectfully at. *adj* not real; pretended. *n* **mockery** /'mɒkərɪ/ *n* act of mocking; thing mocked at.

mock-up /'. ./ *n* roughly made thing of the same size as a (future, planned) aeroplane or fighting machine (etc.), so as to show what it will look like.

mode /məʊd/ *n* **1** custom; manner. **2** manner of dressing.

model /'mɒdl/ *n, adj* **1** small copy of some larger thing, e.g. *A model railway.* **2** small thing made to be copied larger, e.g. *A model for a ship.* **3** thing to be copied, e.g. *He is a model father* = all other fathers should try to be like him. **4** woman who shows off dresses in a shop by wearing them. **5** person employed by painters as an example to paint from. *v* **1** make a model of (something); copy; do modelling. **2** wear (clothes) as a model. **to model oneself on** = try to copy (the work, life, etc. of someone whom one admires).

moderate /'mɒdərət/ *adj* not too great or too small; (of e.g. the wind) not too strong. *n* person with moderate opinions. /'mɒdəreɪt/ *vt* make less strong, great, etc. *n* **moderation** /ˌmɒdə'reɪʃən/.

modern /'mɒdən/ *adj* having to do with the present time; new. *vt* **modernize** /'mɒdənaɪz/ make modern.

modest /'mɒdɪst/ *adj* not thinking too much of one's own powers; not proud. *n* **modesty** /'mɒdɪstɪ/.

modicum /'mɒdɪkəm/ *n* small amount.

modify /'mɒdɪfaɪ/ *vt* make small changes to. *n* **modification** /ˌmɒdɪfɪ'keɪʃən/.

modulate /'mɒdjʊleɪt/ *vt* change the sound of. *n* **modulation** /ˌmɒdjʊ'leɪʃən/.

mohair /'məʊheə/ *n* cloth made from the hair of the Angora goat; cloth like this, but made of a mixture of wool and cotton.

Mohammedan /mə'hæmədən/ *n, adj* Muslim; follower of Mohammed (Muhammad).

moist /mɔɪst/ *adj* damp; wet. *vt* **moisten** /'mɔɪsən/ make damp. *n* **moisture** /'mɔɪstʃə/ dampness; wetness.

molar /'məʊlə ˈ/ n large double tooth at the back of the mouth.

molasses /mə'læsɪz/ n dark sugary liquid.

mole[1] /məʊl/ n small dark growth on the skin.

mole[2]

mole[2] /məʊl/ n small mammal which makes holes in the ground.

mole[3] /məʊl/ n strong sea-wall at the mouth of a harbour.

molecule /'mɒlɪkjuːl/ n smallest amount of any material which can be taken separately and still keep its character. adj **molecular** /mə'lekjʊlə ˈ/.

molehill /'məʊl,hɪl/ n earth thrown up by a MOLE[2]. **to make mountains out of molehills** = be anxious and troubled by small difficulties.

molest /mə'lest/ vt give trouble to; touch in order to harm.

mollify /'mɒlɪfaɪ/ vt calm.

mollusc /'mɒləsk/ n shell-fish.

mollycoddle /'mɒlɪkɒdl/ n one who is too careful of himself. vt take too great care of (e.g. a child).

molten /'məʊltən/ adj liquid as a result of having melted.

moment /'məʊmənt/ n 1 a very short time, e.g. In a moment = very soon. 2 importance, e.g. Of little moment = unimportant. adj **momentary** /'məʊməntrɪ/ lasting only for a short time. adj **momentous** /mə'mentəs/ very important.

momentum /mə'mentəm/ n force of a moving body.

monarch /'mɒnək/ n king or queen. n **monarchy** /'mɒnəkɪ/ office of the monarch; system of government by a monarch.

monastery /'mɒnəstrɪ/ n house in which a group of men live apart from the world, their lives given to God. adj **monastic** /mə'næstɪk/.

Monday /'mʌndɪ/ the second day of the week, following Sunday.

monetary /'mʌnɪtrɪ/ adj having to do with money.

money /'mʌnɪ/ n gold, silver, printed paper, etc., used in buying and selling. **to make money** = gain money. **moneyed** /'mʌnɪd/ adj having a lot of money.

mongoose /'mɒŋguːs/ n small Indian mammal which kills snakes.

mongrel /'mʌŋɡrəl/ n dog of a mixed kind.

monitor /'mɒnɪtə ˈ/ n 1 one who gives a warning or advice. 2 boy who is given charge of younger boys in a school. vt keep a CHECK on (esp. what is said on foreign radio stations).

monk /mʌŋk/ n one of a group of men living apart from the world, their lives given to God.

monkey /'mʌŋkɪ/ n any of various higher mammals, rather like a man in shape; child who plays amusing or troublesome tricks. n **monkey-wrench** /'.. ./ instrument with a movable part so that it can hold things of different sizes, used for holding things very firmly.

mono- /'mɒnəʊ, 'mɒnə, mə'nɒ/ one, e.g. n **monochrome** /'mɒnəkrəʊm/ picture in one colour. n **monorail** /'mɒnəʊreɪl/ railway with only one rail.

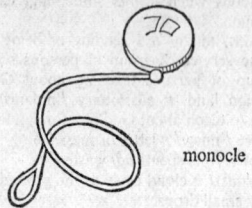

monocle

monocle /'mɒnəkəl/ n glass held in one eye to help the sight.

monogamy /mə'nɒɡəmɪ/ n marriage with only one wife or husband at a time.

monogram /'mɒnəɡræm/ n two or more letters written on top of each other so as to make a single sign.

monograph /'mɒnəɡrɑːf/ n short book on one subject.

monolith /'mɒnəlɪθ/ n pillar made of one large stone. adj **monolithic** /,mɒnə'lɪθɪk/ too large and therefore unable to deal with particular matters in a simple way.

monologue /'mɒnəlɒɡ/ n long speech, as in a play, said by one person.

monoplane /'mɒnəpleɪn/ n aeroplane having only one supporting wing on each side.

monopolize /mə'nɒpəlaɪz/ vt possess the whole of. **to monopolize the conversation** = talk so much that no one else has a chance to talk. n **monopolist** /mə'nɒpəlɪst/ n person or company which alone is able to do trade in a certain article. n **monopoly** /mə'nɒpəlɪ/ possession by one person or company alone of the ability to sell a certain article.

monotonous /mə'nɒtənəs/ adj continuing without change and therefore uninteresting. n **monotony** /mə'nɒtənɪ/. n **monotone** /'mɒnətəʊn/ continued use of a single note in speaking.

monsoon /mɒn'suːn/ n wind which blows in the Indian Ocean, from the south-west in summer, north-east in winter.

monster /'mɒnstə ˈ/ n large unnatural animal or plant; ugly and bad person; anything of unusual size. n **monstrosity** /mɒn'strɒsətɪ/ something big and ugly. adj **monstrous** /'mɒnstrəs/ like a monster; very bad.

month /mʌnθ/ n 1/12 of a year. adj **monthly** /'mʌnθlɪ/ happening once a month. n paper which is printed and sold each month.

monument /'mɒnjʊmənt/ *n* thing built to keep alive the memory of a person or event.

monumental /ˌmɒnjʊ'mentl/ *adj* very large.

moo /muː/ *n, interj* sound made by a cow.

mood /muːd/ *n* state of the mind and feelings.

moody /'muːdɪ/ *adj* sad and ill-tempered.

moon /muːn/ *n* the small heavenly body which goes round our Earth; any small world going round a greater. **once in a blue moon** = almost never. **to moon about** = walk about in a dreamy way. *n* **moonlight** /'muːnlaɪt/ the light of the moon.

moor¹ /mʊə/ *n* large space of waste hilly land.

moor² /mʊə/ *n* fasten a ship with chains or ropes. *n* **moorings** /'mʊərɪŋz/ place where a ship is so fastened.

moose /muːs/ *n* a large North American deer.

moot /muːt/ **a moot point** = doubtful question not yet decided.

mop /mɒp/ *n* lot of strings or narrow pieces of cloth fixed on the end of a stick, used for cleaning floors, etc. **to mop up** = 1 clean up with a mop. 2 look for the remaining soldiers of a beaten enemy army.

mope /məʊp/ *vi* be silent and sad.

moral /'mɒrəl/ *adj* 1 having to do with right or wrong actions. 2 right; good. *n* lesson taught by a story. *n* **morals** ideas as to right and wrong.

morale /mə'rɑːl/ *n* state of mind which makes men able to do great deeds.

morality /mə'rælətɪ/ *n* set of ideas as to duty and good behaviour; goodness. *vi* **moralize** /'mɒrəlaɪz/ tell people what is right and what is wrong.

morass /mə'ræs/ *n* piece of wet ground.

moratorium /ˌmɒrə'tɔːrɪəm/ *n* order of government permitting a delay, e.g. in the payment of debts.

morbid /'mɔːbɪd/ *adj* having to do with disease; unhealthy; sad and unpleasant (thoughts).

mordant /'mɔːdənt/ *adj* (of words) cruel; (of disease) eating away the flesh; (of liquid) destroying material as an acid does. *n* liquid which enables a colour to be fixed firmly into a cloth so that it will not be washed out.

more /mɔː/ *adv, det* greater in quantity or quality.

moreover /mɔː'rəʊvə/ *adj* and also; and I must also say this.

morgue /mɔːg/ *n* place where the bodies of persons found dead are kept in order to discover who they are, or until a doctor can examine them.

moribund /'mɒrɪbənd/ *adj* dying.

morning /'mɔːnɪŋ/ *n* early part of the day.

morocco /mə'rɒkəʊ/ *n* leather with a shiny rough surface often used for book covers.

moron /'mɔːrɒn/ *n* person who lacks the usual power of mind. *adj* **moronic** /mə'rɒnɪk/.

morose /mə'rəʊs/ *adj* very sad and ill-tempered.

morphia /'mɔːfɪə/, **morphine** /'mɔːfiːn/ *n* white powder which causes sleep and lessens pain.

morse /mɔːs/ **morse code** /ˌ. './ = way of sending

messages by long and short sounds or flashes of light.

morsel /'mɔːsəl/ *n* small piece of food.

mortal /'mɔːtl/ *adj* that will die; causing death. *n* man, not a god or fairy.

mortar-board

mortar¹ /'mɔːtə/ *n* mixture of sand and lime to which water is added, used to join together bricks in building. *n* **mortar-board** /ˈ. ../ flat black hat worn with university dress.

mortar² /'mɔːtə/ *n* 1 stone or metal bowl in which things are beaten into powder. 2 large short gun which shoots high up in the air.

mortgage /'mɔːgɪdʒ/ *n* money lent to someone so that he may buy a house, to be repaid over many years.

mortify /'mɔːtɪfaɪ/ *vt* cause pain to; punish. *vi* (e.g. of a wound) go bad. *n* **mortification** /ˌmɔːtɪfɪ'keɪʃən/ feeling of anger and shame.

mortise, mortice /'mɔːtɪs/ *n* hole cut in a piece of wood into which another piece fits, in order to join the two.

mortuary /'mɔːtʃʊərɪ/ *n* building where dead bodies are kept before they are put in the grave.

mosaic /məʊ'zeɪ-ɪk/ *n* picture made up of small pieces of coloured glass or stone.

Moslem /'mʊzlɪm, 'mɒzləm/ *n* MUSLIM.

mosque /mɒsk/ *n* place where MUSLIMS pray to God.

mosquito /mə'skiːtəʊ/ *n* flying insect which bites and drinks blood, and sometimes causes fever.

moss /mɒs/ *n* small plant which spreads over stones, trees, or wet ground. **a rolling stone gathers no moss** = a restless person who often changes his employment will not get wealth.

most /məʊst/ *adv, det* greatest number or amount, etc. *adj* very, e.g. *That's most interesting.*

mostly /'məʊstlɪ/ *adv* generally; usually.

mote /məʊt/ *n* very small bit, e.g. of dust.

motel /məʊ'tel/ *n* hotel for people who are travelling by car.

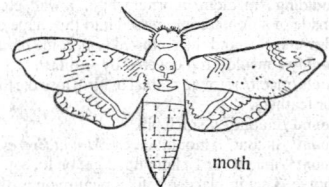

moth

moth /mɒθ/ *n* insect with powdery wings which eats into cloth. *n* **moth-ball** /ˈ. ./ ball of strong-smelling substance which keeps moths out of clothes.

mother /ˈmʌðə/ n woman who has given birth to a child. **mother country** = country in which one was born. **one's mother tongue** = one's own native language.

mother-of-pearl /ˌ. . . '. / n hard shining material found in the inside of certain shells.

motif /məʊˈtiːf/ n chief idea in a work of art.

motion /ˈməʊʃən/ n **1** act of moving. **2** something put forward at a meeting for those present to VOTE on. **to set in motion** = cause to move. vt make a sign to.

motivate /ˈməʊtɪveɪt/ vt cause (someone) to wish to work or act in a certain way. n **motivation** /ˌməʊtɪˈveɪʃən/.

motive /ˈməʊtɪv/ n feeling or desire which causes an action. **motive power** = power that causes a thing to move.

motley /ˈmɒtlɪ/ adj made up of different colours, or different kinds of things.

motor /ˈməʊtə/ n machine which changes power into movement. n **motorcar** /ˈməʊtəkɑː/ car. n **motorist** /ˈməʊtərɪst/ one who drives a car. n

motorcycle

motorcycle /ˈməʊtəˌsaɪkəl/ two-wheeled motor-driven vehicle. n **motorway** /ˈməʊtəweɪ/ special wide road on which many people may drive long distances at high speed.

motor park /'. . ./ West African n place where MAMMY-WAGONS or other motor vehicles start out from and return to.

mottle /ˈmɒtl/ vt mark with spots.

motto /ˈmɒtəʊ/ n saying or word used as a rule of life; saying or word painted below a shield.

mould[1] /məʊld/ n rich soil.

mould[2] /məʊld/ n hollow form into which liquid (e.g. hot metal) is poured. vt give a desired shape to.

mould[3] /məʊld/ n substance that grows on wet cloth, old bread, etc.

moulder /ˈməʊldə/ vi fall to pieces through age or decay.

moulding /ˈməʊldɪŋ/ n ornament on a wall, etc., made of soft material pressed into the shape of flowers, etc., and then allowed to become hard.

mouldy /ˈməʊldɪ/ adj covered by MOULD[3].

moult /məʊlt/ vi (of an animal or bird) lose the fur or feathers.

mound /maʊnd/ n small hill.

mount[1] /maʊnt/ n mountain, e.g. Mount Everest.

mount[2] /maʊnt/ vt **1** climb up. **2** get on to, e.g. a horse. **3** set in place, e.g. fix a picture on a stiff card. **to mount up** = increase. n card upon which a picture is fixed; frame in which a jewel is held in a ring or other ornament.

mountain /ˈmaʊntɪn/ n very high hill. n **moun-**
taineer /ˌmaʊntɪˈnɪə/ mountain-climber. adj **mountainous** /ˈmaʊntɪnəs/ (of country) having many mountains.

mourn /mɔːn/ v be sad, show grief, esp. for a dead person n **mourning** /ˈmɔːnɪŋ/.

mouse /maʊs/ (pl **mice** /maɪs/) n small mammal with a long tail found in houses, caught by cats.

mousse /muːs/ n sweet dish made by beating eggs and cream.

moustache /məˈstɑːʃ/ n hair growing on the upper lip.

mouth /maʊθ/ n **1** opening in the face which contains the teeth. **down in the mouth** = sad. **2** opening of anything. /maʊð/ vt show that one is saying (a word) by moving the lips, but without making a noise. n **mouthful** /ˈmaʊθfʊl/ quantity of food that can be taken into the mouth.

mouth-organ /'. ˌ. ./ n small musical instrument held in the hand and played by passing it across the lips while blowing.

mouthpiece /ˈmaʊθpiːs/ n **1** that part of a pipe or musical instrument to which the mouth is put. **2** person who expresses the opinions of others.

move /muːv/ vi go from one place to another vt **1** cause (something) to go from one place to another. **2** cause (someone) to have deep or tender feelings. n **movement** /ˈmuːvmənt/ **1** act of moving. **2** part of a longer piece of music. **3** united action for a purpose, e.g. A movement to preserve the countryside.

movie /ˈmuːvɪ/ infml n cinema film.

mow /məʊ/ v cut (grass).

Mr /ˈmɪstə/ n form of address for a man. n **Mrs** /ˈmɪsɪz/ form of address for a married woman.

much /mʌtʃ/ adv, det great in amount; greatly. **to make much of** = treat (a person) as if very important. **I don't think much of** = think to be of little value.

muck /mʌk/ n dirt; MESS.

mucous /ˈmjuːkəs/ adj of soft wet skin inside the mouth, nose, throat, etc. n **mucus** /ˈmjuːkəs/ liquid given out by such skin.

mud /mʌd/ n soft wet soil. adj **muddy** /ˈmʌdɪ/.

muddle /ˈmʌdl/ n disorderly heap. vt make disorder; cause (a plan) to fail. adj **muddled** not clear; not well arranged. **to muddle along** = be busy without a clear plan.

muezzin /muːˈezɪn/ n man who calls out the hour of prayer for Muslims.

muff[1] /mʌf/ n piece of fur or cloth inside which the hands are put to keep them warm out of doors.

muff[2] /mʌf/ vt do (something) badly; miss (e.g. a catch).

muffin /ˈmʌfɪn/ n light flat cake eaten hot with butter.

muffle /ˈmʌfəl/ vt put cloth round (something) to keep it warm; make (sound) less loud.

muffler /ˈmʌflə/ n warm cloth worn round the neck.

mufti /ˈmʌftɪ/ n plain clothes worn by soldiers, etc., when off duty.

mug (1)

mug /mʌg/ n **1** drinking-cup with a handle. **2** sl face. **3** person who is easily deceived by others.

muggy /'mʌgɪ/ adj (of weather) hot and airless.

mulatto /mju:'lætəʊ/ n person of mixed race.

mulberry /'mʌlbərɪ/ n tree bearing a dark red fruit; this fruit.

mulct /mʌlkt/ vt punish by taking money from; take money from.

mule /mju:l/ n animal produced from a male donkey and a female horse; person who is difficult to control, who will not listen to reason adj **mulish** /'mju:lɪʃ/.

mull /mʌl/ vt make (wine) hot.

mullet /'mʌlɪt/ n kind of fish.

multi- /'mʌltɪ/ adj many, e.g. **multi-coloured** /ˌ. ' . ./ having many colours.

multifarious /ˌmʌltɪ'feərɪəs/ adj various.

multilateral /ˌmʌltɪ'lætərəl/ adj many sided.

multiple /'mʌltɪpəl/ adj having a large number of parts. n number which contains another number an exact number of times. n **multiplicity** /ˌmʌltɪ'plɪsətɪ/ great number of different things.

multiply /'mʌltɪplaɪ/ vi (of animals) make many more of the same kind, by bearing young. vt add (some quantity) to itself a number of times. n **multiplication** /ˌmʌltɪplɪ'keɪʃən/.

multitude /'mʌltɪtju:d/ n large number; great crowd.

mum /mʌm/ **to keep mum** = be silent, not tell a secret.

mumble /'mʌmbəl/ v speak through closed lips.

mummer /'mʌmə/ n one who acts a silent play; actor.

mummy[1] /'mʌmɪ/ n dead body kept from decay by cleaning, drying and tying up in cloth—as in ancient Egypt.

mum(my)[2] /'mʌm(ɪ)/ infml n child's name for mother.

mumps /mʌmps/ n disease which causes swelling at the sides of the neck.

munch /mʌntʃ/ v eat with much movement of the mouth and some noise.

mundane /mʌn'deɪn/ adj of this world.

municipal /mju:'nɪsɪpəl/ adj having to do with the business of the city owned by the city-government. n **municipality** /mju:ˌnɪsɪ'pælɪtɪ/ city or part of a city.

munificent /mju:'nɪfɪsənt/ adj generous. n **munificence** /mju:'nɪfɪsəns/.

munitions /mju:'nɪʃənz/ n things used in making war, esp. explosives and shot for guns.

mural /'mjʊərəl/ n, adj (painting) on a wall.

murder /'mɜːdə/ vt kill (someone) on purpose. n

murderer /'mɜːdərə/. adj **murderous** /'mɜːdərəs/.

murky /'mɜːkɪ/ adj (e.g. of water) not clear; very dark.

murmur /'mɜːmə/ vi, n (make) a low sound as of running water, or low quiet talk, or bees.

muscle /'mʌsəl/ n part of the body which causes movement, e.g. of the limbs. **muscular** /'mʌskjʊlə/ adj strong, having powerful muscles.

muse /mju:z/ vi think deeply, taking no notice of things around.

museum /mju:'zɪəm/ n building containing a collection of interesting or beautiful things as examples of history, or of some special part of man's life or work.

mush /mʌʃ/ n soft paste. adj **mushy** /'mʌʃɪ/ like soft paste.

mushroom

mushroom /'mʌʃrʊm/ n white plant used for food—shaped like a T with a round top, and having no flowers or leaves. **a mushroom growth** = sudden very rapid growth (e.g. of a town). vi grow rapidly.

music /'mju:zɪk/ n art of producing sweet sounds; sound so produced. adj **musical** /'mju:zɪkəl/. n **musician** /mju:'zɪʃən/ one who produces music.

musk /mʌsk/ n brown sweet-smelling matter obtained from a certain kind of deer; smell like this.

musket /'mʌskɪt/ n light gun carried by a soldier in ancient times. n **musketeer** /ˌmʌskɪ'tɪə/ soldier who carried a musket. n **musketry** /'mʌskɪtrɪ/ art of shooting as taught to soldiers.

Muslim /'mʊzlɪm/ n follower of the religion taught by Muhammad.

muslin /'mʌzlɪn/ n fine cloth made of cotton.

mussel /'mʌsəl/ n a small shellfish.

must /mʌst/ v be forced to; find it necessary to; be unable not to, e.g. *You must go now* = it is necessary for you to go now. **a must** = something necessary.

mustang /'mʌstæŋ/ n half-wild horse in America.

mustard /'mʌstəd/ n yellow powder made from the seeds of a plant, mixed with water and eaten with meat.

muster /'mʌstə/ vt gather together. n soldiers gathered together. **to pass muster** = be just good enough.

musty /'mʌstɪ/ adj made useless or unpleasant by age and damp.

mutable /'mju:təbəl/ adj changeable. n **mutation** /mju:'teɪʃən/ change.

mute /mju:t/ adj **1** silent; unable to speak. (of a

letter) not sounded in saying the word. *n* **1** person who cannot speak. **2** thing used to lessen the sound of a stringed instrument of music.

mutilate /'mju:tɪleɪt/ *vt* cut off or badly damage part of (someone)'s body, to cut off a limb; to damage. *n* **mutilation** /ˌmju:tɪ'leɪʃən/.

mutineer /ˌmju:tɪ'nɪə/ *n* seaman or soldier who will not obey orders and fights against his officers. *n* **mutiny** /'mju:tɪnɪ/ rising of men against their officers. *adj* **mutinous** /'mju:tɪnəs/.

mutter /'mʌtə/ *n* speak in a low voice without moving the lips.

mutton /'mʌtn/ *n* meat of a sheep.

mutual /'mju:tʃʊəl/ *adj* given to or done for or to each other, e.g. *Mutual help.*

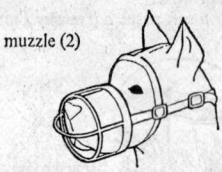

muzzle (2)

muzzle /'mʌzəl/ *n* **1** mouth and nose of an animal. **2** thing put over the mouth of an animal to prevent biting. **3** mouth or opening of a gun.

vt fix a wire or leather cage over the mouth of (an animal); force (someone) to be silent.

my /maɪ/ *det* belonging to me.

myopic /maɪ'ɒpɪk/ *adj* unable to see distant things clearly.

myriad /'mɪrɪəd/ *n* very large number.

myrrh /mɜ:/ *n* matter obtained from a tree which has a sweet smell.

myrtle /'mɜ:tl/ *n* a kind of bush with sweet-smelling white flowers.

mystery /'mɪstərɪ/ *n* a secret; a thing beyond man's understanding; secret knowledge or magic made known only to chosen persons. **a mystery play** = play showing a Bible story. *adj* **mysterious** /mɪ'stɪərɪəs/.

mystic /'mɪstɪk/ *adj* having to do with secret teachings and magic. *n* one who believes that he can enter into direct touch (understanding) with God. *adj* **mystical** /'mɪstɪkəl/.

mystify /'mɪstɪfaɪ/ *vt* make (someone) unable to understand. *n* **mystification** /ˌmɪstɪfɪ'keɪʃən/.

myth /mɪθ/ *n* story of gods, fairies, etc., often showing through these persons some fact of nature; any widely believed but in fact untrue story. *adj* **mythical** /'mɪθɪkəl/ not real, known only in myths. *n* **mythology** /mɪ'θɒlədʒɪ/ story of myths; body of myths. *adj* **mythological** /ˌmɪθə'lɒdʒɪkəl/.

N

nab /næb/ *vt infml* seize.

nadir /'neɪdɪə/ *n* lowest point, e.g. of hope.

nag[1] /næg/ *n* small horse.

nag[2] /næg/ *v* scold continually.

nail /neɪl/ *n* **1** piece of metal with a point and head, used for joining pieces of wood. **2** horny growth on the ends of the fingers. *vt* fix with a nail.

naive /naɪ'i:v/ *adj* simple and natural in speech and manner. *n* **naiveté, naivety** /naɪ'i:vətɪ/.

naked /'neɪkɪd/ *adj* without clothes; not kept secret; open, uncovered. **to see with the naked eye** = without the help of a glass.

name /neɪm/ *n* word by which a person or thing is known. **one's good name** = high opinion held by others of one. *vt* give a name to. *adj* **nameless** /'neɪmləs/ not named; too bad to be spoken of. *adv* **namely** /'neɪmlɪ/ that is to say; I mean. *n* **namesake** /'neɪmseɪk/ person having the same name as another.

nanny /'nænɪ/ *n* one paid to look after children. *n* **nanny-goat** /'. . ./ female goat.

nap[1] /næp/ *n, vi* (have a) short sleep. **caught napping** = surprised when not keeping watch.

nap[2] /næp/ *n* mass of short hairs on the surface of cloth.

nape /neɪp/ *n* back of the neck.

naphtha /'næfθə/ *n* light oil obtained from coal.

naphthalene /'næfθəli:n/ *n* white glassy material

with a strong smell, obtained from coal, used to keep insects out of clothes.

napkin /'næpkɪn/ *n* **1** small cloth used when eating to keep the clothing clean, also to clean the hands and mouth. **2** cloth tied round a baby.

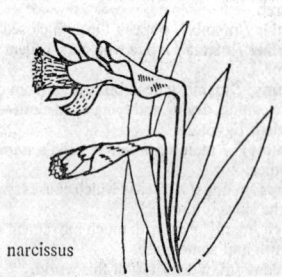

narcissus

narcissus /nɑ:'sɪsəs/ *n* a kind of flower, usually white or yellow.

narcotic /nɑ:'kɒtɪk/ *n, adj* medicine (or other substance) which produces sleep.

narrate /nə'reɪt/ *vt* tell (a story). *adj, n* **narrative** /'nærətɪv/ (of or like a) story. *n* **narrator** /nə'reɪtə/. *n* **narration** /nə'reɪʃən/ *n* telling of a story.

narrow /'nærəʊ/ *adj* not broad or wide. **narrow-**

minded /ˌ. ' . ./ = not able to take in great ideas or to understand other people's opinions. *adv*

narrowly /'nærəʊlɪ/ only just.

nasal /'neɪzəl/ *adj* having to do with the nose or with sounds produced through the nose.

nasty /'nɑːstɪ/ *adj* unpleasant; dirty.

natal /'neɪtl/ *adj* having to do with birth.

nation /'neɪʃən/ *n* race of people under one government. *n* **nationalism** /'næʃənəlɪzəm/ strong feeling for one's nation; demand for the freedom of one's nation. *n* **nationalist** /'næʃənəlɪst/. *n* **nationality** /ˌnæʃə'nælətɪ/ fact of belonging to a nation; state of being a nation. *vt* **nationalize** /'næʃənəlaɪz/ cause to belong to the nation. *n* **nationalization** /ˌnæʃənəlaɪ'zeɪʃən/.

native /'neɪtɪv/ *adj, n* (one) born in a certain place.

nativity /nə'tɪvətɪ/ *n* birth. **the Nativity** = Birth of Jesus Christ.

natural /'nætʃərəl/ *adj* **1** according to the usual laws which govern events in the world; usual and to be expected. **2** produced by the forces of the earth and weather, not by man. *adv* **naturally** /'nætʃərəlɪ/ **1** according to nature. **2** of course. *n* **naturalist** /'nætʃərəlɪst/ *n* one who studies plants, animals, insects, etc. *adj* **naturalized** /'nætʃərəlaɪzd/ having obtained a nationality by law, not by birth, e.g. *Naturalized Frenchman* = French by law but not by birth.

nature /'neɪtʃə/ *n* **1** character of a thing. **2** the power which causes changes in the world. **3** world of plants, animals and matter as a whole.

naught /nɔːt/ *pron* nothing.

naughty /'nɔːtɪ/ *adj* giving trouble, e.g. *A naughty child.*

nausea /'nɔːsɪə/ *n* feeling of being sick in the stomach. *v* **nauseate** /'nɔːsɪeɪt/ cause a feeling of sickness. *adj* **nauseating** /'nɔːsɪeɪtɪŋ/ very nasty.

nautical /'nɔːtɪkəl/ *adj* having to do with ships and seamen. **nautical mile** = measure of distance, about 6080 feet or 1·85 kilometres.

naval /'neɪvəl/ *adj* having to do with the NAVY.

nave /neɪv/ *n* main part of a church.

navel /'neɪvəl/ *n* the little hollow in the middle of the front of the body.

navigate /'nævɪgeɪt/ *v* use instruments to set the course of (a ship). *adj* **navigable** /'nævɪgəbəl/ river up which a ship can pass, *n* **navigation** /ˌnævɪ'geɪʃən/.

navvy /'nævɪ/ *n* unskilled workman employed for digging, for making roads, railways, etc.

navy /'neɪvɪ/ *n* warships of a country; officers and men of these ships. **navy blue** = very dark blue.

nay /neɪ/ *interj* no.

neap /niːp/ **neap tide** = smaller rise and fall of the sea in the first and third quarters of the moon (see SPRING[1]).

near /nɪə/ *adj, prep* close; not far away.

nearly /'nɪəlɪ/ *adv* not far from (being), e.g. *I*

nearly *lost it* = I didn't lose it but I was near to losing it.

neat /niːt/ *adj* **1** clean and in good order. **2** careful. e.g. *Neat writing.* **3** skilful, e.g. *A neat piece of work. adj, adv* (of a drink) without water added.

nebula /'nebjʊlə/ *n* cloud of brightly burning gas or small stars seen in the sky. *adj* **nebulous** /'nebjʊləs/ cloudy, not clearly seen or understood.

necessary /'nesəsərɪ/ *adj* needed; which must be; must be done or obtained. *adv* **necessarily** /ˌnesə'serəlɪ, 'nesəsərɪlɪ/ as must be the case. *n* **necessity** /nɪ'sesətɪ/ something which makes one act in a certain way; need; a thing needed. *vt* **necessitate** /nɪ'sesɪteɪt/ make necessary.

neck /nek/ *n* part of the body between the head and the shoulders. **neck and neck** = (e.g. of runners in a race) coming in equal.

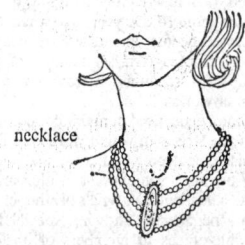

necklace

necklace /'nekləs/ *n* string of jewels (or other small ornamental objects) worn round the neck.

necktie /'nektaɪ/ *n* band of coloured silk worn by a man round the neck.

nectar /'nektə/ *n* **1** wine of the Greek gods. **2** sweet liquid found in plants.

née /neɪ/ born, e.g. *Jane Smith, née Jones* = her name before marriage was Jones.

need /niːd/ *n* necessity; lack (e.g. of money). *vt* **1** have to have, e.g. *I need a lot of sleep.* **2** have to; must, e.g. *Nobody needs to go,* or *Nobody need go. adj* **needful** /'niːdfəl/ needed.

needle /'niːdl/ *n* instrument used for joining cloth together with thread; any sharp pointed object.

needless /'niːdləs/ *adj* not necessary.

needy /'niːdɪ/ *adj* poor.

nefarious /nɪ'feərɪəs/ *adj* unlawful; very bad.

negation /nɪ'geɪʃən/ *n* act of saying No.

negative /'negətɪv/ *adj, n* (of) a word or sentence meaning that something is not true. *adj* (of a number) less than **0**. *n* photograph in which all the light parts are dark and dark parts light—used for printing copies of the picture.

neglect /nɪ'glekt/ *vt* **1** take no care of. **2** fail to do. *adj* **neglectful** /nɪ'glektfəl/ not careful. *adj* **negligible** /'neglɪdʒəbəl/ not worth troubling about. *adj* **negligent** /'neglɪdʒənt/ not taking care. *n* **negligence** /'neglɪdʒəns/.

negotiate /nɪ'gəʊʃɪeɪt/ *v* try to reach an agreement with someone on (something); give or get money for. *adj* **negotiable** /nɪˈgəʊʃəbəl/ which may be bought or sold. *n* **negotiation** /nɪˌgəʊʃɪˈeɪʃən/.

negro /ˈniːgrəʊ/ *n* man of the black races of Africa or their descendants. *n* **negress** /ˈniːgrəs/ female negro. *adj* **negroid** /ˈniːgrɔɪd/ having some of the character or appearance of a negro.

neigh /neɪ/ *n* cry of a horse.

neighbour /ˈneɪbə/ *n* person who lives near one. *n* **neighbourhood** /ˈneɪbəhʊd/ country or streets near any particular place; people in that part. *adj* **neighbouring** /ˈneɪbərɪŋ/ near. *adj* **neighbourly** /ˈneɪbəlɪ/ friendly.

neither /ˈnaɪðə, ˈniːðə/ *pron, det* not either. **neither—nor** not this and not that, e.g. *He neither ate nor drank* = didn't eat, and didn't drink either.

nemesis /ˈneməsɪs/ *n* fate which brings punishment.

neo- /ˈniːəʊ, ˈniːə/ new, e.g. *adj* **neolithic** /ˌniːəˈlɪθɪk/ of the time some 10,000 years ago when the new and better stone instruments were made.

neologism /niːˈɒlədʒɪzəm/ *n* making of a new word; using words in a new way; new word or new use of words.

neon /ˈniːɒn/ *n* gas used in making those electric signs in the streets in which words are formed by a glass pipe filled with light.

nephew /ˈnevjuː/ *n* son of one's brother or sister, or of one's husband's or wife's brother or sister.

nepotism /ˈnepətɪzəm/ showing special favour and giving offices to members of one's own family.

nerve /nɜːv/ *n* **1** thread-like parts of the body which carry feelings to the brain, or carry messages which produce action in the limbs, etc. **2** courage. *n* (*pl*) **nerves** anxiety. *adj* **nerveless** /ˈnɜːvləs/ without strength or courage. *adj* **nervous** /ˈnɜːvəs/ having to do with the nerves; in an unhealthy state of mind, easily excited or frightened. **a nervous breakdown** = illness of the mind caused by anxiety or overwork. *n* **nervousness** /ˈnɜːvəsnəs/ a state of fear and excitement.

nest /nest/ *n* place built by a bird in which it lays its eggs. *vi* make a nest. **to feather one's nest** = make oneself rich, sometimes dishonestly. *n* **nest-egg** store of money laid up for the future.

nestle /ˈnesəl/ *vi* lie closely and comfortably against someone or something.

nestling /ˈneslɪŋ/ *n* young bird not yet able to leave the nest.

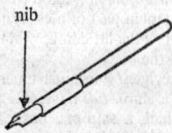

net¹

net¹ /net/ *n* knotting of string into squares, used, e.g. to catch fish. *vt* catch with a net; cover with a net.

net² /net/ *adj* real, e.g. *Net gain* = that amount left when all costs, etc., have been taken off; *Net weight* = weight without the box, paper or packing.

nether /ˈneðə/ *adj* lower.

netting /ˈnetɪŋ/ *n* net; cloth made like net.

nettle /ˈnetl/ *n* plant which, when touched, causes pain and redness of the skin. **nettled** /ˈnetld/ *adj* made angry.

network /ˈnetwɜːk/ *n* system of many lines crossing each other, e.g. *A network of railways*.

neuralgia /njuˈrældʒə/ *n* pain in the nerves.

neurotic /njuˈrɒtɪk/ *adj* excitable and uncontrolled.

neuter /ˈnjuːtə/ *adj* **1** neither male nor female. **2** (of a word) of that form which means neither a male nor female thing.

neutral /ˈnjuːtəl/ *adj* **1** taking neither side in a war; belonging to neither of two classes. **2** of no recognizable character. **in neutral** = with the engine of the car not in any GEAR. *n* **neutrality** /njuːˈtrælətɪ/ state of being neutral. *vt* **neutralize** /ˈnjuːtrəlaɪz/ make neutral; stop (something) from having any effect.

never /ˈnevə/ *adv* not at any time.

nevermore /ˌnevəˈmɔː/ *adv* never again.

nevertheless /ˌnevəðəˈles/ *adv* in spite of all that.

new /njuː/ *adj* not old; fresh; not seen before; lacking experience.

new-fangled /ˌnjuːˈfæŋgəld/ *derog adj* of a new kind.

news /njuːz/ *n* report of events which have happened lately. *n* **newspaper** /ˈnjuːsˌpeɪpə/ a paper giving the news. *n* **newsreel** /ˈnjuːzriːl/ cinema film showing the news of the day or week.

newt /njuːt/ *n* small water creature with four legs and a long tail.

next /nekst/ *adj, adv* nearest, coming after this one; following (this).

nib

nib /nɪb/ *n* metal point of a pen.

nibble /ˈnɪbəl/ *v* take little bites of (food).

nice /naɪs/ *adj* **1** pleasing. **2** difficult to judge, e.g. *A nice point of law.*

nicety /ˈnaɪsətɪ/ *n* very small difference.

niche /nɪʃ/ *n* hollow place in a wall, usually meant to contain a stone figure; any place specially suited for something.

nick /nɪk/ *n* small V-shaped cut in (a stick) made by cutting out a piece. **in the nick of time** = just in time. *vt* make such a mark in (a stick).

nickel /'nɪkəl/ *n* hard white metal used as a covering for spoons, boxes, etc.

nickname /'nɪkneɪm/ *n* name used by friends instead of one's real name. *vt* call by such a name.

nicotine /'nɪkəti:n/ *n* active substance found in TOBACCO.

niece /ni:s/ *n* daughter of one's brother or sister or of one's husband's or wife's brother or sister.

niggardly /'nɪgədlɪ/ *adj* ungenerous; too careful with money.

nigger /'nɪgə[r]/ *derog n* NEGRO.

nigh /naɪ/ *adj, adv* near.

night /naɪt/ *n* time of darkness. *n* **nightcap** /'naɪtkæp/ drink taken just before going to bed. *n* **nightfall** /'naɪtfɔ:l/ end of the day.

nightingale /'naɪtɪŋgeɪl/ *n* small bird which sings beautifully at night.

nightmare /'naɪtmeə[r]/ *n* frightening dream.

nihilist /'naɪ-ɪlɪst/ *n* one who has no values.

nil /nɪl/ *n* nothing.

nimble /'nɪmbəl/ *adj* quick in movement; active.

nincompoop /'nɪŋkəmpu:p/ *n* fool.

nine /naɪn/ *det, n* number following eight, often written 9.

ninepins /'naɪn͵pɪnz/ *n* game in which a ball is thrown at nine pieces of wood, in order to knock them down.

nineteen /͵naɪn'ti:n/ *det, n* number following eighteen, often written 19. *det, n* **ninety** /'naɪntɪ/ number often written 90, being nine times ten.

nip /nɪp/ *vt* 1 press a small piece of skin between the fingers, causing pain. 2 stop the growth of (a plant), e.g. *Nipped by the frost; Nipped in the bud* = killed before the flower opened. **there's a nip in the air** = it is cold. *infml* **to nip off** = run away. *n* **nipper** /'nɪpə[r]/ 1 thing used for nipping, e.g. *The nippers of a shellfish.* 2 *infml* small boy.

nipple /'nɪpəl/ *n* point of the breast; anything so shaped.

nippy /'nɪpɪ/ *adj* quick in movement.

nirvana /nɪə'vɑ:nə/ *n* state after death in which the spirit of a man becomes united with God.

nitrogen /'naɪtrədʒən/ *n* colourless gas found in the air and very necessary to the life of plants.

nitwit /'nɪt͵wɪt/ *infml n* foolish person.

no /nəʊ/ *interj* that is not so; I do not agree. *det* not any. *pron* **no one** /'. ./ no person.

noble /'nəʊbəl/ *adj* of very fine character; high in social rank *n* **nobleman** /'nəʊbəlmən/ person of high social rank; lord. *n* **nobility** /nəʊ'bɪlətɪ/. **the nobility** = all the persons of high rank and birth.

nobody /'nəʊbədɪ/ *pron* no person.

nocturnal /nɒk'tɜ:nəl/ *adj* happening at night; (of an animal) active at night.

nod /nɒd/ *v* bend (the head) down as a sign of agreement or greeting, or because one is feeling sleepy. **to nod off** = fall asleep without meaning to.

node /nəʊd/ *n* 1 place on a stem at which a leaf is joined on. 2 hard swelling on a muscle or bone. 3 point at which a curve crosses another curve, or where a curve turns and crosses itself.

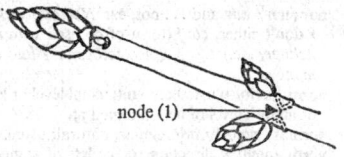

node (1)

Noel /nəʊ'el/ *n* Christmas.

noise /nɔɪz/ *n* sound, esp. if too loud or for some other reason unwanted. *adj* **noisy** /'nɔɪzɪ/.

noisome /'nɔɪsəm/ *adj* very harmful and unpleasant.

nomad /'nəʊmæd/ *n* one of a wandering people. *adj* **nomadic** /nəʊ'mædɪk/.

nomenclature /nəʊ'meŋklətʃə[r]/ *n* system of names.

nominal /'nɒmɪnəl/ *adj* 1 having to do with names. 2 in name only, e.g. *A nominal leader.*

nominate /'nɒmɪneɪt/ *vt* put forward (someone)'s name so that he may be chosen for an office. *n* **nomination** /͵nɒmɪ'neɪʃən/. *n* **nominee** /͵nɒmɪ'ni:/ person nominated.

non- /nɒn/ not, e.g. *adj* **non-fiction** /͵. '. ./ (of a book) telling of facts, not stories.

nonchalant /'nɒnʃələnt/ *adj* not very concerned.

noncommittal /͵nɒnkə'mɪtl/ *adj* not telling what one intends to do.

nonconformist /͵nɒnkən'fɔ:mɪst/ *n* one who refuses to act or believe as others do, esp. in matters of belief in God.

nondescript /'nɒndɪskrɪpt/ *adj* not easily described; very ordinary.

none /nʌn/ *pron* no person or persons; no thing or things. *adv* not at all; not, e.g. *He is none the worse for it.*

nonentity /nɒ'nentətɪ/ *n* person of no importance.

nonplus /nɒn'plʌs/ *vt* surprise (someone) so much that he does not know what to say or do.

nonsense /'nɒnsəns/ *n* not sense; silly talk.

nonsequitur /͵nɒn'sekwɪtə[r]/ *Latin n* bad piece of reasoning which does not lead up to the judgment intended.

noodle /'nu:dl/ *n* little flat stick made from egg and flour, cooked in soup.

nook /nʊk/ *n* sheltered corner.

noon /nu:n/ *n* midday.

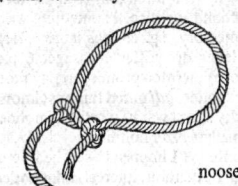

noose

noose /nu:s/ *n* circle of rope which becomes tight when one end is pulled—used for hanging people.

nor /nɔː/ *adv* and ... not, e.g. *Nor do I* = And I don't either. *conj* (form of **or** used with *not*, *neither*, etc.) e.g. *Neither John nor I had any money.*

norm /nɔːm/ *n* usual amount, usual level or kind of action; level of action aimed at.

normal /'nɔːməl/ *adj* regular; natural; usual.

north /nɔːθ/ *n* direction to the left of someone facing east. *adj* **northern** /'nɔːðən/ in or of the north. *adj* **northerly** /'nɔːðəlɪ/ to the north; (of winds) from the north. *adj, adv* **northwards** /'nɔːθwədz/ towards the north.

nose /nəʊz/ *n* that part of the face with which we smell; anything of that shape. *adj* **nosy, nosey** /'nəʊzɪ/ interested in other people's business. **a Nosey Parker** = nosy person.

nosegay /'nəʊzgeɪ/ *n* handful of sweet-smelling flowers tied together.

nostalgia /nɒ'stældʒə/ *n* sadness at being away from home; sad looking back on the past.

nostril /'nɒstrəl/ *n* one of the two openings in the nose.

not /nɒt/ *adv* (word added to a sentence to express the opposite of that sentence) e.g. *He is not dead* = he is alive.

notable /'nəʊtəbəl/ *adj* worthy of notice; worth remembering; likely to be remembered. *adv* **notably** /'nəʊtəblɪ/ specially.

notary /'nəʊtərɪ/ *n* man who does certain kinds of law business.

notation /nəʊ'teɪʃən/ *n* written signs standing for numbers (*The Roman system of notation, V, X, L, C*), sounds (PHONETIC *notation*) etc.

notch

notch /nɒtʃ/ *n* V-shaped cut.

note /nəʊt/ *n* **1** sign standing for a certain musical sound; the musical sound; a key (= piece of bone or wood) struck to produce a musical sound. **2** fame, good name, e.g. *A man of note* = a famous man. **3** attention. **to take note of** = pay attention to; notice. **4** something written to help the memory, e.g. *To take notes of a speech.* **5** short letter or written message. **6** piece of paper money; written promise to pay money. *vt* attend to; notice. *adj* **noted** famous; known. *adj* **noteworthy** /'nəʊtˌwɜːðɪ/ worthy of notice.

nothing /'nʌθɪŋ/ *pron* no thing.

notice /'nəʊtɪs/ *vt* **1** happen to see, hear, etc. **2** attend to. *n* **1** attention; interest. **take notice of** = pay attention to. **2** act of telling someone working for one that they will not be employed after a certain date. **3** piece of paper, etc., telling of some event.

notify /'nəʊtɪfaɪ/ *vt* make known; make public; warn. *n* **notification** /ˌnəʊtɪfɪ'keɪʃən/.

notion /'nəʊʃən/ *n* idea.

notorious /nəʊ'tɔːrɪəs/ *adj* well known for something bad. *n* **notoriety** /ˌnəʊtə'raɪətɪ/.

notwithstanding /ˌnɒtwɪð'stændɪŋ/ *prep* in spite of. *conj* although.

nougat /'nuːgɑː, 'nʌgət/ *n* soft white sweet with dried fruit in it.

nought /nɔːt/ *n* the number **0**; ZERO.

noun /naʊn/ *n* word used as the name of a thing.

nourish /'nʌrɪʃ/ *vt* give food to. *n* **nourishment** /'nʌrɪʃmənt/.

novel[1] /'nɒvəl/ *adj* new and strange; new and interesting. *n* **novelty** /'nɒvəltɪ/.

novel[2] /'nɒvəl/ *n* long imaginary story written in a book. *n* **novelist** /'nɒvəlɪst/ one who writes novels.

November /nə'vembə, nəʊ-/ *n* the eleventh month of the year.

novice /'nɒvɪs/ *n* beginner; one new to the work. *n* **novitiate** /nə'vɪʃɪət/ **1** novice. **2** state or time of being a novice.

now /naʊ/ *adv* at this time. **now and again, now and then** = sometimes; from time to time. **now, now!** = warning, e.g. to stop children making too much noise. *adv* **nowadays** /'naʊədeɪz/ in these times.

nowhere /'nəʊweə/ *adv* at or to no place.

noxious /'nɒkʃəs/ *adj* harmful.

nozzle /'nɒzəl/ *n* pointed end of a pipe used to direct a stream of liquid.

nuance /'njuːɒns/ *n* very slight difference in the meaning of a word; slight difference in colour, in the quality of a feeling, etc.

nub /nʌb/ *n* point of a story or chief point in a difficulty.

nubile /'njuːbaɪl/ *adj* (of a girl) old enough for marriage.

nucleus /'njuːklɪəs/ *n* centre part about which matter collects or grows; any central part. *adj* **nuclear** /'njuːklɪə/.

nude /njuːd/ *adj* uncovered; having no clothes on. *n* (painting of a) person with no clothes on.

nudge /nʌdʒ/ *n, vt* touch with the ELBOW.

nudist /'njuːdɪst/ *n* person who believes in the value of wearing no clothes for health.

nugget /'nʌgɪt/ *n* rough piece of gold as found in the ground.

nuisance /'njuːsəns/ *n* harmful or troublesome thing or person.

null /nʌl/ *adj* of no effect. **null and void** = having no force according to the law.

nullify /'nʌlɪfaɪ/ *vt* make of no effect, of no force.

numb /nʌm/ *adj* having no feeling, e.g. because of cold.

number /'nʌmbə/ *n* **1** quantity or amount. **2** figure, e.g. 1, 2, 3, etc. **3** copy of a newspaper. *vt* **1** count. **2** write numbers on. **3** amount to. *adj* **numberless** /'nʌmbələs/ very many.

numeral /'njuːmərəl/ *n, adj* word or figure (expressing a number).

numerate /'nju:mərət/ *adj* able to work with numbers.

numerical /nju:'merɪkəl/ *adj* having to do with numbers.

numerous /'nju:mərəs/ *adj* many in number.

numskull /'nʌmskʌl/ *n* fool.

nun /nʌn/ *n* woman living, with a group of other women, a life given to God. *n* **nunnery** /'nʌnərɪ/ house for nuns.

nuptial /'nʌpʃəl/ *adj* having to do with marriage.

nurse /nɜ:s/ *n* person trained to take care of the young, or sick persons, helping a doctor. *vt* take care of (a child or sick person). **a wet nurse** = woman who gives milk to another's child.

nursery /'nɜ:sərɪ/ *n* **1** room for the use of children. **2** place where young plants are grown, esp. for selling. *n* **nurseryman** /'nɜ:sərɪmən/ one who owns such a place.

nurture /'nɜ:tʃə/ *n* training and care of the young. *vt* take care of (e.g. a child).

nut¹ /nʌt/ *n* seed of a tree, contained in a hard shell. *infml* fool.

nut² /nʌt/ *n* small block of metal with a hole in it which may be screwed on to a bar.

nutmeg /'nʌtmeg/ *n* hard seed of a Malayan tree used, when powdered, to give a pleasant taste to

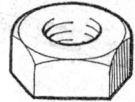

nut²

food, esp. to foods made from milk.

nutriment /'nju:trɪmənt/ *n* food. *n* **nutrition** /nju:'trɪʃən/ giving or receiving of food. *adj* **nutritious** /nju:'trɪʃəs/ providing good food value; useful as food, supplying power of growth to the body. *n* **nutrient** /'nju:trɪənt/.

nutshell /'nʌt-ʃel/ **in a nutshell** = in as few words as possible.

nutty /'nʌtɪ/ *adj* having a taste like nuts.

nuzzle /'nʌzəl/ *vt* push with the nose, as a dog does.

nylon /'naɪlɒn/ *n* very strong silk-like thread used for ladies' STOCKINGS and dresses. *n* **nylons** (*pl*) stockings made of nylon.

nymph /nɪmf/ *n* female god living in rivers, forests, etc.

nymphomaniac /ˌnɪmfə'meɪnɪæk/ *n* woman who has uncontrollable or unusually strong sexual desires.

O

oaf /əʊf/ *n* ungraceful foolish fellow.

oak /əʊk/ *n* a kind of tree which grows to a great age and has very hard wood.

oakum /'əʊkəm/ *n* loose material got by opening up old rope, used for filling cracks between the boards on a ship.

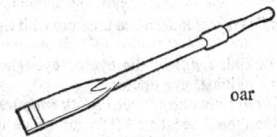

oar

oar /ɔ:/ *n* one of a pair of long bars of wood with flat ends used for rowing a boat.

oasis /əʊ'eɪsɪs/ (*pl* **oases** /əʊ'eɪsi:z/) *n* place in a desert where there are trees and water.

oath /əʊθ/ *n* **1** promise, esp. to tell the truth. **2** disrespectful use of the name of God or any holy name.

oats /əʊts/ *n* grain seeds used for food.

oba /'əʊbə/ *n* chief or ruler in parts of Nigeria.

obdurate /'ɒbdʒʊrət/ *adj* not easily moved from an opinion.

obedient /ə'bi:dɪənt/ *adj* willing to do as ordered. *n* **obedience** /ə'bi:dɪəns/.

obeisance /ə'beɪsəns/ **to make an obeisance** = bend oneself down as a sign of respect.

obelisk /'ɒbəlɪsk/ *n* tall pointed stone with flat sides.

obese /əʊ'bi:s/ *adj* very fat. *n* **obesity** /əʊ'bi:sətɪ/.

obey /ə'beɪ/ *v* do as ordered; act according to (a rule or law).

obituary /ə'bɪtʃʊərɪ/ *n* notice of death.

object¹ /'ɒbdʒɪkt/ *n* **1** thing. **2** word telling the person or thing to whom an action is done. **3** purpose.

object² /əb'dʒekt/ *vi* not agree. *n* **objection** /əb'dʒekʃən/ disagreement. *adj* **objectionable** /əb'dʒekʃənəbəl/ nasty; unpleasant.

objective /əb'dʒektɪv/ *adj* that is real; outside the mind. *n* purpose; aim, e.g. aim of an attack by soldiers.

obligatory /ə'blɪgətərɪ/ *adj* which must be done.

obligation /ˌɒblɪ'geɪʃən/ *n* **1** duty. **2** state of being in debt or of thankfulness to another person who has helped one.

oblige /ə'blaɪdʒ/ *vt* **1** force (someone) to act. **2** do a kindness to. *adj* **obliging** /ə'blaɪdʒɪŋ/ kind and eager to help.

oblique /ə'bli:k/ *adj* indirect; in a sideways direction.

obliterate /ə'blɪtəreɪt/ *vt* rub out (e.g. a word); destroy. *n* **obliteration** /əˌblɪtə'reɪʃən/.

oblivion /ə'blɪvɪən/ *n* act of forgetting; state of being forgotten. *adj* **oblivious** /ə'blɪvɪəs/ forgetting completely; taking no notice (of something).

oblong /'ɒblɒŋ/ *n, adj* (having a) shape like a square but with two sides longer than the ends.

obnoxious /əb'nɒkʃəs/ *adj* unpleasant.

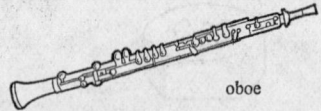

oboe

oboe /'əʊbəʊ/ *n* a wooden musical instrument played with the breath.

obscene /əb'si:n/ *adj* nasty and dirty (in idea). *n* **obscenity** /əb'senətɪ/.

obscure /əb'skjʊə/ *adj* dark; not easily understood; not well known. *vt* make dark, or difficult to understand. *n* **obscurity** /əb'skjʊərətɪ/.

obsequies /'ɒbsɪkwɪz/ *n* ceremonies performed at a funeral.

obsequious /əb'si:kwɪəs/ *adj* too eager to obey and serve.

observation /ˌɒbzə'veɪʃən/ *n* **1** act of watching. **2** power of noticing. **3** something noticed or report of something noticed.

observatory /əb'zɜːvətərɪ/ *n* place from which scientists watch the stars.

observe /əb'zɜːv/ *vt* **1** keep or act according to, e.g. *Observe the laws.* **2** watch; notice. **3** say. *n* **observance** /əb'zɜːvəns/ act of observing (a law, etc.). *adj* **observant** /əb'zɜːvənt/ *adj* having good powers of OBSERVATION.

obsession /əb'seʃən/ *n* fixed idea from which the mind cannot be freed. *vt* **obsess** /əb'ses/ (of an idea) to be an obsession for (someone); fill the mind with ——.

obsolete /'ɒbsəli:t/ *adj* no longer in use; of an old kind not such as is now used. *adj* **obsolescent** /ˌɒbsə'lesənt/ becoming obsolete.

obstacle /'ɒbstəkəl/ *n* something which stands in the way and prevents action or movement.

obstinate /'ɒbstɪnət/ *adj* not giving up an opinion; not moved by reasoning; unwilling to obey. *n* **obstinacy** /'ɒbstɪnəsɪ/.

obstreperous /əb'strepərəs/ *adj* noisy and uncontrollable, e.g. children.

obstruct /əb'strʌkt/ *vt* get in the way of; stop up or block (e.g. a path). *n* **obstruction** /əb'strʌkʃən/.

obtain /əb'teɪn/ *vt* get; gain possession of. *vi* be in use; be the case.

obtrusive /əb'truːsɪv/ *adj* pushing forward and causing oneself, or some object, to be noticed. *vi* **obtrude** /əb'truːd/ push oneself forward.

obtuse /əb'tjuːs/ *adj* **1** not sharp. **2** (of an angle) greater than ninety degrees. **3** slow of understanding.

obviate /'ɒbvɪeɪt/ *vt* clear away (a difficulty) from the path.

obvious /'ɒbvɪəs/ *adj* clearly noticed.

occasion /ə'keɪʒən/ *n* **1** event. **2** chance. **3** time. *vt* cause. *adj* **occasional** /ə'keɪʒənəl/ happening from time to time.

occidental /ˌɒksɪ'dentl/ *adj* of the West.

occult /ə'kʌlt/ *adj* hidden; secret; having to do with magic.

occupant /'ɒkjʊpənt/ *n* person holding land or living in a house.

occupation /ˌɒkjʊ'peɪʃən/ *n* **1** act of OCCUPYING. **2** employment. *adj* **occupational** /ˌɒkjʊ'peɪʃənəl/ (of, e.g. a disease or danger) caused or made more probable by a particular occupation.

occupy /'ɒkjʊpaɪ/ *vt* **1** take and hold possession of. **2** hold (an enemy's country). **3** live in (a house). **4** fill (a certain space), e.g. *Occupy a house.* **5** employ, e.g. *Occupy oneself in* = work at.

occur /ə'kɜː/ *vi* happen; be found. **to occur to one** = (of an idea) come to one. *n* **occurrence** /ə'kʌrəns/ happening.

ocean /'əʊʃən/ *n* great sea.

ochre /'əʊkə/ *n* yellow earth used as a colouring matter, e.g. in paints.

o'clock /ə'klɒk/ *adv* as shown on the clock, e.g. *Seven o'clock.*

octa- /'ɒktə/ eight, e.g. *adj* **octagonal** /ɒk'tægənəl/ eight-sided. *n* **octave** /'ɒktɪv/ eight musical notes above or below a certain note.

octane /'ɒkteɪn/ number which shows the power and quality of PETROL; 100 octane petrol is very good.

October /ɒk'təʊbə/ *n* the tenth month of the year.

octopus

octopus /'ɒktəpəs/ *n* deep-sea creature with eight arms.

ocular /'ɒkjʊlə/ *adj* of the eye or eyesight. *n* **oculist** /'ɒkjʊlɪst/ eye-doctor.

odd /ɒd/ *adj* **1** not one of a set, e.g. *An odd shoe* = only one shoe. **2** peculiar. **3** (of a number) which cannot be divided by 2. *n* **oddity** /'ɒdətɪ/ peculiarity; an unusual person. **the odds are 2 to 1 on** = there are two chances to one in favour of. **odds and ends** = loose bits of things left over.

ode /əʊd/ *n* song or poem of a solemn kind.

odious /'əʊdɪəs/ *adj* hateful.

odium /'əʊdɪəm/ *n* widespread hatred.

odour /'əʊdə/ *n* smell.

of /əv; *strong* ɒv/ *prep* **1** belonging to, e.g. *The handle of the door.* **2** having; with, e.g. *A man of courage.* **3** made from, e.g. *A bar of iron.* **4** which is, e.g. *The city of Rome.* **5** from; from among, e.g. *Four of them came.*

off /ɒf/ *adj, adv, prep* **1** at or to a distance, e.g. *Be off!* = go away; *Five miles off* = five miles away. **2** not on; (so as to be) no longer on, e.g. *Take that coat off; Turn off the radio; Switch off the lights; Get him off the train.*

offal /'ɒfəl/ n waste part of animal killed for food.

offence /ə'fens/ n unlawful act. **to take offence** = be displeased. **to give offence** = displease.

offend /ə'fend/ v do wrong; displease.

offensive /ə'fensɪv/ adj 1 unpleasant, e.g. *An offensive smell.* 2 causing anger, e.g. *Offensive remarks* = sayings that displease. 3 having to do with attack, e.g. *Offensive weapons* = weapons used in attack. **to take the offensive** = to attack.

offer /'ɒfə/ vt 1 hold out as a gift; give a chance of accepting, e.g. *I offer £100 for your car.* 2 say that one is prepared to (do something), e.g. *I offered to walk.* n thing offered. n **offering** /'ɒfərɪŋ/ gift, e.g. to a god. n **offertory** /'ɒfətərɪ/ n money given by the people at a church service.

offhand /ɒf'hænd/ adv at once; without preparation. adj (of a person's manner) careless and disrespectful.

office /'ɒfɪs/ n 1 employment and special duties, e.g. *The office of headmaster.* 2 house or room used as a place of business, for writing letters, etc. n **officer** /'ɒfɪsə/ one who holds an office or is employed by the government, e.g. *An officer in the army.* adj **official** /ə'fɪʃəl/ having to do with an office; having to do with the government. n one employed by the government or a company, etc., to deal with the public or with matters of public importance. vi **officiate** /ə'fɪʃɪeɪt/ do the work of an officer who is away or ill; carry out a ceremony in a church. adj **officious** /ə'fɪʃəs/ (e.g. of an official) taking charge in a rude and unpleasant way, giving unnecessary orders, etc.

offing /'ɒfɪŋ/ **in the offing** = 1 (of a ship) at a distance from the shore but still in sight. 2 (of any event) which will probably happen soon.

offset /'ɒfset/ v weigh equally against (some other thing).

offspring /'ɒfsprɪŋ/ n children.

often /'ɒfən, ɒftn/ adv many times.

ogle /'əʊgəl/ v look at (someone) with desire.

ogre /'əʊgə/ n imaginary man-eating GIANT.

ohm /əʊm/ n measure of the difficulty with which electricity passes along a certain wire.

oil /ɔɪl/ n fatty liquid, used for burning, for making machines run easily, and for cooking. vt put oil on the parts of (a machine) so that it may run easily.

oilcake /'ɔɪlkeɪk/ n mass of seeds from which the oil has been pressed, used to feed cattle.

oilskin /'ɔɪl,skɪn/ n cloth specially treated with oil to keep out rain.

ointment /'ɔɪntmənt/ n medicine made up with fat to be rubbed on the skin.

O.K., Okay /əʊ'keɪ/ infml interj yes. adj, adv in a satisfactory way or condition.

okra, okro /'ɒkrə/ n (plant with a) long green fruit used as a vegetable.

old /əʊld/ adj 1 having lived for a long time. 2 much used; not new. 3 belonging to an earlier time. derog **old maid** = old unmarried woman.

okra

an old hand = experienced person. adj **olden** /'əʊldən/ of earlier times.

oligarchy /'ɒlɪgɑːkɪ/ n government by a few.

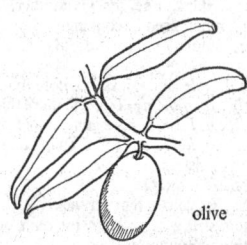

olive

olive /'ɒlɪv/ n tree (grown especially in Italy) which has a small egg-shaped fruit, used also for its oil; the fruit of this tree. n, adj (of) the green colour of this fruit.

omelette /'ɒmlət/ n dish consisting of eggs beaten together with salt and pieces of pleasant-tasting leaves, etc., and cooked with butter.

omen /'əʊmən/ n sign showing that something is going to happen. adj **ominous** /'ɒmɪnəs/ showing future evil.

omit /ə'mɪt/ vt miss out, e.g. not write or say a certain word or not read a certain part of a book. **to omit to** = fail to; not do. n **omission** /ə'mɪʃən/.

omni- /'ɒmnɪ/ all; for all.

omnibus /'ɒmnɪbəs/ n public motor vehicle, usually BUS.

omnipotent /ɒm'nɪpətənt/ adj able to do anything. n **omnipotence** /ɒm'nɪpətəns/.

omniscient /ɒm'nɪsɪənt/ adj all-knowing. n **omniscience** /ɒm'nɪsɪəns/.

omnivorous /ɒm'nɪvərəs/ adj eating all kinds of food—meat, plants, etc.

on /ɒn/ prep 1 at the upper surface of, e.g. *On the table.* 2 at the time or date of, e.g. *On Monday.* 3 travelling in, e.g. *We came on the train.* 4 about, e.g. *A talk on Italian glass.* adv, adj in a working or active condition, e.g. *The lights are on; Turn on the tap.* **on and on** = continuing without stopping. **off and on** = from time to time. **and so on** = etc.

once /wʌns/ adv at one time; some time ago. **all at once** = all together. **at once** = now; without waiting.

one /wʌn/ n, det the first number, written **1.** pron a person, e.g. *One doesn't generally do that sort of thing* = people do not generally do that sort of thing.

onerous /'ɒnərəs/ adj heavy; troublesome.

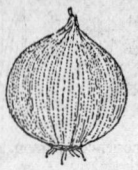

onion

onion /'ʌnɪən/ n a round white vegetable made up of many skins, one inside another, strong smelling, much used in cooking.

onlooker /'ɒnlʊkə/ n one who looks on as others act.

only /'əʊnlɪ/ adv alone; just; no more than, e.g. *I saw only two of them* = I saw no more than two. conj but, e.g. *I would have gone, only I couldn't find the car keys.* adj (of a child) having no brothers or sisters.

onset /'ɒnset/ n attack.

onslaught /'ɒnslɔːt/ n fierce attack.

onus /'əʊnəs/ n weight; duty. **the onus of proof lies with you** = you must prove it.

onward /'ɒnwəd/ adv forward; towards the front.

onyx /'ɒnɪks/ n precious stone having lines of various colours in it.

ooze /uːz/ vi (of liquid) pass slowly through or out of something.

opal /'əʊpəl/ n a precious stone of the colour of milk-and-water.

opaque /əʊ'peɪk/ adj not allowing light to pass through. n **opacity** /əʊ'pæsɪtɪ/.

open /'əʊpən/ adj **1** not shut; free. **2** (of a question or problem) unanswered or undecided. **3** (of a person) keeping nothing secret. v become or cause to become open; start. n **opening** /'əʊpnɪŋ/ break or hole in a wall, the side of a box, etc. adj **open-handed** /ˌəʊpən'hændɪd/ generous. adv **openly** /'əʊpənlɪ/ not secretly.

opera /'ɒpərə/ n musical play of a serious kind. adj **operatic** /ˌɒpə'rætɪk/. n **opera glasses** /'... ͵. ./ glasses used in a theatre to see the actors as if nearer.

operate /'ɒpəreɪt/ v work or cause to work; have an effect. vi cut (the body) in order to set right a diseased part. n **operation** /ˌɒpə'reɪʃən/ **1** working; the way a thing works. **2** cutting of the body by a doctor. adj **operative** /'ɒpərətɪv/ having power to work. n workman. n **operator** /'ɒpəreɪtə/ one who operates a piece of equipment, esp. a telephone SWITCHBOARD.

opiate /'əʊpɪət/ n a sleep-producing medicine.

opinion /ə'pɪnjən/ n what one thinks about a subject. adj **opinionated** /ə'pɪnjəneɪtɪd/ very sure of the rightness of one's own opinions.

opium /'əʊpɪəm/ n sleep-producing material made from the seed of the white POPPY.

opponent /ə'pəʊnənt/ n person who takes the other side in a game, talk or fight.

opportune /'ɒpətʃuːn/ adj coming just at the right time.

opportunity /ˌɒpə'tjuːnɪtɪ/ n chance to do something.

oppose /ə'pəʊz/ vt to stand or fight against (a person or idea).

opposite /'ɒpəzɪt/ adj facing one. n, adj (thing) most different from something, e.g. *Black is the opposite of white.*

opposition /ˌɒpə'zɪʃən/ n state or act of fighting or struggling against someone or something.

oppress /ə'pres/ vt rule in a hard and cruel way; cause to feel ill or sad. n **oppression** /ə'preʃən/. adj **oppressive** /ə'presɪv/.

opprobrious /ə'prəʊbrɪəs/ adj rude (word), showing disrespect.

opprobrium /ə'prəʊbrɪəm/ n shame; thing or words which cause a feeling of shame.

optic /'ɒptɪk/ adj having to do with the eyes. adj **optical** /'ɒptɪkəl/ having to do with light and eyesight. n **optician** /ɒp'tɪʃən/ one who makes or sells glasses for the eyes.

optimism /'ɒptɪmɪzəm/ n belief that everything will come right, will end happily; hopefulness. n **optimist** /'ɒptɪmɪst/ one who believes that all will be well. adj **optimistic** /ˌɒptɪ'mɪstɪk/.

optimum /'ɒptɪməm/ n, adj the best possible.

option /'ɒpʃən/ n choice. adj **optional** /'ɒpʃənəl/ which may or may not be done, at one's own choice.

opulent /'ɒpjʊlənt/ adj rich.

or /ɔː/ conj (word used to join sentences when saying that at least one of them is true) e.g. *Either John or Bill was married* = John and Bill weren't both unmarried.

oracle /'ɒrəkəl/ n place where a god was believed to speak to people; person through whom the god was believed to speak. adj **oracular** /ə'rækjʊlə/ as of an oracle.

oral /'ɔːrəl/ adj by mouth; of the mouth.

orange /'ɒrɪndʒ/ n a very common sweet golden-coloured fruit. n, adj (of the) colour (roughly) of this fruit. n **orangeade** /ˌɒrɪn'dʒeɪd/ drink made from oranges.

orang-outang /ɔːˌræŋ uː'tæŋ/ adj a large Asian monkey-like creature with no tail.

oration /ɔː'reɪʃən/ n solemn speech. n **orator** /'ɒrətə/ good public speaker. adj **oratorical** /ˌɒrə'tɒrɪkəl/ of an orator.

oratorio /ˌɒrə'tɔːrɪəʊ/ n long piece of music and singing, esp. one telling a Bible story.

oratory /'ɒrətərɪ/ n **1** art of speaking. **2** small house of prayer.

orb /ɔːb/ n round thing, ball; star or world.

orbit /'ɔːbɪt/ n path of a star or other world in the sky which moves round another star. v move round (another thing) thus.

orchard /'ɔːtʃəd/ n field of fruit trees.

orchestra /'ɔːkɪstrə/ n group of persons who play music together. adj **orchestral** /ɔː'kestrəl/.

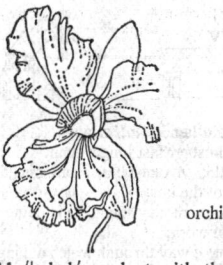

orchid

orchid /'ɔːkɪd/ n plant with three brightly coloured PETALS often curiously shaped, found usually in hot countries.

ordain /ɔː'deɪn/ vt 1 order, e.g. *God has ordained it*. 2 make (someone) a priest.

ordeal /ɔː'diːl/ n difficult or painful experience. **trial by ordeal** = judging a person by giving him a painful or frightening experience.

order /'ɔːdə/ n 1 arrangement, e.g. *In alphabetical order*. 2 neat arrangement. 3 state of law and good control. 4 healthy state, e.g. *My stomach is out of order*. 5 class. **the lower orders** = common people. 6 command. 7 act of asking for particular things, e.g. in a shop. vt 1 arrange in order. 2 command. 3 ask (e.g. a shop) to have something supplied. adj **orderly** /'ɔːdəlɪ/ well arranged; loving good arrangement; peace-loving and well behaved. n soldier who carries orders from one officer to another.

ordinal /'ɔːdɪnəl/ adj showing order, e.g. *The ordinal numbers are first, second, third, etc.*

ordinance /'ɔːdɪnəns/ n rule or law.

ordinary /'ɔːdənərɪ/ adj usual; of a sort commonly found.

ordination /ˌɔːdɪ'neɪʃən/ n act and ceremony of making a man a priest.

ordnance /'ɔːdnəns/ n guns and army stores.

ore /ɔː/ n rock from which metal is obtained.

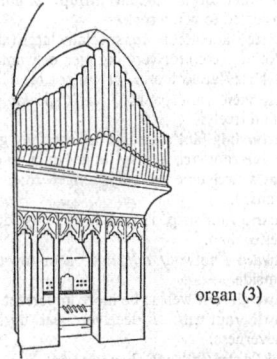

organ (3)

organ /'ɔːgən/ n 1 part of a plant or animal which does some special work. 2 anything thought of

as doing some special work. 3 a musical instrument made of many pipes blown by air—much used in churches.

organic /ɔː'gænɪk/ adj 1 having to do with some ORGAN of the body. 2 (of a substance) found in living things.

organism /'ɔːgənɪzəm/ n living thing.

organize /'ɔːgənaɪz/ vt arrange (people or things) so that they may work together to make an active whole. n **organization** /ˌɔːgənaɪ'zeɪʃən/ 1 act or way of organizing. 2 large organized group of people, such as a business company.

orgy /'ɔːdʒɪ/ n gathering of people to enjoy sex, drink, etc. in an uncontrolled way.

Orient /'ɔːrɪənt/ n the East. adj **oriental** /ˌɔːrɪ'entl/ of the east. n native of an Eastern country, e.g. China.

orientate /'ɔːrɪənteɪt/ vt show or find the position or direction of (something), esp. with respect to the points of the compass. n **orientation** /ˌɔːrɪən'teɪʃən/.

orifice /'ɒrɪfɪs/ n opening; the small mouth of a large hole.

origin /'ɒrədʒɪn/ n place from which a thing began; first beginning of a thing.

original /ə'rɪdʒənəl/ adj 1 earliest. 2 new, not like any other. n **originality** /əˌrɪdʒɪ'nælətɪ/ power of thinking out new ideas. v **originate** /ə'rɪdʒɪneɪt/ begin; come or bring into being.

ornament /'ɔːnəmənt/ n thing used to add beauty to something else. adj **ornamental** /ˌɔːnə'mentl/.

ornate /ɔː'neɪt/ adj having many ornaments; ornamented too much.

ornithology /ˌɔːnɪ'θɒlədʒɪ/ n scientific study of birds.

orphan /'ɔːfən/ n young child whose father and mother are dead. n **orphanage** /'ɔːfənɪdʒ/ home for orphans.

orthodox /'ɔːθədɒks/ adj holding accepted opinions. n **orthodoxy** /'ɔːθədɒksɪ/.

orthography /ɔː'θɒgrəfɪ/ n 1 correct SPELLING. 2 system of writing.

oscillate /'ɒsɪleɪt/ vi swing from side to side. n **oscillation** /ˌɒsɪ'leɪʃən/.

osier /'əʊzɪə/ n a tree whose smaller branches are used to make baskets.

ostensible /ɒ'stensəbəl/ adj seeming or pretended.

ostentation /ˌɒsten'teɪʃən/ n unnecessary show. adj **ostentatious** /ˌɒsten'teɪʃəs/ making much show.

osteopathy /ˌɒstɪ'ɒpəθɪ/ n art of treating diseases by pressing, pulling (etc.) the bones with the hands, e.g. pressing up the bones in the arch of the foot to end pain in walking.

ostler /'ɒslə/ n man who took care of horses.

ostracize /'ɒstrəsaɪz/ vt drive out (someone) from a group of people.

ostrich /'ɒstrɪtʃ/ n a very large bird with long legs and a long neck, which runs very quickly, found in Africa, Arabia and Syria.

185

ostrich

outhouse

other /ˈʌðə/ adj different; not the same; further.

otherwise /ˈʌðəwaɪz/ adv 1 in a different way. 2 if this is not so.

otter /ˈɒtə/ n a fish-eating mammal with beautiful brown fur.

ottoman /ˈɒtəmən/ n long soft seat without back or arms.

ought /ɔːt/ **ought to** = should, e.g. You ought to help others.

ounce /aʊns/ n measure of weight = $\frac{1}{16}$th of a pound, 28·35 grams.

our /ˈaʊə/ det belonging to us. **pron ours** /ˈaʊəz/ something belonging to us.

oust /aʊst/ vt push (someone) out of—e.g. out of employment, favour, etc.

out /aʊt/ adv 1 not in; away from the inside. e.g. He ran out of the house; I'm afraid he's out. 2 not on; off, e.g. Turn the light out. **out of** = 1 not in, e.g. Out of reach = not able to be obtained. 2 through a feeling of pity, e.g. Don't do it out of pity. 3 no longer having, e.g. We're out of bread. **to run out of bread** = come to have no more bread left.

outbid /aʊtˈbɪd/ vt offer more than.

outboard /ˈaʊtbɔːd/ adj (of a motor) fixed on to the outside of a boat to drive it.

outbreak /ˈaʊtbreɪk/ n sudden widespread breaking out of something, e.g. a disease.

outburst /ˈaʊtbɜːst/ n sudden angry speech.

outcast /ˈaʊtkɑːst/ n homeless, friendless person.

outclass /aʊtˈklɑːs/ vt be better than.

outcome /ˈaʊtkʌm/ n result.

outcrop /ˈaʊtkrɒp/ n rock which stands up out of the ground.

outcry /ˈaʊtkraɪ/ n show of anger by the people.

outdistance /aʊtˈdɪstəns/ vt go farther or faster than.

outdo /aʊtˈduː/ vt do better than.

outdoors /aʊtˈdɔːz/ adv not in the house. adj **outdoor** /ˈaʊtdɔː/.

outlying /ˈaʊtlaɪ-ɪŋ/ adj lying away from the main /ˈaʊtməʊst/ farthest outside.

outfit /ˈaʊtfɪt/ n all the things necessary for a certain piece of work; set of clothes worn together.

outgrow /aʊtˈɡrəʊ/ vt grow too large for.

outgrowth /ˈaʊtɡrəʊθ/ n something growing out of something else.

outhouse /ˈaʊthaʊs/ n small building in the grounds or garden of a house.

outing /ˈaʊtɪŋ/ n short pleasure-journey.

outlandish /aʊtˈlændɪʃ/ adj strange.

outlast /aʊtˈlɑːst/ vt last longer than.

outlaw /ˈaʊtlɔː/ n one who is put outside the protection of the law.

outlay /ˈaʊtleɪ/ n money spent, e.g in doing a certain piece of work.

outlet /ˈaʊtlet/ n way through which a thing may go out; good chance for using one's powers.

outline /ˈaʊtlaɪn/ n line showing the shape of a thing; general idea of something. vt draw the shape of; give a general idea of.

outlive /aʊtˈlɪv/ n live longer than.

outlook /ˈaʊtlʊk/ n 1 view seen from a window. 2 general appearance of future events.

outlying /ˈaʊtlaɪ-ɪŋ/ adj lying away from the main or central part of an area.

outnumber /aʊtˈnʌmbə/ vt be more in number than.

outpost /ˈaʊtpəʊst/ n position held at some distance from the main army for keeping watch while the army is at rest, e.g. during the night.

output /ˈaʊtpʊt/ n amount of work done or of articles made.

outrage /ˈaʊt-reɪdʒ/ n very wrong or cruel act which causes great anger. vt attack; seem to (people) to be very wrong. adj **outrageous** /aʊtˈreɪdʒəs/ 1 very bad; causing great anger. 2 most unusual.

outright /ˈaʊt-raɪt/ adv 1 at once. 2 freely and truthfully.

outset /ˈaʊtset/ n beginning.

outside /aʊtˈsaɪd/ adv, adj, prep not inside; not included in, e.g. Come outside = come out of the house with me. n outside part or area; surface.

outsider /aʊtˈsaɪdə/ n 1 person who is not a member of a certain group. 2 horse not expected to win a race.

outsize /ˈaʊtsaɪz/ n, adj specially large (article of clothing, etc.) for very big men or women.

outskirts /ˈaʊtskɜːts/ n (pl) outer edge of a town.

outspoken /aʊtˈspəʊkən/ adj speaking one's mind freely.

outstanding /aʊtˈstændɪŋ/ adj specially good.

outstay /aʊtˈsteɪ/ vt stay longer than. **to outstay one's welcome** = stay longer than one is wanted.

outstrip /aʊtˈstrɪp/ vt pass in running; do much better than.

outward /ˈaʊtwəd/ adj, adv on or towards the outside.

outweigh /aʊtˈweɪ/ vt be more important than.

outwit /aʊtˈwɪt/ vt deceive; beat by greater cleverness.

oval /ˈəʊvəl/ adj egg-shaped.

ovary /ˈəʊvərɪ/ n 1 egg-producing organ. 2 seed-producing organ in a plant.

ovation /əʊˈveɪʃən/ n joyful welcome given by the people to some person greatly admired.

oven /ˈʌvən/ n box used for baking.

over[1] /ˈəʊvə/ prep 1 above. 2 across; on the other side of. 3 more than. adv, adj finished, e.g. The day is over.

over[2] /ˈəʊvə/ too much, e.g. **overeat** /ˌəʊvəˈriːt/ vi eat too much.

overalls

overall(s)[1] /ˈəʊvərɔːl(z)/ n loose dress covering the usual clothes and protecting them during work.

overall[2] /ˌəʊvəˈrɔːl/ adj complete; whole.

overawe /ˌəʊvəˈrɔː/ adj fill a person with fear so that he obeys.

overbalance /ˌəʊvəˈbæləns/ vi fall over. vt 1 cause to fall over. 2 be greater in weight or value than.

overbearing /ˌəʊvəˈbeərɪŋ/ adj taking no notice of other people's ideas or feelings.

overboard /ˈəʊvəbɔːd/ adv over the side of a ship.

overcast /ˌəʊvəˈkɑːst/ adj very cloudy.

overcoat /ˈəʊvəkəʊt/ n warm coat to wear in the street.

overcome /ˌəʊvəˈkʌm/ vt conquer.

overdo /ˌəʊvəˈduː/ vt 1 do too much, e.g. to be foolishly eager in an attempt; work too hard at. 2 cook (meat) too much.

overdraw /ˌəʊvəˈdrɔː/ n take more money from a bank than one put in. n **overdraft** /ˈəʊvədrɑːft/ amount overdrawn.

overdue /ˌəʊvəˈdjuː/ adj late, too late.

overflow /ˌəʊvəˈfləʊ/ vi flow over, e.g. the sides of a river, the edge of a glass, etc. /ˈəʊvəfləʊ/ n amount of liquid which overflows; special place for such liquid.

overgrown /ˌəʊvəˈgrəʊn/ adj (e.g. of a path) made difficult to pass along or through because of a thick growth of plants.

overhang /ˌəʊvəˈhæŋ/ vt stick out over.

overhaul /ˌəʊvəˈhɔːl/ vt examine and repair thoroughly /ˈəʊvəhɔːl/ n.

overhead /ˌəʊvəˈhed/ adj placed above the head. n **overheads** /ˈəʊvəhedz/ regular costs of carrying on a business.

overhear /ˌəʊvəˈhɪə/ vt hear by accident.

overjoyed /ˌəʊvəˈdʒɔɪd/ adj very pleased.

overlap /ˌəʊvəˈlæp/ v lie partly covering (something else).

overlook /ˌəʊvəˈlʊk/ vt 1 look over, e.g. The windows overlooked the street = one could look out over the street from those windows. 2 look at and fail to see. 3 pretend not to see; forgive.

overnight /ˌəʊvəˈnaɪt/ adv during the night. /ˈəʊvənaɪt/ adj lasting or staying the night.

overpower /ˌəʊvəˈpaʊə/ vt conquer by greater power. adj **overpowering** /ˌəʊvəˈpaʊərɪŋ/ more than one can bear.

overrate /ˌəʊvəˈreɪt/ vt think too highly of.

overreach /ˌəʊvəˈriːtʃ/ **to overreach oneself** = fail by trying to do too much or to be too clever.

override /ˌəʊvəˈraɪd/ vt take no notice of (another person's orders, claims, etc.); give opposite orders from (those of another person).

overrule /ˌəʊvəˈruːl/ vt change the ruling of.

overrun /ˌəʊvəˈrʌn/ vt spread all over (a place).

overseas /ˌəʊvəˈsiːz/ adv, n to or in (places) beyond the seas.

overseer /ˈəʊvəsɪə/ n one who watches to see that work is properly done.

oversight /ˈəʊvəsaɪt/ n mistake.

oversleep /ˌəʊvəˈsliːp/ vi sleep on past the proper time for waking.

overstate /ˌəʊvəˈsteɪt/ vt claim more for (something) than is correct.

overstep /ˌəʊvəˈstep/ vt step beyond.

overt /əʊˈvɜːt/ adj open, not secret.

overtake /ˌəʊvəˈteɪk/ v come up and pass (someone) from behind.

overthrow /ˌəʊvəˈθrəʊ/ vt turn over; remove (esp. by force) (e.g. a government). /ˈəʊvəθrəʊ/ n act of overthrowing.

overtime /ˈəʊvətaɪm/ n 1 time worked beyond the regular working hours. 2 payment for such work.

overture /ˈəʊvətʃʊə/ n piece of music played at the beginning of a musical play.

overturn /ˌəʊvəˈtɜːn/ vi turn or cause to turn over in falling.

overwhelm /ˌəʊvəˈwelm/ vt cover or swallow up completely.

overwrought /ˌəʊvəˈrɔːt/ adj tired and too excited.

owe /əʊ/ vt be in debt; feel that one should be grateful to. **owing** /ˈəʊɪŋ/ **owing to** = because of.

owl /aʊl/ n night-bird with large eyes, supposed to be very wise.

own /əʊn/ adj possessed by oneself. **to hold one's**

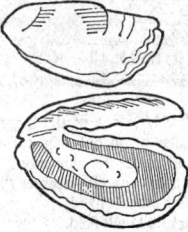

oysters

own = be able to stand against attack; (in illness) not lose strength. **on one's own** = alone. **to do it on one's own** = without help. *vt* possess; agree that an opinion is right. **to own up (to)** = say that one did a wrong act. *n* **owner** /'əʊnə⁷/ one who owns something. *n* **ownership** /'əʊnəʃɪp/.

ox /ɒks/ *n* male form of cattle which cannot cause the production of young. *pl* **oxen**

/'ɒksən/.

oxide /'ɒksaɪd/ *n* substance containing OXYGEN. *v* **oxidize** /'ɒksɪdaɪz/ (cause to) unite with OXYGEN.

oxygen /'ɒksɪdʒən/ *n* a gas necessary for all animal life.

oyster /'ɔɪstə⁷/ *n* a flat shell-fish.

ozone /'əʊzəʊn/ *n* 1 special form of OXYGEN. 2 very pleasant air, e.g at the seaside.

P

pa /pɑː/ *infml n* (child's word for) father.

pace /peɪs/ *n* 1 step. 2 speed. *vi* walk, e.g. *He paced up and down the room.*

pacify /'pæsɪfaɪ/ *vt* make peaceable. *adj* **pacific** /pə'sɪfɪk/ peaceful, peace-loving. *n* **pacification** /ˌpæsɪfɪ'keɪʃən/. *n* **pacifist** /'pæsɪfɪst/ one who desires to put an end to all war.

pack /pæk/ *n* 1 set of things tied or fastened together; load carried on the back or on an animal. 2 group of animals, e.g. *A pack of hounds.* 3 set of playing-cards. *vt* fit closely into a box; cover with material so as to protect from damage. *infml adj* **packed** /pækt/ (e.g. of a room) very crowded.

packet /'pækɪt/, **package** /'pækɪdʒ/ *n* small collection or amount tied up together usually in paper. *n* **packing** /'pækɪŋ/ 1 soft material used for putting round things which are sent in boxes. 2 material used to make a joint tight in an engine.

pact /pækt/ *n* agreement.

pad /pæd/ *n* 1 piece of soft material, e.g. one used to protect the body from blows. 2 number of sheets of writing-paper fixed together on a piece of card. 3 soft round part on the bottom of some animals' feet, e.g. cats. *vt* add padding to. *n* **padding** /'pædɪŋ/ 1 matter used to fill a pad or make chairs, etc., soft. 2 useless words in a book.

paddle /'pædl/ *n* wooden blade used to move a boat along in the water. *v* move (a boat) with a paddle. *vi* walk in water having no shoes on the feet.

paddle-steamer

paddle-wheel /'.. ./ *n* one of the large wheels fixed to the sides of an old ship, turned by a steam-engine to make the ship move forward through the water. *n* **paddle-steamer** /'..,.../ a ship having such wheels fixed.

paddock /'pædək/ *n* small field.

paddy /'pædɪ/ *n* rice growing in a field. *n* **paddy field** /'.. ,./ rice field.

padlock /'pædlɒk/ *n* lock, not fixed to the door, but passed through rings.

padre /'pɑːdrɪ/ *n* priest.

pagan /'peɪgən/ *n, adj* (person) who is not a Christian.

page[1] /peɪdʒ/ *n* one side of a piece of paper in a book.

page[2] /peɪdʒ/ *n* boy servant.

pageant /'pædʒənt/ *n* fine show or public performance; acting in the open air of scenes from the history of a town. *n* **pageantry** /'pædʒəntrɪ/ fine or useless shows and ceremonies.

pagoda /pə'gəʊdə/ *n* tall Asian tower, used for religion.

pail /peɪl/ *n* open vessel with handle used for carrying liquids.

pain /peɪn/ *n* suffering of body or mind. *adj* **painful** /'peɪnfəl/ causing pain. *adj* **painless** /'peɪnləs/ causing no pain. *adj* **painstaking** /'peɪnzteɪkɪŋ/ careful.

paint /peɪnt/ *n* liquid colouring matter laid on with a brush. *v* 1 put paint on to (e.g. walls). 2 use paint to make a picture (of). *n* **painting** /'peɪntɪŋ/ painted picture.

painter /'peɪntə⁷/ *n* 1 one who paints. 2 rope at the front of a boat with which it is tied to the shore.

pair /peə⁷/ *n* set of two things. *v* arrange or be arranged in pairs.

pal /pæl/ *infml n* friend.

palace /'pæləs/ *n* house of a king or other ruler; any large fine house.

palatable /'pælətəbəl/ *adj* pleasing to the taste.

palate /'pælət/ *n* 1 top part of the inside of the mouth. 2 sense of taste.

palatial /pə'leɪʃəl/ *adj* of or like a palace.

palaver /pə'lɑːvə⁷/ *n* 1 a talk, at which many people sit round in a circle. 2 unimportant talk. 3 unnecessary activity.

pale /peɪl/ *adj* having little colour; white.

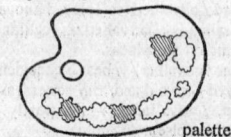

palette

palette /'pælət/ *n* board with a hole for the thumb, on which a painter of pictures mixes his paints.

palisade /ˌpælɪ'seɪd/ *n* fence used in defending against attack.

pall[1] /pɔːl/ *n* ornamental covering of cloth or silk thrown over a box in which a dead body is carried.

pall[2] /pɔːl/ *vi* become uninteresting.

pallet /'pælət/, **palliasse** /'pælɪæs/ *n* STRAW MATTRESS.

palliate /'pælɪeɪt/ *vt* **1** make (something) seem less wrong. **2** lessen (pain) without setting right the cause. *n* **palliative** /'pælɪətɪv/ something which lessens pain or removes a difficulty for a short time only, without attacking the cause.

pallid /'pælɪd/ *adj* (of the skin) white; bloodless. *n* **pallor** /'pælə/.

palm[1] /pɑːm/ *n* flat inside of the hand. **to palm off** = pass (something) off in a deceiving way.

palm[2] /pɑːm/ *n* tree with broad leaves growing out of the top.

palmist /'pɑːmɪst/ *n* one who tells character and the future from lines on the hand.

palm-oil /'. ./ *n* oil obtained from the nuts of the West African palm tree.

palm wine /ˌ. './ *n* (in West Africa) strong drink made of liquid from the palm tree.

palpable /'pælpəbəl/ *adj* which can be felt or noticed.

palpitate /'pælpəteɪt/ *vi* (e.g. of the heart) move quickly, *n* **palpitation** /ˌpælpə'teɪʃən/.

paltry /'pɔːltrɪ/ *adj* worthless.

pamper /'pæmpə/ *vt* treat (e.g. a child) too kindly.

pamphlet /'pæmflət/ *n* small book.

pan[1] /pæn/ *n* flat open pot.

pan-[2] /pæn/ all, for all, e.g. *n* **panacea** /ˌpænə'siːə/ medicine for all diseases.

pancake /'pænkeɪk/ *n* thin, flat cake.

pandemonium /ˌpændɪ'məʊnɪəm/ *n* scene of great noise and disorder.

pander /'pændə/ **to pander to** = help (someone) to satisfy bad desires.

pane /peɪn/ *n* sheet of glass, e.g. in a window.

panegyric /ˌpænɪ'dʒɪrɪk/ *n* speech in praise of someone or something.

panel /'pænəl/ *n* **1** large board set in a door, or fixed to the wall. **2** list of names. **3** list of people chosen to deal with a certain sort of question, e.g. *A panel of doctors*. **panel game** = radio game in which three or four people (the panel) try to guess the right answer. *n* **panelling** /'pænəlɪŋ/ wooden covering of a wall.

pang /pæŋ/ *n* sudden great pain.

panic /'pænɪk/ *n* sudden fear spreading through a crowd. *vi* experience a sudden fear. *adj* **panicky** /'pænɪkɪ/.

pannier /'pænɪə/ *n* one of a pair of baskets carried on a donkey or horse; any basket.

panoply /'pænəplɪ/ *n* complete set of armour; any complete set of equipment.

panorama /ˌpænə'rɑːmə/ *n* view all round; a picture painted on a long narrow piece of material which is unrolled from one end and rolled up on the other. *adj* **panoramic** /ˌpænə'ræmɪk/.

pansy /'pænzɪ/ *n* small plant with broad flat flowers.

pant /pænt/ *vi* breathe quickly. *n* quick breath.

pantheism /'pænθɪ-ɪzəm/ *n* belief that the whole world is God.

pantheon /'pænθɪən/ *n* **1** large hall, e.g. one built in honour of many gods or of famous men. **2** all the gods of a certain nation.

panther /'pænθə/ *n* large wild cat.

pantomime /'pæntəmaɪm/ *n* fairy play acted at Christmas in the theatre.

pantry /'pæntrɪ/ *n* store-room for cups, plates, knives, spoons, etc., in a house; a serving-room for meals.

pants /pænts/ *n* garments worn on the legs, either trousers or garments worn under the trousers.

pap /pæp/ *n* soft food for babies.

papa /pə'pɑː/ *n* child's name for father.

papacy /'peɪpəsɪ/ *n* office of POPE. *adj* **papal** /'peɪpəl/.

papaya /pə'paɪə/, **pa(w)paw** /'pɔːpɔː/ *n* fruit of tree which grows in hot countries, green outside, yellow inside, with black seeds and a sweet-salt taste.

paper /'peɪpə/ *n* **1** material on which a book is printed. **2** newspaper. **3** written or printed paper; written examination. *vt* stick paper on to (e.g., a wall).

papier mâché /ˌpæpɪeɪ 'mæʃeɪ/ *n* paper boiled into a soft mass and used for making boxes, ornamental figures, etc.

papist /'peɪpɪst/ *derog n* Roman Catholic.

papyrus /pə'paɪərəs/ *n* leaf of a plant used by ancient Egyptians for paper.

par /pɑː/ *n* state of being equal. **at par** = equal to its usual or correct value. **on a par with** = equal to, level with.

parable /'pærəbəl/ *n* short story teaching some lesson about God or goodness.

parabola /pə'ræbələ/ *n* curve made by the flight of a ball when thrown.

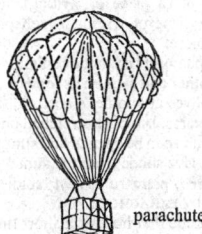

parachute

parachute /'pærəʃuːt/ *n* large circle of thin cloth which opens to let a man fall slowly through the air. *vi* let oneself down from an aeroplane with the help of a parachute.

parade

parade /pə'reɪd/ n **1** show consisting of people walking or marching together. **2** raised road along the sea-front. vi be a part of a parade. vt make a show of.

paradise /'pærədaɪs/ n place to which the souls of good people go after death; any very happy place.

paradox /'pærədɒks/ n saying that seems foolish yet may be true. adj **paradoxical** /ˌpærə'dɒksɪkəl/.

paraffin /'pærəfɪn/ n **1** oil used in lamps; fat from this oil used in making candles. **2** KEROSENE.

paragon /'pærəgən/ n example of goodness which all should copy.

paragraph /'pærəgrɑːf/ n block of writing or printing of which the first word is set a little inwards to the right.

parallel /'pærəlel/ adj (of lines) running side by side yet never meeting.

parallelogram /ˌpærə'leləgræm/ n four-sided figure whose opposite sides are equal and PARALLEL.

paralysis /pə'ræləsɪs/ n disease causing loss of power and feeling in part of the body. vt **paralyse** /'pærəlaɪz/ make unable to move. adj **paralytic** /ˌpærə'lɪtɪk/.

paramount /'pærəmaʊnt/ adj of the highest importance.

paranoia /ˌpærə'nɔɪə/ n form of madness in which the mad person thinks that he is very great, e.g. a king, Napoleon, etc. adj **paranoid** /'pærənɔɪd/.

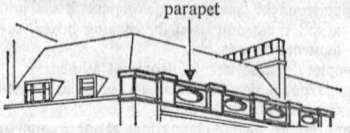

parapet

parapet /'pærəpɪt/ n wall at the edge of a roof or at the side of a bridge.

paraphernalia /ˌpærəfə'neɪlɪə/ n many and various things belonging to a person, or used in some work.

paraphrase /'pærəfreɪz/ vt say or write the meaning of (a piece of writing), using other words. n piece of writing which paraphrases another piece.

parasite /'pærəsaɪt/ n plant or animal which joins on to another and lives on its food or blood; person who lives at another's cost.

parasol /'pærəsɒl/ n cloth stretched on a frame of metal, which can be opened and shut, carried by a lady to give shade from the sun.

paratrooper /'pærəˌtruːpə/ n soldier who is dropped by PARACHUTE.

parboil /'pɑːbɔɪl/ vt boil for a short time.

parcel /'pɑːsəl/ n something covered with paper as for the post or for carrying. **to parcel out** = divide into shares.

parch /pɑːtʃ/ vi **1** burn slightly. **2** dry up. adj **parched** /pɑːtʃt/ very thirsty.

parchment /'pɑːtʃmənt/ n animal skin used for writing on.

pardon /'pɑːdn/ vt forgive. n forgiveness. **I beg your pardon** = I am sorry; allow me to trouble you; forgive me for troubling you.

pare /peə/ vt cut away the outside or edge of.

parent /'peərənt/ n father or mother. adj **parental** /pə'rentl/.

parenthesis /pə'renθəsɪs/ (pl **parentheses** /pə'renθəsiːz/) n either of a pair of BRACKETS; whatever is enclosed between them; words put inside marks like ( ) to keep them separate from the words round them. adj **parenthetical** /ˌpærən'θetɪkəl/.

parish /'pærɪʃ/ n area served by one church. n **parishioner** /pə'rɪʃənə/ one who lives in a parish.

parity /'pærətɪ/ n state of being equal.

park /pɑːk/ n large piece of enclosed ground used by the public, or lying round a great man's house. v put a car in an open place where it may be left safely, e.g. in a quiet street.

parlance /'pɑːləns/ n way of speaking.

parley /'pɑːlɪ/ vi talk with an enemy so as to make peace.

parliament /'pɑːləmənt/ n group of persons elected by the people to make laws. adj **parliamentary** /ˌpɑːlə'mentərɪ/.

parlour /'pɑːlə/ n sitting-room.

parlous /'pɑːləs/ adj dangerous, very bad.

parochial /pə'rəʊkɪəl/ adj having to do with a PARISH narrow in opinion.

parody /'pærədɪ/ vt write or speak in the manner of another person so as to make others laugh at him. n thing said or written with this purpose; a laughable copy of a thing.

parole /pə'rəʊl/ n promise given by a prisoner not to try to escape.

paroxysm /'pærəksɪzəm/ n sudden fierce attack, e.g. of pain.

parquet /'pɑːkeɪ/ n (of a floor) made of blocks of wood fitted together like bricks.

parricide /'pærɪsaɪd/ n **1** killing of one's father or near relative. **2** one who has done this.

parrot /'pærət/ n bird which is able to speak. vt say (words) learnt without thought of their meaning.

parry /'pærɪ/ vt turn aside (e.g. a blow).

parse /pɑːz/ vt describe (a word) showing its relation to other words in a sentence.

parsimonious /ˌpɑːsɪ'məʊnɪəs/ adj too careful with money. n **parsimony** /'pɑːsɪmənɪ/.

parsley /'pɑːslɪ/ n vegetable whose leaves are put on food to make it look nice, used in cooking.

parsnip /'pɑːsnɪp/ n sweet yellow root, boiled for food.

parson /'pɑːsən/ n priest. n **parsonage** /'pɑːsənɪdʒ/ house in which the priest of a church lives.

part /pɑːt/ n **1** one of the pieces into which a thing is divided. **2** character played by an actor in a play or film. **to take part in** = help in; join in

patch

with. *v* separate. **to part with** = give up; allow to go or be given away.

partake /pɑːˈteɪk/ *vi* take part; have a share.

partial /ˈpɑːʃəl/ *adj* **1** not complete. **2** in favour, e.g. *She is partial to sweets* = she likes sweets. *n* **partiality** /ˌpɑːʃiˈæləti/.

participate /pɑːˈtɪsɪpeɪt/ *vi* share in some activity. *n* **participant** /pɑːˈtɪsɪpənt/ one who participates. *n* **participation** /pɑːˌtɪsɪˈpeɪʃən/.

participle /pɑːˈtɪsɪpəl/ *n* part of a verb used as an adjective.

particle /ˈpɑːtɪkəl/ *n* **1** very small piece. **2** word which is used only with other words and does not have a separate meaning.

particular /pəˈtɪkjʊlə/ *adj* **1** special or separate and different from others, e.g. *Each works in his own particular way.* **in a particular case** = in one special example. **2** difficult to please, e.g. *Very particular about one's food.* *n* single point or part, e.g. *Correct in every particular.* *vt* **particularize** /pəˈtɪkjʊləraɪz/ give a list of all the special parts of. *adv* **particularly** /pəˈtɪkjʊləli/ specially; especially.

parting (2)

parting /ˈpɑːtɪŋ/ *n* **1** act of separating. **2** line from which one's hair is brushed to right and left.

partisan /ˌpɑːtɪˈzæn/ *n* eager supporter of a group or of a set of ideas.

partition /pɑːˈtɪʃən/ *n* **1** thin dividing wall. **2** cutting up into parts.

partner /ˈpɑːtnə/ *n* one who works or plays with another. *vt* be a partner of. *n* **partnership** /ˈpɑːtnəʃɪp/.

partridge /ˈpɑːtrɪdʒ/ *n* a kind of bird, shot and used for food.

party /ˈpɑːti/ *n* **1** group of persons who share the same opinion. **2** small group. **3** gathering of friends for food and amusement. **4** person. **to be a party to** = help in (something bad).

partook /pɑːˈtʊk/ *p.t.* of **partake**.

pass /pɑːs/ *v* go past (something); go. *vt* **1** hit, kick or throw (esp. a ball) to another player in a game. **2** allow (e.g. a law) to come into being. **3** cause (something) to go along or down something. **4** succeed in (an examination). *vi* **1** (of time) go by. **2** make no move at one's turn in a game. **to pass away** = die. **to pass out** = faint. **to pass oneself off as** = pretend to be. *n* **1** act of passing. **2** paper which allows one to pass through a door or gate. **3** road through mountains. *adj* **passable** /ˈpɑːsəbəl/ just good enough.

passage /ˈpæsɪdʒ/ *n* **1** act of passing. **2** journey by sea. **3** way by which one passes. **4** narrow way joining the rooms of a house. **5** part of a book.

passbook /ˈpɑːsbʊk/ *n* book showing money paid into and taken out of one's bank.

passenger /ˈpæsɪndʒə/ *n* traveller by train, ship, car etc.

passion /ˈpæʃən/ *n* strong feeling; eager desire. **the Passion** = the sufferings of Christ on the cross, *adj* **passionate** /ˈpæʃənət/.

passive /ˈpæsɪv/ *adj* suffering; without taking action. *n, adj* (of a) form of the verb used to show that the subject suffers the action. *n* **passivity** /pəˈsɪvəti/.

Passover /ˈpɑːsəʊvə/ *n* feast of the Jews in memory of their escape from Egypt.

passport /ˈpɑːspɔːt/ *n* paper allowing one to visit a foreign country.

password /ˈpɑːswɜːd/ *n* word which, when spoken to the guard, allows one to pass.

past /pɑːst/ *adj* no longer present. *adv, prep* by; beyond.

paste /peɪst/ *n* soft matter, such as a mixture of flour and water; such matter used for sticking papers together. *vt* stick with paste

pasteboard /ˈpeɪstbɔːd/ *n* stiff thick paper.

pastel /ˈpæstl/ *n* one of a set of sticks of dry colour used for drawing.

pasteurize /ˈpɑːstʃəraɪz/ *vt* heat (milk) so as to kill all seeds of disease in it.

pastille /ˈpæstɪl/ *n* small sweet containing medicine for the throat.

pastime /ˈpɑːstaɪm/ *n* amusement.

pastor /ˈpɑːstə/ *n* priest in charge of a church. *adj* **pastoral** /ˈpɑːstərəl/ of country life; of church duties.

pastry /ˈpeɪstri/ *n* flour, water, butter, etc., mixed and baked.

pasture /ˈpɑːstʃə/ *n* grassland for cattle.

pasty[1] /ˈpeɪsti/ *adj* (of a face) white and unhealthy-looking.

pasty[2] /ˈpæsti/ *n* pastry cooked with meat in it.

pat /pæt/ *vt* touch lightly with the flat hand. **to pat oneself on the back** = be pleased at one's own cleverness. *n* **1** small piece of butter. **2** act of patting.

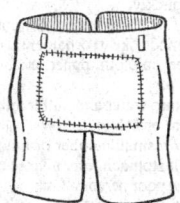
patch (n)

patch /pætʃ/ *n* piece of material fixed on to or into another material to repair it. *vt* fix a patch on. **to patch up** = fix by patching; sort out (something) that has gone wrong. *adj* **patchy** /ˈpætʃi/ irregular in colour; not all of one quality.

191

pate /peɪt/ *n* head.

patent /ˈpeɪtənt/ *adj* open; clear to see. *n* government order giving to one person or one group of people only, the right to make a certain article for sale. *vt* get such an order. *n* **patentee** /ˌpeɪtənˈtiː/ person who owns a patent.

paternal /pəˈtɜːnəl/ *adj* of a father; like a father. *n* **paternity** /pəˈtɜːnəti/ fatherhood.

path /pɑːθ/ *n* 1 narrow road for walking on. 2 line of action. 3 track followed by a moving object.

pathetic /pəˈθetɪk/ *adj* 1 causing a feeling of pity. 2 *infml* very poor in quality.

pathology /pəˈθɒlədʒi/ *n* study of the signs, causes and treatment of disease. *adj* **pathological** /ˌpæθəˈlɒdʒɪkəl/.

pathos /ˈpeɪθɒs/ *n* power of causing pity.

patience /ˈpeɪʃəns/ *n* 1 power of suffering without complaining. 2 card game for one person. *adj* **patient** /ˈpeɪʃənt/ bearing trouble without complaining. *n* sick person being treated by a doctor.

patriarch /ˈpeɪtrɪɑːk/ *n* father and ruler of a family.

patrician /pəˈtrɪʃən/ *n* nobleman of ancient Rome.

patrimony /ˈpætrɪməni/ *n* (*sing*) land, money, etc., handed down to descendants.

patriot /ˈpeɪtrɪət/ *n* one who loves and defends his country. *adj* **patriotic** /ˌpætrɪˈɒtɪk/. *n* **patriotism** /ˈpætrɪətɪzəm/ quality of being patriotic; idea that one's own country is better than others.

patrol /pəˈtrəʊl/ *n* small group of men who march about and guard a place. *v* go round and guard a place.

patron /ˈpeɪtrən/ *n* helper and protector; rich man who helps a writer, painter, etc.; one who buys regularly at a certain shop. *n* **patronage** /ˈpætrənɪdʒ/ state of being a patron. *vt* **patronize** /ˈpætrənaɪz/ 1 act as protector and helper towards. 2 show that one thinks (someone) lower and less important than oneself.

patter /ˈpætə^r/ *n* 1 sound of a number of quick light blows or short steps. 2 special talk of a certain class, e.g. thieves. *vi* 1 make a pattering sound. 2 talk quickly.

pattern /ˈpætən/ *n* thing made so that other things may be made like it; ornamental drawing made or printed on cloth, paper, etc., e.g. *The pattern on a cup.*

patty /ˈpæti/ *n* flour, water and butter mixed, and baked with meat or fish in it.

paucity /ˈpɔːsəti/ *n* small number or amount.

paunch /pɔːntʃ/ *n* stomach, esp. a large one.

pauper /ˈpɔːpə^r/ *n* poor person.

pause /pɔːz/ *n*, *vi* stop or rest.

pave /peɪv/ *vt* cover with stone. **to pave the way** **for** = prepare for, help to arrive or happen. *n* **pavement** /ˈpeɪvmənt/ the path at the side of a street used by people walking.

pavilion /pəˈvɪljən/ *n* big tent; tent-shaped building.

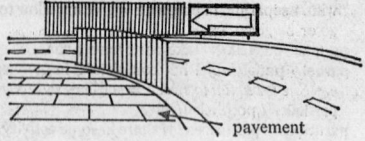

pavement

paw /pɔː/ *n* soft foot of an animal. *vt* touch with the paw or hand.

pawn[1] /pɔːn/ *vt* get money by leaving (an article of value) which will be given back when the money is repaid. *n* **pawnbroker** /ˈpɔːnˌbrəʊkə^r/ one who lends money on things so offered.

pawn[2] /pɔːn/ *n* smallest piece in the game of CHESS; unimportant person used by another.

pawpaw /ˈpɔːpɔː/ see **papaya.**

pay /peɪ/ *vt* give (money) to someone for something. *vi* produce gain, e.g. *The shop is not paying* = it is not bringing in enough money. **to pay a call** = go to a person's house and visit him. *n* money paid for work done. *adj* **payable** /ˈpeɪəbəl/ to be paid. *n* **payee** /peɪˈiː/ one to whom money is paid. *n* **payment** /ˈpeɪmənt/ act of paying; amount paid.

payroll /ˈpeɪrəʊl/ *n* list of workers with the amount paid to each.

pea /piː/ *n* small round green seed which grows in a green seed case, eaten as a vegetable; the kind of plant which produces this food.

peace /piːs/ *n* 1 calm; quietness. 2 freedom from war. *adj* **peaceable** /ˈpiːsəbəl/ liking peace. *adj* **peaceful** /ˈpiːsfəl/ calm; quiet.

peach /piːtʃ/ *n* a soft fruit with a rough stone.

peacock

peacock /ˈpiːkɒk/ *n* a bird with a big brightly coloured tail.

peak /piːk/ *n* 1 pointed top, e.g. of a rock or hill. 2 front part of a cap which stands out over the eyes.

peal /piːl/ *n* loud and continuous ringing of bells.

peanut /ˈpiːnʌt/ *n* hard-shelled seed, white outside, yellow inside, grown under the ground.

pear /peə^r/ *n* a fruit.

pearl /pɜːl/ *n* jewel, white and round, found in shell-fish.

peasant /ˈpezənt/ *n* small farmer or worker on a farm. *n* **peasantry** /ˈpezəntri/ people who work on farms.

peat /piːt/ *n* mass of decayed plants, leaves, etc., cut from the ground and used for burning.

pebble /ˈpebəl/ n small stone.

peccadillo /ˌpekəˈdɪləʊ/ n small unimportant fault.

peck[1] /pek/ n a measure of grain = 7¼ litres.

peck[2] /pek/ v strike at with a pointed thing, as a bird in eating. adj **peckish** /ˈpekɪʃ/ slightly hungry.

peculiar /pɪˈkjuːlɪə/ adj 1 one's own. 2 not like any other; strange. n **peculiarity** /pɪˌkjuːlɪˈærətɪ/ peculiar quality of something.

pecuniary /pɪˈkjuːnɪərɪ/ adj of money.

pedagogue /ˈpedəgɒg/ n teacher. n **pedagogy** /ˈpedəgɒdʒɪ/ art of teaching.

pedal /ˈpedl/ n part of a machine pressed by the foot. v move the pedals of (a machine) with the foot or feet.

pedant /ˈpedənt/ n one is interested in words and rules rather than in making wise use of knowledge. n **pedantry** /ˈpedəntri/. adj **pedantic** /pɪˈdæntɪk/.

peddle /ˈpedl/ vt sell from door to door.

pedestal /ˈpedɪstəl/ n square or round block upon which a stone figure or pillar stands.

pedestrian /pɪˈdestrɪən/ n one travelling on foot.

pedigree /ˈpedɪgriː/ n line of persons (e.g. father, grandfather, etc.) from whom one is descended; such a line in the case of animals.

pedlar /ˈpedlə/ n one who sells from door to door.

peek /piːk/ vi look at something quickly or secretly. n quick or secret look.

peep /piːp/ vi look at something or someone secretly and for a moment.

peer[1] /pɪə/ vi look with half-closed eyes.

peer[2] /pɪə/ n 1 one of equal rank. 2 nobleman. adj **peerless** /ˈpɪələs/ without equal. n **peerage** /ˈpɪərɪdʒ/ rank of nobleman; all the noblemen; list of noblemen.

peevish /ˈpiːvɪʃ/ adj easily angered like a child.

peg /peg/ n wooden nail. vt fix with a peg.

pelican /ˈpelɪkən/ n a bird with a very large beak.

pellet /ˈpelɪt/ n little ball, e.g. of bread pressed together in the fingers.

pell-mell /ˌpel ˈmel/ adv in a disorderly rush.

pelmet /ˈpelmɪt/ n narrow band of curtain across the top of a window.

pelt[1] /pelt/ n skin of an animal.

pelt[2] /pelt/ vt throw many things at. vi rain heavily.

pelvis /ˈpelvɪs/ n large bone at the bottom of the body to which the legs join.

pen[1] /pen/ n enclosed place for sheep, pigs, or other animals.

pen[2] /pen/ n instrument for writing with ink. vt write.

penalty /ˈpenəltɪ/ n punishment. adj **penal** /ˈpiːnəl/ having to do with punishment. vt **penalize** /ˈpiːnəlaɪz/ punish.

penance /ˈpenəns/ n suffering given to oneself as a sign of sorrow for wrongdoing.

pence /pens/ pl of penny.

pencil /ˈpensəl/ n instrument for writing with,

containing hard black material which is able to mark paper.

pendant /ˈpendənt/ n hanging ornament, e.g. jewelled ornament hanging round the neck.

pending /ˈpendɪŋ/ prep during; waiting for. adj not yet settled.

pendulous /ˈpendʒʊləs/ adj hanging down.

pendulum /ˈpendʒʊləm/ n weight swinging from side to side, e.g. on a large clock.

penetrate /ˈpenɪtreɪt/ vt enter into; make a hole in. n **penetration** /ˌpenɪˈtreɪʃən/.

penguin

penguin /ˈpeŋgwɪn/ n bird with short legs, not able to fly, found in very cold countries.

penicillin /ˌpenɪˈsɪlɪn/ n a substance that kills BACTERIA.

peninsula /pəˈnɪnsjʊlə/ n piece of land with water nearly all round it, joined to the shore by a narrow neck of land. adj **peninsular** /pəˈnɪnsjʊlə/.

penitent /ˈpenɪtənt/ adj sorry for wrong done. n **penitence** /ˈpenɪtəns/.

penitentiary /ˌpenɪˈtenʃərɪ/ n prison.

penknife /ˈpen-naɪf/ n small knife in the pocket.

pennon /ˈpenən/, **pennant** /ˈpenənt/ n long, narrow, three-cornered flag.

penny /ˈpenɪ/ n small metal piece of money = 1/100 th of a pound.

pension /ˈpenʃən/ n money paid to an officer, worker, etc., from the time he gives up work until his death.

pensive /ˈpensɪv/ adj thoughtful.

pentagon /ˈpentəgən/ n five-sided figure. **the Pentagon** = war office of U.S.A. in Washington.

penthouse /ˈpenthaʊs/ n 1 specially nice set of rooms for living in at the top of a tall building. 2 sloping roof over a window. 3 hut built against a wall or on the top of a flat roof.

pent-up /ˌpent ˈʌp/ adj enclosed tightly in.

penultimate /peˈnʌltɪmət/ adj last but one.

penury /ˈpenjʊərɪ/ n state of being very poor. adj **penurious** /pɪnˈjʊərɪəs/.

people /ˈpiːpəl/ n persons. n nation.

pep /pep/ n quickness; activity; interest.

pepper /ˈpepə/ n hot-tasting powder, white, black or red, made from a seed and used with food. **to pepper (something) with** = hit with many small shots of.

peppermint

peppermint /'pepə,mint/ *n* oil used for giving a taste to sweets—tasting hot at first, cold afterwards.

peppery /'pepəri/ *adj* hot-tasting; easily angered.

per /pɜː^r, pə^r/ *prep* by; for each, e.g. *per head* = for each person. *adv* **per cent** /pə 'sent/ in each hundred, e.g. ⅖ = *40 per cent,* often written 40%, *n* **percentage** /pə'sentɪdʒ/ number per cent.

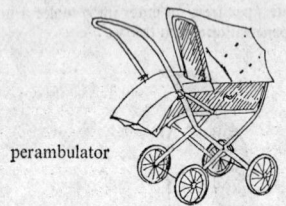

perambulator

perambulator /pə'ræmbjʊleɪtə^r/ *n* carriage for a baby, pushed by hand.

perceive /pə'siːv/ *vt* see, feel, hear, taste, or smell; understand. *adj* **perceptible** /pə'septəbəl/ which can be perceived. *n* **perception** /pə'sepʃən/ power of perceiving. *adj* **perceptive** /pə'septɪv/.

perch¹ /pɜːtʃ/ *n* fresh-water fish.

perch² /pɜːtʃ/ *n* bar on which a bird stands in a cage. *vi* stand on a branch or bar like a bird.

percolate /'pɜːkəleɪt/ *vi* (of liquid) to pass through—as through sand. *n* **percolator** /'pɜːkəleɪtə^r/ instrument used for making coffee.

percussion /pə'kʌʃən/ *n* 1 act of striking one thing against another. 2 (medical) striking the chest and listening to discover what part (if any) is diseased. **percussion instrument** = musical instrument which is struck or shaken, like a drum.

perdition /pɜː'dɪʃən/ *n* ruin; loss of hopes of heaven.

peremptory /pə'remptərɪ/ *adj* sharp and allowing no answer.

perennial /pə'renɪəl/ *adj* lasting from year to year; lasting all through the year. *n* plant which lives more than two years.

perfect /'pɜːfɪkt/ *adj* finished; which cannot be better. *vt* **perfect** /pə'fekt/ make perfect. *n* **perfection** /pə'fekʃən/.

perfidy /'pɜːfɪdɪ/ *n* disloyalty; unfaithfulness. *adj* **perfidious** /pə'fɪdɪəs/.

perforate /'pɜːfəreɪt/ *vt* make a hole through. *n* **perforation** /,pɜːfə'reɪʃən/ small hole.

perform /pə'fɔːm/ *vt* 1 carry out (e.g. a ceremony). 2 do in a solemn ceremonial way or in public. *v* act (a part) in a play or film; sing, dance, etc. in public. *n* **performance** /pə'fɔːməns/.

perfume /'pɜːfjuːm/ *n* pleasant smell; pleasant smelling liquid. /pɜː'fjuːm/ *vt* add a pleasant smell to.

perfunctory /pə'fʌŋktərɪ/ *adj* done quickly and badly as an unpleasant duty.

perhaps /pə'hæps/ *adv* possibly.

perimeter /pə'rɪmɪtə^r/ *n* measure round the outside of an area.

peril /'perəl/ *n* great danger. *adj* **perilous** /'perələs/.

period /'pɪərɪəd/ *n* 1 certain length of time. 2 mark '.' used at the end of a sentence. *adj* **periodic** /,pɪərɪ'ɒdɪk/ happening regularly. *n* **periodical** /,pɪərɪ'ɒdɪkəl/ newspaper or book of stories, etc., printed from time to time, e.g. every month.

periscope →

periscope /'perɪskəʊp/ *n* instrument used in SUB-MARINES for seeing above the water.

perish /'perɪʃ/ *vi* die; decay. *adj* **perishable** /'perɪʃəbəl/ (of goods) tending to become useless if left too long, e.g. eggs.

perjury /'pɜːdʒərɪ/ *n* act of breaking a promise; act of saying, in the name of God, things which **are not true.** *vt* **perjure** /'pɜːdʒə^r/ **to perjure oneself** = perform an act of perjury.

perky /'pɜːkɪ/ *adj* full of life, active in an amusing way, e.g. a bird.

permanent /'pɜːmənənt/ *adj* continuing unchanged. *n* **permanence** /'pɜːmənəns/.

permeate /'pɜːmɪeɪt/ *vt* spread through, as a smell through the air of a room. *adj* **permeable** /'pɜːmɪəbəl/ allowing, e.g. water, to pass through.

permit /pə'mɪt/ *vt* allow. /'pɜːmɪt/ *n* written paper allowing a certain act. *adj* **permissible** /pə'mɪsəbəl/ permitted. *n* **permission** /pə'mɪʃən/ act of allowing. *adj* **permissive** /pə'mɪsɪv/.

pernicious /pɜː'nɪʃəs/ *adj* harmful.

peroration /,perə'reɪʃən/ *n* end of a long speech.

perpendicular /,pɜːpən'dɪkjʊlə^r/ *adj* (of lines) at right angles.

perpetrate /'pɜːpɪtreɪt/ *vt* perform (an unlawful act).

perpetual /pə'petʃʊəl/ *adj* continuing for ever. *vt* **perpetuate** /pə'petʃʊeɪt/ cause to continue for ever.

perplex /pə'pleks/ *vt* cause difficulty in understanding.

perquisite /'pɜːkwɪzɪt/ *n* extra payment or gain beyond one's regular pay.

persecute /'pɜːsɪkjuːt/ *vt* continue to treat cruelly, e.g. because of some belief. *n* **persecution** /,pɜːsɪ'kjuːʃən/.

persevere /ˌpɜːsɪˈvɪə/ *v* go on trying; continue to try. *n* **perseverance** /ˌpɜːsɪˈvɪərəns/.

persist /pəˈsɪst/ *vi* continue steadily in a course of action in spite of difficulty. *adj* **persistent** /pəˈsɪstənt/.

person /ˈpɜːsən/ *n* man, woman or child. *adj* **personable** /ˈpɜːsənəbəl/ good-looking. *n* **personage** /ˈpɜːsənɪdʒ/ person of importance. *adj* **personal** /ˈpɜːsənəl/ of one's own, *n* **personality** /ˌpɜːsəˈnælətɪ/ character. *n* **personnel** /ˌpɜːsəˈnel/ persons employed in a business, on a ship, etc. *vt* **personify** /pəˈsɒnɪfaɪ/ speak of a quality as if it were a person, e.g. 'Come, Mercy, and speak to the hearts of men'. *n* **personification** /pəˌsɒnɪfɪˈkeɪʃən/.

perspective /pəˈspektɪv/ *n* art of drawing in such a way as to show depth and distance. **to see things in perspective** = have a true judgment of the relative importance of events.

perspicacious /ˌpɜːspɪˈkeɪʃəs/ *adj* having good understanding and judgment. *n* **perspicacity** /ˌpɜːspɪˈkæsətɪ/.

perspire /pəˈspaɪə/ *vi* pass liquid out through the skin when hot. *n* **perspiration** /ˌpɜːspəˈreɪʃən/ this natural act; liquid so passed.

persuade /pəˈsweɪd/ *vt* bring (someone) round to one's opinion, or get him to do as one wishes. *adj* **persuasive** /pəˈsweɪsɪv/ able to persuade. *n* **persuasion** /pəˈsweɪʒən/ **1** act of persuading. **2** belief.

pert /pɜːt/ *adj* (of a child) who tries to amuse but forgets to show respect to his elders.

pertain /pəˈteɪn/ *vi* belong or have to do with (something).

pertinacious /ˌpɜːtɪˈneɪʃəs/ *adj* holding firmly to an opinion; not giving up work begun.

pertinent /ˈpɜːtɪnənt/ *adj* well fitted to the subject.

perturb /pəˈtɜːb/ *vt* make anxious or afraid.

peruse /pəˈruːz/ *vt* read carefully. *n* **perusal** /pəˈruːzəl/.

pervade /pəˈveɪd/ *vt* spread through. *adj* **pervasive** /pəˈveɪsɪv/ spreading everywhere.

perverse /pəˈvɜːs/ *adj* seeming to go against all reason, other people's ideas, etc.

pervert /pəˈvɜːt/ *vt* turn to a wrong use. /ˈpɜːvɜːt/ *n* person turned away from right and natural behaviour, esp. in sexual matters. *n* **perversion** /pəˈvɜːʃən/.

pessimism /ˈpesɪmɪzəm/ *n* belief that the worst will always happen. *n* **pessimist** /ˈpesɪmɪst/ one who always expects the worst to happen. *adj* **pessimistic** /ˌpesɪˈmɪstɪk/.

pest /pest/ *n* thing that causes trouble or harm; spreading disease.

pester /ˈpestə/ *vt* continue to trouble.

pestilence /ˈpestɪləns/ *n* dangerous disease that spreads widely.

pestle /ˈpesəl/ *n* striker used for breaking things to powder in a strong stone or metal bowl (MORTAR).

pet /pet/ *n* animal kept in the house as a plaything. *n, adj* favourite. *vt* play lovingly with.

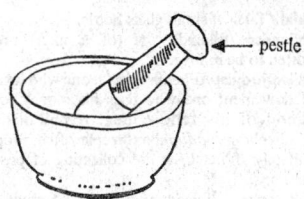
← pestle

petal /ˈpetl/ *n* coloured part of a flower.

peter /ˈpiːtə/ **to peter out** = slowly end or disappear.

petition /pɪˈtɪʃən/ *n* letter from a lower to a higher officer asking for some favour; letter signed by many making some demand of the government. *vt* give such a letter to.

petrify /ˈpetrɪfaɪ/ *vt* **1** change into stone. **2** greatly frighten. *n* **petrifaction** /ˌpetrɪˈfækʃən/.

petrol /ˈpetrəl/ *n* light oil used in car engines.

petroleum /pɪˈtrəʊlɪəm/ *n* heavy oil obtained from the earth.

petticoat /ˈpetɪkəʊt/ *n* woman's garment worn under a skirt or dress.

petty /ˈpetɪ/ *adj* unimportant. **petty cash** = small amounts of money spent on various small matters.

petulant /ˈpetʃʊlənt/ *adj* impatient and ill-tempered. *n* **petulance** /ˈpetʃʊləns/.

pew /pjuː/ *n* line of seats in a church.

pewter /ˈpjuːtə/ *n* mixture of tin and lead used for making drinking pots.

phalanx /ˈfælæŋks/ *n* **1** soldiers standing or moving close together. **2** bone of the fingers or TOES.

phantasm /ˈfæntæzəm/ *n* supposed appearance of the spirit of an absent person.

phantasy /ˈfæntəsɪ/ see **fantasy**.

phantom /ˈfæntəm/ *n* appearance of a dead person seen by a living person.

pharmacy /ˈfɑːməsɪ/ *n* shop which sells medicines. *adj* **pharmaceutical** /ˌfɑːməˈsjuːtɪkəl/ of or for medicines.

phase /feɪz/ *n* part of the time during which something lasts; appearance of a thing as seen in one state of growth. **to phase out** = have (something) slowly stopped.

pheasant /ˈfezənt/ *n* bird with a very long tail, shot for food.

phenomenon /fəˈnɒmɪnən/ *n* natural event as seen or felt by the senses; uncommon event. *adj* **phenomenal** /fəˈnɒmɪnəl/ strange and unusual.

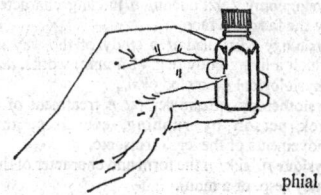
phial

195

phial /'faɪəl/ *n* small glass bottle.

philander /fɪ'lændə/ *vi* (of a man) pretend often to be in love.

philanthropist /fɪ'lænθrəpɪst/ *n* one who loves his fellow men; one who uses his money for the good of his fellow men. *n* **philanthropy** /fɪ'lænθrəpɪ/. *adj* **philanthropic** /ˌfɪlən'θrɒpɪk/.

philately /fɪ'lætəlɪ/ *n* the collecting of postage-stamps.

philologist /fɪ'lɒlədʒɪst/ *n* one who studies the history of language *n* **philology** /fɪ'lɒlədʒɪ/ this study.

philosophy /fɪ'lɒsəfɪ/ *n* **1** study of certain very general matters such as the nature of know-ledge, experience, thought, time, God, etc. **2** any set of general ideas, such as govern a person's behaviour. *n* **philosopher** /fɪ'lɒsəfə/ **1** one who studies philosophy. **2** one who always takes things calmly as they come. *adj* **philosophical** /ˌfɪlə'sɒfɪkəl/.

phlegm /flem/ *n* thick liquid which comes from the nose and throat. *adj* **phlegmatic** /fleg'mætɪk/ slow to act.

phobia /'fəʊbɪə/ *n* unreasoned fear or dislike.

phone /fəʊn/ shortened form of **telephone**.

phoney /'fəʊnɪ/ *adj* pretending; not real.

phonetics /fə'netɪks/ *n* study of the sounds of speech. *adj* **phonetic**.

phosphate /'fɒsfeɪt/ *n* any of a number of sub-stances containing phosphorus. *n* **phosphorus** /'fɒsfərəs/ a poisonous wax-like material which gives out light in the dark. *n* **phosphorescent** /ˌfɒsfə'resənt/ the giving out by a substance of light.

photo /'fəʊtəʊ/ shortened form of **photograph**.

photogenic /ˌfəʊtə'dʒenɪk/ *adj* looking well when photographed, e.g. for the cinema.

photograph /'fəʊtəgrɑːf/ *n* picture made by light passing through a piece of glass on to a film covered with a special preparation of silver. *vt* make such a picture of. *n* **photography** /fə'tɒgrəfɪ/ *n* this art or science. *adj* **photo-graphic** /ˌfəʊtə'græfɪk/.

phrase /freɪz/ *n* small group of words. *vt* express in words. *n* **phraseology** /ˌfreɪzɪ'ɒlədʒɪ/ manner of expression.

physical /'fɪzɪkəl/ *adj* having to do with the body; having to do with the natural world.

physician /fɪ'zɪʃən/ *n* doctor.

physics /'fɪzɪks/ *n* study of matter and the forces of the natural world. *n* **physicist** /'fɪzɪsɪst/ one who studies physics.

physiognomy /ˌfɪzɪ'ɒnəmɪ/ *n* judging character by the face; the face.

physiology /ˌfɪzɪ'ɒlədʒɪ/ *n* study of the way in which a living body (e.g. of a man) works. *adj* **physiological** /ˌfɪzɪə'lɒdʒɪkəl/.

physiotherapy /ˌfɪzɪəʊ'θerəpɪ/ *n* treatment of a sick person by rubbing, exercises, and movements of the legs, arms, etc.

physique /fɪ'ziːk/ *n* the form and character of the body (esp. of a man).

piano /pɪ'ænəʊ/ *n* musical instrument with strings which are hit by little hammers when the keys are pressed. *n* **pianist** /'pɪənɪst/ one who plays the piano.

piassava /pɪə'sɑːvə/ *n* material obtained from a palm tree, used for making ropes, etc.

piccolo /'pɪkələʊ/ *n* musical instrument making a very high whistling sound.

pick[1] /pɪk/, **pickaxe** /'pɪkæks/ *n* pointed iron cross-bar with a wooden handle, used for breaking the earth. *vt* break up (earth, etc.) with a pick.

pick[2] /pɪk/ *vt* **1** choose. **2** gather (e.g. fruit). **to pick up** = take up with the hands. **to pick on** = single out (someone) for specially unpleasant treatment.

picket /'pɪkɪt/ *n* **1** wooden post fixed in the ground. **2** small group of soldiers acting as a guard. **3** any group of persons acting as a guard, e.g. a group of workers trying to keep others from going into the place of work. *v* make a picket to guard (a place).

pickle /'pɪkəl/ *vt* put (food) in salt water to keep it for eating. *n* food so treated.

pickpocket /'pɪkˌpɒkɪt/ *n* one who secretly steals things from people's pockets.

picnic /'pɪknɪk/ *vi*, *n* (go on a) short journey taken for pleasure, with a meal eaten out of doors.

picture /'pɪktʃə/ *n* drawing, painting, or photograph. *vt* **1** make a picture of. **2** imagine. *adj* **picturesque** /ˌpɪktʃə'resk/ such as would make a good picture. *adj* **pictorial** /pɪk'tɔːrɪəl/.

pie /paɪ/ *n* dish of fruit or meat with pastry above or below it.

piebald /'paɪbɔːld/ *adj* (of a horse) having irregular markings in two colours.

piece /piːs/ *n* part; bit. **to piece together** = put the pieces of (something) together. *adv* **piecemeal** /'piːs-miːl/ bit by bit. *n* **piecework** /'piːs-wɜːk/ work paid for according to the amount done (not by time).

pier /'pɪə/ *n* **1** strong post, e.g. of iron. **2** road, built out into the sea on iron posts, for landing from a ship or for use as a place of amusement.

pierce /pɪəs/ *vt* make a hole through.

piety /'paɪətɪ/ *n* goodness in doing one's duty towards God and the Church.

pig /pɪg/ *n* a fat animal used for food; person who behaves like a pig, eating too much and in a rude way, etc. **to make a pig of oneself** = eat too much.

pigeon /'pɪdʒən/ *n* bird which has a wonderful power of finding its way home, also used for food.

pigeonhole /'pɪdʒənhəʊl/ *n* one of a set of small open boxes in which papers are put.

pigheaded /ˌpɪg'hedɪd/ *adj* unwilling to listen to reason.

pig-iron /'. ˌ. / *n* iron in rough square masses.

pigment /'pɪgmənt/ *n* colouring matter.

pigmy /'pɪgmɪ/ *n* see **pygmy**.

pigtail /'pɪgteɪl/ *n* chain of hair twisted together

pigtail

prettily at the back of a girl's head.

pike¹ /paɪk/ n long spear.

pike² /paɪk/ n a large fresh-water fish.

pilchard /'pɪltʃəd/ n a small sea-fish.

pile¹ /paɪl/ n, v heap.

pile² /paɪl/ n soft hair, e.g. on cloth.

pile³ /paɪl/ n large post driven into the ground on which a building is built.

piles /paɪlz/ n soft swellings in the bowel.

pilfer /'pɪlfə/ vi steal small things.

pilgrim /'pɪlgrɪm/ n one who goes to a holy place; a wanderer. n **pilgrimage** /'pɪlgrɪmɪdʒ/ journey to a holy place.

pill /pɪl/ n small ball of medicine.

pillage /'pɪlɪdʒ/ vt take away things from (a house or town) seized in war.

pillar /'pɪlə/ n strong post made of stone, brick, or iron.

pillion /'pɪlɪən/ n seat to carry a second person behind a rider.

pillory /'pɪlərɪ/ n bar with holes in it in which the head and hands were fixed as a punishment.

pillow /'pɪləʊ/ n case full of feathers or other soft material for putting under the head. n **pillowcase** /'... ./ covering for a pillow.

pilot /'paɪlət/ n man who controls an aeroplane or guides a ship through difficult places.

pimple /'pɪmpəl/ n small poisoned spot on the skin.

pin /pɪn/ n very small metal bar with a point and head used for fastening cloth, papers, etc. vt

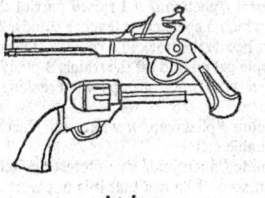

pistols

fasten with a pin. **pins and needles** = feeling in the arms or legs as if needles were being pushed into the skin. **to pin up** = stick up (e.g. a picture) with pins.

pinafore /'pɪnəfɔː/ n loose outer covering worn by children to protect their clothes in play.

pincers /'pɪnsəz/ n (pl) instrument used for holding things tightly. n **pincer-movement** /'.. ,. ./ movement of two armies curving in to meet behind an enemy.

pinch /pɪntʃ/ vt 1 press a small amount between the finger and thumb (or between any two small surfaces). 2 sl steal. n small amount (e.g. of salt).

pine¹ /paɪn/ n tree with needle-like leaves and white soft wood.

pine² /paɪn/ vi waste away with grief.

pineapple /'paɪnæpəl/ n large yellow fruit with pointed leaves growing out of the top, found in hot countries.

pinion¹ /'pɪnɪən/ n wing of a bird. vt hold or tie up the arms of.

pinion² /'pɪnɪən/ n small toothed wheel which joins with another wheel and turns it (or is turned by it).

pink /pɪŋk/ n, adj (of the) colour made by mixing red and white; a flower.

pinnacle /'pɪnəkəl/ n pointed piece of stonework on a building; pointed piece of rock.

pinpoint /'pɪnpɔɪnt/ vt hit exactly (the place aimed at); find the exact place of.

pioneer /ˌpaɪə'nɪə/ n one who goes in front, e.g. of an army, and prepares the way; one who goes first into a new country or into a new subject or branch of study. vt be a pioneer in (something).

pious /'paɪəs/ adj loving to serve God and the Church.

pip /pɪp/ n small seed in a fruit.

pipe /paɪp/ n 1 round bar with a hole through it, used to carry liquid or gas from one place to another. 2 a musical instrument. 3 instrument used for smoking TOBACCO. n **piping** /'paɪpɪŋ/ 1 set of pipes. 2 round fold used to make an edge or ornament on cloth. **piping hot** = very hot. **pipe down!** = do not talk so much—not make so much noise!

pipeline /'paɪp-laɪn/ n long pipe carrying oil, e.g. from the oil well to the sea and ships.

piper /'paɪpə/ n Scotsman playing the BAGPIPES.

piquant /'piːkənt/ adj 1 having a pleasant sharp taste. 2 clever and amusing.

pique /piːk/ vt 1 to hurt the PRIDE of. 2 interest.

pirate /'paɪərət/ n one who attacks and steals from ships. n **piracy** /'paɪərəsɪ/.

pirouette /ˌpɪru:'et/ vi turn round on the point of the foot.

pistol /'pɪstl/ n short gun fired with one hand.

piston /'pɪstn/ n round block inside a pipe which is pushed forward and backward by a gas or steam in an engine.

pit /pɪt/ n deep hole in the ground. **the pit** = back

seats on the lowest floor of a theatre. **to pit against** = set (someone) to fight against.

pitch¹ /pɪtʃ/ n black sticky material used to stop cracks between the boards of ships. **pitch dark** = very dark; black.

pitch² /pɪtʃ/ vt 1 set up (a tent). 2 throw (a ball). vi move with force, esp. (of a ship) up and down. n 1 field for playing a game on. 2 level of a musical note or a speech sound.

pitcher /'pɪtʃə‸/ n large pot with handle.

pitchfork

pitchfork /'pɪtʃfɔːk/ n instrument with two metal fingers used for moving dried grass, etc.

piteous /'pɪtɪəs/ adj worthy of pity.

pitfall /'pɪtfɔːl/ n covered hole for catching animals; trap.

pith /pɪθ/ n soft centre of a stick; most important part of a speech or book.

pitiful /'pɪtɪfəl/ adj worthy of pity; very poor in quality.

pittance /'pɪtəns/ n small amount of food or money. **a mere pittance** = very little, just enough to keep one alive.

pitted /'pɪtɪd/ adj having many small hollows in it, e.g. the skin after an illness.

pity /'pɪtɪ/ n sorrow for the pain of others. **it's a pity that** = I am sorry because. adj **pitiless** /'pɪtɪləs/ having no pity.

pivot /'pɪvət/ n point upon which anything turns; centre bar upon which a wheel turns. vi turn on a pivot.

placard /'plækɑːd/ n public notice stuck on a wall.

placate /plə'keɪt/ vt take away the anger of.

place /pleɪs/ n 1 point in space; area or part of an area. 2 open space in a town. vt 1 put. 2 find a place for, e.g. get employment for.

placid /'plæsɪd/ adj calm; peaceful. n **placidity** /plə'sɪdətɪ/.

plagiarize /'pleɪdʒəraɪz/ vt take (ideas) from another's writings as if they were one's own. n **plagiarism** /'pleɪdʒərɪzəm/.

plague /pleɪg/ n easily spread dangerous disease. vt trouble.

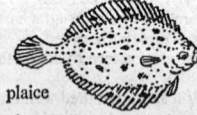

plaice

plaice /pleɪs/ n a flat sea-fish much used as food.

plaid /plæd/ n cloth of various bright colours, the colours showing to what family group a Scotsman belongs.

plain¹ /pleɪn/ adj 1 flat. 2 easily understood. 3 without ornament; not beautiful.

plain² /pleɪn/ n low flat area in a country.

plaintiff /'pleɪntɪf/ n one who makes or begins a claim in a law court.

plaintive /'pleɪntɪv/ adj sad; asking for pity.

plait /plæt/ vt join three or more strings of (esp. hair) together by turning each over the other in turn. n line of plaited hair.

plan /plæn/ n 1 map of anything, e.g. a machine, house. 2 way of acting thought out for the future.

plane¹ /pleɪn/ n tree with large leaves.

plane² /pleɪn/ n instrument for making wood smooth. vt make (wood) smooth. adj flat and level.

plane³ /pleɪn/ n aeroplane.

planet /'plænɪt/ n world going round the sun.

plank /plæŋk/ n wooden board.

plankton /'plæŋktən/ n very small animals and plants in the sea on which fishes feed.

plant¹ /plɑːnt/ n living thing which is not an animal: flower, tree, etc. vt set (a seed or plant) in the ground to grow.

plant² /plɑːnt/ n (sing) buildings, machines, etc., used for any special purpose.

plantain¹ /'plæntɪn/ n common wild plant with broad leaves.

plantain² /'plæntɪn/ n tree which produces fruit like BANANAS.

plantation /plɑːn'teɪʃən/ n wood planted by man; large amount of land on which tea, sugar, etc., is grown. n **planter** /'plɑːntə‸/ man in charge of a plantation.

plaque /plæk/ n flat piece of metal or other material used as an ornament.

plaster /'plɑːstə‸/ n 1 material spread over the walls of buildings to make them smooth. 2 material of this kind used for shaping into figures as ornaments. 3 cloth covered with sticky matter used to protect a wound. vt spread plaster over (e.g. the walls of a room).

plastic /'plæstɪk/ adj soft and able to be shaped. n, adj (made of) substance which, heated and pressed into shape, becomes hard.

plate /pleɪt/ n 1 flat thin sheet of metal. 2 flat open dish from which food is eaten. vt cover (a common metal) with a more valuable one, e.g. Silver plated. n **plate glass** /ˌ ˈ./ glass in large thick sheets, like those in large shop windows.

plateau /'plætəʊ/ n level high land.

platform /'plætfɔːm/ n 1 raised part of the floor on which a speaker or teacher stands. 2 raised part beside the track in a railway station where people get on and off the trains. 3 plans offered by a POLITICAL group when asking to be elected.

platinum /'plætɪnəm/ n white, soft, heavy, very valuable metal.

platitude /'plætɪtjuːd/ n uninteresting fact or opinion so well known that it is not worth saying again.

platoon /plə'tuːn/ *n* group of about 35 soldiers.

platter /'plætə[r]/ *n* large flat dish, esp. a wooden one.

plausible /'plɔːzəbəl/ *adj* seeming to be just or true, but perhaps not so.

play /pleɪ/ *v* 1 amuse oneself; join in (a game). 2 act (a part) in a theatre. 3 make music on (an instrument). *n* 1 free movement, e.g. *There is too much play in this joint* = it is loose, it shakes. 2 amusement. 3 piece in a theatre. *adj* **playful** /'pleɪfəl/ liking play; playing. *n* **plaything** /'pleɪ,θɪŋ/ something or someone used by another for playing with. *n* **playwright** /'pleɪraɪt/ one who writes plays.

plea /pliː/ *n* 1 something begged for. 2 what the prisoner in a law-court says in defending himself.

plead /pliːd/ *v* make a PLEA (of).

pleasant /'plezənt/ *adj* enjoyable; comforting.

pleasantry /'plezəntrɪ/ *n* speech or talk that causes laughter.

please /pliːz/ *vt* give enjoyment to. *interj* (used in forming polite commands) e.g. *Please do it* = I ask you to do it.

pleasure /'pleʒə[r]/ *n* enjoyment. *adj* **pleasurable** /'pleʒərəbəl/ giving pleasure.

pleat /pliːt/ *n* part of the cloth in a garment which is folded down flat. *adj* **pleated** /'pliːtɪd/ having many flat folds.

plebeian /plɪ'biːən/ *adj* belonging to the common people.

plebiscite /'plebɪsɪt/ *n* giving of an opinion by all the people in a country to decide a question of government.

pledge /pledʒ/ *n* thing given by A to B to be held by B so as to make sure that A carries out a promise; a promise. *vt* give as a pledge; promise.

plenary /'pliːnərɪ/ *adj* full; complete. **plenary session** = meeting of all the members.

plenipotentiary /,plenɪpə'tenʃərɪ/ *adj*, *n* (person) having full powers, e.g. to act for his government.

plenty /'plentɪ/ *n* amount which is more than enough. *adj* **plenteous** /'plentɪəs/. *adj* **plentiful** /'plentɪfəl/.

plethora /'pleθərə/ *n* 1 too large an amount; over-fullness. 2 diseased state of the body caused by too much blood.

pleurisy /'plʊərəsɪ/ *n* disease of the outer covering of the LUNGS.

pliable /'plaɪəbəl/, **pliant** /'plaɪənt/ *adj* easily bent; (of a person) easily controlled, readily changing his opinion to suit the wishes of others.

pliers /'plaɪəz/ *n* (*pl*) instrument used for holding things tightly, also for bending and cutting wire.

plight /plaɪt/ *n* unfortunate state.

plinth /plɪnθ/ *n* raised floor of stone or brick on which a house or tall stone figure stands.

plod /plɒd/ *vi* walk or work steadily on.

plot¹ /plɒt/ *n* small piece of land.

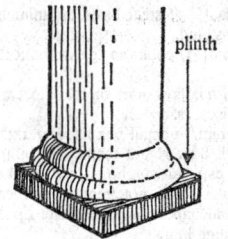

plinth

plot² /plɒt/ *n* 1 plan of a story. 2 secret plan against a person. *vi* make secret plans.

plough /plaʊ/ *n* instrument used for turning up the soil before planting seeds. *vt* turn up (soil) with a plough. **the Plough** = a certain group of stars in the sky shaped like a plough. *n* **ploughshare** /'plaʊʃeə[r]/ iron blade of a plough.

pluck /plʌk/ *vt* pull off (the feathers of a bird, flowers of a plant, etc.); give a sudden pull at. *infml adj* **plucky** /'plʌkɪ/ brave.

plug /plʌg/ *n* something that fits into a hole to prevent liquid flowing out. *vt* stop or block up (a hole).

plum /plʌm/ *n* red or blue-red fruit with a stone in it.

plumage /'pluːmɪdʒ/ *n* (*sing*) feathers.

plumb /plʌm/ *n* ball of lead on a string used to find whether a wall is upright, or to find how deep water is. *vt* get to the bottom of; study thoroughly.

plumber /'plʌmə[r]/ *n* man who fits or repairs pipes used for the water supply, gas supply, etc., in a house. *n* (*sing*) **plumbing** /'plʌmɪŋ/ all the pipes which have to do with the water and gas supply in a house.

plume /pluːm/ *n* feather; ornament made of feathers.

plump¹ /plʌmp/ *adj* nicely fat.

plump² /plʌmp/ *vi* sit or fall suddenly. **to plump for** = give all one's support to (one person) in an election.

plunder /'plʌndə[r]/ *v* steal openly or by force.

plunge /plʌndʒ/ *vi* fall or jump, e.g. into water.

plural /'plʊərəl/ *n*, *adj* (of a) form of a word expressing "more than one".

plus /plʌs/ *prep* added to (often written +).

plush /plʌʃ/ *adj*, *n* (made of or covered with) soft cloth made of wool with short hairs standing up on one side.

plutocrat /'pluːtəkræt/ *n* man who has power because of his wealth. *n* **plutocracy** /pluː'tɒkrəsɪ/ rule by such persons.

ply /plaɪ/ *vt* work at (a trade).

plywood /'plaɪwʊd/ *n* wood consisting of thin pieces of wood stuck together to make one strong board.

pneumatic /njuː'mætɪk/ *adj* containing air; (of a machine) worked by air.

pneumonia /njuː'məʊnɪə/ *n* serious illness of the LUNGS.

poach

poach¹ /pəʊtʃ/ *vi* steal birds or animals from someone's land.

poach² /pəʊtʃ/ *vt* cook (an egg) without the shell in water.

pock /pɒk/ *n* hollow mark on the skin, caused by certain diseases.

pocket /'pɒkɪt/ *n* small bag fixed in a garment; any small bag. *vt* put (something) into one's pocket, esp. in stealing it. *n* **pocketbook** /'pɒkɪtbʊk/ small notebook; small case for money and papers. *n* **pocketknife** /'pɒkɪtnaɪf/ small folding knife.

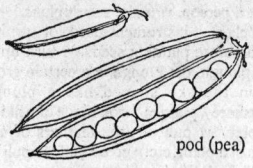

pod (pea)

pod /pɒd/ *n* long seed-vessel of a plant.

podgy /'pɒdʒɪ/ *adj* fat; thick.

poetry /'pəʊɪtrɪ/ *n* beautiful language arranged in lines of regular length and form. *n* **poem** /'pəʊɪm/ one example of such writing. *n* **poet** /'pəʊɪt/ one who writes poetry. *adj* **poetic(al)** /pəʊ'etɪk(əl)/.

poignant /'pɔɪnjənt/ *adj* moving the feelings; sharp.

point /pɔɪnt/ *n* **1** sharp end. **2** exact place or time. **3** idea. **4** purpose. *v* aim (a finger or stick, etc.) at something. **a pointed remark** = saying aimed at some one person. *adj* **pointless** /'pɔɪntləs/ foolish and meaningless. *adv* **point-blank** /ˌ. './ (shooting) straight at a thing when close to it. *n* **points** movable RAILS used for sending trains in different directions. *n* **pointer** /'pɔɪntə/ **1** thing used for pointing, e.g. a long stick. **2** dog used to show where birds or animals are when one is out shooting.

poise /pɔɪz/ *vt* place (something) so that it stays steady. *n* way of holding the head and body; calmness and good judgment.

poison /'pɔɪzən/ *n* matter which causes harm if allowed to enter the body. *vt* give poison to (someone). *adj* **poisonous** /'pɔɪzənəs/.

poke /pəʊk/ *vt* push with the finger or with a stick. **to poke fun at** = try to make people laugh at.

poker /'pəʊkə/ *n* **1** iron bar used to break up coals in a fire. **2** card game played for money.

poky /'pəʊkɪ/ *adj* (of e.g. a room) too small.

pole¹ /pəʊl/ *n* long strong stick.

pole² /pəʊl/ *n* farthest north (or south) point of the earth. *adj* **polar** /'pəʊlə/.

polemic /pə'lemɪk/ *n* attack in speech or writing.

police /pə'liːs/ *n* set of men who keep order in a country. *n* **policeman** /pə'liːsmən/ one of these men.

policy /'pɒləsɪ/ *n* plan, esp. of government. **an in-**surance policy = agreement to pay a certain amount of money in a certain event, e.g. accident or death.

polish /'pɒlɪʃ/ *vt* rub smooth and shining. *n* wax-like substance used in polishing. **to polish off** = finish quickly.

polite /pə'laɪt/ *adj* pleasing in manner; acting like a gentleman. *n* **politeness** /pə'laɪtnəs/.

politic /'pɒlɪtɪk/ *adj* having to do with government; wise, carefully thought out. *adj* **political** /pə'lɪtɪkəl/ having to do with the art of government or with public business. *n* **politician** /ˌpɒlɪ'tɪʃən/ **1** one who takes part, or wants to take part, in the government of a country. **2** one who is more interested in the success of his political party than in the wellbeing of the people. *n* **politics** /'pɒlɪtɪks/ art of government; one's opinion about matters of government.

poll /pəʊl/ *n*, *vi* VOTE.

pollen /'pɒlən/ *n* yellow dust in a flower which makes the seed begin to grow.

pollute /pə'luːt/ *vt* make dirty. *n* **pollution** /pə'luːʃən/.

polo /'pəʊləʊ/ *n* game played with a ball and sticks on horses.

poly- /'pɒlɪ, pə'lɪ/ many, e.g. *n* **polygamy** /pə'lɪgəmɪ/ act or custom of having more than one wife. *n* **polyglot** /'pɒlɪglɒt/ one having many languages. *n* **polygon** /'pɒlɪgən/ many-sided figure. *n* **polytechnic** /ˌpɒlɪ'teknɪk/ school teaching many arts and sciences.

pomade /pə'mɑːd/ *n* thick oily material rubbed on the hair.

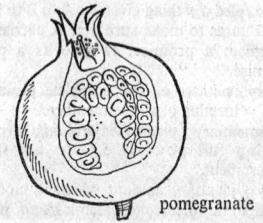

pomegranate

pomegranate /'pɒmɪgrænət/ *n* large fruit containing many red seeds.

pommel /'pʌməl/ *n* **1** round end of the handle of a sword. **2** front of a SADDLE. *vt* continue to hit with the hands.

pomp /pɒmp/ *n* solemn ceremonial show. *adj* **pompous** /'pɒmpəs/ behaving in a foolishly solemn way.

pond /pɒnd/ *n* hole in the ground with water in it, e.g. where cattle drink and ducks live.

ponder /'pɒndə/ *v* think carefully and for a long time about (a question).

ponderous /'pɒndərəs/ *adj* heavy; (of a person or manner) slow and too solemn and serious.

pontoon /pɒn'tuːn/ *n* **1** flat boat used to support a bridge. **2** a card game.

pony /'pəʊnɪ/ n small horse.

poodle /'puːdl/ n dog which usually has its hair cut in a special way.

pooh /puː/ interj sound showing that one feels a thing is of no value or importance. vt **pooh-pooh** /ˌ·'·/ express this feeling about (something).

pool¹ /puːl/ n 1 small hole in the ground with water in it. 2 place built or set aside for swimming in.

pool² /puːl/ n 1 American game played with balls on a table. 2 amount of money made up of payments from each person taking part in a game or business. vt put together (amounts of money or something else) taken from many different people. **football pool** = a lot of people pay money into one large amount; this money is divided up among those who say correctly the results of games of football next week.

poor /pʊə/ adj 1 having little money. 2 unhappy; unfortunate. 3 bad, e.g. *A poor speaker*; *Poor soil.* adj **poorly** /'pʊəlɪ/ not feeling well.

pop¹ /pɒp/ n, interj, vi (make the) sound of opening a bottle. **to pop up** = come up or appear suddenly. **to pop in** = come in suddenly. **to pop out** = go out for a short time.

pop² /pɒp/ short for **pop music** = a kind of popular music.

Pope /pəʊp/ n head of the Roman Catholic Church.

poplar /'pɒplə/ n very tall tree often grown along the sides of rivers or roads.

poplin /'pɒplɪn/ n cloth made of silk and wool, not smooth, but with raised lines on it.

poppy /'pɒpɪ/ n a red (or white) flower.

populace /'pɒpjʊləs/ n the common people.

popular /'pɒpjʊlə/ adj liked by many people. n **popularity** /ˌpɒpjʊ'lærɪtɪ/. vt **popularize** /'pɒpjʊləraɪz/ make popular.

population /ˌpɒpjʊ'leɪʃən/ n all the people in a country; number of people in a country. adj **populous** /'pɒpjʊləs/ thickly populated.

porcelain /'pɔːsəlɪn/ n fine CHINA.

porch /pɔːtʃ/ n raised floor covered with a roof built outside the front door of a house, church, etc.

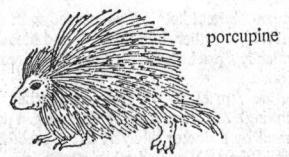

porcupine

porcupine /'pɔːkjʊpaɪn/ n animal like a rat covered with long prickles.

pore¹ /pɔː/ **to pore over** = fix the eyes and mind upon.

pore² /pɔː/ n one of the many small openings in the skin from which liquid comes when the body is hot.

pork /pɔːk/ n meat obtained from a pig.

porous /'pɔːrəs/ adj allowing liquid to pass through.

porpoise /'pɔːpəs/ n large fish-like sea mammal which swims about in groups, going over and under the water in curves.

porridge /'pɒrɪdʒ/ n grain boiled in water to a thick mass, eaten by Scottish people and others.

port¹ /pɔːt/ n 1 harbour; town with a harbour. 2 left-hand side of a ship as one faces forward.

port² /pɔːt/ n a sweet thick wine.

portable /'pɔːtəbəl/ adj of a kind which can be carried easily.

portage /'pɔːtɪdʒ/ n place where boats or goods have to be carried from one stream to another.

portal /'pɔːtl/ n grand gate or door.

portcullis /pɔːt'kʌlɪs/ n network of iron bars hung above the gate of a castle and lowered during attack.

portend /pɔː'tend/ vt be a sign of (a future event). n **portent** /'pɔːtent/ such a sign. adj **portentous** /pɔː'tentəs/ very important; (of a person) pretending to be very important.

porter /'pɔːtə/ n 1 door-keeper. 2 man who carries goods.

portfolio /pɔːt'fəʊlɪəʊ/ n 1 case for papers. 2 office of a member of the government.

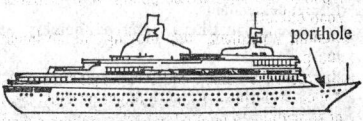

porthole

porthole /'pɔːthəʊl/ n round window in the side of a ship.

portico /'pɔːtɪkəʊ/ n roof supported by pillars covering a path, or built outside the entrance to a building.

portion /'pɔːʃən/ n part or share.

portly /'pɔːtlɪ/ adj solemn and important-looking; fat.

portmanteau /pɔːt'mæntəʊ/ n large bag for carrying clothes when travelling.

portrait /'pɔːtrɪt/ n picture of a person. vt **portray** /pɔː'treɪ/ make a picture of; describe. n **portrayal** /pɔː'treɪəl/ description.

pose /pəʊz/ vt put (a question). vi stand still holding the body in a certain way while a picture is made. **to pose as** = pretend to be. n **poseur** /pəʊ'zɜː/ one who behaves in an unnatural way so as to appear clever or important.

posh /pɒʃ/ infml of the richer social classes.

position /pə'zɪʃən/ n 1 way in which a thing is placed. 2 state. 3 employment. 4 place to be defended. 5 set of one's opinions or ideas.

positive /'pɒzətɪv/ adj 1 very sure. 2 (of a number) greater than 0. adv **positively** /'pɒzətɪvlɪ/ certainly; undoubtedly.

possess /pə'zes/ vt own. adj **possessed** /pə'zest/

under the control of evil spirits. *adj* **self-possessed** calm and sure of oneself. *n* **possession** /pə'zeʃən/ **1** something owned. **2** state of being possessed. *adj* **possessive** /pə'zesɪv/ **1** eager to own or show that one owns. **2** that form of a word which shows possession, e.g. Man's.

possible /'pɒsəbəl/ *adj* which can be done; which can or may happen. *n* **possibility** /ˌpɒsə'bɪlətɪ/ state of being possible; something possible. *adv* **possibly** /'pɒsəblɪ/ perhaps.

post /pəʊst/ *n* **1** bar of wood, metal or stone fixed upright in the ground. **2** letters sent or received. **3** place to which an officer is sent for his work. **4** group of houses where trade is done. *vt* **1** fix up (a notice) in public. **2** send (a man) to work in a certain place. **3** to put (a letter) in the letter-box. **post office** /'. ˌ. ./ building where letters are sorted, stamps are sold, etc. *adj* **postal** /'pəʊstl/.

postage /'pəʊstɪdʒ/ *n* cost of sending a letter by post.

postdate /ˌpəʊst'deɪt/ *vt* write a date on (something) later than the real one.

poster /'pəʊstə/ *n* public notice, e.g. for selling goods.

posterior /pɒ'stɪərɪə/ *adj* later; farther back. *n* back part of the body on which one sits.

posterity /pɒ'sterətɪ/ *n*, (*sing*) people in the future; descendants.

posthaste /ˌpəʊst'heɪst/ *adv* as quickly as possible.

posthumous /'pɒstʃʊməs/ *adj* (of a book) printed after the death of (the writer).

postmortem /ˌpəʊst'mɔːtəm/ *n* examination of a body after death to find the cause of death.

postpone /pə'spəʊn/ *vt* delay till a later date.

postscript /'pəʊst,skrɪpt/ *n* writing added afterwards to a letter or book.

postulate /'pɒstʃʊleɪt/ *vt* take (a fact) as known or as true in order to reason from it. /'pɒstʃʊlət/ *n*.

posture /'pɒstʃə/ *n* way of standing or of holding the body.

posy /'pəʊzɪ/ *n* a few flowers tied together.

pot /pɒt/ *n* vessel, usually of baked earth, used for holding liquid for cooking or eating, or with soil, for plants, etc. *vt* put (a plant) into a pot. *infml* **to go to pot** = be ruined. *infml adj* **potty** /'pɒtɪ/ mad.

potash /'pɒtæʃ/ *n* white powder used in making glass and soap.

potassium /pə'tæsɪəm/ *n* metal substance contained in POTASH.

potato /pə'teɪtəʊ/ *n* root very commonly used as a vegetable.

potency /'pəʊtənsɪ/ *n* power. *adj* **potent** /'pəʊtənt/ powerful. *n* **potentate** /'pəʊtənteɪt/ powerful ruler.

potential /pə'tenʃəl/ *adj* possible; that might be. **electric potential** = possible amount of work a certain electric flow can do.

pothole /'pɒthəʊl/ *n* **1** hole in the road which will shake a car going over it. **2** deep underground

cave. **to go potholing** = go into such caves.

potion /'pəʊʃən/ *n* liquid to be drunk.

potter[1] /'pɒtə/ *vi* work in a lazy careless way.

potter[2] /'pɒtə/ *n* man who makes pots, cups, etc., out of baked earth. *n* **pottery** /'pɒtərɪ/ such cups, plates, etc.; the place where they are made; the art of making them.

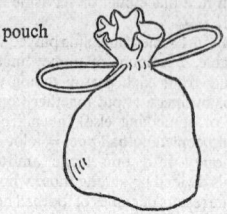

pouch

pouch /paʊtʃ/ *n* small bag.

poultice /'pəʊltɪs/ *n* mass of hot material put on the skin as a medicine.

poultry /'pəʊltrɪ/ *n* hens and other birds kept for eggs and food. *n* **poulterer** /'pəʊltərə/ one who sells birds for food.

pounce /paʊns/ *vi* jump suddenly upon someone or something.

pound[1] /paʊnd/ *vt* break up into powder; hit heavily and often.

pound[2] /paʊnd/ *n* place in which wandering cattle, horses, etc., are imprisoned.

pound[3] /paʊnd/ *n* **1** measure of weight. **2** amount of English money = 100 pence.

pour /pɔː/ *v* flow or cause (liquid) to flow. *vi* rain heavily.

pout /paʊt/ *vi* push out the lips as a sign of being displeased. *n* such an expression of the face.

poverty /'pɒvətɪ/ *n* state of having little money.

powder /'paʊdə/ *n* any dry material broken into very small pieces. *vt* **1** make into a powder. **2** put powder on, e.g. the face.

power /'paʊə/ *n* **1** strength; force. **2** powerful country. *adj* **powerful** /'paʊəfəl/ strong. *adj* **powerless** /'paʊələs/ without power.

practicable /'præktɪkəbəl/ *adj* which can be done or used.

practical /'præktɪkəl/ *adj* concerned with doing real things, rather than thinking and ideas.

practically /'præktɪkəlɪ/ *adv* **1** usefully. **2** really. **3** almost.

practice /'præktɪs/ *n* **1** doing (rather than thinking). **2** custom. **3** act of practising. **4** people served by a doctor, lawyer, etc. *n* **practitioner** /præk'tɪʃənə/ *n* one who has a practice, e.g. *A doctor is a medical practitioner.*

practise /'præktɪs/ *v* do (something) often so as to learn and become skilful. *vt* put into action, e.g. *Practise what you preach* = do yourself what you advise others to do.

prairie /'preərɪ/ *n* grass-land without trees.

praise /preɪz/ *vt* say that one admires; speak in honour of. *n* act of praising.

pram /præm/ *n* 1 short for **perambulator**. 2 small flat-bottomed boat.

prance /prɑːns/ *vt* jump along.

prank /præŋk/ *n* childish trick.

prate /preɪt/ *vi* talk meaninglessly and too much.

prattle /'prætl/ *vi* talk a lot, like a child.

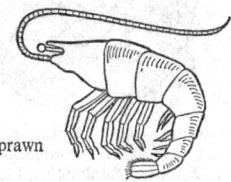

prawn

prawn /prɔːn/ *n* small water-creature with a soft shell which becomes red when boiled.

pray /preɪ/ *vi* 1 ask eagerly or solemnly. 2 ask God for something. *n* **prayer** /preə'/ an act of praying; words said in praying, e.g. to God.

pre- /priː/ *before*, e.g. *adj* **pre-war** /ₗ.'./ before the war.

preach /priːtʃ/ *vi* talk solemnly—as a priest in a church.

preamble /'priːæmbəl/ *n* first part, e.g. of a law, giving reasons for making it.

precarious /prɪ'keərɪəs/ *adj* uncertain; dangerous.

precaution /prɪ'kɔːʃən/ *n* care taken before an event in order to prevent it happening or in order to cause it to happen without doing harm. *adj* **precautionary** /prɪ'kɔːʃənərɪ/.

precede /prɪ'siːd/ *vt* come before; go in front of. *n* **precedence** /'presɪdəns/ greater importance.

precedent /'presɪdənt/ *n* something done or settled before, which is now used as an example or rule.

precept /'priːsept/ *n* rule of behaviour.

precinct /'priːsɪŋkt/ *n* land round a church, school, government office, etc.

precious /'preʃəs/ *adj* 1 of great value. 2 (in art or writing) too careful about little things, not natural.

precipice /'presəpɪs/ *n* very steep cliff.

precipitate /prɪ'sɪpəteɪt/ *vt* 1 throw down. 2 cause a thing to happen at once. 3 cause the solid part of a liquid to separate out and fall to the bottom. *n* **precipitation** /prɪ,sɪpə'teɪʃən/.

precipitous /prɪ'sɪpətəs/ *adj* very steep.

précis /'preɪsiː/ *n* (*sing*) ideas of a long speech or book written down in as few words as possible.

precise /prɪ'saɪs/ *adj* exact. *n* **precision** /prɪ'sɪʒən/.

preclude /prɪ'kluːd/ *vt* prevent; shut off from.

precocious /prɪ'kəʊʃəs/ *adj* growing up too soon; (child) unusually clever for one so young.

preconceived /ₗpriːkən'siːvd/ *adj* (of an idea) formed before one has really looked at the matter. *n* **preconception** /ₗpriːkən'sepʃən/ such an idea.

precursor /priː'kɜːsə'/ *n* something which comes or happens before, e.g. *A red sky is the precursor of a storm.*

predatory /'predətərɪ/ *adj* (of an animal) living by hunting and killing other animals.

predecessor /'priːdɪsesə'/ *n* one who came before, e.g. in office or employment.

predestined /priː'destɪnd/ *adj* already settled by fate.

predicament /prɪ'dɪkəmənt/ *n* dangerous or unpleasant difficulty.

predicate /'predɪkeɪt/ *vt* say (something) about a subject. *n* **predicate** /'predɪkət/ something said of a subject.

predict /prɪ'dɪkt/ *vt* say that (an event) will happen. *n* **prediction** /prɪ'dɪkʃən/.

predilection /ₗpriːdɪ'lekʃən/ *n* great liking for.

predispose /ₗpriːdɪ'spəʊz/ *vt* have such an effect on (the body or mind) as to make a certain event probable, e.g. *To predispose the body to disease.* *n* **predisposition** /ₗpriːdɪspə'zɪʃən/.

predominate /prɪ'domɪneɪt/ *vi* be greater in number, strength, etc. *adj* **predominant** /prɪ'domɪnənt/ most important.

preen /priːn/ *vt* (of a bird) set its (feathers) in order.

prefabricate /ₗpriː'fæbrɪkeɪt/ *vt* make it ready before it is put in place, as e.g. the walls, floor, roof, etc., of a prefabricated house are made in a factory and then put together on the land.

preface /'prefəs/ *n* note written at the beginning of a book.

prefect /'priːfekt/ *n* 1 officer of government in ancient Rome. 2 schoolboy set to keep other boys in order.

prefer /prɪ'fɜː'/ *vt* like better. *adj* **preferable** /'prefərəbəl/ better; more suitable. *n* **preferment** /prɪ'fɜːmənt/ rising to a higher office in the Church. *n* **preference** /'prefərəns/. *adj* **preferential** /ₗprefə'renʃəl/.

prefix /'priːfɪks/ *vt* fix in front. *n* group of letters fixed in front of the root of a word, e.g. *un* in *unhappy*.

pregnant /'pregnənt/ *adj* 1 full of meaning. 2 (of a woman) in the state before childbirth.

prehensile /priː'hensaɪl/ *adj* able to seize and hold.

prehistoric /ₗpriːhɪ'storɪk/ *adj* having happened or lived long ago, before there were any historical writings.

prejudice /'predʒʊdɪs/ *n* opinion formed before examining the facts. **to the prejudice of** = so as to cause harm to. *vt* make (someone) form such an opinion.

prelate /'prelət/ *n* high officer of the Church.

preliminary /prɪ'lɪmɪnərɪ/ *adj*, *n* (something) done in order to prepare for something else.

prelude /'preljuːd/ *n* piece of music which leads up to another; any act or performance which is meant to lead on to something else.

premature /'premətʃə'/ *adj* happening or done before the proper time.

premeditate

premeditate /priːˈmedɪteɪt/ *vt* think over (something) before doing it. *n* **premeditation** /priːmedɪˈteɪʃən/.

premier /ˈpremɪə/ *adj* first, of highest rank. *n* the chief of government.

premise /ˈpremɪs/ *n* something used as a starting point to reason from *n* (*pl*) **premises** house or building with all that belongs to it.

premium /ˈpriːmɪəm/ *n* **1** special payment. **2** money paid to a teacher by a learner. **3** money paid for an INSURANCE. **at a premium** = costing more than the usual price.

premonition /ˌpreməˈnɪʃən/ *n* feeling that a certain event is going to happen.

preoccupied /priːˈɒkjʊpaɪd/ *adj* thinking of other things.

prepare /prɪˈpeə/ *v* get ready before. *adj* **preparatory** /prɪˈpærətərɪ/ getting ready. *n* **preparation** /ˌprepəˈreɪʃən/.

preponderate /prɪˈpɒndəreɪt/ *vi* be in greater weight or power.

preposition /ˌprepəˈzɪʃən/ *n* word such as *to*, *by*, *with*, etc.

prepossessing /ˌpriːpəˈzesɪŋ/ *adj* such as produces a good opinion at first sight.

preposterous /prɪˈpɒstərəs/ *adj* very foolish or unbelievable.

prerogative /prɪˈrɒgətɪv/ *n* special power or right, e.g. of a king.

presage /ˈpresɪdʒ/ *vt* be a sign of (a future event).

prescience /ˈpresɪəns/ *n* knowledge of what will happen in the future.

prescribe /prɪˈskraɪb/ *vt* order the use of (e.g. a book or medicine). *n* **prescription** /prɪˈskrɪpʃən/ **1** list of things to be mixed to make up a medicine. **2** order.

present[1] /ˈprezənt/ *adj* **1** here. **2** now. *n* **presence** /ˈprezəns/ **in the presence of** = being with (someone); standing in front of. **presence of mind** = quickness in thinking and acting when in danger.

present[2] /prɪˈzent/ *vt* **1** bring (one person) before another and make him known. **2** give. **to present arms** = (of soldiers) hold the guns upright in honour of a high officer. *n* **present** /ˈprezənt/ gift. *n* **presentation** /ˌprezənˈteɪʃən/ act of presenting.

presentiment /prɪˈzentɪmənt/ *n* feeling that something bad is going to happen.

presently /ˈprezəntlɪ/ *adv* soon; after a little time.

preserve /prɪˈzɜːv/ *vt* keep from harm or decay. *n* fruit preserved from decay by cooking it in sugar. *n* **preservation** /ˌprezəˈveɪʃən/ *n* act of preserving. *adj, n* **preservative** /prɪˈzɜːvətɪv/ (substance) added to food in order to preserve it.

preside /prɪˈzaɪd/ *vi* act as head of and control (a meeting). *n* **president** /ˈprezɪdənt/ head and controller of a business company, government, etc. *adj* **presidential** /ˌprezɪˈdenʃəl/.

press /pres/ *vt* **1** push down; push down on. **2** make (clothes) flat and neat. **3** urge (someone to

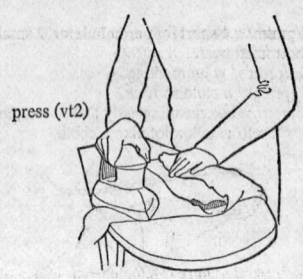

press (vt2)

act). **to press on** = hurry forward. **to press for** = continue to ask for. *n* **1** instrument used for pressing. **2** piece of furniture used for storing clothes. **3** printing machine. **the Press** = newspapers.

pressure /ˈpreʃə/ *n* **1** act of pressing; force with which one thing presses against another, e.g. *The pressure of gas in a container.* **2** state of difficulty.

pressurized /ˈpreʃəraɪzd/ *adj* (of an aeroplane) with the air inside kept at about the same pressure as the pressure of air on the ground.

prestige /preˈstiːʒ/ *n* power because of one's fame.

presume /prɪˈzjuːm/ *vt* take as being known to be true, or as allowed to be done; guess. *vi* be too bold in behaviour. *n* **presumption** /prɪˈzʌmpʃən/ *n* act of presuming; a thing taken as known; boldness of behaviour. *adj* **presumptuous** /prɪˈzʌmptʃʊəs/ bold and bad-mannered.

pretend /prɪˈtend/ *v* act in such a way as to make people believe (something untrue). *adj* **pretentious** /prɪˈtenʃəs/ pretending to be very important.

pretext /ˈpriːtekst/ *n* pretended but not real reason for an action.

pretty /ˈprɪtɪ/ *adj* nice to look at; beautiful in a simple way. *adv* quite, e.g. *Pretty far* = quite a long way.

prevail /prɪˈveɪl/ *vi* win; become generally accepted as a custom. **the prevailing wind** = most usual wind at some time of year. *adj* **prevalent** /ˈprevələnt/ widespread; generally found or accepted.

prevaricate /prɪˈværɪkeɪt/ *vi* try to hide the truth by refusing to give straight or clear answers to questions. *n* **prevarication** /prɪˌværɪˈkeɪʃən/.

prevent /prɪˈvent/ *vt* stop (something) from happening. *n* **prevention** /prɪˈvenʃən/.

preview /ˈpriːvjuː/ *n* showing of a film before it is shown generally to the public.

previous /ˈpriːvɪəs/ *adj* happening before.

prey /preɪ/ *n* animal (or bird) which is hunted by other animals (birds). *vi* hunt animals. **to prey on his mind** = continue to make him sad and anxious.

price /praɪs/ *n* money for which a thing is sold. *vt* give a price to. *adj* **priceless** /ˈpraɪsləs/ of great value.

prick /prɪk/ *vt* make a small hole with a sharp point in (something). *n* act of pricking.

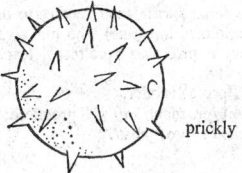

prickly

prickle /'prɪkəl/ *n* sharp needle-like part of a plant or animal. *adj* **prickly** /'prɪklɪ/ covered in prickles.

pride /praɪd/ *n* feeling of being proud.

priest /priːst/ *n* one who has the right to lead prayers and perform ceremonies in a church.

prig /prɪg/ *n* person who makes a show of goodness or wisdom.

prim /prɪm/ *adj* stiff in manner and behaviour, like an old lady.

primacy /'praɪməsɪ/ *n* state of being the most important person or thing in a group.

prima donna /ˌpriːmə 'dɒnə/ *n* chief woman singer.

primary /'praɪmərɪ/ *adj* **1** first in order. **2** simplest. **3** (in matters having to do with teaching) of young children. **of primary importance** = more important than anything else.

primate¹ /'praɪmət/ *n* head of the Church of England.

primate² /'praɪmət/ *n* one of that class of animals which includes men and monkeys.

prime /praɪm/ *adj* **1** first in order, chief, e.g. *Of prime importance; The Prime Minister* = highest officer of government. **2** very good, e.g. *In prime condition.* **3** (of a number) which cannot be divided except by itself and the number 1, e.g. 1, 2, 3, 5, etc. *n* the best time (esp. of a person's life). *vt* prepare for use or action, e.g. put gunpowder ready for firing a gun; tell (someone) facts so as to prepare him to make a speech.

primer /'praɪmə'/ *n* child's first book.

primitive /'prɪmɪtɪv/ *adj* of the earliest times; simple.

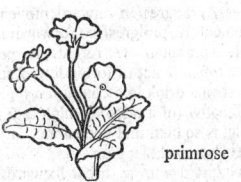

primrose

primrose /'prɪmrəʊz/ *n* yellow wild flower.

prince /prɪns/ *n* son of a king; ruler. *n* **princess** /prɪn'ses/ daughter of a king; wife of a prince.

principal /'prɪnsəpəl/ *adj* most important. *n* head of a school.

principality /ˌprɪnsə'pælətɪ/ *n* country ruled by a prince.

principle /'prɪnsəpəl/ *n* general truth or law at the bottom of other laws; general reason for action; idea according to which one guides one's life.

print /prɪnt/ *vt* produce (a book, paper, etc.) by pressing letters covered in ink on to the page with the use of a machine. *v* write (words) by forming each letter separately. *n* **1** printed letters. **2** any mark made by pressing. **3** one copy of a photograph or picture.

prior /'praɪə'/ *adj* earlier. *n* head of a house in which men lead lives given to God. *n* **prioress** /'praɪəres/ head of a priory for women. *n* **priory** /'praɪərɪ/ *n* such a house.

priority /praɪ'ɒrətɪ/ *n* **1** the right to get something or have something done before other people can get it or have it done. **2** idea of what is most important.

prise /praɪz/ **to prise open** = open by force.

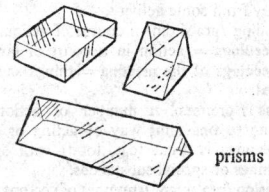

prisms

prism /'prɪzəm/ *n* block of regular shape with three or more flat sides; piece of glass with three sides used for breaking up light into its colours.

prison /'prɪzən/ *n* building in which law-breakers are shut up. *n* **prisoner** /'prɪzənə'/ person put into prison.

pristine /'prɪstiːn/ *adj* belonging to the earliest times; in its first simple and pure state.

privacy /'prɪvəsɪ/ *n* state of being alone, of being secret.

private /'praɪvət/ *adj* belonging to one person; not public. *n* common soldier.

privateer /ˌpraɪvə'tɪə'/ *n* ship which does not belong to the government but is allowed to attack enemy ships.

privation /praɪ'veɪʃən/ *n* lack of food and comforts.

privilege /'prɪvəlɪdʒ/ *n* special favour or right. *adj* **privileged** /'prɪvəlɪdʒd/.

privy /'prɪvɪ/ *adj* having special knowledge of (a secret). **Privy Council** = body of special advisers to the king or queen. *n* place where one leaves the waste matter of the body.

prize /praɪz/ *n* something given as a return for, or as a sign of, very good work—e.g. given to one who is first in a race, or who is head of his class in school. *vt* value greatly.

pro /prəʊ/ shortened form of PROFESSIONAL.

pro- /prəʊ/ in favour of, e.g. *pro-German.*

pros and cons *n* (*pl*) reasons for and against.

probable /'prɒbəbəl/ *adj* which is thought to be

true, though it cannot be proved; expected to happen. *n* **probability** /ˌprɒbə'bɪlətɪ/.

probate /'prəʊbeɪt/ *n* examining of a person's will after his death to see that it is in order and according to law.

probation /prə'beɪʃən/ *n* **1** time when one is doing certain work to show others that one is good enough to be employed in that work. **2** time when a prisoner is allowed to remain out of prison if he behaves well.

probe /prəʊb/ *n* **1** thin bar of metal used by a doctor to feel for a shot (etc.) in a wound. **2** space vehicle sent to make discoveries. *v* examine into (something).

probity /'prəʊbətɪ/ *n* honesty.

problem /'prɒbləm/ *n* difficult question. *adj* **problematic** /ˌprɒblə'mætɪk/ doubtful.

procedure /prə'siːdʒəˈ/ *n* way of going forward; way of carrying out a business.

proceed /prə'siːd/ *vi* go forward; carry on work; come out from. *n* (*pl*) **proceeds** /'prəʊsiːdz/ money from some activity.

proceeding /prə'siːdɪŋ/ *n* course of action. **legal proceedings** = action in a court of law. **the proceedings of the meeting** = things said and settled.

process /'prəʊses/ *n* number of actions all leading to one aim; way of acting or doing something. *vt* treat (e.g. food) with special machines or special substances.

procession /prə'seʃən/ *n* number of persons going along in line, in a fixed order, e.g. at a marriage or funeral.

proclaim /prə'kleɪm/ *vt* make public. *n* **proclamation** /ˌprɒklə'meɪʃən/ thing made known to the public; act of proclaiming.

proclivity /prə'klɪvətɪ/ *n* leaning towards (a certain sort of behaviour).

procrastinate /prəʊ'kræstɪneɪt/ *vi* delay. *n* **procrastination** /prəʊˌkræstɪ'neɪʃən/.

procure /prə'kjʊəˈ/ *vt* obtain; buy; cause a result to happen.

prod /prɒd/ *vt* push with a pointed object; urge to action.

prodigal /'prɒdɪgəl/ *adj* wasteful; careless in spending.

prodigy /'prɒdɪdʒɪ/ *n* wonder; person who has some wonderful power. *adj* **prodigious** /prə'dɪdʒəs/ unusual; very big; wonderful.

produce /prə'djuːs/ *vt* **1** bring forward. **2** bear or yield, e.g. *The soil produces corn.* **3** be the cause of, e.g. *My work has produced no result.* **4** make, e.g. *To produce cars.* *n* (*sing*) **produce** /'prɒdjuːs/ things produced, e.g. crops. *n* **product** /'prɒdʌkt/ **1** thing produced; result. **2** result of MULTIPLYING two numbers together. *n* **production** /prə'dʌkʃən/ act of producing something; something produced.

profane /prə'feɪn/ *adj* not holy; having to do with this life (not the life after death); disrespectful to God. *n* **profanity** /prə'fænətɪ/.

profess /prə'fes/ *vt* say openly; make a claim to;

claim to be able to do; pretend. *n* **profession** /prə'feʃən/ **1** declaration. **2** learned employment, e.g. doctor, teacher, lawyer. *adj* **professional** /prə'feʃənəl/ having to do with a profession. *n, adj* (one) who plays games for money. *n* **professor** /prə'fesəˈ/ teacher in a university.

proffer /'prɒfəˈ/ *vt* offer.

proficient /prə'fɪʃənt/ *adj* well practised; clever. *n* **proficiency** /prə'fɪʃənsɪ/.

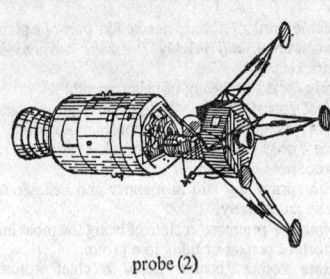

probe (2)

profile /'prəʊfaɪl/ *n* line round the edge of a thing, e.g. of a face seen from the side.

profit /'prɒfɪt/ *n* gain, e.g. of money. *vi* gain a profit. *vt* to be of use to. *adj* **profitable** /'prɒfɪtəbəl/ providing a profit; useful. *n* **profiteer** /ˌprɒfɪ'tɪəˈ/ one who gains a lot of money in time of war or difficulty.

profligate /'prɒflɪgət/ *n, adj* (one) given up to bad ways.

profound /prə'faʊnd/ *adj* deep; very learned. *n* **profundity** /prə'fʌndətɪ/.

profuse /prə'fjuːs/ *adj* plentiful; giving or given out freely. *n* **profusion** /prə'fjuːʒən/.

progeny /'prɒdʒənɪ/ *n* descendants.

prognosticate /prɒg'nɒstɪkeɪt/ *vt* tell that (some future event) will happen. *n* **prognosis** /prɒg'nəʊsɪs/ probable result of a disease.

program(me) /'prəʊgræm/ *n* **1** list of things which will be done in public, e.g. of songs, etc., in a public show. **2** separate television or radio show.

progress /'prəʊgres/ *n* onward movement; improvement. *vi* /prə'gres/ go forward; improve.

prohibit /prə'hɪbɪt/ *vt* forbid. *n* **prohibition** /ˌprəʊɪ'bɪʃən/ **1** act of forbidding. **2** forbidding of all strong drink in a country. *adj* **prohibitive** /prə'hɪbətɪv/ (of a price) so high that it forbids buying, is so high that one cannot buy.

project[1] /'prɒdʒekt/ *n* plan.

project[2] /prə'dʒekt/ *vt* throw forward. *vi* stand out. *n* **projectile** /prə'dʒektaɪl/ thing shot forward, e.g. from a gun. *n* **projector** /prə'dʒektəˈ/ instrument for throwing pictures on a SCREEN by means of a bright light.

proletariat /ˌprəʊlə'teərɪət/ *n* all the common people; all the workers.

prolific /prə'lɪfɪk/ *adj* fruitful; producing much.

prolix /'prəʊlɪks/ *adj* using many words to express little meaning.

prologue /'prəʊlɒg/ *n* speech made before a play begins.

prolong /prə'lɒŋ/ *vt* make longer.

promenade /ˌprɒmə'nɑːd/ *n* 1 quiet walk. 2 road along the sea-front.

prominent /'prɒmɪnənt/ *adj* standing out; easily seen; well known to all.

promiscuous /prə'mɪskjʊəs/ *adj* 1 mixed; of all classes. 2 having sexual relations with many different people.

promise /'prɒmɪs/ *v* say that one will do something; cause a person to hope. *n* act of promising; thing promised. *adj* **promising** /'prɒmɪsɪŋ/ causing one to hope.

promissory /'prɒmɪsərɪ/ *adj* (of a note) saying that money will be paid on a certain date.

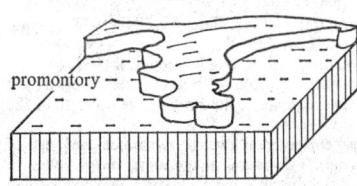

promontory

promontory /'prɒməntrɪ/ *n* point of high land standing out into the sea.

promote /prə'məʊt/ *vt* 1 move up to a higher rank or place; help to start (e.g. a business). *n* **promotion** /prə'məʊʃən/.

prompt¹ /prɒmpt/ *adj* ready; done at once.

prompt² /prɒmpt/ *vt* 1 move or urge (someone) to action. 2 help (an actor) who has forgotten his words.

promulgate /'prɒmʌlgeɪt/ *vt* make known to the public (e.g. a law, news).

prone /prəʊn/ *adj* lying face downward; sloping towards. **prone to** = tending to.

prong /prɒŋ/ *n* sharp point of an instrument.

pronoun /'prəʊnaʊn/ *n* word standing for a noun, such as *I, you, he*, etc. *adj* **pronominal** /prəʊ'nɒmɪnəl/.

pronounce /prə'naʊns/ *vt* 1 say solemnly. 2 form (the sounds of a language). *n* **pronunciation** /prəˌnʌnsɪ'eɪʃən/ way of saying words or of forming the sounds of a language. *adj* **pronounced** /prə'naʊnst/ strongly marked; clear, e.g. *His fear was very pronounced.*

proof /pruːf/ *n* 1 that which shows a thing to be true. 2 first printing which the writer will correct.

prop /prɒp/ *n, vt* support.

propaganda /ˌprɒpə'gændə/ *n* (*sing*) arrangements for spreading a certain belief; beliefs so spread.

propagate /'prɒpəgeɪt/ *vt* cause to increase, e.g. plants; spread an idea among people. *n* **propagation** /ˌprɒpə'geɪʃən/.

propel /prə'pel/ *vt* push forward. *n* **propeller** /prə'pelə/ set of sloping blades which drive a ship or aeroplane forward.

propensity /prə'pensətɪ/ *n* leaning towards a certain kind of behaviour.

proper /'prɒpə/ *adj* right and fitting; polite. **a proper noun** = name of a person or place.

property /'prɒpətɪ/ *n* 1 that which is owned. 2 special and peculiar character of a thing.

prophecy /'prɒfɪsɪ/ *n* telling of a future event. *vt* **prophesy** /'prɒfɪsaɪ/ tell the future. *n* **prophet** /'prɒfɪt/ one who declares the will of God to men, who tells the future. *adj* **prophetic** /prə'fetɪk/.

propitiate /prə'pɪʃɪeɪt/ *vt* gain the favour of; lessen the anger of.

propitious /prə'pɪʃəs/ *adj* favourable; fortunate.

proportion /prə'pɔːʃən/ *n* size of a thing when considered as a part of a whole.

propose /prə'pəʊz/ *vt* offer an idea for consideration. *vi* offer marriage. *n* **proposal** /prə'pəʊzəl/ offer of marriage. *n* **proposition** /ˌprɒpə'zɪʃən/ offer. 2 idea expressed in a sentence.

propound /prə'paʊnd/ *vt* put forward (an idea) for consideration.

proprietor /prə'praɪətə/ *n* owner. *adj* **proprietary** /prə'praɪtrɪ/ *adj* (medicine) made by a business company, not specially ordered by a doctor; in the manner of an owner.

propriety /prə'praɪətɪ/ *n* state of being proper, or according to the rules of good behaviour.

propulsion /prə'pʌlʃən/ *n* act of PROPELLING or being PROPELLED.

prosaic /prəʊ'zeɪ-ɪk/ *adj* containing no new or interesting ideas.

prose /prəʊz/ *n* writing which is not poetry.

prosecute /'prɒsɪkjuːt/ *vt* follow (a plan); take action against or make a claim against in a court of law. *n* **prosecution** /ˌprɒsɪ'kjuːʃən/.

prosody /'prɒsədɪ/ *n* laws that govern the regular arrangement of sounds in poetry.

prospect /'prɒspekt/ *n* scene; looking forward or expecting. /prə'spekt/ *vi* look for, e.g. gold. *adj* **prospective** /prə'spektɪv/ expected.

prospectus /prə'spektəs/ *n* plan or short description.

prosper /'prɒspə/ *vi* be successful; do well in business. *n* **prosperity** /prɒ'sperətɪ/. *adj* **prosperous** /'prɒspərəs/.

prostitute /'prɒstɪtjuːt/ *vt* use for a bad purpose. *n* woman who offers herself for money. *n* **prostitution** /ˌprɒstɪ'tjuːʃən/.

prostrate /'prɒstreɪt/ *adj* lying stretched out. *vt* /prɑ'streɪt/ throw (oneself) down on the ground as a sign of great respect. *n* **prostration** /prɒ'streɪʃən/.

protagonist /prəʊ'tægənɪst/ *n* chief actor; leader.

protect /prə'tekt/ *vt* guard; shelter from evil. *n* **protection** /prə'tekʃən/. *adj* **protective** /prə'tektɪv/. *n* **protector** /prə'tektə/ *n* one who protects; ruler of a kingdom while the king is too young. *n* **protectorate** /prə'tektərət/ such rule; weaker country placed in charge of a stronger one.

protégé /'prɒtɪʒeɪ/ n one who is under protection.

protein /'prɒuti:n/ n kind of body-building food, contained in, e.g., meat, egg—not in fat or sugar.

protest /prə'test/ vi say that one is not in favour of something; say that a thing should not be done. n **protest** /'prəutest/.

Protestant /'prɒtɪstənt/ n one of a group of Christians who separated themselves from the Church of Rome.

protocol /'prəutəkɒl/ n (sing) rules of behaviour fixed by custom.

prototype /'prəutətaɪp/ n first example according to which other later things are made.

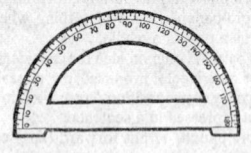

protractor

protract /prə'trækt/ vt make long. n **protractor** /prə'træktə⁷/ instrument used for measuring angles.

protrude /prə'tru:d/ vi stand out.

protuberance /prə'tju:bərəns/ n swelling out. adj **protuberant** /prə'tju:bərənt/.

proud /praud/ adj holding a high opinion of oneself or of one's possessions.

prove /pru:v/ vt show that (something) is true; try to see whether a thing is true.

provender /'prɒvəndə⁷/ n food for cattle.

proverb /'prɒvɜ:b/ n short wise saying. adj **proverbial** /prə'vɜ:bɪəl/ famous from a proverb.

provide /prə'vaɪd/ vt supply. **provided that** = if.

providence /'prɒvɪdəns/ n care and preparation for the future; the care of God for man. adj **provident** /'prɒvɪdənt/ caring for the future. adj **providential** /,prɒvɪ'denʃəl/ very fortunate.

province /'prɒvɪns/ n part of a country; area within which a certain person or thing has power. adj **provincial** /prə'vɪnʃəl/.

provision /prə'vɪʒən/ n 1 supply. 2 preparation. n **provisions** food. adj **provisional** /prə'vɪʒənəl/ serving for the present time only, but able to be changed later.

proviso /prə'vaɪzəu/ n condition.

provoke /prə'vəuk/ vt make angry. adj **provocative; provoke** /prə'vɒkətɪv/. n **provocation** /,prɒvə'keɪʃən/.

provost /'prɒvəst/ n head of a COLLEGE; holder of an office in the Church; chief officer of Scottish cities.

prow /prau/ n front of a ship.

prowess /'prauɪs/ n courage.

prowl /praul/ vt wander about like a hunting animal.

proximity /prɒk'sɪmətɪ/ n nearness.

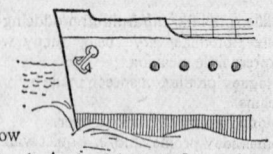

prow

proxy /'prɒksɪ/ n the right to act for another person. **to vote by proxy** = show one's opinion (e.g. at a meeting) through someone else although one is not oneself present.

prude /pru:d/ n woman who is over-correct and careful in her behaviour. adj **prudish** /'pru:dɪʃ/.

prudent /'pru:dənt/ adj wise and careful. n **prudence** /'pru:dəns/.

prune¹ /pru:n/ n dried PLUM.

prune² /pru:n/ vt cut off parts of (a tree) to make it grow better.

prurient /'pruərɪənt/ adj interested in unpleasant things.

pry /praɪ/ vi look into something which is not one's concern.

psalm /sɑ:m/ n song in honour of God.

pseudo /'sju:dəu/ adj not real, pretending to be. n **pseudonym** /'sju:dənɪm/ name other than the real name.

psychiatry /saɪ'kaɪətrɪ/ n science and art of curing disorders of the mind. adj **psychiatric** /,saɪkɪ'ætrɪk/. n **psychiatrist** /saɪ'kaɪətrɪst/ psychiatric doctor.

psychic /'saɪkɪk/ adj of the soul; having to do with the spirits of the dead.

psychology /saɪ'kɒlədʒɪ/ n scientific study of the mind. adj **psychological** /,saɪkə'lɒdʒɪkəl/.

psychopath /'saɪkəupæθ/ n person of rather disordered mind, but not mad.

psychosis /saɪ'kəusɪs/ n disorder of the mind.

ptomaine /'təumeɪn/ n poisonous matter in bad food.

pub /pʌb/ n inn; PUBLIC HOUSE.

puberty /'pju:bətɪ/ n earliest age at which it is possible to become a parent.

pubic /'pju:bɪk/ adj having to do with that part of the body where the sexual ORGANS are.

public /'pʌblɪk/ n people in general, not just those in some special work, etc. adj open to the public; owned by the public. **a public house** = building where people may go to buy strong drink. **a public school** = (in England) school which a parent must pay to send his child to.

publican /'pʌblɪkən/ n owner of a PUBLIC HOUSE.

publication /,pʌblɪ'keɪʃən/ n printed thing, e.g. a book; act of printing and selling books.

publicity /pʌ'blɪsətɪ/ n making something widely known.

publish /'pʌblɪʃ/ vt 1 make known. 2 print and sell (a book or paper).

puce /pju:s/ n, adj (of the) colour made by mixing red, blue and brown.

puck /pʌk/ n small round, flat piece of rubber used instead of a ball in playing HOCKEY on the ice.

pucker /'pʌkə'/ *vt* gather into small folds.

pudding /'pʊdɪŋ/ *n* **1** sweet dish served at the end of a meal. **2** meat boiled inside a thin pipe-like skin; meat cooked inside pastry.

puddle /'pʌdl/ *n* small quantity of water lying in a hollow, e.g. in the road.

puerile /'pjʊəraɪl/ *adj* childish; silly.

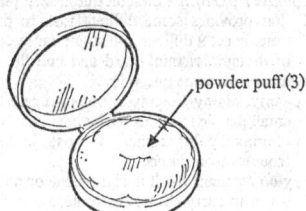

powder puff (3)

puff /pʌf/ *n* **1** short sharp breath of wind. **2** small cloud of smoke. **3** any soft round object, e.g. one made of feathers used to put powder on the face. *vi* send out puffs, e.g. of smoke. *adj* **puffy** /'pʌfɪ/ soft and swollen.

pugnacious /pʌg'neɪʃəs/ *adj* loving to fight.

pull /pʊl/ *vt* draw towards oneself. *n* act or force of pulling. **to pull a face** = make the face look ugly as a sign of disrespect. **to pull up** = stop.

pullet /'pʊlɪt/ *n* young hen.

pulley /'pʊlɪ/ *n* wheel over which a rope passes, used to raise weights.

pullover /'pʊləʊvə'/ *n* woollen garment pulled on to the body by passing it over the head.

pulmonary /'pʌlmənərɪ/ *adj* having to do with the LUNGS.

pulp /pʌlp/ *n* soft inside material of a plant or fruit.

pulpit /'pʊlpɪt/ *n* raised place in a church from which a priest speaks to his people.

pulsate /pʌl'seɪt/ *vi* beat, like the heart.

pulse¹ /pʌls/ *n* heart-beat.

pulse² /pʌls/ *n* seeds of plants such as beans.

pulverize /'pʌlvəraɪz/ *vt* make into powder.

puma /'pjuːmə/ *n* fierce animal like a large cat.

pumice /'pʌmɪs/ *n* light stone with little holes in it used for cleaning the hands.

pummel /'pʌməl/ *vt* strike many times with the hands.

pump /pʌmp/ *n* machine for raising liquid, or pressing air into things or for taking liquid or air out. *vt* use a pump to raise (liquid), force (air) into, etc.

pumpkin /'pʌmpkɪn/ *n* very large round yellow fruit which grows on the ground and is used for food.

pumps /pʌmps/ *n* special shoes used in the past for dancing.

pun /pʌn/ *n* play on words.

punch¹ /pʌntʃ/ *vt* strike with the closed hand. *n* act of punching.

punch² /pʌntʃ/ *vt* make a small hole in. *n* instrument for this purpose.

punch³ /pʌntʃ/ *n* strong drink made of spirits (e.g. whisky), hot water, sugar, etc.

punctilious /pʌŋk'tɪlɪəs/ *adj* very careful over small matters of politeness.

punctual /'pʌŋktʃʊəl/ *adj* coming at the exact time. *n* **punctuality** /ˌpʌŋktʃʊ'ælətɪ/.

punctuate /'pʌŋktʃʊeɪt/ *vt* put the marks ; : . etc. into (writing). *n* **punctuation** /ˌpʌŋktʃʊ'eɪʃən/.

puncture /'pʌŋktʃə'/ *vt* make a hole in; make a hole and let out the air, e.g. from the wheel of a car. *n* such a hole.

pundit /'pʌndɪt/ *n* learned man.

pungent /'pʌndʒənt/ *adj* strong-smelling; sharp and painful.

punish /'pʌnɪʃ/ *vt* cause pain or discomfort to a person as a return for wrongdoing; treat roughly. *n* **punishment** /'pʌnɪʃmənt/.

punitive /'pjuːnətɪv/ *adj* punishing.

punt /pʌnt/ *n* flat boat pushed along with a pole. *vi* move along in a punt.

punter /pʌntə'/ *n* one who risks money on horse-races.

puny /'pjuːnɪ/ *adj* small and weak.

pupil /'pjuːpəl/ *n* **1** person being taught. **2** black opening in the centre of the eye.

puppet /'pʌpɪt/ *n* small wooden figure moved by strings to make it dance; person who is completely under the control of another.

puppy /'pʌpɪ/ *n* young dog.

purchase /'pɜːtʃəs/ *vt* buy. *n* something bought.

pure /pjʊə'/ *adj* not mixed with anything else; simple; clean. *n* **purity** /'pjʊərətɪ/. *adv* **purely** /'pjʊəlɪ/ completely.

purée /'pjʊəreɪ/ *n* thick SOUP; MASH of vegetables etc.

purgative /'pɜːgətɪv/ *n* medicine used to drive waste matter downwards from the body.

purgatory /'pɜːgətərɪ/ *n* place in which souls after death are made pure and fit to enter heaven.

purge /pɜːdʒ/ *vt* make pure and clean.

purify /'pjʊərɪfaɪ/ *vt* make pure. *n* **purification** /ˌpjʊərɪfɪ'keɪʃən/. *n* **purist** /'pjʊərɪst/ one who demands great correctness in language.

puritan /'pjʊərɪtən/ *n* one who leads a very plain simple life and believes that church services should be performed in a very plain way.

purloin /pɜː'lɔɪn/ *vt* steal.

purple /'pɜːpəl/ *n*, *adj* (of the) colour obtained by mixing red and blue.

purport /'pɜːpət/ *n* the meaning, /pə'pɔːt/ *vi* seem to be; pretend.

purpose

purpose /'pɜːpəs/ *n* aim; desire; plan.

purr /pɜː/ *n* low sound made by a cat when pleased. *vi* make this sound.

purse[1] /pɜːs/ *n* small bag for money; amount of money given or collected for some purpose.

purse[2] /pɜːs/ *vt* draw (the lips) together into a small round shape.

purser /'pɜːsə/ *n* officer in charge of the money and stores on a ship.

pursuance /pə'sjuːəns/ **in pursuance of** = while performing.

pursue /pə'sjuː/ *vt* run after and try to catch. *n* **pursuit** /pə'sjuːt/.

purvey /pə'veɪ/ *vt* provide; supply.

pus /pʌs/ *n* liquid which comes out of a poisoned wound.

push /pʊʃ/ *vt* press forward; cause (something) to move forward or away. *n* act of pushing. **to get the push** = be sent away from one's employment. *sl n* **pusher** one who sells unlawful DRUGS.

puss /pʊs/, **pussy** /'pʊsɪ/ *n* name used in calling a cat.

put /pʊt/ *vt* **1** move into a certain place or cause to remain in a certain place, e.g. *To put a book on the table* = set down. **2** bring into a certain state; cause, e.g. *To put a stop to* = cause to end; *Put things right* = cause things to be right; *Put to death* = kill. **to put about** = spread (a story) round. **to put across** = help people to understand. **to put forward** = suggest. **to put off** = **1** delay. **2** cause (someone) to think badly of one. **to put out** = cause (a light) to cease burning. **to be put out** = angry. **to put together** = arrange or fix together. **to put (someone) up** = take (him) in as a visitor. **to put up with** = TOLERATE.

putrefy /'pjuːtrɪfaɪ/ *vi* decay. *n* **putrefaction** /ˌpjuːtrɪ'fækʃən/. *adj* **putrescent** /pjuː'tresənt/ decaying. *adj* **putrid** /'pjuːtrɪd/ decayed.

putt /pʌt/ *n* a gentle stroke in the game of GOLF. *v* hit (the ball) in making such a stroke.

putty /'pʌtɪ/ *n* white powder and oil mixed to make a soft material used for fixing glass in windows.

puzzle /'pʌzəl/ *n* **1** difficult question. **2** plaything that provides some difficult task to pass the time. *vt* set a difficult question; cause difficulty of thought. *vi* think hard and find the correct answer to some question.

pygmy, pigmy /'pɪgmɪ/ *n* one of a race of very small people found in Africa.

pyjamas /pə'dʒɑːməz/ *n* loose jacket and trousers worn in bed.

pylon /'paɪlən/ *n* tall upright stone or post; steel tower to carry electric wires across country.

pyramids

pyramid /'pɪrəmɪd/ *n* thing square at the bottom and pointed at the top (or of this shape but having three or more sides). **the Pyramids** = great buildings of this shape in Egypt in which the dead bodies of kings were put in ancient times.

pyre /paɪə/ *n* heap of wood on which a dead body is burned.

pyrotechnics /ˌpaɪrəʊ'tekniks/ *n* FIREWORKS.

python /'paɪθən/ *n* large snake which kills by twisting itself tightly round the body of an animal.

Q

quack[1] /kwæk/ *n, vi* (make the) cry of a duck.

quack[2] /kwæk/ *n* person who pretends to have knowledge (esp. of medicine) which he does not possess.

quadrangle /'kwɒdræŋgəl/ *n* figure with four sides, e.g. a square; square courtyard.

quadrant /'kwɒdrənt/ *n* **1** one quarter of a circle. **2** instrument used for measuring angles.

quadrilateral /ˌkwɒdrɪ'lætərəl/ *adj, n* (of a) figure with four sides.

quadruped /'kwɒdrʊped/ *n* animal with four legs.

quadruple /'kwɒdrʊpəl/ *adj* four times.

quaff /kwɒf/ *v* drink.

quagmire /'kwægmaɪə/ *n* very soft piece of ground.

quail /kweɪl/ *vi* draw back in fear.

quaint /kweɪnt/ *adj* pleasing because old or unusual.

quake /kweɪk/ *vi* shake.

quadrant

Quaker /'kweɪkə/ *n* member of a group of Christians holding certain special beliefs in God and very much against war.

qualification /ˌkwɒlɪfɪ'keɪʃən/ *n* **1** act of QUALIFYING. **2** something which QUALIFIES a person for something (e.g. for certain work).

qualify /'kwɒlɪfaɪ/ *v* get or give the qualities necessary for, e.g. *To become qualified as a doctor* = pass the necessary examinations. *vt* make less or weaker, e.g. *To qualify what one has said* = add something which makes one's words less strong or less general.

qualitative /'kwɒlɪtətɪv/ *adj* having to do with quality.

quality /'kwɒlətɪ/ *n* **1** character; that which makes a person or thing different from others. **2** goodness or badness. **3** good character.

qualm /kwɑːm/ *n* sudden feeling, e.g. of sickness or faintness.

quandary /'kwɒndərɪ/ *n* state of doubt or difficulty.

quantity /'kwɒntətɪ/ *n* amount.

quarantine /'kwɒrəntiːn/ *n* separation from other animals or people for fear of spreading disease.

quarrel /'kwɒrəl/ *n, vi* (have a) disagreement.

quarry¹ /'kwɒrɪ/ *n* place from which stone is got.

quarry² /'kwɒrɪ/ *n* hunted animal; anything which is eagerly searched for or followed.

quart /kwɔːt/ *n* measure of liquid = 1.136 litres.

quarter /'kwɔːtə ʳ/ *n* **1** one fourth part of a whole. **2** one of the four limbs of an animal, e.g. *The hind quarters* = back legs. **3** one of the four points of the compass, e.g. *From every quarter* = from all sides. **4** part of a town, e.g. *The Chinese quarter* = that part where the Chinese live. *vt* cut into four parts.

quarters /'kwɔːtəz/ *n* place given to soldiers to live in. **at close quarters** = near.

quarterly /'kwɔːtəlɪ/ *adj* happening four times a year. *n* a paper printed and sold four times a year.

quartermaster /'kwɔːtəˌmɑːstə ʳ/ *n* army officer who supplies food, clothes, etc.; seaman with special duties, e.g. at the ship's wheel.

quartet /kwɔːˈtet/ *n* set of four, esp. of musicians.

quartz /kwɔːts/ *n* hard rock in which gold is sometimes found.

quasi- /'kweɪzaɪ/ almost; seeming as if, e.g. *adj* **quasi-official** /ˌ . . ' . ./ official in appearance only.

quatrain /'kwɒtreɪn/ *n* four lines of poetry.

quaver /'kweɪvə ʳ/ *vi* shake. *n* short note of music.

quay /kiː/ *n* place where ships are loaded or unloaded.

queasy /'kwiːzɪ/ *adj* feeling sick; easily made sick.

queen /kwiːn/ *n* wife of a king; woman ruler of a country.

queer /kwɪə ʳ/ *adj* **1** unusual; peculiar. **2** *sl n* HOMOSEXUAL.

quell /kwel/ *vt* put down; cause to cease (e.g. a rising against the government).

quench /kwentʃ/ *vt* put an end to (thirst or fire) by means of water.

querulous /'kwerʊləs/ *adj* full of complaints; eager to quarrel.

query /'kwɪərɪ/ *n, vt* question.

quest /kwest/ *n* search.

question /'kwestʃən/ *n* **1** something asked. **2** difficult matter. **out of the question** = impossible; not to be considered. *vt* **1** express doubt about. **2** ask (someone questions). *adj* **questionable** /'kwestʃənəbəl/ doubtful. *n* **questionnaire** /ˌkwestʃəˈneə ʳ, ˌkes-/ set of printed questions sent out to many persons in order to get facts on a certain subject.

queue

queue /kjuː/ *n* line of people waiting, e.g. to get into a theatre. *vi* (of people) form such a line.

quibble /'kwɪbəl/ *vi, n* (give an) answer intended to deceive—or to escape from telling the truth.

quick /kwɪk/ *adj* swift; keen; active; thinking or moving fast. *n* **quicklime** /'kwɪk-laɪm/ powder which, with water, boils and becomes building lime. *n* **quicksand** /'kwɪksænd/ soft sand which swallows up ships. *n* **quicksilver** /'kwɪkˌsɪlvə ʳ/ = MERCURY.

quid /kwɪd/ *n* **1** piece of TOBACCO kept in the mouth. **2** *sl* £1.

quiescent /kwaɪˈesənt/ *adj* resting.

quiet /'kwaɪət/ *adj* free from noise or movement; calm; (of colours) not bright. *n* **quietness** /'kwaɪətnəs/. *v* **quieten** /'kwaɪətən/ make or become quiet.

quill /kwɪl/ *n* central stem of a feather; feather used as a pen; any sharp pointed object.

quilt /kwɪlt/ *n* bed-covering filled with wool or feathers. *adj* **quilted** /'kwɪltɪd/ made like a quilt.

quince /kwɪns/ *n* hard fruit like an apple.

quinine /'kwɪniːn/ *n* bitter medicine used for fever.

quintessence /kwɪnˈtesəns/ *n* real nature of a thing; perfect example of something.

quip /kwɪp/ *n, vi* (make a) clever saying.

quire /'kwaɪə ʳ/ *n* twenty-four sheets of paper.

quit /kwɪt/ *v* **1** go away from. **2** leave (employment).

quite /kwaɪt/ *adv* **1** completely; in all ways. **2** almost; rather. *interj* I agree.

quiver¹ /'kwɪvə ʳ/ *n* case in which arrows are carried.

quiver² /'kwɪvə ʳ/ *vi* shake.

quixotic /kwɪkˈsɒtɪk/ *adj* **1** generous. **2** full of imagination and taking no care of one's own business interests.

quiz /kwɪz/ *vt* question (someone). *n* game in which each of two groups of people tries to

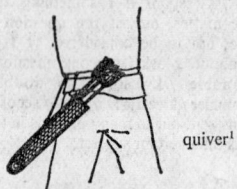

quiver[1]

answer more questions than the other group.

quizzical /'kwɪzɪkəl/ *adj* secretly laughing.

quoit /kɔɪt/ *n* ring for throwing over a small post as part of a game.

quorum /'kwɔːrəm/ *n* number of persons who must be present at a meeting according to the rules.

quota /'kwəʊtə/ *n* share that one must receive or pay; amount of goods which one nation may send into a certain foreign country.

quote /kwəʊt/ *vt* repeat the words of (another person) saying whose words they are; speak of (some person) as a supporter of one's opinion, or tell (some fact or event) which serves as an example. *n* **quotation** /kwəʊ'teɪʃən/ act of quoting; words quoted. **quotation marks** = the marks 'and' or "and" used to separate off words quoted.

quotient /'kwəʊʃənt/ *n* number of times one number can be divided into another.

R

rabbi /'ræbaɪ/ *n* Jewish teacher or priest.

rabbit /'ræbɪt/ *n* small common mammal with long ears, which lives in a hole in the ground.

rabble /'ræbəl/ *n* crowd of low noisy people.

rabid /'reɪbɪd/ *adj* 1 having rabies. 2 mad, e.g. mad with anger. *n* **rabies** /'reɪbiːz/ serious illness caused by the bite of a mad dog.

race[1] /reɪs/ *n* an attempt to move faster than another, e.g. *Horse-races*. *v* try to win by running faster than; move very quickly.

race[2] /reɪs/ *n* group of people or animals of the same blood. *adj* **racial** /'reɪʃəl/ having to do with race.

rack /ræk/ *vt* stretch; cause great pain to. *n* frame fixed to the wall on which things are kept, e.g. for drying; frame of wood and string on which light bags, etc., are put in a railway carriage.

racket[1] /'rækɪt/ *n* 1 noisy talk and play. 2 dishonest way of getting money. *n* **racketeer** /,rækɪ'tɪə/ one who makes money thus.

racket[2], **racquet** /'rækɪt/ *n* instrument used for hitting the ball in games like TENNIS.

racy /'reɪsɪ/ *adj* full of life.

radar /'reɪdɑː/ *n* equipment for seeing aeroplanes, etc., by means of radio waves.

radiate /'reɪdɪeɪt/ *vt* send out (light or heat). *adj* **radiant** /'reɪdɪənt/ 1 sending out such waves. 2 showing great happiness. *n* **radiation** /,reɪdɪ'eɪʃən/ act of radiating.

radiator /'reɪdɪeɪtə/ *n* 1 instrument for sending out heat in a house. 2 instrument for cooling the engine of a car.

radio

radical /'rædɪkəl/ *adj* from or of the root. *n, adj* (one) wanting or working for great changes, e.g. in laws or the form of government.

radio /'reɪdɪəʊ/ *n* instrument for receiving music, speech or messages sent through the air by means of electrical waves. *adj* **radioactive** /,reɪdɪəʊ'æktɪv/ (of a substance) giving off a dangerous form of ENERGY. *n* **radioactivity** /,reɪdɪəʊæk'tɪvətɪ/. *n* **radiography** /,reɪdɪ'ɒgrəfɪ/ taking X-RAY photographs. *n* **radium** /'reɪdɪəm/ a radioactive metal.

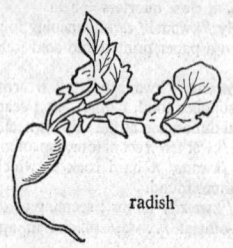

radish

radish /'rædɪʃ/ *n* red root with a hot taste.

radius /'reɪdɪəs/ *n* straight line from the centre of a circle to the edge.

raffia /'ræfɪə/ *n* (*singæ* long pieces of soft paperlike substance from a plant, used to make baskets, mats, etc.

raffle /'ræfəl/ *n* sale in which each person pays a small part of the value of a thing and a name is drawn by chance to decide who shall become the owner.

raft /rɑːft/ *n* large pieces of wood joined together to make a rough flat boat.

rafter /'rɑːftə/ *n* one of the main beams of a roof.

rag /ræg/ *n* bit of cloth. *adj* **ragged** /'rægɪd/ torn; dressed in bad torn clothes. *n* **ragamuffin** /'rægəmʌfɪn/ boy dressed in ragged clothes.

rage /reɪdʒ/ *n* wild uncontrolled anger.

raid /reɪd/ *n* sudden attack. *vt* make a raid on.

rail[1] /reɪl/ *n* **1** cross-bar of a fence. **2** one of the iron bars on which a train runs. **to go by rail** = go by train. *n* **railing** /'reɪlɪŋ/ bars put up to stop people from falling off stairs, off a cliff, etc.

rail[2] /reɪl/ *vi* speak angrily to or about a person.

raillery /'reɪlərɪ/ *n* laughing at a person in a good-tempered way.

railway /'reɪlweɪ/, **railroad** /'reɪlrəʊd/ *n* lines and track on which a train runs; lines, trains, stations and all things used in carrying people and goods by train.

rain /reɪn/ *n* water falling from the clouds. **it's raining** = rain is falling. *adj* **rainy** /'reɪnɪ/.

rainbow /'reɪnbəʊ/ *n* many-coloured arch of light in the sky.

raise /reɪz/ *vt* **1** lift up. **2** produce or cause to grow. **3** increase.

raisin /'reɪzən/ *n* dried GRAPE.

raja(h) /'rɑːdʒə/ *n* Indian ruler.

rake[1] /reɪk/ *n* instrument with teeth fixed to a cross-bar, used for drawing together leaves, dry grass, etc. *vt* to use a rake on (e.g. grass). **to rake out** = discover by searching. **to rake up** = cause people to remember (things better forgotten).

rake[2] /reɪk/ *n* slope of a floor or MAST.

rake[3] /reɪk/ *n* man of bad character.

rally /'rælɪ/ *v* bring or come together for united action against something. *n* large meeting.

ram[1] /ræm/ *n* male sheep.

ram[2] /ræm/ *n* any heavy instrument used for pushing or striking with great force. *vt* strike with a ram; push into.

ramble /'ræmbəl/ *vi* walk about in the country; talk in a foolish wandering way. *n* **rambler** /'ræmblə/ climbing rose-tree with groups of small flowers.

ramify /'ræmɪfaɪ/ *vi* spread out in branches. *n* **ramification** /ˌræmɪfɪ'keɪʃən/ one of many branches; one of many effects of something.

ramp /ræmp/ *n* sloping place, e.g. in a fort.

rampage /ræm'peɪdʒ/ *vi* act wildly. **to be on the rampage** = run about wildly in great excitement. *adj* **rampant** /'ræmpənt/ **1** standing upon the back feet. **2** not controlled, e.g. *Disease is rampant in that part of the town.*

rampart /'ræmpɑːt/ *n* bank made to defend a fort or castle against attack.

ramrod /'ræmrod/ *n* stick used for pushing gunpowder and shot into an old kind of gun.

ramshackle

ramshackle /'ræmʃækəl/ *adj* (of a house) nearly falling down.

ran /ræn/ *p.t.* of **run**.

ranch /rɑːntʃ/ *n* large cattle farm. *vt* put in a rank; have an opinion as to the value of. **to rank with** = take place among, be considered equal to.

rancid /'rænsɪd/ *adj* (of fat or oil) bad; decayed.

rancour /'ræŋkə/ *n* deep-rooted, unforgiving hatred.

random /'rændəm/ *adj* without order or plan; happening by chance.

rang /ræŋ/ *p.t.* of **ring**.

range /reɪndʒ/ *vt* set in line, e.g. *He ranged his soldiers in order of size.* *vi* **1** be stretched out, e.g. *The forest ranges from A to B.* **2** wander about, e.g. *Beasts ranging in the forest.* **3** change between certain fixed points, e.g. *The prices range from 5p to 50p.* *n* **1** line, e.g. *A range of mountains.* **2** distance a gun can shoot; difference, e.g. distance anything can reach or travel. **3** *A wide range of prices* = many different prices. **4** large iron fire-place used for cooking.

ranger /'reɪndʒə/ *n* forest guard.

rank[1] /ræŋk/ *n* **1** single line of soldiers. **2** certain class or level. **rank and file** = common soldiers, people, etc.

rank[2] /ræŋk/ *adj* growing roughly and in plenty, e.g. grass in a wet place; bad smelling. **rank dishonesty** = complete, very bad dishonesty.

rankle /'ræŋkəl/ *v* continue to cause anger or pain.

ransack /'rænsæk/ *vt* search thoroughly.

ransom /'rænsəm/ *n* money paid so as to set a prisoner free.

rant /rænt/ *n* noisy meaningless speech. *vi* speak in a noisy and meaningless way.

rap /ræp/ *v* strike with a sharp quick blow. *sl* **I don't care a rap** = not at all.

rapacious /rə'peɪʃəs/ *adj* seizing by force; seizing everything possible.

rape[1] /reɪp/ *vt* force (a woman) to have sexual relations with one. *n* act of raping.

rape[2] /reɪp/ *n* a seed from which oil is made.

rapid /'ræpɪd/ *adj* moving quickly. *n* place in a stream where the water is swift and rough.

rapier /'reɪpɪə/ *n* long thin sword.

rapport /ræ'pɔː/ *n* close relationship with, and understanding of, each other.

rapt /ræpt/ *adj* lost in thought.

rapture /'ræptʃə/ *n* delight; great joy.

rare /reə/ *adj* **1** (e.g. of air) thin, **2** not often found and therefore valuable. **3** (of meat) lightly cooked. *adv* **rarely** /'reəlɪ/ not often.

rascal /'rɑːskəl/ *n* bad man; (used playfully) fellow.

rash[1] /ræʃ/ *adj* foolishly daring.

rash[2] /ræʃ/ *n* redness of the skin caused by illness.

rasher /'ræʃə/ *n* thin piece of BACON.

rasp /rɑːsp/ *n* instrument used for rubbing away or smoothing wood, metal, etc. *adj* **rasping** /'rɑːspɪŋ/ rough sounding.

raspberry /'rɑːzbərɪ/ *n* small red fruit containing many seeds.

rat /ræt/ *n* mammal like a mouse, but larger. **to rat on** = desert (one's friends).

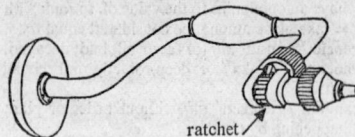

ratchet

ratchet /'rætʃɪt/ *n* toothed wheel with a bar resting on it allowing it to go round only in one direction.

rate[1] /reɪt/ *n* **1** amount of one thing measured in relation to another, e.g. *The birth rate* = number of births considered in relation to the number of people. **2** speed. **the rates** = money paid by householders to the government of the town in which the house is. **-rate**, e.g. *First-rate* = very good; *Second-rate* = not very good. *vt* consider; decide the quality of.

rate[2] /reɪt/ *vt* speak angrily to.

rather /'rɑːðə/ *adv* not very; quite. **I would rather have this than that** = I like this better; I want this more than that.

ratify /'rætɪfaɪ/ *vt* settle; fix, e.g. a written agreement. *n* **ratification** /ˌrætɪfɪ'keɪʃən/.

rating /'reɪtɪŋ/ *n* class to which a thing (e.g. a ship) belongs. **naval ratings** = men other than officers on a warship.

ratio /'reɪʃɪəʊ/ *n* number of times one quantity contains another, e.g. *The ratio of 2 and 8 is one to four, or a quarter.*

ration /'ræʃən/ *n* fixed amount of (e.g. food) given each (day). *vt* give a fixed quantity of (e.g. food) each (day).

rational /'ræʃənəl/ *adj* reasonable; having common sense.

rattle /'rætl/ *v* make a noise as of shaking stones in a tin. **to rattle along** = go fast. **to rattle off** = do quickly; say quickly. *n* instrument for making a rattling noise. *n* **rattlesnake** /'rætlsneɪk/ American snake which makes a noise with its tail.

raucous /'rɔːkəs/ *adj* unpleasant-sounding like the tired voice of one who has been shouting.

ravage /'rævɪdʒ/ *vt* destroy everything in (a country).

rave /reɪv/ *vi* talk and behave in a mad way. **to rave about** = say that (someone or something) is wonderful. *n* **ravings** /'reɪvɪŋz/.

ravel /'rævəl/ *vt* twist together (threads).

raven /'reɪvən/ *n* large very black bird.

raven

ravenous /'rævənəs/ *adj* very hungry.

ravine /rə'viːn/ *n* long deep narrow valley.

ravish /'rævɪʃ/ *vt* carry away by force. *adj* **ravishing** /'rævɪʃɪŋ/ very charming.

raw /rɔː/ *adj* uncooked; unprepared; (of a part of the body) having no skin on it, painful; (of weather, wind) cold and wet.

ray /reɪ/ *n* **1** beam of light. **2** large flat sea-fish.

rayon /'reɪɒn/ *n* silk-like material, obtained by special treatment of wood made into a liquid by acid, and pressed through very small holes.

raze /reɪz/ *vt* level to the ground.

razor /'reɪzə/ *n* knife used for cutting hair off the face; electrical machine for doing this.

re[1] /riː/ *prep* concerning; on the subject of.

re-[2] /riː/ *vt* again, e.g. retell /riː'tel/ to tell again.

reach /riːtʃ/ *v* **1** obtain by stretching out the hand. **2** arrive at (a place). **3** be stretched out as far as, e.g. *The garden reaches down to the river.* **beyond my reach** = too far for me to reach; not obtainable.

react /rɪ'ækt/ *vi* act in return; to act as the result of an act. *n* **reaction** /rɪ'ækʃən/ movement coming as a result of, or an answer to, some exciting cause. *adj, n* **reactionary** /rɪ'ækʃənərɪ/ (one) who wishes to return to things as they were.

read /riːd/ *v* (p.t. and p.p read /red/) *v* get ideas from print or writing; study. *adj* **readable** /'riːdəbəl/ easy to read. *n* **reading** /'riːdɪŋ/ ability to read.

ready /'redɪ/ *adj* **1** prepared. **2** near at hand; easily obtained. *n* **readiness** /'redɪnəs/.

real /rɪəl/ *adj* actual; true. *n* **realist** /'rɪəlɪst/ one who believes in painting or describing things exactly as they really are. *n* **realism** /'rɪəlɪzəm/. *adj* **realistic** /rɪə'lɪstɪk/. *n* **reality** /rɪ'ælətɪ/ state of being real; real, not imaginary, thing. *adv* **really** /'rɪəlɪ/ truly; in fact.

realize /'rɪəlaɪz/ *v* **1** make real. **2** understand as being real. *n* **realization** /ˌrɪəlaɪ'zeɪʃən/.

realm /relm/ *n* kingdom; large area.

ream /riːm/ *n*, 480 sheets of paper. *vt* make (a hole in metal) larger.

reap /riːp/ *vt* cut and gather in a crop.

rear[1] /rɪə/ *n* back part of anything.

rear[2] /rɪə/ *vt* **1** set up on end. **2** nurse and bring up (young). *vi* rise up on the back legs, as a horse does.

reason /'riːzən/ *n* **1** cause for belief. **2** power of thinking. *v* consider facts and get from them (some meaning, idea or result). *adj* **reasonable** /'riːzənəbəl/ having common sense; willing to listen to reasoning; not too much, e.g. in price.

reassure /ˌriːə'ʃʊə/ *vt* cause (someone) to have trust; cause (someone) not to worry. *n* **reassurance** /ˌriːə'ʃʊərəns/.

rebate /'riːbeɪt/ *n* small lessening of the price.

rebel /'rebəl/ *n* one who fights, e.g. against the government. *vi* **rebel** /rɪ'bel/ fight against (the government). *n* **rebellion** /rɪ'beljən/ rising up of people against the government. *adj* **rebellious** /rɪ'beljəs/ tending to rebel.

red

rebound /rɪˈbaʊnd/ *vi* jump back from, e.g. a ball from a wall. *n* /ˈriːbaʊnd/.

rebuff /rɪˈbʌf/ *n* rude treatment received when one is trying to be friendly.

rebuke /rɪˈbjuːk/ *vt* find fault with. *n* blame.

rebut /rɪˈbʌt/ *vt* push back; prove (what has been said) to be wrong.

recalcitrant /rɪˈkælsɪtrənt/ *adj* refusing to obey.

recall /rɪˈkɔːl/ *vt* remember.

recant /rɪˈkænt/ *v* say that one no longer believes in (a former opinion). *n* **recantation** /ˌriːkænˈteɪʃən/.

recapitulate /ˌriːkəˈpɪtʃʊleɪt/ *vi* repeat the chief ideas of a speech in a few words. *n* **recapitulation** /ˌriːkəpɪtʃʊˈleɪʃən/.

recede /rɪˈsiːd/ *vi* go back; slope back.

receipt /rɪˈsiːt/ *n* act of receiving; paper showing that money has been paid.

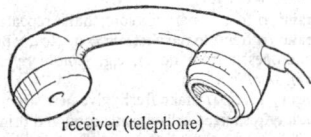

receiver (telephone)

receive /rɪˈsiːv/ *vt* take; get; accept. *n* **receiver** /rɪˈsiːvə⁷/ instrument or part of an instrument that receives messages, e.g. the part of a telephone that one lifts up.

recent /ˈriːsənt/ *adj* happening not long ago.

receptacle /rɪˈseptɪkəl/ *n* any vessel or container.

reception /rɪˈsepʃən/ *n* 1 act of receiving. 2 meeting at which many guests are received. *adj* **receptive** /rɪˈseptɪv/.

receptionist /rɪˈsepʃənɪst/ *n* man or woman who greets people in a hotel; woman who greets those visiting a doctor etc.

recess /rɪˈses/ *n* 1 space hollowed out. 2 break in school work when the children go out to play.

recession /rɪˈseʃən/ *n* weakening of trade.

recipe /ˈresəpɪ/ *n* piece of paper telling how to mix and make a cake or other form of food.

recipient /rɪˈsɪpɪənt/ *n* one who receives.

reciprocal /rɪˈsɪprəkəl/ *adj* done or given to each other.

reciprocate /rɪˈsɪprəkeɪt/ *v* have an effect upon each other; give and take.

recite /rɪˈsaɪt/ *vt* say from memory; tell. *n* **recital** /rɪˈsaɪtl/ performance of music by one person, or of the music of one writer; reading of poetry in public. *n* **recitation** /ˌresɪˈteɪʃən/.

reckless /ˈrekləs/ *adj* careless about the results; not caring about danger.

reckon /ˈrekən/ *vt* count; consider; make accounts; calculate. *n* **reckoning** /ˈrekənɪŋ/.

reclaim /rɪˈkleɪm/ *vt* bring back (e.g. a person from wrong, land from the sea). *n* **reclamation** /ˌrekləˈmeɪʃən/.

recline /rɪˈklaɪn/ *vi* lie down.

recluse /rɪˈkluːs/ *n* person who lives alone and does not like meeting people.

recognize /ˈrekəgnaɪz/ *vt* 1 know again. 2 accept as true or real, or as belonging to oneself. *n* **recognition** /ˌrekəgˈnɪʃən/.

recoil /rɪˈkɔɪl/ *vi* 1 (of a gun) spring backwards after firing. 2 draw back from something.

recollect /ˌrekəˈlekt/ *vt* remember. *n* **recollection** /ˌrekəˈlekʃən/.

recommend /ˌrekəˈmend/ *vt* speak in favour of; advise. *n* **recommendation** /ˌrekəmenˈdeɪʃən/.

recompense /ˈrekəmpens/ *n* something given as a return for good (or evil) done to the giver.

reconcile /ˈrekənsaɪl/ *vt* make friends again with; cause (two people) to become friends or come to an agreement. *n* **reconciliation** /ˌrekənsɪlɪˈeɪʃən/.

recondite /ˈrekəndaɪt/ *adj* very learned and difficult to understand.

reconnoitre /ˌrekəˈnɔɪtə⁷/ *n* look round (a place) to find out where the enemy is, his numbers, the general nature of the land, etc. *n* **reconnaissance** /rɪˈkɒnəsəns/.

 record (n1)

record /rɪˈkɔːd/ *vt* 1 set down in writing. 2 set down (sounds) on a flat plate. *n* **record** /ˈrekɔːd/ 1 such a plate. 2 writing that records some past event. 3 something done better, quicker, etc., than anyone else has done it. **record player** GRAMOPHONE.

recount[1] /riːˈkaʊnt/ *v* count again. /ˈkiːkaʊnt/ *n* second count.

recount[2] /rɪˈkaʊnt/ *vt* tell (a story).

recoup /rɪˈkuːp/ *vt* get back (money lost); make a gain that pays back (a former loss).

recourse /rɪˈkɔːs/ **to have recourse to** = turn to (something) for help.

recover /rɪˈkʌvə⁷/ *vt* get back again. *vi* become well again after illness. *n* **recovery** /rɪˈkʌvərɪ/.

recreation /ˌrekrɪˈeɪʃən/ *n* rest or amusement after work.

recrimination /rɪˌkrɪmɪˈneɪʃən/ *n* act of blaming people after something has gone wrong.

recruit /rɪˈkruːt/ *n* person who has just joined, esp. the army. *vt* get (soldiers) for the army; collect (helpers).

rectangle /ˈrektæŋgəl/ *n* four-sided figure, having opposite sides equal, and four equal angles.

rectify /ˈrektɪfaɪ/ *vt* set right (e.g. a mistake). *n* **rectification** /ˌrektɪfɪˈkeɪʃən/.

rectitude /ˈrektɪtjuːd/ *n* honesty.

rector /ˈrektə⁷/ *n* 1 man in charge of a church. 2 head of a large school or university.

recumbent /rɪˈkʌmbənt/ *adj* lying down.

recuperate /rɪˈkjuːpəreɪt/ *vi* get well after an illness. *n* **recuperation** /rɪˌkjuːpəˈreɪʃən/.

recur /rɪˈkɜː⁷/ *vi* come back again; happen again. *adj* **recurrent** /rɪˈkʌrənt/. *n* **recurrence** /rɪˈkʌrəns/.

red /red/ *n, adj* (of the) colour of blood. **Red Cross** = sign used by those who care for the

redeem

wounded in war. **red tape** = mass of silly rules delaying business. **to catch (someone) red-handed** = catch him actually doing some bad deed. **in the red** = owing money to the bank.

redeem /rɪ'diːm/ *vt* **1** bring back. **2** pay off (a debt). **3** save from the punishment of evil-doing. **a redeeming feature** = something good in a thing that is bad in all other ways. *n* **redemption** /rɪ'dempʃən/.

redolent /'redələnt/ *adj* smelling of something.

redoubt /rɪ'daʊt/ *n* small fort.

redoubtable /rɪ'daʊtəbəl/ *adj* to be feared or respected.

redound /rɪ'daʊnd/ **it redounds to his credit** = it adds to his good name.

redress /rɪ'dres, 'riːdres/ *n* setting right of a wrong, or repayment for loss caused by it.

reduce /rɪ'djuːs/ *vt* make less or fewer. *n* **reduction** /rɪ'dʌkʃən/.

redundant /rɪ'dʌndənt/ *adj* **1** more than is necessary. **2** no longer employed by a firm. *n* **redundancy** /rɪ'dʌndənsɪ/.

reed /riːd/ *n* **1** tall grass-like plant found in wet places. **2** (in a wind instrument of music) that part which makes the sound when the breath passes over it.

reef /riːf/ *n* **1** part of a sail that can be rolled up. **2** line of rocks in the sea.

reek /riːk/ *vi* smell strongly of something.

reel /riːl/ *n* **1** frame or roller on which string (or any long band) is kept. **2** a kind of dance. **to reel off** = **1** pull quickly off a reel. **2** tell something quickly and easily. **to reel along** = walk as if drunk.

refectory /rɪ'fektərɪ/ *n* large room in which meals are served to many people.

refer /rɪ'fɜː/ *vt* pass on a matter to some person, e.g. *Let us refer the matter to Mr. X* = ask Mr. X to settle it. **to refer to** = be a name of; describe; be about. *n, v* **referee** /,refə'riː/ judge, e.g. in a game. *n* **reference** /'refərəns/ act of referring; thing referred to. **reference book** = book to which one turns to find facts, e.g. dictionary, book of maps, etc. *n* **referendum** /,refə'rendəm/ asking all the people of a country to give an opinion on a law or question of government.

refine /rɪ'faɪn/ *vt* make pure. *adj* **refined** (of a person) very polite; having a nice mind. *n* **refinement** /rɪ'faɪnmənt/.

reflect /rɪ'flekt/ *v* throw back (light) as from a looking-glass. *vi* think. *n* **reflection** /rɪ'flekʃən/ act of reflecting. *adj* **reflective** /rɪ'flektɪv/ reflecting.

reflex /'riːfleks/ *adj* bent back. *n* action done without meaning to do it and without power to prevent it, e.g. shutting the eyes at a flash of light.

reflexive /rɪ'fleksɪv/ *adj* (of a pronoun) showing that the object of the verb is the same as the subject, as, for example, 'myself' in 'I could see myself in the mirror'; (of a verb) used only with such pronouns.

reform /rɪ'fɔːm/ *vt* change and make better. *n* **reformatory** /rɪ'fɔːmətərɪ/ school for young wrongdoers. *n* **reformation** /,refə'meɪʃən/.

refract

refract /rɪ'frækt/ *vt* bend (a beam of light), e.g. by passing it through a three-sided glass. *n* **refraction** /rɪ'frækʃən/.

refractory /rɪ'fræktərɪ/ *adj* troublesome and unwilling to obey.

refrain¹ /rɪ'freɪn/ *n* part of a song that is repeated.

refrain² /rɪ'freɪn/ **to refrain from** = not to do; prevent oneself from doing, e.g. *Kindly refrain from smoking.*

refresh /rɪ'freʃ/ *vt* make fresh; give new strength to. *n* **refreshment** /rɪ'freʃmənt/ food and drink.

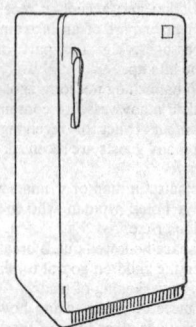

refrigerator

refrigerate /rɪ'frɪdʒəreɪt/ *vt* keep (e.g. food) cold, esp. in a refrigerator. *n* **refrigerator** /rɪ'frɪdʒəreɪtə/ machine that keeps food cold.

refuge /'refjuːdʒ/ *n* shelter. *n* **refugee** /,refju'dʒiː/ one who seeks shelter from danger, e.g. in a foreign land.

refund /rɪ'fʌnd/ *vt* pay back, /'riːfʌnd/ *n* amount refunded.

refuse¹ /rɪ'fjuːz/ *v* be unwilling to do or give what is asked. *n* **refusal** /rɪ'fjuːzəl/.

refuse² /'refjuːs/ *n* waste matter.

refute /rɪ'fjuːt/ *vt* prove (something) not to be true. *n* **refutation** /,refjʊ'teɪʃən/.

regal /'riːgəl/ *adj* as of a king. *n* **regalia** /rɪ'geɪlɪə/ signs of kingship used when a king is crowned, e.g. the crown, jewelled sword, etc., etc.

regale /rɪ'geɪl/ *v* supply with and cause to enjoy (e.g. food, music).

regard /rɪ'gɑːd/ *vt* consider. *n* respect. **in regard to** = in respect of; concerning. **one's regards** = one's good wishes. *adj, adv* **regardless** /rɪ'gɑːdləs/ without thinking, careless of, e.g. of the cost.

regatta /rɪ'gætə/ *n* meeting of many people for boat races.

regenerate /rɪ'dʒenəreɪt/ *vt* make better after decay; cause to grow again and better.

regent /'riːdʒənt/ *n* one who rules a country until a young king is old enough to rule it himself or if the real king is mad.

régime /reɪ'ʒiːm/ *n* way of governing; government.

regiment /'redʒɪmənt/ *n* group of four companies of soldiers—about 1,000 men. *vt* **regiment** /'redʒɪment/ arrange (people) in groups, make them obey many rules, etc. *n* **regimentation** /ˌredʒɪmen'teɪʃən/.

region /'riːdʒən/ *n* part of the country; space round a certain place. *adj* **regional** /'riːdʒənəl/.

register /'redʒɪstə/ *n* **1** written list, e.g. *A register of births* = book in which births are written; list of births. **2** instrument for showing an amount, e.g. of heat, light, etc. **3** range of the voice. *vt* **1** write (something) in a register. **2** show an expression of (some feeling) on the face. **3** pay an amount of money so that (a valuable letter) may be taken through the post with special care. *n* **registrar** /'redʒɪstrɑː/ officer who registers. *n* **registry** /'redʒɪstrɪ/ office for registering. **registry office** = place where people may be married, also keeping a list of births and deaths. *n* **registration** /ˌredʒɪ'streɪʃən/ act of registering.

regret /rɪ'gret/ *n* grief for a mistake or wrong done. *vt* be sorry about.

regular /'regjʊlə/ *adj* **1** according to rule; not changing; usual. **2** always happening at the same time. *n* **regularity** /ˌregjʊ'lærətɪ/. *vt* **regularize** /'regjʊləraɪz/.

regulate /'regjʊleɪt/ *vt* control; make according to rule. *n* **regulation** /ˌregjʊ'leɪʃən/ act of regulating; rule.

regurgitate /rɪ'gɜːdʒəteɪt/ *vt* pour out again, e.g. from the stomach.

rehabilitate /ˌriːə'bɪləteɪt/ *vt* put (someone) back in his former office, or into a former state, e.g. of health.

rehearse /rɪ'hɜːs/ *vt* repeat aloud; practise (a play). *n* **rehearsal** /rɪ'hɜːsəl/.

reign /reɪn/ *vi* rule as a king. *n* time of a king's rule.

reimburse /ˌriːɪm'bɜːs/ *vt* pay back.

rein /reɪn/ *n* one of the leather bands used in driving a horse.

reincarnation /ˌriːɪnkɑː'neɪʃən/ *n* idea that a person may be born again after dying.

reindeer /'reɪndɪə/ *n* kind of deer with large horns, found in cold parts of northern Asia and northern Europe.

reinforce /ˌriːɪn'fɔːs/ *vt* bring up new forces to

reindeer

help; make stronger. *n* **reinforcement** /ˌriːɪn'fɔːsmənt/.

reinstate /ˌriːɪn'steɪt/ *vt* put back as before.

reiterate /ˌriː'ɪtəreɪt/ *vt* repeat. *n* **reiteration** /ˌriːɪtə'reɪʃən/.

reject /rɪ'dʒekt/ *vt* throw back (something) as not being good enough; refuse. *n* **rejection** /rɪ'dʒekʃən/.

rejoice /rɪ'dʒɔɪs/ *vi* feel or show gladness.

rejoin /rɪ'dʒɔɪn/ *vt* **1** return to (someone) after being separated. **2** answer. *n* **rejoinder** /rɪ'dʒɔɪndə/ answer.

rejuvenate /rɪ'dʒuːvəneɪt/ *vt* make young again. *n* **rejuvenation** /rɪˌdʒuːvə'neɪʃən/.

relapse /rɪ'læps/ *vi, n* fall back into evil or illness.

relate /rɪ'leɪt/ *vt* **1** tell (a story). **2** show the relation between. *n* **relation** /rɪ'leɪʃən/ **1** joining of two things, e.g. *The relation between cause and effect; The relation of the weather to the quality of crops.* **2** way in which persons are united, or the effect which they have on each other, e.g. *My relations with him are quite friendly.* **3** member of one's family. *n* **relative** /'relətɪv/ member of one's family. *adj* being in some way joined to; having an effect on or resulting from; having to do with. **relatively large** = large when considered with other things. *n* **relativity** /ˌrelə'tɪvətɪ/ state of being relative.

relax /rɪ'læks/ *v* rest; loosen; become loose. *n* **relaxation** /ˌriːlæk'seɪʃən/ rest; amusement.

relay /'riːleɪ/ *n* supply of fresh men or horses to take over work from tired ones. *vt* **relay** /'riːleɪ, rɪ'leɪ/ receive and send on (e.g. a message) again.

release /rɪ'liːs/ *vt* **1** set free; give up. **2** allow (something) to be made public.

relegate /'relɪgeɪt/ *vt* send away; put in a lower place. *n* **relegation** /ˌrelə'geɪʃən/.

relent /rɪ'lent/ *vi* become less hard or cruel. *adj* **relentless** /rɪ'lentləs/ without pity.

relevant /'relɪvənt/ *adj* concerned with the matter being considered. *n* **relevance** /'relɪvəns/.

reliable /rɪ'laɪəbəl/ *adj* able to be trusted. *n* **reliance** /rɪ'laɪəns/ act or state of trusting. *adj* **reliant** /rɪ'laɪənt/.

relic /'relɪk/ *n* something left over from a past age.

217

relief[1]

relief[1] /rɪˈliːf/ **figures cut in relief** = shapes of men, etc., made to stand out from the surface of stone by cutting away the rest of the surface. **a relief map** = map in which the mountains stand out, and seas, lakes, etc., are shown as below the surface.

relief[2] /rɪˈliːf/ *n* 1 lessening of pain or trouble. 2 help given to the poor. 3 driving away of an enemy which is attacking a town. 4 being set free from a duty. 5 person who takes over one's work to set one free.

relieve /rɪˈliːv/ *vt* 1 make (pain or trouble) less. 2 drive away an enemy attacking (a town). 3 set (someone) free from duty.

religion /rɪˈlɪdʒən/ *n* all those acts, feelings and beliefs that are concerned with doing one's duty to God. *adj* **religious** /rɪˈlɪdʒəs/.

relinquish /rɪˈlɪŋkwɪʃ/ *vt* yield; give up.

relish /ˈrelɪʃ/ *vt* enjoy; enjoy the taste of. *n* 1 something used to give taste to food. 2 enjoyment.

reluctant /rɪˈlʌktənt/ *adj* unwilling. *n* **reluctance** /rɪˈlʌktəns/.

rely /rɪˈlaɪ/ *vi* depend on (someone); trust, e.g. *I am relying on you.*

remain /rɪˈmeɪn/ *v* 1 be left after part has been taken or destroyed. 2 continue to be. *n* **remains** parts left. *n* **remainder** /rɪˈmeɪndə[r]/ the rest; what is left.

remand /rɪˈmɑːnd/ *vt* send back to prison until the trial is carried on again.

remark /rɪˈmɑːk/ *vt* 1 notice. 2 make the remark that. *n* saying drawing attention to something. *adj* **remarkable** /rɪˈmɑːkəbəl/ specially good; worthy of notice.

remedy /ˈremədɪ/ *n* anything used to cause a person to get well from illness; setting right of a wrong. *vt* set right. *adj* **remedial** /rɪˈmiːdɪəl/.

remember /rɪˈmembə[r]/ *v* have in mind; not to forget. *n* **remembrance** /rɪˈmembrəns/ act of remembering; thing that causes one to remember.

remind /rɪˈmaɪnd/ *vt* cause to remember. *n* **reminder** /rɪˈmaɪndə[r]/ something to remind one of something.

reminiscence /ˌremɪˈnɪsəns/ *n* remembering of long-past events. *adj* **reminiscent** /ˌremɪˈnɪsənt/ causing one to remember. *vi* **reminisce** /ˌremɪˈnɪs/.

remiss /rɪˈmɪs/ *adj* careless; not attending to duty.

remission /rɪˈmɪʃən/ *n* freeing from debt; forgiveness.

remit /rɪˈmɪt/ *vt* forgive. **to remit money** = send. *n* **remittance** /rɪˈmɪtəns/ sending of money; money sent.

remnant /ˈremnənt/ *n* small piece left over.

remonstrate /ˈremənstreɪt/ *vi* complain (against); show reasons against. *n* **remonstrance** /rɪˈmɒnstrəns/.

remorse /rɪˈmɔːs/ *n* grief for one's wrongdoing.

remote /rɪˈməʊt/ *adj* distant.

remove /rɪˈmuːv/ *vt* move to another place; take away, e.g. a cause of pain. *n* **removal** /rɪˈmuːvəl/.

remunerate /rɪˈmjuːnəreɪt/ *vt* pay for work or loss. *n* **remuneration** /rɪˌmjuːnəˈreɪʃən/. *adj* **remunerative** /rɪˈmjuːnərətɪv/ paying well.

renaissance /rɪˈneɪsəns/ *n* new birth of anything. **the Renaissance** = that time when a new interest in learning arose in Europe, about 1300 to 1500.

rend /rend/ *vt* tear.

render /ˈrendə[r]/ *vt* 1 give, e.g. *Render good for evil; Render an account of* = tell about. 2 make, e.g. *Render it useless.*

rendezvous /ˈrɒndeɪvuː/ *n* agreed place of meeting.

renegade /ˈrenɪgeɪd/ *n* one who deserts the group or army to which he belonged.

renew /rɪˈnjuː/ *vt* make fresh and new again. *n* **renewal** /rɪˈnjuːəl/.

renounce /rɪˈnaʊns/ *vt* say that one does not own; give up all claim to.

renovate /ˈrenəveɪt/ *vt* make like new. *n* **renovation** /ˌrenəˈveɪʃən/.

renown /rɪˈnaʊn/ *n* fame.

rent[1] /rent/ *n* tear, e.g. in cloth.

rent[2] /rent/ *n* money paid for the use of a house. *vt* 1 pay rent for the use of (a house). 2 take rent from those using (one's house). *n* **rental** /ˈrentl/ the amount demanded as rent.

renunciation /rɪˌnʌnsɪˈeɪʃən/ *n* giving up.

repair /rɪˈpeə[r]/ *vt* put in good condition again after being damaged. *n* act of repairing; state of being repaired. *adj* **reparable** /ˈrepərəbəl/ that can be repaired. *n* **reparation** /ˌrepəˈreɪʃən/ payment to set right damage done.

repartee /ˌrepɑːˈtiː/ *n* quick, clever answer.

repast /rɪˈpɑːst/ *n* meal.

repatriate /riːˈpætrɪeɪt/ *vt* send (someone) back to his own country. *n* **repatriation** /riːˌpætrɪˈeɪʃən/.

repay /rɪˈpeɪ/ *vt* pay (someone) back. *n* **repayment** /rɪˈpeɪmənt/.

repeal /rɪˈpiːl/ *vt* make (a law) of no further force; end it. *n* act of repealing.

repeat /rɪˈpiːt/ *vt* say or do again. *adv* **repeatedly** /rɪˈpiːtɪdlɪ/ again and again; often.

repel /rɪˈpel/ *vt* drive back (an enemy); push back. *adj* **repellent** /rɪˈpelənt/ causing dislike.

repent /rɪˈpent/ *v* feel sorry for having done (wrong). *n* **repentance** /rɪˈpentəns/. *adj* **repentant** /rɪˈpentənt/.

repercussion /ˌriːpəˈkʌʃən/ *n* 1 beating back; act of coming back after going out, e.g. when a ball strikes a wall. 2 far-reaching effect.

repertoire /ˈrepətwɑː[r]/, **repertory** /ˈrepətərɪ/ *n* set of plays that a company of actors has ready for acting.

repetition /ˌrepɪ'tɪʃən/ n saying or doing again.

replace /rɪ'pleɪs/ vt 1 put (something) back in its former place. 2 give in the place of a thing lost or damaged. n **replacement** /rɪ'pleɪsmənt/.

replenish /rɪ'plenɪʃ/ vt fill up again.

replete /rɪ'pliːt/ adj full. n **repletion** /rɪ'pliːʃən/.

replica /'replɪkə/ n exact copy of a work of art.

reply /rɪ'plaɪ/ n, v answer.

report /rɪ'pɔːt/ n, vt (give) an account of (something). n noise, e.g. of a gun. n **reporter** /rɪ'pɔːtə'/ one who gathers news for a newspaper.

repose /rɪ'pəʊz/ vt rest; lie still.

repository /rɪ'pɒzətərɪ/ n shop; storehouse.

reprehensible /ˌreprɪ'hensəbəl/ adj worthy of blame.

represent /ˌreprɪ'zent/ vt 1 cause to be present in the mind; cause one to think of, or be a sign of, e.g. *A picture representing a ship; This mark on the map represents a city.* 2 act for, e.g. *Mr. X will represent me at the meeting.* n **representation** /ˌreprɪzen'teɪʃən/. n **representative** /ˌreprɪ'zentətɪv/ one who acts for another.

repress /rɪ'pres/ vt beat down; put under control. n **repression** /rɪ'preʃən/. adj **repressive** /rɪ'presɪv/.

reprieve /rɪ'priːv/ vt free from punishment.

reprimand /'reprɪmɑːnd/ vt scold; blame for a fault.

reprisal /rɪ'praɪzəl/ n wrong done as repayment or punishment for wrong.

reproach /rɪ'prəʊtʃ/ vt blame sadly or angrily. n act of reproaching; thing that brings shame upon one.

reproduce /ˌriːprə'djuːs/ vt 1 cause to be seen or heard again. 2 make a perfect copy of. vi bring children (or young) into the world. n **reproduction** /ˌriːprə'dʌkʃən/. adj **reproductive** /ˌriːprə'dʌktɪv/.

reprove /rɪ'pruːv/ vt speak to (someone) blaming him; scold. n **reproof** /rɪ'pruːf/.

reptile

reptile /'reptaɪl/ n cold-blooded egg-laying creature, e.g. a snake.

republic /rɪ'pʌblɪk/ n country governed not by a king but by persons elected by the people. adj **republican** /rɪ'pʌblɪkən/.

repudiate /rɪ'pjuːdɪeɪt/ vt say that a thing is not one's own; be unwilling to accept a gift; be un-

willing to claim; say that one does not owe a debt. n **repudiation** /rɪˌpjuːdɪ'eɪʃən/.

repugnant /rɪ'pʌgnənt/ adj greatly disliked; hateful. n **repugnance** /rɪ'pʌgnəns/.

repulse /rɪ'pʌls/ vt drive back; treat with coldness a person who tries to be friendly. n **repulsion** /rɪ'pʌlʃən/ feeling that something is repulsive. adj **repulsive** /rɪ'pʌlsɪv/ very ugly or unpleasant.

reputation /ˌrepjʊ'teɪʃən/ n fame, good or bad. adj **reputable** /'repjʊtəbəl/ having a good name; worthy of trust. n **repute** /rɪ'pjuːt/ fame. **reputed** /rɪ'pjuːtɪd/ **reputed to be** = thought to be.

request /rɪ'kwest/ vt ask for. n thing asked for; act of asking.

requiem /'rekwɪəm/ n service of prayer for a dead person,

require /rɪ'kwaɪə'/ vt need. n **requirement** /rɪ'kwaɪəmənt/. n, adj **requisite** /'rekwɪzɪt/ (something) necessary. vt **requisition** /ˌrekwɪ'zɪʃən/ demand (supplies) for the use of, e.g., an army.

requite /rɪ'kwaɪt/ vt pay back good with good or evil with evil.

rescind /rɪ'sɪnd/ vt put an end to; cause (a law) to have no more force.

rescue /'reskjuː/ vt save from danger. n act of rescuing.

research /rɪ'sɜːtʃ/ n scientific study in order to discover new facts. v do research (on).

resemblance

resemble /rɪ'zembəl/ vt look like. n **resemblance** /rɪ'zembləns/.

resent /rɪ'zent/ vt show anger about. n **resentment** /rɪ'zentmənt/.

reserve /rɪ'zɜːv/ vt 1 keep back for future use, e.g. *Reserve one's strength.* 2 keep for the use of a particular person, e.g. *To reserve a seat in a theatre.* n 1 piece of country kept for a special purpose, e.g. for wild animals, e.g. in Africa. 2 self-control in hiding one's feelings. n **reservation** /ˌrezə'veɪʃən/ 1 part of the country set aside for a special people, e.g. Red Indians in America. 2 a place or seat reserved, e.g. in an aeroplane. 3 condition, on which one's agreement to something depends. adj **reserved** /rɪ'zɜːvd/ not showing one's feelings; quiet. n **reservoir** /'rezəvwɑː'/ large container built to hold water, e.g. all the water for a city.

reside /rɪ'zaɪd/ vi have one's home in a place. n **residence** /'rezɪdəns/ house. n, adj **resident** /'rezɪdənt/ (one) living or staying in a place. adj **residential** /ˌrezɪ'denʃəl/ (e.g. of an area) where there are houses, not shops.

residue

reservoir

residue /'rezɪdju:/ *n* what is left. *adj* **residual** /rɪ'zɪdʒʊəl/.

resign /rɪ'zaɪn/ *v* give up (one's office). **to resign oneself to** = accept and suffer calmly. *n* **resignation** /ˌrezɪg'neɪʃən/ calm suffering without complaint.

resilient /rɪ'zɪlɪənt/ *adj* springing back to its former place, like a stick bent and let go. *n* **resilience** /rɪ'zɪlɪəns/.

resin /'rezɪn/ *n* sticky material that comes out of trees and later becomes hard, like yellow glass.

resist /rɪ'zɪst/ *vt* stand against; try to prevent. *n* **resistance** /rɪ'zɪstəns/ act of resisting.

resolute /'rezəlu:t/ *adj* firmly decided.

resolve /rɪ'zɒlv/ *vt* decide. *adj* **resolved** /rɪ'zɒlvd/ firmly decided. *n* **resolution** /ˌrezə'lu:ʃən/.

resonant /'rezənənt/ *adj* deep sounding; sending sounds back as in a large empty hall. *n* **resonance** /'rezənəns/.

resort /rɪ'zɔːt/ **to resort to** = go to; turn to for help. **a seaside resort** = place near the sea to which people go for health and enjoyment.

resound /rɪ'zaʊnd/ *vi* ring with; send sounds back as in a large empty hall.

resource /rɪ'sɔːs/ *n* cleverness in finding a way of doing a thing. **my resources** = my money and all the things that may help me in doing what I want. *adj* **resourceful** /rɪ'sɔːsfəl/ cleverly finding a way of carrying out one's plans.

respect /rɪ'spekt/ *n* **1** attention to, care of, e.g. *We should have respect for his wishes* = do as he wishes. **2** honour, e.g. *To pay one's respects to* = visit and greet a person of higher rank. **3** part of something's character. **in respect of** = concerning. *n* **self-respect** /ˌ. . ./ proper regard for one's character and position. *adj* **respectable** /rɪ'spektəbəl/ worthy of honour; of such size or importance as to be worth notice; of good character. *n* **respectability** /rɪˌspektə'bɪlətɪ/. *adj* **respectful** /rɪ'spektfəl/ showing respect. *prep* **respecting** /rɪ'spektɪŋ/ concerning.

respective /rɪ'spektɪv/ *adj* of each, e.g. *Let each go to his respective place* = to the place that belongs to him. *adv* **respectively** in that order, e.g. *John and Bill took Mary and Jane, respectively* = John took Mary and Bill took Jane.

respire /rɪ'spaɪə/ *vi* breathe. *n* **respiration** /ˌrespɪ'reɪʃən/.

respite /'respaɪt/ *n* short pause in, e.g. work, pain, etc.

resplendent /rɪ'splendənt/ *adj* shining, very fine, splendid.

respond /rɪ'spɒnd/ *vi* give an answer. *n* **response** /rɪ'spɒns/ answer.

responsible /rɪ'spɒnsəbəl/ *adj* **1** trusted to do; in charge of, e.g. *He is responsible for it* = he will be blamed if things go wrong, he is trusted to make things go right. **2** able to be trusted. *n* **responsibility** /rɪˌspɒnsə'bɪlətɪ/ **1** state of being responsible. **2** something for which one is responsible.

responsive /rɪ'spɒnsɪv/ *adj* answering; showing results, e.g. showing feeling when spoken to with deep feeling.

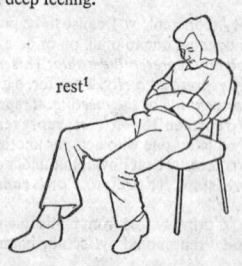

rest[1]

rest[1] /rest/ *vi, n* pause in work so as to get new strength. *n* instrument used to support or steady the hand. **to rest on** = be supported by. *adj* **restful** /'restfəl/ quiet; making rest easy.

rest[2] /rest/ **the rest** = that which still remains.

restaurant /'restərã, 'restərənt/ *n* place where people can eat meals if they pay for them.

restitution /ˌrestɪ'tju:ʃən/ *n* payment for damage done.

restive /'restɪv/, **restless** /'restləs/ *adj* not willing or not able to stay still.

restore /rɪ'stɔː/ *vt* put (something) back as it was; build up again. *n* **restoration** /ˌrestə'reɪʃən/.

restrain /rɪ'streɪn/ *vt* hold back; control. *n* **restraint** /rɪ'streɪnt/.

restrict /rɪ'strɪkt/ *vt* keep within a certain space or amount. *n* **restriction** /rɪ'strɪkʃən/.

result /rɪ'zʌlt/ *n* that which is produced by a cause. *vi* **1** have as a result, e.g. *Disease resulting in death*. **2** be the result, e.g. *Death resulting from disease*.

resume /rɪ'zju:m/ *vt* begin again. *vi* continue after a pause. *n* **resumption** /rɪ'zʌmpʃən/.

résumé /reɪ'zju:meɪ/ *n* short account of a speech, book etc.

resurrect /ˌrezə'rekt/ *vt* cause (someone or something) to be born again. *n* **resurrection** /ˌrezə'rekʃən/ rising again from the dead.

resuscitate /rɪ'sʌsəteɪt/ *vt* bring to life (one who is almost dead). *n* **resuscitation** /rɪˌsʌsə'teɪʃən/.

retail /'ri:teɪl'/ vt sell (goods) in small quantities, as in a shop. adj **retail** selling only in small quantities.

retain /rɪ'teɪn/ vt keep for or within oneself. n **retainer** /rɪ'teɪnə⁷/ 1 servant. 2 money paid, e.g., to a lawyer so that one may be sure that he will work for one when necessary.

retaliate /rɪ'tælɪeɪt/ vi do evil to others as they have done to you. n **retaliation** /rɪ,tælɪ'eɪʃən/.

retard /rɪ'tɑːd/ vt cause a delay in. adj **retarded** /rɪ'tɑːdɪd/ not having the same abilities as someone else of the same age.

retch /retʃ/ vi make movements as if about to be sick.

retention /rɪ'tenʃən/ n act of RETAINING. adj **retentive** /rɪ'tentɪv/ able to retain or keep, e.g. *A retentive memory* = good power of remembering.

reticent /'retɪsənt/ adj not telling; keeping things secret. n **reticence** /'retɪsəns/.

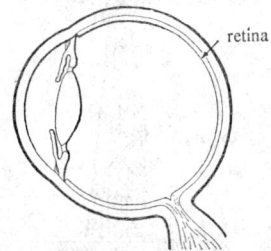

retina

retina /'retɪnə/ n back of the eye where light falls on the nerve-endings.

retinue /'retɪnjuː/ n followers and servants of a prince or nobleman.

retire /rɪ'taɪə⁷/ vi 1 go back; go to bed; go away. 2 give up one's work when one is old. n **retirement** /rɪ'taɪəmənt/.

retort[1] /rɪ'tɔːt/ vt, n (give) a quick or angry answer.

retort[2] /rɪ'tɔːt/ n bottle with a bent neck.

retouch /,riː'tʌtʃ/ vt improve or repair a picture by small touches.

retrace /riː'treɪs/ vt go back over. **to retrace one's footsteps** = go back along the path by which one came.

retract /rɪ'trækt/ vt take back (something said); say that it was not meant or was not true.

retreat /rɪ'triːt/ vi go back from a battle. n 1 act of going back, esp. from an enemy. 2 place to which one goes for peace and quiet.

retrench /rɪ'trentʃ/ v arrange to spend less money (on).

retribution /,retrɪ'bjuːʃən/ n punishment.

retrieve /rɪ'triːv/ vt get back (something lost). n **retriever** /rɪ'triːvə⁷/ dog that brings back shot birds to its master.

retro- /'retrəʊ/ backwards, e.g. adj **retrograde** /'retrəgreɪd/ moving backwards. n **retrogres-sion** /,retrə'greʃən/. a moving backwards. n **retrospect** /'retrəspekt/ considering the past.

return /rɪ'tɜːn/ vi come or go back. vt give back; send back. **in return for** = as thanks for, as a payment of.

reunion /riː'juːnɪən/ n meeting of people who have not seen each other for a long time.

reveal /rɪ'viːl/ vt make known (what was hidden).

reveille /rɪ'vælɪ/ n music that wakens soldiers in the morning.

revel /'revəl/ vi feast merrily. n **revelry** /'revəlrɪ/ merrymaking and feasting.

revelation /,revə'leɪʃən/ n act of REVEALING; something revealed.

revenge /rɪ'vendʒ/ n doing wrong to another as a punishment for wrong done by him to oneself.

revenue /'revənjuː/ n money coming in, e.g. to the government.

reverberate /rɪ'vɜːbəreɪt/ vi (of sound) be thrown back; continue to sound as in a large empty hall. n **reverberation** /rɪ,vɜːbə'reɪʃən/.

revere /rɪ'vɪə⁷/ vt feel great respect for. n **reverence** /'revərəns/ feeling of great respect.

reverend /'revərənd/ n title of a priest, e.g. *Rev. George Smith*. adj worthy of great respect.

reverent /'revərənt/ adj feeling or showing great respect.

reverie /'revərɪ/ n day-dream.

reverse /rɪ'vɜːs/ vt turn the wrong way up; turn the other way round. v move (one's car) backwards. **the reverse side** = the back. **the reverse of** = opposite of. n **reversal** /rɪ'vɜːsəl/. adj **reversible** /rɪ'vɜːsəbəl/ able to be reversed.

revert /rɪ'vɜːt/ vi go back to a former condition or subject. n **reversion** /rɪ'vɜːʃən/ giving back to the first owner; becoming as before.

review /rɪ'vjuː/ vt 1 look over (something) again. 2 write an opinion on (a book). n 1 weekly, monthly or three-monthly paper that gives opinions on new books, public events, etc. 2 piece of writing in which a book is reviewed.

revile /rɪ'vaɪl/ vt use unkind language to; call cruel names.

revise /rɪ'vaɪz/ v make sure that one has learnt (everything one must know) for an examination; look over and correct (something written). n **revision** /rɪ'vɪʒən/.

revive /rɪ'vaɪv/ v bring or come fully back to life. n **revival** /rɪ'vaɪvəl/.

revoke /rɪ'vəʊk/ vt take back (an order one has given). vi (in playing cards) play a card of the wrong kind even though one has one of the kind needed. n **revocation** /,revə'keɪʃən/.

revolt /rɪ'vəʊlt/ vt (of a people) to rise against the government. n rising of the people against the government. adj **revolting** /rɪ'vəʊltɪŋ/ very nasty.

revolution /,revə'luːʃən/ n 1 turning, e.g. of a wheel. 2 sudden change of government. adj, n **revolutionary** /,revə'luːʃənərɪ/ (one) working for revolution; having to do with revolution. adj (e.g. of an idea) very new.

revolve /rɪ'vɒlv/ *v* turn round and round.

revolver /rɪ'vɒlvə/ *n* hand-gun that holds six or more shots in a barrel which turns round after each shot is fired.

revue /rɪ'vju:/ *n* amusing musical play with no story in it.

revulsion /rɪ'vʌlʃən/ *n* sudden change of feeling, esp. from love to hate.

reward /rɪ'wɔːd/ *n* something given in return for service, or as a sign that one is grateful. *vt* give a reward to.

rhapsody /'ræpsədɪ/ *n* poem or piece of music written when very excited.

rhetoric /'retərɪk/ *n* art of good writing or speaking. *adj* **rhetorical** /rɪ'tɒrɪkəl/ **1** having to do with rhetoric. **2** (of a question) asked only for effect, not in order to receive an answer.

rheumatism /'ruːmətɪzəm/ *n* disease causing pain in muscles and joints. *adj* **rheumatic** /ruː'mætɪk/.

rhinoceros

rhinoceros /raɪ'nɒsərəs/ *n* a large mammal.

rhubarb /'ruːbɑːb/ *n* garden plant, boiled and eaten.

rhyme /raɪm/ *vi* (of a word) end in the same sound as another word, as at the end of a line of poetry. *n* pair of rhyming words.

rhythm /'rɪðəm/ *n* regular beat of poetry, music, or dancing. *adj* **rhythmic(al)** /'rɪðmɪk(əl)/.

rib /rɪb/ *n* one of the curved bones of the breast; any narrow curved piece of material, e.g. as part of a boat or building; any narrow raised part of a surface. *adj* **ribbed** /rɪbd/ formed in such raised parts.

ribald /'rɪbəld/ *adj* (e.g. of a song) showing disrespect in a rude and unpleasant way.

ribbon /'rɪbən/ *n* narrow band, e.g. of silk.

rice /raɪs/ *n* white grain boiled for food, very common in India and China.

rich /rɪtʃ/ *adj* **1** having a lot of money. **2** producing much, e.g. *Rich soil*. **3** of great cost or value, e.g. *Rich silks*. **4** (of food) fat, oily. **5** (of colour) deep. *n* (*pl*) **riches** /'rɪtʃɪz/ wealth. *n* **richness** /'rɪtʃnəs/.

rick /rɪk/ *n* heap of hay shaped like a small house.

rickets /'rɪkɪts/ *n* disease in which the bones of children become soft.

rickety /'rɪkɪtɪ/ *adj* not steady.

ricochet /'rɪkəʃeɪ/ *n* jumping of a BULLET when it hits the ground. *vi* jump back thus.

rid /rɪd/ **to get rid of** = remove; get free of. *n* **riddance** /'rɪdəns/ **good riddance** = I am glad to be free of it, you, etc.

ridden /'rɪdn/ *p.p.* of **ride.**

riddle[1] /'rɪdəl/ *n* difficult or amusing question.

riddle[2] /'rɪdəl/ *n* vessel with many holes in the bottom for shaking small things through and keeping back the larger. *vt* make many holes in.

ride /raɪd/ *v* be carried on or in a vehicle, etc.

rider[1] /'raɪdə/ *n* something added to, e.g., a written paper.

rider[2] /'raɪdə/ *n* one who rides.

ridge /rɪdʒ/ *n* long narrow hill; any long narrow raised object.

ridicule /'rɪdɪkjuːl/ *vt* laugh at. *n* laughing at someone. *adj* **ridiculous** /rɪ'dɪkjʊləs/ silly; laughable.

rife /raɪf/ *adj* (of something unpleasant) found everywhere.

riff-raff /'rɪf ræf/ *n* low common people.

rifle[1] /'raɪfəl/ *n* long gun such as a soldier uses.

rifle[2] /'raɪfəl/ *vt* search through (things) in order to steal.

rift /rɪft/ *n* crack; separation.

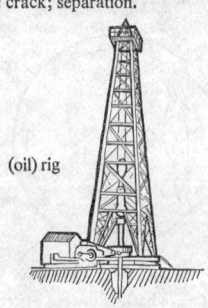

(oil) rig

rig /rɪg/ *n* arrangement of sails on a ship; any equipment. **to rig out** = equip or dress. **oil rig** = place for machines and men taking oil out of the ground.

rigging /'rɪgɪŋ/ *n* (*sing*) ropes that hold up the sails and MASTS on a ship.

right /raɪt/ *adv* **1** straight, e.g. *Go right on* = go straight on. **2** completely, e.g. *Turn right over*. **right here, right now** = just here, just now. *adj* **1** on the opposite side from the heart, e.g. *Right hand*. **2** just; fair; according to law and good behaviour. **3** correct; proper. **a right angle** = angle of ninety degrees, as at the corner of a square. *n* just claim, e.g. *I have a right to speak*. *vt* make right; set up in the correct way, e.g. *To right a boat*. *adj* **rightful** /'raɪtfəl/ owned according to law; proper. *adj* **righteous** /'raɪtʃəs/ just and good.

rigid /'rɪdʒɪd/ *adj* stiff. *n* **rigidity** /rɪ'dʒɪdətɪ/.

rigmarole /'rɪgmərəʊl/ *n* long meaningless talk.

rigour /'rɪgə/ *n* hardness; unmercifulness. *adj* **rigorous** /'rɪgərəs/.

rile /raɪl/ *vt* make angry.

rill /rɪl/ *n* little stream.

rim /rɪm/ *n* edge, e.g. of a cup.

rime /raɪm/ *n* (*sing*) frozen drops of water seen on leaves or on the grass (etc.) in winter.

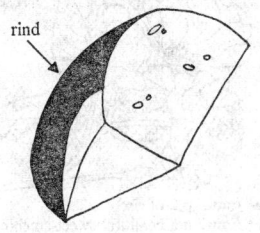

rind

rind /raɪnd/ n outer covering of a fruit, of meat, or cheese.

ring¹ /rɪŋ/ n 1 circular band, e.g. of gold, worn on the finger, 2 circle of any metal or material. 3 place closed in with ropes in which two men BOX.

ring² /rɪŋ/ vt cause (a bell) to sound. vi (of a bell) to sound; sound out clearly like a bell. to ring true = show by sign or sound that it is true. to ring up = call on a telephone.

ringleader /ˈrɪŋˌliːdə ʲ/ n leader of a group joined together for wrongdoing.

ringlet /ˈrɪŋlət/ n small curl of hair.

ringworm /ˈrɪŋwɜːm/ n disease usually on the skin of the head causing circular hairless rings.

rink /rɪŋk/ n sheet of ice for SKATING on.

rinse /rɪns/ vt wash soap off; wash lightly.

riot /ˈraɪət/ n noise, disorder, and unlawful acts of a crowd; disorderly behaviour. vi (of a crowd) behave thus. adj riotous /ˈraɪətəs/.

rip /rɪp/ v, n tear.

ripe /raɪp/ adj (of a fruit) ready to be eaten. v ripen /ˈraɪpən/ make or become ripe.

ripple /ˈrɪpəl/ n small wave.

rise /raɪz/ v p.t. rose /rəʊz/. p.p. risen /ˈrɪzən/. 1 go up; get out of bed. 2 increase, e.g. The river is rising. 3 begin, e.g. The river rises in those mountains. to rise again = come back from being dead. to rise to an occasion = show oneself able to deal with a specially difficult matter. to rise up against the government = begin to fight against. n a rise of prices = an increase. a gentle rise = small hill. to give rise to = cause. to take a rise out of = deceive and laugh at (a person).

risk /rɪsk/ n danger. vt take a chance on; endanger a thing. adj risky /ˈrɪskɪ/.

rissole /ˈrɪsəʊl/ n meat cut small and made into a roll.

rite /raɪt/ n fixed form of prayer and song as in a church; any set of actions fixed by custom. n ritual /ˈrɪtʃʊəl/ set of rites or fixed forms. adj having to do with rites.

rival /ˈraɪvəl/ n one who tries to do better than another, or to win something desired also by another.

river /ˈrɪvə ʲ/ n wide stream.

rivet /ˈrɪvɪt/ n thing like a nail with an end that is not very hard. vt put a rivet through (two pieces of metal) and beat the soft end flat to hold them together.

rivulet /ˈrɪvjʊlət/ n little river.

road /rəʊd/ n hard prepared way for carriages, etc. n roadhog /ˈrəʊdhɒg/ one who drives a car in a selfish way, not considering other drivers on the road. n (sing) road-metal [ˈ. ˌ.] stones used in road-making.

roadstead /ˈrəʊdsted/ n place near the shore where ships ANCHOR.

roam /rəʊm/ vi wander.

roar /rɔː ʲ/ n, vi (make a) loud deep cry, as of a lion.

roast /rəʊst/ v cook in front of an open fire or in an OVEN. n piece of meat cooked in this way.

rob /rɒb/ vt steal from, esp. by force. n robber /ˈrɒbə ʲ/ thief. n robbery /ˈrɒbərɪ/.

robe /rəʊb/ n long indoor garment.

robin /ˈrɒbɪn/ n common small bird with a red breast.

robot /ˈrəʊbɒt/ n machine made in the form of a man which works as a slave; any machine-like worker.

robust /rəʊˈbʌst/ adj strong and healthy.

rock¹ /rɒk/ n large mass of stone. on the rocks = 1 being in money difficulties. 2 (of a drink) served with ice.

rock² /rɒk/ v move from side to side or backwards and forwards. rock and roll = a kind of music, usually fast, specially liked by young /ˈrɒbə ʲ/ thief. n robbery /ˈrɒbərɪ/.

rockery /ˈrɒkərɪ/ n heap of stones or small rocks with flowers among them, as part of a garden.

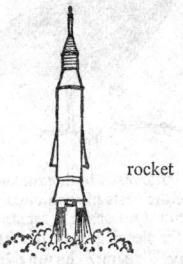

rocket

rocket /ˈrɒkɪt/ n 1 stick shot into the air which lets out stars of coloured flame when it gets high up. 2 object driven by burning gases, used as a weapon or to carry things or men into space. n rocketry /ˈrɒkɪtrɪ/.

rod /rɒd/ n straight bar or stick.

rode /rəʊd/ p.t. of ride.

rodent /ˈrəʊdənt/ n any small mammal with an arrangement of sharp teeth like mice and rats.

rodeo /ˈrəʊdɪəʊ/ n gathering together of cattle; show of riding by COWBOYS.

roe¹ /rəʊ/ n small deer; female red deer. n roebuck /ˈrəʊbʌk/ male deer.

roe² /rəʊ/ n eggs of a fish.

223

rogue /rəʊg/ *n* dishonest fellow; troublesome but playful child. *adj* **roguish** /'rəʊgɪʃ/.

role /rəʊl/ *n* part taken by an actor; behaviour called for by a person's position, e.g. *A father's role.*

roll /rəʊl/ *vi* move along by turning over and over. *vt* **1** cause to roll, e.g. *To roll one's eyes* = move the eyes round. **2** flatten with a roller, e.g. *To roll the grass.* **to roll in** = come in large numbers. **to roll up** = **1** form paper, etc., into a shape like a pipe. **2** arrive unexpectedly. *n* **1** pipe of paper. **2** very small loaf of bread. **3** list. **roll call** = reading of all the names on a list to see if all are present. *n* **rolled gold** /ˌ. ˈ./ metal with a thin covering of gold on it.

roller /'rəʊlə^r/ *n* solid, pipe-shaped piece of iron or metal used for flattening grass or a path, or as a part of a machine.

rollicking /'rɒlɪkɪŋ/ *adj* noisy and merry.

rolling pin /ˈ. . ./ *n* round piece of wood used for rolling out paste for cooking.

romance /rə'mæns/ *n* **1** love between a man and a woman. **2** fanciful story, e.g. of knights; a love story. **a romance language** = language which comes from Latin. *adj* **romantic** /rə'mæntɪk/ fanciful; dealing with love.

romp /rɒmp/ *vi* (of children) play noisily. *n* **rompers** /'rɒmpəz/ clothes of a small child, made in one piece.

roof /ruːf/ *n* outside upper covering of a house.

rook

rook /rʊk/ *n* large black bird. *n* **rookery** /'rʊkərɪ/ collection of the nests of such birds.

room /rʊm, ruːm/ *n* **1** space. **2** separate part of a house, e.g. for sleeping in, or for eating in, etc. *adj* **roomy** /'ruːmɪ/ having plenty of space.

roost /ruːst/ *n* bar on which hens sit at night. *vi* sit and sleep thus. *n* **rooster** /'ruːstə^r/ male form of hen. **to rule the roost** = be a leader and force others to obey.

root /ruːt/ *n* **1** underground part of a plant; that from which something grows; first cause or beginning. **2** that part of a word to which endings are added to make other words.

rope /rəʊp/ *n* very strong string-like thing, as used in ships. **to know the ropes** = know the customs and arrangements.

rosary /'rəʊzərɪ/ *n* string of BEADS used for counting the number of prayers said.

rose²

rose¹ /rəʊz/ *p.t.* of **rise**.

rose² /rəʊz/ *n* a beautiful sweet-smelling flower.

rosemary /'rəʊzmərɪ/ *n* sweet-smelling bush.

rosette /rəʊ'zet/ *n* piece of silk material in the shape of a rose to be fixed to the coat as an ornament, or sign of office; piece of stone so cut and shaped.

rosewood /'rəʊzwʊd/ *n* a hard dark wood.

roster /'rɒstə^r/ *n* list of persons showing the order in which they will do work.

rostrum /'rɒstrəm/ *n* raised place for a speaker.

rosy /'rəʊzɪ/ *adj* of light red colour. **the future is rosy** = seems hopeful.

rot /rɒt/ *n, vi* decay. *n sl* foolish talk.

rotary /'rəʊtərɪ/ *adj* turning round. *v* **rotate** /rəʊ'teɪt/ turn round. *n* **rotation** /rəʊ'teɪʃən/. **rotation of crops** = planting different things in a field each year, so as not to use up the food in the soil.

rote /rəʊt/ **by rote** = (e.g. said) from memory without thought of the meaning.

rotor /'rəʊtə^r/ *n* part inside a machine that turns round and round.

rotten /'rɒtn/ *adj* **1** decayed. **2** *infml* very bad.

rotund /rəʊ'tʌnd/ *adj* round and fat. *n* **rotundity** /rəʊ'tʌndətɪ/.

rouge /ruːʒ/ *n* red matter put on their faces by women.

rough /rʌf/ *adj* **1** not smooth; not level, e.g. *Rough country.* **2** not exact, e.g. *A rough idea of the number; Roughly 50 people came.* **3** full of uncontrolled force, e.g. *A rough sea.* **a rough game** = noisy fighting sort of game. **4** not polite. **a rough diamond** = impolite person who is really kind. **5** unfinished, unpolished, e.g. *A rough draft of a letter* = first writing that will be made better later.

roughcast /'rʌfkɑːst/ *adj* covered with very rough PLASTER.

roughshod /'rʌfʃɒd/ **to ride roughshod over** = treat (someone) roughly and with disrespect.

roulette /ruː'let/ *n* game played with a wheel and a small ball falling into holes opposite numbers, the person who guesses the number winning money.

round /raʊnd/ *adj* shaped like a circle. **a round number** = number ending in 0. **a round trip** = journey to a place and back. *n* **1** course from house to house done each day (e.g. by a doctor or postman). **2** one of the parts into which an arranged fight is divided. **3** BULLET. *adv, prep* around; about. *adj* **roundabout** /'raʊndəbaʊt/

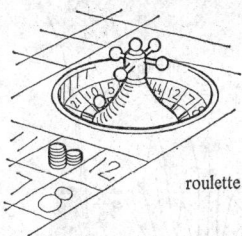

roulette

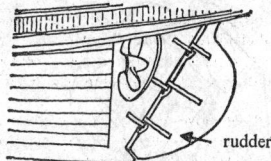

rudder

not in the straight and shortest way. *adv* **round-ly** /'raʊndlɪ/ with great force, e.g. *To scold a person roundly.*

rouse /raʊz/ *vt* wake up; excite; drive to action.

rout /raʊt/ *n* disorderly crowd; army driven back in disorder. *vt* drive back in disorder.

route /ruːt/ *n* track; road. **a route march** = a march done by soldiers for exercise.

routine /ruːˈtiːn/ *n* regular order of work. *adj* too regular to be interesting.

rove /rəʊv/ *vi* wander about.

row¹ /rəʊ/ *v* move (a boat) forward by means of OARS.

row² /raʊ/ *n* noise. *n, vi* quarrel. *adj* **rowdy** /'raʊdɪ/ noisy. *n* **rowdyism** /'raʊdɪ-ɪzəm/ rowdy behaviour.

row³ /rəʊ/ *n* line of things.

royal /'rɔɪəl/ *adj* of a king; splendid. *n* **royalty** /'rɔɪəltɪ/ **1** state of being a king; persons of the king's family. **2** part of the price of a book paid to the writer on every book sold; a similar payment made to those who write plays, music, etc.

rub /rʌb/ *v* press down and move something over (a surface), e.g. in order to clean or polish. **to rub out** = cause (e.g. pencil marks) to disappear by rubbing. *n* some small thing on the ground that prevents a ball from rolling straight; any small difficulty.

rubber /'rʌbə/ *n* **1** material obtained from a tree grown in hot countries, used for the wheels of cars, over-shoes, etc. **2** piece of rubber or similar material used for rubbing out pencil marks.

rubbish /'rʌbɪʃ/ *n* unwanted useless things or matter; silly talk or writing.

rubble /'rʌbəl/ *n* mass of broken rocks, bricks, etc. from old or destroyed buildings.

rubicund/ /'ruːbɪkənd/ *adj* red in the face.

ruby /'ruːbɪ/ *n* red precious stone.

ruck /rʌk/ *n* small fold. *vt* make such folds in.

rucksack /'rʌksæk, 'rʊksæk/ *n* bag carried on the back, e.g. by campers.

rudder /'rʌdə/ *n* movable blade at the back of a boat or ship used to guide it.

ruddy /'rʌdɪ/ *adj* red and healthy-looking.

rude /ruːd/ *adj* rough; not gentle; not polite. *n* **rudeness** /'ruːdnəs/.

rudiment /'ruːdɪmənt/ *n* one of the earliest things taught; simplest and most important part of a

study. *adj* **rudimentary** /ˌruːdɪˈmentərɪ/ very simple.

rue /ruː/ *vi* be sorry. *n* pity.

ruff /rʌf/ *n* circle of stiff material standing out round the neck as part of a dress.

ruffian /'rʌfɪən/ *n* rough lawless fellow.

ruffle /'rʌfəl/ *vt* make (the feathers of a bird or the hair on a man's head) stand up. *n* cloth gathered together to make a loose edge to a garment, e.g. round the neck or at the end of the arm.

rug /rʌg/ *n* thick floor-covering made usually of wool; large piece of thick woollen material used to cover the legs when travelling.

rugby /'rʌgbɪ/ *n* form of football in which the ball is touched with the hands as well as the feet.

rugged /'rʌgɪd/ *adj* rough and unpolished; (of a man) strong and rough.

ruin /'ruːɪn/ *n* **1** condition of complete loss or destruction. **2** old building in bad repair. *vt* destroy completely. *n* **ruination** /ˌruːɪˈneɪʃən/. *adj* **ruinous** /'ruːɪnəs/.

rule /ruːl/ *n* **1** law or custom followed by all. **2** piece of straight wood used for measuring. *vt* **1** govern; control. **2** (e.g. of a judge) decide that something should be the case. **to rule lines** = make straight lines with the help of a straight edge. **to rule out** = say that (something) may not be considered. *n* **ruler** /'ruːlə/ **1** person who rules. **2** straight edge used in ruling lines. *n* **ruling** /'ruːlɪŋ/ judgment given by a judge or by the chief man in a meeting.

rum¹ /rʌm/ *n* strong drink made from sugar.

rum² /rʌm/ *adj* strange; unusual.

rumble /'rʌmbəl/ *vi, n* (make) a noise like distant thunder.

ruminate /'ruːmɪneɪt/ *vi* bite food over and over again, like a cow; think.

rummage /'rʌmɪdʒ/ *vi* search thoroughly. **a rummage sale** = selling of various used articles so as to get money for a good cause.

rumour /'ruːmə/ *n* common talk, probably untrue.

rump /rʌmp/ *n* tail end of an animal.

rumple /'rʌmpəl/ *vt* gather up (a smooth thing) in a careless way, causing marks of bending or folding.

rumpus /'rʌmpəs/ *n* noisy quarrelling or scolding.

run /rʌn/ *vi* **1** move quickly on the legs. **2** move or travel, e.g. *A train runs.* **3** change and become mixed, as the colours in some kinds of cloth when washed. *vt* be in charge of (e.g. a business). **to run down (run over)** = knock

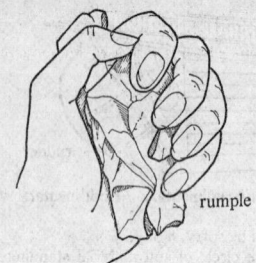

rumple

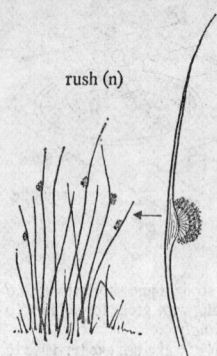

rush (n)

(someone) down while driving a car. **run down** = weak and tired. **to run out of** = finish the last of (e.g. food or other supplies). *n* **1** act of moving quickly, e.g. *Go for a run.* **2** distance moved, e.g. *London is an hour's run from here.* **3** time during which a thing lasts, e.g. *The play had a run of 100 days.* **4** enclosed place for animals, e.g. *A sheep run.* **in the long run** = in the end.

rung¹ /rʌŋ/ p.p. of **ring²**.

rung² /rʌŋ/ *n* cross-bar, e.g. between long bars of a LADDER.

runner /'rʌnə'/ *n* **1** person who runs. **2** long cloth for a table. **3** kind of plant that climbs up walls, trees, etc. **4** one of the two iron bars on which a wheel-less carriage slides over snow. *n* **runner-up** /ˌ.ˈ./ person next after the winner in a race.

runway /'rʌnweɪ/ *n* hard surface in an air-field from which aeroplanes go up or on which they come down.

rupee /ruːˈpiː/ *n* a silver coin in India (etc.).

rupture /'rʌptʃə'/ *n* **1** bursting or breaking; a quarrel. **2** the pushing out of a part of the bowel through a weak place in the muscles of the front of the body. *v* break or burst.

rural /'rʊərəl/ *adj* of the country.

ruse /ruːz/ *n* trick.

rush¹ /rʌʃ/ *n* tall grass-like plant that grows in wet places.

rush² /rʌʃ/ *vi* move rapidly forward. *vt* **1** seize by a sudden attack. **2** hurry (someone) into deciding.

rusk /rʌsk/ *n* piece of bread baked hard.

russet /'rʌsɪt/ *adj* red-brown.

rust /rʌst/ *n* **1** red coating formed on iron left in a wet place. **2** a disease of plants. *n, adj* (of a) reddish-brown colour. *vi* (of a metal) become covered in rust.

rustic /'rʌstɪk/ *adj* of the country people. *n* man from the country.

rustle /'rʌsəl/ *n, v* (make) a noise as of dead leaves.

rut /rʌt/ *n* deep track of a wheel. **to be in a rut** = be unable to do anything or think anything new.

ruthless /'ruːθləs/ *adj* merciless.

rye /raɪ/ *n* a grain-bearing plant.

S

Sabbath /'sæbəθ/ *n* holy day for the Jews, Saturday; for Christians, Sunday.

sable /'seɪbəl/ *n* small meat-eating animal; valuable dark brown fur.

sabotage /'sæbətɑːʒ/ *n* damage to machines, materials, bridges etc., to stop work, or movement in war. *vt* do such damage to; wreck. *n* **saboteur** /ˌsæbəˈtɜː/.

sabre /'seɪbə'/ *n* curved sword.

sachet /'sæʃeɪ/ *n* small bag containing sweet-smelling material.

sack¹ /sæk/ *n* large bag of strong cloth. *vt* put into sacks. *n* **sacking** /'sækɪŋ/ rough cloth of which such bags are made.

sack² /sæk/ *vt* attack a town and carry off everything of value.

sack³ /sæk/ *infml vt* send away from employment, cease to employ. **to get the sack** = lose one's employment.

sacrament /'sækrəmənt/ *n* important religious ceremony of the Christian Church, regarded as a sign of grace. *adj* **sacramental** /ˌsækrəˈmentl/.

sacred /'seɪkrɪd/ *adj* **1** holy. **2** solemn, e.g. *A sacred promise.*

sacrifice /'sækrɪfaɪs/ *v* make an offering to God; give up a thing for some noble reason; sell goods at a loss. *n* act of sacrificing; a thing sacrificed. *adj* **sacrificial** /ˌsækrɪˈfɪʃəl/.

sacrilege /'sækrɪlɪdʒ/ *n* doing a disrespectful act to a holy thing. *adj* **sacrilegious** /ˌsækrɪˈlɪdʒəs/.

sacrosanct /'sækrəʊsæŋkt/ *adj* very holy, and therefore protected from harm.

sad /sæd/ *adj* feeling sorrow, unhappy; causing sorrow. *n* **sadness** /'sædnəs/. *v* **sadden** /'sædn/ make or become sad.

saddle /'sædl/ *n* **1** leather seat fixed on a horse for riding. **2** back of an animal used as meat. **3** high piece of land rising at each end to a high point.

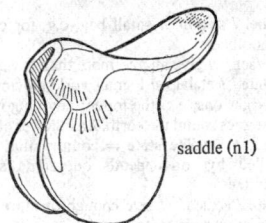

saddle (n1)

vt fix a saddle on. **to saddle with** = lay as a load or duty upon, e.g. *To saddle with debts. n* **saddler** /'sædlə/ maker of saddles and other leather goods.

sadism /'seɪdɪzəm/ *n* love of cruelty; being cruel for pleasure. *n* **sadist** /'seɪdɪst/ one who gets pleasure from cruelty. *adj* **sadistic** /sə'dɪstɪk/.

safari /sə'fɑːrɪ/ *n* a journey hunting wild animals, esp. in Africa.

safe /seɪf/ *adj* **1** out of danger; unhurt. **2** not dangerous. **3** trustworthy, on which one can depend. *n* strong box for valuables. *n* **safeguard** /'seɪfgɑːd/ protection. *vt* keep safe, protect. *n* **safety** /'seɪftɪ/ state of being safe. *n* **safety pin** /'.. ,./ pin that has a cover for its point when closed.

sag /sæg/ *vi* hang down in the middle.

saga /'sɑːgə/ *n* story of brave deeds, esp. those of great men of old in Norway, Denmark, Sweden, and Iceland; any long story about a family or group over many years.

sagacious /sə'geɪʃəs/ *adj* wise, clever, e.g. *A sagacious animal. n* **sagacity** /sə'gæsɪtɪ/.

sage[1] /seɪdʒ/ sweet-smelling plant, used in cooking.

sage[2] /seɪdʒ/ *adj* wise. *n* wise man.

said /sed/ p.t. and p.p. of **say.**

sail /seɪl/ *n* stretched cloth used to catch wind and so drive a ship forward. *v* **1** travel on the water. **2** control (a boat or ship). **3** set out on water. **to set sail** = leave the harbour to begin a journey. *n* **sailor** /'seɪlə/ seaman.

saint /seɪnt/ *n* holy person. *adj* **saintly** /'seɪntlɪ/.

sake /seɪk/ **for the sake of** = in order to help or please; because of a desire for.

salaam /sə'lɑːm/ *n* greeting used in the East.

salad /'sæləd/ *n* uncooked vegetables used as food.

salary /'sælərɪ/ *n* payment for regular employment, expressed as so much a year.

sale /seɪl/ *n* **1** act of selling. **2** special selling at low prices. *n* **salesman** /'seɪlzmən/ person who sells goods in a shop, or to shopkeepers. *n* **salesmanship** /'seɪlzmənʃɪp/ art of selling.

salient /'seɪlɪənt/ *adj* easily seen or noticed; most important.

saline /'seɪlaɪn/ *adj* containing salt.

saliva /sə'laɪvə/ *n* liquid that naturally comes in the mouth when eating.

sallow /'sæləʊ/ *adj* (of the skin) of a yellow-white colour.

sand

salmon /'sæmən/ *n* large fish with light red meat used for food.

salon /'sælɒn/ *n* large room in which guests are received.

saloon /sə'luːn/ *n* **1** large room; sitting-room in a ship or train. **2** closed car. **3** place for buying and drinking strong drink.

salt /sɒlt, sɔːlt/ *n* white substance, present in sea water, commonly eaten with food, or added to preserve it. *vt* add salt to. *adj* **salty** /'sɒltɪ, sɔːltɪ/ containing or tasting of salt.

salubrious /sə'luːbrɪəs/ *adj* resulting in good health.

salutary /'sæljʊtərɪ/ *adj* having a good effect.

salute /sə'luːt/ *v* greet; raise the hand in greeting like a soldier. *n* (act of) greeting. *n* **salutation** /ˌsæljʊ'teɪʃən/.

salvage /'sælvɪdʒ/ *n* **1** payment for saving a ship. **2** goods so saved. **3** act of saving goods or a ship. *vt* save from loss in a fire, wreck, etc.

salvation /sæl'veɪʃən/ *n* saving of the soul; that which saves.

salver /'sælvə/ *n* silver or metal plate used by servants for carrying small things, e.g. glasses.

salvo /'sælvəʊ/ *n* firing of many guns at the same time.

same /seɪm/ *adj* not different, not another; exactly alike; unchanged. **the same** = the same thing; the same way. **to be all the same to** = make no difference to. **all the same** = in spite of that. **at the same time** = however, yet.

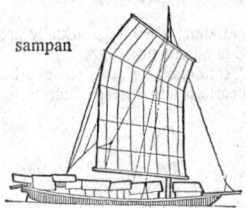

sampan

sampan /'sæmpæn/ *n* flat-bottomed boat used in China.

sample /'sɑːmpəl/ *n* example (of goods for sale); part of a thing that shows what the rest is like. *vt* take a sample of.

sanctify /'sæŋktɪfaɪ/ *vt* make holy. *n* **sanctification** /ˌsæŋktɪfɪ'keɪʃən/.

sanctimonious /ˌsæŋktɪ'məʊnɪəs/ *adj* pretending to be very holy.

sanction /'sæŋkʃən/ *n* **1** right or permission to do something; support (of behaviour, etc.) by general custom. **2** punishment for breaking an agreement (esp. between nations). *vt* allow.

sanctity /'sæŋktɪtɪ/ *n* holiness.

sanctuary /'sæŋktʃʊərɪ/ *n* holy place; place that gives protection to people (or animals) who need it.

sand /sænd/ *n* very fine grains of broken stone and shells, as on the sea-shore. **the sands** = sandy shore.

sandal /'sændl/ *n* kind of open shoe, held on to the foot with strings or leather bands.

sandalwood /'sændlwʊd/ *n* kind of sweet-smelling red wood.

sandwich /'sænwɪdʒ,-wɪt/ *n* meat, etc., between two pieces of bread. *vt* put (a thing or person) tightly between two others.

sane /seɪn/ *adj* **1** not mad. **2** having good sense; according to common sense.

sang /sæŋ/ p.t. of **sing**.

sang-froid /ˌsɑŋ 'frwɑː/ *French n* calmness in face of danger.

sanguinary /'sæŋgwɪnərɪ/ *adj* bloody, with much killing.

sanguine /'sæŋgwɪn/ *adj* **1** hopeful. **2** red-faced.

sanitary /'sænətərɪ/ *adj* **1** concerned with the protection of health. **2** free from dirt and therefore from disease.

sanity /'sænətɪ/ *n* state of being SANE.

sank /sæŋk/ p.t. of **sink**.

sap¹ /sæp/ *n* liquid in a plant.

sap² /sæp/ *v* **1** weaken (a wall, etc.) by digging under it. **2** use up (one's strength); destroy (one's faith, etc.).

sapling /'sæplɪŋ/ *n* young tree.

sapper /'sæpə⁷/ *n* soldier who has to do with digging, building bridges, etc.

sapphire /'sæfaɪə⁷/ *n* blue jewel.

sarcasm /'sɑːkæzəm/ *n* bitter words meant to hurt the feelings. *adj* **sarcastic** /sɑː'kæstɪk/.

sarcophagus /sɑː'kɒfəgəs/ *n* stone box for a dead body.

sardine /sɑː'diːn/ *n* small fish usually preserved for food in oil in a tin.

sardonic /sɑː'dɒnɪk/ *adj* (of a smile or laughter) bitter, heartless and disrespectful.

sari

sari /'sɑːrɪ/ *n* dress of an Indian woman.

sarong /sə'rɒŋ/ *n* dress of people in Malaysia.

sartorial /sɑː'tɔːrɪəl/ *adj* having to do with making (men's) clothes.

sash¹ /sæʃ/ *n* broad band of silk worn round the waist or over the shoulder.

sash² /sæʃ/ *n* window frame.

sat /sæt/ p.t. of **sit**.

Satan /'seɪtən/ *n* the chief evil spirit, the Devil. *adj* **satanic** /sə'tænɪk/.

satchel /'sætʃəl/ *n* small bag, e.g. for carrying schoolbooks.

sate /seɪt/ *vt* give all and more than is wanted.

satellite /'sætəlaɪt/ *n* **1** small world moving round a larger one, e.g. the moon; anything in space that goes round the earth. **2** a follower of a great man. **a satellite state** = country that is controlled by, or depends on, some stronger country.

satiate /'seɪʃɪeɪt/ *vt* give enough or more than is desired. *n* **satiety** /sə'taɪətɪ/.

satin /'sætɪn/ *n* silk material which is smooth and shiny on one side.

satire /'sætaɪə⁷/ *n* (piece of) writing meant to make something seem foolish and laughable. *adj* **satirical** /sə'tɪrɪkəl/. *vt* **satirize** /'sætɪraɪz/ attack with satire.

satisfy /'sætɪsfaɪ/ *vt* **1** supply a need; fulfil a wish; be enough for. **2** make contented; give what is claimed. **3** free from doubt. *n* **satisfaction** /ˌsætɪs'fækʃən/ something that satisfies; state of being satisfied; feeling of pleasure. *adj* **satisfactory** /ˌsætɪs'fæktərɪ/ that satisfies; good enough (but not very good).

saturate /'sætʃəreɪt/ *vt* make as wet or full of liquid as possible. *n* **saturation** /ˌsætʃə'reɪʃən/.

Saturday /'sætədɪ/ *n* the seventh day of the week, following Friday.

sauce /sɔːs/ *n* **1** pleasant-tasting liquid added to food. **2** *infml* rudeness, disrespect.

saucepan /'sɔːspən/ *n* round cooking pot with a handle.

saucer /'sɔːsə⁷/ *n* small curved plate on which a cup is placed.

saucy /'sɔːsɪ/ *infml adj* disrespectful to elders; rude.

saunter /'sɔːntə⁷/ *vi* walk slowly. *n* slow walk.

sausage /'sɒsɪdʒ/ *n* meat cut small and put into a tube-like skin.

savage /'sævɪdʒ/ *adj* **1** in a state of nature. **2** wild; fierce; cruel. *n* savage person. *n* **savagery** /'sævɪdʒrɪ/.

savanna(h) /sə'vænə/ *n* plain with only a few trees, found in hot countries.

save /seɪv/ *v* **1** take out of danger. **2** keep for future use. **3** not use up; prevent waste of. *prep* except. *n* (*pl*) **savings** /'seɪvɪŋz/ money put aside for future use.

saviour /'seɪvjə⁷/ *n* one who saves. **Our Saviour** = Jesus Christ.

savour /'seɪvə⁷/ *n* pleasant taste or smell. *vt* taste, enjoy the taste of. *adj* **savoury** /'seɪvərɪ/ pleasant tasting, but not sweet.

saw¹ /sɔː/ *n* tool with toothed blade, used for cutting. *v* cut with a saw; use a saw. *n* **sawdust** /'sɔːdʌst/ dust that falls when wood is sawn.

saw² /sɔː/ p.t. of **see**.

saxophone /'sæksəfəʊn/ *n* musical wind instrument, made of metal.

say /seɪ/ *vt* speak (words); express (a thought) in words. **to have a say in** = have what one says about (a matter) taken into account. *n* **saying**

saxophone

/'seɪ-ɪŋ/ fixed form of words commonly used to express an idea, such as 'Every cloud has a silver lining'.

scab /skæb/ *n* hard mass of dried blood formed on a wound. *adj* **scabby** /'skæbɪ/.

scabbard /'skæbəd/ *n* case for the blade of a sword.

scabies /'skeɪbiːz/ *n* kind of skin disease.

scaffold /'skæfəld/ *n* raised floor of wood upon which evil-doers were killed in public. *n* **scaffolding** /'skæfəldɪŋ/ frame put up round a building that is being built or repaired.

scald /skɔːld/ *vt* **1** burn with hot liquid or steam. **2** clean with boiling water. **3** heat but not boil (e.g. milk).

scale¹ /skeɪl/ *vt* climb.

scale² /skeɪl/ *n* **1** set of musical notes of any particular key. **2** set of marks for measuring. **3** system of steps or differences. **4** size of a map, plan, etc., in relation to the thing it stands for. **5** amount; relative size.

scale³ /skeɪl/ *n* one of the thin flat plates on the skin of a fish, snake, etc.

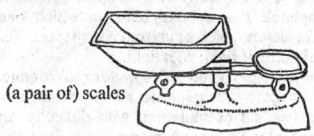

(a pair of) scales

scales /skeɪlz/ **a pair of scales** = instrument used for weighing.

scallop /'skæləp, 'skɒləp/ *n* kind of shell-fish.

scalp /skælp/ *n* skin and hair of the top of the head. *vt* cut off the scalp (as a sign of victory).

scalpel /'skælpəl/ *n* small knife used by a doctor.

scamp /skæmp/ *vt* do (work) carelessly and in a hurry. *n* lazy worthless person.

scamper /'skæmpə/ *vi* run about quickly, e.g. as children playing.

scan /skæn/ *v* **1** look carefully at every part of. **2** look through quickly. **3** divide up poetry according to its regular beat.

scandal /'skændl/ *n* **1** spreading of evil reports about a person. **2** action likely to cause such reports or public anger. *adj* **scandalous** /'skændələs/ very bad, such as will cause scandal. *vt* **scandalize** /'skændəlaɪz/ shock; make angry by doing something wrong.

scant /skænt/ *adj* not enough. *adj* **scanty** /'skæntɪ/ very small.

scapegoat /'skeɪpgəʊt/ *n* one who is made to bear the blame for the wrongdoing of others.

scar /skɑː/ *n* mark left on the skin by an old wound. *vt* mark with a scar or scars.

scarab /'skærəb/ *n* insect with a hard skin, once considered very holy in Egypt.

scarce /skeəs/ *adj* few and hard to find. *adv* **scarcely** /'skeəslɪ/ nearly not, hardly; not quite. *n* **scarcity** /'skeəsɪtɪ/.

scare /skeə/ *vt* frighten. *n* fright; general feeling of fear.

scarecrow /'skeəkrəʊ/ *n* wooden figure dressed in old clothes used to frighten birds.

scarf /skɑːf/ *n* long piece of cloth worn round the neck.

scarlet /'skɑːlət/ *n, adj* (of a) bright red colour. *n* **scarlet fever** /ˌ.. '../ disease that causes red marks on the skin and pain in the throat.

scathing /'skeɪðɪŋ/ *adj* (of a speech etc.) very bitter and wounding.

scatter /'skætə/ *v* throw loosely about; drive in different directions; go in different directions. *adj* **scattered** /'skætəd/ not near one another.

scavenger /'skævəndʒə/ *n* **1** animal that feeds on waste food, etc. **2** street-cleaner.

scenario /sɪ'nɑːrɪəʊ/ *n* written plan of a story for a play, film, etc.

scene /siːn/ *n* **1** view; that which is seen by the eye. **2** place where an event happened. **3** part of a play. **4** one set of painted pictures used in a theatre. **5** noisy quarrel.

scenery /'siːnərɪ/ *n* **1** general appearance of the country. **2** painted pictures used in showing a play in a theatre. *adj* **scenic** /'siːnɪk/.

scent /sent/ *n* **1** (liquid that has a) pleasant smell. **2** that smell left by an animal on the ground which enables other animals to follow it. *vt* cause to smell; smell.

sceptic /'skeptɪk/ *n* one who doubts the truth of something. *adj* **sceptical** /'skeptɪkəl/ doubtful. *n* **scepticism** /'skeptɪsɪzəm/.

sceptre /'septə/ *n* ornamental bar of gold carried by a king as a sign of power.

schedule /'ʃedjuːl/ *n* list, esp. of times for doing things. **according to schedule** = as planned. *vt* plan; arrange.

scheme /skiːm/ *n* **1** arrangement. **2** plan. **3** secret or dishonest plan. *vi* make plans (esp. dishonest ones).

schism /'sɪzəm/ *n* division of opinion in the Church. *adj* **schismatic** /sɪz'mætɪk/.

scholar /'skɒlə/ *n* **1** one who goes to school. **2** one who has won a scholarship. **3** learned person. *n* **scholarship** /'skɒləʃɪp/ **1** money given to a promising learner to enable him to go on learning. **2** knowledge gained by studying. *adj* **scholastic** /skə'læstɪk/.

school¹ /skuːl/ *n* **1** place in which the young are taught; any place of teaching. **2** group of people who share certain ideas or ways of doing things, e.g. *A school of painters.* *vt* teach; train; bring under control.

school² /skuːl/ *n* large group of fish swimming together.

schooner /ˈskuːnə ʸ/ *n* kind of sailing ship.

science /ˈsaɪəns/ *n* **1** knowledge of facts (e.g. of the nature of matter, of natural forces) obtained by careful study. **2** a branch of such knowledge. *n* **scientist** /ˈsaɪəntɪst/ one who studies science. *adj* **scientific** /ˌsaɪənˈtɪfɪk/ having to do with science.

scintillate /ˈsɪntɪleɪt/ *vi* shine like a star, SPARKLE. *adj* **scintillating** /ˈsɪntɪleɪtɪn/ (of speech, etc.) very clever and amusing.

scissors /ˈsɪzəz/ *n* (*pl*) instrument with two blades used for cutting cloth, etc. (Often **a pair of scissors**).

scoff /skɒf/ *vi* laugh disrespectfully (at someone, an idea, etc.).

scold /skəʊld/ *v* blame angrily, find fault with.

scone /skəʊn, skɒn/ *n* kind of flat, plain cake, often eaten hot with butter.

scoop /skuːp/ *vt* make a hole in; lift (up), get out (from a hole, etc.). *n* **1** instrument for scooping. **2** important piece of news printed by only one newspaper.

scooter (motor)

scoot /skuːt/ *infml vi* move (away) quickly. *n* **scooter** /ˈskuːtə ʸ/ **1** toy with two wheels, moved along by using one foot. **2** kind of motor bicycle with small wheels.

scope /skəʊp/ *n* range of view; field of action.

scorch /skɔːtʃ/ *v* slightly burn, burn the outside of.

score¹ /skɔː ʸ/ *v* **1** make marks on a surface with a sharp point, e.g. *He scored the table with a nail.* **2** win points in a game; keep a note of (points scored, etc.). *n* **1** points won in a game. **2** printed music in which the parts for the different instruments and kinds of voice are shown on sets of lines one above another. **to pay off old scores** = punish those who have harmed one.

score² /skɔː ʸ/ *n* (set of) twenty.

scorn /skɔːn/ *vt* **1** feel no respect for. **2** refuse (to do something) because it is wrong or unworthy. *n* lack of respect for; feeling that a thing is bad and worthless. *adj* **scornful** /ˈskɔːnfəl/ feeling or showing scorn.

scorpion /ˈskɔːpɪən/ *n* small creature with eight legs having poison in its tail.

Scotch /skɒtʃ/ *adj* (of things) from Scotland. *n* WHISKY (from Scotland).

scot-free /ˌskɒt ˈfriː/ *adj* without having been harmed or punished.

scoundrel /ˈskaʊndrəl/ *n* very bad man.

scorpion

scour /ˈskaʊə ʸ/ *vt* **1** clean; polish; rub away. **2** quickly search all over for.

scourge /skɜːdʒ/ *n* **1** number of strings tied together used for beating as a punishment. **2** anything that causes great suffering, e.g. a widespread disease. *vt* **1** beat with a scourge. **2** bring suffering to.

scout /skaʊt/ *n* **1** person, aeroplane etc., sent in front of an army to get news of the enemy. **2** member of the Boy Scouts. *vi* act as a scout. **to scout round** = search.

scowl /skaʊl/ *vi* pull down the muscles above the eyes as a sign of anger. *n* such a look.

scraggy /ˈskrægɪ/ *adj* thin and bony.

scramble /ˈskræmbəl/ *vi* **1** climb using the hands and knees. **2** struggle against others for something. **scrambled eggs** = eggs beaten and cooked in butter. *n* **1** short climb. **2** disorderly struggle.

scrap¹ /skræp/ *n* **1** small piece. **2** waste material. **scrap iron** = pieces of waste iron to be melted down. *vt* throw away or give up as useless. *n* **scrapbook** /ˈskræpbʊk/ book in which one sticks pictures, pieces cut from newspapers, etc.

scrap² /skræp/ *infml vi, n* fight.

scrape /skreɪp/ *v* **1** rub with a knife or sharp edge. **2** damage by scraping. **to scrape through** = pass (e.g. an examination) with difficulty. **to scrape up** = gather (e.g. money) with difficulty. *n* **1** act or sound of scraping. **2** difficult situation; trouble.

scratch /skrætʃ/ *v* **1** make marks on a surface with a pointed object. **2** rub or SCRAPE with the nails. **3** strike out (e.g. from the list of players in a game). *n* **1** act of scratching. **2** sound or mark made by scratching. *adj* collected or prepared in a hurry, e.g. *A scratch dinner.* **to start from scratch** = start from the beginning. **not up to scratch** = not good enough.

scrawl /skrɔːl/ *v* write in a bad, careless way; make meaningless marks. *n* something scrawled.

scream /skriːm/ *v* **1** give a loud long cry, e.g. of pain. **2** say in a loud voice. *n* loud, sharp cry or noise.

screech /skriːtʃ/ *v* make a loud high noise. *n* high loud cry or noise.

screen /skriːn/ *vt* **1** protect; hide. **2** test and examine a person to see if he is trustworthy. *n* **1** frame covered with cloth, paper or other material used to hide or protect; anything used for this purpose. **2** surface on which cinema films are shown or television pictures appear. **3** net-like instrument used to separate larger pieces from smaller pieces (e.g. of coal or earth).

screw /skru:/ *n* **1** thing like a nail that is driven into wood etc., by being turned round and round. **2** set of blades at the back of a ship that turn to drive it forward. *v* **1** join together or fix with a screw. **2** twist, turn round.

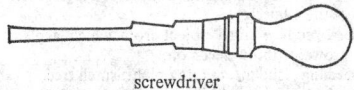

screwdriver

screwdriver /'skru:draɪvə ʔ/ *n* instrument with a flat end used to drive in screws.

scribble /'skrɪbəl/ *v* write quickly and carelessly.

scribe /skraɪb/ *n* writer in ancient times.

scrimmage /'skrɪmɪdʒ/ *n* disorderly struggle.

script /skrɪpt/ *n* **1** writing done by hand. **2** written words from which a film is made or which are to be spoken on radio.

scripture /'skrɪptʃə ʔ/ *n* holy book or writing. **the Holy Scriptures** = the Bible.

scroll /skrəʊl/ *n* long piece of paper or skin rolled up on two rollers; ancient book written on a scroll.

scrub[1] /skrʌb/ *n* (land covered with) low trees and bushes. *adj* **scrubby** /'skrʌbɪ/ small and unpleasant.

scrub[2] /skrʌb/ *v* clean by rubbing with a brush.

scruff /skrʌf/ *n* back of the neck. *adj* **scruffy** /'skrʌfɪ/ rough and dirty in appearance.

scruple /'skru:pəl/ *n* **1** small weight = 1.3 grammes. **2** feeling of doubt as to the rightness of what one is asked to do. *adj* **scrupulous** /'skru:pjʊləs/ **1** very careful and afraid of doing wrong. **2** paying great attention to small points.

scrutinize /'skru:tənaɪz/ *vt* examine very carefully. *n* **crutiny** /'skru:tənɪ/.

scuffle /'skʌfəl/ *n, vi* (take part in a) disorderly fight.

scull /skʌl/ *n* one of two OARS used to row a boat. *vt* row using sculls.

scullery /'skʌlərɪ/ *n* room in which plates, etc., are washed.

sculptor /'skʌlptə ʔ/ *n* one who makes figures of men, etc., from stone, wood or other materials. *n* **sculpture** /'skʌlptʃə ʔ/ figure made from stone, etc.; this art.

scum /skʌm/ *n* mass of dirt that collects on the top of boiling liquid. **the scum of the earth** = bad, worthless people.

scupper /'skʌpə ʔ/ *n* opening in a ship's side that allows the water from waves falling on the ship to flow back into the sea.

scurf /skɜ:f/ *n* small pieces of dry skin found among the hairs on the head.

scurrilous /'skʌrɪləs/ *adj* using low and rude language in speaking against a person.

scurry /'skʌrɪ/ *vi* run or move hastily.

scurvy /'skɜ:vɪ/ *n* disease caused by lack of fresh fruit.

scuttle[1] /'skʌtl/ *n* coal box.

scuttle[2] /'skʌtl/ *vi* run hastily away.

scuttle[3] /'skʌtl/ *vt* (a ship) let water in so as to sink it on purpose.

scythe /saɪð/ *n* tool with a long curved blade, used for cutting grass.

sea /si:/ *n* mass of water, not land. *n* **seasickness** /'si:ˌsɪknəs/ illness caused by the movement of a ship. *n* **seaman** /'si:mən/ (*pl* **seamen** /'si:mən/) man who works on a ship. *n* **seamanship** /'si:mənʃɪp/ art of guiding and controlling a ship. *n, adj* **seaside** /'si:saɪd/ (place) by the sea. *n* **seaweed** /'si:wi:d/ plant(s) growing in the sea.

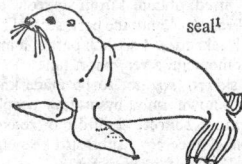

seal[1]

seal[1] /si:l/ *n* large sea animal hunted for its skin.

seal[2] /si:l/ *vt* **1** close a letter (with hot wax); print a mark upon hot wax. **2** close up tightly so as to keep out air. **3** settle; decide and make firm. *n* instrument or mark used to seal; anything that seals.

seam /si:m/ *n* **1** joining-line of two pieces of cloth. **2** part of a rock containing coal or metal. *n* **seamstress** /'semstrəs/ needlewoman. *adj* **seamy** /'si:mɪ/ unpleasant, e.g. *The seamy side of life.*

sear /sɪə ʔ/ *vt* burn the outside of, esp. with a hot iron.

search /sɜ:tʃ/ *v* look in a place in order to find; examine in order to find. *n* act of examining or looking for something. *n* **searchlight** /'sɜ:tʃlaɪt/ electric lamp throwing a very powerful beam.

season /'si:zən/ *n* **1** one of the four parts of the year, summer, winter, etc.; part of the year different because of the weather. **2** time suitable for doing a thing; short time. *v* **1** (of wood, etc.) make or become fit for use. **2** give a good taste to food. *adj* **seasonable** /'si:zənəbəl/ **1** well fitted for the time of the year. **2** done at the right time. *adj* **seasonal** /'si:zənəl/ lasting only during a certain season. *n* **seasoning** /'si:zənɪŋ/ substance used to give a good taste. *n* **season ticket** /ˈ.. ˌ.ˌ./ card tht gives one the right to travel between two places as often as one likes for a certain time.

seat /si:t/ *n* **1** piece of furniture on which one sits. **2** part of a chair etc. on which one sits. **3** place where a thing happens or is done, e.g. *The seat of government.* **4** place paid for in a theatre or train. *vt* **1** give a chair to. **2** have enough room for, e.g. *This hall seats 500 people.* **be seated** = please sit down.

secede /sɪ'siːd/ vi leave, cease to be a member of. n **secession** /sɪ'seʃən/.

seclude /sɪ'kluːd/ vt shut away from. adj **secluded** /sɪ'kluːdɪd/ quiet; untroubled. n **seclusion** /sɪ'kluːʒən/ being alone and shut off from others.

second¹ /'sekənd/ adj, n next after the first; another. n person who helps another in a fight. vt support. **to second a motion** = say that one agrees with an opinion already expressed by another person in a meeting. vt **second** /sɪ'kɒnd/ take someone from his usual work and give him some special duty. adj **secondary** /'sekəndərɪ/ coming later; of less importance. **secondary school** = school for children aged about 11 to 18. adj **secondhand** /ˌsekənd'hænd/ not new, already used; obtained from someone else. adj **second-rate** /ˌ. . '.ˌ/ not the best; second best.

second² /'sekənd/ n 1 sixtieth part of a minute. 2 infml a moment, a very short time.

secret /'siːkrət/ adj not to be made known to others; known only by a few people. n 1 something secret. 2 hidden reason for something. n **secrecy** /'siːkrəsɪ/ 1 keeping things secret. 2 state of being secret.

secretary /'sekrətərɪ/ n helper who writes letters, etc., and does duties for the employer. adj **secretarial** /ˌsekrə'teərɪəl/.

secretion /sɪ'kriːʃən/ n a liquid formed in the body for a certain use, etc.

secrete /sɪ'kriːt/ vt 1 hide; keep secret. 2 make a SECRETION.

secretive /'siːkrətɪv/ adj liking to keep things secret.

sect /sekt/ n group of persons holding a particular set of opinions in religion, etc. adj **sectarian** /sek'teərɪən/ belonging to a certain small party.

section /'sekʃən/ n 1 part cut off. 2 part of something. adj **sectional** /'sekʃənəl/.

sector /'sektə/ n 1 part of a circle between two lines drawn from the centre to the edge. 2 part of something, divided for control purposes.

secular /'sekjʊlə/ adj concerned with this world and material things rather than religious matters.

secure /sɪ'kjʊə/ vt 1 make safe, protect from danger. 2 fasten well. adj 1 safe. 2 well fastened. n **security** /sɪ'kjʊərətɪ/ 1 safeness. 2 something valuable given to a person who lends one money, to be kept by him if the money is not paid back. **securities** = papers which prove that one owns shares in a business, land, etc.

sedate /sɪ'deɪt/ adj calm and serious. vt make calm by giving medicine to.

sedative /'sedətɪv/ n calming medicine. n **sedation** /sɪ'deɪʃən/ condition caused by a sedative.

sedentary /'sedntərɪ/ adj done sitting down; spending much time sitting down.

sediment /'sedɪmənt/ n matter that settles at the bottom of a liquid.

sedition /sɪ'dɪʃən/ n words or acts intended to make people disobey the government. adj **seditious** /sɪ'dɪʃəs/.

seduce /sɪ'djuːs/ vt lead a person into wrong-doing; get a person to have sexual relations with one. n **seduction** /sɪ'dʌkʃən/. adj **seductive** /sɪ'dʌktɪv/ very charming, ATTRACTIVE.

sedulous /'sedjʊləs/ adj working steadily and carefully; not giving up easily.

see¹ /siː/ v 1 use the eyes; notice with the eyes. 2 understand. 3 meet; visit. **to see to** = attend to.

see² /siː/ n area under the control of a high officer of the Church.

seed /siːd/ n small object from which a plant grows. vt throw seeds on.

seedling /'siːdlɪŋ/ n young plant; small tree.

seedy /'siːdɪ/ infml adj ill; not taken care of.

seek /siːk/ vt look for; try to get. **to seek to** = try to.

seem /siːm/ vi appear to be.

seemly /'siːmlɪ/ adj proper; correct.

seen /siːn/ p.p. of **see**.

seep /siːp/ vi (of liquid) pass slowly through. n **seepage** /'siːpɪdʒ/.

seer /sɪə/ n one who sees and tells the future.

seesaw

seesaw /'siːsɔː/ n 1 board laid over a barrel or other object (a child sits on each end and they move up and down). 2 up-and-down movement. vi move in this way.

seethe /siːð/ vi 1 boil. 2 feel something (e.g. anger) very strongly.

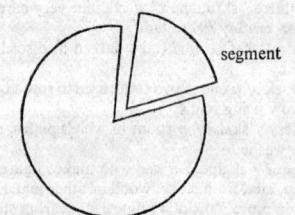

segment

segment /'segmənt/ n one of the parts into which a fruit etc. is divided; part cut off.

segregate /'segrɪgeɪt/ vt keep separate from others. n **segregation** /ˌsegrɪ'geɪʃən/.

seize /siːz/ v 1 take hold of suddenly and by force. 2 take possession of. 3 become fixed (e.g. a machine when overheated). n **seizure** /'siːʒə/ 1 act of seizing. 2 sudden attack of illness (esp. of the heart).

seldom /'seldəm/ adv not often.

select /sɪ'lekt/ vt choose. adj **1** carefully chosen. **2** not open to everyone. n **selection** /sɪ'lekʃən/ **1** act of selecting. **2** thing(s) selected or group from which one can choose. adj **selective** /sɪ'lektɪv/ choosing only the best.

self¹ /self/ n person's nature, special qualities, etc.; one's own interests, wishes etc.

self-² /self/ concerning oneself (no other person); done by oneself, itself, e.g. n **self-pity** /ˌ. '. ./ pitying oneself. adj **self-conscious** /ˌ. '. ./ SHY because unable to forget oneself when in the company of others. adj **self-contained** /ˌself kən'teɪnd/ (of a house) complete in itself; (of a person) self-controlled. adj **selfish** /'selfɪʃ/ thinking only of one's own interests. adj **self-possessed** /ˌself pə'zest/ calmly sure of one's own behaviour. adj **self-willed** /ˌself 'wɪld/ determined to have things done according to one's own wishes; refusing to be guided by others.

-self³ /self/, **-selves** /selvz/ (used in forming reflexive pronouns such as **myself, ourselves,** etc.)

sell /sel/ v **1** give in return for money. **2** (of goods) be sold. **to sell off** = sell cheaply.

selvedge, selvage /'selvɪdʒ/ n edge of cloth made specially strong to prevent threads coming out.

semantics /sɪ'mæntɪks/ n (scientific) study of the meaning of words. adj **semantic** /sɪ'mæntɪk/.

semaphore /'seməfɔː/ n way of sending messages by holding the arms up in various ways, each way meaning a letter.

semblance /'semblans/ n likeness; appearance.

semester /sɪ'mestə/ n half-year in a school.

semi- /'semɪ/ prefix **1** half. **2** partly; not completely.

semicolon /ˌsemɪ'kəʊlən/ n the mark (;).

seminar /'semɪnɑː/ n small group of learners studying the more difficult parts of a subject under a teacher.

seminary /'semɪnərɪ/ n school where priests are trained.

semitic /sɪ'mɪtɪk/ adj having to do with the Jews.

senate /'senət/ n **1** meeting of law-givers in ancient Rome. **2** meeting of persons for law-making in some governments (e.g. the United States). **3** meeting that controls a university. n **senator** /'senətə/ member of a senate.

send /send/ vt cause to go. **to send for** = ask for someone to come, something to be brought.

senile /'siːnaɪl/ adj old and weak. n **senility** /sɪ'nɪlətɪ/.

senior /'siːnɪə/ adj older; higher in rank; longer in service. n **seniority** /ˌsiːnɪ'ɒrətɪ/.

sensation /sen'seɪʃən/ n **1** feeling. **2** great excitement. adj **sensational** /sen'seɪʃənəl/ causing great excitement.

sense /sens/ n **1** power to feel, see, hear, etc. **2** feeling. **3** power to understand and judge. **4** meaning. vt feel. **to make sense** = have a meaning that can be understood. **common sense** = good judgment. n (pl) **senses** /'sensɪz/

usual healthy state of mind. adj **senseless** /'senslas/ foolish, meaningless.

sensibility /ˌsensə'bɪlətɪ/ n power of feeling; possession of fine feelings.

sensible /'sensəbəl/ adj **1** having good judgment. **2** enough to be noticed.

sensitive /'sensətɪv/ adj **1** having keen powers of feeling. **2** (of a person) whose feelings are easily hurt. **3** (of an instrument) able to note very small changes. n **sensitivity** /ˌsensə'tɪvətɪ/.

sensory /'sensərɪ/ adj having to do with the senses (hearing, sight, etc.).

sensual /'sensjʊəl/ adj **1** having to do with the pleasures of the body. **2** too much interested in the pleasures of the body. adj **sensuous** /'sensjʊəs/ working on, noticed, or caused by the feelings of the body.

sentence /'sentəns/ n **1** group of words forming a complete statement, question, or command. **2** punishment given by a judge to a wrongdoer. vt give such punishment to.

sententious /sen'tenʃəs/ adj trying to sound wise.

sentiment /'sentɪmənt/ n **1** feeling; (show of) tender feeling. **2** expression of feeling. **3** opinion. adj **sentimental** /ˌsentɪ'mentl/ having or showing too much feeling, intended to have an effect on the feelings. n **sentimentality** /ˌsentɪmen'tælətɪ/.

sentinel /'sentɪnəl/, **sentry** /'sentrɪ/ n soldier on guard.

separate /'sepərət/ adj apart; not joined. v /'sepəreɪt/ **1** make, become or keep apart. **2** (of people) go different ways. n **separation** /ˌsepə'reɪʃən/.

sepia /'siːpɪə/ n, adj dark brown (paint).

September /sep'tembə/ n the ninth month of the year.

septic /'septɪk/ adj poisoned by disease, INFECTED.

sepulchre /'sepəlkə/ n grave cut in the rock or built of stone, TOMB. adj **sepulchral** /sɪ'pʌlkrəl/ **1** of a sepulchre. **2** (of a voice, etc.) deep and solemn.

sequel /'siːkwəl/ n **1** that which follows or is the result of (something earlier). **2** book, film etc. that continues the story of an earlier one.

sequence /'siːkwəns/ n number of things following each other.

sequester /sɪ'kwestə/ vt keep apart from other people.

sequin /'siːkwɪn/ n very small plate of bright metal fixed on a dress as an ornament.

seraph /'serəf/ n ANGEL, messenger from God. pl **seraphim** /'serəfɪm/. adj **seraphic** /sɪ'ræfɪk/.

serenade /ˌserə'neɪd/ n playing or singing by a lover outside a lady's window in the evening; quiet piece of music. v sing or play a serenade (to).

serene /sɪ'riːn/ adj calm and peaceful. n **serenity** /sɪ'renətɪ/.

serf /sɜːf/ n slave; (in ancient times) a land-worker who was not allowed to leave his land.

serge /sɜːdʒ/ n strong rough woollen cloth.

sergeant /'sɑːdʒənt/ n rank in the army or police force.

serial /'sɪərɪəl/ adj 1 happening in, or as part of, a SERIES. 2 (of a story, etc.) appearing in parts once weekly, monthly, etc. n serial story.

series /'sɪəriːz/ n number of things coming one after another.

serious /'sɪərɪəs/ adj 1 solemn; thoughtful. 2 important, perhaps dangerous. 3 meaning what one says. n seriousness /'sɪərɪəsnəs/.

sermon /'sɜːmən/ n speech given by a priest in a church.

serpent /'sɜːpənt/ n snake.

serrated

serrated /sɪ'reɪtɪd/ adj having a toothed edge (like a saw).

serried /'serɪd/ adj (of people in rows) closely packed together.

serum /'sɪərəm/ n 1 white liquid of the blood. 2 liquid taken from the blood of an animal that has had a disease and put into men's bodies to protect them from that disease.

servant /'sɜːvənt/ n one who works for another for pay, esp. one who works at housework.

serve /sɜːv/ v 1 work for another; do something for. 2 supply (with goods or services). 3 bring food or drink (to). 4 be useful; be good enough. **that serves him right** = that is what he deserves.

service /'sɜːvɪs/ n 1 act of serving; work done for another. 2 branch of public work; people employed by the government. 3 arrangement that supplies public needs. 4 religious ceremony; form of prayer to God. 5 set of dishes. 6 work done by servants, WAITERS, etc. **at your service** = ready to do what you want. adj **serviceable** /'sɜːvɪsəbəl/ 1 useful. 2 strong and lasting.

serviette /ˌsɜːvɪ'et/ n cloth used for mouth or fingers while eating.

servile /'sɜːvaɪl/ adj behaving like a slave. n **servility** /sɜː'vɪlətɪ/.

servitude /'sɜːvɪtjuːd/ n condition of being a slave. **penal servitude** = forced work in a prison.

session /'seʃən/ n meeting, e.g. of a law-court; number of such meetings.

set¹ /set/ v 1 put in a place; put in the proper place or condition. 2 fix. 3 give something to a person. 4 cause to be in a certain condition. 5 (of liquids etc.) become hard or solid. 6 (of the sun) go down in the evening. **to set off** = 1 begin a journey. 2 cause to explode. **to set out** = start on a journey. **to set to** = 1 eagerly begin to do something. 2 fight; quarrel. **to set up** = 1 start (a business, etc.). 2 place in position.

set² /set/ n 1 group or collection of things or people that go together. 2 instrument for receiving

radio, television etc. 3 scene or SCENERY of a play, film etc. n **setback** /'setbæk/ some accident that causes loss, esp. of time.

settee

settee /se'tiː/ n long seat.

setting /'setɪŋ/ n place, scene etc. in which some event, story etc. takes place.

settle /'setl/ v 1 fix in one place. 2 decide. 3 (cause to) come to rest. 4 make one's home (in). 5 pay (a debt etc.). 6 make or become calm or comfortable. 7 sink down. n **settler** /'setlə/ one who makes a home in a new country. n **settlement** /'setlmənt/ 1 way in which a quarrel has been ended. 2 place where people are starting to live. 3 payment.

seven /'sevən/ det, n number following six, often written 7. det, n **seventeen** /ˌsevən'tiːn/ number following sixteen, often written 17. det, n **seventy** /'sevəntɪ/ number often written 70, being seven times ten.

sever /'sevə/ v 1 cut off, break off. 2 come apart. n **severance** /'sevərəns/.

several /'sevərəl/ det, pron more than two but not many.

severe /sɪ'vɪə/ adj 1 plain, without ornament. 2 (of disease, etc.) dangerous. 3 hard and merciless. n **severity** /sɪ'verətɪ/.

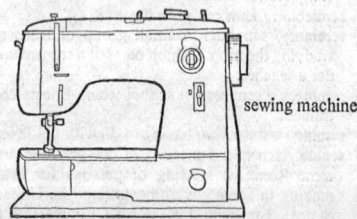

sewing machine

sew /səʊ/ v 1 join with a needle and thread. 2 make (clothes) by using a needle and thread. n **sewing** /'səʊɪŋ/ work done with a needle and thread. n **sewing machine** /'.. ../.

sewage /'suːɪdʒ/ n waste matter of a house or city.

sewer /suːə/ n pipe carrying away waste matter from a house or city.

sex /seks/ n 1 condition of being male or female. 2 males or females as a group. 3 PHYSICAL love. adj **sexual** /'sekʃʊəl/ having to do with sex or the sexes.

sexton /'sekstən/ n one who has charge of a church building and graveyard.

shabby /'ʃæbɪ/ adj 1 badly dressed. 2 (of a garment) much worn and bad. 3 (of behaviour) low, ungenerous.

shack /ʃæk/ n roughly built hut.

shackle /'ʃækəl/ n 1 iron ring on a chain for fastening a prisoner, etc. 2 something that prevents freedom of action. vt 1 put shackles on. 2 prevent from acting freely.

shade /ʃeɪd/ v 1 protect from direct light; cover. 2 make darker (drawing, etc.). 3 change by small amounts. n 1 place or area protected from the full light. 2 lighter or darker kinds of colour. 3 something that shuts out light or makes it less bright. 4 slight difference or amount.

shadow /'ʃædəʊ/ n dark form thrown on the ground by something that cuts off direct light. vt 1 darken. 2 follow secretly.

shady /'ʃeɪdɪ/ adj 1 (place) protected from the heat of the sun. 2 *infml* (person) dishonest.

shaft /ʃɑːft/ n 1 stem of an arrow or spear. 2 any long handle of an instrument. 3 bar turning round and round to carry power. 4 one of the poles of a carriage between which the horse runs. 5 deep hole in the ground leading to a MINE. 6 narrow beam of light.

shaggy /'ʃægɪ/ adj having rough hair.

shake /ʃeɪk/ v 1 (cause to) move quickly from side to side or up and down, TREMBLE. 2 make less firm, e.g. *To shake one's belief.* adj **shaky** /'ʃeɪkɪ/.

shale /ʃeɪl/ n soft rock that breaks easily into thin sheets.

shall /ʃəl; strong ʃæl/ v 1 (form of will used after *I* and *we*.) 2 (used to express the speaker's determination that something is to be the case), e.g. *He shall never marry my daughter.*

shallot /ʃə'lɒt/ n small strong-tasting vegetable.

shallow /'ʃæləʊ/ adj not deep (water or container); not serious.

sham /ʃæm/ v pretend. n something meant to deceive, FALSE.

shamble /'ʃæmbəl/ v to walk in an ungraceful way.

shambles /'ʃæmbəlz/ n state of disorder.

shame /ʃeɪm/ n 1 painful feeling of having done wrong. 2 dishonour. v cause this feeling in another. **it's a shame** = it is unfair (that).

shampoo /ʃæm'puː/ n special soap, etc., for washing the hair. vt wash the hair.

shamrock

shamrock /'ʃæmrɒk/ n plant with leaves in sets of three.

shank /ʃæŋk/ n 1 leg. 2 part of an instrument between the working part and the handle.

shanty /'ʃæntɪ/ n 1 poorly built hut. 2 seaman's song.

shape /ʃeɪp/ n form; appearance. v 1 give a certain form to. 2 take on a certain shape. adj **shapeless** /'ʃeɪpləs/ not having a regular shape. adj **shapely** /'ʃeɪplɪ/ of good shape; well formed.

share /ʃeə/ n 1 part of something that belongs to a person; part taken by someone (in an action, etc.). 2 one of the parts into which the ownership of a business company is divided. v 1 divide up (among), give a share of to others. 2 have or use with others. 3 take part (in).

shark

shark /ʃɑːk/ n 1 large fish that eats other fish and can be dangerous. 2 person who tricks people out of money.

sharp /ʃɑːp/ adj 1 having a keen edge or fine point. 2 sudden, changing direction quickly. 3 (of feeling, taste) keen, acid. 4 (of sounds) high and loud. 5 (in music) above the true note. 6 clever. **two o'clock sharp** = 2 exactly at 2 o'clock.

shatter /'ʃætə/ v 1 break into small pieces. 2 shock; destroy (one's hopes etc.).

shave /ʃeɪv/ v 1 cut the hair from the skin with a RAZOR. 2 cut very thin pieces off something. n act of shaving (the face). **a close shave** = a fortunate escape from harm.

shavings /'ʃeɪvɪŋz/ n (pl) very thin pieces that are cut off when smoothing wood.

shawl /ʃɔːl/ n loose square cloth worn over the shoulders or head by women.

she /ʃɪ; strong ʃiː/ pron (used in speaking of a woman), e.g. *My daughter is a good girl—she always obeys me.*

sheaf /ʃiːf/ n number of objects, e.g. pieces of paper, corn STALKS, etc., gathered and tied together.

shea nut /'ʃeɪ, 'ʃiː/ n nut from an African tree, used for its fat.

shear /ʃɪə/ vt cut (the wool off a sheep) using shears. n (pl) **shears** large instrument with two blades used for cutting branches, the wool of sheep, etc.

sheath /ʃiːθ/ n case or covering, e.g. one to hold a blade. vt **sheathe** /ʃiːð/ put into a sheath.

shed[1] /ʃed/ n hut for keeping things in.

shed[2] /ʃed/ vt 1 cause to fall (e.g. tears, leaves, etc.æ. 2 give out.

sheen /ʃiːn/ n brightness.

sheep /ʃiːp/ n animal useful for its wool, and also for food. adj **sheepish** /'ʃiːpɪʃ/ foolish and afraid in the company of others.

sheer[1] /ʃɪə/ *adj* **1** very steep. **2** (of cloth) very fine. **3** thorough, complete, e.g. *Sheer foolishness*.

sheer[2] /ʃɪə/ *vi* suddenly change direction.

sheet /ʃiːt/ *n* **1** large piece of cloth (of cotton, etc.) for a bed. **2** thin flat piece of paper, metal, glass, etc. **3** rope tied to the corner of a sail.

sheik(h) /ʃeɪk/ *n* Arab chief.

shelf /ʃelf/ *n* **1** board (fixed to the wall, etc.) on which things are put, e.g. books. **2** shelf-like piece of rock.

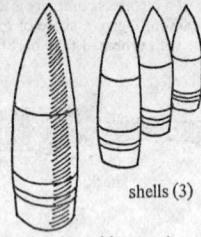

shells (3)

shell /ʃel/ *n* **1** hard outside covering of eggs, fish, nuts etc. **2** frame. **3** metal case full of explosive material fired from a big gun. *vt* **1** take off the shell from (an egg, a nut, ec.). **2** fire shells at.

shelter /ʃeltə/ *v* **1** protect. **2** take cover or protection (from something). *n* **1** thing that protects. **2** protection, cover.

shelve /ʃelv/ *vi* slope slowly down. *vt* las aside a problem, etc.) to be dealt with later.

shepherd /ʃepəd/ *n* one who takes care of sheep. *vt* direct or guide.

sheriff /ʃerɪf/ *n* chief officer of the law in a particular part of the country.

sherry /ʃerɪ/ *n* kind od strong yellow wine.

shield /ʃiːld/ *n* **1** piece of armour carried on the arm or in the hand. **2** any plate that protects, e.g. windshield, etc. *vt* protect.

shift /ʃɪft/ *v* (cause to) move from one place to another. *n* **1** movement. **2** group of workers who work in turn with other groups. *adj* **shiftless** /ʃɪftləs/ lazy and careless. *adj* **shifty** /ʃɪftɪ/ untrustworthy; deceiving.

shilling /ʃɪlɪŋ/ *n* formerly a piece of money worth 5 new pence.

shimmer /ʃɪmə/ *vi* shine with a soft, unsteady light.

shin /ʃɪn/ *n* front of the lower part of the leg. **to shin up** limb.

shine /ʃaɪn/ *v* give out light; (cause to) be bright. *n* brightness.

shingle[1] /ʃɪŋgəl/ *n* small smooth stones on (or from) the seashore.

shingle[2] /ʃɪŋgəl/ *n* flat bits of wood used in making a roof.

shiny /ʃaɪnɪ/ *adj* shining.

ship /ʃɪp/ *n* large sea-going vessel. *vt* send (goods) by ship. *n* **shipment** /ʃɪpmənt/ act of sending goods by ship; amount of goods sent.

shipshape /ʃɪpʃeɪp/ *adj* in good order.

shire /ʃaɪə/ *n* one of the areas into which England is divided (usually only in a name, e.g. Yorkshire /jɔːkʃə/).

shirk /ʃɜːk/ *v* try to escape (from doing a duty); not to do one's work.

shirt /ʃɜːt/ *n* garment worn over the upper part of the body.

shiver[1] /ʃɪvə/ *vi* shake with cold or fear.

shiver[2] /ʃɪvə/ *vi* break into small pieces.

shoal /ʃəʊl/ *n* large group of fish.

shock[1] /ʃɒk/ *n* **1** sudden blow or shaking. **2** (loss of strength or disorder of mind caused by) sudden great pain or sorrow. **3** effect produced by passing electricity through the body. *vt* give a shock to; fill with surprise, fear, DISGUST, etc. *adj* **shocking** /ʃɒkɪŋ/ very bad; shameful.

shock[2] /ʃɒk/ *n* a shock of hair = mass of thick disarranged hair.

shod /ʃɒd/ p.p. of **shoe. well shod** = wearing good shoes.

shoddy /ʃɒdɪ/ *adj* made of bad materials or poorly done.

shoe /ʃuː/ *n* covering for the foot. *vt* put shoes on (esp. a horse). *n* **shoelace** /ʃuːleɪs/, **shoestring** /ʃuːstrɪŋ/ string used to tie up a shoe. *infml* **on a shoestring** = with very little money.

shone /ʃɒn/ p.t. and p.p. of **shine**.

shook /ʃʊk/ p.t. of **shake**.

shoot /ʃuːt/ *v* **1** fire a gun, let fly an arrow; hurt someone in this way. **2** move or send out very quickly or suddenly, e.g. *He shot out his arm.* *n* new young branch on a tree, plant, etc.

shop /ʃɒp/ *n* **1** room or building in which one buys things. **2** place where things are made or repaired by machines. *vi* go to the shops and buy. **to talk shop** = talk about one's own business interests. *n* **shoplifter** /ʃɒplɪftə/ one who steals things from a shop. *n* **shopwalker** /ʃɒpwɔːkə/ person who walks about in a shop to see that all the people are being served properly.

shore[1] /ʃɔː/ *n* land on the edge of the sea or lake.

shore[2] /ʃɔː/ **to shore up** = support with wooden posts or beams.

shorn /ʃɔːn/ p.p. of **shear**.

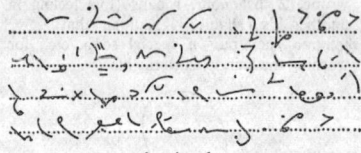

shorthand

short /ʃɔːt/ *adj* **1** not long; not tall. **2** not enough; less than the correct amount. **a short cut** = a way of getting somewhere, doing something, more quickly than usual. *n* **shortage** /ʃɔːtɪdʒ/ lack of, not enough of. *n* **shortcoming** /ʃɔːtkʌmɪŋ/ fault, weakness. *v* **shorten** /ʃɔːtn/ make or become shorter. *n* **shortening** /ʃɔːtnɪŋ/ fat put into cakes, pastry, etc. *n* **shorthand**

/'ʃɔːthænd/ quick way of writing down speech using special signs. *adv* **shortly** /'ʃɔːtlɪ/ **1** soon. **2** in a few words. *n* (*pl*) **shorts** /ʃɔːts/ kind of trousers with short legs. *adj* **short-sighted** /ˌʃɔːt 'saɪtɪd/ not able to see distant objects clearly. *adj* **short-tempered** /ˌʃɔːt 'tempəd/ easily made angry.

shot[1] /ʃɒt/ p.t. and p.p. of **shoot**.

shot[2] /ʃɒt/ *n* **1** (*sing*) metal balls shot from a gun. **2** sound of a gun; firing of a gun. **3** attempt to do something, e.g. *To have a shot at it* = make an attempt. *n* **shotgun** /'ʃɒtgʌn/ gun used for firing shot.

should /ʃʊd/ *v* **1** ought to. **2** form of **would** used after *I* and *we*.

shoulder /'ʃəʊldə/ *n* part of the body between the neck and the top of the arm. *vt* **1** put on the shoulder. **2** push with the shoulder.

shout /ʃaʊt/ *n* loud cry. *v* give a loud cry; say something loudly.

shove /ʃʌv/ *infml v, n* push.

shovel /'ʃʌvəl/ *n* instrument with a broad blade fixed in the end of a handle, used for moving coal, snow, etc. *v* move (something) with a shovel.

show /ʃəʊ/ *v* **1** cause or allow to be seen. **2** make something clear; direct, guide. **to show off** = make a show of one's abilities, importance, etc. **to show up at** = be present at. *n* **1** thing shown; showing, e.g. of horses, flowers. **2** things meant to be noticed by other people. **3** public performance. *adj* **showy** /'ʃəʊɪ/ bright, such as will be noticed—but probably not good.

shower /'ʃaʊə/ *n* **1** slight fall of rain. **2** instrument for washing with, which SPRAYS water like rain. **3** number of things falling or arriving at once, e.g. *A shower of letters.*

shown /ʃəʊn/ p.p. of **show**.

shrank /ʃræŋk/ p.t. of **shrink**.

shrapnel /'ʃræpnəl/ *n* kind of shell that explodes in the air and scatters pieces of metal, etc.

shred /ʃred/ *vt* tear or cut into small pieces. *n* piece so torn or cut off; small piece of anything.

shrew /ʃruː/ *n* **1** bad-tempered, scolding woman. **2** kind of field-mouse.

shrewd /ʃruːd/ *adj* having a keen mind, sharp in business matters. *n* **shrewdness** /'ʃruːdnəs/.

shriek /ʃriːk/ *v, n* (give a) high loud cry.

shrill /ʃrɪl/ *adj* (of sounds) sharp; high and loud, e.g. *A shrill whistle.*

shrimp /ʃrɪmp/ *n* small shell-fish with ten legs, used for food.

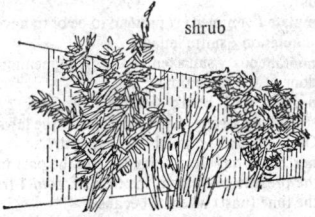
shrub

shrine /ʃraɪn/ *n* **1** case containing holy things; the grave of a holy man. **2** building considered holy.

shrink /ʃrɪŋk/ *v* **1** make or become smaller (esp. of cloth through washing). **2** draw back from a dangerous or unpleasant thing. *n* **shrinkage** /'ʃrɪŋkɪdʒ/ amount by which a thing becomes smaller.

shrivel /'ʃrɪvəl/ *v* (cause to) become curled and bent through the action of heat, dryness etc.

shroud /ʃraʊd/ *n* sheet put round a dead body. *v* cover with a sheet, or as with a sheet, e.g. *Shrouded in mist.*

shrub /ʃrʌb/ *n* low bush; kind of small low tree. *n* **shrubbery** /'ʃrʌbərɪ/ low bushes, esp. where planted round a house.

shrug /ʃrʌg/ *v* draw up (the shoulders) to show that one does not know or does not care.

shrunk /ʃrʌŋk/ p.p. of **shrink**. *adj* **shrunken** /'ʃrʌŋkən/.

shudder /'ʃʌdə/ *vi* shake with fear or cold. *n* this movement.

shuffle /'ʃʌfəl/ *v* **1** walk rubbing the feet along the ground. **2** mix up playing-cards before a new game.

shun /ʃʌn/ *vt* keep away from, try not to meet.

shunt /ʃʌnt/ *v* move (a train) from one track to another.

shut /ʃʌt/ *v* close; be closed. *infml* **to shut up** = stop talking.

shutters

shutter /'ʃʌtə/ *n* wooden covering for a window used to keep out light.

shuttle /'ʃʌtl/ *n* instrument that carries the thread from side to side in making cloth. *v* move backwards and forwards like a shuttle.

shy[1] /ʃaɪ/ *adj* **1** easily frightened; careful. **2** not sure of oneself in the company of others. *vi* (of a horse) turn aside suddenly (in fear).

shy[2] /ʃaɪ/ *infml v, n* throw.

sick /sɪk/ *adj* unwell; ill. **to be sick** = throw up food from the stomach. **sick of** = tired of. *v* **sicken** /'sɪkən/ became sick, make sick, make tired of. *adj* **sickening** /'sɪkənɪŋ/ DISGUSTING. *adj* **sickly** /'sɪklɪ/ **1** not having strong health. **2** causing a sick feeling. **3** (of colour, etc.) weak and unpleasant. *n* **sickness** /'sɪknəs/ bad health; disease.

sickle /'sɪkəl/ *n* instrument with a curved blade used for cutting corn, grass, etc.

side /saɪd/ *n* **1** edge, border, e.g. *The side of a square.* **2** surface, e.g. *One side of a sheet of paper.* **3** one of the surfaces of something that is

sideboard

not the back or front, e.g. *The side of a house.* **4** group. **to take sides** = set against another (e.g. in a game etc). **to side (with)** = support (in a quarrel etc.).

sideboard \/ˈsaɪdbɔːd/ *n* piece of furniture in a dining-room in which plates, knives, etc. are kept.

sideline /ˈsaɪdlaɪn/ *n* work that is not one's main employment.

sidelong /ˈsaɪdlɒŋ/ *adj* to or from the side, e.g. *A sidelong glance.*

sidetrack /ˈsaɪdtræk/ *vt* turn (someone) away from his main purpose to something less important.

siding /ˈsaɪdɪŋ/ *n* short railway track at the side of the main line, where carriages are kept when not in use.

sidle /ˈsaɪdl/ **to sidle up (to)** = move towards (a person) as if afraid.

siege /siːdʒ/ *n* the placing of an army all round a town in order to take it. **to lay siege to (a town)** = keep an army round a town and attack it in order to take it.

siesta /sɪˈestə/ *n* short midday sleep.

sieve /sɪv/ *n* round frame with a wire net at the bottom used for separating solids from liquids, small things from large, etc.

sift /sɪft/ *v* **1** pass through a SIEVE. **2** examine very carefully.

sigh /saɪ/ *vi* take or let out a deep breath as when sad, tired, or no longer anxious.

sight /saɪt/ *n* **1** (power of) seeing. **2** something seen (esp. something worth seeing), e.g. *The sights of the city.* **3** instrument for guiding the eye, e.g. *The sights of a gun.* **at sight, on sight** = as soon as seen. *v* **1** notice. **2** look carefully at as when aiming.

sign /saɪn/ *n* **1** mark or letter or movement that stands for an idea, etc. **2** something that shows the future, e.g. *Clouds are a sign of rain.* *v* **1** express an idea using some kind of movement. **2** write one's name (on something). *n* **signboard** /ˈsaɪnbɔːd/ board having a sign or notice on it. *n* **signpost** /ˈsaɪnpəʊst/ sign showing the places to which roads go.

signal[1] /ˈsɪɡnəl/ *n* sound, movement, sign, etc., that carries an order or idea to another person. *v* **1** make signs. **2** express (something) by using a signal etc.

signal[2] /ˈsɪɡnəl/ *adj* worthy of notice; OUTSTANDING. *vt* **signalize** /ˈsɪɡnəlaɪz/ draw attention to.

signatory /ˈsɪɡnətərɪ/ *n* person who signs an agreement.

signature /ˈsɪɡnətʃə/ *n* name of a person written by himself.

significant /sɪɡˈnɪfɪkənt/ *adj* having special meaning; important. *n* **significance** /sɪɡˈnɪfɪkəns/.

signify /ˈsɪɡnɪfaɪ/ *v* **1** show by a sign. **2** mean. **3** be important. *n* **signification** /ˌsɪɡnɪfɪˈkeɪʃən/ meaning; sense.

silent /ˈsaɪlənt/ *adj* **1** not speaking or making a

noise; quiet. **2** saying little or nothing. *n* **silence** /ˈsaɪləns/.

silhouette /ˌsɪluˈet/ *n* **1** picture in black showing only the shape. **2** dark shape seen against something light.

silica /ˈsɪlɪkə/ *n* hard substance found in sand and many glass-like kinds of stone.

silk /sɪlk/ *n* fine soft thread made by a special insect; cloth made from this. *adj* **silky** /ˈsɪlkɪ/ (as) of silk.

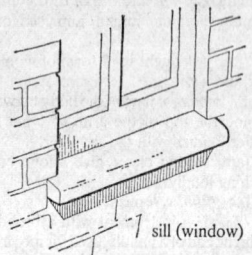

sill (window)

sill /sɪl/ *n* flat shelf at the bottom of a window.

silly /ˈsɪlɪ/ *adj* foolish.

silo /ˈsaɪləʊ/ *n* tower in which grass, etc., is put in order that it may change into a dark, strong-smelling food for cattle. *n* **silage** /ˈsaɪlɪdʒ/ food so made.

silt /sɪlt/ *n* fine earth and sand left on the land by a river. *v* (cause to) become stopped up with silt.

silver /ˈsɪlvə/ *n* white metal used for money; colour of this metal. *n* **silverware** /ˈsɪlvəweə/ silver instruments and vessels, e.g. knives, spoons, plates, etc.

similar /ˈsɪmələ/ *adj* of the same sort, like. *n* **similarity** /ˌsɪməˈlærətɪ/.

simile /ˈsɪmɪlɪ/ *n* saying that a thing is like something else, e.g. "Her teeth are like pearls".

simmer /ˈsɪmə/ *v* boil gently. **to simmer with anger** = only just control one's anger.

simper /ˈsɪmpə/ *n* silly smile. *vi* smile in a silly way.

simple /ˈsɪmpəl/ *adj* **1** easy. **2** plain, unmixed. **3** easily understood, not COMPLICATED. **4** not clever; foolish. *n* **simpleton** /ˈsɪmpəltən/ fool. *n* **simplicity** /sɪmˈplɪsətɪ/ condition of being simple. *vt* **simplify** /ˈsɪmplɪfaɪ/ make simpler or easier. *n* **simplification** /ˌsɪmplɪfɪˈkeɪʃən/. *adv* **simply** /ˈsɪmplɪ/ **1** in a plain way. **2** quite, very. **3** only.

simulate /ˈsɪmjʊleɪt/ *vt* pretend to be or to have. *n* **simulation** /ˌsɪmjʊˈleɪʃən/.

simultaneous /ˌsɪməlˈteɪnɪəs/ *adj* happening or done at the same time.

sin /sɪn/ *vi* **1** break the laws of God. **2** do something wrong. *n* act that breaks the laws of God. *adj* **sinful** /ˈsɪnfəl/ wrong, bad.

since /sɪns/ *adv* from some time in the past until the present. *prep* from the time of. *conj* **1** from the time (past) when. **2** because.

sincere /sɪnˈsɪə/ *adj* 1 (of feeling) not pretended, real. 2 (of a person) meaning what one says. *n* **sincerity** /sɪnˈserəti/.

sinecure /ˈsɪnɪkjʊə/ *n* paid office in which the duties are very light.

sinew /ˈsɪnjuː/ *n* kind of strong string in the body fixing a muscle on to a bone. *n* (*pl*) **sinews** muscles; strength.

sing /sɪŋ/ *v* make musical sounds with the voice.

singe /sɪndʒ/ *v* burn slightly (esp. hair).

single /ˈsɪŋɡəl/ *adj* 1 one only. 2 for one person only. 3 not married. **in single file** = one behind the other. **to single out** = choose from among others. *adj* **single-handed** /ˌsɪŋɡəl ˈhændɪd/ without help from others. *adj* **single-minded** /ˌsɪŋɡəl ˈmaɪndɪd/ giving all one's attention to one purpose only.

singlet /ˈsɪŋɡlət/ *n* light, tight-fitting garment worn under the shirt.

singly /ˈsɪŋɡli/ *adv* separately; one at a time.

singular /ˈsɪŋɡjʊlə/ *adj* 1 (in GRAMMAR) of the form used in speaking of only one person or thing. 2 unusual; strange. *n* **singularity** /ˌsɪŋɡjʊˈlærəti/.

sinister /ˈsɪnɪstə/ *adj* being a sign of future evil looking as if intending to do evil.

sink (n)

sink /sɪŋk/ *v* 1 go slowly down; (cause to) go down to the bottom of water. 2 become worse or weaker. 3 go deep into. *n* square container with a waste pipe at the bottom, used for washing dishes, etc. *n* **sinker** /ˈsɪŋkə/ weight on a string used in fishing.

sinuous /ˈsɪnjʊəs/ *adj* twisting, with many bends.

sip /sɪp/ *v* drink, taking a small quantity each time.

siphon /ˈsaɪfən/ *n* 1 bent tube with a longer downward arm used to draw liquid up over the edge and down out of a vessel. 2 bottle filled with water that can be forced out by gas which is in it.

sir *n* 1 /sɜː/ respectful form of address for a man. 2 /sə/ title of a knight.

sire /ˈsaɪə/ *n* 1 father. 2 old form of **SIR**. *vt* (of a horse or other animal) father.

siren /ˈsaɪərən/ *n* instrument that makes a loud noise to give warning of something.

sirloin /ˈsɜːlɔɪn/ *n* best meat from part of the back of cattle.

sisal /ˈsaɪzəl/ *n* plant that is used for making rope, etc.

sissy /ˈsɪsi/ *infml n* boy who behaves like a girl.

sister /ˈsɪstə/ *n* 1 girl born from the same father and mother as oneself. 2 nurse in charge of a room in a hospital. *n* **sisterhood** /ˈsɪstəhʊd/ number of women joined together for the purpose of doing good works.

sit /sɪt/ *vi* 1 rest the body on the BUTTOCKS. 2 (of a court, etc.) hold meetings. 3 (of clothes) fit, e.g. *This coat sits well*. **to sit up (all night)** = not to go to bed.

site /saɪt/ *n* piece of ground on which a building might be built or is built; place where something happened or will happen.

situated /ˈsɪtʃʊeɪtɪd/ *adj* placed. *n* **situation** /ˌsɪtʃʊˈeɪʃən/ 1 place. 2 condition. 3 employment.

six /sɪks/ *det, n* number following five, often written 6. *det, n* **sixteen** /ˌsɪksˈtiːn/ number following fifteen, often written 16. *det, n* **sixty** /ˈsɪksti/ number often written 60, being six times ten.

sizable /ˈsaɪzəbəl/ *adj* rather large.

size /saɪz/ *n* 1 largeness or smallness of something. 2 measure of the fit of clothes, etc. *vt* arrange in order of size. **to size up** = understand thoroughly.

sizzle /ˈsɪzəl/ *vi* make a sound as of something cooking in fat.

skate[1] /skeɪt/ *n* kind of large flat fish.

skate[2] /skeɪt/ *vi* move over ice on iron blades fixed to the boots. *n* such a blade.

skein /skeɪn/ *n* quantity of wool or thread tied up loosely together.

skeleton /ˈskelətən/ *n* 1 bony frame of the body. 2 general plan (of action, etc.).

sketch /sketʃ/ *n* 1 rough unfinished drawing or painting. 2 short account of anything. 3 short play. *adj* **sketchy** /ˈsketʃi/ done roughly; incomplete.

skewer /ˈskjuːə/ *n* pin of iron or wood put through meat to hold it together.

ski /skiː/ *n* one of a pair of long pieces of wood, etc., fastened to the boots for going over snow.

skid /skɪd/ *vi* (esp. a car) slip on a wet road. *n* piece of wood or iron put under a cart wheel to prevent it turning.

skiff /skɪf/ *n* kind of small boat.

skill /skɪl/ *n* ability to do something well (through practice). *adj* **skilful** /ˈskɪlfəl/ having skill.

skim /skɪm/ *v* 1 remove (SCUM, etc.) from the top of liquid. 2 move lightly over the surface of. 3 read hastily. **skim milk** /ˌ. ˈ./ milk from which the fatty part has been removed.

skimp /skɪmp/ *v* not supply enough of; not use enough material or labour in a piece of work. *adj* **skimpy** /ˈskɪmpi/ not large enough; not using or giving enough.

skin /skɪn/ *n* outer covering, e.g. of the body, of a fruit. *vt* take the skin off. *adj* **skinny** /ˈskɪni/ (of a person, etc.) very thin.

skip /skɪp/ *v* 1 lightly jump a short distance. 2 swing a rope under the feet and jump over it. 3 pass quickly from one thing to another. 4 miss out (esp. parts in reading).

skip (2)

skipper /'skɪpə/ *n* master or captain (of a ship).

skirmish /'skɜːmɪʃ/ *n* (unplanned) fight between small groups (of soldiers, etc.).

skirt /skɜːt/ *n* **1** woman's dress from the waist downward. **2** border, edge. *vt* lie or go along the edge of.

skit /skɪt/ *n* short piece of writing copying something in order to make people laugh at it.

skittish /'skɪtɪʃ/ *adj* playful, easily excited (e.g. a horse).

skittles /'skɪtlz/ *n* (*sing*) game in which one throws a ball to knock down bottle-shaped pieces of wood. *n* **skittle** one of these pieces of wood.

skulk /skʌlk/ *vi* hide so as to escape danger or work.

skull /skʌl/ *n* bony frame of the head.

skunk /skʌŋk/ *n* **1** small American animal that gives off a very nasty smell. **2** *sl* nasty person.

sky /skaɪ/ *n* space above the earth where clouds, stars, etc., are seen.

skylark /'skaɪlɑːk/ *n* small bird that sings as it flies upwards.

skylight /'skaɪlaɪt/ *n* window in a roof.

skyscraper /'skaɪˌskreɪpə/ *n* very high building.

slab /slæb/ *n* large flat block of stone, etc.

slack /slæk/ *adj* **1** not tight. **2** lazy and careless. **3** not busy. *n* (*pl*) **slacks** kind of trousers. *v* **slacken** /'slækən/ make or become slower or looser.

slag /slæg/ *n* waste matter left from melted metal.

slain /sleɪn/ *p.p.* of **slay.**

slake /sleɪk/ *vt* satisfy (thirst).

slam /slæm/ *v* shut (a door, etc.) with noise; throw down with force.

slander /'slɑːndə/ *n* untrue report spoken to damage a person's character. *vt* make such a report about someone.

slang /slæŋ/ *n* words, meanings, etc. commonly used in speech but not always considered suitable. *vt* scold.

slant /slɑːnt/ *v, n* slope.

slap /slæp/ *vt* **1** strike with the flat of the hand. **2** put down with a slapping noise. *n* blow with the open hand.

slapdash /'slæpdæʃ/ *adj* careless.

slash /slæʃ/ *v* **1** make cuts in (something) with a quick movement. **2** hit with a thin stick or WHIP. *n* long cut.

slat /slæt/ *n* thin narrow board.

slate /sleɪt/ *n* **1** blue-grey rock that breaks easily into sheets, used for roofs. **2** piece of slate (for writing on).

slattern /'slætən/ *n* woman who is careless and dirty in her dress, etc.

slaughter /'slɔːtə/ *n* act of killing. *v* kill in large numbers; (of animals) kill for food.

slave /sleɪv/ *n* unpaid servant owned by a master. *vi* work very hard. *n* **slavery** /'sleɪvərɪ/ state of being a slave.

slay /sleɪ/ *vt* kill; murder.

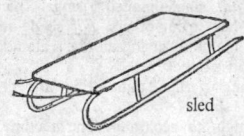

sled

sled /sled/, **sledge** /sledʒ/ *n* carriage that slides over the snow on metal or wooden blades.

sledgehammer /'sledʒˌhæmə/ *n* heavy hammer.

sleek /sliːk/ *adj* **1** (of hair) smooth and shiny. **2** (of a person) too neat.

sleep /sliːp/ *vi* be in a state of complete rest—as in bed at night. *vt* (of a hotel, etc.) have enough beds for. *n* condition of sleeping. *n* **sleeper** /'sliːpə/ **1** railway carriage with beds in it. **2** wooden crosspiece under railway lines.

sleet /sliːt/ *n* snow and rain mixed.

sleeve /sliːv/ *n* that part of a garment which covers the arm. **to laugh up one's sleeve** = be secretly amused.

sleigh /sleɪ/ *n* SLEDGE, esp. one pulled by a horse.

sleight /slaɪt/ **sleight of hand** = cleverness of the hand, esp. in doing magic tricks that deceive the eye.

slender /'slendə/ *adj* **1** long and thin; graceful. **2** slight, not enough.

slept /slept/ *p.t.* & *p.p.* of **sleep.**

slew[1] /sluː/ *p.t.* of **slay.**

slew[2], **slue** /sluː/ *v* turn or twist round, SKID.

slice /slaɪs/ *n* thin flat piece cut off something, e.g. bread *vt* cut into slices.

slick /slɪk/ *adj* (of a person) too smooth or clever.

slid /slɪd/ *p.t.* & *p.p.* of **slide.**

slide /slaɪd/ *v* **1** move smoothly over; move quietly. **2** pass without noticing or being noticed. *n* **1** stretch of ice, etc., on which to slide. **2** picture on glass, etc., to be shown on a SCREEN. **3** something that slides. *n* **slide rule** /'. ˌ./ instrument used for calculating.

slight /slaɪt/ *adj* **1** thin; weak. **2** small in amount; unimportant. *vt* treat rudely, as if of no importance. *adv* **slightly** /'slaɪtlɪ/ a little.

slim /slɪm/ *adj* **1** thin. **2** small, e.g. *A slim chance.*

slime /slaɪm/ *n* nasty soft sticky matter; soft mud.

sling /slɪŋ/ *v* **1** throw with force. **2** support (something) so that it can swing or be lifted. *n* **1** piece of cloth or leather used for throwing a

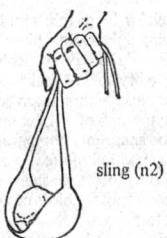

sling (n2)

stone. **2** band passed round a thing (e.g. a broken arm) so as to lift or support it.

slink /slɪŋk/ *vi* move quietly and secretly.

slip /slɪp/ *v* **1** slide by accident, e.g. *He slipped and fell on the ice.* **2** move quickly or quietly, without being noticed. **3** escape from; fall from. **to slip up** = make a mistake. **to slip on** (a dress) = put on quickly. *n* **1** small mistake. **2** garment worn by women under their outer clothes. **3** loose covering. **4** long thin piece of paper.

slipper /ˈslɪpə/ *n* kind of loose comfortable shoe.

slippery /ˈslɪpərɪ/ *adj* very smooth, likely to cause slipping.

slipshod /ˈslɪpʃɒd/ *adj* careless (esp. in dress, etc.).

slit /slɪt/ *n* long cut; narrow hole. *v* make a long narrow cut in.

slither /ˈslɪðə/ *vi* slide; slip.

sliver /ˈslɪvə/ *n* thin narrow piece.

slobber /ˈslɒbə/ *vi* allow liquid to run from the mouth.

slog /slɒg/ *v* **1** hit (a ball) hard. **2** *infml* work hard.

slogan /ˈsləʊgən/ *n* easily remembered saying used (in trading, etc.) to get the attention of the public.

sloop

sloop /sluːp/ *n* kind of small sailing-ship.

slop /slɒp/ *v* (of liquids) (let) flow over the edge of a pot, etc. *n* (*pl*) **slops 1** liquid food for sick persons. **2** waste water from a kitchen, etc.

slope /sləʊp/ *v* (cause to) lean or be at an angle. *n* surface that is neither flat nor upright (e.g. the side of a hill).

sloppy /ˈslɒpɪ/ *adj* **1** wet and dirty. **2** careless. **3** weak and silly.

slot /slɒt/ *n* long narrow hole. *vt* make a slot in; put in a slot. *n* **slot machine** /ˈ. ,/ machine from which something is obtained when a piece of money is put into the slot.

sloth /sləʊθ/ *n* **1** laziness. **2** type of large South American animal which lives in trees.

slouch /slaʊtʃ/ *n* lazy ungraceful way of walking

or standing. *vi* walk or stand in this way.

slough¹ /slaʊ/ *n* very wet muddy land.

slough² /slʌf/ *v* (of a snake) throw off the old dead skin. *n* piece of dead skin that comes off.

slovenly /ˈslʌvənlɪ/ *adj* dirty, untidy and careless.

slow /sləʊ/ *adj* **1** not fast. **2** not clever. **3** uninteresting. **4** (of a clock) behind the right time. *n* **slowness** /ˈsləʊnəs/.

sludge /slʌdʒ/ *n* **1** thick oily mud. **2** thick waste liquid from houses, etc.

slue /sluː/ see **slew²**.

slug¹ /slʌg/ *n* slow-moving creature like a SNAIL, but without a shell.

slug² /slʌg/ *n* small piece of metal used as a shot. *infml* hit hard.

sluggard /ˈslʌgəd/ *n* lazy person. *adj* **sluggish** /ˈslʌgɪʃ/ slow-moving, lazy.

sluice /sluːs/ *n* kind of gate that can be opened or shut to control the flow of water in a river, etc. *vt* pour water over.

slum /slʌm/ *n* poor dirty crowded street or building in a city.

slumber /ˈslʌmbə/ *vi, n* sleep.

slump /slʌmp/ *vi* fall heavily; fall suddenly. *n* sudden drop in business activity, etc.

slung /slʌŋ/ *p.t.* & *p.p.* of **sling**.

slunk /slʌŋk/ *p.t.* & *p.p.* of **slink**.

slur /slɜː/ *v* say in a careless unclear way. *n* something said against someone; a cause of blame.

slush /slʌʃ/ *n* half-melted snow; watery dirt.

slut /slʌt/ *n* dirty careless woman.

sly /slaɪ/ *adj* deceiving cleverly and secretly.

smack¹ /smæk/ *n* slight taste. *vi* **1** taste of. **2** give a faint idea of.

smack² /smæk/ *vt* strike with the open hand. *n* such a blow.

smack³ /smæk/ *n* kind of small sailing-boat used for fishing.

small /smɔːl/ *adj* **1** not large, little. **2** unimportant. **to look (feel) small** = appear (feel) foolish, ashamed. *n* (*pl*) **small-arms** /ˈ. ,/ weapons that can be carried easily.

smallpox /ˈsmɔːlpɒks/ *n* dangerous easily spread disease causing spots on the skin.

smart¹ /smɑːt/ *vi* feel a sharp pain (in the body or mind). *n* such a pain.

smart² /smɑːt/ *adj* **1** quick. **2** skilful, clever. **3** neat in appearance; new-looking. **4** FASHIONABLE. *n* **smartness** /ˈsmɑːtnəs/. *v* **smarten** /ˈsmɑːtn/ make or become neater.

smash /smæʃ/ *v* **1** break to pieces; destroy. **2** (of a business) to be ruined. *n* **1** serious accident. **2** very hard blow; (sound of) smashing.

smattering /ˈsmætərɪŋ/ **a smattering of** = a slight knowledge of (a subject).

smear /smɪə/ *v* mark (by spreading) with something oily, sticky or dirty. *n* such a mark.

smell /smel/ *n* that which is noticed by means of the nose (as unpleasant). *v* **1** notice by means of the nose. **2** give out a (bad) smell. **to smell out** = discover by using the sense of smell.

smelt

smelt[1] /smelt/ vt melt the metal out of rock.

smelt[2] /smelt/ p.t. & p.p. of **smell**.

smile /smaɪl/ vi turn up the corners of the mouth showing pleasure or amusement. n act of smiling.

smirch /smɜːtʃ/ vt make dirty; harm (someone's good name).

smirk /smɜːk/ vi smile in a silly, self-satisfied way. n such a smile.

smite /smaɪt/ v strike; hit.

smith /smɪθ/ n 1 worker in metal. 2 (blacksmith) worker in iron, maker of horseshoes. n **smithy** /'smɪðɪ/ place in which a blacksmith works.

smitten /'smɪtn/ p.p. of **smite**.

smock

smock /smɒk/ n loose outer garment.

smoke /sməʊk/ n cloud of gases given off by something burning. v 1 give off smoke. 2 draw in smoke from (a cigarette, etc.). 3 (of meat, etc.) dry and preserve with smoke.

smolder /'sməʊldə/ see **smoulder**.

smooth /smuːð/ adj 1 not rough. 2 (of movement) easy and without shaking. v make smooth; free from difficulties, etc.

smote /sməʊt/ p.t. of **smite**.

smother /'smʌðə/ vt 1 keep air from (and so cause the death of). 2 cover completely or thickly (with).

smoulder, smolder /'sməʊldə/ vi burn slowly without flame.

smudge /smʌdʒ/ n mark made by rubbing writing while it is still wet; dirty mark. v make a smudge on.

smug /smʌg/ adj very self-satisfied.

smuggle /'smʌgəl/ v 1 take in or out secretly. 2 take goods secretly and unlawfully into a country.

smut /smʌt/ n dirt that falls down out of coal smoke. adj **smutty** /'smʌtɪ/ (of language, etc.) not proper.

snack /snæk/ n light hasty meal.

snag /snæg/ n hidden danger; unexpected difficulty.

snail

snail /sneɪl/ n small slow-moving creature with a shell on its back.

snake /sneɪk/ n long, thin reptile with no legs, often having a poisonous bite.

snap /snæp/ v 1 break suddenly with a sharp noise, like a dry stick. 2 make a sudden bite (at). 3 open or close with a sharp sound. 4 quickly take a photograph of. n 1 act or sound of snapping. 2 (or **snapshot**) photograph. adj **snappy** /'snæpɪ/ quick; full of life.

snapshot /'snæpʃɒt/ n see **snap**.

snare /sneə/ n trap for birds or animals. vt catch in such a trap.

snarl /snɑːl/ n sound of an angry dog. vi make this sound.

snatch /snætʃ/ vt 1 seize suddenly and without asking. 2 get quickly or when one has the chance, e.g. *To snatch a meal*.

sneak /sniːk/ vi move quietly and secretly.

sneer /snɪə/ vi smile or speak in such a way as to show disrespect. n such a smile or expression.

sneeze /sniːz/ n sudden outburst of breath through the nose and mouth which one cannot control. vi give a sneeze.

sniff /snɪf/ v 1 draw air noisily up the nose. 2 smell.

snigger /'snɪgə/ vi laugh quietly, often disrespect-fully or at something not proper.

snip /snɪp/ v cut with SCISSORS. n **snippet** /'snɪpɪt/ 1 very small piece cut off. 2 small piece of writing, news, etc.

snipe[1] /snaɪp/ n small bird with a very long beak which lives in wet or muddy ground.

snipe[2] /snaɪp/ v shoot (someone) from a place where one cannot be seen. n **sniper** /'snaɪpə/ soldier who shoots from a hiding-place.

snivel /'snɪvəl/ vi to cry with liquid running from the nose.

snob /snɒb/ n one who has too great a respect for persons of wealth and rank. n **snobbery** /'snɒbərɪ/. adj **snobbish** /'snɒbɪʃ/.

snoop /snuːp/ vi inquire secretly into other people's business.

snooze /snuːz/ vi, n (take a) short sleep.

snore /snɔː/ vi breathe with a loud unpleasant noise while sleeping.

snort /snɔːt/ vi blow out air through the nose with a loud noise.

snout /snaʊt/ n nose of an animal, e.g. of a pig.

snow /snəʊ/ n water frozen in a soft white form like wool. vi (of snow) come down from the sky. adj **snowy** /'snəʊɪ/ covered with snow; white like snow.

snowdrop /'snəʊdrɒp/ n kind of small white flower.

snub /snʌb/ vt behave rudely and coldly to; refuse to notice

snuff[1] /snʌf/ v 1 draw in through the nose. 2 powder (TOBACCO) drawn up the nose.

snuff[2] /snʌf/ v 1 cut off the black burnt top of a candle. 2 put out (a candle).

snuffle /'snʌfəl/ vi breathe noisily.

snug /snʌg/ adj warm and comfortable.

snuggle /'snʌgəl/ vi move and lie close (to

snowdrop

somebody) for warmth and comfort, e.g. *The child snuggled up to its mother.*

so /səʊ/ *adv* 1 to such a point, e.g. *He was so tired that he fell asleep.* 2 in this (that) way. 3 also. 4 very; very much, e.g. *He is so kind.* 5 about, e.g. *A mile or so* = about a mile. 6 the same, e.g. *I told you so* = that is what I told you. *conj* therefore, e.g. *He was tired, so he went to bed.* *n* **so-and-so** /'. . ./ some person whose name is not given.

soak /səʊk/ *v* 1 become wet through. 2 make very wet.

soap /səʊp/ *n* fatty substance used with water to clean the hands, etc. *adj* **soapy** /'səʊpɪ/ like soap; covered with soap. *n* (*pl*) **soap-suds** /'. ,./ soap mixed with water.

soar /sɔː/ *vi* 1 fly up in the air. 2 rise very quickly, e.g. prices.

sob /sɒb/ *vi* draw in the breath while weeping.

sober /'səʊbə/ *adj* 1 not drunk. 2 calm, self-controlled, serious. 3 (of colours, etc.) not bright. *n* **sobriety** /sə'braɪətɪ/.

soccer /'sɒkə/ *n* Association Football, a form of the game in which the ball may not be touched with the hands, except by the player who guards the goal.

sociable /'səʊʃəbəl/ *adj* interested in meeting others; friendly.

social /'səʊʃəl/ *adj* 1 living in groups. 2 having to do with SOCIETY.

socialist /'səʊʃəlɪst/ *n* one who believes that all means of producing wealth (all land, works, etc.) should be owned by the government. *n* **socialism** /'səʊʃəlɪzm/ this belief.

society /sə'saɪətɪ/ *n* 1 way in which men live together ordering their lives according to law and custom. 2 any group of men so living together. 3 particular group joined together for some special purpose, e.g. *A scientific society.* 4 persons of wealth and high rank. 5 company of others, e.g. *To enjoy the society of one's friends.*

sociology /ˌsəʊsɪ'ɒlədʒɪ/ *n* study of the nature and growth of SOCIETY. *adj* **sociological** /ˌsəʊsɪə'lɒdʒɪkəl/.

sock /sɒk/ *n* short covering for the foot and part of the leg. *vt infml* hit.

socket /'sɒkɪt/ *n* hollow in which something turns; hole into which something fits.

sod /sɒd/ *n* mass of growing grass cut from the earth with its roots.

soda /'səʊdə/ *n* white substance used in making soap, washing etc. *n* **soda, soda water** /'. . ,. ./ water filled with gas, used as a pleasant drink.

sodden /'sɒdn/ *adj* very wet.

sodium /'səʊdɪəm/ *n* white metal found in salt, etc.

sofa /'səʊfə/ *n* long seat with a back and arms.

soft /sɒft/ *adj* 1 not hard. 2 (of colour) not bright. 3 (of sound) not loud. 4 (of lines in a picture) not sharp, not clear. 5 (of speech) gentle. 6 (of persons) kind, weak. 7 (of water) not chalky. *v* **soften** /'sɒfən/ make or become soft. *n* **softness** /'sɒftnəs/.

soggy /'sɒgɪ/ *adj* heavy with water, e.g. wet earth.

soil[1] /sɔɪl/ *n* that part of the earth in which plants grow.

soil[2] /sɔɪl/ *v* make or become dirty.

sojourn /'sɒdʒɜːn/ *vi, n* stay for a time in a place.

solace /'sɒləs/ *vt, n* comfort in trouble.

solar /'səʊlə/ *adj* of the sun.

sold /səʊld/ *p.t. & p.p. of* sell.

solder /'səʊldə/ *n* easily melted metal used for joining other metals. *vt* join with solder.

soldier /'səʊldʒə/ *n* fighting man in an army.

sole[1]

sole[1] /səʊl/ *n* under part of the foot or a shoe, etc.

sole[2] /səʊl/ *n* kind of flat sea-fish used for food.

sole[3] /səʊl/ *adj* one and only; single.

solecism /'sɒlɪsɪzəm/ *n* mistake in the use of language or the rules of good behaviour.

solemn /'sɒləm/ *adj* slow, serious, performed with ceremony. *n* **solemnity** /sə'lemnətɪ/. *vt* **solemnize** /'sɒləmnaɪz/ carry out a ceremony, e.g. *The marriage was solemnized in the church.*

solicit /sə'lɪsɪt/ *v* invite; ask for, beg for.

solicitor /sə'lɪsɪtə/ *n* one who advises on law and prepares law cases for a BARRISTER.

solicitous /sə'lɪsɪtəs/ *adj* 1 eager (to do something). 2 anxious about. *n* **solicitude** /sə'lɪsɪtjuːd/.

solid /'sɒlɪd/ *adj* 1 not liquid. 2 firm, hard, strong. 3 of the substance in every part, e.g. *Solid gold.* 4 that can be depended on. *n* **solidarity** /ˌsɒlɪ'dærətɪ/ being united by common aims, interests, etc. *v* **solidify** /sə'lɪdɪfaɪ/ make or become solid. *n* **solidity** /sə'lɪdətɪ/ quality of being solid.

solid

243

soliloquize

soliloquize /sə'lɪləkwaɪz/ *vi* speak one's thoughts aloud. *n* **soliloquy** /sə'lɪləkwɪ/ such a speech.

solitary /'sɒlətərɪ/ *adj* living or being alone; single. *n* **solitude** /'sɒlətjuːd/.

solo /'səʊləʊ/ *n* piece of music played or sung by one person.

soluble /'sɒljʊbəl/ *adj* that can be made liquid by adding to a liquid, e.g. *Salt is soluble in water.*

solution /sə'luːʃən/ *n* **1** the act of mixing with a liquid; liquid in which something is mixed, e.g. salt water. **2** answer (to a question, etc.).

solve /sɒlv/ *vt* find the answer to (a problem or difficulty).

solvent /'sɒlvənt/ *n* liquid in which certain matter is SOLUBLE. *adj* able to pay one's debts.

sombre /'sɒmbə/ *adj* dark; sad.

some *det, pron* **1** /sʌm/ a certain; not known, e.g. *I read it in some book (or other).* **2.** /səm; *strong* sʌm/ a certain amount or number (of), e.g. *Some water, Some friends.* **3.** /sʌm/ about; quite a large number or amount of, e.g. *He was gone for some time.* *pron* **somebody** /'sʌmbədɪ/, **someone** /'sʌmwʌn/ some person or other. *adv* **somehow** /'sʌmhaʊ/ in one way or another. *pron* **something** /'sʌmθɪŋ/ some thing or other. *adv* **sometime** /'sʌmtaɪm/ at some time (past or future). *adv* **sometimes** /'sʌmtaɪmz/ from time to time. *adv* **somewhat** /'sʌmwɒt/ to a certain point; rather. *adv* **somewhere** /'sʌmweə/ in or to some place unknown.

somersault /'sʌməsɔːlt/ *n, vi* (act of) jumping, and turning the body completely over.

somnambulism /sɒm'næmbjʊlɪzəm/ *n* sleep-walking.

somnolent /'sɒmnələnt/ *adj* sleepy, almost asleep. *n* **somnolence** /'sɒmnələns/.

son /sʌn/ *n* male child.

sonata /sə'nɑːtə/ *n* piece of music divided into three or four parts, and played by one or two instruments.

song /sɒŋ/ *n* music produced by the voice; words and music written for the voice.

songster /'sɒŋstə/ *n* singer; singing bird.

sonic /'sɒnɪk/ *adj* having to do with sound.

sonnet /'sɒnɪt/ *n* poem of 14 lines arranged in a special way.

sonorous /'sɒnərəs/ *adj* producing a deep and beautiful sound. *n* **sonority** /sə'nɒrətɪ/.

soon /suːn/ *adv* **1** in a short time. **2** early. **as soon as** = at the moment when.

soot /sʊt/ *n* black powder which is left by smoke. *adj* **sooty** /'sʊtɪ/.

soothe /suːð/ *vt* **1** calm (an excited person). **2** make less painful.

sop /sɒp/ *n* **1** bread that has been put in water, milk or other liquid. **2** something given to a person to please him or to keep him quiet for a time. *adj* **sopping** /'sɒpɪŋ/ wet through.

sophist /'sɒfɪst/ *n* one whose reasoning is clever but not true. *n* **sophism** /'sɒfɪzəm/.

sophisticated /sə'fɪstɪkeɪtɪd/ *adj* not natural; too wise in the ways of the world. *n* **sophistication** /sə,fɪstɪ'keɪʃən/.

soporific /,sɒpə'rɪfɪk/ *adj* causing sleep.

soprano /sə'prɑːnəʊ/ *n, adj* (person having the) highest kind of singing voice in boys or women.

sorcerer /'sɔːsərə/ *n* one who can do things by magic. *n* **sorcery** /'sɔːsərɪ/ art of magic.

sordid /'sɔːdɪd/ *adj* **1** poor; dirty. **2** ungenerous.

sore /sɔː/ *adj* **1** painful. **2** causing anger, etc. *n* painful place on the body.

sorrow /'sɒrəʊ/ *n* (a cause of) grief or sadness. *adj* **sorrowful** /'sɒrəʊfəl/.

sorry /'sɒrɪ/ *adj* **1** sad, because of loss or wrongdoing, etc. **2** poor, pitiful. **to feel sorry for** = pity.

sort /sɔːt/ *n* kind, class. *v* arrange each according to its kind.

sortie /'sɔːtɪ/ *n* attack made by soldiers in a defended town, etc., on those outside it.

SOS /,es əʊ 'es/ *n* message sent (by a ship, etc.) calling for help.

sot /sɒt/ *n* one who always drinks too much.

sought /sɔːt/ p.t. & p.p. of **seek**.

soul /səʊl/ *n* **1** the spiritual part of a human being. **2** a person's real nature or character. **3** human being, e.g. *I did not meet a soul* = I did not meet anyone. *adj* **soulful** /'səʊlfəl/ seeming to be full of fine feelings. *adj* **soulless** /'səʊl-ləs/ not having any fine feelings.

sound¹ /saʊnd/ *adj* **1** complete, unbroken. **2** healthy; strong. **3** (of sleep) deep.

sound² /saʊnd/ *n* that which can be heard. *v* **1** (cause to) make a noise. **2** examine by listening (e.g. someone's chest).

sound³ /saʊnd/ *v* measure the depth of water. **to sound out** = get someone's opinion (on something).

sound⁴ /saʊnd/ *n* long narrow piece of water, e.g. between an island and the mainland.

soup /suːp/ *n* liquid food made by boiling meat, vegetables, etc., in water.

sour /'saʊə/ *adj* **1** acid-tasting. **2** having gone bad. **3** bad-tempered.

source /sɔːs/ *n* **1** spring from which a river comes. **2** first cause of anything; place from which something (e.g. news, etc.) is obtained.

souse /saʊs/ *vt* **1** throw into water. **2** preserve (food) in salt water.

south /saʊθ/ *n* direction to the right of someone facing east. *adj* **southern** /'sʌðən/ in or of the south. *adj* **southerly** /'sʌðəlɪ/ to the south; (of winds) from the south. *adj, adv* **southward(s)** /'saʊθwəd(z)/ towards the south.

souvenir /,suːvə'nɪə/ *n* thing kept in memory of a place, person or event.

sovereign /'sɒvrɪn/ *n* chief ruler; king or queen. *adj* **1** (of power) highest. **2** (of a country, etc.) not ruled by another.

soviet /'səʊvɪət/ *n* one of the elected groups (of workers, etc.) that form the government of Russia. *adj* of Russia.

sow¹ /saʊ/ *n* female pig.

sow² /səʊ/ *v* scatter or plant (seeds).

sow²

spa /spɑ:/ *n* **1** spring whose water is used as medicine. **2** place where there is such a spring.

space /speɪs/ *n* **1** any emptiness in which things are put, or might be put, or through which a thing might move, e.g. *There are many stars in space.* **2** distance, amount of space, between objects, etc. **3** length of time, e.g. *In the space of an hour.* *vt* set out with regular spaces between. *adj* **spacious** /'speɪʃəs/ with plenty of room; large. *n* **spacecraft** /'speɪskrɑ:ft/, **spaceship** /'speɪsʃɪp/ kind of vehicle for travelling through space.

spade (2)

spade /speɪd/ *n* **1** instrument used for digging. **2** one sort of playing-card.

spaghetti /spə'geti/ *n* (*sing*) long thin sticks made from flour, cooked and eaten.

span /spæn/ *vt* stretch across from side to side. *n* **1** distance between the ends of the little finger and thumb when stretched out. **2** distance between supports (esp. of a bridge). **3** stretch of time.

spangle /'spæŋgəl/ *n* any small bright object used as an ornament. *vt* ornament with spangles.

spaniel

spaniel /'spænjəl/ *n* kind of dog with long hair and long ears.

spank /spæŋk/ *vt* strike with the open hand, to punish (esp. a child).

spanner /'spænə/ *n* instrument used for tightening or loosening NUTS on screws, etc.

spar¹ /spɑ:/ *n* pole used on a ship for supporting sails.

spar² /spɑ:/ *vi* practise the blows used in BOXING.

spare¹ /speə/ *adj* **1** not in plenty. **2** (of persons) thin. **3** more than is necessary, kept for future use, e.g. *A spare wheel.* *n* part of a machine kept to be used when repairing.

spare² /speə/ *vt* **1** keep from using something that one has. **2** give away, do without, e.g. *He cannot be spared* = he is needed. **3** show pity, e.g. *Spare my life* = do not kill me. **4** protect or save from, e.g. *I will spare you the painful story.* *adj* **sparing** /'speərɪŋ/ careful; not giving freely.

spark /spɑ:k/ *n* very small piece of burning matter; flash made by electricity jumping from one wire to another. *vi* give off sparks.

sparkle /'spɑ:kəl/ *vi* give out quick flashes of light.

sparrow

sparrow /'spærəʊ/ *n* small common grey-brown bird.

sparse /spɑ:s/ *adj* thinly scattered.

spasm /'spæzəm/ *n* sudden tightening of the muscles of the face or body; any sudden great feeling, e.g. *A spasm of fear.* *adj* **spasmodic** /spæz'mɒdɪk/ happening suddenly at any time.

spastic /'spæstɪk/ *n* person who cannot control his limbs because of damage to the brain before birth.

spat /spæt/ *p.t.* & *p.p.* of **spit**.

spate /speɪt/ *n* sudden rush or flow (of water, etc.).

spatter /'spætə/ *v* scatter liquid over.

spatula /'spætʃʊlə/ *n* **1** flat instrument used to mix paint or powders, etc. **2** instrument used by doctors to hold down the tongue when looking down the throat.

spawn /spɔ:n/ *v* (of fish) produce (eggs). *n* (*sing*) the eggs produced.

speak /spi:k/ *v* **1** say in words; talk. **2** be able to use (a language). **3** address a meeting, etc. **to speak up** = talk louder. **nothing to speak of** = very little. **so to speak** = as one might say. *n* **speaker** /'spi:kə/ person who speaks (esp. in public).

spear /spɪə/ *n* weapon with a metal point fixed to a long stick. *vt* push a spear through.

special /'speʃəl/ *adj* not general; not for general use; not the usual. *n* **specialist** /'speʃəlɪst/ one who has made particular study of one subject (esp. in medicine). *n* **specialty** /'speʃəltɪ/, **speciality** /ˌspeʃɪ'ælətɪ/ thing that one does particularly well; one kind of goods, work etc. for which a person, place, etc. is well known. *v* **specialize** /'speʃəlaɪz/ become a specialist (in); give special study to a particular subject, etc.

specie /'spiːʃɪ/ *n* money made of metal.

species /'spiːʃiːz/ *n* kind, sort.

specific /spɪ'sɪfɪk/ *adj* having to do with one particular thing; exact.

specify /'spesɪfaɪ/ *vt* name a particular thing; give the particulars of. *n* **specification** /ˌspesɪfɪ'keɪʃən/ careful description of something to be done (and the materials to be used).

specimen /'spesɪmən/ *n* thing, or part of a thing, used as an example.

specious /'spiːʃəs/ *adj* seeming to be good or right but not really.

speck /spek/ *n* very small spot or mark. *adj* **speckled** /'spekəld/ covered with small spots of colour.

spectacles (glasses)

spectacle /'spektəkəl/ *n* show, grand sight; something that makes people look. *n* (*pl*) **spectacles** glasses worn in front of the eyes to correct the eyesight.

spectacular /spek'tækjʊlə/ *adj* very grand; providing a fine show.

spectator /spek'teɪtə/ *n* one who looks on at a public show.

spectre /'spektə/ *n* spirit of a dead person appearing to a living person. *adj* **spectral** /'spektrəl/.

spectrum /'spektrəm/ *n* bands of colour into which light can be divided when passed through a PRISM.

speculate /'spekjʊleɪt/ *vi* 1 consider (without full knowledge); guess. 2 buy shares in business companies in the hope of gaining money by selling them again later. *n* **speculation** /ˌspekjʊ'leɪʃən/.

sped /sped/ *p.t.* & *p.p.* of **speed.**

speech /spiːtʃ/ *n* 1 ability to speak; way of speaking. 2 talk given in public. *adj* **speechless** /'spiːtʃləs/ unable to speak (because of anger, etc.).

speed /spiːd/ *n* 1 swiftness. 2 movement measured against time. *v* (cause to) go quickly. **to speed up** = (cause to) go more quickly.

speedometer /spiː'dɒmɪtə ; 'spiːdɒmɪtə / *n* instrument that shows how fast a car, etc., is going.

spell[1] /spel/ *n* (magic) charm; words supposed to have magic power.

spell[2] /spel/ *n* short time, e.g. *A spell of bad weather.*

spell[3] /spel/ *v* 1 say or write a word using the correct letters. 2 mean, e.g. *This news spells danger.*

spelt /spelt/ *p.t.* & *p.p.* of **spell.**

spend /spend/ *v* 1 pay out (money). 2 use up (esp. time).

spent /spent/ *p.t.* & *p.p.* of **spend.** *adj* tired out, with no force left.

spendthrift /'spendˌθrɪft/ *n* one who wastes money.

sperm /spɜːm/ *n* liquid from male animals that causes females to have young.

spew /spjuː/ *v* throw out of the mouth or up from the stomach.

sphere /sfɪə/ *n* 1 body shaped like a ball. 2 range of interests, activities, etc., e.g. *One's proper sphere.* *adj* **spherical** /'sferɪkəl/ shaped like a sphere.

sphinx /sfɪŋks/ *n* 1 imaginary creature with the head of a woman, body of a lion, and wings. **the Sphinx** great stone image of this in Egypt. 2 strange person about whom little is known.

spice /spaɪs/ *n* 1 substance used to give a pleasant taste to food. 2 excitement, interest. *vt* add spice to. *adj* **spicy** /'spaɪsɪ/.

spick /spɪk/ **spick and span** = clean and neat.

spider /'spaɪdə / *n* creature with eight legs which makes a fine net to catch insects for food.

spied /spaɪd/ *p.t.* and *p.p.* of **spy.**

spike /spaɪk/ *n* (something with a) sharp point.

spill[1] /spɪl/ *v* 1 (of liquids, etc.) (cause to) flow over. 2 (cause to) fall off, out of something. *n* fall from a horse, bicycle, etc.

spill[2] /spɪl/ *n* thin piece of wood or paper used for lighting a candle, etc.

spilt /spɪlt/ *p.t.* & *p.p.* of **spill**[1].

spin /spɪn/ *v* 1 twist wool or cotton so as to make it into a thread. 2 make from threads. 3 (cause to) go round quickly, like a wheel. *n* 1 spinning movement. 2 short ride in a car, etc. **to spin out** = make (something) last a long time.

spinach /'spɪnɪdʒ/ *n* kind of green vegetable.

spindle /'spɪndl/ *n* 1 bar on to which thread is rolled or twisted. 2 thin bar or pin upon which something turns.

spine /spaɪn/ *n* 1 backbone. 2 any needle-like part of a plant or animal which pricks. *adj* **spinal** /'spaɪnəl/ of the spine. *adj* **spineless** /'spaɪnləs/ 1 having no spine. 2 weak-willed.

spinster /'spɪnstə / *n* unmarried woman.

spiral

spiral /'spaɪərəl/ *adj* going round and round and up and up, like a screw. *n* anything having this form. *vi* move in a spiral.

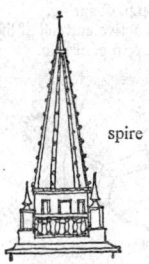

spire

spire /spaɪə/ n tall pointed roof on a tower (esp. a church).

spirit[1] /'spɪrɪt/ n (often pl) strong drink, e.g. WHISKY, etc.

spirit[2] /'spɪrɪt/ n 1 soul. 2 being without a body. 3 fairy. 4 quality of courage, etc. 5 real meaning or intention, e.g. *The spirit of the law.* 6 state of mind, e.g. *In high spirits* = full of life and happiness. *adj* **spirited** /'spɪrɪtɪd/ full of force and feeling; courageous. *adj* **spiritual** /'spɪrɪtʃʊəl/ having to do with the soul, religion, etc. n **spiritualist** /'spɪrɪtʃʊəlɪst/ one who believes that the souls of the dead can be made to appear to and send messages to the living.

spit[1] /spɪt/ n 1 pin or bar on which meat is cooked in front of or over a fire. 2 narrow piece of land standing out into the sea.

spit[2] /spɪt/ v 1 throw out (liquid) from the mouth. 2 make a noise as of spitting.

spite /spaɪt/ n ill will; hatred and anger. *vt* hurt or make angry because of spite. **in spite of** = not caring about, not to be prevented by.

spittle /'spɪtl/ n liquid of the mouth.

splash /splæʃ/ n 1 noise made by something falling into water. 2 water thrown out by an object falling in. *v* cause a splash; fall with a splash.

splay /spleɪ/ v slope outwards; make or become wider. *adj* (of feet) turned outwards.

spleen /spliːn/ n 1 part of the body found just behind the stomach which causes changes in the blood. 2 bad temper.

splendid /'splendɪd/ *adj* wonderful, fine; to be admired; bright. n **splendour** /'splendə/.

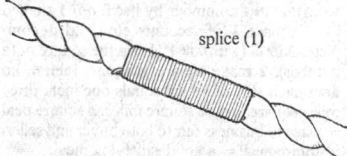

splice (1)

splice /splaɪs/ *vt* 1 join two ropes by working the threads of one into the threads of the other. 2 join wood by putting a tongue of one piece into the other.

splint /splɪnt/ n thin piece of wood, etc., used to hold a broken bone in place.

splinter /'splɪntə/ n thin sharp piece of wood, glass, etc., broken off (or standing out from) a larger piece.

split /splɪt/ v 1 divide into parts; break (a piece of wood) from end to end, etc. 2 tear, burst open suddenly. **to split hairs** = make much of very small and unimportant differences (in reasoning, etc.).

splutter /'splʌtə/ v speak quickly and unclearly from excitement, etc. (often with liquid thrown from the mouth).

spoil /spɔɪl/ v 1 damage and make useless. 2 allow (a child) to have his own way too much. 3 (of food) become unfit for use. n **spoils** gains; stolen goods.

spoke[1] /spəʊk/, **spoken** /'spəʊkən/ p.t. & p.p. of **speak**.

spoke[2] /spəʊk/ n one of the bars joining the outer part of a wheel to the centre.

spokesman /'spəʊksmən/ n one who speaks for others.

sponge /spʌndʒ/ n 1 kind of soft, yellow, simple sea animal that takes in water and lets it out when pressed. 2 this or any substance like it used for cleaning, etc. *vt* clean with a sponge. *infml* **to sponge on a person** = live at his cost. *adj* **spongy** /'spʌndʒɪ/ soft like a sponge.

sponsor /'spɒnsə/ n 1 person who promises to take charge of another person. 2 person who puts forward and supports an idea, etc. 3 business man who supports a television production, etc., to advertise his goods.

spontaneous /spɒn'teɪnɪəs/ *adj* happening without any outside cause. *adv* **spontaneously**. **to act spontaneously** = act without being asked or ordered to do so. n **spontaneity** /spɒntə'niːətɪ/.

spool /spuːl/ n small roller on which thread, wire, photographic film, etc., is wound.

spoon /spuːn/ n instrument with a small flat bowl on the end of a handle used in eating liquids, etc.

spoor /spʊə, spɔː/ n track of a wild animal.

sporadic /spə'rædɪk/ *adj* happening in scattered places or from time to time.

spore /spɔː/ n kind of seed.

sport /spɔːt/ n 1 amusement. 2 game or outdoor exercise for amusement. 3 *infml* person who plays honestly; one who is not angry when he loses. *v* 1 play about. 2 wear with pride. n **sportsman** /'spɔːtsmən/ one who loves sport. *adj* **sporting** /'spɔːtɪŋ/ 1 having to do with sport. 2 willing to take a risk of losing.

spot /spɒt/ n 1 particular place. 2 small mark. 3 small red mark on the skin. *vt* 1 make a mark on. 2 see or recognize. *adj* **spotted** /'spɒtɪd/, **spotty** /'spɒtɪ/ covered with spots. *adj* **spotless** /'spɒtləs/ without spots; (esp.) very clean. n **spotlight** /'spɒtlaɪt/ (lamp giving a) strong light directed at a particular person or place (esp. in a theatre).

spouse /spaʊz/ n husband or wife.

spout /spaʊt/ v 1 (of liquid) come or send out with

spouts (n)

force. **2** *infml* speak in a self-important manner. *n* pipe, etc., from which liquid is poured.

sprain /sprem/ *vt* pull or turn (a limb) with such force as to cause damage. *n* damage so caused.

sprang /spræŋ/ *p.t.* of **spring**.

sprat /spræt/ *n* kind of small sea-fish.

sprawl /sprɔːl/ *vi* **1** spread out the limbs ungracefully. **2** (of writing, etc.) spread out in disorder.

spray /spreɪ/ *n* **1** fine drops of water flying through the air; liquid forced out of a pipe into a fine mist. **2** small branch of a tree with its leaves. *vt* direct a stream of fine drops of liquid upon.

spread /spred/ *v* **1** cover the surface of (with), e.g. *Spread butter on bread*. **2** stretch out (in space or time). **3** (cause to) cover a large area; (cause to) pass to more people, e.g. *Flies spread disease*. *n* **1** breadth; distance something stretches. **2** growth, spreading to a larger area, etc. **3** something that is spread.

spree /spriː/ to have a spree = have a merry time. **to go out on a spree** = go out for drinking and amusement.

sprig /sprɪg/ *n* part of a branch of a tree or of a plant bearing a few leaves or flowers.

sprightly /ˈspraɪtlɪ/ *adj* gay and amusing.

spring[1] /sprɪŋ/ *v* **1** jump or move suddenly. **2** produce or cause suddenly. **to spring up** = appear or grow suddenly. **to spring a leak** = (of a ship) begin to let in water through the side or bottom. **spring tide** = higher rise and fall of the sea in the second and fourth quarters of the moon (see NEAP).

spring[2] /sprɪŋ/ *n* **1** (place where there is) water coming out of the earth. **2** cause or starting point of something. **to spring from** = arise from, be caused by.

spring[3] /sprɪŋ/ *n* piece of metal which, when bent, pulled, uncurled, etc., returns to its former shape or position. *adj* **springy** /ˈsprɪŋɪ/.

spring[4] /sprɪŋ/ *n* the season after winter; the season of the year when plants begin to grow.

sprinkle /ˈsprɪŋkəl/ *v* scatter (drops of liquid, sand, etc.) over something.

sprint /sprɪnt/ *vi* run as fast as possible.

sprite /spraɪt/ *n* kind of fairy.

sprout /spraʊt/ *v* (cause to) begin to grow. *n* **1** shoot, very young plant. **2** small group of young leaves on a plant (esp. a kind of CABBAGE).

spruce[1] /spruːs/ *adj* neat, well and carefully dressed. **to spruce oneself up** = set one's hair, clothes, etc., in order.

spruce[2] /spruːs/ *n* kind of tree; its wood.

sprung /sprʌŋ/ *p.p.* of **spring**.

spry /spraɪ/ *adj* active and full of life.

spun /spʌn/ *p.t.* & *p.p.* of **spin**.

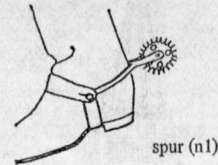

spur (n1)

spur /spɜː/ *n* **1** sharp instrument worn on the back of the foot, used to make a horse go faster. **2** sharp point on the back of a bird's leg. **3** hill standing out from a range of hills. **4** something that urges a person on to try harder, etc. *vt* **1** drive on faster. **2** urge a person (on) to do something.

spurious /ˈspjʊərɪəs/ *adj* not real, but made to look like the real thing.

spurn /spɜːn/ *vt* refuse to accept; kick away; treat as worthless or bad.

spurt /spɜːt/ *v* **1** (of liquid) (cause to) rush out suddenly and with force. **2** (in a race, etc.) try very hard for a short time. *n* **1** sudden stream of liquid, e.g. from a pipe. **2** short sudden try or activity.

spy /spaɪ/ *n* one who goes secretly to find out about the enemy, etc. *v* see (at a distance). **to spy on** = watch secretly.

squabble /ˈskwɒbəl/ *vi* quarrel noisily about an unimportant matter.

squad /skwɒd/ *n* small group, e.g. of soldiers, working together.

squadron /ˈskwɒdrən/ *n* **1** group of 120–200 horse-soldiers. **2** number of warships or aeroplanes acting together.

squalid /ˈskwɒlɪd/ *adj* dirty and unpleasant because uncared for. *n* **squalor** /ˈskwɒlə/.

squall /skwɔːl/ *vi* (of a baby) cry loudly. *n* **1** loud cry. **2** sudden storm.

squander /ˈskwɒndə/ *vt* waste (time, money, etc.); spend carelessly.

square /skweə/ *n* **1** figure with four equal sides and four equal angles. **2** open space in a town with buildings round it. **3** result obtained by MULTIPLYING a number by itself. *adj* **1** shaped like a square. **2** (of accounts, etc.) settled; complete. **3** level (with). *vt* **1** obtain the square of (a number). **2** make square. **a square inch** = an area each side of which equals one inch. **three miles square** = nine square miles. **a square deal** = piece of business fair to both buyer and seller. **a square meal** = a good satisfying meal.

squash /skwɒʃ/ *v* **1** flatten by pressing; press (together) into a small space. **2** stop; silence. *n* **1** group of people squashed together. **2** drink made from squashed fruit, e.g. *Orange squash*.

squat /skwɒt/ *vi* sit down on one's HEELS. *adj* (of a person) short and thick,

squatter /'skwɒtə/ *n* person who settles on public land, in an empty building, etc., without having the right to do so.

squaw /skwɔː/ *n* American-Indian woman or wife.

squawk /skwɔːk/ *vi, n* (give a) short cry of pain or fear, esp. of a hen, etc.

squeak /skwiːk/ *vi, n* (make a) short high cry (e.g. of a mouse) or noise (e.g. of an unoiled door).

squeal /skwiːl/ *vi, n* (give a) long high cry (esp. in pain or terror).

squeamish /'skwiːmɪʃ/ *adj* feeling sick, e.g. on a ship; easily made to feel sick.

squeeze /skwiːz/ *v* press into a smaller space or different shape, esp. in order to get out the liquid; get (money) with difficulty or by force. *n* act of squeezing; condition of being squeezed; close fit.

squelch /skweltʃ/ *v, n* (make a) noise as when walking in sticky mud.

squint /skwɪnt/ *vi* 1 look cross-eyed (the two eyes not pointing in the same direction). 2 look from the side or with half-closed eyes.

squire /'skwaɪə/ *n* 1 country gentleman. 2 (in former times) servant of a knight.

squirm /skwɜːm/ *vi* twist the body like a snake (when feeling shame, etc.).

squirrel /'skwɪrəl/ *n* kind of small animal with a large bushy tail.

squirt /skwɜːt/ *v* (of liquids) force out, be forced out in a thin stream. *n* 1 instrument used for this. 2 something squirted.

stab /stæb/ *v* wound with a pointed weapon. *n* stabbing blow.

stable[1] /'steɪbəl/ *adj* firm, steady; not easily changed. *vt* **stabilize** /'steɪbəlaɪz/ make steady. *n* **stability** /stə'bɪlətɪ/ steadiness.

stable[2] /'steɪbəl/ *n* building in which horses are kept.

staccato /stə'kɑːtəʊ/ *adj* (of notes in music) short, sharp and not joined to other notes; sounding like this.

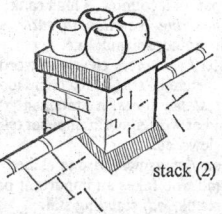

stack (2)

stack /stæk/ *n* 1 neat heap of wood, bricks, etc. 2 (also **chimney stack** /'.. ./) tall chimney, or several chimneys together. *vi* form into a stack.

stadium /'steɪdɪəm/ *n* open space for games with seats all round it.

staff[1] /stɑːf/ *n* stick used in walking, or as a sign of office.

staff[2] /stɑːf/ *n* 1 group of persons working under a head or chief, e.g. *The staff of a school* = all

the teachers. 2 group of army officers who help to draw up plans, etc. *vt* supply with helpers or workers.

stag /stæg/ *n* male deer.

stage /steɪdʒ/ *n* 1 raised part of a hall or theatre on which the performers stand. **to go on the stage** = become an actor. 2 journey, distance between two stopping-places along a road, etc. 3 certain point in growth or change, e.g. *At an early stage in our history*. *vt* put (a play) on the stage; arrange (an event).

stagger /'stægə/ *v* 1 (cause to) walk unsteadily. 2 shock; surprise greatly. 3 arrange (office hours, etc.) so that they start and finish at different times.

stagnant /'stægnənt/ *adj* 1 (of water) not flowing, therefore dirty. 2 (of trade, etc.) not busy; unchanging. *vi* **stagnate** /stæg'neɪt/ be or become stagnant; lose interest. *n* **stagnation** /stæg'neɪʃən/.

staid /steɪd/ *adj* (of a person) steady and serious.

stain /steɪn/ *v* 1 change the colour of; make a coloured or dirty mark on. 2 become a different colour or dirty. *n* dirty mark. *adj* **stainless** /'steɪnləs/ 1 without a stain; pure. 2 (esp. of certain metals) that does not stain or become RUS-TY, e.g. *Stainless steel*.

stair /steə/ *n* (often *pl*) (any one of a) number of steps one above the other, for going up and down in a building. *n* **staircase** /'steəkeɪs/, **stairway** /'steəweɪ/ set of stairs inside or outside a building.

stake /steɪk/ *n* 1 pointed post (to be) driven into the ground. 2 money risked on the result of a future event. *vt* 1 mark (out) with stakes. 2 support with a stake. 3 risk, place (money, etc. on something). **at stake** = risked, in danger of being lost.

stale /steɪl/ *adj* 1 (of food) not fresh. 2 (of news, etc.) uninteresting because heard before.

stalemate /'steɪlmeɪt/ *n* state in which neither person or side can win or nothing more can be done.

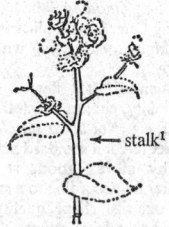

← stalk[1]

stalk[1] /stɔːk/ *n* stem of a plant on which the leaves and flowers grow; stick of a leaf or fruit that joins it on to the plant.

stalk[2] /stɔːk/ *v* 1 hunt an animal by moving slowly and carefully towards it. 2 walk proudly or stiffly.

stall /stɔːl/ *n* **1** part of a cow-house or stable in which one cow, horse, etc., is kept. **2** small lightly built shop, e.g. *The bookstall in a railway station.* **3** seat in a theatre or church. *v* **1** (of an engine) (cause to) stop running through lack of power to do its work. **2** delay so as to gain time.

stallion /'stæljən/ *n* male horse.

stalwart /'stɔːlwət/ *adj* firm; strong and brave.

stamen /'steɪmən/ *n* male part of a flower, bearing POLLEN.

stamina /'stæmɪnə/ *n* strength that enables a person or animal to work hard for a long time.

stammer /'stæmə/ *v* speak with difficulty, repeating the same sounds, e.g. "I m-m-must g-go".

stamp /stæmp/ *v* **1** print or press a mark (upon). **2** bring the foot down heavily. *n* **1** instrument used for printing marks on. **2** small piece of paper stuck to a letter to pay for sending it. **to stamp out** = put out, put an end to (a fire, disease, etc.).

stampede /stæm'piːd/ *n* sudden rush of frightened animals or people.

stanch /stɑːntʃ/ see **staunch**.

stand /stænd/ *v* **1** be, become, remain upright (on); place (something) upright. **2** be in a certain place or condition, e.g. *As things now stand.* **3** remain without change, e.g. *My decision stands.* **4** bear, put up with. **to stand by** = **1** stand to one side and do nothing. **2** be ready (for action). **3** be faithful to (e.g. a friend). **to stand for** = **1** mean, be a sign of, e.g. *£ stands for 'pound'.* **2** try to be elected to (an office, etc.). **to stand out** = **1** be easily seen among others. **2** continue firm (against or for something). **to stand up for** = support, fight for. **to stand up to** = **1** face boldly. **2** not be damaged by. *n* **1** piece of furniture or support on which things may be placed, e.g. *A hatstand.* **2** rows of seats rising behind each other on which people sit to watch a game. *n* **stand-in** /'. ./ person who takes the place of someone (often an actor). *n* **standby** /'stændbaɪ/ replacement that is ready if needed. *n* **standing** /'stændɪŋ/ **1** length of time, e.g. *He is a doctor of long standing* = he has been a doctor for a long time. **2** rank, place in society, e.g. *A man of high standing.* *adj* without change, PERMANENT.

standard /'stændəd/ *n* **1** flag. **2** fixed weight, measure, quality, etc., to which things must be made equal, e.g. *Not up to standard* = not as good as is required. **a standard author** = writer accepted by all as good. *vt* **standardize** /'stændədaɪz/ fix according to a standard so as to make of one size, shape, quality, etc. *n* **standardization** /ˌstændədaɪ'zeɪʃən/.

standpoint /'stændpɔɪnt/ *n* point of view, way of considering something.

standstill /'stændˌstɪl/ *n* stop; state of rest.

stank /stæŋk/ *p.t.* of **stink**.

stanza /'stænzə/ *n* group of lines in a poem.

staple[1] /'steɪpəl/ *n* U-shaped nail pointed at both ends, used to fasten something.

staple[2] /'steɪpəl/ *adj, n* most produced, main (food, crop, etc.), e.g. *Rice is the staple (crop) of this country* = rice is the chief food product.

star /stɑː/ *n* **1** other worlds and suns seen shining in the sky at night. **2** figure of this shape (★). **3** famous actor or singer, etc.

starboard /'stɑːbəd/ *n* right side of a ship when one faces forward.

starch /stɑːtʃ/ *n* **1** white food substance found in bread, grain, etc. **2** this substance (as a powder) mixed with water and used to make clothes stiff.

stare /steə/ *v* look steadily (at) with wide-open eyes.

stark /stɑːk/ *adj* **1** stiff. **2** complete. *adv* quite, completely, e.g. *Stark naked* = wearing no clothes at all.

starling

starling /'stɑːlɪŋ/ *n* kind of small noisy bird.

starry /'stɑːrɪ/ *adj* shining like a star, covered with stars. *adj* **starry-eyed** /ˌstɑːrɪ 'aɪd/ thinking of beautiful but impossible plans.

start /stɑːt/ *v* **1** (cause to) begin; set going. **2** set out on a journey. **3** jump with sudden fear, surprise, etc. *n* **1** sudden jump because of fear, etc. **2** beginning (of a journey, etc.). **3** amount by which someone is in front. **by fits and starts** = not regularly, from time to time.

startle /'stɑːtl/ *vt* surprise and frighten.

starve /stɑːv/ *v* (cause to) die or suffer from hunger. *n* **starvation** /stɑː'veɪʃən/.

state[1] /steɪt/ *n* **1** condition. **2** self-governing country or part of a country. **3** high rank; ceremony, e.g. *The King travelled in state.* *adj* **stately** /'steɪtlɪ/ grand, solemn, fine.

state[2] /steɪt/ *vt* express clearly in words, say as a fact. *adj* **stated** /'steɪtɪd/ fixed and made known, e.g. *At stated times.* *n* **statement** /'steɪtmənt/ fact said or written; written paper telling certain facts, views, etc.

statesman /'steɪtsmən/ *n* one skilled in government and who takes an important part in it.

static /'stætɪk/ *adj* standing still.

station /'steɪʃən/ *n* **1** place where something is done, esp. a place where the police, etc., have their offices, e.g. *A fire station.* **2** stopping-place for railway trains, etc. **3** one's place in life or social standing. *vt* put in a place for a certain purpose.

stationary /'steɪʃənərɪ/ *adj* **1** not moving. **2** not meant to be moved about.

stationery /'steɪʃənərɪ/ *n* writing materials, e.g.

paper, pens, etc. *n* **stationer** /'steɪʃənə/ person who sells stationery.

statistics /stə'tɪstɪks/ *n* (*pl*) facts shown by numbers. *n* **statistician** /ˌstætɪs'tɪʃən/ one who deals with statistics. *adj* **statistical** /stə'tɪstɪkəl/.

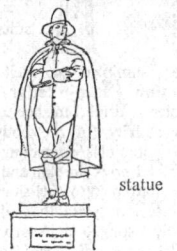

statue

statue /'stætʃuː/ *n* figure of a person, animal, etc., cut out of stone or made in metal, etc. *adj* **statuesque** /ˌstætʃʊ'esk/ (beautiful and calm) like a statue. *n* **statuette** /ˌstætʃʊ'et/ small statue.

stature /'stætʃə/ *n* **1** height of the body. **2** importance.

status /'steɪtəs/ *n* social rank or place in relation to others. *n* **status quo** /ˌsteɪtəs 'kwəʊ/ same state as now or before a certain date.

statute /'stætʃuːt/ *n* law passed by a law-making body. *adj* **statutory** /'stætʃʊtərɪ/ fixed, demanded by statute.

staunch¹ /stɔːntʃ/ *vt* stop the flow of blood from (a wound).

staunch² /stɔːntʃ/ *adj* (of a friend, etc.) firm, loyal.

stave /steɪv/ *n* **1** curved piece of wood forming part of a barrel. **2** five lines on which music is written. **to stave in** = break a hole in, e.g. a boat, etc. **to stave off** = keep off, delay.

stay¹ /steɪ/ *v* **1** stop or delay (action). **2** remain in the same place, condition etc. (for a time); not leave. **3** be able to continue. *n* (length of time of) staying; visit.

stay² /steɪ/ *n* support; strong rope or wire holding up a post. *n* (*pl*) **stays** stiff body support worn by women.

steadfast /'stedfɑːst/ *adj* firm; not changing; loyal.

steady /'stedɪ/ *adj* **1** firmly fixed; not shaking. **2** regular. **3** unchanging. *v* make or become steady. *n* **steadiness** /'stedɪnəs/.

steak /steɪk/ *n* thick piece of meat or fish.

steal /stiːl/ *v* **1** take away secretly and unlawfully a thing that belongs to another. **2** move quietly.

stealthy /'stelθɪ/ *adj* done, or acting, in such a way as not to be noticed; secret. *n* **stealth** /stelθ/.

steam /stiːm/ *n* gaseous form of water (as a result of boiling). *v* **1** give out steam. **2** move under the power of steam. **3** cook by steam. *n* **steamer** /'stiːmə/ **1** ship driven by steam. **2** pot used for cooking food by steam.

steel /stiːl/ *n* hard metal made from iron mixed with CARBON (used for knives, machinery, etc.). *vt* make (oneself, one's will) determined; harden (one's feelings).

steep¹ /stiːp/ *adj* having a sharp slope.

steep² /stiːp/ *v* make or become wet through, e.g. *To steep vegetables in water.*

steeple /'stiːpəl/ *n* church tower with a tall pointed roof.

steeplechase /'stiːpəltʃeɪs/ *n* horse-race or race on foot across the country, over walls, streams, etc.

steer¹ /stɪə/ *v* guide the course of (a ship, car, etc.). **to steer clear of** = keep away from.

steer² /stɪə/ *n* young BULLOCK raised for meat.

steerage /'stɪərɪdʒ/ *n* **1** act of steering. **2** that part of a ship in which one may travel at least cost.

stellar /'stelə/ *adj* having to do with the stars.

stem¹ /stem/ *n* main or central stick of a plant; part of a leaf, flower or fruit joining it to the branch, etc. **2** anything that joins like a stem, e.g. *The stem of a wine-glass.* **3** main part of a word to which different beginnings and endings are added.

stem² /stem/ *vt* **1** stop the flow of (water). **2** go forward against.

stench /stentʃ/ *n* very bad smell.

stencil /'stensəl/ *n* piece of paper or metal with holes in it through which ink is pressed, as a way of printing copies of letters, etc.

stenographer /stə'nɒɡrəfə/ *n* one who can write speech very quickly using special signs. *n* **stenography**/stə'nɒɡrəfɪ/.

step¹ /step/ *v* move the foot in walking. *n* **1** one movement of the foot; distance so moved. **2** sound made by someone walking. **3** place to put one's foot when going up or down stairs, etc. **4** something done (next) to bring something else about. **in step with** = **1** putting the right foot down at the same time as (everyone else marching, etc.). **2** behaving the same as (other people).

step² /'step/ related by later marriage. *n* **stepchild, stepson, stepdaughter** child of an earlier marriage of one's husband or wife. *n* **stepfather, stepmother** one's parent's later husband, wife. *n* **stepbrother, stepsister** child of an earlier or later marriage of one's mother or father.

steppe /step/ *n* broad treeless plain (esp. in Russia).

stereotyped /'sterɪətaɪpt, 'stɪə-/ *adj* (of ideas, answers, etc.) fixed in form; repeated without change; without meaning.

sterile /'steraɪl/ *adj* **1** unable to produce crops, children, etc. **2** completely free from the seeds of disease. **3** without result; useless. *vt* **sterilize** /'sterəlaɪz/ make sterile. *n* **sterilization** /ˌsterəlaɪ'zeɪʃən/.

sterling /'stɜːlɪŋ/ *adj* **1** of fixed value, pure. **2** trustworthy; of good quality. *n* British money.

stern¹ /stɜːn/ *adj* very serious in manner and without mercy.

251

stern² /stɜːn/ *n* back end of a ship.

stethoscope /'steθəskəʊp/ *n* instrument for listening to sounds in the body, especially the breathing or the heart.

stevedore /'stiːvədɔː/ *n* man in charge of loading or unloading a ship.

stew /stjuː/ *v* cook (meat and vegetables) in liquid in a closed pot. *n* dish so made.

steward /'stjuːəd/ *n* **1** man who looks after people travelling on a ship or aeroplane. **2** man in charge of the food and living arrangements in a large house, etc. **3** person giving help at a public meeting, dance, etc. *n* **stewardess** /'stjuːədəs/ woman steward (1).

stick¹ /stɪk/ *n* **1** long thin branch cut or broken from a plant or tree. **2** long thin piece of anything, e.g. *A stick of chalk.*

stick² /stɪk/ *v* **1** push a pointed thing into; remain (in something) by the point. **2** put, e.g. *To stick out one's tongue.* **3** fasten with paste or similar substance, e.g. *To stick a stamp on a letter.* **4** be or become fixed or not able to move, e.g. *This door sticks.* **5** = stand, as in **to stick out, to stick up for**, etc. **to stick to** = stand by (a promise, etc.).

stickler /'stɪklə/ *n* one who is stiff in his opinions about unimportant matters.

sticky /'stɪkɪ/ *adj* **1** that sticks or tends to stick. **2** difficult, e.g. *A sticky problem.*

stiff /stɪf/ *adj* **1** unbending; not easily moved. **2** difficult. **3** (of drink, wind, etc.) strong. *v* **stiffen** /'stɪfən/ make or become stiff(er). *n* **stiffness** /'stɪfnəs/.

stifle /'staɪfəl/ *v* **1** prevent from breathing; make breathing difficult. **2** (try to) stop, keep from being heard.

stigma /'stɪgmə/ *n* mark of shame; any small mark on the body. *vt* **stigmatize** /'stɪgmətaɪz/ mark as shameful; say that a thing is bad.

stile

stile /staɪl/ *n* step or steps for getting over a fence.

stiletto /stɪ'letəʊ/ *n* kind of small pointed weapon.

still¹ /stɪl/ *adj, adv* not moving; silent, peaceful. *vt* make calm.

still² /stɪl/ *adv* **1** (even) up till now; (even) up till then. **2** yet; even; to a greater degree, e.g. *I like this still better.* **3** however.

still³ /stɪl/ *n* equipment used for making strong drink.

stillborn /'stɪlbɔːn/ *adj* born dead.

stilt /stɪlt/ *n* one of two long poles with supports for the feet so made that one is able to walk at a height above the ground. *adj* **stilted** /'stɪltɪd/ (of behaviour, writing, etc.) stiff and solemn; not natural.

stilts

stimulate /'stɪmjʊleɪt/ *vt* excite; drive on. *n* **stimulation** /ˌstɪmjʊ'leɪʃən/. *n* **stimulant** /'stɪmjʊlənt/ drink, medicine, etc., that increases activity (of the body or mind). *n* **stimulus** /'stɪmjʊləs/ something that stimulates.

sting /stɪŋ/ *v* **1** prick the skin and drive in poison. **2** cause sharp pain to; feel sharp pain. *n* **1** part of an insect or plant that stings. **2** swelling caused by a sting. **3** any sharp pain.

stingy /'stɪndʒɪ/ *adj* mean; too careful with money.

stink /stɪŋk/ *vi, n* (give out a) very bad smell.

stint /stɪnt/ *v* keep (oneself) to a small allowance; not give enough of. *n* fixed amount of work, e.g. for one day.

stipulate /'stɪpjʊleɪt/ *v* make certain necessary conditions; arrange specially as part of an agreement. *n* **stipulation** /ˌstɪpjʊ'leɪʃən/.

stir /stɜː/ *v* **1** (begin to) move; cause to move. **2** excite. **3** move (liquid) round with a spoon. *n* general feeling of interest, etc.

stirrup /'stɪrəp/ *n* D-shaped piece of iron, etc., in which one puts one's foot when riding a horse.

stitch /stɪtʃ/ *v* join with a needle and thread. *n* **1** single in-and-out action of a needle. **2** amount of thread between two holes made in the material.

stock /stɒk/ *n* **1** main stem of a tree. **2** family or birth, e.g. *He is of good stock.* **3** support or handle of an instrument or gun, etc. **4** store of goods for use or for selling in a shop. **to take stock** = count and make a list of such goods; consider what has to be done. **5** liquid of boiled bones and meat kept for use in cooking. **6** money lent to the government for interest; shares in a business company. **7** (also **livestock**) farm animals. *vt* supply (with goods); keep a store of (goods in a shop, etc.).

stockade /stɒ'keɪd/ *n* (place encircled by a) wall made of upright posts.

stockbroker /'stɒkˌbrəʊkə/ *n* one who buys and sells shares in business companies.

stock exchange /ˈ. ˌ./ *n* place where shares in business companies are bought and sold.

stocking /'stɒkɪŋ/ *n* tight-fitting garment of wool, silk, cotton, etc., pulled over the foot and leg.

stock-in-trade /ˌ. . ˈ./ *n* (*sing*) things needed in carrying on a business, trade etc.

stockpile /'stɒkpaɪl/ *n* big store of some important substance (e.g. cotton, wheat, oil) kept in case of special need, e.g. a future war. *vt* store up for this purpose.

stock-still /ˌ. ˈ./ *adv* completely still, not moving.

stocky /'stɒkɪ/ *adj* (of persons, etc.) short and strong.

stodgy /'stɒdʒɪ/ *adj* **1** (of food) solid and heavy. **2** (of books, etc.) uninteresting.

stoic /'stəʊɪk/ *n* person who accepts pleasure and pain equally calmly. *adj* **stoical** /'stəʊɪkəl/. *n* **stoicism** /'stəʊɪsɪzəm/.

stoke /stəʊk/ *v* put coal, etc., on a (closed) fire (esp. a large fire giving heat for an engine).

stole¹ /stəʊl/, **stolen** /'stəʊlən/ *p.t. & p.p.* of **steal**.

stole²

stole² /stəʊl/ *n* long band of silk worn by a priest; long band of fur or feathers worn by a woman.

stolid /'stɒlɪd/ *adj* not easily excited.

stomach /'stʌmək/ *n* **1** bag-like part of the body into which food goes. **2** lower front part of the body. *vt* bear without complaining.

stone /stəʊn/ *n* **1** hard substance of rock (not metal); small piece of rock. **2** hard centre in a fruit. **3** measure of weight equal to 14 pounds (6·356 kg). **4** jewel. *vt* **1** throw stones at. **2** take fruit-stones out. **stone-blind** /ˌ·'·/ = completely unable to see.

stood /stʊd/ *p.t. & p.p.* of **stand**.

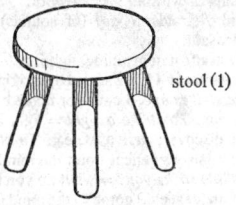

stool (1)

stool /stuːl/ *n* **1** small seat with no back. **2** *West African* seat of a chief which is the sign of his office; THRONE.

stoop /stuːp/ *v* bend the body forward and down. **to stoop to** = not be too proud to do (something wrong).

stop /stɒp/ *v* **1** put an end to (a movement or activity); come to rest; cease (an activity). **2** prevent. **3** fill or close (a hole, etc.). **4** refuse to give (payment of), e.g. *He has stopped my pay.* **5** stay, remain, e.g. *To stop at home.* *n* **1** act of stopping, e.g. *To put a stop to* = end. **2** place where BUSES, etc., stop regularly. **3** (also **full stop**) the mark '.' as used at the end of a sentence. **4** instrument that stops or controls, e.g. *A door stop.* *n* **stopgap** /'stɒpgæp/ thing or person filling the place of another for a time. *n*

stoppage /'stɒpɪdʒ/ condition of being stopped (up); blockage. *n* **stopper** /'stɒpə/ round block of glass, etc., used to close the mouth of a bottle.

store /stɔː/ *vt* keep for future use; keep a supply ready for use. *n* **1** supply so kept; (*pl*) different goods so kept. **2** place where goods are kept. **3** large shop that sells all kinds of things; any shop. **to set great store by** = value greatly.

storey, story /'stɔːrɪ/ *n* floor or level of a building.

stork /stɔːk/ *n* large bird with very long legs.

storm /stɔːm/ *n* **1** bad weather, with wind, rain, thunder, etc., e.g. *A snowstorm* = a storm with snow. **2** any great show of strong feelings. *v* **1** express strong feelings. **2** attack strongly and seize, e.g. a fort. *adj* **stormy** /'stɔːmɪ/.

story /'stɔːrɪ/ *n* account of events, real or imagined. **to tell stories** = tell untruths.

stout /staʊt/ *adj* **1** strong and thick. **2** brave. **3** (of a person) rather fat. *n* kind of strong dark brown bitter drink, made from grain.

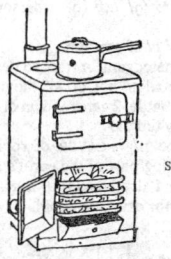

stove¹

stove¹ /stəʊv/ *n* enclosed fire used for cooking or heating.

stove² /stəʊv/ *p.t. & p.p.* of **stave**.

stow /stəʊ/ *vt* pack carefully and tightly (into); load on to a ship.

stowaway /'stəʊəweɪ/ *n* one who hides on a ship so as to travel without paying.

straddle /'strædl/ *v* stand or sit with one's legs far apart (over something).

straggle /'strægl/ *vi* **1** spread out too much in a disorderly way. **2** fall behind the others (on a march, etc). *n* **straggler** /'stræglə/.

straight /streɪt/ *adj* **1** without a bend. **2** in a line. **3** in good order. **4** (of a person) honest. *adv* by the shortest way; directly, e.g. *Straight away* = at once. *v* **straighten** /'streɪtn/ make or become straight. *adj* **straightforward** /ˌstreɪt'fɔːwəd/ **1** honest. **2** simple; without difficulties.

strain /streɪn/ *v* **1** pull very tight. **2** make the greatest possible use of (one's powers, oneself, etc.). **3** damage by using too much. **4** try very hard. **5** pass liquid through a cloth or wire in order to get out solid matter. *n* **1** state of being strained. **2** something that strains one's powers, etc. **3** way of speaking or writing. **4** tendency in someone's character. *n* **strainer** /'streɪnə/ instrument used for straining liquid.

strait

strait /streɪt/ *adj* narrow. *n* (often *pl*) narrow piece of water open at both ends. *vt* **straiten** /'streɪtn/ make narrow. **in straightened circumstances** = having very little money.

strand¹ /strænd/ *n* one of the threads that make up a string or rope.

strand² /strænd/ *n* shore. *v* (of a ship) run on the shore, etc. *adj* **stranded** /'strændɪd/ left without money, friends, etc., when in difficulty, e.g. *To be left stranded in a foreign country.*

strange /streɪndʒ/ *adj* not one's own; not well known; foreign; peculiar. **to be strange to** = not be accustomed to. *n* **strangeness** /'streɪndʒnəs/. *n* **stranger** /'streɪndʒə/ foreigner; person from another place.

strangle /'stræŋgəl/ *vt* 1 kill by holding the throat tightly. 2 make (breathing) difficult (for). *n* **strangulation** /ˌstræŋgjʊ'leɪʃən/.

strap /stræp/ *n* leather band; any narrow band used for fastening. *vt* 1 fasten or hold in place with a strap. 2 beat with a strap.

strapping /'stræpɪŋ/ *adj* (of a person) big and strong.

strata /'strɑːtə/ *pl* of **stratum**.

stratagem /'strætədʒəm/ *n* trick to deceive.

strategy /'strætədʒɪ/ *n* 1 art of moving armies, etc., before a battle. 2 general plan of action. *adj* **strategic** /strə'tiːdʒɪk/.

stratum /'strɑːtəm/ *n* LAYER of rock or other material forming part of the earth's surface.

straw /strɔː/ *n* 1 dry stem(s) of a grain-bearing plant. 2 tube for drinking liquid.

strawberries

strawberry /'strɔːbərɪ/ *n* kind of small red fruit with little seeds on its surface.

stray /streɪ/ *vi* wander from the path; go wrong. *n, adj* (animal or child) having strayed.

streak /striːk/ *n* 1 line of colour. 2 unexpected presence (of a quality in a person), e.g. *He has a mean streak.*

stream /striːm/ *n* 1 small river. 2 flowing of any liquid or gas. 3 crowd of people or things all moving in one direction.

streamer /'striːmə/ *n* long narrow flag or band of paper, etc.

streamlined /'striːmlaɪnd/ *adj* (of a car, etc.) shaped so that the air may flow easily over its surface.

street /striːt/ *n* road in a town.

strength /streŋθ/ *n* 1 quality of being strong. 2 number of persons present or that can be used. *v* **strengthen** /'streŋθən/ make or become strong(er).

strenuous /'strenjʊəs/ *adj* needing great strength, using much strength, e.g. *A strenuous game.*

stress /stres/ *vt* lay special weight on; say with special force, e.g. *He stressed the word "If".* *n* 1 pressure; difficult conditions, e.g. *Times of stress* = times of trouble and danger. 2 weight; importance; force given to a word or part of a word.

stretch /stretʃ/ *v* 1 make larger or longer by pulling; pull tight. 2 (lie) spread out, e.g. *The plain stretches for miles.* 3 make (a rule, word, etc.) go further or cover more than it should. *n* 1 act of stretching, etc. 2 unbroken length of time or piece of country, etc.

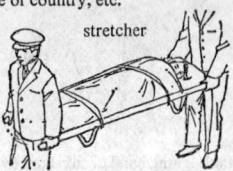

stretcher

stretcher /'stretʃə/ *n* frame used for carrying sick persons.

strew /struː/ *vt* scatter.

stricken /'strɪkən/ *adj* struck by; overcome, e.g. *Stricken with age* = very old.

strict /strɪkt/ *adj* 1 unyielding; demanding to be obeyed. 2 exact.

stricture /'strɪktʃə/ *n* blame, finding many faults with something.

stride /straɪd/ *vi* 1 take long steps. 2 pass (over) with one step. *n* (distance covered in) such a step. **to take it in one's stride** = do it without pausing or without special work.

strident /'straɪdənt/ *adj* (of sounds) high and unpleasant.

strife /straɪf/ *n* quarrelling, fighting.

strike /straɪk/ *v* 1 hit. 2 sound by striking, e.g. *The clock strikes one.* 3 cause or make by some action, e.g., *To strike a light* = light a match. 4 find; discover; arrive at, e.g. *To strike oil.* 5 have a (strong) effect upon the mind, e.g. *How does this strike you?* = what do you think of it? 6 (of an idea, etc.) come to the mind (suddenly). 7 (of a flag, tent, etc.) lower; take down. 8 (of workers) refuse to continue working, in order to get better pay or conditions, etc. *n* 1 refusal to continue work. 2 sudden discovery (e.g. of gold). 3 attack (esp. by aeroplanes). **to strike up** = begin (music, a friendship). **to strike out** = 1 cut out (a word) by drawing a line through it. 2 set off in a certain direction. **to strike out for oneself** = begin to work unhelped, set up one's own business. *adj* **striking** /'straɪkɪŋ/ surprising; unusual.

string /strɪŋ/ *n* 1 strong thread; any long and narrow thing used for tying. 2 stretched string or wire of a musical instrument. 3 thread on which things are arranged in a line; any line of things, e.g. *A string of cars.* *v* 1 fix a string on to. 2 put on a string (e.g. jewels); hang on a string.

stringent /'strɪndʒənt/ *adj* **1** that must be obeyed exactly. **2** needing great care because of a lack of (esp. money). *n* **stringency** /'strɪndʒənsɪ/.

strip /strɪp/ *v* **1** pull off the outer covering, e.g. from a tree. **2** take everything off, esp. clothes; take away (the possessions, rights, etc., of someone). *n* long narrow piece of something.

stripe /straɪp/ *n* long narrow band or mark, e.g. on cloth.

strive /straɪv/ *v* struggle; try hard.

strode /strəʊd/ p.t. of **stride**.

stroke[1] /strəʊk/ *n* **1** one of a number of regularly repeated movements (e.g. in swimming, of an engine). **2** single movement of the arms or made by a pen, etc. **3** attack of illness caused by the sudden bursting of a blood vessel in the brain. **4** something caused suddenly by effort or accident, e.g. *A stroke of luck.* = a piece of good fortune **5** one sound of a bell, e.g. *On the stroke of nine o'clock.*

stroke[2] /strəʊk/ *vt* rub gently; move the hand gently over.

stroll /strəʊl/ *vi* walk in an unhurried way.

strong /strɒŋ/ *adj* **1** powerful; firm; forceful. **2** having a powerful effect. **3** (of liquids, taste) not weakened. **strong drink** = drink containing ALCOHOL. *n* **stronghold** /'strɒŋhəʊld/ fort.

strove /strəʊv/ p.t. of **strive**.

struck /strʌk/ p.t. and p.p. of **strike**.

structure /'strʌktʃə/ *n* **1** thing built or fitted together. **2** way in which a thing is built up, its inner form. *adj* **structural** /'strʌktʃərəl/.

struggle /'strʌgəl/ *vi* try hard; fight.

strum /strʌm/ *vi* play a stringed instrument in a noisy careless way.

strung /strʌŋ/ p.t. and p.p. of **string**. **highly strung** = (of a person) easily excited.

strut[1] /strʌt/ *vi* walk in a stiff proud manner.

strut[2] /strʌt/ *n* piece of wood or metal used as a support.

stub /stʌb/ *n* short remaining end of something (e.g. a pencil, etc.). **to stub one's toe** = strike one of the front parts of the foot against a stone, etc.

stubble /'stʌbəl/ *n* **1** the cut ends of corn remaining in the field after the corn has been cut. **2** short growth of hair on the face looking like this.

stubborn /'stʌbən/ *adj* fixed in purpose or opinion.

stubby /'stʌbɪ/ *adj* short and thick.

stuck /stʌk/ p.t. & p.p. of **stick**.

stud[1] /stʌd/ *n* **1** thick nail with a large head. **2** object like a BUTTON that passes through two holes, used to fasten shirt-fronts, etc.

stud[2] /stʌd/ *n* collection of horses kept for racing or producing young.

student /'stju:dənt/ *n* person who studies.

studio /'stju:dɪəʊ/ *n* **1** room in which a painter, photographer, etc., works. **2** room from which plays, etc., shown on television (or heard on the radio) are sent out.

study /'stʌdɪ/ *v* work at (a subject) in order to

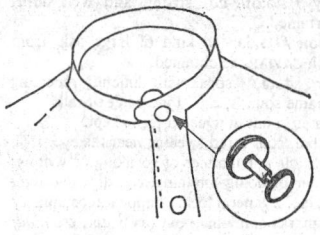

stud[1] (2)

learn it; give careful attention to. *n* **1** studying; subject studied; result of study. **2** room used for study or writing.

stuff /stʌf/ *n* **1** substance. **2** something of which the name is not known, uncertain or unimportant. *vt* **1** fill tightly (with); pack tightly. **2** put a nice-tasting mixture into the inside of a bird, etc., before cooking it. **3** fill the skin of a dead animal with wool, etc., so as to make it look as in life.

stuffy /'stʌfɪ/ *adj* hot and airless.

stultify /'stʌltɪfaɪ/ *v* make a thing useless; make it seem foolish.

stumble /'stʌmbəl/ *vi* **1** make a wrong step and fall forward. **2** make a mistake, esp. in speaking. **to stumble on** = find by accident.

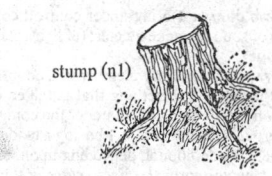

stump (n1)

stump /stʌmp/ *n* **1** part of a tree that remains in the ground after the tree has been cut down. **2** broken or useless end of anything. **3** (in cricket) one of the three sticks put upright in the ground. *v* **1** walk heavily. **2** be too difficult for, e.g. *Stumped* = not knowing what to do. *adj* **stumpy** /'stʌmpɪ/ short and thick.

stun /stʌn/ *vt* **1** make senseless by a blow on the head. **2** shock. *adj* **stunning** /'stʌnɪŋ/ very surprising or beautiful.

stung /stʌŋ/ p.t. & p.p. of **sting**.

stunk /stʌŋk/ p.p. of **stink**.

stunt[1] /stʌnt/ *vt* stop the growth of.

stunt[2] /stʌnt/ *n* something difficult done to get attention.

stupefy /'stju:pɪfaɪ/ *vt* make foolish or unable to think clearly. *n* **stupefaction** /ˌstju:pɪ'fækʃən/.

stupendous /stju:'pendəs/ *adj* very great; very surprising.

stupid /'stju:pɪd/ *adj* slow of understanding; foolish. *n* **stupidity** /stu:'pɪdətɪ/.

stupor /'stju:pə/ *n* deep sleep-like condition caused by medicine, serious illness, shock, etc.

sturdy /'stɜːdɪ/ *adj* strong and well built; determined.

sturgeon /'stɜːdən/ *n* kind of large fish, from which CAVIARE is obtained.

stutter /'stʌtə/ *v* speak with difficulty repeating the same sounds, e.g. "I c-c-can't t-t-talk".

sty[1] /staɪ/ *n* hut in which a pig is kept.

sty[2], **stye** /staɪ/ *n* red swelling near the eye.

style /staɪl/ *n* 1 manner of speaking or writing; manner of doing anything, e.g. drawing, dancing, etc. 2 general form or appearance; quality that marks something out (as better, etc.). *adj* **stylish** /'staɪlɪʃ/ having style; showing good style (esp. of clothes). *n* **stylist** /'staɪlɪst/ person who pays great attention to style. *adj* **stylistic** /staɪ'lɪstɪk/.

suave /swɑːv/ *adj* agreeably polite, with smooth easy manners.

sub- /sʌb/ under; less than; below, e.g. *adj* **substandard** /sʌb'stændəd/ below the accepted quality.

subaltern /'sʌbəltən/ *n* army officer of lower rank than a captain.

subconscious /sʌb'kɒnʃəs/ *adj* having to do with those activities of the mind of which we have no knowledge.

subcutaneous /ˌsʌbkjʊ'teɪnɪəs/ *adj* under the skin.

subdivide /ˌsʌbdɪ'vaɪd/ *v* divide again into more parts.

subdue /səb'djuː/ *vt* 1 bring under control; conquer. 2 (of sounds) make quieter; (of light, etc.,) make softer.

subject /'sʌbdʒɪkt/ *n* 1 any member of a country except the ruler. 2 something that is talked or written about, or studied. *adj* under the control of; governed by. **subject to** = 1 having a tendency to (get). 2 conditional, depending upon, e.g. *Subject to your approval* = if you agree or think it good. /səb'dʒekt/ *vt* 1 cause to happen to. 2 bring under control. *n* **subjection** /səb'dʒekʃən/.

subjective /səb'dʒektɪv/ *adj* giving, concerned with, the thoughts and feelings of one particular person only.

subjugate /'sʌbdʒʊgeɪt/ *vt* conquer, bring under control. *n* **subjugation** /ˌsʌbdʒʊ'geɪʃən/.

sublet /sʌb'let/ *v* let to someone else (a room, etc.) that one has rented oneself.

sublime /sə'blaɪm/ *adj* of the highest sort, causing wonder; very grand and very noble. *n* **sublimity** /sə'blɪmətɪ/.

submarine (n)

submarine /'sʌbməriːn, ˌsʌbmə'riːn/ *n, adj* (ship able to travel) under the surface of the sea.

submerge /səb'mɜːdʒ/ *v* go under, put under water.

submit /səb'mɪt/ *v* 1 yield; put under the control of. 2 ask a person to consider. *n* **submission** /səb'mɪʃən/. *adj* **submissive** /səb'mɪsɪv/ ready to yield; willing to do as ordered.

subordinate /sə'bɔːdɪnət/ *n, adj* (person who is) lower in rank or importance. /sə'bɔːdɪneɪt/ *vt* treat as or make subordinate. *n* **subordination** /səˌbɔːdɪ'neɪʃən/.

subpoena /səb'piːnə/ *n* paper ordering a person to appear in a court of law.

subscribe /səb'skraɪb/ *v* 1 sign one's name at the bottom of a paper. 2 agree to pay (money) in common with others (to a cause, etc.). 3 agree with; support. **to subscribe to a newspaper** = place an order for it. *n* **subscription** /səb'skrɪpʃən/.

subsequent /'sʌbsɪkwənt/ *adj* later; next.

subside /səb'saɪd/ *vi* sink down to a lower level; become quiet. *n* **subsidence** /səb'saɪdəns/.

subsidiary /səb'sɪdʒərɪ/ *adj* giving help or support; secondary. **a subsidiary company** = one controlled by a larger one.

subsidy /'sʌbsədɪ/ *n* money given by government to help a company, etc., keep going or keep prices down. *vt* **subsidize** /'sʌbsədaɪz/ give a subsidy to.

subsist /səb'sɪst/ *vi* stay alive; continue to live. *n* **subsistence** /səb'sɪstəns/ means of staying alive.

substance /'sʌbstəns/ *n* 1 material of which a thing is made; real nature of a thing. 2 chief ideas of a speech or book. 3 firmness; solidity. *adj* **substantial** /səb'stænʃəl/ 1 solid; strong; large. 2 real. 3 wealthy. *vt* **substantiate** /səb'stænʃɪeɪt/ prove that a thing is real; give facts to support (a claim, etc.).

substitute /'sʌbstɪtjuːt/ *n* thing used in place of something else; person who works in place of someone else. *v* put (a person or thing) in place of another. *n* **substitution** /ˌsʌbstɪ'tjuːʃən/.

subterfuge /'sʌbtəfjuːdʒ/ *n* something done to escape blame or difficulty; trick.

subterranean /ˌsʌbtə'reɪnɪən/ *adj* under the earth.

subtle /'sʌtl/ *adj* 1 fine; difficult to feel or to understand. 2 clever. *n* **subtlety** /'sʌtltɪ/.

subtract /səb'trækt/ *vt* take (a number or quantity) away from.

suburb /'sʌbɜːb/ *n* outlying part of a city. *adj* **suburban** /sə'bɜːbən/ living in or having to do with a suburb.

subvert /səb'vɜːt/ *vt* overturn or destroy (e.g. a set of beliefs, a government) by destroying people's faith in it. *adj* **subversive** /səb'vɜːsɪv/ tending to subvert.

subway /'sʌbweɪ/ *n* underground way; underground railway.

succeed /sək'siːd/ *v* 1 come after and take the place of. 2 do what one has planned and wished to do. 3 do well; have a good result. *n* **success** /sək'ses/ 1 things happening as planned or hoped. 2 person, activity, etc., that succeeds.

adj **successful** /sək'sesfəl/. *n* **succession** /sək'seʃən/ (of persons or things) the coming of one after another; number of things coming after another. *adj* **successive** /sək'sesɪv/ coming one after the other. *n* **successor** /sək'sesə⁷/ someone or something that succeeds (1) another.

succinct /sək'sɪŋkt/ *adj* clearly expressed in few words.

succour /'sʌkə⁷/ *vt, n* help.

succulent /'sʌkjʊlənt/ *adj* (of fruit, etc.) full of liquid, pleasing to the taste. *n* **succulence** /'sʌkjʊləns/.

succumb /sə'kʌm/ *vi* yield (to); die.

such /sʌtʃ/ *det* **1** of the same kind or degree (as). **2** of a kind (already mentioned), e.g. *Such is my wish.* **3** so much; so great, etc., e.g. *He is such a kind man.*

suck /sʌk/ *v* draw (liquid) into the mouth using the lips; take in; pull in.

suckle /'sʌkəl/ *vt* give milk to (a baby etc.) from the breast.

suction /'sʌkʃən/ *n* **1** act of SUCKING. **2** force that holds two things together when the air between them is taken away.

sudden /'sʌdn/ *adj* happening quickly and unexpectedly. *n* **suddenness** /'sʌdn-nəs/.

suds

suds /sʌdz/ *n (pl)* white mixture of soap, air and water that floats on top of soapy water.

sue /suː/ *v* **1** make a claim against (a person) in a court of law. **2** ask (for mercy, etc.).

suede /sweɪd/ *n* kind of soft leather.

suet /'suːɪt/ *n* hard fat of animals, used in cooking.

suffer /'sʌfə⁷/ *v* **1** bear (pain); feel or meet (pain, loss, etc.). **2** allow; not try to stop. *n* **sufferance** /'sʌfərəns/ **he is here on sufferance** = he has no right to be here but is allowed to remain. *n* **suffering** /'sʌfərɪŋ/.

suffice /sə'faɪs/ *v* be enough; satisfy.

sufficient /sə'fɪʃənt/ *adj* enough. *n* **sufficiency** /sə'fɪʃənsɪ/ sufficient quantity (of).

suffix /'sʌfɪks/ *n* ending added to a word (e.g. *-ly* in *quickly*).

suffocate /'sʌfəkeɪt/ *v* have or cause difficulty in breathing; kill by so doing. *n* **suffocation** /ˌsʌfə'keɪʃən/.

suffrage /'sʌfrɪdʒ/ *n* right to take part in electing a person; act of so doing.

suffuse /sə'fjuːz/ *vt* spread slowly over the surface of, e.g. *The sky was suffused with light.*

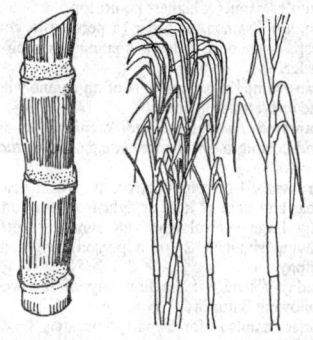

sugar-cane

sugar /'ʃʊgə⁷/ *n* substance commonly used to give a sweet taste. *n* **sugar-cane** /'.. ./, **sugar-beet** /'.. ./ plants from which sugar is obtained.

suggest /sə'dʒest/ *vt* **1** cause an idea to arise in the mind. **2** put forward (a plan, idea, etc.) for consideration. *n* **suggestion** /sə'dʒestʃən/ **1** idea, plan, etc., that is suggested. **2** slight sign (of). *adj* **suggestive** /sə'dʒestɪv/ tending to suggest.

suicide /'suːɪsaɪd/ *n* act of killing oneself; one who kills himself. *adj* **suicidal** /ˌsuːɪ'saɪdl/.

suit /suːt/ *v* **1** satisfy; be right for; be well fitted to. **2** (esp. of clothes) look well when worn. *n* **1** set of clothes made of the same material. **2** claim made in a law court. **3** one of the four sets of playing cards. **to be suited for** = be of the right kind for, be fit for.

suitable /'suːtəbəl/ *adj* right for the purpose; well fitted for. *n* **suitability** /ˌsuːtə'bɪlətɪ/.

suitcase /'suːtkeɪs/ *n* flat-sided case for clothes, carried in the hand.

suite /swiːt/ *n* **1** group of servants. **2** set of rooms; set of tables, chairs, etc., all of the same kind.

sulk /sʌlk/ *vi* be silently bad-tempered. *adj* **sulky** /'sʌlkɪ/.

sullen /'sʌlən/ *adj* **1** (tending to be) silently bad-tempered. **2** (of the sky, etc.) dark.

sully /'sʌlɪ/ *vt* make dirty.

sulphur /'sʌlfə⁷/ *n* yellow substance that burns with a blue flame and a very bad smell.

sultan /'sʌltən/ *n* Muslim ruler.

sultana /sʌl'tɑːnə/ *n* **1** wife of a sultan. **2** small yellow dried fruit used in cakes.

sultry /'sʌltrɪ/ *adj* hot and airless.

sum /sʌm/ *n* **1** whole amount resulting from adding. **2** amount of money. **3** calculation (e.g. adding, dividing, etc.). **to sum up** = **1** add up. **2**

express (the important ideas of a speech, etc.) in a few words. *n* **summary** /'sʌmərɪ/ short account of the main points of a book, etc. *adj* done quickly or without delay. *vt* **summarize** /'sʌməraɪz/.

summer /'sʌmə/ *n* season, usually the hottest of the year.

summit /'sʌmɪt/ *n* highest point; top.

summon /'sʌmən/ *vt* order (a person) to come (esp. to a court of law). *n* **summons** such an order.

sump /sʌmp/ *n* bottom part of an engine where the dirty, used oil collects.

sumptuous /'sʌmptʃuəs/ *adj* comfortable; fine and costing a lot of money, e.g. *A sumptuous meal.*

sun /sʌn/ *n* 1 heavenly body that gives the earth heat and light. 2 heat or light from the sun. 3 any large central star. *adj* **sunny** /'sʌnɪ/ 1 having sunlight. 2 (of a person) bright and happy.

Sunday /'sʌndɪ/ *n* the first day of the week, following Saturday.

sunder /'sʌndə/ *v* force apart; separate.

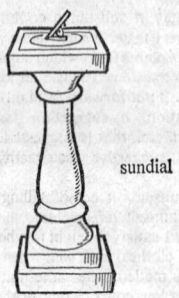

sundial

sundial /'sʌndaɪəl/ *n* instrument on which the shadow of a bar thrown by the sun shows the time.

sundry /'sʌndrɪ/ *adj* various.

sunflower /'sʌnflauə/ *n* kind of plant with large yellow flowers.

sung /sʌŋ/ p.p. of sing.

sunk /sʌŋk/ p.p. of sink. *adj* **sunken** /'sʌŋkən/ below the surface of something else; hollow.

sunstroke /'sʌnstrəuk/ *n* illness caused by the heat of the sun on the head.

super[1] /'suːpə/ *infml adj* very good; fine.

super-[2] /'suːpə/ *prefix* above; more than; greater than usual.

superb /suː'pɜːb/ *adj* very grand and beautiful.

supercilious /ˌsuːpə'sɪlɪəs/ *adj* proud, treating other people as if they were not so good as oneself.

superficial /ˌsuːpə'fɪʃəl/ *adj* 1 on the surface only, not deep. 2 with no depth of knowledge or feeling.

superfine /'suːpəfam/ *adj* very fine.

superfluous /suː'pɜːfluəs/ *adj* more than is necessary. *n* **superfluity** /ˌsuːpə'fluːɪtɪ/.

superimpose /ˌsuːpərɪm'pəuz/ *vt* put on the top of something else.

superintend /ˌsuːpərɪn'tend/ *v* watch (people working) to see that they do things well and correctly; have charge of. *n* **superintendent** /ˌsuːpərɪn'tendənt/ one who superintends.

superior /suː'pɪərɪə/ *adj* 1 higher, better, or greater. 2 not giving way (to). *n* person of higher rank or who is better, etc. *n* **superiority** /suːˌpɪərɪ'ɒrɪtɪ/.

superlative /suː'pɜːlətɪv/ *adj* of the highest degree or quality.

supermarket /'suːpəˌmɑːkɪt/ *n* large shop where customers collect their goods themselves and pay on the way out.

supernatural /ˌsuːpə'nætʃərəl/ *adj* spiritual; not controlled by the laws of nature.

supersede /ˌsuːpə'siːd/ *vt* put in the place of; be used instead of. *n* **supersession** /ˌsuːpə'seʃən/.

supersonic /ˌsuːpə'sɒnɪk/ *adj* faster than the speed of sound.

superstition /ˌsuːpə'stɪʃən/ *n* unreasonable belief in, or fear of, magic or what is unknown. *adj* **superstitious** /ˌsuːpə'stɪʃəs/.

supervise /'suːpəvaɪz/ *v* watch over (persons working) to see that something is done; direct (work, etc.). *n* **supervision** /ˌsuːpə'vɪʒən/.

supine /'suːpaɪn/ *adj* 1 lying on the back, face upwards. 2 lazy.

supper /'sʌpə/ *n* last meal of the day.

supplant /sə'plɑːnt/ *vt* take the place of.

supple /'sʌpəl/ *adj* easily bent or moved.

supplement /'sʌplɪment/ *vt* improve or complete by adding something. *n* **supplement** /'sʌplɪmənt/. *adj* **supplementary** /ˌsʌplɪ'məntərɪ/ added.

supply /sə'plaɪ/ *vt* bring or give (what is wanted or needed). *n* 1 supplying; that which is supplied. 2 store of things needed.

support /sə'pɔːt/ *vt* 1 bear the weight of; hold up. 2 help (to continue). 3 provide (a person) with food, clothes, etc. *n* supporting or being supported; someone or something that supports. *n* **supporter** /sə'pɔːtə/.

suppose /sə'pəuz/ *vt* 1 imagine to be true; take it as a fact that. 2 think; guess. *adj* **supposed** /sə'pəuzd/ regarded as being so. *adv* **supposedly** /sə'pəuzɪdlɪ/. *n* **supposition** /ˌsʌpə'zɪʃən/.

suppress /sə'pres/ *vt* 1 put an end to; put down (e.g. a rising of the people). 2 prevent from being known. *n* **suppression** /sə'preʃən/.

suppurate /'sʌpjʊreɪt/ *vi* produce PUS.

supreme /suː'priːm/ *adj* highest in power or rank; greatest or best possible. *n* **supremacy** /suː'preməsɪ/.

surcharge /'sɜːtʃɑːdʒ/ *n* money to be paid beyond what has been paid already.

sure /ʃʊə/ *adj* 1 free from doubt; certain. 2 proved; trustworthy. *adv* **surely** /'ʃʊəlɪ/ 1 certainly. 2 as expected; if experience can be trusted.

surety /'ʃʊərətɪ/ n one who promises to make sure that another pays his debt or does as ordered.

surf /sɜːf/ n (sing) waves breaking where the sea runs up on the land.

surface /'sɜːfɪs/ n 1 outside part of any object, etc. 2 outward appearance. 3 top of a liquid.

surfeit /'sɜːfɪt/ n too much of anything, esp. eating or drinking.

surge /sɜːdʒ/ vi move forward like waves. n such a movement or rush.

surgeon /'sɜːkʒən/ n skilled doctor who cuts away diseased parts of the body, sets right broken bones, etc. n **surgery** /'sɜːdʒərɪ/ 1 treatment of disease, etc., by a surgeon. 2 room in which a doctor gives advice, etc. adj **surgical** /'sɜːdʒɪkəl/.

surly /'sɜːlɪ/ adj rude and bad-tempered.

surmise /sə'maɪz/ v suppose; guess. /'sɜːmaɪz/ n.

surmount /sə'maʊnt/ v 1 climb over, get over; overcome (difficulties, etc.). 2 be above. adj **surmountable** /sə'maʊntəbəl/ able to be overcome.

surname /'sɜːneɪm/ n family name, e.g. John's surname is Smith.

surpass /sə'pɑːs/ vt do or be better than.

surplice

surplice /'sɜːplɪs/ n loose white garment worn in church by a priest.

surplus /'sɜːpləs/ n amount above what is needed.

surprise /sə'praɪz/ n feeling caused by something sudden and unexpected. vt 1 cause this feeling. 2 catch unprepared; attack suddenly. adj **surprising** /sə'praɪzɪŋ/ causing surprise.

surrender /sə'rendə/ v give up (something); yield; hand over to the power of someone.

surreptitious /ˌsʌrəp'tɪʃəs/ adj done secretly.

surround /sə'raʊnd/ vt be on all sides of, shut in on all sides. adj **surroundings** /sə'raʊndɪŋz/ everything that is round about (a person or place).

surveillance /sə'veɪləns/ n careful watch.

survey /sə'veɪ/ vt 1 consider as a whole. 2 examine carefully. 3 measure land and make a plan of it. /'sɜːveɪ/ n 1 general view. 2 measurement of land.

survive /sə'vaɪv/ v 1 live longer than. 2 remain alive; continue to live. n **survival** /sə'vaɪvəl/ 1 act of surviving. 2 something left over from a former time. n **survivor** /sə'vaɪvə/ person who has survived.

susceptible /sə'septəbəl/ adj 1 easily moved by feelings. 2 susceptible to = easily affected by. n **susceptibility** /sə,septə'bɪlətɪ/.

suspect /sə'spekt/ vt 1 have a general idea or feeling (that). 2 have doubt about. 3 think that someone may have done wrong. /'sʌspekt/ n. person suspected. adj doubtful; deserving to be suspected.

suspend /sə'spend/ vt 1 hang (something) up (from). 2 delay; stop for a time. **to be suspended** = remain in place as if hanging. n **suspension** /sə'spenʃən/ 1 suspending or being suspended. 2 the part of a car, etc., that makes it run smoothly over rough places.

suspense /sə'spens/ n feeling of fear and uncertainty whether a thing will happen or not.

suspicion /sə'spɪʃən/ 1 act of SUSPECTING; feeling that something is wrong. 2 slight taste or small sign (of). adj **suspicious** /sə'spɪʃəs/ having or causing suspicion.

sustain /sə'steɪn/ vt 1 hold up. 2 support or keep alive. 3 (in law) decide in favour of; agree with. 4 suffer; bear. n **sustenance** /'sʌstənəns/ food and drink.

suzerain /'suːzəreɪn/ n king, ruler; country having control of another.

swab /swɒb/ n 1 piece of cloth tied to a handle for cleaning floors, etc. 2 piece of cotton-wool, etc., for medical use.

swagger /'swægə/ vi walk or behave in a proud self-satisfied way.

swallow¹ /'swɒləʊ/ n kind of small bird with long wings and a V-shaped tail.

swallow² /'swɒləʊ/ v 1 take (food) down the throat into the stomach. 2 take in; use up. 3 accept too easily; hide, e.g. To swallow one's anger = not to show it.

swam /swæm/ p.t. of **swim**.

swamp /swɒmp/ n soft, very wet land. v (of a boat, etc.) fill with water and sink. **to be swamped with** = receive too much of (something).

swan

swan /swɒn/ n kind of large beautiful water bird with a long neck.

swap /swɒp/ see **swop**.

swarm /swɔːm/ n large crowd of insects, birds, etc., moving together; large moving crowd of

swarthy

people. *vi* move in crowds; be crowded, e.g. *The place is swarming with people* = there are large crowds in the place.

swarthy /'swɔːðɪ/ *adj* (esp. of skin) dark.

swat /swɒt/ *vt* hit quickly and kill (flies, etc.).

swathe /sweɪð/ *vt* bind tightly (with cloth).

sway /sweɪ/ *v* **1** (cause to) move unsteadily in different directions. **2** have an effect on or control over. *n* **1** swaying movement. **2** power; control, e.g. *To hold sway over* = rule.

swear /sweə/ *v* **1** promise or say solemnly in the name of God. **2** use bad language.

sweat /swet/ *n* **1** liquid that comes out of the skin when one is hot. **2** *infml* hard work. *v* **1** produce sweat. **2** (cause to) work hard. *adj* **sweaty** /'swetɪ/.

sweater /'swetə/ *n* woollen covering for the upper part of the body.

sweep /swiːp/ *v* **1** clear away (dirt, etc.) with a brush; clean in this way. **2** (cause to) move quickly (taking away anything in the way), e.g. *The storm swept all before it.* **3** stretch over a large area or in a curve. *n* **1** sweeping movement, e.g. of the arm. **2** unbroken stretch (of country, etc.), esp. in a curve. **3** (also **chimney sweep** /'.. ../ man who cleans chimneys. *adj* **sweeping** /'swiːpɪŋ/ **1** far-reaching. **2** with no attention to details; too general.

sweepstake(s) /'swiːpsteɪk(s)/ *n* kind of GAMBLING, esp. on a horse-race.

sweet /swiːt/ *adj* **1** tasting of sugar. **2** fresh; pleasant; nice. *n* **1** sweet-tasting dish in a meal. **2** small piece of boiled sugar, CHOCOLATE, etc. *v* **sweeten** /'swiːtn/ make or become sweet(er).

sweetheart /'swiːthɑːt/ *n* dearly loved person.

swell /swel/ *v* (cause to) become larger; be blown out with air, gas or liquid; (of music) become louder. *n* **1** increase of sound. **2** rise and fall of the sea. *n* **swelling** /'swelɪŋ/ swollen place on the body.

swelter /'sweltə/ *vi* feel very hot and uncomfortable.

swept /swept/ *p.t.* & *p.p.* of **sweep**.

swerve /swɜːv/ *v* turn aside suddenly (e.g. a car).

swift¹ /swɪft/ *adj* quick; rapid.

swift² /swɪft/ *n* kind of small bird.

swill /swɪl/ *v* **1** wash out (a pot, etc.). **2** drink large quantities (of). *n* pigs' food (mostly liquid).

swim /swɪm/ *v* **1** move through the water (like a fish, etc.); cross by swimming. **2** be full of, e.g. *Eyes swimming with tears.* **3** seem to be going round and round, e.g. *My head swims.*

swindle /'swɪndl/ *v* get money (from someone) by deceiving. *n* **swindler** /'swɪndlə/.

swine /swaɪn/ *n* pig.

swing /swɪŋ/ *v* **1** (cause to) move from side to side or backwards and forwards (e.g. a door opening and shutting, etc.). **2** (cause to) turn quickly. *n* seat hanging by ropes as a child's plaything. **the play went with a swing** = was a success with no trouble. **the party was in full swing** = going on well, at its height.

swing (n1)

swipe /swaɪp/ *vt, n* **1** (hit at with a) swinging blow. **2** *infml* steal.

swirl /swɜːl/ *v* (cause to) move quickly like liquid turning in circles as it flows on.

swish /swɪʃ/ *n* sound made by a stick, etc., moving very quickly through the air; sound made by a skirt, etc., moving over the floor. *v* move and make such a sound.

switch¹ /swɪtʃ/ *n* very thin stick. *v* hit with a thin stick; move (a tail) quickly.

switch² /swɪtʃ/ *v* **1** send (a train) on to another line. **2** send (electricity) along another wire; turn (on or off). **3** turn or change suddenly. *n* instrument for turning electricity on or off. *n*

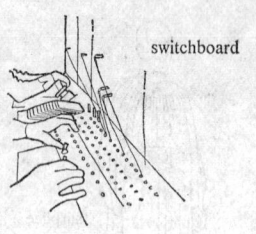

switchboard

switchboard /'swɪtʃbɔːd/ a collection of electrical switches on a board, esp. one for use with telephones.

swivel /'swɪvəl/ *n* ring fixed to a pin so that both can turn freely.

swollen /'swəʊlən/ *p.p.* of **swell**.

swoon /swuːn/ *vi, n* faint.

swoop /swuːp/ *vi* come (down on) with a rush; attack, e.g. *A bird swoops down on an animal to kill it.*

swop, swap /swɒp/ *infml v* give something and receive something else for it.

sword /sɔːd/ *n* kind of weapon with a long sharp blade fixed in a handle.

swore /swɔː/, **sworn** /swɔːn/ *p.t.* & *p.p.* of **swear**.

swum /swʌm/ *p.p.* of **swim**.

swung /swʌŋ/ *p.t.* & *p.p.* of **swing**.

sycamore /'sɪkəmɔː/ *n* a kind of tree.

sycophant /'sɪkəfænt/ *n* one who tries to win favour by behaving in a slave-like way.

syllable /'sɪləbəl/ *n* sound group (or letter group) with one VOWEL, into which a word can be divided. *adj* **syllabic** /sɪ'læbɪk/.

syllabus /ˈsɪləbəs/ *n* course of study in a school or university; written list of subjects to be studied.

syllogism /ˈsɪlədʒɪzəm/ *n* piece of reasoning set out in three parts, e.g. (1) *all insects have 6 legs*, (2) *this creature has 8 legs*, (3) *therefore it is not an insect.*

sylph /sɪlf/ *n* fairy; thin and graceful young woman.

symbol /ˈsɪmbəl/ *n* sign; mark, e.g. *The Cross is the symbol of Christianity. adj* **symbolic** /sɪmˈbɒlɪk/. *vt* **symbolize** /ˈsɪmbəlaɪz/ be a symbol of; make use of a symbol for.

symmetry /ˈsɪmətrɪ/ *n* exact agreement of opposite sides of a figure to each other; (beauty resulting from) right relation of parts. *adj* **symmetrical** /sɪˈmetrɪkəl/.

sympathize /ˈsɪmpəθaɪz/ *vi* share the feelings of another, e.g. be glad when he is glad, etc.; feel pity or tenderness (with). *n* **sympathy** /ˈsɪmpəθɪ/. *adj* **sympathetic** /ˌsɪmpəˈθetɪk/ having or showing sympathy; caused by sympathy.

symphony /ˈsɪmfənɪ/ *n* piece of music for an ORCHESTRA.

symptom /ˈsɪmptəm/ *n* sign of the presence of something (esp. of a disease in the body). *adj* **symptomatic** /ˌsɪmptəˈmætɪk/.

synagogue /ˈsɪnəgɒg/ *n* house of prayer of the Jews.

synchronize /ˈsɪŋkrənaɪz/ *v* (cause to) agree as to time; (cause to) happen at the same time. *n* **synchronization** /ˌsɪŋkrənaɪˈzeɪʃən/.

syndicate /ˈsɪndɪkət/ *n* number of people or business companies united for a certain pur-

pose, usually one needing a large amount of money. /ˈsɪndɪkeɪt/ *vt* join together into a syndicate; print a story in many (**syndicated**) newspapers at the same time.

synod /ˈsɪnəd/ *n* meeting of officers of the Church.

synonym /ˈsɪnənɪm/ *n* word that has (almost) the same meaning as another word, e.g. *'Start' and 'Begin' are synonyms. adj* **synonymous** /sɪˈnɒnɪməs/.

synopsis /sɪˈnɒpsɪs/ *n* short account of a book, play, etc.

syntax /ˈsɪntæks/ *n* (rules for) putting words together correctly to make sentences. *adj* **syntactic** /sɪnˈtæktɪk/.

synthesis /ˈsɪnθəsɪs/ *n* (*pl* **syntheses** /ˈsɪnθəsiːz/) a putting together of several parts into a whole; result of doing this. *adj* **synthetic** /sɪnˈθetɪk/ **1** of synthesis. **2** (of materials, etc.) man-made.

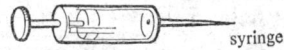

syringe

syringe /sɪˈrɪndʒ/ *n* instrument for pushing liquid out through a small needle-like tube (used for putting medicine into a blood-vessel, etc.).

syrup /ˈsɪrəp/ *n* very sweet, thick liquid.

system /ˈsɪstəm/ *n* **1** a grouping of things or ideas so as to make one well-ordered whole, e.g. *A system of thought.* **2** number of things arranged to make one working whole; way things are arranged; plan for arranging. **3** the human body. *adj* **systematic** /ˌsɪstəˈmætɪk/ orderly; done or arranged according to a system.

T

ta /tɑː/ *infml interj* thank you.

tab /tæb/ *n* small piece of cloth or paper fixed on to the edge of a larger piece (e.g. a coat, dress, etc.), used for hanging it up, for showing whose it is, etc.

table /ˈteɪbəl/ *n* **1** piece of furniture with a flat top and which stands on legs. **2** clear arrangement or list of figures or facts. *n* **tablecloth** /ˈteɪbəlklɒθ/ cloth spread over a table. *n* **tablespoon** /ˈteɪbəlspuːn/ kind of large spoon used for serving food.

table d'hôte /ˌtɑːblə ˈdəʊt/ *French n* meal served in a hotel, etc., at a fixed price, giving a choice of only a certain number of dishes.

tablet /ˈtæblət/ *n* **1** small flat surface with words cut or written on it. **2** piece of soap; small amount of powdered medicine pressed together in a flat piece.

taboo /təˈbuː/ *n, adj* (something that is) regarded by religion or custom as forbidden, not to be spoken of, etc.

tabulate /ˈtæbjʊleɪt/ *vt* arrange (facts, figures, etc. in a list or table. *adj* **tabular** /ˈtæbjʊlə/

arranged in the form of a table. *n* **tabulation** /ˌtæbjʊˈleɪʃən/.

tacit /ˈtæsɪt/ *adj* understood without anything being said, e.g. *A tacit agreement.*

taciturn /ˈtæsɪtɜːn/ *adj* (of a person) saying very little. *n* **taciturnity** /ˌtæsɪˈtɜːnətɪ/.

tack[1] /tæk/ *n* small nail with a flat head. *vt* **1** fasten with tacks. **2** join loosely with needle and thread.

tack[2] /tæk/ *vi* (make a ship) sail from side to side so as to move against the wind.

tackle /ˈtækəl/ *n* **1** ropes, etc., used on a ship. **2** equipment needed for a certain game or piece of work, e.g. *Fishing tackle. v* **1** begin (a difficult piece of work, etc.) with determination. **2** seize, try to stop (a thief, a football player who has the ball).

tacky /ˈtækɪ/ *adj* feeling sticky when touched.

tact /tækt/ *n* power of understanding other people's feelings and of doing or saying just the right thing at the right moment. *adj* **tactful** /ˈtæktfəl/. *adj* **tactless** /ˈtæktləs/ having no tact.

tactics /ˈtæktɪks/ *n* (*pl*) art of moving and

tactile

placing forces for or during a battle; any clever plans. *adj* **tactical** /'tæktɪkəl/.

tactile /'tæktaɪl/, **tactual** /'tæktʃʊəl/ *adj* having to do with touch.

tadpole /'tædpəʊl/ *n* first form of a FROG before it is fully grown.

tag /tæg/ *n* small card fastened to something (e.g. to show the price of it, or to show where it is to be sent).

tail (of coat)

tail /teɪl/ *n* **1** movable part at the lower end of the back of an animal, bird, fish, etc. **2** something like a tail, e.g. *The tail of a coat.* **3** opposite side of a COIN from that which shows the head of the king or ruler. *v* follow behind (often secretly). **to tail off** = become smaller in number, size, loudness, etc.

tailor /'teɪlə/ *n* person who cuts out, makes and sells outer garments (esp. for men).

taint /teɪnt/ *n* unpleasant quality, smell or taste. *v* (cause to) become decayed.

take /teɪk/ *v* **1** seize or hold; remove or steal. **2** get; have, e.g. *To take a bath.* **3** win; gain. **4** receive; accept, e.g. *He took the bad news well.* **5** carry; move; go with, e.g. *To take a friend home.* **6** make (a note of something), e.g. *He took my name and address.* **7** need, e.g. *This work will take two days.* **8** think; suppose, e.g. *I take it that you agree.* **9** (of treatment, etc.) have effect. **to take after** = look like. **to take for** = consider to be. **to take in** = **1** understand. **2** (of clothes, etc.) make smaller. **3** deceive. **4** receive as a guest. **to take off** = **1** copy the behaviour of (a person) so as to make others laugh. **2** leave the ground. **to take on** = accept; begin to have. **to take over** = take control (of); accept someone else's duties. **to take to** = begin doing something regularly; begin to like. **to take up** = **1** begin; become interested in. **2** (of time, space, etc.) use; fill. **3** start to deal with. *adj* **taking** /'teɪkɪŋ/ pleasing, ATTRACTIVE. *n* (*pl*) **takings** money taken by a shop, a business, etc.; gains.

talc /tælk/ *n* natural material that can be made into a powder for the skin. *n* **talcum** /'tælkəm/ **(powder)** fine powder made from talc.

tale /teɪl/ *n* story; report, account. **to tell tales** = tell of a person's wrongdoing.

talent /'tælənt/ *n* natural power to do something; ability, e.g. *A talent for music.* *adj* **talented** /'tæləntɪd/ having talent.

talisman /'tælɪzmən/ *n* a charm; thing supposed to possess magic power.

talk /tɔːk/ *v* say things; speak (about); have the power of speech. *n* talking; speech. *adj* **talkative** /'tɔːkətɪv/ liking to talk a lot.

tall /tɔːl/ *adj* high (esp. of persons). **a tall order** = piece of work difficult to carry out. **a tall story** = a story that is difficult to believe.

tallow /'tæləʊ/ *n* kind of hard fat, usually of animals, used in making candles, etc.

tally /'tælɪ/ *n* account, list of charges etc. *vi* agree exactly; be the same.

talon /'tælən/ *n* long hooked CLAW of certain birds.

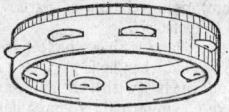

tambourine

tambourine /ˌtæmbə'riːn/ *n* light drum with pieces of metal at the sides, shaken or beaten with the hand.

tame /teɪm/ *adj* **1** (of animals) used to humans; not wild or fierce. **2** spiritless; uninteresting.

tamper /'tæmpə/ *vi* change dishonestly or in such a way as to damage, e.g. *To tamper with a machine* = put it out of working order.

tan /tæn/ *v* **1** make (the skin of an animal) into leather. **2** make or become brown (with the sun). *n, adj* (of a) yellow-brown colour.

tandem /'tændəm/ *n* kind of bicycle for two riders.

tang /tæŋ/ *n* sharp, strong taste, e.g. *The air has a tang of the sea.*

tangent /'tændʒənt/ *n* straight line touching a curve at one point only. **to fly off at a tangent** = suddenly talk of, or start doing, something else.

tangerine /ˌtændʒə'riːn/ *n* kind of small orange.

tangible /'tændʒəbəl/ *adj* that can be touched; real.

tangle /'tæŋgəl/ *n* disorderly mass of threads, string, etc. *v* mix up, become mixed up, in a disorderly way.

tango /'tæŋgəʊ/ *n* kind of slow dance for two persons.

tank /tæŋk/ *n* **1** (large) metal container for gas or liquid. **2** heavy armoured vehicle with a gun, used in battle.

tankard /'tæŋkəd/ *n* large drinking-pot.

tanker /'tæŋkə/ *n* ship or vehicle used for carrying oil.

tantalize /'tæntəlaɪz/ *vt* keep (a person) always hoping for something that he will never obtain.

tantamount /'tæntəmaʊnt/ *adj* equal in effect (to).

tantrum /'tæntrəm/ *n* sudden burst of bad temper.

tap¹ /tæp/ *n* instrument fitted on the end of a pipe that controls the flow of liquid or gas. *vt* **1** let liquid out from (e.g. a barrel). **2** try to obtain (money, news, etc.).

tap² /'tæp/ v strike lightly (with). n quick, light blow.

tape /teɪp/ n 1 long narrow piece of cloth used for tying or fastening. 2 narrow band of some material for a special purpose, e.g. *Adhesive tape* = sticky band for fastening things. n **tape measure** /'. ,. ./ long narrow band of cloth used

tape-recorder

for measuring. n **tape recorder** /'. ,. ./ piece of equipment that preserves sound by means of special MAGNETIC tape.

taper¹ /'teɪpə/ n kind of thin candle.

taper² /'teɪpə/ v (cause to) become narrower towards one end.

tapestry /'tæpɪstrɪ/ n large piece of cloth whose threads make a picture; cloth picture.

tapioca /ˌtæpɪ'əʊkə/ n kind of food (in the form of white grains) obtained from the root of a plant.

tar /tɑː/ n black oily substance obtained from wood or coal, used for making roads, etc. vt cover with tar. adj **tarry** /'tɑːrɪ/.

tardy /'tɑːdɪ/ adj late; slow. n **tardiness** /'tɑːdɪnəs/.

target /'tɑːgɪt/ n 1 object to be aimed at with a gun, etc. 2 aim or end one is trying to reach.

tariff /'tærɪf/ n 1 list of goods on which money must be paid when brought into a country. 2 list of charges, esp. for food, etc., in a hotel.

tarmac /'tɑːmæk/ n mixture of TAR and small stones used for the surfaces of roads, etc.

tarnish /'tɑːnɪʃ/ v (of metal, etc.) (cause to) lose its brightness or shine.

tarpaulin /tɑː'pɔːlɪn/ n cloth treated with TAR to make it keep out water.

tarry¹ /'tærɪ/ vi delay; stay; wait.

tarry² /'tɑːrɪ/ adj see tar.

tart¹ /tɑːt/ adj acid; sharp.

tart² /tɑːt/ n fruit, etc., cooked in a dish with pastry above or below it.

tartan /'tɑːtn/ n woollen cloth with coloured squares, worn in Scotland.

tartar /'tɑːtə/ n hard covering formed on dirty teeth. **to catch a Tartar** = have to deal with a very difficult or hot-tempered person.

task /tɑːsk/ n piece of work that must be done. **to take to task** = scold or blame. n **task force** /'. ,. / small army, a few warships, etc., sent to do some special piece of work. n **taskmaster** /'tɑːsk,mɑːstə/ person who makes others perform hard tasks.

tassel /'tæsəl/ n number of threads tied together at the upper end, hanging down from a cap, flag, etc., as an ornament.

taste /teɪst/ n 1 the sense that we get only through the tongue; quality of substances noticed by this sense, e.g. *The taste of sugar.* 2 good choice or judgment in matters of art, behaviour, etc. 3 small quantity (of something to eat or drink). 4 liking (for), e.g. *To my taste* = as I like it. v 1 have a taste. 2 notice or try the taste of (something). 3 experience. adj **tasteful** /'teɪstfəl/ showing good taste (2). adj **tasteless** /'teɪstləs/ 1 without taste. 2 showing bad taste (2). adj **tasty** /'teɪstɪ/ having a pleasant taste.

tatters /'tætəz/ n (pl) torn pieces of cloth, paper, etc. **in tatters** = torn in many places. adj **tattered** /'tætəd/ badly torn.

tattle /'tætl/ n unimportant talk.

tattoo¹ /tə'tuː/ n, vt (mark someone with a) coloured picture drawn on the skin by pricking it and rubbing colouring matter into the holes.

tattoo² /tə'tuː/ n 1 beating of the drum calling soldiers back for the night. 2 public show given by a large number of soldiers, usually at night.

taught /tɔːt/ p.t. & p.p. of **teach**.

taunt /tɔːnt/ vt say cruel things so as to hurt a person's feelings. n something said to taunt.

taut /tɔːt/ adj stretched tight.

tautology /tɔː'tɒlədʒɪ/ n the saying of the same thing again in different words. adj **tautological** /ˌtɔːtə'lɒdʒɪkəl/.

tavern /'tævən/ n drinking place; inn.

tawdry /'tɔːdrɪ/ adj bright and showy but of bad quality.

tawny /'tɔːnɪ/ adj of a yellow-brown colour.

tax /tæks/ n 1 money that has to be paid to the government. 2 something that is difficult to bear; a STRAIN (on). vt 1 put a tax on; make (someone) pay taxes. 2 be a tax (2) on, e.g. *This work taxes my powers* = it is almost too hard for me. **to tax with** = say that a person has done some wrong, e.g. *They taxed him with being lazy.* adj **taxable** /'tæksəbəl/ that can be taxed. n **taxation** /tæk'seɪʃən/ means of raising money by taxes; money paid as taxes.

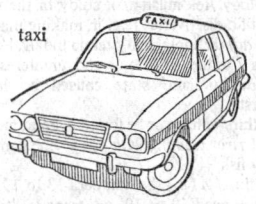

taxi

taxi /'tæksɪ/ n car for hire with a machine showing the amount to be paid. vi (of an aeroplane) run along the ground. n **taximeter** /'tæksɪˌmiːtə/ instrument fitted to a taxi that shows the amount to be paid.

taxidermist /'tæksɪˌdɜːmɪst/ n one who fills the skins of dead birds or animals and sets them up to look like live ones. n **taxidermy** /'tæksɪˌdɜːmɪ/ this art.

tea

tea /tiː/ n **1** drink made by pouring hot water on tea-leaves. **2** time when tea is drunk; light meal eaten in the afternoon. n **teacloth** /'tiːklɒθ/ cloth used for drying dishes. n **teaspoon** /'tiːspuːn/ small spoon used in serving tea, etc.

teach /tiːtʃ/ v try to make a person learn and help him in so doing; give lessons (as one's work). n **teacher** /'tiːtʃə/. n **teaching** work of teaching; that which is taught.

teak /tiːk/ n (large Indian tree with) hard red-brown wood used in making furniture, ship-building, etc.

team /tiːm/ n **1** two or more horses, dogs, etc., pulling a cart, SLEDGE, etc., together. **2** group of persons working or playing together (on one side).

tear¹ /teə/ v **1** damage or break by pulling apart (e.g. cloth). **2** remove suddenly by pulling sharply, e.g. *To tear out a page from a book.* **3** become torn or damaged. **4** move very quickly. **to tear up** = tear to pieces, destroy. n place that has been torn.

tear² /tɪə/ n drop of water coming from the eyes (esp. as a sign of grief). n **tearful** /'tɪəfəl/ crying; wet with tears.

tease /tiːz/ vt **1** laugh at (someone) playfully or unkindly; trouble or ANNOY in this way. **2** make a hairy surface on cloth. n **teaser** /'tiːzə/ difficult question.

teat /tiːt/ n part of the breast from which a child draws out milk; anything so shaped.

technical /'teknɪkəl/ adj having to do with some special art or skill; having to do with machines and making things by machines. n **technicality** /ˌteknɪ'kælətɪ/ technical word, phrase, point, etc.; something that is only important in this sense.

technician /tek'nɪʃən/ n person trained in a particular skill (esp. one concerned with machines, etc.).

technique /tek'niːk/ n skilled way or art of doing some special thing.

technology /tek'nɒlədʒɪ/ n study of the uses of scientific discoveries (e.g. in making machines, etc.). adj **technological** /ˌteknə'lɒdʒɪkəl/.

tedious /'tiːdɪəs/ adj long and uninteresting. n **tedium** /'tiːdɪəm/ state caused by lack of interest.

teem /tiːm/ vi have or be found in great numbers, e.g. *A river teeming with fish* = one containing many fish.

teens /tiːnz/ n (pl) the numbers 13 to 19. **in her teens** = aged 13 to 19. adj **teenage** /'tiːneɪdʒ/ having to do with young persons in their teens. n **teenager** /'tiːnˌeɪdʒə/ young person in his (her) teens.

teeth /tiːθ/ pl of **tooth**. vi **teethe** /tiːð/ produce the first teeth in childhood.

teetotal /tiː'təʊtl/ adj refusing to take, not allowing, wine or strong drink.

tele- /'telɪ/ far, e.g. n **telecommunication** /ˌtelɪkəmjuːnɪ'keɪʃən/ sending messages over a distance by using electricity.

telegram /'telɪɡræm/ n message sent in signs (not spoken) by electricity along a wire or by radio. n **telegraph** /'telɪɡrɑːf/ equipment for doing this. v send messages thus. n **telegraphy** /tə'leɡrəfɪ/ use, science of the telegraph. adj **telegraphic** /ˌtelɪ'ɡræfɪk/.

telepathy /tə'lepəθɪ/ n power of passing thought direct from one mind to another without speaking or making signs. adj **telepathic** /ˌtelɪ'pæθɪk/.

telephone /'telɪfəʊn/ n instrument for sending and receiving sound of the voice on an electric wire or by radio. v send such messages; speak to (someone) by telephone. adj **telephonic** /ˌtelɪ'fɒnɪk/.

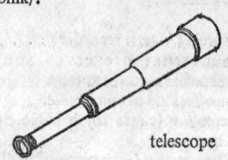
telescope

telescope /'telɪskəʊp/ n instrument used for seeing distant objects, using one eye. adj **telescopic** /ˌtelɪ'skɒpɪk/ **1** having to do with telescopes. **2** made with parts that can be closed by pushing one into another.

television /'telɪvɪʒən/ n sending and receiving of pictures by radio waves; equipment for receiving television pictures. vt **televise** /'telɪvaɪz/ send by television.

tell /tel/ v **1** make known; say (a story); express or show, e.g. *A clock tells the time.* **2** know; judge; discover; notice the difference between, e.g. *I can't tell which is which.* **3** order, e.g. *Tell him to go.* **4** have an effect, e.g. *The hard work is beginning to tell on him.* adj **telling** /'telɪŋ/ having great effect.

teller /'telə/ n one who counts or pays out money in a bank.

telltale /'telteɪl/ adj, n (person) making known a secret, something hidden, etc.

temerity /tɪ'merətɪ/ n daring, boldness.

temper /'tempə/ v treat (metal or other material) so as to make it of just the right hardness. n **1** hardness so obtained. **2** general condition of the feelings, e.g. *Bad-tempered* = easily angered; *Good-tempered* = calm and pleasant. **to lose one's temper** = become angry.

temperament /'tempərəmənt/ n general character, especially in regard to the feelings. adj **temperamental** /ˌtempərə'mentl/ easily excited.

temperance /'tempərəns/ n self-control in speech, behaviour or (esp.) the use of strong drink.

temperate /'tempərət/ adj **1** self-controlled; not eating or drinking too much. **2** (of parts of the earth) not very hot or very cold.

temperature /'tempərəʃə/ n degree of heat or cold. **to have a temperature** = have a fever.

tempest /ˈtempɪst/ n violent storm. adj **tempestuous** /temˈpestʃʊəs/.

template, templet /ˈtemplət/ n shaped plate used as a guide when cutting something out.

temple¹ /ˈtempəl/ n building in which prayers are said to a god.

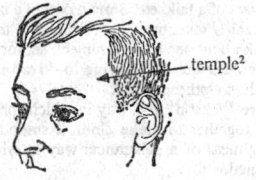

temple²

temple² /ˈtempəl/ n part of the head just above and in front of the ear.

templet /ˈtemplət/ see **template**.

tempo /ˈtempəʊ/ n speed at which music is played; speed of any activity.

temporal /ˈtempərəl/ adj 1 of time. 2 having to do with this world only; not spiritual.

temporary /ˈtempərərɪ/ adj lasting for or intended to be used for a short time only. adv **temporarily** /ˈtempərerəlɪ/.

temporize /ˈtempəraɪz/ vi behave in such a way as to gain time; delay doing an important action.

tempt /tempt/ vt 1 try to make a person do something (esp. something wrong) by promises. 2 excite desire in. n **temptation** /tempˈteɪʃən/.

ten /ten/ det, n number following nine, often written 10.

tenable /ˈtenəbəl/ adj 1 that can be held (for a certain time). 2 that can be defended successfully.

tenacious /təˈneɪʃəs/ adj holding on tightly; not letting go. n **tenacity** /təˈnæsətɪ/.

tenant /ˈtenənt/ n person who holds and pays rent for the use of a house, land, etc. n **tenancy** /ˈtenənsɪ/ state or time of being a tenant.

tend¹ /tend/ vt watch over, take care of (e.g. the sick).

tend² /tend/ vi turn, lean towards (a particular kind of thought or action), e.g. He tends to be cruel; be likely to, e.g. Wars tend to settle nothing = wars usually settle nothing. n **tendency** /ˈtendənsɪ/.

tender¹ /ˈtendə/ v offer (e.g. one's services); make an offer (to supply goods, etc.) at a certain price. n such an offer. **legal tender** = form of money that must (according to law) be accepted in payment.

tender² /ˈtendə/ adj 1 soft; easily eaten. 2 easily damaged; easily hurt; painful when touched. 3 kind and loving.

tendon /ˈtendən/ n strong string-like part of the body that joins a muscle on to a bone.

tendril /ˈtendrɪl/ n thin outgrowth of a climbing plant that holds the plant to the wall, stick, support, etc., up which it grows.

tenement /ˈtenəmənt/ n large building containing many sets of rooms for different families (often poor).

tenet /ˈtenɪt/ n belief.

tennis /ˈtenɪs/ n game played by two or four players hitting a ball backwards and forwards over a net.

tenor /ˈtenə/ n 1 general direction or course; general meaning. 2 (person who sings with the) highest male voice (in the usual range).

tense¹ /tens/ n form of a verb that shows time, e.g. The past tense.

tense² /tens/ adj 1 tightly stretched. 2 showing or feeling excitement; nervous. n **tension** /ˈtenʃən/ 1 state or degree of being tense. 2 condition when feelings are tense and relations STRAINED.

tent /tent/ n cloth shelter, supported by poles and ropes.

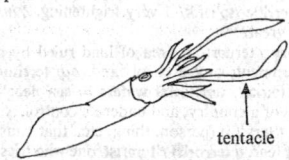

tentacle

tentacle /ˈtentəkəl/ n long easily bent limb of certain animals with no bone in it.

tentative /ˈtentətɪv/ adj not fixed, but said or done as a trial, to see the effect, e.g. A tentative suggestion = one made in order to hear what people say in answer.

tenterhooks /ˈtentəhʊks/ **on tenterhooks** = very anxious or excited.

tenuous /ˈtenjʊəs/ adj very fine and thin.

tenure /ˈtenjʊə/ n act of holding, or right to hold, land or a house; time during which a house, land, or office is held.

tepid /ˈtepɪd/ adj slightly warm. n **tepidity** /teˈpɪdətɪ/.

tercentenary /ˌtɜːsənˈtiːnərɪ/ n 300th year after an event.

term /tɜːm/ n 1 part of the school year; time during which a law-court sits; any fixed length of time, e.g. time to be spent in prison. 2 word(s) with a particular meaning (esp. in a branch of study), e.g. A medical term. 3 (pl) conditions offered or agreed to. **to come to terms** = reach an agreement. 4 (pl) words, e.g. In terms of praise. **to be on good terms with someone** = be friendly with him. vt call; name.

terminal /ˈtɜːmɪnəl/ adj of, or forming, the end of something (esp. someone's life). n 1 station in a town for people travelling by air. 2 point to which the end of an electric wire is joined.

terminate /ˈtɜːmɪneɪt/ v finish; come or bring to an end. n **termination** /ˌtɜːmɪˈneɪʃən/.

terminology /ˌtɜːmɪˈnɒlədʒɪ/ special words used in a particular science or art.

terminus /ˈtɜːmɪnəs/ n railway station, etc., at the end of a line.

termite /'tɜ:maɪt/ n a kind of white ant-like insect that destroys wood (often called a white ant).

terrace /'terəs/ n 1 level piece of ground outside a house, or cut into the side of a hill, 2 row of houses joined together. adj **terraced** /'terəst/ cut into terraces; forming a terrace.

terra-cotta /ˌterə 'kɒtə/ Italian n kind of hard, red-brown POTTERY.

terra firma /ˌterə 'fɜ:mə/ Latin n dry land.

terrain /tə'reɪn/ n area of land (esp. when considered as a place for a battle).

terrestrial /tə'restrɪəl/ adj having to do with this earth; of, living on, dry land.

terrible /'terəbəl/ adj 1 causing great fear or sorrow. 2 infml very bad. infml adv **terribly** /'terəblɪ/ very.

terrier /'terɪə/ n kind of small active dog.

terrify /'terɪfaɪ/ vt fill with fear; frighten greatly. adj **terrific** /tə'rɪfɪk/ 1 very frightening. 2 infml very great.

territory /'terɪtərɪ/ n area of land ruled by one government; any area of land. adj **territorial** /ˌterɪ'tɔ:rɪəl/. **territorial waters** = sea near the coast of a country, and under its control.

terror /'terə/ n (person, thing, etc., that causes) great fear. n **terrorist** /'terərɪst/ one who tries to bring about a change in the government by acts intended to cause terror, e.g. murder of government officers. n **terrorism** /'terərɪzəm/.

terse /tɜ:s/ adj (of speech, speakers, etc.) short; using few words.

tertiary /'tɜ:ʃərɪ/ adj third in rank or order of importance.

test /test/ n examination or trial. vt 1 put to the test; examine. 2 be a test of.

testament /'testəmənt/ **the Old Testament, the New Testament** = the two main parts of the Bible. **last will and testament** = paper showing what is to be done with goods, land and other possessions after the owner is dead.

testify /'testɪfaɪ/ v 1 declare solemnly as the truth. 2 give EVIDENCE (in a court of law). **to testify to** = be a sign of. n **testimony** /'testɪmənɪ/.

testimonial /ˌtestɪ'məʊnɪəl/ n 1 letter giving an opinion as to a person's character and ability. 2 something given (usually by a group of people) to someone to show their thanks for services.

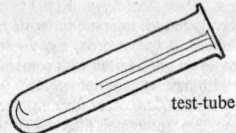

test-tube

test-tube /'. ./ n small glass tube closed at one end, used in scientific work.

testy /'testɪ/ adj bad-tempered; easily angered.

tetanus /'tetənəs/ n disease that causes stiffening of the muscles.

tête-à-tête /ˌteɪt ɑː 'teɪt/ French n PRIVATE talk between two people.

tether /'teðə/ vt tie (an animal) with a rope or chain so that it cannot run away. n rope or chain used in this way. **at the end of one's tether** = at the end of one's power or self-control; not knowing what to do.

text /tekst/ n 1 words actually used by a writer. 2 small piece chosen (esp. out of the Bible) as the subject of a talk, etc. 3 main part of a book. adj **textual** /'tekstjʊəl/. n **textbook** /'tekstbʊk/ book about one special subject, set for study.

textile /'tekstaɪl/ adj having to do with making cloth. n cloth; material.

texture /'tekstʃə/ n 1 way in which threads are put together to make cloth. 2 smoothness or roughness of a substance; way in which it is formed.

than /ðən; strong ðæn/ conj (used in comparing one thing with another), e.g. He is taller than you = you are not as tall as he is.

thank /θæŋk/ vt say that one is grateful to a person. interj, n (pl) **thanks** /θæŋks/ expression, or words, used to show that one is grateful (to a person who has given one something, etc.). interj **Thank you** /'. ./ expression of thanks. **thanks to** = because of. adj **thankful** /'θæŋkfəl/. adj **thankless** /'θæŋkləs/ ungrateful; (of an action) for which no thanks are given.

that¹ /ðæt/ det, pron the one over there, e.g. I want that book, not this one; the words just spoken, the thing just done, e.g. Who did that?

that² /ðət; strong ðæt/ pron (relative pronoun often used instead of who, whom, which, when) e.g. The man that I saw was your father. conj 1 (used to join two parts of a sentence), e.g. I will make sure that it is done. 2. with the following result, e.g. It was so heavy that I dropped it. 3 because, e.g. He is delighted that you could come. **so that** = for this purpose, e.g. He shouted so that everyone could hear.

thatch

thatch /θætʃ/ n roof made of dry grass, leaves, etc. vt cover (a roof, etc.) with thatch.

thaw /θɔ:/ v 1 (of ice and snow) melt; (cause to) become soft. 2 (of persons) (cause to) become more friendly.

the /ðə (before consonants), ðɪ (before vowels); strong ðɪː/ det 1 one or more particular known persons or things. 2 a particular class of persons or things, e.g. The poor must be helped. adv by so much; by that amount, e.g. The sooner the better.

theatre /'θɪətə/ n 1 public hall in which plays are acted. 2 scene of important events. adj

theatrical /θɪˈætrɪkəl/ **1** of the theatre. **2** (of behaviour, etc.) like an actor; showy; meant for effect.

theft /θeft/ *n* act of stealing.

their /ðeə⁷/ *det* belonging to them. *pron* **theirs** /ðeəz/ something belonging to them.

them /ðem/ *strong* ðem/ *pron* (from of **they** used after verbs and prepositions), e.g. *They like me, and I like them.*

theme /θiːm/ *n* **1** idea that is the subject of thought, speech or writing. **2** certain set of notes often repeated in a piece of music. *adj* **thematic** /θɪˈmætɪk/.

then /ðen/ *adv* **1** at that time (past or future) **2** next; afterwards, e.g. *He did his work and then went out.* **3** if that is so; in that case, e.g. *If he is ill, then he must go home.*

thence /ðens/ *adv* from there.

theocracy /θiːˈɒkrəsɪ/ *n* government by priests.

theodolite /θiːˈɒdəlaɪt/ *n* instrument used in measuring angles when making a map, etc.

theology /θiːˈɒlədʒɪ/ *n* study of the nature of God and of religious beliefs. *adj* **theological** /ˌθiːəˈlɒdʒɪkəl/. *n* **theologian** /ˌθiːəˈləʊdʒɪən/ person who has a great knowledge of theology.

theorem /ˈθɪərəm/ *n* STATEMENT that has to be proved by reasoning.

theory /ˈθɪərɪ/ *n* **1** general idea put forward to explain a certain set of facts. **2** the general laws (not practice) of an art or science, e.g. *All very well in theory* = good as an idea but not possible in fact. *adj* **theoretic(al)** /ˌθɪəˈretɪk(əl)/. *vi* **theorize** /ˈθɪəraɪz/ make theories (about). *n* **theorist** /ˈθɪərɪst/ person who forms theories.

therapy /ˈθerəpɪ/ *n* medical treatment (of diseases). *adj* **therapeutic** /ˌθerəˈpjuːtɪk/.

there *adv* **1** /ðeə⁷/ in, at, or to that place. **2** /ðə⁷; *strong* ðeə⁷/ (used with **is, appear, seem,** etc., at the beginning of a sentence) e.g. *There is nobody at home* = no one is at home. *adv* **thereabouts** /ˈðeərəbaʊts/ near that place, number or quantity. *adv* **thereby** /ðeəˈbaɪ/ in that way; by that means. *adv* **therefore** /ˈðeəfɔː⁷/ for that reason. *adv* **thereupon** /ˌðeərəˈpɒn/ then; as a result of that.

therm /θɜːm/ *n* measure of amount of heat.

thermal /ˈθɜːməl/ *adj* having to do with heat.

thermometer /θəˈmɒmɪtə⁷/ *n* instrument for measuring the degree of heat or cold.

these /ðiːz/ *pl* of **this.**

thesis /ˈθiːsɪs/ *n* (*pl* **theses** /ˈθiːsiːz/) idea that is the subject of a piece of reasoning, esp. a book written in order to get a degree.

they /ðeɪ/ *pron* (used in speaking of people or things) e.g. *I asked the men to leave but they refused.*

thick /θɪk/ *adj* **1** not thin; wide, broad. **2** placed close together, e.g. *A thick wood* = one where the trees are close together. **3** (of liquids) not flowing freely. **4** hard to see through, e.g. *A thick mist.* **5** *infml* not able to understand. *n* **thickness** /ˈθɪknəs/ **1** degree or quality of being

thick. **2** sheet, e.g. *A single thickness of wood.* *v* **thicken** /ˈθɪkən/ make or become thick.

thicket /ˈθɪkɪt/ *n* place where there are many trees and bushes growing close together.

thick-skinned /ˌ ˈ ./ *adj* (of a person) who does not notice (or does not care about) other people's bad opinion of him; not easily hurt.

thief /θiːf/ *n* (*pl* **thieves** /θiːvz/) person who steals. *v* **thieve** /θiːv/ be a thief; steal.

thigh /θaɪ/ *n* thick upper part of the leg, above the knee.

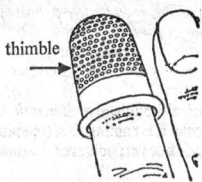

thimble

thimble /ˈθɪmbəl/ *n* metal cap worn on the finger to protect it when using a needle.

thin /θɪn/ *adj* **1** not thick, not deep, not broad, e.g. *A thin sheet of paper.* **2** (of persons) not fat, having little fat, e.g. *Thin and hungry-looking.* **3** (of liquids) watery; easily poured. *v* make or become thin.

thing /θɪŋ/ *n* **1** any material object; an idea, event, act, e.g. *That was a terrible thing to do.* **2** (*pl*) general conditions, e.g. *Things are getting better.* **3** (*pl*) belongings.

think /θɪŋk/ *v* **1** use the mind; get an idea. **2** have an opinion; believe. **to think up** = make (a plan); find (an answer). **to think better of** = think about (doing something) and then decide not to.

third /θɜːd/ *adj, n* next after the second. *n* one of three equal parts.

third rate /ˌ ˈ ./ *adj* of poor quality.

thirst /θɜːst/ *n* **1** desire for drink; feeling or suffering caused by lack of drink. **2** any strong desire (e.g. for knowledge). *adj* **thirsty** /ˈθɜːstɪ/.

thirteen /θɜːˈtiːn/ *det, n* number following twelve, often written **13**. *det, n* **thirty** /ˈθɜːtɪ/ number often written **30**, being three times ten.

this /ðɪs/ *det, pron* the one here, e.g. *This book belongs to me*; (that) which follows, e.g. *Listen to this* = listen to what I am going to say.

thistle /ˈθɪsəl/ *n* kind of wild plant with leaves that prick the skin.

thong /θɒŋ/ *n* thin leather band.

thorax /ˈθɔːræks/ *n* that part of the body between the neck and the stomach.

thorn /θɔːn/ *n* sharp part of a plant, growing out of the stem, which pricks the skin. *adj* **thorny** /ˈθɔːnɪ/ **1** having thorns. **2** (of questions, etc.) difficult; causing trouble.

thorough /ˈθʌrə/ *adj* complete; careful and exact. *n, adj* **thoroughbred** /ˈθʌrəbred/ (animal, esp. a horse) of pure BREED; (person) of good birth. *n* **thoroughfare** /ˈθʌrəfeə⁷/ public road or street, much used.

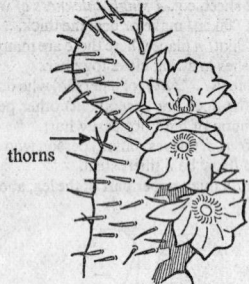

thorns

threshold (1)

those /ðəʊz/ *pl* of **that**[1].

though /ðəʊ/ *conj* although, e.g. *Though it is raining, I shall go* = it is raining, but (in spite of that) I shall go. *adv* but yet; however. **as though** = as if.

thought /θɔːt/ *p.t. & p.p.* of **think**. *n* 1 (power, act, way, of) thinking. 2 idea, opinion, intention formed by thinking. *adj* **thoughtful** /'θɔːtfəl/ 1 full of thought; showing thought. 2 thinking of; showing concern for others. *adj* **thoughtless** /'θɔːtləs/ careless; not considering others.

thousand /'θaʊzənd/ *n* number often written 1000, being a hundred times ten.

thrash /θræʃ/ *v* 1 beat (with a stick, etc.). 2 win against. **to thrash out** (a question, etc.) = talk over thoroughly and settle. *n* **thrashing** /'θræʃɪŋ/.

thread /θred/ *n* 1 very fine single long piece of silk, cotton, etc. 2 chain or line (of thought), e.g. *The thread of his thoughts* = the general direction of his thinking. 3 SPIRAL raised part of a screw. *v* put a thread through (e.g. a needle). **to thread one's way** = go slowly and carefully, finding one's path with difficulty (e.g. through a crowd of people). *adj* **threadbare** /'θredbeə/ (of cloth, etc.) worn very thin.

threat /θret/ *n* 1 declaration of an intention to harm or punish someone (esp. if he does not agree to do something). 2 sign of danger or trouble to come. *v* **threaten** /'θretn/ 1 make threats (against). 2 be a danger to; give warning of. 3 (of something unpleasant) seem probable.

three /θriː/ *det, n* number following two, often written 3.

thresh /θreʃ/ *v* beat the grain out of corn; beat (corn, etc.) to get out the grain.

threshold /'θreʃhəʊld/ *n* 1 stone or board under a door; entrance to a house. 2 start, beginning.

threw /θruː/ *p.t.* of **throw**.

thrice /θraɪs/ *adv* three times.

thrift /θrɪft/ *n* carefulness in the use of money or goods. *adj* **thrifty** /'θrɪftɪ/.

thrill /θrɪl/ *n* (experience causing a) sudden feeling of excitement. *v* (cause to) have a thrill. *n* **thriller** /'θrɪlə/ exciting story, play or film.

thrive /θraɪv/ *vi* be successful; grow strong and healthy.

thriven /'θrɪvən/ *p.p.* of **thrive**.

throat /θrəʊt/ *n* front part of the neck; pipe in the neck that leads from the back of the mouth to the stomach and LUNGS.

throb /θrɒb/ *vi* 1 beat or work regularly like the heart, e.g. *A throbbing pain* = a pain that comes and goes in a regular way. 2 (of the heart, etc.) beat more rapidly or strongly than usual.

throe /θrəʊ/ *n* sharp pain. **in the throes of** = struggling with.

throne /θrəʊn/ *n* ceremonial seat of a king, queen, etc.

throng /θrɒŋ/ *n, v* crowd.

throttle /'θrɒtl/ *vt* prevent (someone) from breathing by pressing the throat. *n* part of a car, etc., that controls the flow of PETROL, etc., into the engine.

through /θruː/ *prep* 1 from one end or side to the other, e.g. *The road through the town.* 2 from beginning to end of, e.g. *Through the night.* 3 because of; by means of, e.g. *He succeeded through working hard.* *adv* 1 from end to end, side to side, or beginning to end. 2 to the end; till complete, e.g. *To see the business through.* 3 by way of; all the way, e.g. *This train goes through to London.* **to be through with** = be finished with. *prep, adv* **throughout** /θruː'aʊt/ in every part (of); during the whole time (of).

throve /θrəʊv/ *p.t.* of **thrive**.

throw /θrəʊ/ *v* 1 cause to move through the air by a strong movement of the arm or a machine. 2 move, do something, quickly and with force, e.g. *He threw out his arm.* 3 cause to fall down or fall off, e.g. *The horse threw its rider.* *n* act of throwing; distance something is thrown. **to throw away** = 1 put aside as useless. 2 lose by being careless. **to throw off** = become free from. **to throw on** = put on (clothes, etc.) quickly or carelessly. **to throw over** = desert; give up (a plan, a friend). **to throw up** = be sick.

thrush /θrʌʃ/ *n* a kind of small singing bird.

thrust /θrʌst/ *v* push suddenly and with force.

thud /θʌd/ *n* sound made by a soft thing falling. *vi* make such a sound.

thug /θʌg/ *n* person who is dangerous and violent.

thumb /θʌm/ *n* short thick inside finger of the hand, separate from the others.

thump /θʌmp/ *n* (sound of a) heavy blow, esp. one given with the closed hand. *v* give such a blow (to); make such a sound.

thunder /ˈθʌndə/ *n* loud sound heard in the sky during a storm. *vi* make a noise of or like thunder. *n* **thunderclap** /ˈθʌndəklæp/ noise of thunder. *adj* **thunderous** /ˈθʌndərəs/ making a noise like thunder. *adj* **thunderstruck** /ˈθʌndəstrʌk/ very surprised. *adj* **thundery** /ˈθʌndəri/ (of weather) giving signs of thunder.

Thursday /ˈθɜːzdi/ *n* the fifth day of the week, following Wednesday.

thus /ðʌs/ *adv* in this way; so.

thwart¹ /θwɔːt/ *vt* prevent (a person) from doing what he wishes.

thwart² /θwɔːt/ *n* board across a boat, used as a seat.

thyme /taɪm/ *n* kind of sweet-smelling plant, used in cooking.

tiara /tɪˈɑːrə/ *n* small jewelled crown worn by ladies.

tic /tɪk/ *n* uncontrolled movement of the muscles of the face.

tick¹ /tɪk/ *n* very small creature that fixes itself on to the skin and drinks the blood.

tick² /tɪk/ *n* 1 light regular sound of a clock, etc. 2 small mark (often ✓) showing that something is correct or has been noted. *v* 1 make a ticking sound. 2 put a tick against.

ticket /ˈtɪkɪt/ *n* small card showing that the holder has the right to travel by train, etc., or enter a cinema, theatre, etc.; card showing the price of a thing in a shop.

tickle /ˈtɪkəl/ *v* 1 cause (a person) to laugh by touching his skin lightly (e.g. under the arms). 2 have, give, this feeling. 3 amuse, please. *adj* **ticklish** /ˈtɪklɪʃ/ 1 (of a person) easily made to laugh when tickled. 2 (of a piece of work, a problem, etc.) difficult, needing careful treatment.

tide /taɪd/ *n* 1 regular rise and fall of the sea, caused by the moon. 2 (of opinion, public feeling, etc.) flow or general direction. **to tide over** = (help to) get over (a time of difficulty, etc.). *adj* **tidal** /ˈtaɪdl/.

tidings /ˈtaɪdɪŋz/ *n* (*pl*) news.

tidy /ˈtaɪdi/ *adj* neat; in good order. **a tidy sum** = quite a large amount of money. *v* make tidy; set in order. *n* **tidiness** /ˈtaɪdɪnəs/.

tie /taɪ/ *v* 1 fasten with rope, string, thread, etc. 2 make (a knot). 3 LIMIT the freedom of. 4 (of sides in a game) make the same number of points. *n* 1 fastening; something that holds people together, e.g. *Ties of friendship.* 2 something that keeps one busy and gives one less freedom. 3 band of cloth, tied in a knot, worn round the neck.

tier /tɪə/ *n* row of things one above another (esp. seats).

tiff /tɪf/ *n* slight quarrel.

tiger /ˈtaɪɡə/ *n* large fierce animal of the cat family found in Asia.

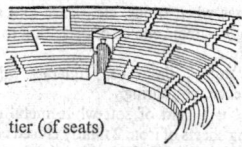

tier (of seats)

tight /taɪt/ *adj* 1 fully stretched. 2 firmly held; not easily loosened. 3 fixed; fitting closely. 4 (of money, etc.) difficult to get; not enough. *v* **tighten** /ˈtaɪtn/ make or become tight(er). *n* (*pl*) **tights** close-fitting garment covering the feet, legs and lower part of the body, worn by women, dancers, etc.

tile /taɪl/ *n* flat piece of baked earth, etc., used to cover roofs, floors or walls.

till¹ /tɪl/ *prep, conj* up to (the time when).

till² /tɪl/ *n* small box or DRAWER where money is kept in a shop.

till³ /tɪl/ *vt* prepare (land) for planting seeds. *n* **tillage** /ˈtɪlɪdʒ/ tilling of land; land so tilled.

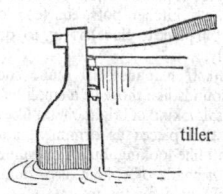

tiller

tiller /ˈtɪlə/ *n* bar fixed to the top of the blade with which one guides a small boat.

tilt /tɪlt/ *v, n* (cause to) slope.

timber /ˈtɪmbə/ *n* 1 wood prepared for building. 2 trees to be used for building.

timbre /ˈtæmbə/ *n* particular quality of the sound of a voice or musical instrument.

time /taɪm/ *n* 1 the whole of the past, present and future; the passing of hours, days, years, etc., e.g. *Only time will tell who is right.* 2 number of minutes, hours, days, etc., that an action or condition lasts, e.g. *He was gone a long time.* 3 measure of time stated in hours and minutes, e.g. *What time is it?* 4 particular moment or date when something happens, e.g. *The last time he came I was out.* 5 speed at which a piece of music is played. 6 life; age, e.g. *In ancient times.* 7 (*pl*) MULTIPLYING, e.g. *Two times three are six.* **to have a good time** = enjoy oneself. *vt* 1 measure the amount of time taken to do something. 2 choose or arrange time for something to happen, e.g. *To time one's blows* = hit at just the right moment. **in good time** = not late, with no need for haste. **at the same time** = 1 together. 2 yet, however. *adj* **timeless** /ˈtaɪmləs/ unending. *adj* **timely** /ˈtaɪmli/ happening, coming, just at the right time. *n* **timetable** /ˈtaɪmteɪbəl/ list of times of lessons in a school, or of times when certain things will be done, or of times when trains, etc., leave and arrive. *n*

timing /'taɪmɪŋ/ choice of or setting to the correct time.

timid /'tɪmɪd/, **timorous** /'tɪmərəs/ *adj* easily frightened, not daring.

tin /tɪn/ *n* **1** kind of soft white metal used for coating sheets of iron. **2** tightly closed container for food, etc., made from thin iron plate covered with tin. *vt* **1** coat with tin. **2** pack (food, etc.) in tins in order to keep it from decay. *adj* **tinny** /'tɪnɪ/ like tin; making a sound like a tin when struck.

tinder /'tɪndə/ *n* dry material used for starting a fire. *n* **tinderbox** /'tɪndəbɒks/ instrument formerly used for making fire.

tinge /tɪndʒ/ *vt* **1** colour slightly. **2** change slightly by adding a small amount of something, e.g. *His words were tinged with anger.* *n* slight colouring or quality (of).

tingle /'tɪŋgəl/ *vi, n* (have a) pricking feeling in the skin (e.g. of blood coming back into the skin after being cold).

tinker /'tɪŋkə/ *n* person who repairs things made of metal, e.g. kitchen pots, etc. (esp. one who travels from place to place). *vi* (try to) do repairs unskilfully.

tinkle /'tɪŋkəl/ *v* (cause to) make short high ringing sounds like those of a small bell.

tinsel /'tɪnsəl/ *n* kind of bright, metal-like material used in thin pieces as ornaments; anything bright and fine-looking, but of no value.

tint /tɪnt/ *n* shade of colour (esp. faint); slight colour (of). *vt* give a tint to.

tiny /'taɪnɪ/ *adj* very small.

tip[1] /tɪp/ *n* **1** point or end. **2** small piece put on the end of something.

tip[2] /tɪp/ *v* **1** touch or strike slightly. **2** (cause to) slope, or rise on one side, or turn over; empty (what is inside something) by tipping. *n* **1** light blow. **2** place where waste matter may be thrown.

tip[3] /tɪp/ *n* **1** small gift of money made to a servant, etc., for services. **2** piece of advice (e.g. about which horse is going to win a race, how to do something, etc.). *n* **tipster** /'tɪpstə/ person who gives tips about races.

tipple /'tɪpəl/ *v* drink (wine, etc.) too often.

tipsy /'tɪpsɪ/ *adj* having had too much strong drink.

tiptoe /'tɪptəʊ/ *vi, adv* (walk quietly) on the toes.

tirade /taɪ'reɪd/ *n* long angry speech.

tire[1] /taɪə/ see **tyre**.

tire[2] /'taɪə/ *v* (cause to) become in need of rest, uninterested. *adj* **tired** /'taɪəd/ in need of rest. **tired of** = having already had too much of, and so not wanting any more. *n* **tiredness** /'taɪədnəs/. *adj* **tireless** /'taɪələs/ not easily tired; never stopping. *adj* **tiresome** /'taɪəsəm/ causing one to be tired or angry.

tiro, tyro /'taɪərəʊ/ *n* beginner; inexperienced person.

tissue /'tɪʃuː, 'tɪʃjuː/ *n* **1** any very fine light material.

2 substance such as skin or muscle forming part of an animal or plant. *n* **tissue paper** /'.. ,. ./ very thin soft paper.

titbit /'tɪt,bɪt/ *n* specially nice piece of food, news, breast from which milk comes. **3** *sl* breast. **4 tit for tat** = blow for blow, doing to others as they have done to you.

titanic /taɪ'tænɪk/ *adj* very large.

titbit /'tɪt,bɪt/ *n* specially nice piece of food, news, etc.

titillate /'tɪtɪleɪt/ *vt* excite in a pleasant way.

title /'taɪtl/ *n* **1** name of a book, poem, etc. **2** word used to show a person's rank or his work, e.g. *Sir, Lord, Professor.* **to have a title to** = have a right to. *adj* **titled** /'taɪtld/ having a noble title. *n* **title-deed** /'.. ,. / paper showing one's right to hold land.

titter /'tɪtə/ *vi, n* (give a) silly, quiet laugh.

tittle-tattle /'tɪtl ,tætl/ *n* foolish and careless talk about other people.

titular /'tɪtʃʊlə/ *adj* having the title but not the power of an office.

to /tə/ (*before consonants*) tʊ (*before vowels*); *strong* tuː/ *prep* **1** in the direction of; towards. **2** as far as, e.g. *From end to end.* **3** on; against, e.g. *He fixed it to the wall.* **4** (of time) until; before, e.g. *The time is a quarter to five.* **5** (to show a second object) e.g. *Please give it to me.* **6** against, e.g. *We won by six points to three.* **7** (used to show the INFINITIVE) e.g. *I have work to do* = I have work that must be done. *adv* in or reaching a particular state, e.g. *To push the door to* = close the door. **to and fro** = backwards and forwards.

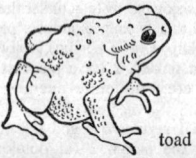

toad

toad /təʊd/ *n* small cold-blooded jumping animal which lives in wet cool places and eats insects.

toadstool /'təʊdstuːl/ *n* kind of T-shaped FUNGUS, usually poisonous.

toast[1] /təʊst/ *n* piece of bread made brown and hard on the surface by being held in front of a fire, etc. *v* **1** make toast (from). **2** warm (one's body) before a fire.

toast[2] /təʊst/ *vt* drink in honour of, to the health of (a person). *n* act of toasting; person toasted.

tobacco /tə'bækəʊ/ *n* kind of plant, the leaves of which are used for smoking (e.g. in a cigarette). *n* **tobacconist** /tə'bækənɪst/ person who sells tobacco.

toboggan /tə'bɒgən/ *n* flat wooden frame, curved up at the front, on which one slides down a snow-covered hill.

today /tə'deɪ/ *adv, n* (on) this day; (at) the present time.

toddle /'tɒdl/ *vi* walk with short unsteady steps as a baby does. *n* **toddler** /'tɒdlə'/ baby who can toddle.

to-do /tə du:/ *infml n* noise and excitement.

toe /təʊ/ *n* **1** one of the five parts at the end of the foot. **2** end of a shoe, etc., which covers the toes. *vt* touch with the toes. **to toe the line** = do exactly as ordered (as a member of a group).

toffee /'tɒfɪ/ *n* kind of sweet which is a boiled mixture of sugar and butter.

together /tə'geðə'/ *adv* in one group; in company; one with another; at the same time. **together with** = along with, as well as.

toil /tɔɪl/ *vi* work hard; move with difficulty. *n* hard work.

toilet /'tɔɪlət/ *n* **1** act of washing oneself, dressing, brushing one's hair, etc. **2** room for washing; small room where waste matter from the body is washed down a pipe by water.

token /'təʊkən/ *n* sign; something used instead of money. **a token payment** = payment of a very small part of what is owed so as to show that one agrees to pay the whole amount. **in token of** = in order to show.

told /təʊld/ p.t. & p.p. of **tell**.

tolerate /'tɒləreɪt/ *vt* suffer a thing that one does not like; allow such a thing to continue though one does not like it. *adj* **tolerable** /'tɒlərəbəl/ **1** that can be tolerated. **2** fairly good. *adj* **tolerant** /'tɒlərənt/ allowing others to think or act as they please even when they seem to be wrong. *n* **tolerance** /'tɒlərəns/, **toleration** /ˌtɒləˈreɪʃən/.

toll¹ /təʊl/ *v* (of a bell) ring with slow, regular strokes (e.g. as a sign that someone has died). *n* sound made by a bell ringing in this way.

toll² /təʊl/ *n* **1** money paid for going along a road or over a bridge, e.g. *A toll-bridge* = bridge at which one has to pay. **2** damage; loss, e.g. *To take a heavy toll of* = destroy a great part of.

tomahawk

tomahawk /'tɒməhɔːk/ *n* kind of small axe used by North American Indians.

tomato /tə'mɑːtəʊ/ *n* kind of (plant with a) soft red fruit, often used in cooking.

tomb /tuːm/ *n* place in which the dead are put; grave.

tomboy /'tɒmbɔɪ/ *n* girl who behaves like a boy.

tomcat /'tɒmkæt/ *n* male cat.

tome /təʊm/ *n* large book.

tomorrow /tə'mɒrəʊ/ *adv, n* (on) the day after today.

tomtom /'tɒmtɒm/ *n* Indian drum.

ton /tʌn/ *n* measure of weight equal to 2,240 pounds or 1016 kg (2,000 pounds or 907 kg in America). *infml* **tons of** = a great quantity of.

tone /təʊn/ *n* **1** (quality of) sound of a voice or of a musical instrument. **2** shade of colour, degree of light. **3** general spirit, e.g. *The tone of a school*; condition (e.g. of muscles, etc.). **4** (in music) space between one note of a SCALE and the next. *v* **1** give a particular sound or colour to. **2** (of colours) agree with. **to tone down** = make softer, kinder, etc.

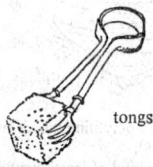

tongs

tongs /tɒŋz/ *n* (*pl*) instrument with two arms joined at one end used for picking up and holding something (e.g. coal, sugar, etc.).

tongue /tʌŋ/ *n* **1** movable thing inside the mouth with which we talk and taste. **2** language, e.g. *My mother tongue* = my native language. **3** anything shaped like a tongue, e.g. *The tongue of a shoe*.

tonic /'tɒnɪk/ *n* **1** something (esp. a medicine) used to excite or give strength to the body. **2** (in music) keynote.

tonight /tə'naɪt/ *n, adv* (on) this night (coming).

tonnage /'tʌnɪdʒ/ *n* **1** weight of goods that a ship can carry. **2** tonnage of all the ships of a country.

tonsil /'tɒnsəl/ *n* one of two small masses at the back of the throat (which sometimes become diseased and have to be removed). *n* **tonsillitis** /ˌtɒnsəˈlaɪtɪs/ disease of the tonsils.

tonsure /'tɒnʃə'/ *n* top of a priest's head from which all the hair has been cut as a mark of his office; act of cutting the hair in this way.

too /tuː/ *adv* **1** also; as well. **2** more than enough; to a greater degree than is needed, e.g. *Too much; Too big.* **I was too tired to speak** = I was so very tired that I could not speak.

took /tʊk/ p.t. of **take**.

tool /tuːl/ *n* **1** any instrument used in doing work, usually held in the hands (e.g. a hammer, an axe, etc.). **2** person used like a tool, e.g. *He used him as a tool* = made him do work that he did not wish to do himself.

toot /tuːt/ *n* short sound of a horn. *v* (cause to) give such a sound.

tooth /tuːθ/ *n* (*pl* **teeth** /tiːθ/) **1** one of the small white bony objects in the mouth with which we bite. **2** anything so shaped, e.g. teeth on a wheel

271

by which it turns another wheel. **armed to the teeth** = heavily armed. **to fight tooth and nail** = fight very fiercely.

top[1] /tɒp/ *n* **1** highest part or point, e.g. *At the top of one's voice* = as loudly as possible. **2** upper surface of something, e.g. *A table top. adj* highest; most important, e.g. *At top speed; The top man. vt* **1** cover; be a top to. **2** reach the top of; be at the top of; be higher or better than. **3** cut the top(s) off (e.g. trees).

top[2]

top[2] /tɒp/ *n* child's plaything which turns round on its pointed end.

topaz /'təʊpæz/ *n* kind of jewel, usually yellow.

topic /'tɒpɪk/ *n* subject of a talk. *adj* **topical** /'tɒpɪkəl/ concerned with matters of present-day interest.

topography /tə'pɒgrəfi/ *n* careful description of a place; special character of a place. *adj* **topographical** /ˌtɒpə'græfɪkəl/.

topple /'tɒpəl/ *v* (cause to) be unsteady and fall over.

topsy-turvy /ˌtɒpsɪ 'tɜːvɪ/ *adj* upside-down; in great disorder.

torch /tɔːtʃ/ *n* **1** piece of wood treated with oil, etc., burnt to give light. **2** small electric hand light.

tore /tɔː/ p.t. of *tear.*

torment /tɔː'ment/ *vt* cause great pain or suffering to. /'tɔːment/ *n* (cause of) great pain or suffering.

torn /tɔːn/ p.p. of *tear.*

tornado /tɔː'neɪdəʊ/ *n* violent storm in which the wind blows round and round.

torpedo /tɔː'piːdəʊ/ *n* long round metal shell pointed at each end, filled with explosive material and sent through the water to destroy a ship.

torpid /'tɔːpɪd/ *adj* heavy mad and slow; inactive. *n* **torpidity** /tɔː'pɪdətɪ/, **torpor** /'tɔːpə/.

torque /tɔːk/ *n* twisting force such as makes a wheel go round; turning power or movement of an engine.

torrent /'tɒrənt/ *n* violent rushing stream, e.g. *The rain fell in torrents. adj* **torrential** /tə-'renʃəl/ of or like a torrent.

torrid /'tɒrɪd/ *adj* (of the weather or a country) hot and dried up by the sun.

torsion /'tɔːʃən/ *n* act or force of twisting or being twisted.

torso /'tɔːsəʊ/ *n* the human body without the limbs or head.

tortoise /'tɔːtəs/ *n* kind of slow-moving animal with a hard shell from which only the head, legs and tail come out.

tortuous /'tɔːtʃʊəs/ *adj* **1** (of a road, etc.) having many twists and bends. **2** (of a piece of reasoning) difficult to understand. **3** (of character or action) dishonest, full of tricks.

torture /'tɔːtʃə/ *vt* cause great pain to. *n* great pain; act of torturing someone as a punishment, etc. *n* **torturer** /'tɔːtʃərə/.

toss /tɒs/ *v* **1** throw. **2** (cause to) move restlessly up and down or from side to side. *n* tossing movement. **to toss off** = finish (something) quickly and easily. **to toss up** = throw a penny to settle a question according to which side of the penny falls upwards.

tot[1] /tɒt/ *n* **1** very young child. **2** small measure of strong drink.

tot[2] /tɒt/ **to tot up** = add up.

total /'təʊtl/ *n* complete or whole amount. *adj* complete, making up a whole. *v* amount to; add up.

totalitarian /təʊˌtælə'teərɪən/ *adj* of, having, government by one party, no other party being allowed.

totem /'təʊtəm/ *n* animal or plant taken as the sign of a family group of North American Indians, and considered as being a member of the group; tall pole cut with signs and so used.

totter /'tɒtə/ *vi* **1** walk unsteadily as if about to fall. **2** be about to fall.

touch /tʌtʃ/ *v* **1** (cause to) be not completely separate from; put one's hand, finger, etc., on or against (something). **2** reach. **3** concern; have an effect on, e.g. *I was touched by his kindness.* **4** be as good as, be equal to, e.g. *As an actor, no one can touch him.* **to touch at** = (of a ship) visit for a short time. **to touch down** = (of an aeroplane, etc.) land, return to earth. **to touch (up)on** = speak of or deal with (a subject) in a few words. **to touch up** = improve (something) slightly by making small changes to it. *n* **1** act of touching. **2** (sense of) feeling. **3** slight amount (of), e.g. *A touch of fever* = a slight fever. **in touch with** = receiving news from and giving news to; regularly meeting; having news or knowledge of. **to lose touch with** = not to keep in touch with. *adj* **touch-and-go** /ˌ. . '. ./ very uncertain. *infml* **touched** /tʌtʃt/ mad, e.g. *He is slightly touched. adj* **touchy** /'tʌtʃɪ/ easily angered. *n* **touchiness** /'tʌtʃɪnəs/. *prep* **touching** /'tʌtʃɪŋ/ concerning. *adj* moving the feelings, esp. pity, e.g. *A touching story.*

touchstone /'tʌtʃstəʊn/ *n* something used as a test (of purity, etc.) or measure by which something else is judged.

tough /tʌf/ *adj* **1** not easily torn, broken or cut; difficult to eat. **2** (of a person) strong and daring; not easily tired or hurt. **3** (of work, etc.) difficult. *v* **toughen** /'tʌfən/ make or become tough.

toupée /'tuːpeɪ/ *n* piece of hair worn to hide a

place on the head on which there is no hair growing.

tour /tʊə/ *n* round journey, stopping at various places. *v* make a tour (of). *n* **tourist** /'tʊərɪst/ one who travels for pleasure. *n* **tourism** /'tʊərɪzəm/ business depending on tourists.

tournament /'tʊənəmənt, 'tɔː-/ *n* number of games played between different players to see who is best.

tourniquet /'tʊənɪkeɪ, tɔː-/ *n* band twisted tightly round a limb to stop the flow of blood.

tousle /'taʊzəl/ *vt* put the hair in disorder by rubbing it, running the fingers through it, etc.

tout /taʊt/ *n* person who goes about asking people to buy from him (esp. one who sells TIPS about horse races).

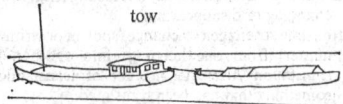

tow

tow /təʊ/ *vt* pull (a ship, car, etc.) along by a rope or chain. *n* towing or being towed. **to have in tow** = be towing (a boat, etc.); have charge of (a person).

toward(s) /tə'wɔːd(z)/ *prep* **1** in the direction of. **2** (of time) near; just before. **3** as a help in getting, e.g. *Put this money towards a new car*. **4** with regard to.

towel /'taʊəl/ *n* cloth used for drying the hands or body after washing.

tower /'taʊə/ *n* tall narrow building or part of a building (esp. a church or castle, etc.). *vi* rise very high. **a towering rage** = state of great anger.

town /taʊn/ *n* **1** group of houses and buildings larger than a village. **2** the people of a town. **3** the centre of a town where the shops, offices, etc., are. **4** nearest important town (esp. London). *n* **town hall** /ˌ. './ building used by the officials of a town and also for public events.

toxic /'tɒksɪk/ *adj* poisonous. *n* **toxin** /'tɒksɪn/ poison produced in an animal or plant.

toy /tɔɪ/ *n* child's plaything. **to toy with** = play with; consider, but not seriously.

trace /treɪs/ *n* track or mark left by something that has passed or that shows where something has been. **a trace of** = a very small amount of. *vt* **1** follow the tracks of (something) in order to find it. **2** copy (a picture, etc.) by drawing on a thin piece of paper laid over it. *n* **tracing** /'treɪsɪŋ/ copy of a map, etc., made by tracing.

track /træk/ *n* **1** line or mark left on the ground by something that has passed. **2** rough road or path. **3** course or way specially prepared for something, e.g. *A race track; A railway track*. **4** endless band on which a TANK, etc., runs instead of on wheels. **off the beaten track** = away from towns, busy roads, etc. *vt* follow the tracks of.

tract /trækt/ *n* **1** stretch or area of country. **2** short printed article or book on a particular subject, esp. a religious one.

tractable /'træktəbəl/ *adj* easily controlled.

traction /'trækʃən/ *n* (power used in) pulling something along.

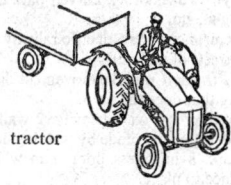

tractor

tractor /'træktə/ *n* powerful vehicle used for pulling farm machinery, carts, etc.

trade /treɪd/ *n* **1** business of buying and selling. **2** work, employment of any kind (esp. skilled work). **3** persons employed in a certain business, e.g. *The building trade*. *v* buy and sell; have as a business. **to trade (up)on** = use (something) unfairly for one's own ends. *n* **trademark** /'treɪdmɑːk/ special mark put on goods to show who made them. *n* **tradesman** /'treɪdzmən/ shopkeeper. *n* **trade union** /ˌ. '. './ joining together of the men in one employment so as to get better pay, improve conditions, etc.

tradition /trə'dɪʃən/ *n* passing on of history, beliefs or customs from age to age; old custom, story or belief so passed on. *adj* **traditional** /trə'dɪʃənəl/.

traduce /trə'djuːs/ *vt* speak badly about the character of (a person).

traffic /'træfɪk/ *n* **1** movement of people and vehicles along roads, of ships over the sea, etc. **2** trading. **to traffic in** = trade in.

tragedy /'trædʒɪdɪ/ *n* **1** serious and solemn play, usually with a sad ending. **2** any sad event or experience. *n* **tragedian** /trə'dʒiːdɪən/ writer of, or actor in, tragedies. *adj* **tragic** /'trædʒɪk/ of tragedy; very sad, ruinous.

trail /treɪl/ *n* **1** line, mark or track left by something that has passed. **2** path through rough country. *v* **1** follow the trail of. **2** pull, be pulled along, behind. **3** walk slowly because one is tired.

trailer /'treɪlə/ *n* vehicle (e.g. a cart) pulled along by another.

train[1] /treɪn/ *v* **1** prepare for a special purpose by teaching and exercising. **2** aim; point at. *n* **trainee** /treɪ'niː/ person who is being trained. *n* **trainer** /'treɪnə/ person who trains horses, football players, etc. *n* **training** /'treɪnɪŋ/. **in training for** = practising and getting ready for.

train[2] /treɪn/ *n* **1** group of followers. **2** number of railway carriages pulled along by an engine. **3** part of a lady's dress that lies on the floor behind her. **4** number of things joined together and following one after another, e.g. *A train of events; A train of thought*.

trait

trait /treɪt/ n special and peculiar quality or point of character.

traitor /'treɪtə/ n person who is unfaithful to his friends, who does harm to his own country by helping an enemy, etc. *adj* **traitorous** /'treɪtərəs/.

trajectory /trə'dʒektərɪ/ n curved path of a shot from a gun, etc.

tram /træm/ n car of an electric railway running in the streets of a town.

trammel /'træməl/ vt make movement difficult. n anything that does this.

tramp /træmp/ v 1 walk heavily. 2 walk a long distance. n 1 sound made by walking heavily. 2 long walk. 3 homeless poor man who walks from place to place.

trample /'træmpəl/ v walk heavily (on) and so damage (e.g. flowers in a garden).

trance /trɑːns/ n unnatural sleep-like condition in which people sometimes see or do strange things.

tranquil /'træŋkwɪl/ adj quiet; calm. n **tranquillity** /træŋ'kwɪlɪtɪ/.

trans- /trænz, træns/ across; on the other side of, e.g. *adj* **transatlantic** /ˌtrænzət'læntɪk/ crossing, or lying on the other side of, the Atlantic Ocean.

transact /træn'zækt/ vt (of business) do, settle. n **transaction** /træn'zækʃən/ (transacting a) piece of business.

transcend /træn'send/ vt go beyond (usual experience, etc.); be better than. *adj* **transcendent** /træn'sendənt/.

transcribe /træn'skraɪb/ vt copy written or printed matter on to another paper. n **transcript** /'trænskrɪpt/ something that has been transcribed. n **transcription** /træn'skrɪpʃən/ act of transcribing; something transcribed.

transept /'trænsept/ n part of a church that is built at right angles across the main hall.

transfer /træn'sfɜː/ v move from one place to another; hand over. /'trænsfɜː/ n act of transferring; something or someone transferred. n **transference** /'trænsfərəns/.

transfigure /træn'sfɪgə/ v change the appearance of (esp. so as to make more beautiful). n **transfiguration** /ˌtrænsfɪgə'reɪʃən/.

transfix /træn'sfɪks/ vt 1 push a knife, sword, etc., right through. 2 cause (somebody) to be unable to move or think.

transform /træn'sfɔːm/ vt change the shape, appearance, nature or quality of; change from one form into another. n **transformation** /ˌtrænsfə'meɪʃən/.

transfuse /træn'sfjuːz/ vt pass (blood) from one living body into another. n **transfusion** /træns'fjuːʒən/.

transgress /træns'gres/ v break (a rule, etc.); go beyond the law, do wrong, n **transgression** /træns'greʃən/. n **transgressor** /træns'gresə/ wrongdoer.

transient /'trænzɪənt/ adj soon passing away, not lasting long. n **transience** /'trænzɪəns/.

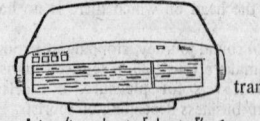
transistor (2)

transistor /træn'zɪstə, -'sɪstə/ n 1 very small piece of equipment used in radio and television sets, etc. 2 small raido set having transistors.

transit /'trænzɪt/ n a moving through or across. **in transit** = (goods) being carried from one place to another.

transition /træn'zɪʃən/ n change from one condition to another. *adj* **transitional** /træn'zɪʃənəl/.

transitive /'trænzətɪv/ adj (of a verb) that takes a direct object.

transitory /'trænzətərɪ/ adj not lasting long, soon changing or disappearing.

translate /trænz'leɪt/ v change (spoken or written matter) from one language into another. n **translation** /trænz'leɪʃən/ act of translating; something that has been translated.

translucent /trænz'luːsənt/ adj that allows light to pass through, although one may not be able to see through it.

transmit /trænz'mɪt/ vt send or pass on; allow to pass through, e.g. *Wires transmit electricity.* n **transmission** /trænz'mɪʃən/ 1 transmitting or being transmitted. 2 part of a car, etc., that carries the power from the engine to the wheels.

transmute /trænz'mjuːt/ vt change into another form or substance, e.g. *Transmute lead into gold.*

transparent /træn'spærənt/ adj 1 that can be seen through, e.g. glass. 2 clear; easily understood. n **transparency** /træn'spærənsɪ/ 1 state of being transparent. 2 photographic SLIDE (2).

transpire /træn'spaɪə/ vi (of an event, a secret, etc.) become known.

transplant /træn'splɑːnt/ vt take (growing plants, part of the body, etc.) from one place and make them grow in another. /'trænsplɑːnt/ n something transplanted; OPERATION to transplant something.

transport /træn'spɔːt/ vt carry from one place to another. /'trænspɔːt/ n transporting; means of transporting. **transports of delight** = feelings of great joy.

transpose /træn'spəʊz/ vt 1 cause (two or more things) to change places. 2 change the order of words. 3 (of music) change the key. n **transposition** /ˌtrænspə'zɪʃən/.

transverse /'trænzvɜːs/ adj placed or lying across.

trap /træp/ n 1 instrument for catching animals, e.g. mice; plan or trick to catch someone (out). 2 kind of small horse-carriage with two wheels. vt catch in a trap or by a trick. n **trap-door** /'. ./ small door in a floor or roof.

trapeze /trə'piːz/ n short bar hanging by two ropes on which people perform clever tricks or do exercises.

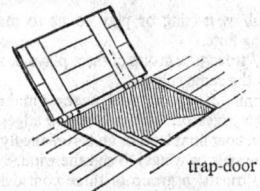

trap-door

trapezium /trə'piːzɪəm/ n irregular four-sided figure.

trapper /'træpə/ n person who traps animals to get their skins.

trappings /'træpɪŋz/ n (pl) ornaments, esp. as a sign of rank.

trash /træʃ/ n worthless material; worthless writing.

travel /'trævəl/ v 1 move. 2 make a journey, esp. to other countries. n 1 travelling. 2 (pl) journeys. n **traveller** /'trævələ/ n 1 person who travels. 2 travelling salesman.

traverse /trə'vɜːs/ vt pass across. /'trævɜːs/ n (esp. in climbing) way across; movement across.

travesty /'trævəstɪ/ n very poor copy or wrong description of something (often made on purpose). vt make a travesty of.

trawl /trɔːl/ n kind of large fishing net pulled along the bottom of the sea. n **trawler** /'trɔːlə/ ship that pulls such a net.

tray /treɪ/ n flat piece of wood, metal, etc., with a raised edge on which cups or other light things are carried, etc.

treacherous /'tretʃərəs/ adj 1 disloyal. 2 deceiving; not to be trusted. n **treachery** /'tretʃərɪ/ disloyal act.

treacle /'triːkəl/ n kind of thick, sticky, sugary liquid.

tread /tred/ v press with the foot; walk, step. n 1 part of a TYRE that touches the road. 2 part of a stair on which one sets one's foot.

treadle /'tredl/ n part of a machine on which the foot presses in order to drive it.

treason /'triːzən/ n disloyalty; helping persons to attack one's ruler or government. adj **treasonable** /'triːzənəbəl/.

treasure /'treʒə/ n store of precious things; thing of great value; dearly loved person. vt value greatly. n **treasurer** /'treʒərə/ officer in charge of money. n **treasury** /'treʒərɪ/ 1 place where treasures are kept. 2 government office that deals with a country's public money.

treat /triːt/ v 1 act upon; behave towards, e.g. *Treat him kindly* = be kind to him. 2 consider, e.g. *To treat the matter as serious.* 3 deal with; talk or write about. 4 give medical care to. 5 buy something; pay for someone, e.g. *He treated me to a dinner* = paid for a dinner for me. n unusual pleasure. n **treatment** /'triːtmənt/ 1 (way of) treating someone or something. 2 (particular kind of) medical attention.

treatise /'triːtɪz/ n serious book or writing about a particular subject.

treaty /'triːtɪ/ n agreement between nations (e.g. to end a war).

treble¹ /'trebəl/ adj, v (make or become) three times as much.

treble² /'trebəl/ n (voice that can sing) the highest part in music. adj of or for the treble.

tree /triː/ n large plant from which we get wood. **family tree** /ˌ...'./ = list of one's father, father's father, mother's father, and other relations from whom one is descended.

trek /trek/ vi, n (go on a) long journey (esp. in a cart pulled by cattle).

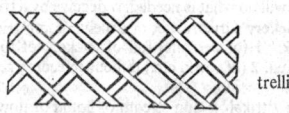

trellis

trellis /'trelɪs/ n frame made of pieces of wood crossing each other and nailed together (e.g. for supporting climbing plants).

tremble /'trembəl/ vi shake (with fear, anger, cold, etc.); be afraid.

tremendous /trɪ'mendəs/ adj very great; very large.

tremor /'tremə/ n short shaking movement (e.g. of the limbs, or the earth).

tremulous /'tremjʊləs/ adj shaking; nervous, afraid.

trench /trentʃ/ n long deep hole dug in the ground (e.g. as protection for soldiers).

tranchant /'trentʃənt/ adj (of speech, etc.) keen, clever and often unkind.

trend /trend/ vi go, bend or slope in a certain direction. n general direction; tendency.

trepidation /ˌtrepɪ'deɪʃən/ n state of fear and excitement.

trespass /'trespəs/ vi 1 go unlawfully on to another's land. 2 do wrong. n 1 act of trespassing. 2 wrong act.

tress /tres/ n number of long hairs taken together, e.g. one long curl.

trestle /'tresəl/ n wooden frame shaped like an A, used to support a table top, etc.

tri- /traɪ/ three.

trial /'traɪəl/ n 1 act of trying something out to see if it is suitable, etc. 2 examining of a prisoner in a court of law to see if he has done wrong. 3 something that gives trouble or difficulty.

triangle /'traɪˌæŋgəl/ n figure with three angles and three straight sides. adj **triangular** /traɪ'æŋgjʊlə/ three-sided.

tribe /traɪb/ n group of families of one race; class or kind. adj **tribal** /'traɪbəl/.

tribulation /ˌtrɪbjʊ'leɪʃən/ n (cause of) great grief or trouble.

tribunal /traɪ'bjuːnəl/ n court of law; court set up for a special purpose (e.g. to hear complaints about rents, etc.).

tributary /'trɪbjʊtəri/ *n, adj* **1** (river) flowing into a larger river. **2** (country, ruler, etc.) paying money to some more powerful country or ruler.

tribute /'trɪbjuːt/ *n* **1** payment that one government or ruler forces another to make. **2** something said or done to show respect or express thanks, e.g. *To pay tribute to a person* = tell of the good he has done.

trice /traɪs/ **in a trice** = in a moment, very quickly.

trick /trɪk/ *n* **1** act done to deceive, to amuse, or to make a person appear foolish. **2** (in card games) cards played in one round, e.g. *To take a trick* = win one round. **that will do the trick** = that will do what is needed. *vt* deceive by a trick. *n* **trickery** /'trɪkəri/ act of deceiving. *adj* **tricky** /'trɪki/ **1** (of persons) full of tricks; not to be trusted. **2** (of work, etc.) difficult; needing great skill.

trickle /'trɪkəl/ *n* thin stream of liquid or flow of drops. *v* (cause to) flow in a trickle.

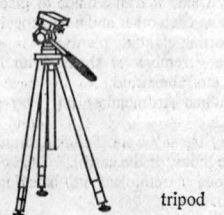
tripod

trickster /'trɪkstə'/ *n* one who tricks.

tricolour /'trɪkələ'/ *n* flag with three bands of colour (e.g. that of France).

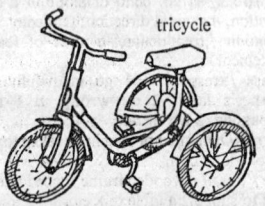
tricycle

tricycle /'traɪsɪkəl/ *n* vehicle with three wheels, driven by the feet.

tried /traɪd/ p.t. and p.p. of **try**. *adj* proved true or good; dependable.

triennial /traɪ'eniəl/ *adj* lasting for three years; happening once every three years.

trifle /'traɪfəl/ *n* **1** something of little value or importance. **2** kind of sweet dish made from CREAM, cake and fruit. *v* play with, treat lightly; speak or act lightly, not seriously. *adj* **trifling** /'traɪflɪŋ/ of little importance.

trigger /'trɪgə'/ *n* part of a gun pulled with the finger in order to fire it.

trigonometry /ˌtrɪgə'nɒmɪtri/ *n* branch of science that deals with TRIANGLES.

trill /trɪl/ *v, n* (sing or play so as to make a) shaking note.

trilogy /'trɪlədʒi/ *n* group of three plays or stories about the same subject.

trim /trɪm/ *adj* in good order; neat. *v* **1** make neat; cut the edges of. **2** ornament the edges of. **3** make a boat float level or an aeroplane fly level; set (the sails or wings) to suit the wind.

trinity /'trɪnəti/ *n* group of three considered as one. **the Trinity** (Christian teaching of) God the Father, Jesus Christ the Son, and the Holy Spirit, considered as one God.

trinket /'trɪŋkɪt/ *n* small jewelled ornament of little value.

trio /'triːəʊ/ *n* piece of music for three voices or instruments; group of three persons.

trip[1] /trɪp/ *v* **1** run with quick short steps; dance. **2** catch one's foot and (nearly) fall. **3** (cause to) make a mistake. **4** cause (a person) to fall by catching his foot. *n* fall; mistake.

trip[2] /trɪp/ *n* short journey, esp. for pleasure.

tripe /traɪp/ *n* **1** part of a cow's stomach used as food. **2** *infml* worthless or foolish talk or writing.

triple /'trɪpəl/ *v* make or become three times greater. *adj* **1** three times as much or as many. **2** made up of three persons or parts.

triplet /'trɪplət/ *n* **1** set of three. **2** one of three children born together to the same mother.

triplicate /'trɪplɪkət/ *adj* of which there are three alike made. *n* third copy. **in triplicate** = one written paper and two copies.

tripod /'traɪpɒd/ *n* support with three legs.

tripper /'trɪpə'/ *n* one who goes out on a short journey for pleasure.

trisect /traɪ'sekt/ *vt* divide into three parts (usually equal).

trite /traɪt/ *adj* (of ideas, etc.) not fresh or new; used too often, e.g. *A trite saying*.

triumph /'traɪəmf/ *n* (joy at) victory; feeling of great success. *vi* be successful, win a victory (over); show joy at winning. *adj* **triumphal** /traɪ'ʌmfəl/. *adj* **triumphant** /traɪ'ʌmfənt/ (expressing joy at) having triumphed.

trivial /'trɪviəl/ *adj* of little value; unimportant.

trod /trɒd/ p.t. of **tread**.

trodden /'trɒdn/ p.p. of **tread**.

trolley /'trɒli/ *n* **1** light cart pushed by hand. **2** small low four-wheeled vehicle running on lines.

trombone

trombone /trɒm'bəʊn/ *n* kind of large brass musical instrument with a sliding tube.

troop /truːp/ *n* **1** large group of people (esp. when moving). **2** small group of horse soldiers. *vi* move in a large group. *n* **trooper** /'truːpə'/ horse soldier. *n* (*pl*) **troops** soldiers; army. *n* **troopship** /'truːp,ʃɪp/ ship that carries soldiers.

trophy /'trəʊfi/ *n* something given to the winner of a race, etc.; sign of victory.

tropics /'trɒpɪks/ n (pl) the hot parts of the earth. adj **tropical** /'trɒpɪkəl/.

trot /trɒt/ n movement of a horse quicker than walking; quick walk or slow run of a man. vi go at a trot.

trouble /'trʌbəl/ n 1 difficulty; grief; pain, anxiety. **to get into trouble** = do something that brings trouble or for which one may be punished. 2 special care and attention, e.g. To take trouble over = give special attention to. v cause trouble to; give oneself trouble; take care (to). adj **troublesome** /'trʌbəlsəm/ causing trouble.

trough /trɒf/ n 1 wooden container for the food or water of animals. 2 hollow between two waves.

trounce /traʊns/ vt beat thoroughly.

troupe /tru:p/ n group of actors or performers.

trousers /'traʊzəz/ n (pl) garment covering the lower part of the body and the legs (each separately). (Often **a pair of trousers**.)

trousseau /'tru:səʊ/ n clothes, etc., provided for a woman when she gets married.

trout /traʊt/ n kind of fresh-water fish valued as food.

trowel /'traʊəl/ n 1 instrument with a flat blade fixed in a handle used in laying bricks for building. 2 instrument with a curved blade used for lifting small plants.

truant /'tru:ənt/ n child who stays away from school without good reason. **to play truant** = not attend school when one ought to.

truce /tru:s/ n arrangement to stop a war, battle, etc., for a time.

truck¹ /trʌk/ n low cart used on the road or on a railway line for heavy goods.

truck² /trʌk/ **to have no truck with** = have nothing to do with.

truculent /'trʌkjʊlənt/ adj fierce and eager to fight. n **truculence** /'trʌkjʊləns/.

trudge /trʌdʒ/ vi walk as when one is very tired. n long and tiring walk.

true /tru:/ adj 1 in agreement with fact; correct. 2 actual; real. 3 honest; loyal. adv **truly** /'tru:lɪ/ 1 truthfully. 2 really; certainly.

truism /'tru:ɪzəm/ n something said that is so very clearly true that there should be no need to say it.

trump /trʌmp/ n one of a SUIT of playing-cards given (by agreement) higher value than the rest. **to trump up** = make up (a story, a charge, etc.) that is not true in order to deceive.

trumpet /'trʌmpɪt/ n 1 kind of musical instrument made of brass. 2 anything shaped like a trumpet. v make a sound like a trumpet. **to blow one's own trumpet** = praise oneself. n **trumpeter** /'trʌmpɪtə '/ person who plays a trumpet.

truncate /trʌŋ'keɪt/ vt shorten by cutting off the top or end.

truncheon /'trʌntʃən/ n short stick used by policemen.

trundle /'trʌndl/ v roll (something heavy) along.

trunk /trʌŋk/ n 1 main stem of a tree between the roots and the branches. 2 main part of the body, without the head or limbs. 3 long nose of an elephant. 4 large box used for one's belongings when travelling. **a trunk call** = long distance call by telephone. **a trunk road** = main road.

truss /trʌs/ vt tie up; tie up (a bird) ready for cooking. n 1 mass of HAY, etc., tied together. 2 support for the muscles in front of the body.

trust /trʌst/ v 1 have faith in (another's honesty); believe. 2 give into the care of. 3 hope. n 1 faith; belief. 2 duty. adj **trustful** /'trʌstfəl/ ready to trust in others. adj **trustworthy** /'trʌst,wɜ:ðɪ/ deserving to be trusted; honest; dependable.

truth /tru:θ/ n 1 quality of being true and according to fact. 2 something that is true; fact. adj **truthful** /'tru:θfəl/ 1 (of persons) always telling the truth. 2 true.

try /traɪ/ v 1 make an attempt (to do something). 2 use something, do something, to find out what it is like, e.g. To try a coat on = put a coat on to see if it fits. 3 examine and judge (someone, a case) in a court of law. 4 work as hard as one can, e.g. Try and do it = make every attempt to do it. 5 put a STRAIN on, e.g. This tries my eyes = this is very tiring for my eyes. adj **trying** /'traɪ-ɪŋ/ troublesome; tiring.

tsetse /'tsetsɪ/ n kind of fly found in parts of Africa whose bite causes disease.

tub /tʌb/ n 1 large round (usually wooden) container for liquids, etc. 2 bath. adj **tubby** /'tʌbɪ/ short and fat.

tube /tju:b/ n 1 narrow pipe, esp. of glass or rubber. 2 soft metal container whose contents are pressed out. 3 (in London) underground railway. n **tubing** /'tju:bɪŋ/ length of tube. adj **tubular** /'tju:bjʊlə '/ shaped like a tube.

tuber /'tju:bə '/ n swelling on the root of a plant from which a new plant can grow.

tuberculosis /tjʊ,bɜ:kjʊ'ləʊsɪs/ n kind of serious disease, usually of the LUNGS. adj **tubercular** /tjʊ'bɜ:kjʊlə '/.

tuck /tʌk/ vt push (a piece of cloth, etc.) into a narrow crack (so as to make it neat or firm, or hide it), e.g. To tuck a baby into bed = push the bedclothes tightly around it. n cloth folded over and fixed down, for ornament or so as to make a dress shorter. infml **to tuck in** = (start to) eat a lot.

Tuesday /'tju:zdɪ/ the third day of the week, following Monday.

tuft /tʌft/ n group of hairs, blades of grass, feathers, etc., growing close together.

tug /tʌg/ v pull hard and violently. n 1 sudden hard pull. 2 small powerful ship used to pull larger ones. **tug of war** /,. . './ game where two groups pull opposite ends of a rope to see which can pull harder.

tuition /tju:'ɪʃən/ n act of teaching; taking charge of a child for teaching.

tulip /'tju:lɪp/ n kind of plant with a large bell-shaped flower held upright on a long stem.

tumble

tug (n2)

tumble /'tʌmbəl/ vi fall quickly or heavily. infml **to tumble to** = understand suddenly.

tumbler /'tʌmblə'/ n drinking glass with no stem.

tummy /'tʌmɪ/ infml n stomach.

tumour /'tjuːmə'/ n diseased growth in the body.

tumult /'tjuːmʌlt/ n excitement and noise; disorder. adj **tumultuous** /tjʊ'mʌltʃʊəs/ noisy and excited; violent.

tuna /'tjuːnə/ n kind of large sea fish.

tune /tjuːn/ v **1** set (a musical instrument) so that it gives the right notes. **2** move the controls of (a radio) in order to listen to a particular radio station. n set of musical notes that makes a pleasant sound (and can be easily remembered); music of a song. **in tune with** = in agreement with.

tunic /'tjuːnɪk/ n **1** kind of close-fitting garment worn by soldiers, etc. **2** kind of garment without arms.

tunnel /'tʌnəl/ n, v (make a) long arched hole under the ground, e.g. one cut through a hill for a railway line to pass through.

turban

turban /'tɜːbən/ n covering for the head made from a long piece of cloth bound round it.

turbine /'tɜːbaɪn/ n kind of engine driven by the force of a stream of gas, water, etc., against the blades of a wheel.

turbot /'tɜːbət/ n kind of large flat fish.

turbulent /'tɜːbjʊlənt/ adj moving violently; noisy and uncontrolled. n **turbulence** /'tɜːbjʊləns/.

turf /tɜːf/ n earth covered thickly with short grass; piece of this cut out. **the turf** = horseracing.

turgid /'tɜːdʒɪd/ adj swollen up; foolishly solemn; high-sounding (language, etc.).

turkey /'tɜːkɪ/ n kind of large bird used for food.

turmoil /'tɜːmɔɪl/ n noise and disorder.

turn /tɜːn/ v **1** (cause to) go round and round. **2** change the direction of movement or the place of, e.g. Turn to the right; Turn the stone over. **3** change in nature or quality; become. **the milk has turned** = it has become sour. **4** (with **on, off, out, up, down**) cause (a flow of electricity, water, gas) to begin, stop, increase or become less, e.g. Turn the lights off; Turn the radio down = make it produce less noise. **to turn down** = refuse (an offer etc.). **to turn out** = **1** produce (goods etc.). **2** put out by force. **3** empty (e.g. one's pockets when looking for something). **4** come out for a special reason. **5** become, prove to be in the end, e.g. The weather turned out fine. **to turn up** = arrive (unexpectedly); be found (by chance); appear. n **1** turning movement. **2** change in direction. **3** change in condition. **4** chance, proper time to do something (e.g. a duty). **in turn** = one after another. **to do a good turn** = do a kindness, helpful action (for someone).

turning /'tɜːnɪŋ/ n place where a road turns. n **turning-point** /'.. .,./ time when a great change begins, for better or worse.

turnip /'tɜːnɪp/ n (plant with a) large root used for food.

turnout /'tɜːnaʊt/ n **1** number of people at a meeting. **2** appearance; way one is dressed.

turnover /'tɜːnəʊvə'/ n amount of business done in a certain time.

turnstile /'tɜːnstaɪl/ n gate that turns so that only one person can pass at a time.

turpentine /'tɜːpəntaɪn/ n kind of oil obtained from certain trees, used for mixing paint.

turpitude /'tɜːpɪtjuːd/ n badness (of character).

turquoise /'tɜːkwɔɪz/ n (colour of a) green-blue precious stone. adj of this colour.

turret /'tʌrɪt/ n **1** little tower. **2** armoured house on a ship with guns in it and which can usually move round.

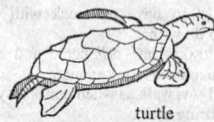

turtle

turtle /'tɜːtl/ n kind of sea animal with hard shell from which only the head, legs and tail come out. **to turn turtle** = (of a ship) turn upside-down.

tusk /tʌsk/ n long pointed tooth (of an elephant, etc.) that sticks out of the mouth.

tussle /'tʌsəl/ vi, n (have a) disorderly fight or struggle.

tutor /'tjuːtə'/ n (PRIVATE or university) teacher. v act as a tutor (to).

twaddle /'twɒdl/ n foolish talk.

twang /twæŋ/ n sound of a musical string being picked with the finger. v (cause to) make this sound.

tweak /twiːk/ vt, n (give a) sharp pull and twist (to).

tweed /twiːd/ n kind of soft woollen cloth, usually of mixed colours.

tweezers /'twiːzəz/ n small instrument with two

narrow arms joined at one end, used for picking up small objects, pulling out hairs, etc.

twelve /twelv/ *det, n* number following eleven, often written **12**. *adj, n* **twelfth** /twelfθ/ next in order after eleventh.

twenty /'twentɪ/ *det, n* number often written **20**, being two times ten.

twice /twaɪs/ *adv* two times.

twiddle /'twɪdl/ *v* aimlessly turn or twist round with the fingers.

twig /twɪg/ *n* thin branch or end of a branch of a tree or bush. *v infml* understand.

twilight /'twaɪlaɪt/ *n* half-light just before sunrise or just after sunset.

twill /twɪl/ *n* kind of strong cotton cloth.

twin /twɪn/ *n* **1** one of two children born together to the same mother. **2** one of two things completely like each other.

twine /twaɪn/ *n* thin string. *v* twist (round).

twinge /twɪndʒ/ *n* sudden sharp pain.

twinkle /'twɪŋkəl/ *vi* shine with an unsteady light as the stars do. *n* **twinkling** /'twɪŋklɪŋ/ **in a twinkling** = at once, without delay.

twirl /twɜːl/ *v* (cause to) turn or twist round quickly.

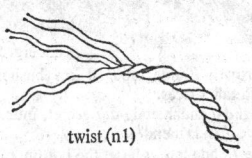

twist (n1)

twist /twɪst/ *v* **1** turn one thing round another; turn one end (of thread, etc.) while holding the other still. **2** change direction suddenly. **3** force a wrong meaning to (someone's words, etc.). *n* **1**

act of twisting; something made by twisting; sudden turn in a road, etc.

twitch /twɪtʃ/ *v* pull or move suddenly. *n* sudden quick pull; sudden uncontrolled movement of a muscle.

twitter /'twɪtə/ *vi* (of birds) make a lot of short, sharp sounds; sound like this when talking. *n* such sounds.

two /tuː/ *det, n* number following one, often written **2**.

tycoon /taɪ'kuːn/ *n* very rich and powerful businessman.

type /taɪp/ *n* **1** one person or thing considered as an example of a class or group. **2** special class or kind. **3** piece of metal with a letter cut on it, used in printing; letters, etc., printed in this way. *v* write on a TYPEWRITER.

typewriter /'taɪprˌaɪtə/ *n* machine with which one prints on paper by pressing keys with the fingers.

typhoid /'taɪfɔɪd/ *n* kind of serious disease of the stomach, etc., common in hot countries.

typhoon /taɪ'fuːn/ *n* violent storm, esp. in the China seas.

typhus /'taɪfəs/ *n* kind of serious disease causing red spots on the body.

typical /'tɪpɪkəl/ *adj* being a good example of a TYPE. *vt* **typify** /'tɪpɪfaɪ/ be an example of.

typist /'taɪpɪst/ *n* person who TYPES.

typography /taɪ'pɒgrəfɪ/ *n* art or manner of printing. *adj* **typographic(al)** /ˌtaɪpə'græfɪk(əl)/.

tyrant /'taɪərnt/ *n* cruel and unjust ruler. *n* **tyranny** /'tɪrənɪ/ rule of a tyrant; state of being under such a ruler. *adj* **tyrannical** /tɪ'rænɪkəl/ like a tyrant. *v* **tyrannize** /'tɪrənaɪz/ rule or behave (towards) like a tyrant.

tyre /'taɪə/ *n* outer ring of a wheel, usually made of rubber.

tyro /'taɪərəʊ/ see **tiro**.

U

ubiquitous /juː'bɪkwətəs/ *adj* found everywhere at the same time.

udder /'ʌdə/ *n* part of a cow (or other animal) from which milk comes.

ugly /'ʌglɪ/ *adj* **1** not beautiful, unpleasant to look at. **2** dangerous.

ulcer /'ʌlsə/ *n* poisoned place on the skin (or in the body) that produces PUS.

ulterior /ʌl'tɪərɪə/ *adj* lying on the further side or beyond. **an ulterior motive** = some reason for behaviour other than that shown or expressed.

ultimate /'ʌltɪmət/ *adj* furthest; last; BASIC.

ultimatum /ˌʌltɪ'meɪtəm/ *n* last demand and warning (e.g. one sent by a government—if it is refused, war may follow).

ultra- /'ʌltrə/ very; more than is usual or reasonable, e.g. *adj* **ultra-careful** /ˌ. . '. ./ very careful; too careful.

ultramarine /ˌʌltrəmə'riːn/ *n, adj* (of a) very bright blue colour.

ultraviolet /ˌʌltrə'vaɪələt/ *adj* (of light) having shorter light-waves than can be seen.

umbrage /'ʌmbrɪdʒ/ **to take umbrage (at)** = feel one has been treated without proper respect, show anger at (something said).

umbrella /ʌm'brelə/ *n* instrument made of a light frame covered with cloth, etc., which can be shut up or opened out, used to keep off the rain.

umpire /'ʌmpaɪə/ *n* person acting as a judge in a game.

umpteen /ʌmp'tiːn/ *sl* large number.

un- /ʌn/ **1** not, e.g. *adj* **unjust** /ʌn'dʒʌst/ not just. **2** do the opposite of, put something back as it was before, e.g. *vt* **untie** /ˌʌn'taɪ/ loosen (something tied).

umbrella

unaccountable /ˌʌnəˈkaʊntəbəl/ *adj* not able to be explained.

unalloyed /ˌʌnəˈlɔɪd/ *adj* (of pleasure, etc.) pure, not SPOILT; not mixed.

unanimous /juːˈnænɪməs/ *adj* being all of one opinion; agreed to by everyone. *n* **unanimity** /ˌjuːnəˈnɪmətɪ/.

unassuming /ˌʌnəˈsjuːmɪŋ/ *adj* not proud; not drawing attention to oneself; quiet in behaviour.

unaware /ˌʌnəˈweəʳ/ *adj* not knowing. *adv* **unawares** /ˌʌnəˈweəz/ by surprise, e.g. *Taken unawares* = surprised by some action for which one was not prepared.

unbalanced /ʌnˈbælənst/ *adj* not balanced. **of unbalanced mind** = mad.

unbecoming /ˌʌnbɪˈkʌmɪŋ/ *adj* not according to good manners; not well-suited, e.g. *She was wearing an unbecoming hat.*

unbend /ʌnˈbend/ *v* become less stiff; behave in an easier manner. *adj* **unbending** /ʌnˈbendɪŋ/ determined.

unbridled /ʌnˈbraɪdld/ *adj* (of anger, temper etc.) violent; uncontrolled.

unburden /ʌnˈbɜːdn/ **to unburden oneself** = make one's troubles easier by telling them to someone.

uncalled for /ʌnˈkɔːld fɔːʳ/ *adj* not necessary or desirable.

uncanny /ʌnˈkænɪ/ *adj* strange, unnatural.

uncle /ˈʌŋkl/ *n* brother of one's father or mother; husband of one's AUNT.

uncouth /ʌnˈkuːθ/ *adj* (of a person, his behaviour) rough and lacking good manners.

unction /ˈʌŋkʃən/ *n* putting on of holy oil.

unctuous /ˈʌŋktʃʊəs/ *adj* pretending to be very polite.

under[1] /ˈʌndəʳ/ *prep* **1** below (in place or rank); covered by. **2** less than, e.g. *Under age* = not (in law) old enough (to do something). **3** while; during; in the condition of, e.g. *Under sail* = while sailing. **under the circumstances** = while (or since) things are in this condition. **under orders** = having received orders.

under-[2] /ˈʌndəʳ/ **1** worn or placed below, e.g. *n* **underclothes** /ˈʌndəkləʊðz/ garments worn next to the skin, under others. **2** not enough, e.g. *vt* **undercharge** /ˌʌndəˈtʃɑːdʒ/ not charge enough in price.

undercurrent /ˈʌndəˌkʌrənt/ *n* hidden movement or feeling below what is first seen.

undercut /ˌʌndəˈkʌt/ *vt* offer goods, services, etc., at a lower price than (others) in order to get more trade.

underdog /ˈʌndədɒg/ *n* person who will probably lose; poor and helpless person treated badly by others.

underdone /ˌʌndəˈdʌn/ *adj* (of food) not completely cooked.

undergo /ˌʌndəˈgəʊ/ *vt* experience; suffer; pass through.

undergraduate /ˌʌndəˈgrædʒʊət/ *n* student at a university who has not yet got a degree.

underground /ˈʌndəgraʊnd/ *adj* below the ground; (of a movement against a government, etc.) secret. *n* underground railway. /ˌʌndəˈgraʊnd/ *adv*.

undergrowth

undergrowth /ˈʌndəgrəʊθ/ *n* low bushes, etc., among taller trees.

underhand /ˈʌndəhænd/ *adj* secret, intended to deceive. /ˌʌndəˈhænd/ *adv*.

underlie /ˌʌndəˈlaɪ/ *vt* be at the bottom of; form the BASIS or cause of.

underline /ˌʌndəˈlaɪn/ *vt* **1** draw a line under. **2** give special force or importance to; call attention to.

underling /ˈʌndəlɪŋ/ *derog n* person holding a low office under another.

undermine /ˌʌndəˈmaɪn/ *vt* **1** make a hole in the ground below (a wall, etc.) so as to weaken it. **2** slowly weaken, e.g. *Health undermined by overwork.*

underneath /ˌʌndəˈniːθ/ *adv, prep* below; under.

underrate /ˌʌndəˈreɪt/ *vt* not value highly enough.

understand /ˌʌndəˈstænd/ *v* **1** know the meaning, nature, etc., of. **2** learn; take to be true; accept as settled. *adj* **understandable** /ˌʌndəˈstændəbəl/ that can be understood. *adj* **understanding** /ˌʌndəˈstændɪŋ/ able to understand clearly someone's difficulties, feelings, etc. *n* **1** power of clear thought; knowledge. **2** agreement, e.g. *To reach an understanding with* = come to an agreement with. **3** condition, e.g. *On the understanding that* = on condition that.

understate /ˌʌndəˈsteɪt/ *vt* not say fully or strongly enough; say less than the truth about. *n* **understatement** /ˌʌndəˈsteɪtmənt/.

understood /ˌʌndəˈstʊd/ *p.t.* and *p.p.* of **understand**.

understudy /ˈʌndəˌstʌdɪ/ *n* one who learns the

part of an actor, etc., so as to be able to take his place if necessary.

undertake /ˌʌndə'teɪk/ vt take a duty upon oneself; promise to do a piece of work. n **undertaker** /'ʌndəteɪkə/ person who arranges funerals. n **undertaking** /ˌʌndə'teɪkɪŋ/ 1 work that one has undertaken. 2 promise.

undertone /'ʌndətəʊn/ n quiet or soft tone of voice or colour.

undertook /ˌʌndə'tʊk/ p.t. of **undertake**.

undertow /'ʌndətəʊ/ n strong backward flow of a wave from the shore.

underwear /'ʌndəweə/ n (sing) clothes worn under one's outer garments, next to one's skin.

underwent /ˌʌndə'went/ p.t. if **undergo**.

underworld /'ʌndəwɜ:ld/ n (sing) 1 (in old beliefs) place of the spirits of the dead. 2 all the lawbreakers in an area.

underwrite /ˌʌndə'raɪt/ vt (esp. of ships) promise to bear part of the possible loss of any business. n **underwriter** /'ʌndəraɪtə/.

undies /'ʌndɪz/ infml n (pl) women's underclothes.

undo /ʌn'du:/ v 1 unfasten, untie (e.g. a knot). 2 destroy the result of (something) and put things back in their former state, e.g. This mistake has undone all your good work. n **undoing** /ʌn'du:ɪŋ/ (cause of someone's) ruin.

undress /ʌn'dres/ vi take off one's clothes.

undue /ʌn'dju:/ adj more than is right or proper.

undulate /'ʌndjʊleɪt/ vi (of surfaces) move like waves; be shaped like a sea covered with waves. n **undulation** /ˌʌndjʊ'leɪʃən/.

unearth /ʌn'ɜ:θ/ vt dig up; discover and bring to light (something hidden).

unearthly /ʌn'ɜ:θlɪ/ adj very strange and frightening; not of this earth. infml **at an unearthly hour** = very early.

uneasy /ʌn'i:zɪ/ adj uncomfortable; anxious. n **uneasiness** /ʌn'i:zɪnəs/.

unfailing /ʌn'feɪlɪŋ/ adj never failing; always to be depended upon.

unfaithful /ʌn'feɪθfəl/ adj not faithful (esp. in marriage).

unfeeling /ʌn'fi:lɪŋ/ adj hard-hearted, unkind.

unfold /ʌn'fəʊld/ v 1 open the folds of. 2 make or become known.

unfounded /ʌn'faʊndɪd/ adj without reason; having no facts to prove it true.

ungainly /ʌn'geɪnlɪ/ adj ungraceful.

unheard-of /ʌn'hɜ:d ɒv/ adj most unusual; never known before.

unicorn /'ju:nɪkɔ:n/ n imaginary horse-like animal having one straight horn in the middle of its head.

uniform /'ju:nɪfɔ:m/ adj having the same form, being the same as others; never changing, e.g. A uniform heat in all parts of the house. n special dress that all members of a group wear, e.g. Soldiers' uniforms. n **uniformity** /ˌju:nɪ'fɔ:mətɪ/.

unify /'ju:nɪfaɪ/ vt make (many things) into one;

uniform

make the same, e.g. We must unify our aims. n **unification** /ˌju:nɪfɪ'keɪʃən/.

unimpeachable /ˌʌnɪm'pi:tʃəbəl/ adj that cannot be questioned or doubted, e.g. Of unimpeachable honesty.

union /'ju:nɪən/ n 1 act of making one; state of being one. 2 group treated as one (often formed for a special purpose), e.g. A trade union. **the Union Jack** = the flag of Great Britain and Northern Ireland.

unionist /'ju:nɪənɪst/ n member of a trade union.

unique /ju:'ni:k/ adj only one of its kind; completely different from all others. n **uniqueness** /ju:'ni:knəs/.

unison /'ju:nɪsən/ n agreement. **in unison** = together, e.g. To sing in unison = all sing the same note at the same time.

unit /'ju:nɪt/ n 1 single person or thing; group considered as one, e.g. A company is one unit in an army. 2 fixed quantity or amount by which measurements are made, e.g. A metre is a unit in measuring length.

unite /jʊ'naɪt/ v make or become one; join together. adj **united** /jʊ'naɪtɪd/. n **unity** /'ju:nətɪ/ state or feeling of being one, of being joined in one group; agreement.

universal /ˌju:nɪ'vɜ:səl/ adj of or for all; having to do with everyone; found everywhere; general, e.g. A universal rule = rule that is always true, or must be kept by all.

universe /'ju:nɪvɜ:s/ n all the suns, stars, etc.—everything that there is everywhere.

university /ˌju:nɪ'vɜ:sətɪ/ n place of higher learning that gives degrees.

unkempt /ʌn'kempt/ adj dirty or badly dressed; (of hair) unbrushed.

unless /ʌn'les/ conj if not; except when.

unlooked-for /ʌn'lʊkt fɔ:/ adj unexpected.

unmistakable /ˌʌnmɪ'steɪkəbəl/ adj about which no mistake can be made; clear.

unmitigated /ʌn'mɪtɪgeɪtɪd/ adj not softened or lessened in any way; complete, e.g. An unmitigated liar = a completely untruthful person.

unnerve /ʌnˈnɜːv/ *vt* cause (someone) to lose his self-control or courage.

unprecedented /ʌnˈpresɪdentɪd/ *adj* having no earlier example.

unravel /ʌnˈrævəl/ *v* **1** untie and straighten out (e.g. a string that is knotted); separate the threads of; become separate. **2** find the answer to or make clear (some difficult or hidden matter).

unremitting /ˌʌnrɪˈmɪtɪŋ/ *adj* unceasing.

unruffled /ʌnˈrʌfəld/ *adj* calm.

unruly /ʌnˈruːlɪ/ *adj* not easily controlled; refusing to obey.

unsavoury /ʌnˈseɪvərɪ/ *adj* unpleasant, nasty.

unsightly /ʌnˈsaɪtlɪ/ *adj* unpleasant to the eye; ugly.

unspeakable /ʌnˈspiːkəbəl/ *adj* that cannot be, unfit to be, put into words.

unthinkable /ʌnˈθɪŋkəbəl/ *adj* that one cannot get any idea of, etc.; not be considered.

until /ənˈtɪl/ *prep, conj* up to (the time when).

untold /ʌnˈtəʊld/ *adj* too great or too many to be measured.

unvarnished /ʌnˈvɑːnɪʃt/ **the unvarnished truth** = the plain truth without any attempt at hiding or making it look less bad.

unwieldy /ʌnˈwiːldɪ/ *adj* difficult to move or use easily (because of size or shape).

unwitting /ʌnˈwɪtɪŋ/ *adj* not knowing; not intending.

up /ʌp/ *prep* towards the top of; along. *adv* **1** in or to a higher place or state; upright. **2** out of bed; on one's feet. **3** close to, nearer, e.g. *He came up to me and asked me the way.* **4** completely, e.g. *Eat up your dinner.* **time's up** = the time allowed is over. **up to** = as far as; equal to, e.g. *Not up to much* = not very good. **it's up to you** = it is your duty; it is for you to decide. **what's he up to?** = what is he doing? **up to no good** = doing something wrong. *infml* **what's up?** = what is the matter? **ups and downs** = changes of fortune; good and bad times.

upbraid /ʌpˈbreɪd/ *vt* scold.

upbringing /ˈʌpbrɪŋɪŋ/ *n* training of a child.

upheaval /ʌpˈhiːvəl/ *n* great and sudden change (e.g. in the government).

uphill /ʌpˈhɪl/ *adv* up a slope. /ˈʌphɪl/ *adj* difficult, e.g. *Uphill work.*

uphold /ʌpˈhəʊld/ *vt* support (e.g. a decision).

upholster /ʌpˈhəʊlstəʳ/ *vt* fix springs and soft material into (chairs, etc.) and cover them with cloth, leather, etc. *n* **upholstery** /ʌpˈhəʊlstərɪ/.

upkeep /ˈʌpkiːp/ *n* (cost of) keeping something (e.g. a house) in good condition.

upland /ˈʌplənd/ *n* (often *pl*) high part(s) of a country.

uplift /ʌpˈlɪft/ *vt* (of thoughts or feelings) raise up to a higher level. /ˈʌplɪft/ *n* improvement of the mind or spirit.

upon /əˈpɒn/ *prep* on.

upper /ˈʌpəʳ/ *adj* higher. *n* upper part of a shoe which covers the top of the foot. *adj, adv* **upper-**

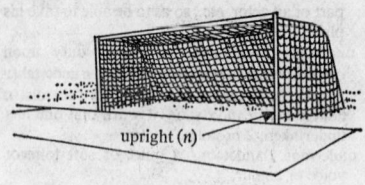

upright (*n*)

most /ˈʌpəməʊst/ highest.

upright /ˈʌpraɪt/ *adj* **1** standing straight up on end; at right angles to the ground. **2** honest and just. *n* upright post, etc.

uprising /ˈʌpraɪzɪŋ/ *n* rising against the government; REVOLT.

uproar /ˈʌprɔːʳ/ *n* excitement and noise. *adj* **uproarious** /ʌpˈrɔːrɪəs/ noisy; with, causing, much loud laughter.

upset /ʌpˈset/ *v* **1** turn over; knock over. **2** put into disorder; ruin, e.g. *This upsets my plans; The food upset me* = it made me ill. **3** trouble; make unhappy, e.g. *I'm very upset about it* = I am troubled and anxious. /ˈʌpset/ *n* upsetting.

upshot /ˈʌpʃɒt/ *n* result.

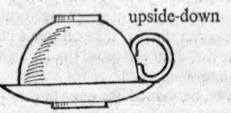

upside-down

upside-down /ˌʌpsaɪd ˈdaʊn/ *adv* with the bottom at the top; in disorder.

upstairs /ʌpˈsteəz/ *adv* to or on the upper floor (of a house). /ˈʌpsteəz/ *adj* on the upper floor.

upstream /ʌpˈstriːm/ *adv* against the flow of a river, stream, etc. /ˈʌpstriːm/ *adj*.

up-to-date /ˌʌp tə ˈdeɪt/ of the latest and newest kind.

upward /ˈʌpwəd/ *adj* going up. *adv* **upward(s)** /ˈʌpwəd(z)/ towards a higher place.

uranium /jʊˈreɪnɪəm/ *n* kind of heavy RADIOACTIVE metal.

urban /ˈɜːbən/ *adj* of or in a town. *vt* **urbanize** /ˈɜːbənaɪz/ make urban.

urbane /ɜːˈbeɪn/ *adj* very polite; with smooth manners. *n* **urbanity** /ɜːˈbænɪtɪ/.

urchin /ˈɜːtʃɪn/ *n* troublesome small boy.

urge /ɜːdʒ/ *vt* **1** push (a person) on to action; drive (an animal) faster. **2** press (upon) the attention of someone. *n* strong desire.

urgent /ˈɜːdʒənt/ *adj* pressing, important; that must be done at once. *n* **urgency** /ˈɜːdʒənsɪ/.

urine /ˈjʊərɪn/ *n* waste liquid from the body. *n* **urinal** /jʊˈraɪnəl/ place where men can go to urinate. *vi* **urinate** /ˈjʊərɪneɪt/ pass urine.

urn /ɜːn/ *n* **1** container used for the ashes of a dead person. **2** large metal container in which tea, coffee, etc., is made or kept warm.

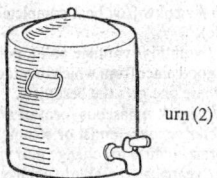

urn (2)

us /əs; *strong* ʌs/ *pron* (form of **we** used after verbs and prepositions).

usage /'juːzɪdʒ, 'juːsɪdʒ/ *n* **1** general custom. **2** way something is used; treatment.

use /juːz/ *vt* **1** employ for a purpose. **2** spend or finish by using. **to use up** = finish completely, e.g. *All the coal is used up* = there is no coal left. /juːs/ *n* **1** purpose; work that something can do. **2** act or condition of using or being used, e.g. *To come into use* = begin to be used. **3** value; worth, e.g. *It's no use waiting for him* = we gain nothing by waiting for him. *adj* **used** /juːzd/ already used; not new, e.g. *A used car*. *v* **used to** /'juːstə/ (*before consonants*), 'juːstʊ (*before vowels*)/ **1** (showing a past custom) e.g. *He used to go swimming every week*. **2** (showing a past state) e.g. *We used to be good friends*. **used to** = accustomed to, e.g. *I'm not used to heights*. *adj* **useful** /'juːsfəl/ such as can be used; helpful. *n* **usefulness** /'juːsfəlnəs/. *adj* **useless** /'juːsləs/ of no use; worthless; not helpful. *n* **uselessness** /'juːsləsnəs/.

usher /'ʌʃə ʸ/ *n* **1** person who shows people to their seats in a theatre, cinema, etc. **2** officer in charge of the door in a law-court, etc. *vt* show (someone) the way, lead (to a seat, room, etc.).

usual /'juːʒʊəl/ *adj* such as commonly happens; according to custom. *adv* **usually** /'juːʒʊəlɪ/ most often.

usurer /'juːʒərə ʸ/ *n* money lender (esp. one who charges high interest).

usurp /juːˈzɜːp/ *vt* seize by force and without right, e.g. *To usurp the throne* = make oneself king by force. *n* **usurper** /juːˈzɜːpə ʸ/.

usury /'juːʒərɪ/ *n* lending of money; high interest; demanding too much from one to whom money is lent.

utensil /juːˈtensəl/ *n* instrument; any container used in the home and kitchen.

utility /juːˈtɪlətɪ/ *n* usefulness, quality of being useful. **public utilities** = public services, supplying of gas, electricity, trains, etc. *adj* **utilitarian** /juːˌtɪləˈteərɪən/ of practical use only (rather than for ornament). *vt* **utilize** /'juːtəlaɪz/ put to use; make use of. *n* **utilization** /ˌjuːtɪlaɪˈzeɪʃən/.

utmost /'ʌtməʊst/ *adj* **1** farthest. **2** greatest. *n* the most that is possible, e.g. *To do one's utmost* = try as hard as possible.

Utopia /juːˈtəʊpɪə/ *n* imaginary perfect form of government. *adj* **Utopian** /juːˈtəʊpɪən/ perfect but imaginary and impossible.

utter[1] /'ʌtə ʸ/ *adj* complete, e.g. *He is an utter fool*.

utter[2] /'ʌtə ʸ/ *vt* say or make a sound with the mouth. *n* **utterance** /'ʌtərəns/ something spoken. **to give utterance to** = express in words.

uttermost /'ʌtəməʊst/ *adj* **1** farthest. **2** greatest.

V

vacancy /'veɪkənsɪ/ *n* emptiness; empty space; office for which a person is to be chosen. *adj* **vacant** /'veɪkənt/ **1** empty; not being filled. **2** showing no signs of interest, e.g. *A vacant look*. *vt* **vacate** /vəˈkeɪt/ leave empty, e.g. *To vacate a house* = cease to live in it.

vacation /vəˈkeɪʃən/ *n* **1** time when schools, law-courts, etc., are closed. **2** HOLIDAYS.

vaccinate /'væksɪneɪt/ *vt* protect against disease (esp. SMALLPOX) by putting vaccine into the body. *n* **vaccination** /ˌvæksɪˈneɪʃən/. *n* **vaccine** /'væksiːn/ substance used to protect people against a disease by giving them the disease in a slight, not dangerous form.

vacillate /'væsəleɪt/ *vi* be unable to decide; be uncertain in opinion.

vacuous /'vækjʊəs/ *adj* empty; showing lack of interest or understanding.

vacuum /'vækjʊəm/ *n* space completely empty of any substance or gas; space from which air has been removed. *n* **vacuum cleaner** /'.. ,. ./ machine that cleans floors, etc., by drawing in air and dust together.

vagabond /'vægəbɒnd/ *adj* moving from place to

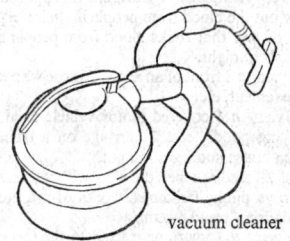

vacuum cleaner

place, without a home. *n* homeless wanderer.

vagary /'veɪgərɪ/ *n* strange idea, etc., for which there seems to be no good reason.

vagrant /'veɪgrənt/ *adj* leading a wandering life. *n* homeless wanderer—usually poor. *n* **vagrancy** /'veɪgrənsɪ/.

vague /veɪg/ *adj* **1** not clear. **2** not certain; not clearly expressed. *n* **vagueness** /'veɪgnəs/.

vain /veɪn/ *adj* **1** valueless; useless; having no result. **2** too proud of one's looks or abilities. **in vain** = without result or success.

valet /ˈvæleɪ/ *n* manservant, with the special duty of looking after his employer's clothes.

valiant /ˈvælɪənt/ *adj* brave.

valid /ˈvælɪd/ *adj* **1** correct according to law; usable, e.g. *A valid ticket.* **2** sound, well-supported, e.g. *A valid argument* = one that can be defended. *vt* **validate** /ˈvælɪdeɪt/ make valid. *n* **validity** /vəˈlɪdətɪ/.

valise /vəˈliːz/ *n* kind of bag used for clothes, etc., when travelling.

valley /ˈvælɪ/ *n* area of low land between mountains or hills.

valour /ˈvælə/ *n* great courage.

value /ˈvæljuː/ *n* **1** usefulness; importance. **2** what something is considered to be worth. *vt* **1** say what something is worth. **2** consider to be of great worth. *adj* **valuable** /ˈvæljʊəbəl/ of great value.

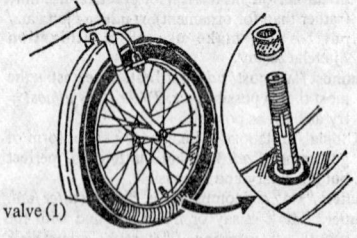

valve (1)

valve /vælv/ *n* **1** part of a machine that allows gas or liquid to flow through it, when opened in one direction only; part of the heart that allows blood to flow in one direction only. **2** glass tube emptied of air, used in radios, etc. (today TRAN-SISTORS are often used instead of valves).

vampire /ˈvæmpaɪə/ *n* **1** evil spirit supposed to draw out the blood from people in their sleep. **2** kind of BAT that sucks blood from people and animals at night.

van[1] /væn/ *n* **1** front of an army. **2** those who lead a movement, etc.

van[2] /væn/ *n* **1** covered motor vehicle used for carrying goods, etc. **2** carriage on a train in which boxes and bags are put.

vandal /ˈvændl/ *n* person who without reason destroys public buildings, works of art, etc. *n* **vandalism** /ˈvændəl-ɪzəm/.

vane /veɪn/ *n* **1** instrument fixed to the top of a building to show which way the wind is blowing. **2** one blade of a wheel turned by air-power or water-power.

vanguard /ˈvænɡɑːd/ *n* that part of an army which marches in front and protects the rest.

vanilla /vəˈnɪlə/ *n* kind of plant whose seeds are used to give a pleasant taste to sweet foods.

vanish /ˈvænɪʃ/ *vi* disappear suddenly.

vanity /ˈvænətɪ/ *n* **1** quality of being too proud of one's looks or abilities. **2** emptiness, worthlessness, e.g. *The vanity of earthly greatness.*

vanquish /ˈvæŋkwɪʃ/ *vt* beat completely (usually in battle).

vantage /ˈvɑːntɪdʒ/ **vantage point, point of van-tage** = good place from which to attack or place from where one gets the best view.

vapour /ˈveɪpə/ *n* gaseous form of a substance, e.g. *Water vapour* = mist or steam. *v* **vaporize** /ˈveɪpəraɪz/ (cause to) change into vapour.

variable /ˈveərɪəbəl/ *adj* able to change; changing easily or often. *n* **variability** /ˌveərɪəˈbɪlətɪ/.

variance /ˈveərɪəns/ **at variance with** = not in agreement with.

variant /ˈveərɪənt/ *adj* different. *n* something different in form though really the same, e.g. another way of writing the same word.

variety /vəˈraɪətɪ/ *n* **1** state of being different, of not always being the same. **2** collection of different things. **3** one sort or kind, e.g. *This is one variety of rose. adj* **various** /ˈveərɪəs/ of many kinds; different; several.

varnish /ˈvɑːnɪʃ/ *n* kind of clear liquid which, when dry, gives a hard, shiny surface to wood, etc. *vt* cover with varnish.

vary /ˈveərɪ/ *v* to change; make one thing unlike another. *n* **variation** /ˌveərɪˈeɪʃən/.

vase /vɑːz/ *n* ornamental pot or container for holding flowers, etc.

vassal /ˈvæsəl/ *n* one who in ancient times held land, and promised (in return for the use of land) to serve his master as a soldier.

vast /vɑːst/ *adj* very large.

vat /væt/ *n* kind of large barrel or other container for holding liquids.

vault[1] /vɔːlt/ *v* jump (over) in one movement, with the help of the hands or a pole.

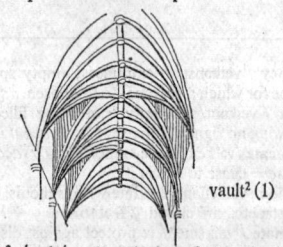

vault² (1)

vault[2] /vɔːlt/ *n* **1** arched roof. **2** underground room (esp. one used as a grave or for keeping wine, etc.). *adj* **vaulted** having an arched roof.

vaunt /vɔːnt/ *v* make a proud show of; speak proudly.

veal /viːl/ *n* meat of very young cattle.

veer /vɪə/ *vi* turn; esp. of the wind) change direction.

vegetable /ˈvedʒtəbəl/ *adj* of, from, having to do with, plants. *n* plant used for food. *n* **vegetarian** /ˌvedʒɪˈteərɪən/ person who does not eat meat. *vi* **vegetate** /ˈvedʒɪteɪt/ live a very uninteresting and inactive life. *n* **vegetation** /ˌvedʒɪˈteɪʃən/ plant life in general; plants growing in one place.

vehement /'viːəmənt/ *adj* having strong feelings and (speaking with) very great force; fierce and eager. *n* **vehemence** /'viːəməns/.

vehicle /'viːɪkəl/ *n* 1 anything that can be used for carrying persons or goods (e.g. cart, carriage, car, bicycle, etc.). 2 means by which thoughts, feelings, etc., can be expressed or passed on. *adj* **vehicular** /vɪ'hɪkjələ/.

veil /veɪl/ *n* 1 covering of fine material for the face or head. 2 anything that hides or covers, e.g. *Hidden behind a veil of mist*. *vt* cover with a veil; hide, e.g. *To veil one's meaning in strange language*.

vein /veɪn/ *n* 1 blood-vessel that carries blood back to the heart. 2 fine line of material or colour that looks like a vein in something, e.g. *The veins on a leaf; Veins of metal in a rock*. 3 state of mind; tone, e.g. *In a more cheerful vein*.

veld(t) /velt/ *n* open grass country in South Africa.

vellum /'veləm/ *n* fine white skin of an animal prepared for writing on.

velocity /və'lɒsətɪ/ *n* speed.

velvet /'velvɪt/ *n* kind of cotton or silk material with short brushed threads standing upright on the surface. *adj* made of velvet; soft like velvet.

venal /'viːnəl/ *adj* (of a person) who can be made to do wrong by being paid money; (of an action) done for money.

vendetta /ven'detə/ *n* quarrel between families (e.g. in Corsica) in which each kills members of the other family.

vendor /'vendə/ *n* person who sells.

veneer /və'nɪə/ *vt* cover cheaper wood with thin sheets of good quality wood. *n* 1 thin sheet so used. 2 surface appearance (e.g. of politeness) that hides the true (and usually bad) nature of something.

venerate /'venəreɪt/ *vt* honour; respect greatly. *adj* **venerable** /'venərəbəl/ worthy of respect (because of age, experience, etc.). *n* **veneration** /ˌvenə'reɪʃən/.

venereal /və'nɪərɪəl/ *adj* (of disease) caused or spread by sexual acts.

vengeance /'vendʒəns/ *n* doing of wrong to another as a punishment for wrong done to oneself; REVENGE. *infml* **with a vengeance** = violently; very thoroughly; very much.

venial /'viːnɪəl/ *adj* (of a mistake or wrong) that may easily be forgiven; not serious.

venison /'venɪsən/ *n* meat of deer.

venom /'venəm/ *n* 1 poison (esp. of a snake, etc.). 2 hate. *adj* **venomous** /'venəməs/ 1 poisonous. 2 full of hatred and anger.

vent /vent/ *n* 1 small hole or outlet for air, gas, liquid, etc. 2 opening in the back of a coat, etc. 3 outlet for one's feelings, eg. *He gave vent to his anger in strong language*. *vt* express a feeling, e.g. *To vent one's anger on* = let out the force of one's anger upon.

ventilate /'ventɪleɪt/ *vt* 1 cause fresh air to flow through (a room, etc.). 2 make (a question,

one's opinions) widely known. *n* **ventilation** /ˌventɪ'leɪʃən/.

venture /'ventʃə/ *n* risky course of action. *v* 1 go into danger; take the risk of danger; be brave enough (to). 2 dare; go so far as (to). *adj* **venturesome** /'ventʃəsəm/ daring; risky.

venue /'venjuː/ *n* place where an event (e.g. a race, a football match) happens.

veracious /və'reɪʃəs/ *adj* true; truthful. *n* **veracity** /və'ræsətɪ/.

verandah

veranda(h) /və'rændə/ *n* covered open place with a floor along the side of a house, etc.

verb /vɜːb/ *n* word used in naming an action or state of the subject, such as 'destroy', 'ask', 'know', etc.

verbal /'vɜːbəl/ *adj* 1 having to do with words. **a verbal message** = one spoken, not written. 2 having to do with a verb.

verbatim /vɜː'beɪtɪm/ *adj, adv* in exactly the same words.

verbose /vɜː'bəʊs/ *adj* using more words than are necessary. *n* **verbosity** /vɜː'bɒsətɪ/.

verdant /'vɜːdənt/ *adj* fresh and green.

verdict /'vɜːdɪkt/ *n* 1 decision reached by a JURY after the facts have been given in a court of law. 2 opinion or judgment given after careful thought, etc.

verdure /'vɜːdʒə/ *n* fresh green grass, etc.; the greenness of growing things.

verge /vɜːdʒ/ *n* edge; border. **on the verge of** = close to; about to (do something). **to verge (up)on** = come near the edge of; be very close to.

verger /'vɜːdʒə/ *n* man in a church who leads people to their seats.

verify /'verɪfaɪ/ *vt* 1 make sure whether something is true or not. 2 show the truth of (e.g. something said); prove. *n* **verification** /ˌverɪfɪ'keɪʃən/.

verisimilitude /ˌverɪsɪ'mɪlɪtjuːd/ *n* appearance of truth.

veritable /'verɪtəbəl/ *adj* true; real.

vermilion /və'mɪlɪən/ *n, adj* (of a) bright red colour.

vermin /'vɜːmɪn/ *n* (*pl*) 1 small animals (e.g. rats) that do damage or harm. 2 insects (e.g. LICE) that live on the bodies of (dirty) animals or people. *adj* **verminous** /'vɜːmɪnəs/ full of vermin; caused by vermin.

vermouth /'vɜːməθ/ *n* kind of bitter wine.

vernacular /və'nækjʊlə/ *adj, n* (of the) local or native language of an area or country.

versatile /'vɜːsətaɪl/ *adj* able to do many different things well. *n* **versatility** /ˌvɜːsə'tɪlətɪ/.

verse /vɜːs/ *n* **1** group of lines in a poem. **2** poetry. **3** short numbered part of a chapter of the Bible.

versed /vɜːst/ **versed in** = clever at; experienced in; knowing much of.

version /'vɜːʃən/ *n* **1** one person's account of certain events, from his point of view. **2** something TRANSLATED from another language.

versus /'vɜːsəs/ *Latin prep* (usually shortened to **v**) against, e.g. *The football match was England v Scotland.*

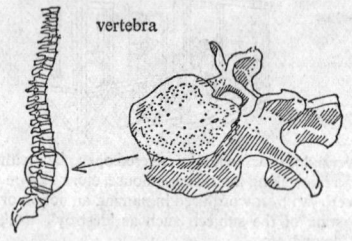

vertebra

vertebra /'vɜːtɪbrə/ *n* (*pl* **vertebrae** /'vɜːtɪbriː/) one of the bones that make up the backbone. *n,* *adj* **vertebrate** /'vɜːtɪbrət/ (animal) that has a backbone.

vertical /'vɜːtɪkəl/ *adj* upright; at right angles to the surface of the earth.

verve /vɜːv/ *n* spirit and force in the work of a writer, painter or musician.

very /'verɪ/ *adv* to a marked degree, more than usually, e.g. *It is very cold. adj* this and no other; exact, e.g. *The very thing I wanted.* **at the very end** = right at the end.

vespers /'vespəz/ *n* (*pl*) evening service in a church; evening prayers.

vessel /'vesəl/ *n* **1** pot or container of any kind (esp. for liquids). **2** ship or large boat.

vest¹ /vest/ *n* garment worn on the upper part of the body next to the skin.

vest² /vest/ **to vest power in** = give right or power to.

vestige /'vestɪdʒ/ *n* mark or sign left behind by something that has now passed on or been destroyed.

vestments /'vestmənts/ *n* (*pl*) official clothes, esp. those worn by a priest when performing a ceremony. *n* **vestry** /'vestrɪ/ room in a church where the priest puts on his vestments.

vet /vet/ *infml n* short form of **veterinary surgeon.** *vt* examine (a plan) before putting it into action; examine (a person) before giving him employment.

veteran /'vetərən/ *n, adj* old and experienced (person), esp. (as) a soldier.

veterinary /'vetrɪnərɪ/ *adj* having to do with the diseases of animals. *n* **veterinary surgeon** /ˌ.... ˈ../ person skilled in treating the diseases of animals.

veto /'viːtəʊ/ *n* right of a person (e.g. king) to forbid a law being made; any right to forbid something. *vt* use a veto against; forbid.

vex /veks/ *vt* trouble; make angry. *n* **vexation** /vek'seɪʃən/ *n* state of being vexed; something that vexes one.

via /'vaɪə/ *prep* by way of; passing through on the way, e.g. *He flew to Rome via Paris.*

viable /'vaɪəbəl/ *adj* **1** able to live. **2** that can be put into practice; workable.

viaduct /'vaɪədʌkt/ *n* long bridge over a valley carrying a road or railway line.

vibrate /vaɪ'breɪt/ *v* **1** (cause to) shake rapidly like the string of a musical instrument. **2** produce sound in this way; sound shaky. *adj* **vibrant** /'vaɪbrənt/ vibrating. *n* **vibration** /vaɪ'breɪʃən/ vibrating movement.

vicar /'vɪkə/ *n* priest in charge of an English church. *n* **vicarage** /'vɪkərɪdʒ/ house in which a vicar lives.

vicarious /vɪ'keərɪəs/ *adj* done or felt by someone in place of someone else.

vice¹ /vaɪs/ *n* serious fault of character; low and bad behaviour.

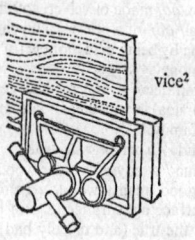

vice²

vice² /vaɪs/ *n* instrument (fixed to a table) used for holding something (e.g. a piece of wood) very tightly while one works on it.

vice-³ /vaɪs/ acting for; working instead of; second in rank to, e.g. *n* **viceroy** /'vaɪsrɔɪ/ governor who rules in place of a king or queen. *adj* **viceregal** /vaɪs'riːgəl/ of a viceroy.

vice versa /ˌvaɪsɪ 'vɜːsə/ *Latin adv* the other way round with the relations considered in the opposite way, e.g. *I hate him, and vice versa* = I hate him and he hates me.

vicinity /vɪ'sɪnətɪ/ *n* nearness; area round about.

vicious /'vɪʃəs/ *adj* **1** of bad character; given up to VICE¹. **2** fierce; intending to harm, e.g. *A vicious dog.* **a vicious circle** = set of bad conditions that act on each other so that the one produces the other, from which there seems to be no escape.

victim /'vɪktɪm/ *n* person, animal who suffers as the result of some force or action beyond his or its control, e.g. *He was the victim of fate. vt* **victimize** /'vɪktɪmaɪz/ make a victim of; cause to suffer. *n* **victimization** /ˌvɪktɪmaɪ'zeɪʃən/.

victor /'vɪktə/ *n* person who conquers; winner.

victory /'vɪktərɪ/ n sucess in battle or in a game. *adj* **victorious** /vɪk'tɔːrɪəs/ having won a victory.

victual /'vɪtl/ v supply with food and drink. n (*pl*) food and drink.

vie /vaɪ/ **to vie with** = try to do better than (someone else); try hard to beat.

view /vjuː/ n **1** sight, e.g. *In full view of all* = seen by all. **2** something looked at, e.g. *A beautiful view* = sight of a stretch of beautiful country. **3** opinion, e.g. *A point of view* = way of looking at a question. **in view of** = because of; considering. **4** purpose; desire; intention, e.g. *I will try to meet your views* = I will try to do what you want. **with a view to** = for the purpose of, with the intention of. *vt* look at; regard; consider.

viewer /'vjuːə/ n person who watches television.

vigil /'vɪdʒɪl/ n act of staying awake to keep watch or to pray, etc. *adj* **vigilant** /'vɪdʒɪlənt/ awake and watchful. n **vigilance** /'vɪdʒɪləns/.

vigour /'vɪgə/ n strength; power of mind or body. *adj* **vigorous** /'vɪgərəs/ full of power; strong; forceful.

vile /vaɪl/ *adj* of very bad character; shameful, DISGUSTING. *vt* **vilify** /'vɪlɪfaɪ/ say evil or vile things about (someone).

villa /'vɪlə/ n kind of house standing in its own garden, in the country or on the edge of a town.

village /'vɪlɪdʒ/ n group of houses, shops, etc., smaller than a town.

villain /'vɪlən/ n bad person; wrongdoer.

vindicate /'vɪndɪkeɪt/ *vt* prove (a claim, etc.) to be just or true; prove to be good (something that has been attacked or questioned). n **vindication** /ˌvɪndɪ'keɪʃən/.

vindictive /vɪn'dɪktɪv/ *adj* unforgiving; desiring to do harm to another as a punishment for harm done to oneself.

vine /vaɪn/ n kind of climbing plant, esp. one that bears GRAPES. n **vineyard** /'vɪnjəd/ area of land planted with vines.

vinegar /'vɪnɪgə/ n kind of very sour liquid, sometimes made from wine, used in cooking and to preserve food.

vintage /'vɪntɪdʒ/ n **1** act of gathering GRAPES; time of gathering grapes. **2** wine produced in a particular year.

viola /vɪ'əʊlə/ n kind of musical instrument with four strings, slightly larger than a VIOLIN.

violate /'vaɪəleɪt/ *vt* break (a promise, an agreement, etc.). **2** treat (something holy) with disrespect, e.g. *To violate a person's grave.* n **violation** /ˌvaɪə'leɪʃən/.

violent /'vaɪələnt/ *adj* **1** showing great or uncontrolled force, e.g. *A violent storm.* **2** caused by force, e.g. *A violent death.* **3** very bad, e.g. *A violent pain.* n **violence** /'vaɪələns/.

violet /'vaɪələt/ n **1** a kind of small flower. **2** blue-red colour. *adj* of this colour.

violin /vaɪə'lɪn/ n kind of musical instrument with four strings, played with a BOW. n **violinist** /vaɪə'lɪnɪst/ person who plays a violin.

violin

viper /'vaɪpə/ n kind of small poisonous snake.

virgin /'vɜːdʒɪn/ n person who has not experienced the sexual act. *adj* **1** pure, untouched. **2** unused (by humans), e.g. *Virgin forests.* *adj* **virginal** /'vɜːdʒɪnəl/ of or like a virgin; pure. n **virginity** /və'dʒɪnətɪ/.

virile /'vɪraɪl/ *adj* having the powers and character of a full-grown man; powerful, active, strong. n **virility** /və'rɪlətɪ/.

virtual /'vɜːtʃʊəl/ *adj* being in fact, though not in name or openly accepted as such, e.g. *The virtual head of the business.*

virtue /'vɜːtʃuː/ n goodness of character; good quality; advantage. **in (by) virtue of** = because of. *adj* **virtuous** /'vɜːtʃʊəs/ having or showing virtue; (sexually) pure.

virulent /'vɪrʊlənt/ *adj* **1** very poisonous; very harmful. **2** full of hatred or bad feeling; bitter. n **virulence** /'vɪrʊləns/.

virus /'vaɪərəs/ n kind of poison (formed by GERMS) that causes and spreads disease.

visa /'viːzə/ n official stamp put on a PASSPORT to show that the owner has permission to enter or leave a particular foreign country.

vis-à-vis /ˌviːz ɑː 'viː/ *prep* **1** face to face with. **2** in relation to.

viscount /'vaɪkaʊnt/ n nobleman next in rank below an EARL.

viscous /'vɪskəs/ *adj* thick; sticky (e.g. thick oil). n **viscosity** /vɪ'skɒsətɪ/.

visible /'vɪzəbəl/ *adj* able to be seen; in sight. n **visibility** /ˌvɪzə'bɪlətɪ/ range within which one can see (according to the weather and light).

vision /'vɪʒən/ n **1** power of seeing; power of imagination. **2** thing believed to be seen, e.g. *A vision of the future.* *adj* **visionary** /'vɪʒənərɪ/ **1** seen in a vision; unreal; imaginary. **2** (of a person) having ideas that cannot be carried out.

visit /'vɪzɪt/ v go to see (a person or place) for a time. n act of visiting; short stay in a place, e.g. *To pay someone a visit.* n **visitor** /'vɪzɪtə/ person who makes a visit. n **visitation** /ˌvɪzɪ'teɪʃən/ **1** official visiting. **2** some terrible event considered as a punishment sent by God.

visor /'vaɪzə/ n **1** iron covering for the face. **2** something that sticks out so as to shade the eyes (e.g. the front part of a cap).

vista /'vɪstə/ n long narrow view; such a view (seen in the mind) of many events one after another.

visual /'vɪʒʊəl/ *adj* having to do with sight. *vt* **visualize** /'vɪʒʊəlaɪz/ call up (something) as a picture in the mind.

vital /'vaɪtl/ *adj* **1** having to do with life; necessary for life. **2** very important; very

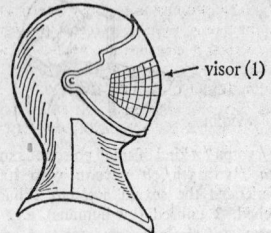

visor (1)

necessary. *n* **vitality** /vaɪ'tælətɪ/ vital force; driving force.

vitamin /'vɪtəmɪn/ *n* substance of various sorts, found in certain foods, that is necessary for health.

vitiate /'vɪʃɪeɪt/ *vt* destroy the force or value of; lower the quality of, e.g. *His book is vitiated by mistakes.*

vitreous /'vɪtrɪəs/ *adj* of or like glass.

vitriol /'vɪtrɪəl/ *n* kind of powerful acid (also called SULPHURIC acid). *adj* **vitriolic** /ˌvɪtrɪ'ɒlɪk/ bitter, full of hatred, e.g. *She has a vitriolic tongue* = she speaks very cruelly.

vituperate /vaɪ'tjuːpəreɪt/ *v* curse; speak angrily about.

vivacious /vɪ'veɪʃəs/ *adj* full of life and spirit. *n* **vivacity** /vɪ'væsətɪ/.

vivid /'vɪvɪd/ *adj* 1 full of life, e.g. *A vivid imagination.* 2 (of colours) bright and clear. 3 giving a clear picture, e.g. *A vivid description.*

vivisect /ˌvɪvɪ'sekt/ *vt* cut open (the body of an animal) while still alive for the purpose of making scientific discoveries. *n* **vivisection** /ˌvɪvɪ'sekʃən/.

vixen /'vɪksən/ *n* female fox.

viz /vɪz/ (short for. Latin, *videlicet* = you may see; often read aloud as "namely" /'neɪmlɪ/) that is, these are, e.g. *Great Britain is divided into three parts, viz. England, Scotland, Wales.*

vizier /vɪ'zɪəʳ/ *n* official of high rank in Muslim countries.

vocabulary /və'kæbjʊlərɪ/ *n* 1 whole set of words known or used by a writer or speaker. 2 list of the words used in a certain book (usually with explanations).

vocal /'vəʊkəl/ *adj* having to do with the voice; using the voice. *n* **vocalist** /'vəʊkəlɪst/ singer.

vocation /vəʊ'keɪʃən/ *n* 1 special calling to or fitness for certain work. 2 person's usual employment. *adj* **vocational** /vəʊ'keɪʃənəl/.

vociferate /və'sɪfəreɪt/ *v* shout. *adj* **vociferous** /və'sɪfərəs/.

vodka /'vɒdkə/ *n* kind of Russian strong drink.

vogue /vəʊg/ *n* that which is admired or liked by many people at a particular time; FASHION, e.g. *Long skirts are in vogue.*

voice /vɔɪs/ *n* sound produced in speaking or singing; ability to make such a sound. **to have a voice in something** = have a right to give one's opinion or help in deciding something. *vt* express in words.

void /vɔɪd/ *adj* 1 empty. 2 of no effect or force, e.g. *The agreement was void* = it was of no value according to law. **void of** = empty of, without.

volatile /'vɒlətaɪl/ *adj* 1 (of a liquid) that changes easily into a gas. 2 (of a person) quickly changing in one's ideas or state of mind.

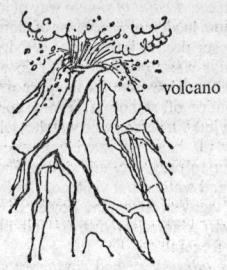

volcano

volcano /vɒl'keɪnəʊ/ *n* mountain with a deep hole in the top from which fire and smoke come out. *adj* **volcanic** /vɒl'kænɪk/.

vole /vəʊl/ *n* kind of small animal like a rat.

volition /və'lɪʃən/ *n* act or power of choosing or using the will.

volley /'vɒlɪ/ *n* number of shots fired at the same time; number of things thrown together or very quickly one after the other, e.g. *A volley of questions.* *v* (in games) hit (a ball) before it touches the ground.

volt /vəʊlt/ *n* measure of electrical force. *n* **voltage** /'vəʊltɪdʒ/ electrical force measured in volts.

voluble /'vɒljʊbəl/ *adj* talking quickly and easily, with a great flow of words. *n* **volubility** /ˌvɒljʊ'bɪlətɪ/.

volume /'vɒljuːm/ *n* 1 book, esp. one of a set. 2 large mass or amount, e.g. *A great volume of water.* 3 amount of space filled by a liquid, gas or a substance. 4 amount of sound that something makes; loudness, e.g. *Please turn down the volume of your radio.* *adj* **voluminous** /və'ljuːmɪnəs/ great in quantity; filling much space.

voluntary /'vɒləntərɪ/ *adj* 1 acting of one's own free will, not forced; done willingly. 2 supported by unpaid work and gifts.

volunteer /ˌvɒlən'tɪəʳ/ *n* 1 person who offers to do something, esp. a difficult or dangerous piece of work, without pay. 2 person who serves as a soldier of his own choice. *v* offer (to do some special piece of work); offer to serve as a soldier.

voluptuous /və'lʌptʃʊəs/ *adj* causing, given up to, pleasures of the senses.

vomit /'vɒmɪt/ *v* 1 throw up (food) from the stomach. 2 send out in great quantities.

voodoo /'vuːduː/ *n* kind of magic practised by certain people in the West Indies.

voracious /və'reɪʃəs/ *adj* having a strong desire for food; difficult to satisfy, e.g. *A voracious reader.* *n* **voracity** /və'ræsətɪ/.

vortex /'vɔːteks/ *n* mass of liquid (e.g. a part of the sea) turning round very quickly, which draws things towards its centre.

votary /'vəʊtərɪ/ *n* person who gives himself up completely to some work of a public or religious kind.

vote /vəʊt/ *v* show one's choice (e.g. in electing a person); show one's opinion in a meeting. *n* **1** expression of one's choice or opinion; right to do so. **2** total number of votes given to a party or person. *n* **voter** /'vəʊtə^r/ person who votes or who has the right to vote.

vouch /vaʊtʃ/ *vi* declare that something is correct or dependable; GUARANTEE, e.g. *To vouch for a person's honesty.*

voucher /'vaʊtʃə^r/ *n* piece of paper showing that money has been paid, or that the holder has a right to goods or service.

vow /vaʊ/ *vi* promise solemnly (usually to God, or in the name of God). *n* solemn promise.

vowel /'vaʊəl/ *n* speech sound made without any blockage or FRICTION in the mouth; letter, etc., standing for such a sound, e.g. *a, e, i, o, u.*

voyage /'vɔɪ-ɪdʒ/ *vi, n* (make a) sea journey.

vulgar /'vʌlgə^r/ *adj* rough, bad-mannered; in bad taste; rude. *n* **vulgarity** /vʌl'gærətɪ/.

vulnerable /'vʌlnərəbəl/ *adj* unprotected against attack; easily damaged or wounded. *n* **vulnerability** /ˌvʌlnərə'bɪlətɪ/.

vulture

vulture /'vʌltʃə^r/ *n* kind of large bird that feeds on the (decaying) bodies of dead animals.

W

wad /wɒd/ *n* small mass of material packed round a thing to prevent it from moving, or used to fill a hole. *n* **wadding** /'wɒdɪŋ/ soft material used for packing.

waddle /'wɒdl/ *vi* walk with short steps, like a duck.

wade /weɪd/ *vi* walk through water. **to wade through a book** = read a long book with difficulty. *n* **waders** /'weɪdəz/ high boots used for walking in water.

wadi /'wɒdɪ/ *n* water-course in North Africa, etc., which is dry in summer.

wafer /'weɪfə^r/ *n* **1** flour, sugar, etc., cooked in the form of a very thin cake. **2** a small round piece of paper or other material stuck on the back of a letter to close it.

waffle[1] /'wɒfəl/ *vi* talk continuously without really saying anything.

waffle[2] /'wɒfəl/ *n* a kind of soft, crisp cake eaten hot.

waft /wɒft/ *v* carry or be carried lightly through the air, as wind carries a leaf.

wag[1] /wæg/ *v* move from side to side or up and down, e.g. *A dog wags its tail.*

wag[2] /wæg/ *n* clever and amusing talker.

wage[1] /weɪdʒ/ *n* amount of money paid for work.

wage[2] /weɪdʒ/ *vt* carry on (a war).

wager /'weɪdʒə^r/ *n* promise made between two persons that Mr. A is to pay Mr. B if a certain event happens, B is to pay A if it does not happen; amount of money so promised. *vt* make such a promise.

waggle /'wægəl/ *v* move slightly backwards and forwards.

wagon, waggon /'wægən/ *n* strong cart; container on wheels used on the railway.

waif /weɪf/ *n* homeless person or animal.

wail /weɪl/ *vi* cry out with grief.

waist /weɪst/ *n* narrow part of the human body just above the legs. *n* **waistcoat** /'weɪskət, 'weɪskəʊt/ close-fitting garment reaching to the waist, worn under a coat.

wait /weɪt/ *vi* **1** stay or stop until something happens or until someone comes. **2** bring food to the table. *n* time spent waiting. *n* **waiter** /'weɪtə^r/ man, e.g. in a RESTAURANT, who brings food to the table. *n* **waitress** /'weɪtrəs/ woman who does this. *n* **lady-in-waiting** /'. . . '. ./ lady of high rank attending on the queen.

waive /weɪv/ *vt* give up, for a time or for ever, e.g. *To waive a claim.*

wake[1] /weɪk/ *n* watching all night by the dead.

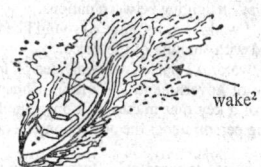

wake[2]

wake[2] /weɪk/ *n* track behind a ship moving through water. **in the wake of** = following.

wake[3] /weɪk/ **wake up, waken** /'weɪkən/ *v* cease

289

cause (someone) to cease sleeping; make or become awake. *adj* **wakeful** /'weɪkfəl/ not sleeping; not feeling desire for sleep.

walk /wɔːk/ *vi* move by putting one foot in front of the other. *vt* take (e.g. a dog) for a walk. *n* act of walking, distance walked. *n* **walkover** /'wɔːk͵əʊvə'/ easy victory. **walk of life** = rank or employment.

wall /wɔːl/ *n* thing built of bricks or stone, e.g. as the side of a house; any flat upright dividing surface. **walls have ears** = others may hear us. **run one's head against a wall** = try to do an impossible thing. **with one's back to the wall** = fighting with no way of escape; **to go to the wall** = be pushed away as useless, be the loser.

wallaby /'wɒləbɪ/ *n* small KANGAROO.

wallet /'wɒlɪt/ *n* bag; pocket-case for money.

wallflower /'wɔːlflaʊə'/ *n* **1** a kind of flower. **2** woman at a party without a man to dance with her.

wallop /'wɒləp/ *n, vt* (strike with a) heavy blow.

wallow /'wɒləʊ/ *vi* roll about in liquid or dirt—as a pig does.

walnut /'wɔːlnʌt/ *n* **1** eatable nut—the shell of a walnut is rough and easily divided into two parts. **2** wood of the walnut tree.

walrus /'wɔːlrəs/ *n* large sea creature with two large teeth standing out from the face with the ends pointing downwards.

waltz /wɒls/ *vi, n* (do a) dance made up of six steps, for two persons dancing together.

wan /wɒn/ *adj* without colour in the face, looking ill and tired.

wand /wɒnd/ *n* thin stick carried in the hand, e.g. by one who does magic tricks.

wander /'wɒndə'/ *vi* move aimlessly from place to place; leave the right path.

wanderlust /'wɒndəlʌst/ *n* restless desire to travel.

wane /weɪn/ *vi* become less, e.g. *The moon is waning.*

wangle /'wæŋgəl/ *sl n, vt* (arrange or obtain by) cleverness or a trick.

want /wɒnt/ *vt* **1** wish for, e.g. *He wants to go now* = he would like to go now. **2** lack; need. *n* something wanted or lacked. *adj* **wanting** /'wɒntɪŋ/ incomplete, lacking something in order to be perfect.

wanton /'wɒntən/ *adj* wild and uncontrolled in behaviour.

war /wɔː'/ *n* fighting between nations.

warble /'wɔːbəl/ *n, vi* (make a) sound like that of a bird with shaking of the voice.

ward[1] /wɔːd/ *n* **1** part of a city divided off for purposes of government. **2** room in a hospital. **3** part of a key that makes it fit only one lock. **4** young person under the protection of a court of law.

ward[2] /wɔːd/ **to ward off** = turn (e.g. an attack) aside.

warden /'wɔːdn/ *n* head or person in control of, e.g. a school.

warder /'wɔːdə'/ *n* prison guard.

wardrobe /'wɔːd-rəʊb/ *n* large upright box, with a door, in which one hangs up clothes; one's whole range of clothes.

wardroom /'wɔːd-rʊm, -ruːm/ *n* officers' room on a warship.

wares /weəz/ *n* (*pl*) goods for selling. *n* **warehouse** /'weəhaʊs/ storehouse.

warfare /'wɔːfeə'/ *n* fighting a war.

warlike /'wɔːlaɪk/ *adj* always wanting or liking to make war.

warm /wɔːm/ *adj* (making one) slightly or pleasantly hot. *v* make or become warm, e.g. *It's beginning to warm up now.* *adj* **warm-hearted** /͵. ˈ. ./ loving; generous. *n* **warmth** /wɔːmθ/.

warmonger /'wɔː͵mʌŋgə'/ *n* person who wants war.

warn /wɔːn/ *vt* tell (someone) about probable danger. *n* **warning** /'wɔːnɪŋ/ act of telling of danger.

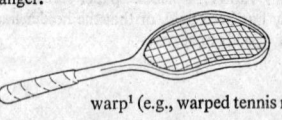

warp[1] (e.g., warped tennis racket)

warp[1] /wɔːp/ *v* bend out of the proper shape, e.g. *Wood warped by the heat.*

warp[2] /wɔːp/ *n* (*sing*) threads running along the length of cloth.

warp[3] /wɔːp/ *n* ship's rope.

warrant /'wɒrənt/ *n* paper giving the right to do something, e.g. put a person in prison; paper giving the right to pay or receive money; right to say or do anything.

warren /'wɒrən/ *n* piece of land in which there are many rabbits.

warrior /'wɒrɪə'/ *n* soldier; experienced fighting man.

wart /wɔːt/ *n* small hard growth on the surface of the skin.

wary /'weərɪ/ *adj* careful; looking out for danger.

wash /wɒʃ/ *v* clean (oneself) with water (or other liquid). *n* act of washing. *n* (*sing*) **washing** /'wɒʃɪŋ/ clothes to be washed. **to wash up** = wash (dishes, etc.) after a meal. *n* **washing machine** = machine for washing clothes.

washer /'wɒʃə'/ *n* round piece of metal or leather with a hole through which a screw passes.

washout /'wɒʃaʊt/ *sl n* failure, e.g. *It was a washout* = it failed completely.

wasp /wɒsp/ *n* an insect, like a bee, but with black and yellow lines on its body.

wastage /'weɪstɪdʒ/ *n* wasting; matter wasted.

waste /weɪst/ *vt* fail to make good use of; use up without getting any good from. *n* **1** act of wasting; thing wasted. **2** unused land. *adj* unused; unwanted; useless. **to waste away** = lose strength, esp. because of disease. *adj* **wasteful** /'weɪstfəl/ showing waste.

watch /wɒtʃ/ *v* keep the eyes on (something); be on

guard. *n* **1** guard. **2** act of watching. **3** time spent in keeping guard (e.g. on a ship). **4** small clock for the pocket or WRIST. *adj* **watchful** /'wɒtʃfəl/ careful in keeping guard. *n* **watchman** /'wɒtʃmən/ one who guards a building. *n* **watchword** /'wɒtʃwɜːd/ word spoken to a guard in time of war to prove that one is not an enemy.

water /'wɔːtə⁷/ *n* a common liquid, colourless when pure, of which rain, the body of seas and rivers, etc., consist. *vt* put water on (e.g. plants in a garden). **to water down** = mix water with (something) so as to make it weaker. *n* **water closet** /'.. ,../ place in which one leaves the waste matter of the body. *n* **watercolour** /'wɔːtəˌkʌlə⁷/ paint to be mixed with water (not oil) used for painting pictures. *n* **watercress** /'wɔːtəkres/ hot-tasting plant grown in water and used as food. *n* **waterfall** /'wɔːtəfɔːl/ water falling straight down over a rock. *n* **waterfront** /'wɔːtəfrʌnt/ part of a town at the edge of the sea. *n* **waterline** /'wɔːtəlaɪn/ one of the lines on the side of a ship to show the level of the water. *adj* **waterlogged** /'wɔːtəlɒgd/ (e.g. of earth) filled with water so that it cannot become wetter; (e.g. of a ship) filled with water so that it cannot float. *n* **watermark** /'wɔːtəmɑːk/ mark of the maker seen on paper when it is held up to the light. *adj* **waterproof** /'wɔːtəpruːf/ (of cloth) that keeps out water. *n* **watershed** /'wɔːtəʃed/ line of hills between two river valleys.

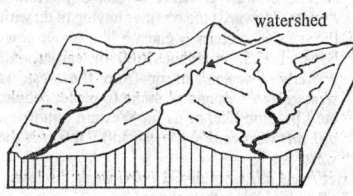
watershed

adj **watertight** /'wɔːtətaɪt/ able to keep water out (or in). a **watertight argument** = piece of reasoning that cannot be proved to be wrong. *n* **waterway** /'wɔːtəweɪ/ path of water along which people sail or goods are carried. *n* **waterworks** /'wɔːtəwɜːks/ place from which water is sent out through pipes to a town or city. *adj* **watery** /'wɔːtəri/ like water; containing much water.

watt /wɒt/ *n* measure of electrical power.

wattle /'wɒtl/ *n* **1** sticks bent in and out between thicker upright sticks so as to form a kind of wall. **wattle and daub** = a wall so made and covered with CLAY **2** red skin hanging down from the neck of a bird.

wave /weɪv/ *n* **1** up and down and rolling movement on the surface of water, e.g. *A wave of the sea.* **2** any movement of the same kind, e.g. *Sound waves, Light waves.* **3** steady forward movement, rapidly spreading change, e.g. *A wave of feeling.* **a cold wave** = short time of cold

weather. *v* move from side to side, e.g. a flag, a branch; move up and down; lie in a hill-and-valley form, e.g. *Hair waves.* *n* **wavelength** /'weɪvleŋθ/.

waver /'weɪvə⁷/ *vi* move unsteadily; change often and be in doubt between two opinions.

wavy /'weɪvi/ *adj* covered with waves; bending from side to side, e.g. *A wavy line* = ～～～～～.

wax¹ /wæks/ *vi* become larger, e.g. *The moon waxes and wanes* = the moon becomes bigger and smaller.

wax² /wæks/ *n* easily melted material made and used by bees in building; also used in making candles. *n* **waxworks** /'wæks-wɜːks/ show of wax figures of well-known persons.

way /weɪ/ *n* **1** road; direction, e.g. *Which way did he go?* = in which direction? **2** distance travelled or to be travelled, e.g. *It is a long way from here to London.* **3** space, e.g. *Make way for the King.* **4** manner, e.g. *The right and the wrong way of doing the work.*

wayfarer /'weɪfeərə⁷/ *n* traveller.

waylay /weɪ'leɪ/ *vt* wait for (someone) in order to attack him or to speak to him.

wayside /'weɪsaɪd/ *n, adj* (of the) side of the road.

wayward /'weɪwəd/ *adj* uncontrolled; not obeying orders.

we /wɪ; *strong* wiː/ *pron* (used in speaking of a group that includes oneself) e.g. *We had to go by car.*

weak /wiːk/ *adj* not strong; not able to stand up against attack; not able to do a thing well. *v* **weaken** /'wiːkən/ make or become weaker. *n* **weakling** /'wiːklɪŋ/ weak person. *n* **weakness** /'wiːknəs/ **1** state of being weak. **2** fault; weak point.

weal¹ /wiːl/ *archaic n* success; good, e.g. *For the public weal* = for the good of the people.

weal² /wiːl/ *n* mark on the skin from the blow of a stick, etc.

wealth /welθ/ *n* state of being rich; riches owned. *adj* **wealthy** /'welθi/.

wean /wiːn/ *vt* accustom (a child) to food other than milk; draw (someone) slowly away from, e.g. make a person slowly begin to be able to do without a former friend, custom, etc.

weapon /'wepən/ *n* instrument used for fighting.

wear /weə⁷/ *vt* have (clothes) on. *n* **1** clothing worn. **2** amount worn away or worn out. **to wear away** = be rubbed away; rub away, e.g. *Water wears away a stone.* **to wear out** = make useless by much wearing (e.g. clothes).

weary /'wɪəri/ *vt* make tired by work; cause loss of interest. *adj* tired, in need of rest; having lost interest in, e.g. *weariness* /'wɪərinəs/. *adj* **wearisome** /'wɪərisəm/ uninteresting.

weasel /'wiːzəl/ *n* small fierce red-brown mammal.

weather /'weðə⁷/ *n* state of the sky and air, e.g. *Bad weather* = rain, storm, etc. *infml* **under the weather** = sad or ill. **to weather a storm** = come

weasel

through safely. *n* **weathercock** / ˈweðəkɒk/ instrument sometimes made in the shape of a bird, fixed to the top of a tower, where it can turn so as to show which way the wind is blowing.

weave /wiːv/ *v* make (something) by forming threads into cloth. *n* **weaver** /ˈwiːvəʳ/.

web /web/ *n* (*sing*) threads laid across each other to form cloth or net. *adj* **web-footed** /ˌ. ˈ. / having feet like those of a duck with skin between the TOES. *n* **webbing** /ˈwebɪŋ/ narrow strong piece of cloth.

wed /wed/ *vt* marry. *n* **wedding** /ˈwedɪŋ/ (church) ceremony and feast at a marriage.

wedge →

wedge /wedʒ/ *n* V-shaped piece of metal (or wood) driven into a piece of material so as to break it into two parts, or driven into a crack between two pieces so as to hold them firmly in place.

wedlock /ˈwedlɒk/ *n* state of being married.

Wednesday /ˈwenzdɪ, ˈwednzdɪ/ *n* the fourth day of the week, following Tuesday.

wee /wiː/ *adj* very small.

weed /wiːd/ *n* useless plant growing where it is not wanted; thin weak person. *vt* pull up weeds. **to weed out** = take out from (a piece of land) the useless things, or people (from a collection).

week /wiːk/ *n* a length of time of 7 days. *adj* **weekly** /ˈwiːklɪ/ appearing or happening once a week, e.g. *A weekly paper*.

weekday /ˈwiːkdeɪ/ *n* any day other than Saturday or Sunday.

weekend /wiːˈkend/ *n* Saturday and Sunday.

weep /wiːp/ *vi* cry, be in tears.

weevil /ˈwiːvəl/ *n* small insect with a hard shell found in fruit and in grain.

weigh /weɪ/ *vt* 1 measure how heavy (something) is. 2 have (a certain weight), e.g. *This weighs a pound*. **to weigh anchor** = pull up the ANCHOR. *n* **weight** /weɪt/ 1 heaviness; importance. 2 heavy mass, e.g. of metal used for measuring how heavy a thing is. *adj* **weighty** /ˈweɪtɪ/ heavy; important; serious.

weir /wɪəʳ/ *n* wall across a stream to make the level of the water higher.

weird /wɪəd/ *adj* strange; not natural.

welcome /ˈwelkəm/ *adj* met or received with pleasure. *vt* meet or receive with pleasure. *n* act of welcoming.

weld /weld/ *vt* join (two pieces of metal) by melting the edges while pressing them together.

welfare /ˈwelfeəʳ/ *n* health; success; good condition.

well[1] /wel/ *n* deep hole made in the ground to get water or oil; spring of water; any deep hole, e.g. in the centre of a high building. **to well up** = (of liquid) come up as from a spring.

well[2] /wel/ *adv* in a good and pleasing way; cleverly; in the right way. *adj* in good health. *interj* (word used with little meaning to begin a sentence), e.g. *Well, what happens next?* **as well** = also. **well off; well-to-do** /ˌ. . ˈ. / = rich.

welt /welt/ *n* piece of leather fixed between the upper part of a shoe and the SOLE.

welter /ˈweltəʳ/ *vi* roll about, e.g. in blood. **a welter of confusion** = great disorder.

wen /wen/ *n* harmless swelling below the skin.

went /went/ *p.t.* of **go**.

wept /wept/ *p.t.* and *p.p.* of **weep**.

were /wə; *strong* wɜː/ *p.t.* of **be** used after *you, we they* and plural nouns.

west /west/ *n, adv* (to the) direction in which the sun sets. *sl* **to go west** = die. *adj* **western** /ˈwestən/ towards the west, or having to do with the west. **a western** = cinema film about cowboys in U.S. in about 1880 or earlier. *adj* **westerly** /ˈwestəlɪ/ in or from the west. *vt* **westernize** /ˈwestənaɪz/ make (a place, people, etc.) become like, or as in, Western countries. *adj, adv* **westward(s)** /ˈwestwəd(z)/ towards the west.

wet /wet/ *adj* 1 not dry. 2 *infml* weak; useless.

wether /ˈweðəʳ/ *n* male sheep.

wet-nurse /ˈ. .ʳ/ *n* woman who gives her milk to another person's child.

whack /wæk/ *interj, n* (sound of a) blow.

whale /weɪl/ *n* largest sea-creature.

wharf /wɔːf/ *n* place built on the edge of water at which ships load or unload. *n* **wharfage** /ˈwɔːfɪdʒ/ money paid for the use of a wharf.

what /wɒt/ *det, pron* which (thing(s)), e.g. *What did you decide to do? I know what I want; What colour is it?*

whatever /wɒˈtevəʳ/ *det, pron* no matter what.

wheat /wiːt/ *n* grain of which bread is made; plant that bears this grain. *adj* **wheaten** /ˈwiːtn/.

wheedle /ˈwiːdl/ *v* get something from a person by making oneself very pleasant to him.

wheel /wiːl/ *n* one of the round objects on which cars, trains, etc., run. *vt* push along (a wheeled vehicle). *n* **wheelbarrow** /ˈwiːlˌbærəʊ/ small cart with one wheel and two handles, used in a garden, etc. *adj* **wheeled** running on wheels.

wheeze /wiːz/ *vi* make a noise in breathing. *adj* **wheezy** /ˈwiːzɪ/.

whelp /welp/ n young of a lion (also of other animals); boy who behaves badly.

when /wen/ adv, pron at which time. conj at the time that.

whenever /wen'evə^r/ conj no matter when.

whence /wens/ adv, pron from which place; from what place.

where /weə^r/ adv, pron to or at which place. conj to or at the place that.

whereabouts /'weərəbauts/ n area where a thing is. adv in what place (as nearly as you can say)? conj **whereas** /weə'ræz/ because; but adv **wherever** /weə'revə^r/ no matter where. conj **whereupon** /ˌweərə'pɒn/ at which moment. n **wherewithal** /'weəwiðɔːl/ the necessary money.

whet /wet/ vt sharpen; excite.

whether /weðə^r/ conj if, e.g. I don't know whether he's coming (or not) = I don't know if he's coming.

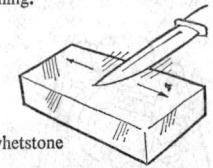
whetstone

whetstone /'wetstəun/ n stone used for sharpening.

whey /wei/ n clear liquid which is left after all the white solid part of milk has been taken away.

which /witʃ/ pron that, e.g. The subject which you mentioned. pron, det (used in asking for the name of a particular thing to be given) e.g. Which house is yours?

whichever /wi'tʃevə^r/ pron no matter which.

whiff /wif/ n a slight breath of air carrying a smell, e.g. A whiff of smoke.

while /wail/ conj 1 during the time that. 2 though; but. n short time. **once in a while** = sometimes, but not often. **worth one's while** = worth the time or work given to it. **to while away time** = pass time. conj **whilst** /wailst/ while.

whim /wim/ n passing idea or wish—usually of a rather strange kind.

whimper /'wimpə^r/ vi cry weakly, like a small baby.

whimsical /'wimzikəl/ adj having many strange ideas which do not last long; strange, unusual.

whine /wain/ vi cry like a dog in pain; complain like a bad child.

whinny /'wini/ n, vi (make the) noise of a horse when pleased.

whip /wip/ n string on the end of a stick used for beating (a horse). vt beat with a whip. **to whip up eggs** = mix thoroughly into a light mass with air enclosed in it.

whippet /'wipit/ n a small dog used for racing.

whir(r) /wɜː^r/ n noise made by anything passing quickly through the air.

whirl /wɜːl/ vi turn round quickly.

wholehearted

whirlpool

whirlpool /'wɜːlpuːl/ n water turning round and round very quickly.

whirlwind /'wɜːlˌwind/ n wind blowing in a circle.

whisk /wisk/ v brush away, e.g. The horse whisked off the flies with its tail. **to whisk eggs** = beat and mix eggs. n thing used for whisking (eggs, etc.).

whisker /'wiskə^r/ n piece of hair growing on the sides of a man's face, or standing out from the face of an animal, e.g. a cat.

whisky, whiskey /'wiski/ n strong drink made from grain.

whisper /'wispə^r/ v speak with the breath only, not using the voice; speak in a low voice. n any such faint sound.

whist /wist/ n a card game.

whistle /'wisəl/ v make a high sound by drawing the lips together and blowing through them; make such a sound by other means. n instrument used for making this sound sl **to wet one's whistle** = to drink.

white /wait/ n, adj (of the) lightest colour, e.g. Snow is white. adj (of a person) having a light skin. v **whiten** /'waitn/ make or become white.

whitewash /'waitwɒʃ/ n mixture of water and lime used as a paint. vt 1 put whitewash on. 2 sl cover up (someone's) wrongdoing.

whither /'wiðə^r/ adv in what (which) direction.

whiting /'waitiŋ/ n 1 small fish usually cooked with the tail bent round into the head. 2 powdered chalk for cleaning silver, or for use as a paint.

Whitsun /'witsən/ n Christian feast (7th Sunday after EASTER).

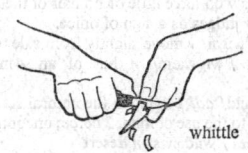
whittle

whittle /'witl/ vt cut thin pieces off (a piece of wood). **to whittle down** = make less.

whiz, whizz /wiz/ n, vi (make the) noise of something passing quickly through the air.

who /huː/ pron which person, e.g. Who was first? The man who won the prize.

whoever /huː'evə^r/ pron no matter who.

whole /həul/ adj complete, e.g. The whole cake = all of the cake.

wholehearted /ˌhəul'hɑːtid/ adj eager; honest.

293

wholesale /'həʊlseɪl/ *n* selling of goods in large quantities, e.g. to shops for selling again. *n* **wholesaler** /'həʊlseɪlə'/.

wholesome /'həʊlsəm/ *adj* good for the health; clean and nice.

wholly /'həʊlɪ/ *adv* completely; thoroughly.

whom /hu:m/ *pron* (form of **who** used after verbs and prepositions).

whoop /hu:p/ *n* loud cry. *n* **whooping cough** /'. . ./ illness of children that causes COUGHING with a voice-sound as the breath is drawn in.

whore /hɔ:'/ *n* woman who offers sex for money.

whorl /wɜ:l/ *n* arrangement of the parts of a flower round a centre; one turn of a SPIRAL shell.

whose /hu:z/ *pron, det* of whom; belonging to whom, e.g. *Whose car is this? Whose is it?*

why /waɪ/ *adv* for what reason; because of what, e.g. *I know why we lost.*

wick /wɪk/ *n* narrow band of cloth that draws up the oil in a lamp; string in the centre of a candle.

wicked /'wɪkɪd/ *adj* (of an act or person) very bad. *n* **wickedness** /'wɪkɪdnəs/.

wicker /'wɪkə'/ *n* basket-work, made of sticks like a basket. *n* **wickerwork** /'wɪkəwɜ:k/ wicker.

wicket /'wɪkɪt/ *n* **1** small door or gate. **2** line of three sticks upright in the ground used in the game of CRICKET.

wide /waɪd/ *adj* broad; having a great distance from one side to the other, e.g. *A very wide river.* **wide awake** = fully awake.

widen /'waɪdn/ *v* make or become wider.

widespread /'waɪdspred/ *adj* found in many places; general.

widow /'wɪdəʊ/ *n* woman whose husband is dead. *n* **widower** /'wɪdəʊə'/ man whose wife is dead.

width /wɪtθ/ *n* measure of how wide something is.

wield /wi:ld/ *vt* have control over; use in the hand, e.g. *To wield a sword.*

wife /waɪf/ *n* woman to whom one is married.

wig /wɪg/ *n* head-covering made of hair, used by persons who have little or no hair of their own, also by judges as a sign of office.

wiggle /'wɪgəl/ *v* move slightly from side to side.

wigwam /'wɪgwæm/ *n* hut of an American Indian.

wild /waɪld/ *adj* **1** living in the natural state; not turned to the use of man. **2** fierce; uncontrolled.

wilderness /'wɪldənəs/ *n* desert.

wildfire /'waɪldfaɪə'/ *n* quickly spreading fire that destroys everything. **like wildfire** = (of something harmful) acting very quickly.

wile /waɪl/ *n* trick.

wilful /'wɪlfəl/ *adj* **1** full of desire to see one's own wishes or plans fulfilled. **2** (of an act) done on purpose, not by accident.

will¹ /l; *strong* wɪl/ *v* (used to form the future) e.g. *He will be there tomorrow.*

will² /wɪl/ *n* **1** power of the mind to decide what to do and what not to do. **2** power of choosing one thing rather than another. **3** self-control and strength of purpose. **4** power of controlling others and making them obey. **5** wish of a person who has power expressed as an order. **6** paper showing to whom a man's possessions are to be given after his death. *n* **willpower** /'wɪlpaʊə/ strength of purpose; self-control.

willing /'wɪlɪŋ/ *adj* ready and eager to act as desired. *n* **willingness** /'wɪlɪŋnəs/.

willow /'wɪləʊ/ *n* tree which grows near water.

willowy /'wɪləʊɪ/ *adj* tall and graceful.

willy-nilly /ˌwɪlɪ 'nɪlɪ/ *adv* whether one wants it or not.

wilt /wɪlt/ *vi* (of flowers) cease to be fresh; fade.

wily /'waɪlɪ/ *adj* full of tricks; deceiving.

win /wɪn/ *v* gain; be successful; reach the place aimed at. *n* act of winning. *n* (*pl*) **winnings** /'wɪnɪŋz/ money won.

wince /wɪns/ *vi* draw back suddenly because of pain or fear.

winch

winch /wɪntʃ/ *n* round, drum-like thing, to which a rope is fixed, for lifting a heavy weight fixed to the rope.

wind¹ /wɪnd/ *n* **1** moving air. **2** air in the stomach. *adj* **winded** /'wɪndɪd/ having difficulty in breathing caused by running too fast, or by being hit in the stomach. **wind instrument** = musical instrument played by blowing. *adj* **windy** /'wɪndɪ/ (of the weather) with the wind blowing hard.

wind² /waɪnd/ *vi* move along a track that bends from side to side, e.g. *A winding road*; move upwards in circles. *vt* turn (a string) round and round on to a stick. **to wind up a clock** = turn round its handle so as to make it go. **to wind up a speech, a business company** = bring to an end.

windfall /'wɪndfɔ:l/ *n* fruit blown down by the wind; unexpected piece of good fortune.

winding-sheet /'. . ./ *n* cloth bound round a dead body.

windlass /'wɪndləs/ *n* WINCH.

window /'wɪndəʊ/ *n* opening in the wall of a building to give light and air.

wine /waɪn/ *n* liquid of fruit so changed that it has an exciting effect upon the mind and the body.

wing /wɪŋ/ *n* **1** limb of a bird with which it flies. **2** part of a building, e.g. *The north wing of the hospital.* *vt* hurt the wing of. **to wing one's way** = go quickly; fly.

wink

wink /wɪŋk/ v shut and open (one eye) quickly without moving the other; give a secret sign to a person in this way.

winnow /'wɪnəʊ/ vt separate off the grain from (the rest of the plant) by means of a stream of air; separate (what is useful) from what is useless.

winter /'wɪntə^r/ n the coldest season. adj **wintry** /'wɪntrɪ/.

wipe /waɪp/ vt pass, e.g. a cloth, over in order to clean. **to wipe out** = destroy; cause to have no more effect. n **wiper** /'waɪpə^r/.

wire /waɪə^r/ n metal thread, e.g. for electrical uses. n (sing) **wiring** /'waɪərɪŋ/ electrical wires, e.g. in a house or machine.

wireless /'waɪələs/ n radio.

wiry /'waɪərɪ/ adj like wire, thin and having strong muscles.

wise[1] /waɪz/ adj having good judgment; having knowledge. n **wisdom** /'wɪzdəm/.

wise[2] /waɪz/ **in any wise** = in any way. adv **lengthwise** /'leŋθwaɪz/ from end to end.

wisecrack /'waɪzkræk/ n amusing play on words; clever saying.

wish /wɪʃ/ n, vt want; desire. adj **wishful** /'wɪʃfəl/.

wishy-washy /'wɪʃɪ ˌwɒʃɪ/ adj thin; tasteless; uninteresting.

wisp /wɪsp/ n handful of grass; a small amount of hair.

wistful /'wɪstfəl/ adj sadly eager for; desiring what can probably not be obtained.

wit /wɪt/ n 1 power of saying clever and amusing things. 2 person who says such things.

witch /wɪtʃ/ n woman who does magic. n **witchcraft** /'wɪtʃkrɑːft/ magic. n **witch-doctor** /ˈ. ˌ./ man who does magic.

with /wɪð/ prep 1 using, e.g. I killed him with a knife. 2 in the company of, e.g. She arrived with her husband. 3 having, e.g. The house with the red car in front.

withdraw /wɪð'drɔː/ v (p.t. **withdrew** /wɪð'druː/. p.p. **withdrawn** /wɪð'drɔːn/). pull back; go back; take away. n **withdrawal** /wɪð'drɔːl/.

wither /'wɪðə^r/ vi dry up and fade.

withhold /wɪð'həʊld/ vt (p.t. and p.p. **withheld** /wɪð'held/.) keep back; not to give.

within /wɪ'ðɪn/ prep, adv in; inside.

without /wɪ'ðaʊt/ prep 1 not with; not having. 2 (formerly) outside.

withstand /wɪð'stænd/ vt (p.t. and p.p. **withstood** /wɪð'stʊd/.) stand against (an attack).

witness /'wɪtnəs/ n 1 person who actually saw an event. 2 what is said by such a person about an event. vt see (an event) and so be able to tell, e.g. a court of law, that it happened.

wits /wɪts/ n (pl) power of mind; cleverness. **to keep one's wits about one** = be on the watch.

witticism /'wɪtɪsɪzəm/ n clever and amusing saying.

wittingly /'wɪtɪŋlɪ/ adv on purpose; knowing what one was doing.

witty /'wɪtɪ/ adj clever and amusing in speech.

wizard /'wɪzəd/ n man who does magic.

wizened /'wɪzənd/ adj dried up; faded; WRINKLED.

wobble /'wɒbəl/ v move unsteadily.

woe /wəʊ/ n grief. adj **woebegone** /'wəʊbɪgɒn/ looking very sad. adj **woeful** /'wəʊfəl/ very sad; causing great sadness.

woke /wəʊk/ p.t. of **wake**. **woken** /'wəʊkən/ p.p. of **wake**.

wolf

wolf /wʊlf/ n wild animal like a dog. **to cry wolf** = warn of danger when there is none.

woman /'wʊmən/ n (pl **women** /'wɪmɪn/) human female. n **womanhood** /'wʊmənhʊd/ state of being a woman. adj **womanly** /'wʊmənlɪ/ like a woman; suiting a woman.

womb /wuːm/ n part of the female body in which the young are formed.

won /wʌn/ p.t. and p.p. of **win**.

wonder /'wʌndə^r/ n feeling of admiring surprise; object that causes this feeling. v 1 feel surprise. 2 wish to know, e.g. I wonder who he is. adj **wonderful** /'wʌndəfəl/ causing wonder; very good. n **wonderment** /'wʌndəmənt/ feeling of wonder.

won't /wəʊnt/ v will not.

wont /wəʊnt/ adj accustomed. adj **wonted** /'wəʊntɪd/ usual.

woo /wuː/ vt try to gain the love of; try to get, e.g. To woo sleep.

wood /wʊd/ n 1 tree-covered land. 2 matter of which a tree is made. adj **wooded** /'wʊdɪd/ (of a place) having trees growing in it. adj **wooden** /'wʊdn/ made of wood.

woodcraft /'wʊdkrɑːft/ n art of living in the forest as a hunter.

woodcut

woodcut /'wʊdkʌt/ n picture printed from a piece of cut wood.

woodland /'wʊdlənd/ n land covered with trees.

woodpecker

woodpecker /'wʊdˌpekə/ n bird that makes little holes in trees in order to get insects.

woodwork /'wʊdwɜːk/ n art of making objects out of wood.

wool /wʊl/ n 1 soft hair of sheep, used in making clothes. 2 any material that looks like wool, e.g. *Cotton-wool* = threads of the cotton plant. *adj* woollen /'wʊlən/ made from wool. *adj* woolly /'wʊlɪ/ 1 made of or looking like wool. 2 not clear.

word /wɜːd/ n sound or group of sounds, a letter or group of letters expressing an idea. to give one's word = promise. *vt* express in words, e.g. *You ought to word your answer differently.* n wording /'wɜːdɪŋ/ way in which something is expressed in words. *adj* word-perfect /ˌ. ˈ. ./ knowing one's words in a play. *adj* wordy /'wɜːdɪ/ expressed in too many words.

wore /wɔː/ p.t. of wear.

work /wɜːk/ n 1 something done for other reasons than pleasure. 2 act of doing things for payment; things so done; employment. 3 something made by an artist, such as a book or painting. *vi* 1 do work; be employed. 2 be successful; (e.g. of a machine) be in good order; be able to be used. *vt* cause to work; use (a machine). worked up = excited. to work out = prepare thoroughly (a plan); find the answer to (a difficult question). *adj* workaday /'wɜːkədeɪ/ such as is used every day; usual. *n* worker /'wɜːkə/ one who works, esp. in INDUSTRY. *n* workman /'wɜːkmən/ one who works, esp. at something needing skill. *adj* workmanlike /'wɜːkmənlaɪk/ well made. *n* workmanship /'wɜːkmənʃɪp/ ability to make things well. *n* workshop /'wɜːkʃɒp/ building in which people make or repair things, esp. machines.

world /wɜːld/ n 1 the earth and sky. 2 great solid mass going round the sun. 3 everything or everyone there is. 4 area of interest. *adj* worldly /'wɜːldlɪ/ not interested in things of the spirit.

worm /wɜːm/ n common small snakelike creature which lives in the ground; other creature of a similar form.

worn /wɔːn/ p.p. of wear.

worry /'wʌrɪ/ v make or be anxious. n something that worries one.

worse /wɜːs/ adv, adj more bad(ly). v worsen /'wɜːsən/ make or become worse.

worship /'wɜːʃɪp/ v show great honour and respect to; praise and pray to God. your Worship = title used in speaking to a MAYOR and certain judges. n worshipper /'wɜːʃɪpə/.

worst /wɜːst/ adj most bad. adv in the most bad way. if the worst comes to the worst = if things become as bad as possible.

worsted /'wʊstɪd/ n fine woollen thread for making into cloth.

worth /wɜːθ/ adj having the value of. worth seeing = good enough to be seen, that should be seen. worth the trouble, worth while = worth the work or money needed. n value. adj worthless /'wɜːθləs/ of no value.

worthy /'wɜːðɪ/ adj deserving of; deserving of honour.

would /d, əd; strong wʊd/ James said that he would go = James said "I will go". I would have left if he hadn't stopped me = I was going to leave when he stopped me. adj would-be /ˈ. ./ wanting to be, e.g. *A would-be poet* = person who wishes to become, wants to be thought, a poet.

wound[1] /waʊnd/ p.t. and p.p. of wind[2].

wound[2] /wuːnd/ vt cause harm to (the body). n harm so caused.

wove /wəʊv/ p.t. of weave. woven /'wəʊvən/ p.p. of weave.

wraith /reɪθ/ n spirit of a dead person (or distant living person) who visits someone to tell of death.

wrangle /'ræŋgəl/ n, vi quarrel.

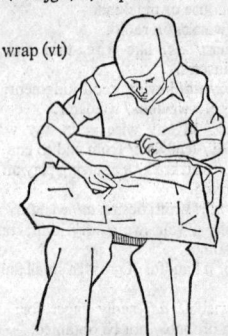
wrap (vt)

wrap /ræp/ vt fold cloth or paper, etc., round. wrapped up in his work = interested in it and in nothing else. n garment to be put loosely round one to keep out the cold. n wrapper /'ræpə/ 1 covering. 2 light loose garment.

wrath /rɒθ/ n anger.

wreak /riːk/ vt put into effect, e.g. *To wreak vengeance on* = do harm to a person as punishment for harm done.

wreath /riːθ/ n circle of leaves and flowers. vt wreathe /riːð/ make into a circle; encircle with.

wreck /rek/ vt ruin; destroy. n something wrecked, esp. a ship destroyed by the sea. n (*sing*) wreckage /'rekɪdʒ/ part of a wreck; act of wrecking.

wren

wren /ren/ *n* a small singing bird.

wrench /rentʃ/ *vt* pull suddenly and with force. *n* **1** pain caused by such a pull. **2** instrument for holding tight and turning things, e.g. for tightening part of a machine.

wrest /rest/ *vt* **1** pull away, e.g. *I wrested the sword from him.* **2** get with difficulty.

wrestle /'resəl/ *vi* struggle with a person and try to throw him down; try hard. *n* **wrestler** /'reslə/.

wretch /retʃ/ *n* sad poor person; bad person. *adj* **wretched** /'retʃɪd/ **1** deserving pity. **2** bad.

wriggle /'rɪgəl/ *vi* move the body about from side to side; move like a snake.

wring /rɪŋ/ *vt* twist, e.g. clothes, so as to get the water out. *n* **wringer** /'rɪŋə/ machine for pressing water out of clothes.

wrinkle /'rɪŋkəl/ *n* small fold in the surface of material, e.g. on the face of an old man. *adj* **wrinkled** /'rɪŋkəld/ covered in wrinkles.

wrist /rɪst/ *n* joint between the arm and the hand.

wristlet /'rɪstlət/ *n* band worn round the WRIST.

writ /rɪt/ *n* written order from the king or from a law-court.

write /raɪt/ *v* draw on a surface signs that make (words). **to write off** = decide that a thing is of no value. **to write up** = give a full account of; praise, e.g. in a newspaper *n* **writer** /'raɪtə/ one who writes books. *n* **writing** /'raɪtɪŋ/ written work.

writhe /raɪð/ *vi* turn the body from side to side as in great pain.

written /'rɪtn/ p.p. of **write**.

wrong /rɒŋ/ *adj* not right; not according to fact; not fitted for the purpose; unjust. *n* something unjust; bad act. *n* **wrongdoer** /'rɒŋ,duːə/ one who does wrong. *adj* **wrongful** /'rɒŋfəl/ unjust; unlawful.

wrote /rəʊt/ p.t. of **write**.

wrought /rɔːt/ *adj* worked. **wrought iron** = iron shaped and beaten when red-hot to make it strong.

wrung /rʌŋ/ p.t. and p.p. of **wring**.

wry /raɪ/ **wry mouthed** = having the mouth pulled to one side. **to make a wry face** = show great dislike, e.g. of a very bitter drink.

X

Xmas /'krɪsməs/ *n* short form (only used in writing) of CHRISTMAS.

X-ray /'eks reɪ/ *n* form of electric light able to pass through solid things. *vt* take an X-ray photograph of.

xylophone /'zaɪləfəʊn/ *n* musical instrument made of pieces of wood or metal, each giving a different note when struck.

xylophone

Y

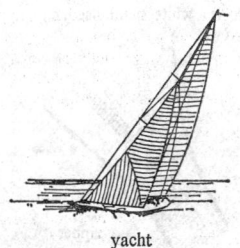

yacht

yacht /jɒt/ *n* ship used for pleasure; sailing ship used for racing. *n* **yachtsman** /'jɒtsmən/ one who sails a yacht.

yak /jæk/ *n* large animal like a cow with long hair.

yam /jæm/ *n* root of an African plant used for food.

yank /jæŋk/ *vt* pull sharply.

Yankee /'jæŋkɪ/ *n* an American (of U.S.A., especially one from the north-east).

yap /jæp/ *vi, n* (make a) short sharp noise as does a dog when very excited.

yard /jɑːd/ *n* **1** pole to which a sail is fixed on a ship. **2** enclosed space near a house; space in which some particular business is carried on, e.g. *A builder's yard*. **3** measure of three feet (0.914 m). *n* **yardstick** /'jɑːd,stɪk/ stick for measuring lengths; anything by which other things are judged.

yarn /jɑːn/ *n* (*sing*) **1** threads of which rope may be made; thread for use in making or repairing cloth. **2** story.

yaw /jɔː/ *vi* (of a ship) move unsteadily and leave the correct course.

yawn /jɔːn/ *vi* open the mouth wide as when tired or uninterested.

yaws /jɔːz/ *n* disease of hot countries causing hard swellings on the skin.

year /jɪə ; jɜː / *n* 365 or 366 days. *n* **yearling** /'jɪəlɪŋ, 'jɜːlɪŋ/ animal one year old. *adj* **yearly** /'jɪəlɪ, jɜːlɪ/ happening each or every year.

yearn /jɜːn/ **to yearn for** = desire greatly.

yeast /jiːst/ *n* material used in making bread and also wine.

yell /jel/ *v* shout loudly on a high note.

yellow /'jeləʊ/ *adj*, *n* (of the) colour of gold, butter, etc.

yelp /jelp/ *n* sudden cry of pain of a dog. *vi* give such a cry.

yeoman /'jəʊmən/ *n* farmer. *n* **yeomanry** /'jəʊmənrɪ/ farmers; certain horse-soldiers in the British Army.

yes /jes/ *interj* that is true; I agree.

yesterday /'jestədɪ, -deɪ/ *n*, *adv* (on the' day before this one.

yet /jet/ *adv* **1** up to this time, up to that time. **2** even; still, e.g. *Yet again, it's happened. conj* even more than this; but.

yew /juː/ *n* a dark green tree often grown near churches.

Yiddish /'jɪdɪʃ/ *n* mixed language spoken by many Jews.

yield /jiːld/ *vt* produce, e.g. *The land yields large crops* = large crops are grown on the land. *vi* give way to force, e.g. *We yielded to the enemy. n* amount or gain produced. *adj* **yielding** /'jiːldɪŋ/ soft; easily bent.

yodel /'jəʊdl/ *vi* sing, quickly changing from a high to a low note, as the Swiss do in the mountains.

yoga /'jəʊgə/ *n* a special Indian way of living and form of prayer, exercise, and breathing, by which a man tries to conquer the IMPULSES of his body and set his soul free. *n* **yogi** /'jəʊgɪ/ one who practises yoga.

yoghourt, yoghurt /'jɒgət/ *n* sour milk used as food.

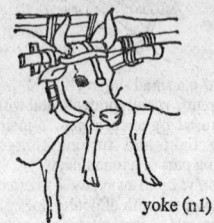
yoke (n1)

yoke /jəʊk/ *n* **1** cross-piece put on the necks of cattle when pulling a cart. **2** part of a dress that lies on the shoulders. *vt* join together.

yokel /'jəʊkəl/ *n* rough or simple man from the country.

yolk /jəʊk/ *n* yellow part of an egg.

yonder /'jɒndə/ *adv* over there.

you /juː/ *pron* **1** (used in speaking of the person(s) one is talking to) e.g. *The decision is for you to make.* **2** one, e.g. *You can't tell what he's going to do next* = it is impossible to know what he's going to do next.

young /jʌŋ/ *adj* not having lived long; not old. *n* **youngster** /'jʌŋstə/ young person; child.

your /jɔː/ *det* belonging to you. *pron* **yours** /jɔːz/ something belonging to you.

youth /juːθ/ *n* **1** early part of life. **2** young man. **3** young men and women. *adj* **youthful** /'juːθfəl/ young; young in spirit.

youth hostel /'. . ./ *n* house where young travellers may sleep and eat cheaply.

yule /juːl/ *n* Christmas. *n*, *adj* **yuletide** /'juːltaɪd/ Christmas time.

Z

zeal /ziːl/ *n* eagerness; keenness. *n* **zealot** /'zelət/ person who is too eager and fixed in his beliefs. *adj* **zealous** /'zeləs/ eager.

zebra /'ziːbrə, 'zebrə/ *n* wild animal shaped like a horse with dark lines on the body, common in Africa. **zebra crossing** /,. '. ./ = part of a road marked with black and white lines where people have the right to walk across and cars must stop to let them pass.

zenith /'zenɪθ/ *n* **1** part of the sky just above one's head. **2** highest point reached.

zero /'zɪərəʊ/ *n* number NOUGHT, written 0; lowest point in measuring.

zest /zest/ *n* **1** something added to give a sharp and pleasant taste, or to add interest. **2** eagerness.

zigzag /'zɪgzæg/ *n*, *adj* shape(d) like a line of Zs.

zinc /zɪŋk/ *n* a white metal, used, e.g., to protect iron from wet.

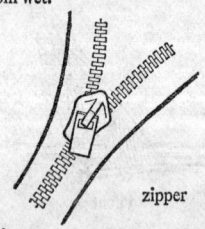
zipper

zip /zɪp/ *n* sound made by an object passing quickly through the air. *n* **zip fastener** /'. ,. ./ **zipper** /'zɪpə/ fastener for joining two pieces of cloth or leather by fitting together two toothed metal edges by passing them through a sliding Y-shaped piece—much used for bags and clothes.

zither /ˈzɪðə/ n musical instrument with strings which are sounded by PLUCKING them.

zodiac /ˈzəʊdɪæk/ n plan of part of the sky divided into twelve parts showing the place of certain stars, in relation to the sun and the earth, used in ASTROLOGY.

zone /zəʊn/ n area; band, e.g. of colour; one of the five bands into which the map of the earth is divided, e.g. *The Arctic zone* = the area north of 66½ degrees N.

zoo /zuː/ n place in which animals of many kinds are kept for show. n zoologist /zuˈɒlədʒɪst, zəʊˈɒ-/ one who studies animals, their different kinds, ways of living, etc. n zoology /zuːˈɒlədʒɪ, zəʊˈɒ-/ this science. adj zoological /ˈzuːəˈlɒdʒɪkəl, zəʊˈɒ-/.

zoom /zuːm/ n deep low sound. vi 1 make such a sound. 2 drive an aeroplane quickly upwards 3 (in filming) make things seem to come nearer.

Zulu /ˈzuːluː/ n member of a native race in South Africa.

In the Preface (p. vii), we tell you how this vocabulary is used in the dictionary. But we do not talk about the little numbers above the words in this list (such as *ball[1]*). They show what meaning of the word has been used in the definitions. To understand the number, you should look at the main part of the dictionary. If you look up *ball*, for example, you will find *ball[1]* defined as "round object used in play; any round thing." This is the meaning of *ball* when it appears in a definition. The word is not used in its other sense (*ball[2]*): "large number of people gathered for dancing."

The Defining Vocabulary

A

a, an
ability
able
about
above
absent
accept
accident
according to
account
accustom
acid
across
act
action
active
actor
actual
add
address
adjective
admire
advise
aeroplane
afraid
after
afternoon
afterwards
again
against
age
ago
agree
aim
air
alive
all
allow
alone
along
aloud
already
also
although
always
among
amount
amuse
ancient
and
anger
angle[2]
angry
animal

answer
ant
anxiety
any
apart
appear
apple
appoint
arch
archway
area
arise
arm
armour
arms
army
around
arrange
arrive
arrow
art
article
as
aside.
ask
at
attack
attempt
attend
attention
autumn
avoid
awake
away
axe

B

baby
back
bad
bag
bake
ball[1]
band
bank[1,2]
bar
barrel
basket
bath
bathe
battle
be
beak
beam

bean
bear[1,2]
beard
beat
beauty
because
become
bed
bee
before
beg
begin
behave
behind
belief
bell
belong
below
bend
best
better
between
beyond
Bible
bicycle
big
bill[1]
bind
bird
birth
bit[1]
bite
bitter
black
blade
blame
bless
block
blood
blow[1,2]
blue
board
boat
body
boil[2]
bold
bone
book
boot
border
both
bowel
bowl[2]
box[1]
boy
brain

branch
brass
brave
bread
breadth
break
breakfast
breast
breath
breathe
brick
bridge[1]
bright
bring
broad
brother
brown
brush
build
burn
burst
bush[1]
bushy
business
busy
but
butter
buy
by

C

cage
cake
calculate
call
calm
camp
can[1]
candle
cap
captain
car
card
care
carriage
carry
cart
case[1,2]
castle
cat
catch
cattle
cause
cave
cease

centi-
centre
ceremony
certain
chain
chair
chalk
chance
change
character
charge
charm
cheap
cheer
cheese
chest
chief
child
chimney
choice
choose
Christmas
church
cigarette
cinema
circle
circular
city
claim
class
clean
clear
clever
cliff
climb
clock
close[1,2]
cloth
clothes
cloud
coal
coast
coat
coffee
cold[2]
collect
colour
come
comfort
command
common
company
companion
compass
complain
complete

concern
condition
conquer
consider
consist
contain
content[1]
continue
continuous
control
cook
cool
copper
copy
corn[1]
corner
correct
cost
costly
cotton
could
count[1]
countless
country
courage
course
court[1]
cover
cow
crack
creature
creep
crop
cross[2]
crowd
crown
cruel
cry
cup
curl
curse
curtain
curve
custom
cut

D

daily
damage
damp
dance
dangerous
dare
dark
date[1]
daughter
day
dead
deal
dear
death

debt
decay
deceive
decide
decision
declare
deed
deep
deer
defend
degree
delay
delight
demand
depend
depth
descend
describe
desert[1,2]
deserve
desire
destroy
determine
devil
die[1]
difference
difficult
dig
dinner
direct
dirt
disappear
discover
disease
dish
distance
divide
do
doctor
dog
donkey
door
doubt
down[1]
draw
dream
dress
drink
drive
drop
drum
dry
duck[1]
during
dust
duty

E

each
eager
ear[1,2]

early
earth
east
easy
eat
edge
effect
egg
either
elder
elect
electricity
elephant
else
empire
employ
empty
end
enemy
engine
enjoy
enough
enter
entrance[1]
equal
equip
escape
especial
even[1,2]
evening
event
ever
every
evil
exact
examine
example
except
excite
exercise
expect
experience
explain
explode
explosion
express
eye

F

face
fact
fade
fail
faint
fair[1]
fairy
faith
fall
fame
family
famous

fancy
far
farm
fast[1,3]
fasten
fat
fate
father
fault
favour
fear
feast
feather
feed
feel
fellow
female
fence
fever
few
field
fierce
fight
figure
fill
film
find
fine[2]
finger
finish
fire
firm[1,2]
first
fish
fit[1,2]
fix
flag[1]
flame
flash
flat
flight[1]
float
floor
flour
flow
flower
fly[1,2]
fold[1]
follow
food
fool
foot[1,2]
for
forbid
force
foreign
forest
forget
forgive
form[2]
former
fort

fortunate
fortune
forward
fox
frame
free
freeze
fresh
friend
fright
from
front
fruit
fulfil
full
funeral
fur
furnish,
  furniture
further
future

G

gain
game
garden
garment
gas
gate
gather
gay
general
generous
gentle
gentleman
get
gift
girl
give
glad
glass
glory
go
goat
god
gold
good
govern
grace
grain
gram
grand[1,2]
grass
grateful
grave[1]
great[1]
green
greet
grey
grief
grieve

ground[2]
group
grow
guard
guess
guest
guide
gun

H

hair
half
hall
hammer
hand
handkerchief
handle
hang[1]
happen
happy
harbour
hard
hardly
harm
haste
hat
hate
have
head
health
heap
hear
heart
heat
heaven
heavy
height
help
hen
here
hide[1]
high
hill
hire
history
hit
hold[2]
hole
hollow
holy
home
honest
honour
hook
hope
horn
horse
hospital
host[1]
hot
hotel

hour
house
how
human
hunger
hunt
hurry
hurt
husband
hut

I

ice
idea
if
ill
imagine
immediate
important
impossible
improve
in
inch
into
include
increase
ink
inn
inquire
insect
inside
instead
instrument
intend
intention
interest
into
invite
iron
island

J

jelly
jewel
join
joint
journey
joy
judge
jump
just[1,2]

K

keen
keep[1]
key
kick
kill
kilo-

kind[1,2]
king
kiss
kitchen
knee
knife
knight
knock
knot
know
knowledge

L

lack
lady
lake
lamb
lamp
land
language
large
last[2,3]
late
laugh
law
lawyer
lay[1]
lazy
lead[1,2]
leaf
lean[2]
learn
least
leather
leave[2]
left[2]
leg
lend
length
less
lesson
let[1,2]
letter
level
lie[1]
life
lift
light[1,2,3]
like[1,2]
likely
limb
lime[1]
line[1]
lion
lip
liquid
list[1]
listen
litre
little
live[1,2]

load
loaf[1]
lock[3]
lodge
log
long[1]
look
loose
lose
loss
lot[1]
loud
love[1]
low[1]
lower
loyal

M

machine
mad
magic
make
male
mammal
main
man
manner
many
map
march
mark[1]
marry
mass
master
match[1]
material
matter
may
meal
mean[1,3]
means
measure
meat
medical
medicine
meet
melt
member
memory
mercy
merry
message
metal
metre
microscope
middle
might[1]
mile
milk
milli-
mind[1,2]

minute[1]
miss[1,2]
mist
mistake
mix
moment
money
monkey
month
moon
more
morning
most
mother
motor
mountain
mouse
mouth
move
Mr
much
mud
murder
muscle
music
must

N

nail
name
narrow
nasty
nation
native
natural
nature
near
nearly
neat
necessary
neck
need
needle
neighbour
neither
nerve
nest
net[1]
never
new
news
next
nice
night
no
noble
noise
none
nor
north
nose

not
note
notice
noun
now
number
nurse
nut[1]

O

obey
object[1]
obtain
ocean
of
off
offer
office
often
oil
old
on
once
only
open
opinion
opposite
or
orange
order
ornament
other
ought
out
outer
outside
over
overflow
owe
own

P

pack
page[1]
pain
paint
pair
palace
paper
parent
part
particular
party
pass
past
paste
pastry
path
pause
pay

peace
peculiar
pen[2]
pencil
penny
people
perfect
perform
perhaps
permit
person
photograph
pick[2]
picture
piece
pig
pillar
pin
pipe
pity
place
plain[1,2]
plan
plant[1]
plate
play
pleasant
please
pleasure
plenty
plural
pocket
poetry
point
poison
pole[1]
police
polite
poor
port[1]
possess
possible
post
pot
pound[3]
pour
powder
power
practice
practise
praise
pray
precious
prepare
present[1]
preserve
press
pretend
pretty
prevent
price
prick

prickle
priest
prince
print
prison
probable
problem
produce
promise
proof
proper
protect
proud
prove
provide
public
pull
punish
pure
purpose
push
put

Q

quality
quantity
quarrel
quarter
queen
question
quick
quiet
quite

R

rabbit
race[1,2]
radio
railway
rain
raise
range
rank[1]
rapid
rat
rather
reach
read
read
real
reason
receipt
receive
recognize
red
refuse[1]
regard
regular
rejoice
relate

religion
remain
remember
rent[2]
repair
repeat
report
reptile
respect
rest[1,2]
result
return
rich
ride
right
ring[1,2]
rise
risk
river
road
rock[1]
roll
roller
roof
room
root
rope
rose[2]
rough
round
row[1,3]
rub
rubber
rude
ruin
rule
run
rush[2]

S

sad
safe
sail
salt
same
sand
satisfy
save
say
scatter
scene
school[1]
science
scold
screw
sea
search
season
seat
second[1,2]
secret

see[1]
seed
seem
seize
self[1,2]
sell
send
sense
separate
serious
servant
serve
service
set[1,2]
settle
several
sex
shade
shadow
shake
shall
shame
shape
share
sharp
sheep
sheet
shelf
shell
shelter
shield
shilling
shine
ship
shirt
shock[1]
shoe
shoot
shop
shore
short
shot
should
shoulder
shout
show
shut
sick
side
sight
sign
silent
silk
silly
silver
similar
simple
since
sing
single
sink
sister

sit	stay[1]	taste	trade	warm
size	steady	tea	train[1,2]	warn
skill	steal	teach	trap	wash
skin	steam	tear[1,2]	travel	waste
skirt	steel	telephone	treat	watch
sky	steep[1]	television	tree	water
slang	stem	tell	trick	wave
slave	step[1]	temper	trouble	wavy
sleep	stick[1,2]	tend[2]	trousers	wax[2]
slide	stiff	tender[2]	true	way
slight	still[1,2]	tense[1]	trust	weak
slip	stomach	tent	truth	wealth
slope	stone	terrible	try	weapon
slow	stop	terror	tube	wear
small	store	than	turn	weather
smell	storm	thank	twist	week
smile	story	that		weep
smoke	straight	the		weigh
smooth	strange	theatre	**U**	welcome
snake	stream	then		well[2]
snow	street	there	ugly	west
so	strength	therefore	under	wet
soap	stretch	these	underneath	what
social	strike	thick	understand	wheel
soft	string	thief	union	when
soil[1]	stroke[1]	thin	unite	where
soldier	strong	thing	university	whether
solemn	struggle	think	up	which
solid	study	third	upon	while
some	subject	thirst	upper	whistle
son	substance	this	upright	white
song	succeed	thorough	upstairs	who
soon	such	those	urge	whole
sorrow	sudden	though	use	wholly
sorry	suffer	thought	usual	why
sort	sugar	thread		wide
soul	suit	throat	**V**	wife
sound[1,2]	summer	through		will[1,2]
sour	sun	throw	valley	willing
south	supper	thumb	value	win
space	supply	thunder	various	wind[1]
speak	support	thus	vegetable	window
spear	suppose	tie	vehicle	wine
special	sure	tight	verb	wing
speech	surface	till[1]	very	winter
speed	surprise	time	vessel	wire
spend	swallow[2]	tin	victory	wise
spirit[2]	sweet	tire[2]	view	wish
spite	swell	title	village	with
splendid	swift[1]	to	violent	without
spoon	swim	today	visit	woman
spot	swing	together	voice	wonder
spread	sword	tomorrow		wood
spring[1,2,3,4]	system	tongue	**W**	wool
square		tonight		word
stair	**T**	too	waist	world
stamp		tooth	wait	work
stand	table	top[1]	wake[3]	worse
star	tail	touch	walk	worst
start	take	towards	wall	worth
state[1]	talk	tower	wander	worthy
station	tall	track	want	would
			war	

wound²	**Y**	yes	young
wreck	yard	yesterday	youth
write	year	yet	
wrong	yellow	yield	

Places and Peoples

Note: Where one form only is given it can be used as an adjective or as a noun, either for a person who lives in the country or (in some cases) for the language spoken there, e.g. *He lives in Russia; He is Russian; He is a Russian; He speaks Russian.* In those cases where more than one form is given, the noun is only used for one who lives in the country; almost always, the language (if there is one) has the same form as the adjective, e.g. *He lives in Poland; He is Polish; He is a Pole; He speaks Polish.* (The main exceptions are *Arabic* and *Czech* which are the only forms used for those languages.)

Afghanistan /æf'gænɪstɑːn/; *Afghan* /'æfgæn/.
Africa /'æfrɪkə/; *African* /'æfrɪkən/.
Albania /æl'beɪnɪə/; *Albanian* /æl'beɪnɪən/.
Algeria /æl'dʒɪərɪə/; *Algerian* /æl'dʒɪərɪən/.
America /ə'merɪkə/; *American* /ə'merɪkən/.
Arabia /ə'reɪbɪə/; *adj Arabian* /ə'reɪbɪən/; *n, adj Arab* /'ærəb/; *n, adj Arabic* /'ærəbɪk/.
Argentina /ˌɑːdʒən'tiːnə/ (also **the Argentine** /'ɑːdʒəntiːn/); *Argentinian* /ˌɑːdʒən'tɪnɪən/.
Asia /'eɪʃə, 'eɪʒə/; *Asian* /'eɪʃən, 'eɪʒən/.
Australia /ɒ'streɪlɪə/; *Australian* /ɒ'streɪlɪən/.
Austria /'ɒstrɪə/; *Austrian* /'ɒstrɪən/.
Belgium /'beldʒəm/; *Belgian* /'beldʒən/.
Brazil /brə'zɪl/; *Brazilian* /brə'zɪlɪən/.
Britain /'brɪtn/; *adj British* /'brɪtɪʃ/; *n Briton* /'brɪtn/.
Bulgaria /bʌl'geərɪə/; *Bulgarian* /bʌl'geərɪən/.
Burma /'bɜːmə/; *Burmese* /bɜː'miːz/.
Canada /'kænədə/; *Canadian* /kə'neɪdɪən/.
Ceylon /sɪ'lɒn/; *Ceylonese* /ˌsiːlə'niːz/ (also *Sinhalese* /ˌsɪnhə'liːz/).
Chile /'tʃɪlɪ/; *Chilean* /'tʃɪlɪən/.
China /'tʃaɪnə/; *Chinese* /tʃaɪ'niːz/.
the Congo /'kɒŋgəʊ/; *Congolese* /ˌkɒŋgə'liːz/.
Cyprus /'saɪprəs/; *Cypriot* /'sɪprɪət/.
Czechoslovakia /ˌtʃekəsləʊ'vækɪə/; *adj Czechoslovakian* /ˌtʃekəsləʊ'vækɪən/; *adj Czechoslovak* /ˌtʃekə'sləʊvæk/; *n, adj Czech* /tʃek/.
Denmark /'denmɑːk/; *adj Danish* /'demɪʃ/; *n Dane* /deɪn/.
Egypt /'iːdʒɪpt/; *Egyptian* /ɪ'dʒɪpʃən/.
England /'ɪŋglənd/; *adj English* /'ɪŋglɪʃ/; *n Englishman* /'ɪŋglɪʃmən/, *Englishwoman* /'ɪŋglɪʃˌwʊmən/.
Ethiopia /ˌiːθɪ'əʊpɪə/; *Ethiopian* /ˌiːθɪ'əʊpɪən/.
Europe /'jʊərəp/; *European* /ˌjʊərə'pɪən/.
Finland /'fɪnlənd/; *adj Finnish* /'fɪnɪʃ/; *n Finn* /fɪn/.
France /frɑːns/; *adj French* /frentʃ/; *n Frenchman* /'frentʃmən/, *Frenchwoman* /'frentʃˌwʊmən/.
Germany /'dʒɜːmənɪ/; *German* /'dʒɜːmən/.
Ghana /'gɑːnə/; *Ghanian* /'gɑːneɪən/.
Greece /griːs/; *Greek* /griːk/.
Holland /'hɒlənd/; *adj Dutch* /dʌtʃ/; *n Dutchman* /'dʌtʃmən/, *Dutchwoman* /'dʌtʃˌwʊmən/.
Hungary /'hʌŋgərɪ/; *Hungarian* /hʌŋ'geərɪən/.
Iceland /'aɪslənd/; *adj Icelandic* /aɪs'lændɪk/; *n Icelander* /'aɪsləndəʳ/.
India /'ɪndɪə/; *Indian* /'ɪndɪən/.
Indonesia /ˌɪndə'niːzə/; *Indonesian* /ˌɪndə'niːʒən/.
Iran /ɪ'rɑːn/; *Iranian* /ɪ'reɪnɪən/.
Iraq /ɪ'rɑːk/; *Iraqi* /ɪ'rɑːkɪ/.
Ireland /'aɪələnd/; *adj Irish* /'aɪərɪʃ/; *n Irishman* /'aɪərɪʃmən/, *Irishwoman* /'aɪərɪʃˌwʊmən/.
Israel /'ɪzreɪəl/; *Israeli* /ɪz'reɪlɪ/.
Italy /'ɪtəlɪ/; *Italian* /ɪ'tælɪən/.
Jamaica /dʒə'meɪkə/; *Jamaican* /dʒə'meɪkən/.
Japan /dʒə'pæn/; *Japanese* /ˌdʒæpə'niːz/.
Jordan /'dʒɔːdn/; *Jordanian* /dʒɔː'deɪnɪən/.
Kenya /'kenjə/; *Kenyan* /'kenjən/.
(the) Lebanon /'lebənən/; *Lebanese* /ˌlebə'niːz/.
Libya /'lɪbɪə/; *Libyan* /'lɪbɪən/.
Malta /'mɔːltə/; *Maltese* /mɔːl'tiːz/.
Mexico /'meksɪkəʊ/; *Mexican* /'meksɪkən/.
Morocco /mə'rɒkəʊ/; *Moroccan* /mə'rɒkən/.
the Netherlands /'neðələndz/ = Holland.
New Zealand /ˌnjuː 'ziːlənd/ (also *adj*); *n New Zealander* /ˌnjuː 'ziːləndəʳ/.
Nigeria /naɪ'dʒɪərɪə/; *Nigerian* /naɪ'dʒɪərɪən/.
Norway /'nɔːweɪ/; *Norwegian* /nɔː'wiːdʒən/.
Pakistan /ˌpɑːkɪ'stɑːn, ˌpækɪ'stɑːn/; *Pakistani* /ˌpɑːkɪ'stɑːnɪ, ˌpækɪ'stɑːnɪ/.
Persia /'pɜːʃə/ (= Iran); *Persian* /'pɜːʃən/.
Peru /pə'ruː/; *Peruvian* /pə'ruːvɪən/.
the Philippines /'fɪlɪpiːnz/; *Filipino* /ˌfɪlɪ'piːnəʊ/.
Poland /'pəʊlənd/; *adj Polish* /'pəʊlɪʃ/; *n Pole* /pəʊl/.
Portugal /'pɔːtʃʊgəl/; *Portuguese* /ˌpɔːtʃʊ'giːz/.
Rumania /rʊ'meɪnɪə/; *Rumanian* /rʊ'meɪnɪən/.
Russia /'rʌʃə/; *Russian* /'rʌʃən/.
Scandinavia /ˌskændɪ'neɪvɪə/; *Scandinavian* /ˌskændɪ'neɪvɪən/.
Scotland /'skɒtlənd/; *adj Scottish* /'skɒtɪʃ/; *adj Scotch* /skɒtʃ/; *n Scot* /skɒt/; *n Scotsman* /'skɒtsmən/, *Scotswoman* /'skɒtsˌwʊmən/.
Spain /speɪn/; *adj Spanish* /'spænɪʃ/; *n Spaniard* /'spænɪəd/.
Sri Lanka /ˌsriː 'læŋkə/ = Ceylon.
Sweden /'swiːdn/; *adj Swedish* /'swiːdɪʃ/; *n Swede* /swiːd/.
Switzerland /'swɪtsələnd/; *Swiss* /swɪs/.
Syria /'sɪrɪə/; *Syrian* /'sɪrɪən/.
Tanzania /ˌtænzə'nɪə/; *Tanzanian* /ˌtænzə'nɪən/.
Thailand /'taɪlænd/; *Thai* /taɪ/.
Tunisia /tjʊ'nɪzɪə/; *Tunisian* /tjʊ'nɪzɪən/.
Turkey /'tɜːkɪ/; *adj Turkish* /'tɜːkɪʃ/; *n Turk*

/tɜːk/.
Uganda /juːˈgændə/: *Ugandan* /juːˈgændən/.
Vietnam /ˌvjetˈnæm/; *Vietnamese* /ˌvjetnəˈmiːz/.
Wales /weɪlz/; *adj Welsh* /welʃ/; *n Welshman*

/ˈwelʃmən/, *Welshwoman* /ˈwelʃˌwʊmən/.
Yugoslavia /ˌjuːgəˈslɑːvɪə/; *Yugoslavian* /ˌjuːgəˈslɑːvɪən/ (also *Yugoslav* /ˈjuːgəʊslɑːv/).
Zambia /ˈzæmbɪə/; *Zambian* /ˈzæmbɪən/.

Common Abbreviations

Note: ABBREVIATIONS are generally PRONOUNCED letter for letter, but where they are simply the beginning of a word, they are usually pronounced as the full word. There are some exceptions when the abbreviation can be spoken as a word; for these the pronunciation is given.

There are no firm rules about the use of full stops in abbreviations, although shortened forms tend to have them more often than those that consist of the first letters of words.

A1	very good; in the highest class	Dec	December
ABC	alphabet; alphabetical order	dept.	department
AC	alternating current	do.	ditto, the same
a/c	account	doz.	dozen
AD	after the birth of Christ	D Phil /ˌdiːˈfɪl/	
a.m.	before midday		Doctor of Philosophy
amp	ampère	Dr	Doctor
anon /əˈnɒn/			
	anonymous		
approx /əˈprɒks/		E	East
	approximately	ed	edited by; editor
Apr	April	EEC	European Economic Community (= the
Aug	August		Common Market)
Ave	Avenue	e.g.	for example
		ER	Queen Elizabeth II
		esp.	especially
b	born	Esq	Esquire
BA	Bachelor of Arts	et al	and others
BBC	British Broadcasting Corporation	etc./ɪtˈsetərə/	
BC	before the birth of Christ		et cetera (= and so on; and the rest)
Bros /brɒs/			
	Brothers		
B Sc	Bachelor of Science	F	Fahrenheit
		Feb	February
		fig.	figure, diagram; figurative
C	Centigrade	Fr	Father; French
c	about; cent(s); centimetre(s); cubic	Fri	Friday
cap	capital letter	ft	foot; feet
cc	cubic centimetres		
cf	compare		
CID	Criminal Investigation Department	g	gram(s)
C in C	Commander in Chief	gal	gallon
cm	centimetre(s)	GB	Great Britain
CO	Commanding Officer	gm	gram(s)
Co.	Company	GP	General Practitioner (= a doctor)
c/o	care of	GPO	General Post Office
COD	cash to be paid on delivery		
C of E	Church of England		
cont'd	continued	H.E.	His Excellency
Co-op /ˈkəʊɒp/		hi-fi /ˈhaɪ faɪ/	
	Co-operative Society		high fidelity (sound)
cu	cubic	HMS	His/Her Majesty's Ship
cwt	hundredweight	Hon	Honourable
		HP	hire purchase
		h.p.	horse power
d	died	HQ	headquarters
DC	direct current	hr	hour
D.D.T	substance used for killing insects	HRH	His/Her Royal Highness

ibid /'ibid, 'ibidem/
in the same place
i/c in charge
i.e. that is
in inch
Inc Incorporated
incl inclusive
IOU I owe you (see the dictionary)
IQ intelligence level
ITV Independent Television

Jan January
jnr, jr, jun
junior
JP Justice of the Peace (= a magistrate)
Jul July
Jun June

kg, kilo /'ki:ləʊ/
kilogram(me)
km kilometre(s)
Kt Knight
kw kilowatt

l left; litre(s)
£ pound sterling (money)
lb pound (weight)
log /lɒg/ logarithm
LP long-playing (record)
Lt. Lieutenant
Ltd Limited (of a business company)

m married; metre(s); mile(s); million(s); minute(s)
MA Master of Arts
Mar March
max /mæks/
maximum
MD Doctor of Medicine
Messrs /'mesəz/
plural of **Mr**
min /min/
minimum; minute[1]
Mon Monday
MP Member of Parliament; Military Police
mpg miles per gallon
mph miles per hour
Mr, Mrs see the dictionary
MS(S), ms(s)
manuscript(s)
Mt mount; mountain

N north
NB, nb note carefully or particularly
No(s), no(s)
number(s)
Nov November
nr near

Oct October
OHMS On His/Her Majesty's Service
OK see the dictionary
oz ounce

p (new) penny/pence; past; page
PA personal assistant
p.a. per year
PC police constable
p.c. per cent
PE physical education
PhD Doctor of Philosophy
pl plural
PM Prime Minister
p.m. after midday
p.p. past participle; in place of
pp pages
pro /prəʊ/
professional
Pro tem /ˌprəʊ 'tem/
for the present time only
PS postscript; also
p.t. past tense
pt pint
PTO please turn over
PVC polyvinyl chloride (= a kind of plastic)

Q Queen
QC Queen's Counsel (= a barrister)
qt quart

r right
RAF Royal Air Force
rep /rep/ representative
Rev. Reverend
rev /rev/ revolution
RIP may he/she rest in peace
RN Royal Navy
rpm revolutions per minute
RSVP please reply (to)

S South
s second; shilling(s)
s.a.e. stamped addressed envelope
Sat Saturday
sec second; secretary
sen, snr senior
Sept September
Sgt Sergeant
sing singular
SOS see the dictionary
Sq square
sr senior
St Saint; Street
st stone (weight)
Sun Sunday
Supt Superintendent

TB	tuberculosis		**VIP**	very important person
tbs	tablespoon		**vol**	volume
tel	telephone		**VSO**	voluntary service overseas
temp /temp/				
	temporary; temperature			
Thurs	Thursday		**W**	West
tsp	teaspoon		**w**	watt; with
Tues	Tuesday		**WC**	water closet
TV	television		**Wed**	Wednesday
			wpm	words per minute
			wt	weight

UFO /'ju:fəʊ, ju: ef. 'əʊ
    unidentified flying object
UK United Kingdom
US, USA United States (of America)   **Xmas** see the dictionary
USSR Union of Soviet Socialist Republics
    (= The Soviet Union)

			yd	yard
			YHA	Youth Hostels Association
v	see; versus; very; volt		**YMCA**	Young Men's Christian Association
VC	Vice-Chancellor		**yr(s)**	year(s); your(s)
VD	veneral disease		**YWCA**	Young Women's Christian Association